MW01001348

# CHILDREN AS VICTIMS, WITNESSES, AND OFFENDERS

# CHILDREN AS VICTIMS, WITNESSES, AND OFFENDERS

*Psychological Science and the Law*

*Edited by*

BETTE L. BOTTOMS
CYNTHIA J. NAJDOWSKI
GAIL S. GOODMAN

THE GUILFORD PRESS
New York      London

© 2009 The Guilford Press
A Division of Guilford Publications, Inc.
72 Spring Street, New York, NY 10012
www.guilford.com

Printed in the United States of America

This book is printed on acid-free paper.

Last digit is print number:  9  8  7  6  5  4  3  2  1

**Library of Congress Cataloging-in-Publication Data**

Children as victims, witnesses, and offenders: psychological science and the law/
edited by Bette L. Bottoms, Cynthia J. Najdowski, and Gail S. Goodman.
    p. cm.
 Includes bibliographical references and index.
 ISBN 978-1-60623-332-0 (hbk.: alk. paper)
1. Children—Crimes against.  2. Child witnesses.  3. Juvenile delinquents.
4. Children—Legal status, laws, etc.  5. Forensic psychology.  6. Criminal
investigation.  I. Bottoms, Bette L.  II. Najdowski, Cynthia J.  III. Goodman, Gail S.
 HV6250.4.C48C4556 2009
 362.88083—dc22

                                         2009018939

*To Gary, my constant support, and to all the students
who make my life richer every day*
—B. L. B.

*To my devoted mother, and to my husband, Jeff,
and son, Jake, who illuminate my days
with their love and laughter*
—C. J. N.

*To Danielle, Lauren, and Phil for their love and support*
—G. S. G.

*To all children who enter the legal system*
—B. L. B., C. J. N., and G. S. G.

# About the Editors

**Bette L. Bottoms, PhD,** is Professor of Psychology at the University of Illinois at Chicago. Her research on child abuse, children's eyewitness testimony, and jurors' perceptions of child victims and of juvenile offenders has been funded by the National Institute of Mental Health and published in numerous scholarly articles. Dr. Bottoms has edited four other books on child maltreatment and children's eyewitness testimony, and she has served on the editorial boards of *Law and Human Behavior*; *Psychology, Public Policy, and Law*; *Journal of Child Sexual Abuse*; *Behavioral Sciences & the Law*; and *Child Maltreatment*. She is a Fellow of the American Psychological Association (APA) and was President of the APA Society for Child and Family Policy and Practice and of the APA Section on Child Maltreatment. In 1998, Dr. Bottoms was a recipient of the APA American Psychology–Law Society Saleem Shah Early Career Award for Contributions to Psychology and Law Research, and of the Today's Chicago Woman Foundation Rising Star Award for career and community contributions in 2003. She has also received eight awards for excellence in graduate and undergraduate teaching and mentoring.

**Cynthia J. Najdowski, BA,** is a doctoral student in social and personality psychology at The University of Illinois at Chicago. She studies issues related to psychology and law, such as factors related to understanding how childhood sexual abuse and rape victims cope with their experiences. Her Master's thesis research considered jurors' perceptions of juvenile offenders. Ms. Najdowski's work has been published in journals such as *Behavioral Sciences & the Law*, *Psychology of Women Quarterly*, and *Addictive Behaviors*. She has received research grants from the Psi Chi National Honor Society and the APA American Psychology–Law Society. In 2006, Ms. Najdowski was the recipient of the Student Poster Award from the

APA Society for Child and Family Policy and Practice and, in 2009, the Christopher B. Keys Award for Early Outstanding Research Achievement from the University of Illinois at Chicago. Ms. Najdowksi serves on the student section of the editorial board for *Law and Human Behavior* and is the Graduate Student Representative for the APA Society for Child and Family Policy and Practice.

**Gail S. Goodman, PhD,** is Distinguished Professor of Psychology and Director of the Center for Public Policy Research at the University of California, Davis. She conducts basic theoretical research on memory development and psycholegal research focusing on children's abilities to provide testimony about events they have experienced or witnessed, especially events related to child abuse; on the psychological effects of testifying in court; and currently on the relations between child maltreatment, revictimization, and juvenile delinquency. Her studies have been cited in U.S. Supreme Court decisions. Dr. Goodman has served on the editorial boards of *Child Development, Law and Human Behavior*, and *Contemporary Psychology*, and as President of the APA's Section on Child Maltreatment, Society for Child and Family Policy and Practice, and American Psychology–Law Society. She was the recipient of the APA's Distinguished Contributions to Research in Public Policy Award and the Distinguished Professional Contributions to Applied Research Award in 2005, and the Urie Bronfenbrenner Award for Lifetime Contribution to Developmental Psychology in the Service of Science and Society in 2008. Dr. Goodman has also been a consultant concerning children in the criminal justice and child protection systems both nationally and internationally.

# Contributors

**Iris Blandón-Gitlin, PhD,** Department of Psychology, California State University, Fullerton, Fullerton, California

**Bette L. Bottoms, PhD,** Department of Psychology, University of Illinois at Chicago, Chicago, Illinois

**Sarah L. Bunnell, MA,** Department of Psychology, University of Kansas, Lawrence, Kansas

**Kay Bussey, PhD,** Department of Psychology, Macquarie University, Sydney, New South Wales, Australia

**Lorinda B.Camparo, PhD,** Department of Psychology, Whittier College, Whittier, California

**Alexia Cooper, MA,** Department of Psychology and Social Behavior, University of California, Irvine, Irvine, California

**Ingrid M. Cordon, PhD,** Center for Public Policy Research, University of California, Davis, Davis, California

**Sacha M. Coupet, PhD, JD,** Civitas ChildLaw Center, School of Law, Loyola University Chicago, Chicago, Illinois

**Emily E. Dunlap, MS,** Department of Psychology, University of Kentucky, Lexington, Kentucky

**James Garbarino, PhD,** Department of Psychology, Loyola University Chicago, Chicago, Illinois

**Jonathan M. Golding, PhD,** Department of Psychology, University of Kentucky, Lexington, Kentucky

**Gail S. Goodman, PhD,** Department of Psychology, University of California, Davis, Davis, California

**Andrea Follmer Greenhoot, PhD,** Department of Psychology, University of Kansas, Lawrence, Kansas

**Tamara M. Haegerich, PhD,** Department of Psychology, University of Illinois at Chicago, Chicago, Illinois

**Emily C. Hodell, MA,** Department of Psychology, University of Kentucky, Lexington, Kentucky

**Saul M. Kassin, PhD,** Department of Psychology, John Jay College of Criminal Justice, New York, New York

**Jessica O. Kostelnik, MA,** Department of Psychology, University of Virginia, Charlottesville, Virginia

**Michael J. Lawler, PhD,** Center for Human Services, University of California, Davis, Davis, California

**Kathryn Levene, MSW,** Child Development Institute, Toronto, Ontario, Canada

**Thomas D. Lyon, PhD, JD,** Gould School of Law, University of Southern California, Los Angeles, California

**Bradley D. McAuliff, PhD, JD,** Department of Psychology, California State University, Northridge, Northridge, California

**Jaime L. Michel, MSW,** Department of Psychology, University of Virginia, Charlottesville, Virginia

**Jillian N. Mongetta, BA,** Center for Public Policy Research, University of California, Davis, Davis, California

**John E. B. Myers, JD,** McGeorge School of Law, University of the Pacific, Sacramento, California

**Cynthia J. Najdowski, BA,** Department of Psychology, University of Illinois at Chicago, Chicago, Illinois

**Debbie Nathan, MA,** Freelance journalist, New York, New York

**M. Teresa Nezworski, PhD,** United States Air Force, Lackland Air Force Base, San Antonio, Texas

**Christin M. Ogle, MA,** Department of Psychology, University of California, Davis, Davis, California

**John Petrila, JD, LLM,** Department of Mental Health Law and Policy, Louis de la Parte Florida Mental Health Institute, University of South Florida, Tampa, Florida

**Kathy Pezdek, PhD,** Department of Psychology, Claremont Graduate University, Claremont, California

**Jodi A. Quas, PhD,** Department of Psychology and Social Behavior, University of California, Irvine, Irvine, California

**Allison D. Redlich, PhD,** School of Criminal Justice, University at Albany, State University of New York, Albany, New York

**N. Dickon Reppucci, PhD,** Department of Psychology, University of Virginia, Charlottesville, Virginia

**Jessica M. Salerno, BA,** Department of Psychology, University of Illinois at Chicago, Chicago, Illinois

**Karen J. Saywitz, PhD,** Department of Pediatrics, University of California School of Medicine, Los Angeles, California

**Christopher Slobogin, JD, LLM,** Vanderbilt University Law School, Nashville, Tennessee

**Margaret C. Stevenson, PhD,** Department of Psychology, University of Evansville, Evansville, Indiana

**Jennifer Anne Titus, MPH,** National Opinion Research Center, University of Illinois at Chicago, Chicago, Illinois

**Patrick H. Tolan, PhD,** Institute for Juvenile Research, University of Illinois at Chicago, Chicago, Illinois

**Natalie R. Troxel, BA,** Department of Psychology, University of California, Davis, Davis, California

**Elizabeth Uhl, MA,** Department of Psychology, University of Texas at El Paso, El Paso, Texas

**Margaret Walsh, BA,** Child Development Institute, Toronto, Ontario, Canada

**Lindsay Wandrey, BA,** Department of Psychology and Social Behavior, University of California, Irvine, Irvine, California

**Cathy Spatz Widom, PhD,** Department of Psychology, John Jay College of Criminal Justice, New York, New York

**Helen W. Wilson, PhD,** Department of Psychology, Rosalind Franklin University of Medicine and Science, North Chicago, Illinois

**James M. Wood, PhD,** Department of Psychology, University of Texas at El Paso, El Paso, Texas

# Contents

## PART II: CHILDREN AS OFFENDERS

# CHILDREN AS VICTIMS, WITNESSES, AND OFFENDERS

# Chapter 1

# Children as Victims, Witnesses, and Offenders

## *An Introduction through Legal Cases*

JILLIAN N. MONGETTA
JESSICA M. SALERNO
CYNTHIA J. NAJDOWSKI
BETTE L. BOTTOMS
GAIL S. GOODMAN

Children become involved in the legal system in myriad ways, including as victims, witnesses, and offenders. Society faces a number of difficulties as it struggles to accommodate these children within the legal context. Ideally, relevant law and policy should be informed by empirical evidence from theoretically sound research. The overarching premise of our book, *Children as Victims, Witnesses, and Offenders: Psychological Science and the Law*, is to identify how social science research can inform the creation, revision, interpretation, and implementation of laws and policy relevant to children.

The chapters in this volume, written by widely respected legal and social science scholars, examine a number of key questions currently at the intersection of psychology and law when children are involved in the legal system. For example, what are children's capacities and competencies as victims, witnesses, and defendants? How vulnerable are children in the context of investigative interviews and interrogations? How do legal players such as jurors perceive child witnesses and child defendants? How does the legal system accommodate—or fail to accommodate—children's special needs

1

and rights? What should future research and policy goals be? What works in other countries and how can the United States learn from other justice systems? Thus, this book serves to increase awareness about a wide variety of issues in great need of theoretical, empirical, and legislative attention.

In this introductory chapter, we discuss a number of actual cases that underscore the theoretical and applied significance of the work reviewed in this volume. These cases illustrate the ways in which children and youth are involved with the law, as victims, witnesses, and offenders. We hope these vivid depictions bring the important topics to life for the reader and set the stage for the chapters that follow.

## CHILDREN AS VICTIMS AND WITNESSES

The first part of our book addresses issues that arise when victimization ushers children into the legal system. Although reports of child physical and sexual abuse are decreasing across the nation (Finkelhor & Jones, 2006), child maltreatment is still a serious societal problem. For example, in 2007, children were abused or neglected at a rate of 10.6 per thousand children in the United States, resulting in an estimated 794,000 victims. These numbers are largely only representative of intrafamilial abuse and reports actually filed. Therefore, the true number of children facing abuse in the United States is likely much higher. Also, in 2007, an estimated 1,760 children died of abuse or neglect, at a rate of 2.35 children per 100,000 in the national population (U.S. Department of Health and Human Services, 2009). In many other countries, the rates are likely much higher.

These statistics do not illustrate the complicated set of psychological issues that arise in individual cases of child abuse, nor do they convey the terrible consequences of individual cases. Consider this one case in particular, which illustrates the severity of child abuse and its devastating effects: The Los Angeles community was shocked upon learning that a 5-year-old boy was hospitalized after being tortured and abused over a 2-year period by his mother and his mother's girlfriend (City News Service, 2008). The young child was starved, repeatedly beaten, burned on his genitals, required to sit in his own urine and feces, and regularly forced to place his hands on a hot stove. Although relatives and neighbors were aware of the abuse, it was never reported until the boy told a stranger who inquired about the severe burns on his hands (Bloomekatz, Dimassa, & Blankstein, 2008). This 5-year-old boy is just one of many children who have faced abuse and will likely appear in the courtroom. A case like this leaves people both saddened and angry about the injustice done to an innocent child. How will this abuse influence the child? How will the case be handled in dependency and criminal court as the child must now recount the abuse to authorities? Next, we discuss these and many other questions that arise after such crimes, questions that are addressed in the chapters of the first section of this book.

## Disclosing Abuse

In the Los Angeles case, a significant concern is whether the boy will be willing and able to talk about the abuse. He disclosed the cause of his burns when asked by a stranger. What compelled him to do so? Will he disclose in the more formal context of a forensic interview? Or will he recant or deny the abuse in an attempt to protect his mother, despite her abusive behavior?

In Chapter 2, Thomas D. Lyon, a developmental psychologist and an attorney, explores factors that influence disclosure, recantation, and denial of abuse. He reviews disclosure research conducted with children as well as with adults who were abused as children. Lyon advises practitioners that although it would be wrong to assume that denial of maltreatment is an indicator that abuse actually occurred, it is also wrong to assume that denials always rule out abuse. Although Lyon focuses largely on child sexual abuse, many of the issues transcend such cases and apply to other types of child maltreatment as well.

## Trauma, Memory, and Suggestibility

Two of the most actively researched topics in the study of child witnesses are children's memory and suggestibility. For example, within the scientific community, there have been heated debates about the effects of trauma on memory, especially about whether special mechanisms (e.g., repression, dissociation) are involved in memory for traumatic childhood events. That is, maltreated children are often traumatized by their experiences, and some such children develop trauma-related psychopathology, such as posttraumatic stress disorder. The 5-year-old boy in Los Angeles surely suffered considerable psychological trauma. Will the trauma affect his memory of what occurred, if not initially perhaps years later? Andrea F. Greenhoot and Sarah L. Bunnell discuss trauma and memory in detail in Chapter 3. The authors review models of trauma memory as well as recent empirical studies of how children and adults remember traumatic events such as child maltreatment.

Scientists have also studied the accuracy of children's memory for maltreatment and abuse as well as children's ability to resist false suggestions that such events occurred. In legal cases, concerns are raised that child victims and child witnesses often fail to provide sufficient information for fact finders to make legal decisions. Concerns are also raised that children are easily led into false reports of child maltreatment or other crimes, even murder, through interviewers' false suggestions. These concerns apply broadly, for example, to interviews by parents or teachers, to therapy sessions by clinicians, to formal child forensic interviews, and to formal courtroom testimony. Scientists have shown that a child's age is consistently related to the completeness and accuracy of children's memory reports and to their resistance to false suggestions. In addition, a wide range of situational and individual difference factors influence children's eyewitness testimony.

In Chapter 4, Iris Blandon-Gitlin and Kathy Pezdek focus on children's eyewitness testimony; specifically, suggestibility, false memory, and individual differences are reviewed as they apply to the legal context. Factors that increase children's accuracy as well as those that increase children's errors are reviewed, and a discussion of individual difference factors (e.g., language ability, quality of attachment) that moderate accuracy/inaccuracy relations is also presented.

In Chapter 5, James M. Wood, Debbie Nathan, M. Teresa Nezworski, and Elizabeth Uhl discuss the lessons learned from forensic interviews and investigative practices in some of the most sensational child sexual abuse cases of the past few decades, in particular the famous McMartin Preschool case in which the children are widely believed to have been led into false reports of abuse. Problematic investigations such as this are far less likely to occur today given that practitioners in the field are adopting science-based interview practices. Karen J. Saywitz and Lorinda B. Camparo, in Chapter 6, identify and discuss improvements in child forensic interviewing over the last two decades. They describe state-of-the-art research-derived interview techniques and protocols for questioning children as well as multidisciplinary approaches to child abuse case investigation. Their call for a "holistic approach" to child interviewing that acknowledges that child interviews are embedded in a larger multisystemic infrastructure is of considerable importance.

Overall, understanding issues of disclosure, trauma, memory, and suggestibility is vital for clinicians, legal professionals, social workers, medical personnel, and laypersons (e.g., parents, potential jurors) who might be involved in child maltreatment cases. Moreover, the topics addressed tap vital theoretical issues of great interest to scientists.

## Children in Court

The 5-year-old boy in Los Angeles was placed in protective custody and removed from his abusive home. His case then went to the dependency division of the juvenile court system. The dependency courts hear cases of child abuse and neglect and determine the best interests of the child, such as whether the child should be returned home or placed in foster care. In Chapter 7, Jodi A. Quas, Alexia Cooper, and Lindsay Wandrey describe the dependency court process and review recent research on children's reactions to dependency court. They review research on children's understanding of this unique legal intervention, children's participation in dependency proceedings, and the effects of removal from home on maltreated children. As the authors point out, it is imperative to study children's understanding of and ability to cope with dependency court so that the trauma of removal from home is not exacerbated by the legal system, by the very system designed to protect children from harm.

The boy in Los Angeles will also likely be involved in the criminal court system. His mother and her partner were criminally charged. In child physical abuse cases, the injuries sometimes speak for themselves, although even then the injuries might have to be linked to the perpetrators through the child victim's testimony. This often requires the child to take the stand and submit to direct and cross-examination in open court. Testifying in court can be an emotional and confusing process for anyone; it can be especially difficult for children already traumatized by crime. In Chapter 8, Natalie R. Troxel, Christin M. Ogle, Ingrid M. Cordon, Michael J. Lawler, and Gail S. Goodman discuss child victims' experiences in the criminal justice system. Specifically, Troxel and colleagues review the short- and long-term effects of legal involvement on child victims and describe special procedures for obtaining and presenting children's evidence in criminal proceedings.

## Jurors and Experts in Legal Cases Involving Child Victims and Witnesses

In 2002, Alejandro Avila was sentenced to death for kidnapping, sexually molesting, and killing 5-year-old Samantha Runnion (CNN, 2002). As Samantha and her friend were playing outside of their apartment complex, Avila approached Samantha and asked her to help him find his dog. He then grabbed her and shoved her into his car. Samantha's body was found less than 24 hours later on the side of a highway. Despite her youth, Samantha's playmate, also 5 years old, provided invaluable information by describing the perpetrator and his car. In this case, a young child's testimony was believed and used in the trial as evidence to convict Avila. A few years earlier, in 2001, however, Avila had been acquitted on charges of molesting two 9-year-old girls. Why did the juries consider the testimony of the 5-year-old girl (a bystander witness) reliable but the testimony of the 9-year-old girls (victim/witnesses) unreliable? Would expert testimony regarding the children's disclosures of abuse and memory accuracy have changed the jurors' perceptions of the child witnesses in the earlier trial? Distinguished legal scholar John E. B. Myers provides readers with an understanding of how the courts view expert testimony. He reviews common uses of psychological testimony related to child sexual abuse cases. Chapter 9 is essential reading for psychologists and others who might be called to court to testify as experts in cases that involve child victims or witnesses.

As the Avila case reminds us, understanding jurors' perceptions of children's testimonies is crucial in cases involving children as victims or witnesses, especially in those with little or no physical evidence. In Chapter 10, Jonathan M. Golding, Emily E. Dunlap, and Emily C. Hodell elaborate on the ways jurors' perceptions are affected by victim factors such as child gender, age, and race and juror factors such as gender. They also review research on the effects of expert testimony on jurors, providing an apt link to Chapter 9.

## Perspectives on Child Victims and Child Witnesses

The first section of the book closes with two chapters that offer broad perspectives on issues of child witnesses in court. In Chapter 11, Kay Bussey provides an international overview of child witness research and legal reform. Protecting children on a global level requires understanding the nuances of culture, government, and history. Countries can benefit from exploring and understanding other cultures and worldviews as they consider their own laws regarding children.

Most countries have ratified international documents on children's rights and protection. In practice, however, enforcement of treaty obligations can be difficult. In China, for example, despite its being a signatory to the United Nations Convention on the Rights of the Child, no formal child protection system exists (Hesketh, Hong, & Lynch, 2000). The complexity of child abuse in China is illustrated by the story of a 12-year-old girl named Ting Ting Hongjie. In 2000, Ting Ting's father, Wang Hongjie, was given full custody of his daughter. From that time forward, Ting Ting was denied education and was verbally and physically abused. Police confirmed that she never received medical attention for her injuries, which included broken bones, crushed fingers from pliers, and burned arms from scalding water. The police chief explained that "at the end of the day she won't be able to prosecute her parents because parents are required to represent their children in court" (Jenkins, 2002). Kay Bussey describes cultural influences on legal systems and the difficulties that children face in the midst of maltreatment throughout numerous countries. She reminds us that accommodating child witnesses is predicated first on having systems in place for reporting child abuse and prosecuting perpetrators.

In Chapter 12, the closing chapter of the first part of the book, Bradley D. McAuliff provides both a legal and a psychological commentary on the child victim and child witness chapters. As an attorney and psychologist, he offers many valuable insights and reviews some of his own research, concluding that social scientists and legal professionals must work side by side to ensure that children can participate in maltreatment proceedings effectively. He also reminds us that, through science-based policy change, society can have a positive impact on maltreated children's lives.

## CHILDREN OFFENDERS

The second part of *Children as Victims, Witnesses, and Offenders: Psychological Science and the Law* turns to issues that arise when children enter the legal system as offenders. One case in particular illustrates many such issues: As widely reported by major newspapers across the nation, in 1997, 11-year-old Nathaniel Abraham was arrested for fatally shooting Ronnie Greene (*People v. Abraham*, 1999). Taken from his fourth-grade classroom into police custody for questioning, Nathaniel admitted that he and a friend had been firing a stolen gun into trees when nearby Ronnie Greene was hit (Robinson, 1999; "Boy, 13, Convicted," 1999). Nathaniel was subsequently arrested and tried as an adult. The defense argued that Nathaniel had been shooting at trees when a bullet unfortunately ricocheted and hit Ronnie Greene in the head, and that Nathaniel was cognitively and emotionally impaired (as a result of both youth and learning disabilities) and, therefore, unable to form the intent to kill. The prosecution, however, claimed that Nathaniel planned to kill someone that day and bragged about it afterward. Ultimately, Nathaniel was convicted and, although eligible for an adult sentence, served time in a juvenile detention center until he turned 21 in 2007. As we elaborate herein, this and other cases demonstrate many of the topics addressed by authors in the second part of this volume.

### How Children Become Offenders

What put Nathaniel on the path to the courtroom as a juvenile offender? Some factors evident in Nathaniel's case include an overworked mother, an uninvolved father, a tough neighborhood, a lack of family supervision, and limited resources (Bailey & Audi, 1999). After Nathaniel's father left his family, they struggled, and Nathaniel moved frequently and was often separated from his siblings. Perhaps as a result of these challenges, Nathaniel began acting out aggressively both at home and in school.

In Chapter 13, readers learn from Cathy Spatz Widom and Helen W. Wilson how these and other factors, such as a history of abuse or neglect, might increase the likelihood that a child will become aggressive and delinquent and consequently enter the justice system as a criminal offender. Clearly, it is important to understand factors that lead children to delinquency so that rehabilitation and prevention efforts can be well informed.

## Police Interrogations and Juveniles' Confessions

Another important question that arises—or should arise—whenever juveniles enter the legal system concerns whether they possess the level of competency required to navigate that system. Based on the belief that juveniles should be protected from their immaturity and inability to make certain decisions, our nation has adopted a number of paternalistic laws such as those preventing children and youth from driving, voting, marrying, and drinking alcohol. Yet when they are criminal suspects, juveniles are expected to be capable of making complex legal decisions that can significantly affect their lives.

Overall, juveniles' rights to justice may be threatened by their developmental immaturity and diminished competencies, such as their inability to understand police interrogation procedures and their heightened suggestibility. When police use questionable tactics to interrogate juvenile suspects, especially young suspects who are actually innocent of crimes, there is considerable risk of miscarriage of justice. Juveniles' heightened suggestibility puts them in particular danger of making false confessions (e.g., Redlich & Goodman, 2003). Consider Marty Tankleff's case to understand the threat to justice posed by juvenile false confessions: As revealed by national news media, including *The Chicago Tribune, The New York Times,* and multiple episodes of CBS's *48 Hours,* 17-year-old Tankleff awoke to find his mother stabbed and bludgeoned to death and his father stabbed and beaten, barely alive. The lead detective, James McCready, spoke with Marty at the scene and, based on the feeling that Marty's demeanor was odd, decided that he had killed his parents. Detective McCready explained in a *48 Hours* interview that he first suspected Marty because he "was sitting calm as calm could be," which violated McCready's expectations that the boy should have been crying, shaking, and upset. On the basis of his impressions, Detective McCready took Marty to the police station, where he was questioned without legal representation. Marty maintained his innocence for 4 hours. Later, the detective told Marty that his father had identified him as the perpetrator. In fact, Marty's father never regained consciousnesss. Confused and traumatized, Marty began to believe that it was possible he had committed the crime, even though he had no memory of it. He asked Detective McCready if he could have blacked out or if he could have been possessed, and McCready replied, "Marty, I think that is what happened to you." A moment later, Marty stated, "It's coming to me," and McCready read Marty his *Miranda* rights (*People v. Tankleff,* 1993). Two minutes later, under the stress of having found his parents murdered a few hours earlier, the exhaustion of persistent and coercive interrogation, and the impression that his father had accused him of this heinous crime, Marty confessed and was charged with the murder of both of his parents. Although Marty recanted almost immediately, refused to sign the confession, and begged to take a polygraph exam, the damage was done. Confessions are extremely persuasive evidence to jurors, who have trouble understanding why people would confess to a crime they did not commit. Marty was sentenced to 50 years to life in prison. After years of appeals arguing that his confession was false, a conclusion supported by psychological evidence, Marty's conviction was overturned 20 years later.

The Tankleff case raises many interesting psychological issues surrounding suggestibility, interrogation tactics, and confessions, issues taken up in Chapter 14 by Allison D. Redlich and Saul M. Kassin. They consider juvenile suspects' vulnerabilities during legal interrogations, the conditions that might induce juveniles to confess to crimes they did not commit, and individual difference factors such as background, suggestibility, maturity, and intellectual and emotional disabilities that can contribute to false confessions. Redlich and Kassin's comprehensive review gives the reader much insight into understanding how people, especially vulnerable juveniles, could confess to crimes they never committed and, therefore, enter the legal system even though they are innocent.

## Children and Youth in Adult versus Juvenile Court: To Punish or Rehabilitate?

Whether falsely convicted or guilty, children and youth enter the legal system via one of two very different routes: (1) the adult criminal court system or (2) the juvenile or family court, which was designed for children more than 100 years ago. The former is becoming more common, as a consequence of juvenile waiver laws, which allow underage juveniles who are suspected of serious crimes to be automatically waived from the juvenile justice system to the adult criminal court system. Eleven-year-old Nathaniel Abraham, for example, was one of the first and youngest children to be charged and tried as an adult as a consequence of legislation enacted in Michigan in 1997. His case sparked national debates about whether children deserve the special protections offered by the rehabilitation-focused juvenile system or whether they should be sentenced with adult time for adult crimes. Judge Eugene Arthur Moore ultimately decided to keep Nathaniel in juvenile court, reportedly criticizing the Juvenile Waiver Law, arguing that the system should be less focused on punishment than rehabilitation to prevent the development of a criminal population in the first place ("Spared a Life Term," 2000; Bradsher, 2000). Others agreed. Amnesty International chose Nathaniel Abraham's face for the cover of a 1999 report claiming that our justice system is too harsh on juveniles ("Boy, 13, Convicted," 1999).

These issues are taken up in detail by N. Dickon Reppucci, Jaime L. Michel, and Jessica O. Kostelnik in Chapter 15. Specifically, as context for their discussion of juveniles' competencies in a variety of domains that are central to the role of defendant and how psychology can assist the courts in the assessment of these competencies, they track the growing trend for juvenile offenders to be tried in adult criminal court instead of family or juvenile court. Reppucci and colleagues review the historical and sociopolitical background that spawned this movement and the implications of putting juveniles into a court system designed for adults. They explain how, since its inception, the juvenile justice system has focused on rehabilitating youthful offenders. They build a powerful, science-based argument that the current trend for harsher juvenile justice policies is misguided and that juveniles, at least those younger than 16, should not be treated as adults.

If juveniles are to be treated in a manner consistent with the goal of rehabilitation, then their cases should be heard in juvenile courts, where they are supposed to receive social and psychological services. There is much concern about the short- and long-term negative psychological effects resulting from juveniles' experiences within the legal system and whether juveniles' mental health needs are being met sufficiently in the juvenile system. The legal system failed to address Nathaniel Abraham's needs in several ways, for example. First, although Nathaniel was suspected in many crimes before he was finally arrested for murder, he never received any assistance or counseling from the justice system (Bradsher, 1999). This was not the case of a neglected child who slipped through the cracks; Nathaniel's mother claimed that she was repeatedly denied assistance when she asked for help from the police (Bradsher, 1999). The police, however, claimed that they tried to get help for Nathaniel by notifying the prosecutor's office about him and by asking the juvenile courts to place Nathaniel in its Youth Assistance Program (Bradsher, 1999). Regardless, Nathaniel's needs were not addressed. Second, the treatment Nathaniel received at the detention center where he awaited trial (a center infamous for serious problems; Kurth & Jackson, 2000; Pardo, 2002) may have been inadequate, even after the judge ordered more therapy sessions. Some fear that the environment at such centers not only ignores youths' mental health needs but also has the potential to inflict psychological damage. In fact, it appears that Nathaniel's sentence did little to rehabilitate him. Only 1 year after his 2007 release from detention, Nathaniel was arrested on drug charges and sentenced to 93 days in jail.

All of these issues fall into the domain of therapeutic jurisprudence, the examination of whether and how the law can be helpful or therapeutic in the life of an offender. How can the mental health needs of juvenile offenders be met within the legal system? Is it possible to rehabilitate youthful offenders through treatment and services? In Chapter 16, Patrick Tolan and Jennifer Anne Titus take up this discussion by reviewing their and others' work on the mental health needs of juvenile offenders. Specifically, these authors review the harmful effects of juvenile defendants' experiences in the legal system as well as the potential for policies and programs to address the mental health needs of juvenile offenders. Such knowledge is invaluable if we are to expect juveniles to exit the legal system with increased potential for contributing to society.

## Girl Offenders

Girls account for more than one-quarter of all juvenile arrests in America (Federal Bureau of Investigation, 2002). Many psychologists have become interested in factors that have contributed to the increasing crime trend among young girls. As the reader learns from Widom and Wilson (Chapter 13), criminal behavior among girls is sometimes the consequence of their own experiences of abuse. For example, Tracie English was convicted of first-degree manslaughter after she shot and killed her father, who she claimed had sexually and physically abused her for most of her life (American Lawyer/Court TV Library Service, 1991). Several years later, however, the governor of Kentucky commuted Tracie's sentence, and she was released on parole (Beattie & Shaughnessy, 2000). In 2007, she was given a full pardon along with several other women who had been convicted of killing their abusers (Kenning, 2007). Child abuse was also cited as a contributing factor in the case of 16-year-old Melinda Loveless, who brutally tortured and murdered 12-year-old Shanda Sharer. The Indiana Supreme Court declared that Melinda's own sexual abuse and her witnessing of her sisters' sexual abuse at the hands of their father should be considered mitigating factors in her sentencing, because those experiences "produce in the developing and dependent child a perverse view of human relationships which made her incapable of recognizing or responding to the pain of others" (*Loveless v. State*, 1994).

Of course, a history of child sexual abuse is not always the root of girls' violent behavior. In Chapter 17, James Garbarino, Kathryn Levene, Margaret Walsh, and Sacha M. Coupet consider the complex constellation of social circumstances that lead to delinquency in girls. They elaborate on the plight of girls who are involved in the legal system as offenders, describe their pathway to crime, and discuss how their needs and circumstances are both different from and the same as those of boys. They provide an example of a treatment program that may be useful in getting girls back on track toward productive lives.

## Perceptions of Juveniles

The ultimate outcome of a legal case will depend not only on actual guilt or innocence but also on the perceived guilt or innocence of a juvenile defendant. As just mentioned, Tracie English was convicted by a jury, who presumably did not find her credible. Yet she was pardoned by a governor who must have perceived the case facts differently. At Nathaniel Abraham's sentencing hearing, the lead defense attorney commented that Nathaniel appeared much older at 13 years than he had as an 11-year-old boy whose prison uniform was too big for him when he was arrested (Robinson, 1999). Would Nathanial's sentence have been as harsh if he still appeared as young at his trial as when he was arrested? Beliefs about Marty Tankleff's guilt were influenced by Detective McCready's perceptions that he was not grieving appropriately.

Perceptions matter throughout a case: The perceptions formed by the first police to arrive at a crime scene determine the course of an investigation; the perceptions formed by prosecutors determine charges filed in a case; the perceptions formed by a judge determine the dispositions levied in juvenile court, whether a case is waived to adult court, and the sentences given in adult court; and the perceptions formed by jurors determine the verdict (and sometimes the sentence) in adult criminal court. In Chapter 18, Margaret C. Stevenson, Cynthia J. Najdowski, Bette L. Bottoms, and Tamara M. Haegerich provide the first comprehensive review of the new but growing body of psychological research on adults' perceptions of child defendants in criminal court. They consider factors that can influence adults' perceptions of juvenile offenders, including juveniles' race, age, gender, history of abuse, and intellectual disability; jurors' gender and preexisting stereotypes about juvenile offenders; and evidence and trial factors such as the presence or absence of confession evidence. It is important to understand these factors to appreciate the full spectrum of forces that can divert the course of justice in a case and to use this knowledge in planning interventions, such as extended voir dire, expert testimony designed to educate jurors, or modified jury instructions.

## International Perspectives on Juvenile Offenders

On August 19, 2008, Reza Hejazi was hanged in an Iranian prison for stabbing a man in a fight. Hejazi was only 15 years old at the time of the murder (Fathi, 2008). This execution was allowed under Iran's Islamic law, wherein boys are punishable from the age of 15 and girls from the age of 9. Iran is a signatory to the International Convention on Civil and Political Rights and the United Nations Convention on the Rights of the Child, neither of which allow the execution of anyone younger than 18 years of age. The United States (in company with only Somalia) has not even signed the Convention on the Rights of the Child, and until very recently youth in the United States who committed crimes when they were younger than 18 years could be sent to death row.

Many countries have considered the human rights issues involved when children and youth commit crime, and internationally there are numerous models of legal approaches to juvenile offenses. Consideration of these systems is clearly needed as the United States and other countries strive for better policy to accommodate child offenders. John Petrila provides this global perspective in Chapter 19. He discusses international standards as well as recent international developments in juvenile justice, making it clear what the United States can learn from other countries and what other countries can learn from the United States in improving the legal response to offenses of children and youth.

## Juvenile Offenders: The Big Picture

In the final chapter, Christopher Slobogin provides an important legal perspective on juvenile justice that serves to integrate the chapters in the second part of the book. He describes four ideal visions of legal response to juvenile offenders: the rehabilitative vision, the adult retribution model, the diminished retribution view, and the individual prevention vision. He then relates these visions to each of the chapters about juvenile offenders. This broadthinking, legally sound commentary provides readers with a wealth of ideas about the implications that should be drawn from research and applied to legal practice and policy and about what is an appropriate agenda for future research that addresses ecologically valid questions of importance when children enter the legal system as offenders.

## CONCLUSION

The cases we have described are only a few examples that illustrate the legal and psychological issues that arise when children and youth are involved in the legal system as victims, witnesses, and offenders. The legal system is complex and often challenging to negotiate, even for intellectually and emotionally mature adults. Numerous factors must be taken into account when working with child victims and child witnesses, such as the accuracy of their memory, their knowledge of the legal system, their emotional needs and level of comfort, and social (e.g., family) forces that surround the children. Similarly, child offenders must be understood in terms of why they offend and, when they do, their competency to navigate the legal system, including police interrogations and courts designed for adults. The issues we highlighted in this introduction are discussed further in the chapters to come, with each chapter providing psychological insights into potential solutions to difficulties that arise when children enter the legal system. Of course, our book cannot cover all of the issues relevant to child victims, child witnesses, and child offenders. Much more research is needed to examine many addi-

tional issues related to children's involvement in the legal system, including
their participation in dependency court hearings, effects of failed foster care,
children's psychological transformation from victims to offenders, and child
victims' increased risk for future victimization (e.g., Arata, 2000; Krinsky
& Rodriguez, 2006; Widom, Czaja, & Dutton, 2008). Even so, this volume
serves as a much-needed forum for information exchange among researchers and professionals interested in issues relating to children and the law
and who share the goal of creating a deeper understanding of how the court
system can better serve and meet the needs of child victims, child witnesses,
and child offenders.

## REFERENCES

American Lawyer/Court TV Video Library Service. (1991). *Kentucky v. English trial story* [Film]. Available from Courtroom Television Network, 600
Third Avenue, New York, NY 10016.

Arata, C. M. (2000). From child victim to adult victim: A model for predicting
sexual revictimization. *Child Maltreatment, 5*, 28–38.

Bailey, R. L., & Audi, T. (1999, November 6). Troubled and alone, Abraham
eluded help: Safety net failed to catch problems as boy headed down wrong
path. *Detroit Free Press*, p. 1A.

Beattie, L. E., & Shaughnessy, M. A. (2000). *Sisters in pain: Battered women
fight back*. Lexington: University Press of Kentucky.

Bloomekatz, A. B., Dimassa, C. M., & Blankstein, A. (2008, June 21). Boy's
abuse was no secret. *Los Angeles Times*. Retrieved January 15, 2009, from
*articles.latimes.com/2008/jun/21/local/me-abuse21*.

Boy, 13, convicted of second-degree murder. (1999, November 17). *Chicago
Tribune*, p. 19.

Bradsher, K. (1999, November 23). Need for counseling unmet in boy who
became a killer. *New York Times*, p. A14.

Bradsher, K. (2000, January 14). Boy who killed gets 7 years; judge says law is
too harsh. *New York Times*, p. A1.

City News Service. (2008, June 17). Woman to face charges in abuse of boy.
*Long Beach Press Telegram*.

CNN. (2002, July 23). Man charged with murder in Samantha case. Retrieved
January 15, 2009, from *archives.cnn.com/2002/us/07/22/girl.abducted/
index.html*.

Fathi, N. (2008, August 28). Iranian execution revives debate over minors.
*New York Times*. Retrieved September 24, 2008, from *www.nytimes.
com/2008/08/21/world/middleeast/21iran.html*.

Federal Bureau of Investigation. (2002). *Crime in the United States—2001*.
Washington, DC: U.S. Department of Justice.

Finkelhor, D., & Jones, L. M. (2006). Why have child maltreatment and child victimization declined? *Journal of Social Issues, 62,* 685–716.

Hesketh, T., Hong, Z. S., & Lynch, M. A. (2000). Child abuse in China: The views and experiences of child health professionals. *Child Abuse and Neglect, 24,* 867–872.

Jenkins, L. (2002, April 28). Tragedy of Ting Ting shows child-abuse failings. *South China Morning Post,* p. 6.

Kenning, C. (2007, December 10). Some abused women get pardons. *The Courier-Journal,* p. 1A.

Krinsky, M. A., & Rodriguez, J. (2006). Giving voice to the voiceless—Enhancing youth participation in court proceedings. *Nevada Law Journal, 6,* 1302–1314.

Kurth, J., & Jackson, I. (2000, December 26). Problems mount at juvenile center. *The Detroit News,* pp. A1, A13.

Loveless v. State, 642 N.E.2d 974 (1994).

Pardo, S. (2002, December 5). Feds investigate juvenile center—Maxey probe focus is alleged civil rights violations. *Detroit News,* p. B1.

People v. Abraham, 234 Mich. App 640; 599 NW2d 736 (1999).

People v. Tankleff, 606 N.Y.S.2d 707 (1993).

Redlich, A. D., & Goodman, G. S. (2003). Taking responsibility for an act not committed: The influence of age and suggestibility. *Law and Human Behavior, 27,* 141–156.

Robinson, B. (1999, September 11). 13- year-old—and Michigan juvenile law—under fire in murder trial. *Court TV archives.* Retrieved August 22, 2007, from *www.courttv.com/archive/trials/abraham/101999_ctv.html.*

Spared a life term, killer at age 11 sent to a juvenile center. (2000, January 14). *Chicago Tribune,* p. 3.

U.S. Department of Health and Human Services. (2009). *Child maltreatment 2007.* Washington, DC: Author.

Widom, C. S., Czaja, S. J., & Dutton, M. A. (2008). Childhood victimization and lifetime revictimization. *Child Abuse and Neglect, 32,* 785–796.

# PART I

# CHILDREN AS VICTIMS AND WITNESSES

# Chapter 2

# Abuse Disclosure
## *What Adults Can Tell*

Thomas D. Lyon

W hether abused children are reluctant to disclose abuse is currently the subject of some controversy (Pipe, Lamb, Orbach, & Cederborg, 2007). The resolution of the controversy has implications for assessing the truthfulness of children's reports. If children are not reluctant to disclose abuse, then a child who denies abuse has not been abused. If children are reluctant to disclose abuse, then denial is evidence against abuse, but it is not conclusive evidence. Reluctance is thus an important factor in assessing the truth of abuse allegations when the alleged victim has been inconsistent in alleging abuse.

Studies examining disclosure rates among children believed to have been abused provide some guidance in understanding children's reluctance to disclose, but they are necessarily hampered by the fact that corroborative evidence for sexual abuse is often lacking. This leads to two problems. First, some claims of sexual abuse may be false. Second, sexually abused children who never disclose their abuse are unlikely to be suspected of being abused ("suspicion bias") and unlikely to be substantiated as having been abused ("substantiation bias"). In earlier work (Lyon, 2007), I examined children known to have been abused without reliance on disclosure to derive realistic assessments of how likely abused children are to disclose abuse. Disclosure rates routinely ran less than 50% among children whose abuse was first suspected because of external evidence of abuse (e.g., gonorrhea). These children can confidently be said to have been abused, thus solving the false allegation problem, and were neither suspected of being abused nor substantiated as having been abused based on disclosure, thus solving the sus-picion and substantiation bias problem.

The fact that substantiated samples of child sexual abuse are made up of children uncommonly willing to disclose abuse has two implications for interviewers. First, if a child who has not previously disclosed abuse denies abuse when first questioned, one cannot say with confidence that suspicions of abuse are unfounded. A subsequent disclosure must be taken seriously and not simply dismissed as the product of suggestion or coercion. On the other hand, it is neither necessary nor wise to ask highly leading questions to elicit reports of abuse from the children seen for evaluation, because most children have previously disclosed and are likely to disclose again (Ceci, Kulkofsky, Klemfuss, Sweeney, & Bruck, 2007). Indeed, it is doubt-ful whether highly leading questions are ever justified, because they risk both creating false allegations and tainting true allegations.

Responding to my argument, advocates of the view that reluctance is uncommon among abused children have challenged research that finds high rates of nondisclosure and recantation as nonrepresentative of abuse victims (London, Bruck, Wright, & Ceci, 2008). They assert, for example, that poor African American children are uncommonly reluctant to dis-close abuse and that this could explain the high rates of denial among children with gonorrhea. Although their claims are subject to question, their call for representative samples of abused children is apt, because a primary concern with research on clinical samples of children believed to have been abused is precisely that they are unrepresentative of abused children in general.

In this chapter, I review population surveys that ask respondents about childhood abuse. These surveys provide support for the proposition that most sexual abuse is not disclosed during childhood, and that, indeed, dis-closure is difficult even for older respondents, and particularly so in cases of intrafamilial abuse.

Surveys enjoy a number of advantages. First, their goal is to question a representative cross-section of the population about their abuse experi-ences and ask whether and when they previously disclosed their abuse. Sec-ond, they are unlikely to elicit false disclosures of abuse. Respondents who acknowledge abuse in population surveys indicate that only about 10% of the abuse they disclosed was ever reported to authorities (Martin, Ander-son, Romans, Mullen, & O'Shea, 1993; Russell, 1983; Smith et al., 2000). Therefore, their reports are unlikely to have been the product of having been suggestively questioned as children by biased adults (either officials or per-haps parents hoping for official intervention). Moreover, only a very small percentage (2%) of women in population surveys who acknowledge abuse report having remembered abuse with the help of a therapist (Wilsnack,

Wonderlich, Kristjanson, Vogeltanz-Holm, & Wilsnack, 2002). Hence, their reports are also unlikely to be the product of suggestion through recovered memory therapy (Geraerts et al., 2009). Third, unlike clinical samples, which enlist participants who already self-identified as former victims, population surveys are potentially able to identify former victims who have never previously disclosed their abuse.

However, to the extent that former abuse victims never disclose their victimization or are inconsistent in their willingness or ability to disclose, population surveys may fall short. Nonreporting of abuse, or "survey reluctance," will have several ill effects. First, estimates of the prevalence of sexual abuse will be biased downward by survey reluctance (Ceci et al., 2007). Second, to the extent that survey reluctance is caused by the same factors that inhibit disclosure more generally, survey reluctance will bias upward estimates of the proportion of abuse victims who previously disclosed their abuse.

This second point has not been generally recognized and, therefore, deserves some explanation. It merely requires the assumption that adults who have previously disclosed abuse are more likely to disclose abuse to a surveyor than adults who have never previously disclosed abuse. If this assumption is true, then adults who acknowledge abuse to surveyors will be disproportionately likely to be those who have previously disclosed. As a result, survey reluctance will lead to inflated estimates of prior disclosure.

As we shall see, survey reluctance offers an alternative explanation for the common finding that younger adults report lower rates of abuse than older adults. Although this is sometimes interpreted as evidence that abuse is declining, it can also reflect differences in survey reluctance between younger and older adults. Moreover, survey reluctance will provide an explanation for the fact that younger respondents often report very high rates of prior disclosure, as high or even higher than older adults. Such a finding flies in the face of logic: Prior disclosure should be higher among older adults because they have had more time to disclose. However, if younger respondents exhibit greater survey reluctance, then younger respondents who acknowledge abuse will be disproportionately likely to have disclosed abuse before the survey.

Hence, this review of population surveys will alleviate some representativeness problems and some false allegation problems, but the false denial problem will remain. Nevertheless, a careful analysis will provide some insights into questions regarding the willingness of abuse victims to disclose their victimization. Most important, despite survey reluctance, the survey research will reveal the difficulties abuse victims face in disclosing. Moreover, survey reluctance is itself evidence of these difficulties.

## OVERVIEW OF THE RESEARCH

I identified seven studies in which representative samples of adults were questioned about whether they had been sexually abused in childhood and when and whether they had disclosed their abuse (see Table 2.1). As can be seen, delayed disclosures are common, and a large percentage of adults across studies report never having told anyone about their abuse before the survey. The one exception is Fergusson, Lynskey, and Horwood's (1996) sample of 18-year-olds. I return to this study later.

I also identified five large-scale surveys of college students (see Table 2.1). College students are quite young. Because they have been given less time to disclose, their nondisclosure rate ought to be higher than that among surveyed older adults. Although there is clear evidence for delayed disclosure, the percentage who had never disclosed is no higher than in the adult population surveys.

College samples have some of the advantages of population surveys, because they include students for whom there are no preexisting suspicions of abuse. However, researchers arguing over the harmful effects of sexual abuse have noted that college students tend to be higher functioning than the general population (Duncan, 2000). How might this affect sexual abuse disclosure? If nondisclosure in general, and nondisclosure of intrafamilial abuse in particular, is associated with poor functioning, then college enrollment might screen out delayed disclosers and nondisclosers. Hence, one must be somewhat cautious in interpreting these numbers.

I found two representative samples of minors questioned about abuse (see Table 2.1). Surveys of children should find higher nondisclosure rates because they are being questioned about abuse that may still be occurring. However, the rates of nondisclosure are not appreciably higher than those of the adult population surveys.

Overall, there is clear support for the proposition that a large proportion of abuse victims never disclose their victimization until questioned by surveyors. However, the percentage of survey respondents who report having never disclosed their abuse does not clearly decrease with age. Indeed, the 10- to 16-year-olds questioned by Boney-McCoy and Finkelhor (1995) reported that 35% of the abuse they disclosed had been reported to authorities, several times the rate found in population surveys of older respondents (Martin et al., 1993; Russell, 1983; Smith et al., 2000). One possible explanation for this curious finding is that younger respondents exhibit higher rates of survey reluctance and this, in turn, generates inflated estimates of the likelihood that abuse was disclosed. I first review the evidence for survey reluctance among survey respondents generally and then consider the evidence that younger respondents are more reluctant to disclose abuse than older respondents.

**TABLE 2.1. Surveys in which Respondents Were Asked about Prior Disclosure of Sexual Abuse**

| Source | Year | N | Population | No prior disclosure | Delayed disclosure |
|---|---|---|---|---|---|
| Population surveys | | | | | |
| Adults | | | | | |
| Finkelhor et al. | 1990 | 2,626 | U.S. | 33% women, 42% men | 59% women, 57% men did not disclose within 1 year |
| Anderson et al. | 1993 | 3,000 | Women, New Zealand | 28% | * |
| Laumann et al. | 1994 | 3,432 | U.S. | * | 74% women, 78% men did not disclose in childhood |
| Fergusson et al. | 1996 | 1,019 | 18-year-old birth cohort, New Zealand | 13% | * |
| Fleming | 1997 | 6,000 | Women, Australia | 48% | 83% did not disclose within 1 year |
| Wyatt et al. | 1999 | 338 | Women, Los Angeles County | 53% African American, 60% White | * |
| Smith et al. | 2000 | 4,009 | U.S. | 28% | 48% did not disclose within 5 years |
| Minors | | | | | |
| Boney-McCoy & Finkelhor | 1995 | 2,000 | 10- to 16-year-olds, U.S. | 36% | * |
| Kogan | 2004 | 4,023 | 12- to 17-year-old women | 26% | * |
| Convenience samples: Students | | | | | |
| Landis | 1956 | 1,800 | U.S. | * | 56% women, 73% men never disclosed to parents |
| Finkelhor | 1980 | 796 | 6 New England colleges and universities | * | 63% women, 75% men did not disclose "at the time" |
| Arata | 1998 | 800 | Women, southeastern U.S. university | * | 69% did not disclose "at the time" |
| Ullman & Filipas | 2005 | 733 | U.S. university | 33% | 64% did not disclose within 1 year |
| Bottoms et al. | 2007 | 1,411 | Women, 3 U.S. colleges and universities | 22% | * |

*Note.* Asterisks (*) indicate information not reported.

23

## SURVEY RELUCTANCE

Three lines of research support the proposition that survey respondents are often reluctant to disclose abuse. First, substantiated abuse is often subsequently denied by survey respondents. Second, more persistent questioning elicits more reports of abuse. Third, respondents surveyed repeatedly are often inconsistent in acknowledging that abuse occurred.

A standard finding in victimization research is that large percentages of respondents known to have been victimized on the basis of official records, such as police reports, hospital records, and court records, will deny it when subsequently questioned (e.g., one-third of rape cases known to police are not reported to surveyors when questioned within 1 year; Turner, 1972). Reviewing the research on retrospective reports of childhood maltreatment, Hardt and Rutter (2004) concluded that "the universal finding [is] that, even with well-documented serious abuse or neglect, about a third of individuals do not report its occurrence when specifically asked about it in adult life" (p. 240).[1]

These rates are likely conservative estimates of the likelihood that former abuse victims fail to disclose their victimization. To the extent that documented childhood abuse is dependent on children's willingness to disclose abuse (Lyon, 2007), studies on documented abuse will enroll large percentages of disclosing children. If there is any consistency between one's willingness to disclose as a child and one's willingness to disclose as an adult, these studies will disproportionately enroll adults who are more willing to disclose.

A second source of evidence for survey reluctance comes from the fact that more respondents acknowledge abuse if more questions, including more direct questions, are asked about sexual abuse. This was first recognized by Russell (1983) in piloting her survey of San Franciscan women, and confirmed by Wilsnack and colleagues in their nationally representative survey of 711 American women (Wilsnack et al., 2002) in which they found that the percentage of respondents reporting abuse doubled (from 15 to 31%) when they asked a greater number of specific questions about sexually abusive experiences. Several reviewers have noted that the most important determinant of prevalence rates in retrospective surveys appear to be the number of questions asked (Finkelhor, 1994; Hardt & Rutter, 2004), an observation formally confirmed in a meta-analysis by Bolen and Scannapieco (1999). Two of the studies examining adult recall of confirmed child abuse cases also had similar findings: Williams, Siegel, and Pomeroy (2000) found that 14 questions were required to elicit all disclosures, with 13% of the abuse disclosures requiring more than five direct questions, and Goodman and colleagues (2003) found that among the nondisclosers, about half (12/26) reported abuse when questioned again.

Of course, to some extent, nonreporting and greater reporting with more persistent questioning reflect memory failure rather than reluctance (Williams et al., 2000). In many cases, however, respondents will subsequently explain that they deliberately withheld information (Femina et al., 1990). A third line of evidence answers the contention that subsequent nonreporting of substantiated abuse is due to forgetting and further supports survey reluctance: Even with shorter delays between initial disclosure of abuse and subsequent questioning, substantial percentages of respondents inconsistently report abuse. Fry and colleagues (1996) interviewed female gynecological clinic patients complaining of chronic pelvic pain at two time periods, 3 months apart. The authors found that 26% of the abuse mentioned at the first interview was not mentioned at the second interview (41/155) and that 16% of the abuse mentioned at the second interview was not mentioned at the first interview (22/136). Although one might suspect that women omitted abuse that was relatively trivial and, therefore, less memorable, the authors found that the "effect is even more striking when the reports of severe (contact) abuse are examined" (p. 727). McGee, Wolfe, Yuen, Wilson, and Carnochan (1995) questioned adolescents from the open caseload of a child protection agency who were substantiated as sexually abused and found that 19% (12/63) denied sexual abuse when individually questioned by two researchers.

## Survey Reluctance among Younger Respondents

If victims surveyed as adults falsely deny abuse, then the rate of abuse will be understated. Evidence that younger respondents are more reluctant to acknowledge abuse can thus be found in the fact that surveys frequently find lower rates of reported abuse among younger respondents. Reviewing five community surveys conducted from 1983 to 1990, Finkelhor (1994) noted that "all five show slightly lower rates for the youngest age group" (p. 44). Although lower rates of abuse among younger respondents in cross-sectional studies are sometimes interpreted as evidence that abuse is declining, Finkelhor noted that "the youngest women may not yet have enough distance from childhood events to feel comfortable talking about them" (p. 44). Wyatt, Loeb, Solis, Carmona, and Romero (1999) directly tested the possibility that there was a decline in sexual abuse from 1984 to 1994 by comparing the rates of their 1994 survey with those of a similar 1984 survey and found no such evidence. Hence, differences in apparent prevalence among age groups in the 1980s are likely to have more to do with differences in reluctance rather than differences in actual prevalence. (Some of the evidence that sexual abuse declined during the 1990s is not subject to this confound because it does not rely on cross-sectional analyses of survey data; Finkelhor & Jones, 2006.)

False denials are also likely to affect the probability that survey respondents who acknowledge abuse will be those who previously disclosed their abuse. It is reasonable to suppose that victims most reluctant to disclose abuse to others will subsequently be most reluctant to disclose abuse to surveyors. If victims who never disclosed their abuse are also less likely to disclose abuse to surveyors, then surveys will miss those victims. As a result, survey respondents who do acknowledge abuse will disproportionately be those abuse victims who previously disclosed their abuse. Hence, underreporting of abuse among younger respondents will mean that among younger respondents who do acknowledge abuse, there will be *higher* rates of reported disclosure. The between-study comparisons are consistent with this effect; one sees relatively high rates of reported disclosure among younger abuse victims. However, because other variables affect disclosure between studies (such as differences in the number of questions), within-study comparisons are more reliable. Here, too, there is some evidence of higher rates of reported disclosure among younger respondents in the surveys of adults: Fleming (1997) grouped the youngest respondents into the 18- to 24-year age category and found a higher percentage of lifetime reported disclosure (83%) compared with 59% for 25- to 35-year-olds, with further declines thereafter. Anderson, Martin, Mullen, Romans, and Herbison (1993) failed to find statistically significant differences in reported disclosure rates based on the age of respondent but grouped the younger respondents into 18- to 39-year-olds, a very large age range (even then, their lifetime disclosure rate was somewhat higher than that of older respondents: 75% vs. 66%). Again, recall that one would expect reported disclosure rates to increase with age because older respondents have had more time to disclose.[2]

The best evidence that high rates of reported prior disclosure among younger respondents is due to reluctance to disclose on surveys can be found in the longitudinal data collected by Fergusson and colleagues (1996). Recall (see Table 2.1) that only 13% of the 18-year-olds acknowledging abuse in that study stated that they had never previously disclosed abuse. At first glance, one might suppose that these young respondents were particularly forthcoming about abuse. On the other hand, perhaps many abuse victims who had never disclosed abuse did not disclose when surveyed. As discussed, one effect of false denial is that prevalence rates will be understated. Fergusson and colleagues (1996) found relatively low prevalence rates and recognized the danger that their young respondents were not ready to disclose. Three years later, Fergusson and colleagues questioned the same individuals when they were 21 (Fergusson, Horwood, & Woodward, 2000). Remarkably, among the respondents who reported sexual abuse at 21, 45% had failed to report abuse at 18 (37/83). Conversely, among the respondents who reported sexual abuse at 18 years of age, more than half (54%) failed to report abuse at age 21 (54/100). In other words, more than half of the respondents who reported abuse at some point did so in only one of the two interviews. The inconsistencies across time suggest that young adults are indecisive with respect to their willingness to disclose abuse. Moreover, the inconsistencies cannot be attributable to uncertainties about whether the reported behaviors were, in fact, sexual abuse, as some have claimed (London, Bruck, Ceci, & Shuman, 2005), because respondents were, if anything, less consistent in their reports of more serious abuse (Fergusson et al., 2000).

To summarize the argument thus far, there is general agreement among researchers that a large percentage of adults sexually victimized as children never disclose the abuse to anyone during their childhood. Prior disclosure is often reported by larger proportions of younger respondents, but this is probably attributable to the fact that a large proportion of younger respondents who experienced abuse are not ready to disclose it to the surveyors. Because those nonreporters are disproportionately abuse victims who have never disclosed their abuse to anyone, their exclusion inflates prior disclosure rates. Reluctance is understated because reluctance makes itself invisible.

It may occur to the reader that this methodological point is analogous to the problem one confronts in examining disclosure rates among children questioned about their abuse. Debates over the need for repeated interviews or direct questions in eliciting abuse reports from children reappear with respect to questioning adult survey respondents about childhood abuse. Disclosure of sexual abuse is never easy, even among adults guaranteed anonymity and questioned long after the abuse has ended.

## Do Survey Respondents Forget Having Disclosed?

One can speculate that there are other possible explanations for differences in the extent to which respondents report having disclosed their abuse. One possibility is that many respondents have simply forgotten that they reported their abuse to others (London et al., 2005, 2008). There is anecdotal evidence that some claims of recovered memory of abuse turn out to have been disclosed to others at the time that the victim claims not to have remembered the abuse (Schooler, Ambadar, & Bendiksen, 1997).

There are a couple of problems with this possibility. Speculation makes it difficult to generate any kind of estimate regarding the likelihood that forgetting of prior disclosure occurs. Moreover, if one is allowed to speculate, then it is just as easy to imagine ways in which respondents' recall of reports would be exaggerated. If one worries about false memories of abuse, then one should also worry about false memories of disclosure. Perhaps more realistically, one should worry about the informativeness of the disclosure that an adult recalls. There is evidence that child disclosures are often less than explicit descriptions of sexual activity ("things were not right at home"; Palmer, Brown, Rae-Grant, & Loughlin, 1999, p. 269). In Ullman and Filipas's (2005) college sample, 75% of the respondents who had previously disclosed abuse characterized their disclosures as a "vague, brief or general reference" (p. 774). This problem replicates a problem one encounters in research on children's disclosure. As stated by Sas and Cunningham, "Sometimes the failure of an adult to catch on to the children's meaning stemmed from the vague terms used by children, words which do not match adult language of sexual abuse" (1995, p. 138). Often children's "disclosures" are, in fact, inconclusive, and counting them as disclosures exaggerates abused children's informativeness (Dubowitz, Black, & Harrington, 1992).

## Victim–Perpetrator Relationship and Disclosure

The assertion that relationships influence the likelihood that victims report their victimization is not new. The same study that found high rates of nondisclosure of rape cases reported to the police found that subsequent nondisclosure to interviewers was three times as likely when the offender was known to the victim as when the offender was a stranger (Turner, 1972). Conversely, it is a standard finding that rape and other sexual offenses committed against adults and reported to surveyors were less likely to have been reported to the police when the victim was close to the offender (Fisher, Daigle, Cullen, & Turner, 2003). Indeed, analysis of Kinsey's large (but possibly nonrepresentative) sample of adult women found the highest rate of reported prior disclosure in the "single-accidental cases," cases in which children were assaulted on one occasion by someone with whom they had no previous contact (Gagnon, 1965, p. 183).

The pattern of results with respect to the victim–perpetrator relationship has to be assessed with caution because the problems noted earlier with respect to survey reluctance, and its effects on both estimated prevalence and rates of reported disclosure, recur. Survey reluctance may be greatest when respondents are asked to discuss intrafamilial abuse. Discussing their sample of 10- to 16-year-olds, Finkelhor and Dzuiba-Leatherman (1994) commented that "it is probably difficult for children even under the best of circumstances to disclose especially intimate victimizations and family abuse to a stranger interviewer, especially if they are under any risk of retaliation by the perpetrator. This is suggested, for example, by the relatively low rate of intrafamily sexual abuse disclosed in this study compared with what is reported by adults retrospectively" (p. 418). Similarly, Martin and colleagues (1993) found, in their interviews with women surveyed via mail by Anderson and colleagues (1993), that "a small core of women had suffered experiences of at least genital touching by a close family member, but chose not to mention the episode to an interviewer. Fifteen percent of women who admitted an incident [child sexual abuse] involving a close family member, reported this only in writing" (p. 389). If respondents' greater reluctance to disclose intrafamilial abuse extends to their survey responses, then this will both decrease the apparent prevalence of intrafamilial abuse and potentially inflate the extent to which acknowledged victims of intrafamilial abuse report having disclosed.

Despite this confound, there is nevertheless clear evidence that disclosure is less likely the closer the relationship between the victim and the perpetrator. Four of the five representative surveys that tested for the effects of relationships on disclosure found that the relationship mattered, with closer relationships leading to lower rates of reported disclosure (Anderson et al., 1993; Kogan, 2004; Smith et al., 2000; Wyatt & Newcomb, 1990; but see Fleming, 1997). Moreover, a study examining the same sample as Smith et al. found that reporting to the police was more likely when the perpetrator was a stranger (Hanson, Resnick, Saunders, Kilpatrick, & Best, 1999). Three of these studies utilized a multivariate design (Kogan, 2004; Smith et al., 2000; Wyatt & Newcomb, 1990), which enabled the researchers to control for possible confounding by interactions between relationship and other characteristics of abuse that might affect reporting.

In contrast, only one of the studies questioning college students found an effect of victim–perpetrator relationship (Landis, 1956). However, although a statistical test comparing all four relationship groups (stranger, acquaintance, relative or stepparent, and parent) was not significant, Arata (1998) found a 10% reporting rate for relatives versus 34% for nonrelatives, a difference that would be statistically significant if it were tested directly, $\chi^2(1)$ = 13.16, $p < .001$. It is probably for this reason that other researchers have cited Arata as supporting such a relation (Hanson et al., 1999).

It seems clear that the best adult evidence supports what is now well accepted in the literature examining children's disclosure rates (London et al., 2008; Lyon, 2007): Relationships matter. Although now conceding this point with respect to research on child samples, London and colleagues (2005, 2008) have argued that the adult evidence is mixed on this point (with five studies finding no effect and two or three studies finding an effect). To their credit, they acknowledged that one must exercise "caution in accepting these null findings because of the relatively small sample sizes" (London et al., 2008, p. 33). Beyond this caveat, however, they made little attempt to assess the quality of the research, cited predominantly clinical samples, and overlooked some of the research reviewed here.[3]

## CONCLUSION

Studying the dynamics of abuse disclosure is a tricky business. Estimates of disclosure are almost inevitably biased by reluctance to disclose. In the case of child samples, this means that we exaggerate the likelihood that abuse victims disclose abuse if we examine samples of children suspected of and substantiated as abuse victims based on interview disclosure. In the case of survey respondents, we similarly exaggerate the likelihood of prior disclosure if we examine samples of respondents known to have been abuse victims because they disclose to surveyors.

Nevertheless, the survey literature shows clear evidence of nondisclosure and supports the link between intrafamilial abuse and reluctance to disclose. The methodological difficulties, such as the evidence for greater reluctance to disclose among younger respondents, themselves support the claim that children find disclosure difficult. Although surveys regarding the disclosure of child abuse have emphasized sexual abuse, similar conclusions are warranted with respect to physical abuse (see, e.g., Bottoms, Rudnicki, & Epstein, 2007; Widom & Shepard, 1996). Indeed, as mentioned earlier, the dynamics discussed in this chapter mirror the larger problem of questioning people about experiences that are intensely embarrassing and painful to disclose.

These difficulties are of obvious importance to practitioners who question children about abuse and researchers who study children's veracity. Practitioners should be cautious in assessing the reports of children who fail to disclose abuse or who inconsistently maintain that abuse occurred. It is obviously wrongheaded to assume that denial is an indicator that abuse occurred, but it is just as wrong to assume that denials conclusively rule out abuse. Unfortunately, practitioners have few tools to encourage disclosure among abused children that do not risk increasing the rate of false allegations. For their part, researchers should be cognizant of the need for questioning methods that increase the willingness of otherwise reluctant children to disclose. They may help create the tools for reassuring children without suggestion, whether those children are survey respondents, clinic patients, or the subject of social services and police investigation.

## ACKNOWLEDGMENT

Preparation of this chapter was supported by National Institute of Child and Human Development Grant No. HD047290-01A2.

## NOTES

1. See Femina, Yeager, and Lewis (1990): 30% (18/61) of incarcerated delinquents disclosing physical abuse questioned 9 years later denied or minimized abuse; Johnson, Cohen, Brown, Smailes, and Bernstein (1999): 74% (23/31) of a social services sample of maltreated children questioned 17 years later denied maltreat-

ment; Widom and Morris (1997): 37% (35/94) of a social services sample of sexually abused children questioned 20 years later denied all sexual abuse; but cf. Goodman et al. (2003): 10% (17/175) of a criminal court sample of sexually abused children questioned 13 years later denied all sexual abuse.

2. Because these data are cross-sectional rather than longitudinal, one cannot conclude that the higher rates of prior disclosure among younger respondents is evidence that victims are becoming more willing to disclose over time; this is the same error as the assertion that lower reported prevalence rates among younger respondents is evidence that sexual abuse is declining. Just as their longitudinal data showed no decrease in sexual abuse prevalence, Wyatt and colleagues (1999) also found no evidence of higher rates of disclosure in 1994 than in 1984.

3. In both articles, London and colleagues (2005, 2008) cite five negative findings (Arata, 1998; Kellogg & Hoffman, 1995; Kellogg & Huston, 1995; Lamb & Edgar-Smith, 1994; Roesler, 1994). As noted, Arata's (1998) findings support a relation between relationship and disclosure. None of the other studies are either representative surveys or large-scale surveys of respondents who had not previously self-identified as abuse victims. Furthermore, Lamb and Edgar-Smith's (1994) sample of 60 women contained no stranger molests whatsoever (p. 315) and the raw numbers are not presented. Interestingly, respondents had disclosed their abuse on average more than 16 times. Studies by Kellogg and Hoffman (1995) and Kellogg and Huston (1995) are, in fact, based on a single sample; the former tested the relation between disclosure and type of perpetrator, the latter the relation between disclosure to an adult and type of perpetrator. The raw numbers are not presented, and it is unclear what "type of perpetrator" entailed. Moreover, because 85% of the respondents had disclosed abuse, this reduced variability, making a statistical test of the relation between relationship and disclosure less powerful. Finally, Roesler (1994) did not, in fact, examine the relation between delay and disclosure, but rather examined the relation between age and disclosure and only compared incest with nonincest cases.

## REFERENCES

Anderson, J., Martin, J., Mullen, P., Romans, S., & Herbison, P. (1993). Prevalence of childhood sexual abuse experiences in a community sample of women. *Journal of the American Academy of Child and Adolescent Psychiatry, 32,* 911–919.

Arata, C. M. (1998). To tell or not to tell: Current functioning of child sexual abuse survivors who disclosed their victimization. *Child Maltreatment, 3,* 63–71.

Bolen, R. M., & Scannapieco, M. (1999). Prevalence of child sexual abuse: A corrective metanalysis. *Social Service Review, 73,* 281–313.

Boney-McCoy, S., & Finkelhor, D. (1995). Psychosocial sequelae of violent victimization in a national youth sample. *Journal of Consulting and Clinical Psychology, 63,* 726–736.

Bottoms, B. L., Rudnicki, A. G., & Epstein, M. A. (2007). A retrospective study of factors affecting the disclosure of childhood sexual and physical abuse. In M.-E. Pipe, M.-E. Lamb, Y. Orbach, & A.-C. Cederborg (Eds.), *Disclosing abuse: Delays, denials, retractions and incomplete accounts* (pp. 175–194). Mahwah, NJ: Erlbaum.

Ceci, S. J., Kulkofsky, S., Klemfuss, Z., Sweeney, C. D., & Bruck, M. (2007). Unwarranted assumptions about children's testimonial accuracy. *Annual Review of Clinical Psychology, 3,* 311–328.

Dubowitz, H., Black, M., & Harrington, D. (1992). The diagnosis of child sexual abuse. *American Journal of Diseases of Children, 146,* 668–693.

Duncan, R. (2000). Childhood maltreatment and college drop-out rates. *Journal of Interpersonal Violence, 15,* 987–995.

Femina, D. D., Yeager, C. A., & Lewis, D. O. (1990). Child abuse: Adolescent records vs. adult recall. *Child Abuse and Neglect, 14,* 227–231.

Fergusson, D. M., Lynskey, M. T., & Horwood, L. J. (1996). Childhood sexual abuse and psychiatric disorder in young adulthood: I. Prevalence of sexual abuse and factors associated with sexual abuse. *Journal of the American Academy of Child and Adolescent Psychiatry, 35,* 1355–1364.

Fergusson, D. M., Horwood, L. J., & Woodward, L. J. (2000). The stability of child abuse reports: A longitudinal study of the reporting behaviour of young adults. *Psychological Medicine, 30,* 529–544.

Finkelhor, D. (1980). Risk factors in the sexual victimization of children. *Child Abuse and Neglect, 4,* 265–273.

Finkelhor, D. (1994). Current information on the scope and nature of child sexual abuse. *Future of Children, 4,* 31–53.

Finkelhor, D., & Dzuiba-Leatherman, J. (1994). Children as victims of violence: A national survey. *Pediatrics, 94,* 413–420.

Finkelhor, D., Hotaling, G., Lewis, I. A., & Smith, C. (1990). Sexual abuse in a national survey of adult men and women: Prevalence, characteristics, and risk factors. *Child Abuse and Neglect, 14,* 19–28.

Finkelhor, D., & Jones, L. M. (2006). Why have child maltreatment and child victimization declined? *Journal of Social Issues, 62,* 685–716.

Fisher, B. S., Daigle, L. E., Cullen, F. T., & Turner, M. G. (2003). Reporting sexual victimization to the police and others: Results from a national-level study of college women. *Criminal Justice and Behavior, 30,* 6–38.

Fleming, J. M. (1997). Prevalence of childhood sexual abuse in a community sample of Australian women. *Medical Journal of Australia, 166,* 65–68.

Fry, R. P. W., Rozewicz, L. M., & Crisp, A. H. (1996). Interviewing for sexual abuse: Reliability and effect of interviewer gender. *Child Abuse and Neglect, 20,* 725–729.

Gagnon, J. H. (1965). Female child victims of sex offenses. *Social Problems, 13,* 176–192.

Geraerts, E., Lindsay, D. S., Merckelbach, H., Jelicic, M., Raymaekers, L., Arnold. M. M., et al. (2009). Cognitive mechanisms underlying recovered-memory experiences. *Psychological Science, 20,* 92–98.

Goodman, G. S., Ghetti, S., Quas, J. A., Edelstein, R. S., Alexander, K. W., Redlich, A. D., et al. (2003). A prospective study of memory for child sexual abuse: New findings relevant to the repressed-memory controversy. *Psychological Science, 14,* 113–118.

Hanson, R. F., Resnick, H. S., Saunders, B. E., Kilpatrick, D. G., & Best, C. (1999). Factors related to the reporting of childhood rape. *Child Abuse and Neglect, 23,* 559–569.

Hardt, J., & Rutter, M. (2004). Validity of adult retrospective reports of adverse childhood experiences: Review of the evidence. *Journal of Child Psychology and Psychiatry, 45,* 260–273.

Johnson, J. G., Cohen, P., Brown, J., Smailes, E. M., & Bernstein, D. P. (1999). Childhood maltreatment increases risk for personality disorders during early adulthood. *Archives of General Psychiatry, 56,* 600–606.

Kellogg, N. D., & Hoffman, T. J. (1995). Unwanted and illegal sexual experiences in childhood and adolescence. *Child Abuse and Neglect, 12,* 1457–1468.

Kellogg, N. D., & Huston, R. L. (1995). Unwanted sexual experiences in adolescents: Patterns of disclosure. *Clinical Pediatrics, 34,* 306–312.

Kogan, S. M. (2004). Disclosing unwanted sexual experiences: Results from a national sample of adolescent women. *Child Abuse and Neglect, 24,* 147–165.

Lamb, S., & Edgar-Smith, S. (1994). Aspects of disclosure: Mediators of outcome of childhood sexual abuse. *Journal of Interpersonal Violence, 9,* 307–326.

Landis, J. T. (1956). Experiences of 500 children with adult sexual deviation. *Psychiatric Quarterly Supplement, 30,* 91–109.

Laumann, E. O., Gagnon, J. H., Michael, R. T., & Michaels, S. (1994). *The social organization of sexuality: Sexual practices in the United States.* Chicago: University of Chicago Press.

London, K., Bruck, M., Ceci, S. J., & Shuman, D. W. (2005). Disclosure of child sexual abuse: What does the research tell us about the ways that children tell? *Psychology, Public Policy, and Law, 11,* 194–226.

London, K., Bruck, M., Wright, D. B., & Ceci, S. J. (2008). Review of the contemporary literature on how children report sexual abuse to others: Findings, methodological issues, and implications for forensic interviewers. *Memory, 16,* 29–47.

Lyon, T. D. (2007). False denials: Overcoming methodological biases in abuse disclosure research. In M. E. Pipe, M. E. Lamb, Y. Orbach, and A. C. Cederborg (Eds.), *Disclosing abuse: Delays, denials, retractions and incomplete accounts* (pp. 41–62). Mahwah, NJ: Erlbaum.

Martin, J., Anderson, J., Romans, S., Mullen, P., & O'Shea, M. (1993). Asking about child sexual abuse: Methodological implications of a two stage survey. *Child Abuse and Neglect, 17,* 383–392.

McGee, R. A., Wolfe, D. A., Yuen, S. A., Wilson, S. K., & Carnochan, J. (1995). The measurement of maltreatment: A comparison of approaches. *Child Abuse and Neglect, 19,* 233–249.

Palmer, S. E., Brown, R. A., Rae-Grant, N. I., & Loughlin, M. J. (1999). Responding to children's disclosure of familial abuse: What survivors tell us. *Child Welfare, 78,* 259–282.

Pipe, M.-E., Lamb, M. E., Orbach, Y., & Cederborg, A.-C. (2007). Seeking resolution in the disclosure wars: An overview. In M. E. Pipe, Y. Orbach, & A. Cederborg (Eds.), *Child sexual abuse: Disclosure, delay, and denial* (pp. 3–10). Mahwah, NJ: Erlbaum.

Roesler, T. A. (1994). Reactions to disclosure of childhood sexual abuse. *Journal of Nervous and Mental Disease, 182,* 618–624.

Russell, D. E. H. (1983). The incidence and prevalence of intrafamilial and extrafamilial sexual abuse of female children. *Child Abuse and Neglect, 7,* 133–146.

Sas, L. D., & Cunningham, A. H. (1995). *Tipping the balance to tell the secret: The public discovery of child sexual abuse.* London, Ontario: London Family Court Clinic.

Schooler, J. W., Ambadar, Z., & Bendiksen, M. A. (1997). A cognitive corroborative case. In J. D. Read & D. S. Lindsay (Eds.), *Recollections of trauma: Scientific research and clinical practice* (pp. 379–388). New York: Plenum.

Smith, D. W., Letourneau, E. J., Saunders, B. E., Kilpatrick, D. G., Resnick, H. S., & Best, C. L. (2000). Delay in disclosure of childhood rape: Results from a national survey. *Child Abuse and Neglect, 24,* 273–287.

Turner, A. (1972). *San Jose Methods Test of Known Crime Victims.* Washington, DC: U.S. Department of Justice, Law Enforcement Assistance Administration, National Institute of Law Enforcement and Criminal Justice.

Ullman, S. E., & Filipas, H. H. (2005). Gender differences in social reactions to abuse disclosures, post-abuse coping, and PTSD of child sexual abuse survivors. *Child Abuse and Neglect, 29,* 767–782.

Widom, C. S., & Morris, S. (1997). Accuracy of adult recollections of childhood victimization: Part 2. Childhood sexual abuse. *Psychological Assessment, 9,* 34–46.

Widom, C. S., & Shepard, R. L. (1996). Accuracy of adult recollection of childhood victimization: Part I. Childhood physical abuse. *Psychological Assessment, 8,* 412–421.

Williams, L. M., Siegel, J. A., & Pomeroy, J. J. (2000). Validity of women's self-reports of documented child sexual abuse. In A. A. Stone, J. S. Turkkan, C. A. Bachrach, J. B. Jobe, H. S. Kurtzman, & V. S. Cain (Eds.), *The science of self-report: Implications for research and practice* (pp. 211–226). Mahwah, NJ: Erlbaum.

Wilsnack, S., Wonderlich, S. A., Kristjanson, A. F., Vogeltanz-Holm, N. D., & Wilsnack, R. W. (2002). Self-reports of forgetting and remembering childhood sexual abuse in a nationally representative sample of US women. *Child Abuse and Neglect, 26,* 139–147.

Wyatt, G. E., Loeb, T. B., Solis, B., Carmona, J. V., & Romero, G. (1999). The prevalence and circumstances of child sexual abuse: Changes across a decade. *Child Abuse and Neglect, 23*, 45–60.

Wyatt, G. E., & Newcomb, M. (1990). Internal and external mediators of women's sexual abuse in childhood. *Journal of Consulting and Clinical Psychology, 58*, 758–767.

# Chapter 3

# Trauma and Memory

ANDREA FOLLMER GREENHOOT
SARAH L. BUNNELL

The involvement of child victims in legal proceedings raises important issues concerning children's memory and testimony about past victimizations. The goal of this chapter is to address questions that revolve around the nature of memory for traumatic experiences like victimization. For instance, how accurate and robust are memories for highly stressful or traumatic childhood experiences like abuse? How prevalent is complete forgetting of such experiences? Does trauma engender special, trauma-specific memory mechanisms (e.g., repression, dissociation)? Might chronic exposure to trauma and associated psychopathology lead to general alterations in memory functioning? There has been considerable scientific and public debate over these issues in the last two decades, and this controversy has prompted a profusion of research on children's memories for stressful events. Although much of this work has focused on nonmaltreated children's memories for one-time stressful experiences, an emerging literature has yielded information about chronically maltreated children's memories for childhood experiences and about the retention of memories for childhood traumatic experiences into adulthood. In this chapter, we discuss the psychological literature on memory for traumatic experiences. We begin with a brief overview of theoretical models of the relation between trauma and memory, followed by a review of the empirical evidence regarding the relations between trauma and memory in three contexts: (1) how normal, healthy children remember traumatic events; (2) how chronically maltreated children, especially those with psychopathology, remember traumatic events; and (3) how adults remember childhood victimization.

## MODELS OF TRAUMA AND MEMORY

A major point of contention in the literature on trauma and memory is the degree to which memory for traumatic events involves special mechanisms that operate in fundamentally different ways from those involved in the memory of nontraumatic experiences. A long-standing idea in the clinical literature is that memories of overwhelmingly stressful events are pushed out of awareness and forgotten through trauma-specific psychological defense mechanisms such as dissociation or repression (e.g., Freud, 1959; Freyd, DePrince, & Zurbriggen, 2001; Terr, 1994; van der Kolk, 1994). The resulting unconscious memories are thought to be indelible and may resurface intact, years later, in the proper retrieval context. Indeed, according to many of these models, the retrieval of submerged memories is critical to the resolution of current psychopathology. In contrast, many cognitive and developmental psychologists question the claim that memory for trauma is dissociated from "ordinary memory." Rather, these formulations suggest that there is considerable continuity in the processes involved in traumatic and nontraumatic memories, although standard memory processes could be attenuated or intensified by emotional processes (e.g., Ornstein, Ceci, & Loftus, 1998; Schooler & Eich, 2000). Even among these models, however, there are varied conceptualizations of stress–memory linkages. For example, some suggest that traumatic events are more memorable than "ordinary" events because they are more distinctive and salient (Howe, Toth, & Cicchetti, 2006). Others propose that traumatic memories involve an orchestration of standard memory mechanisms and special neurological mechanisms that are activated by emotions or stress. According to one such model, high levels of stress activate neurological mechanisms, such as amygdala-based processing, that lead to the formation of especially vivid and durable memories (Cahill, Gorski, & Le, 2003; McGaugh, 2002). A more complex view has been posited by Nadel and Jacobs (1998), who suggested that although trauma activates the amygdala and enhances memory for the emotional attributes of an event, it also disrupts the consolidation functions of the hippocampus, leading to the formation of fragmentary sensory memories.

Any analysis of memory for childhood trauma also requires a consideration of developmental change in memory functioning. First and foremost, the ability to provide coherent verbal recollections seems to emerge between 2 and 3 years of age (e.g., Fivush, Gray, & Fromhoff, 1987), and evidence for the translation of preverbal memories into verbal form is slim (Bauer, Wenner & Kroupina, 2002; Morris & Baker-Ward, 2007; Simcock & Hayne, 2002). Even after children are able to verbally recall their experiences, many of their early memories fail to be retained into later childhood and adulthood. Indeed, although the underlying mechanisms are still a matter of debate, it is well established that adults rarely retain memories of events experienced in the first 3–5 years of life (Sheingold & Tenney, 1982; Usher & Neisser, 1993). A major implication here is that trauma that occurs early in life may be forgotten through ordinary processes related to memory development and childhood amnesia.

## CHILDREN'S MEMORIES
## OF ONE-TIME TRAUMATIC EVENTS

A substantial literature on children's memories for single stressful or traumatic experiences suggests that the core of such events tends to be remembered quite well. Clinical observations of children exposed to acute one-time traumas suggest that these children form vivid memories that are retained over extensive delays. For example, both Malmquist (1986) and Pynoos and Eth (1984) reported that children who had witnessed a parent's murder had vivid, and often intrusive, memories of the episode. Terr (1979, 1983) reported similar patterns in her clinical evaluations of 25 elementary school children who were kidnapped from a school bus, were buried in a tractor trailer, and eventually dug their way to freedom; no child exhibited forgetting of the experience, even when assessed 5 years later.

These clinical observations are corroborated by large-scale investigations of memory for naturally occurring traumatic events. Studies of children's memories for natural disasters, including Hurricane Andrew (Bahrick, Parker, Fivush, & Levitt, 1998; Fivush, Sales, Goldberg, Bahrick, & Parker, 2004), a devastating tornado (Ackil, Van Abbema, & Bauer, 2003), and the 1988 Armenian earthquake (Najarian, Goenjian, Pelcovitz, Mandel, & Najarian, 1996), illustrate that children retain vivid and detailed recollections of these events even after delays of several years. Although memories of natural disasters are not typically externally validated, studies of memory for stressful and frightening medical experiences, which permit precise event documentation, reveal similar patterns (e.g., Burgwyn-Bailes, Baker-Ward, Gordon, & Ornstein, 2001; Merritt, Ornstein, & Spicker, 1994; Peterson & Whalen, 2001; Quas et al., 1999). In their study of 3- to 7-year-olds' recall of a medically indicated invasive radiological procedure, a voiding cystourethrogram (VCUG), Merritt et al. (1994) found that, on average, the children accurately recounted 88% of the features of the procedure, although older children remembered more features than younger children. Furthermore, the children exhibited little forgetting of the procedure after a 6-week delay. Similarly, children have relatively robust memories for traumatic injuries and subsequent emergency room treatment after delays as long as 5 years (Burgwyn-Bailes et al., 2001; Peterson & Whalen, 2001).

Although this research suggests that the core of traumatic events is likely to be remembered over time, traumatic memories are not completely invulnerable to distortion or forgetting. For instance, in a study of elementary schoolchildren's memories for a sniper attack on their school playground, Pynoos and Nader (1989) found that children who were directly exposed to the attack (i.e., were on the playground during the attack) tended to distort their memories so as to reduce their degree of life threat, whereas those who were not directly exposed tended to increase their proximity to the danger in their recollections. Some evidence also suggests that the degree of forgetting and distortion in traumatic memories may vary as a function of the level of stress experienced by the child. Both Merritt et al. (1994) and Quas et al. (1999) found that greater distress during the VCUG predicted poorer recall, although in the Quas et al. study distress also predicted greater resistance to misleading questions. In contrast, Peterson and Whalen (2001) reported that parent ratings of children's stress were associated with *better* recall of emergency room treatment for an injury but were unrelated to memory for the injury itself. Finally, Bahrick et al. (1998) found that 3- to 4-year-olds with low or very severe exposure to Hurricane Andrew recollected less about the storm several months later than those with moderate exposure. After a 6-year delay, this group difference disappeared, but the severe exposure group still required more interviewer prompting than the other groups, suggesting that they were less able or willing to recall their hurricane experiences (Fivush et al., 2004). Therefore, although traumatic and emotional events are generally remembered quite well relative to less emotional events, there is no clear consensus on how the level of stress children experience influences their memories.

Most investigations of memory for one-time traumas have focused on the amount of information retained over time, but a few studies have addressed whether children ever appear to completely forget traumatic experiences. Quas et al. (1999) found that 30% of a sample of children who had experienced a VCUG when they were between 2 and 7 years old showed no memory of the event 8 to 69 months later. Importantly, the vast majority of these children were younger than 5 years at the time of the VCUG, and none of those who were 2 or younger were able to remember the event. The two forgetters who were 5 or older during the VCUG were interviewed after delays of 4 or 5 years. These data illustrate that single traumatic events are sometimes forgotten, particularly when experienced at a very young age. Further, these patterns are quite consistent with research on memory development and childhood amnesia, suggesting that some of this forgetting may be attributable to age-related changes in memory functioning.

Much of the recent research on children's memories for one-time traumas has focused on explaining individual differences in children's recollections. Several researchers have suggested that the inconsistent stress–memory findings may be due to the fact that memory for stressful events cannot be explained by stress alone; rather, it can only be understood by examining stress in conjunction with other variables that might be associated with remembering and forgetting of emotional experiences (e.g., Quas, Qin, Schaaf, & Goodman, 1997). Some of the variation in children's memories for stressful events may be attributable to differences in behavioral responses and coping. For instance, Salmon, Price, and Pereira (2002) found that crying and distraction during a VCUG predicted poorer recall of the procedure, whereas procedural talk predicted greater recall. There is also growing evidence that parent–child relationships may moderate the impact of stress on children's memories. For example, Quas et al. (1999) found that children of parents with insecure attachments have poorer recall of a VCUG than children of secure parents. These differences may have to do with the ways parents help children cope with stressors, which, in turn, have implications for how children remember them.

Taken together, the clinical and experimental literatures provide converging evidence that one-time traumas experienced after infancy and toddlerhood are usually well remembered, even over delays as long as 6 years. At the same time, there is evidence that memories of such experiences are vulnerable to distortion and forgetting. Thus, this work suggests that child victims of a single traumatic event are likely to have vivid and enduring, but not indelible, memories of the core experience. The degree of fallibility, moreover, may depend on the age of the child, the length of the delay, the level of life threat, and individual differences in children's, and perhaps their parents', coping responses. Nevertheless, it is important to note that much of the empirical literature on memory for one-time traumas has focused on natural disasters and medical procedures, and some have questioned the relevance of this work to memory for events involving child maltreatment. Maltreatment may differ from natural disasters and medical events on several dimensions that have implications for remembering, including the level of distress and life threat experienced by the child, and family and community involvement in discussing and coping with the event. Furthermore, this research focuses on otherwise normal and healthy children and, therefore, may not be applicable to children who are chronically stressed or maltreated. We turn to the literature on chronically maltreated children next.

## MALTREATMENT, PSYCHOPATHOLOGY, AND CHILDREN'S MEMORIES OF TRAUMATIC EVENTS

Most studies of traumatic memories have focused on children exposed to one-time traumas. Yet many of the child victims who participate in the legal system, particularly maltreated children, are victimized repeatedly. There are several reasons to believe that chronic maltreatment comprises a different sort of to-be-remembered stimulus than one-time traumas like medical experiences and natural disasters. First and foremost, it is well established in the memory literature that repeated events are better remembered than single events (Baddeley, 1990), although repeated episodes are often blended into a generic memory, making it difficult to retrieve details associated with any individual experience (e.g., Hudson, 1990). In addition, maltreatment may not be discussed in families or communities in the same way as medical events or "public" traumas such as natural disasters. Furthermore, some investigators have argued that abuse may elicit memory mechanisms that are qualitatively different from other traumas. For instance, Terr (1994) suggested that repeated traumas (referred to as type II traumas) are more likely to be forgotten than single traumas (i.e., type I traumas) because they activate defense mechanisms like dissociation, whereas Freyd (e.g., Freyd et al., 2001) has argued that the betrayal of attachment relations induces forgetting of abuse by a family member.

It is also possible that maltreated children may differ in important ways from the majority of children exposed to one-time traumas. Indeed, a considerable body of research suggests that abuse is associated with atypical patterns of social, emotional, and cognitive development (e.g., Arata, Langhinrichsen-Rohling, Bowers, & O'Farrill-Swails, 2005; Coster, Gersten, Beeghly, & Cicchetti, 1989; Hoffman-Plotkin & Twentyman, 1984), and some have suggested that these atypical developmental trends may also extend to memory development. Therefore, in this section, we examine the evidence regarding how maltreated children remember their victimization experiences and whether maltreatment-related stress or associated psychopathology leads to general alterations in memory functioning and development.

## Chronically Maltreated Children's Memories for Victimization

In comparison to research on typical children's memories for one-time traumas, the literature on memory in chronically maltreated children is sparse. Terr's (1988) clinical observations of four children exposed to repeated sexual abuse indicated that two were unable to recall the abuse and the other two provided "spotty" memories. Terr suggested that repetition of the abuse prompted dissociation and, therefore, poor memory (Terr, 1988, 1994), but these findings can also be explained by the well-established patterns of childhood amnesia and memory development discussed earlier; all of the children were younger than 3 years when the abuse occurred. Terr (1988) also reported that all of these children exhibited behavioral indications of their traumas, such as trauma-specific fears, personality changes, or reenactments during play. Similar clinical observations of nonverbal indicators of early trauma in the absence of verbal recall have been reported by Gaensbauer (1995) and Sugar (1992). Although it is possible that these behaviors indicate nonverbal forms of memory of traumatic events, such an interpretation should be made with extreme caution. Behavioral indications of trauma are heavily context dependent, and it is difficult to establish that they are the direct result of past traumatic experiences. As Howe et al. (2006) have argued, "A child's fear of loud noises cannot be inextricably linked to an earlier experience of hearing gunshots while witnessing the murder of his or her parents" (p. 639). More generally, the conclusions that can be drawn about traumatic memories from clinical case studies are limited because of the small samples, lack of controls, and the fact that the therapeutic process itself may influence retention over time.

Several large-scale empirical investigations have examined the forensic interviews of children who reported being sexually abused in the recent past. Consistent with well-established patterns of memory development (e.g., Baker-Ward, Gordon, Ornstein, Larus, & Clubb, 1993; Brainerd, Kingma, & Howe, 1985), this work shows that older children provide more detail about their abuse experiences than younger children (Lamb et al., 2003; Orbach, Hershkowitz, Lamb, Esplin, & Horowitz, 2000; Sternberg, Lamb, & Hershkowitz, 1996). In contrast to Terr's suggestion that repeated abuse should result in dissociation and forgetting (Terr, 1994), children who are victims of multiple incidents actually report more about their experiences than those who are victims of single incidents (Orbach et al., 2000; Sternberg et al., 1996). Without baseline reports or external documentations against which to compare the children's accounts, however, these investigations do not yield information about the accuracy and completeness of children's recollections or about how well their memories are retained over time. Rather, prospective, longitudinal studies of children's memory for maltreatment are necessary to provide information about the accurate retention of such experiences over time.

The seminal prospective study of memory for abuse was conducted by Williams (1994). Her investigation and several that followed examined memory for childhood abuse during adulthood and, as such, are discussed in the final section of this chapter. Greenhoot, McCloskey, and Glisky (2005) conducted the only investigation to date that has examined the long-term retention of abuse memories across childhood and adolescence. These researchers interviewed 12- to 18-year-olds whose exposure to specific acts of mother-directed spousal abuse (e.g., beating, choking) or child-directed abuse and punishment (e.g., hitting with object, burning), or both, had been documented 6 years before. When the teens were asked whether they had been exposed (during childhood) to specific acts of spousal abuse or child abuse and punishment, they forgot or failed to report many of the acts that they disclosed at Year 1, especially when their mothers were the victims.

Thirty-four percent of the teens exposed to spousal violence showed "complete forgetting" in that they failed to remember or report any acts of spousal violence at all, and 20% of those exposed to child-directed aggression failed to recall or report it altogether. Rates of complete forgetting were unrelated to a measure of "nondisclosure tendency," based on discrepancies between teens' and mothers' reports of recent family violence, suggesting that the apparent memory failures do not reflect an unwillingness to disclose family secrets. Furthermore, the teens also forgot or failed to report a number of salient, nonabusive stressors from the same time period (e.g., moving to new home, parent getting arrested), with rates of "complete forgetting" of individual events ranging between 40 and 82%.

The fact that less forgetting was observed for experienced compared with witnessed violence argues against the operation of trauma-specific amnesia mechanisms, which would predict increased forgetting among teens with higher traumatic exposure. These models also cannot easily account for the finding that children exposed to the most severe violence (e.g., kicking, burning, choking) were far *less* likely than other teens to show complete forgetting of their abuse histories but were nonetheless unlikely to recall the severe acts. These findings are consistent with the formulation of Nadel and Jacobs (1998) that traumatic stress leads to vivid but highly fragmented memories or with the argument that children exposed to severe abuse might have been especially likely to blend specific episodes into a schematic memory. In either case, these teens might have had difficulty remembering the details of their abuse histories, yet were highly aware that they were exposed to harsh treatment as children and, therefore, reported the more normative forms of such treatment (e.g., spanking, hitting with object).

Over and above abuse severity, the teens' memories in the Greenhoot, McCloskey, and Glisky (2005) study were related to several well-established predictors from the basic memory literature. Both older age and recent exposure to violence predicted more complete recollections and lower rates of complete forgetting. Recollections of family violence were also positively related to the teens' memories for nonabusive events and to a measure of general autobiographical memory skill, providing direct evidence that memory for abuse is not completely dissociated from other memories. This finding is corroborated by a study of consistency in children's reports of sexual abuse, which found that children's memories of a physical examination were related to across-interview consistency in their accounts (Ghetti, Goodman, Eisen, Qin, & Davis, 2002).

More prospective studies of memory in maltreated children are clearly needed to understand children's long-term memory for abuse, but the existing data do permit some tentative conclusions. First, as observed for nonabusive events, children may have difficulty retaining explicit verbal memories of abuse that occurred during infancy or toddlerhood. Second, most children who are victimized during childhood continue to remember their experiences over time, but it should not be regarded as extraordinary for children to forget these experiences. Third, such forgetting is related to a number of well-established predictors of memory from the basic memory literature, such as child age, reexposure, and generic autobiographical memory skills, suggesting that memory for abuse involves "ordinary" memory mechanisms.

## Global Memory Functioning in Maltreated Children

Although the processes that influence children's memories of nontraumatic events and of victimization appear to be similar, there is some suggestion that chronic maltreatment may lead to global alterations in children's memory functioning. This issue has long been of interest in the clinical literature, but recent attention has been stimulated by evidence of the negative effects of stress on the structure and function of the hippocampus, an area of the brain involved in the consolidation and retrieval of verbal memories (de Quervain, Roozendaal, & McGaugh, 1998; Squire, 1992). In this regard, experimental research with nonhuman animals shows that high or prolonged stress elevates cortisol levels and leads to hippocampal damage and learning impairments (Gould, Tanapat, McEwen, Flugge, & Fuchs, 1998; Sapolsky & McEwen, 1986), and some findings with human adults are consistent with this argument (Bremner, Vermetten, Afzal, & Vythilingam, 2004; Stein, Koverola, Hanna, Torchia, & McClarty, 1997). Yet the neurological and behavioral evidence for maltreatment-related alterations in memory development is mixed. For instance, DeBellis, Hall, Boring, Frustaci, and Moritz (2001) identified no neuroanatomical differences between maltreated children with posttraumatic stress disorder (PTSD) and healthy nonmaltreated children. A study of 3- to 17-year-olds referred to a clinic for evaluation of suspected maltreatment found no differences in memory for an anogenital examination between children for whom abuse or neglect was confirmed and those for whom the claims were judged to be unsubstantiated (Eisen, Qin, Goodman, & Davis, 2002). Similar patterns were observed in an expanded study of this population, although the abused group was more accurate than the neglected group (Eisen, Goodman, Qin, Davis, & Crayton, 2007). Importantly, in both studies, some children in the unsubstantiated group may have actually been abused, thus masking differences in memory as a function of maltreatment status. Finally, no maltreatment-related differences have been found in children's performance on the Deese-Roediger-McDermott paradigm, which examines the tendency to falsely recall nonpresented words that are semantic associates of a set of presented, interrelated words (e.g., Howe, Cicchetti, Toth, & Cerrito, 2004).

On the other hand, abuse-related deficits have been observed in adolescents' performance on an autobiographical memory test (AMT), in which participants are asked to generate specific personal memories in response to cue words. Several studies using the AMT have illustrated that adolescents, as well as adults, with childhood histories of abuse and other traumas have more difficulty recollecting specific autobiographical episodes than individuals without such histories (de Decker, Hermans, Raes, & Eelen, 2003; Johnson, Greenhoot, Glisky, & McCloskey, 2005; Kuyken & Brewin, 1995; Williams et al., 2007). For example, adolescents with recent exposure to family violence have been shown to produce shorter and more overgeneral memories and fewer negative memories on an AMT (Johnson et al., 2005). In addition, teens exposed to family violence in childhood require more interviewer prompting and include fewer emotions in their recollections than teens with no such exposure (Greenhoot, Johnson, & McCloskey, 2005; Johnson et al., 2005). Not all studies, however, have replicated abuse-related memory patterns on the AMT (e.g., Wessel, Meeren, Peeters, Arntz, & Merckelbach, 2001; Startup et al., 2001), and to date none have tested preadolescent samples.

The memory problems sometimes seen in abused teens are unrelated to measures of nonautobiographical memory, suggesting that they are not explained by basic memory or cognitive deficits (de Decker et al., 2003; Johnson et al., 2005). The findings are consistent with the prevailing explanation for trauma-related memory deficits in adults: They reflect affect regulation processes in which the details of past events are avoided so as to blunt potentially negative emotions (Williams et al., 2007). Nevertheless, the literature on maltreated children's memory is still quite limited, and it is not clear how early in development these patterns emerge or whether they are specific to the AMT context (Greenhoot, Bunnell, Curtis, & Beyer, 2008).

There is also evidence that memory functioning may be influenced by trauma-related psychopathology such as PTSD and depression, although neither seems to fully account for trauma-related autobiographical memory disturbances (e.g., de Decker et al., 2003; Johnson et al., 2005). One of the core features of PTSD is the presence of intrusive images and thoughts related to the trauma (e.g., Horowitz, Wilner, Kaltreider, & Alvarez, 1980). Therefore, children with PTSD may have especially vivid and intrusive memories of their traumatic experiences, although they may be fragmentary in nature (e.g., Malmquist, 1986; Pynoos & Nader, 1989). At the same time, intrusive memories and efforts to avoid them may deplete limited cognitive resources and lead to general cognitive and memory deficits. Although PTSD has been linked to more general memory and cognitive deficits in adults (e.g., McNally, Lasko, Macklin, & Pitman, 1995), very little is known about the role of PTSD in traumatized children's cognitive functioning. In Eisen et al.'s (2007) study of maltreated children's memories of an anogenital examination, higher scores on a composite indicator of self-reported trauma symptoms (which included posttraumatic stress symptoms and depressive symptoms) predicted more commission errors to specific and misleading questions but better performance on a photo lineup of the medical staff. On the other hand, an actual diagnosis of PTSD was unrelated to memory performance in this study.

In contrast to PTSD, depression is more consistently linked to memory problems in childhood and adolescence. The autobiographical memory disturbances associated with depression are very similar to those associated with a history of childhood trauma. Adolescents and children who are depressed provide less specific recollections, both in interviews about family disagreements (Orbach, Lamb, Sternberg, Williams, & Dawud-Noursi, 2001) and in response to the AMT, than nondepressed peers (Drummond, Dritschel, Astell, O'Carroll, & Dalgleish, 2006; Johnson et al., 2005; Orbach et al., 2001; Park, Goodyear, & Teasdale, 2002). Some researchers argue that depression may actually be an outcome, rather than a cause, of autobiographical memory problems because the inability to recall specific past experiences impairs problem-solving ability (e.g., Williams et al., 2007).

To summarize, the existing literature provides little support for the hypothesis that maltreatment leads to global memory impairments in children, although further investigation of the role of PTSD is warranted. The data do suggest that maltreatment, as well as depression, may be associated with a reticence or inability to retrieve potentially painful autobiographical memory content, but the underlying mechanisms and their developmental course are not clear. One possibility is that if these memory patterns reflect strategic efforts to blunt affect, they may not appear until late childhood or adolescence, when cognitive strategies for regulating emotions are better developed (Brenner & Salovey, 1997). Nonetheless, because traumatized teens do report some specific memories, and their specificity fluctuates with retrieval conditions such as the type of memory cue (Johnson et al., 2005), they do seem to be capable of encoding and storing specific personal memories. Additional research is needed to evaluate the degree to which these memory problems may be overridden by alternative recall contexts.

## ADULTS' MEMORIES
## OF CHILDHOOD VICTIMIZATION

In contrast to the sparse empirical literature on children's memories for maltreatment, there is a considerable body of research on adults' memories for childhood abuse. The retention of childhood memories of such experiences has been investigated using both retrospective and prospective methodologies, and in the sections that follow we discuss each of these literatures.

## Retrospective Reports of Past Memory for Child Abuse

The most frequently used methodology for studying adult memory for child abuse involves asking participants who currently recall abuse whether they have ever forgotten it. Studies of therapy-seeking adults with self-reported histories of child abuse have shown that 30 to 60% of these individuals report previous periods of forgetting (e.g., Briere & Conte, 1993; Herman & Schatzow, 1987). Retrospective reports of memory failure are also common among nonclinical samples of adults who disclose childhood abuse experiences (e.g., Epstein & Bottoms, 2002; Ghetti et al., 2006). Although these data are commonly cited as evidence for the repression and later recovery of early traumatic memories (e.g., Herman & Schatzow, 1987), recent investigations using more precise questioning techniques suggest that the vast majority of self-reported memory failures reflect common forgetting mechanisms rather than trauma-specific amnesia (Epstein & Bottoms, 2002; Ghetti et al., 2006). Few participants in these studies who reported temporary forgetting described it as complete inaccessibility, and most attributed it to standard mechanisms such as active cognitive avoidance and relabeling. Furthermore, adults are just as likely to retrospectively report prior memory losses for nontraumatic experiences (e.g., vacations and attending music lessons; Read, 1997).

Several concerns also have been raised about the use of this retrospective methodology for tracking long-term memory for abuse. First, adults do not always make accurate metacognitive judgments about past mental states. A recent study showed that adults frequently forgot that they had previously remembered a stimulus in the laboratory, and this effect was especially pronounced in individuals with self-reported recovered memories of sexual abuse (Geraerts et al., 2006). More generally, retrospective reports are often biased by current knowledge, beliefs, mood, and contextual factors (Matt, Vasquez, & Campbell, 1992; Ross, 1989) and, therefore, are not objective measures of forgetting. Finally, retrospective study designs are unable to tell us anything about abuse memories that are currently forgotten.

## Prospective Studies of Adult Memory for Child Abuse

More objective data on the long-term retention of child abuse come from several prospective studies, which involve long-term follow-up assessments of memory in adults whose abuse status was documented during childhood. In the first study of this kind, Williams (1994) interviewed 129 women with sexual abuse histories documented in hospital records 17 years earlier. One in three women failed to report the documented abuse event, although most reported other abuse incidents; 12% denied having been sexually abused altogether. Consistent with research on memory development, participants who were younger than 7 at the time of the abuse were less likely to remember it. Participants who had a closer relationship to the perpetrator were also less likely to remember the event. As Williams (1994) suggested, this finding is consistent with trauma-specific amnesia theories, because abuse by a relative could be more traumatic than abuse by a stranger. On the other hand, this pattern could also reflect the operation of standard memory mechanisms, such as the impact of discussion in maintaining memories over time. In this case, abuse by a relative may be less likely to be discussed in the family than abuse by a stranger. Widom and Morris (1997) observed comparable forgetting rates in a 20-year follow-up of women with court-documented sexual abuse histories, although nearly two-thirds of the men with such histories failed to report it. In a parallel study of memory for physical abuse, 40% of men and women failed to report their abuse, but like the teens in Greenhoot, McCloskey, and Glisky's (2005) study, almost all reported moderate aggression like spanking (Widom & Shepard, 1996).

Goodman and her colleagues' (2003) study of late adolescents and adults with child sexual abuse histories documented in criminal prosecution records elucidates some of the conditions that may lead to forgetting of abuse. They found that 18% of the sample failed to remember or report the abuse, and most of the predictors of forgetting were consistent with traditional principles from the memory literature. For instance, older age and exposure to severe abuse were associated with increased rates of remembering. Participants who had received maternal support following their initial disclosures were also more likely to remember, and the investigators suggested that this legitimization may have increased the likelihood of discussing the abuse years later. A follow-up analysis of the reports of participants who recollected their abuse showed that these participants remembered, on average, 72% of the documented event details (e.g., perpetrator's name; Alexander et al., 2005). Participants' appraisal of the traumatic impact of the event was positively related to memory for event details, whereas abuse frequency was negatively related to memory detail. Given that abuse frequency was unrelated to complete forgetting or failure to report in the Goodman et al. (2003) analysis, this pattern suggests that individuals exposed to frequent abuse may have formed generic memories of their abuse, making it difficult to remember the details of single episodes.

These studies illustrate that most adults remember childhood maltreatment quite well, but that a subset may forget or fail to report such experiences after extensive delays. Both prospective and retrospective studies suggest that such memory losses are not extraordinary and can be at least partially explained by well-established predictors from the memory literature. Thus, memory for abuse seems to involve ordinary memory mechanisms. Nevertheless, as in the literature on adolescents, there is some evidence of atypical memory patterns among adults with childhood maltreatment histories or maltreatment-related psychopathology. For instance, abuse-related PTSD in adults has been associated with hippocampal impairment or verbal declarative memory deficits (e.g., Bremner et al., 2004; Stein et al., 1997). Moreover, a number of studies have shown that adults with maltreatment histories, as well as those with depression, produce overly general memories on the AMT (see Williams et al., 2007, for a review). However, these patterns are not always replicated (e.g., Wessel et al., 2001; Startup et al., 2001), and the differences between individuals with and without abuse histories may be more quantitative than qualitative, because there is considerable variation in specificity on the AMT among healthy, nonmaltreated adults (e.g., Williams et al., 2006). Indeed, recent reviews of this literature suggest that abuse alone cannot explain these atypical memory patterns and that these patterns reflect a flexible response to negative past experiences also influenced by broader emotion management tendencies and cognitive factors (Berliner & Williams, 1994; Greenhoot, Johnson, Legerski, & McCloskey, 2009; Williams et al., 2007). Moreover, as in the developmental literature, it is not clear whether these memory problems generalize beyond the AMT.

## CONCLUSION

The general picture that emerges from the literature reviewed in this chapter is that the core of both nonabusive childhood traumas and child maltreatment tends to be remembered even after delays extending into adulthood, unless the events were experienced during the first 2 to 3 years of life. At the same time, these memories are not indelible and, like more ordinary events, may sometimes be forgotten altogether. Some of the factors associated with the forgetting of these experiences (e.g., Williams's, 1994, finding that abuse by a family member was more likely to be forgotten) are suggestive of trauma-specific memory mechanisms. On the other hand, there are also ordinary memory explanations for these patterns. Indeed, most of the predictors of memory for traumatic experiences are consistent with well-established principles from the basic memory literature. For instance, frequent and severe trauma may accelerate forgetting of episodic details while enhancing memory for the core event, and continued discussion or reexposure may help to maintain memories. Furthermore, the few studies that have looked at memories of maltreatment and of nontraumatic events in the same sample illustrate that individual differences in nontraumatic memory ability predict memories of maltreatment. The most parsimonious interpretation of the existing scientific literature is that many of the same processes are involved in remembering traumatic and nontraumatic events. Thus, memories for childhood trauma may reflect an orchestration of cognitive, social, and emotional processes, each of which may be attenuated or intensified by person-level, event-level, and contextual-level characteristics. If forgetting of trauma involves ordinary mechanisms, a major implication is that once-lost memories that are later remembered are subject to the same sorts of reconstructive processes as ordinary memories (e.g., Bartlett, 1932; Ross, 1989) and, as such, may not necessarily be veridical representations of the experience.

Although there is little evidence that maltreatment and other traumas are processed in an entirely different fashion from other experiences, there is growing evidence that maltreatment may be associated with some atypical patterns of memory functioning. In particular, individuals with abuse histories seem to be less able or willing to recollect episodic details in their memories of personal experiences. These patterns emerge as early as adolescence and appear to be specific to autobiographical memories. Nevertheless, the developmental course of these memory patterns and their significance in contexts outside the laboratory are yet to be determined. There also is some possibility that individuals who have developed PTSD in response to trauma may show more global memory problems, but this issue needs to be more fully explored in the scientific literature. Of importance, these trauma-related memory patterns do not seem to represent a qualitative change in memory processing, but instead should be viewed as an important source of individual differences in memory for experiences, particularly stressful experiences.

## REFERENCES

Ackil, J. K., Van Abbema, D. L., & Bauer, P. J. (2003). After the storm: Enduring differences in mother-child recollections of traumatic and nontraumatic events. *Journal of Experimental Child Psychology, 84,* 286–309.

Alexander, K. W., Goodman, G. S., Quas, J. A., Ghetti, S., Edelstein, R. S., Redlich, A. D., et al. (2005). Traumatic impact predicts long-term memory for documented child sexual abuse. *Psychological Science, 16,* 33–40.

Arata, C. M., Langhinrichsen-Rohling, J., Bowers, D., & O'Farrill-Swails, L. (2005). Single versus multi-type maltreatment: An examination of the long-term effects of child abuse. *Journal of Aggression, Maltreatment and Trauma, 11,* 29–52.

Baddeley, A. D. (1990). *Human memory: Theory and practice.* Boston: Allyn & Bacon.

Bahrick, L. E., Parker, J. F., Fivush, R., & Levitt, M. (1998). The effects of stress on young children's memory for a natural disaster. *Journal of Experimental Psychology: Applied, 4,* 308–331.

Baker-Ward, L., Gordon, B. N., Ornstein, P. A., Larus, D. M., & Clubb, P. A.

(1993). Young children's long-term retention of a pediatric examination. *Child Development, 64,* 1519–1533.

Bartlett, F. C. (1932). *Remembering: A study in experimental and social psychology.* New York: Cambridge University Press.

Bauer, P. J., Wenner, J. A., & Kroupina, M. G. (2002). Making the past present: Later verbal accessibility of early memories. *Journal of Cognition and Development, 3,* 21–47.

Berliner, L., & Williams, L. M. (1994). Memories of child sexual abuse: Response to Lindsay and Read. *Journal of Applied Cognitive Psychology, 8,* 379–387.

Brainerd, C. J., Kingma, J., & Howe, M. L. (1985). On the development of forgetting. *Child Development, 56,* 1103–1119.

Bremner, J. D., Vermetten, E., Afzal, N., & Vythilingam, M. (2004). Deficits in verbal declarative memory function in women with childhood sexual abuse-related posttraumatic stress disorder. *Journal of Nervous and Mental Disease, 192,* 643–649.

Brenner, E. M., & Salovey, P. (1997). Emotion regulation during childhood: Developmental, interpersonal, and individual considerations. In P. Salovey & D. J. Sluyter (Eds.), *Emotional development and emotional intelligence: Educational implications* (pp. 168–192). New York: Basic Books.

Briere, J., & Conte, J. (1993). Self-reported amnesia for abuse in adults molested as children. *Journal of Traumatic Stress, 6,* 21–31.

Burgwyn-Bailes, E., Baker-Ward, L., Gordon, B. N., & Ornstein, P. A. (2001). Children's memory for emergency medical treatment after one year: The impact of individual difference variables on recall and suggestibility. *Applied Cognitive Psychology, 15,* S25-S48.

Cahill, L., Gorski, L., & Le, K. (2003). Enhanced human memory consolidation with post-learning stress: Interaction with the degree of arousal at encoding. *Learning and Memory, 10,* 270–274.

Coster, W. J., Gersten, M. S., Beeghly, M., & Cicchetti, D. (1989). Communicative functioning in maltreated toddlers. *Developmental Psychology, 25,* 1020–1029.

de Decker, A., Hermans, D., Raes, F., & Eelen, P. (2003). Autobiographical memory specificity and trauma in inpatient adolescents. *Journal of Clinical Child and Adolescent Psychology, 32,* 22–31.

de Quervain, D. J. F., Roozendaal, B., & McGaugh, J. L. (1998). Stress and glucocorticoids impair retrieval of long-term spatial memory. *Nature, 394,* 787–790.

DeBellis, M. D., Hall, J., Boring, A. M., Frustaci, K., & Moritz, G. (2001). A pilot longitudinal study of hippocampal volumes in pediatric maltreatment-related posttraumatic stress disorder. *Biological Psychiatry, 50,* 305–309.

Drummond, L. E., Dritschel, B., Astell, A., O'Carroll, R. E., & Dalgleish, T. (2006). Effects of age, dysphoria, and emotion-focusing on autobiographical memory specificity in children. *Cognition and Emotion, 20,* 488–505.

Eisen, M. L., Goodman, G. S., Qin, J., Davis, S., & Crayton, J. (2007). Maltreated children's memory: Accuracy, suggestibility, and psychopathology. *Developmental Psychology, 43,* 1275–1294.

Eisen, M. L., Qin, J., Goodman, G. S., & Davis, S. L. (2002). Memory and suggestibility in maltreated children: Age, stress arousal, dissociation, and psychopathology. *Journal of Experimental Child Psychology, 83,* 167–212.

Epstein, M. A., & Bottoms, B. L. (2002). Explaining the forgetting and recovery of abuse and trauma memories: Possible mechanisms. *Child Maltreatment, 7,* 210–225.

Fivush, R., Gray, J. T., & Fromhoff, F. A. (1987). Two-year-olds talk about the past. *Cognitive Development, 2,* 393–409.

Fivush, R., Sales, J. M., Goldberg, A., Bahrick, L. E., & Parker, J. F. (2004). Weathering the storm: Children's long-term recall of Hurricane Andrew. *Memory, 12,* 104–118.

Freud, A. (1959). Clinical studies in psychoanalysis: Research project of the Hampstead Child Therapy Clinic. *The Psychoanalytic Study of the Child, 14,* 122–131.

Freyd, J. J., DePrince, A. P., & Zurbriggen, E. L. (2001). Self-reported memory for abuse depends upon victim-perpetrator relationship. *Journal of Trauma and Dissociation, 2,* 5–17.

Gaensbauer, T. J. (1995). Trauma in the preverbal period: Symptoms, memories, and developmental impact. *The Psychoanalytic Study of the Child, 50,* 122–149.

Geraerts, E., Arnold, M. M., Lindsay, D. S., Merckelbach, H., Jelicic, M., & Hauer, B. (2006). Forgetting of prior remembering in persons reporting recovered memories of childhood sexual abuse. *Psychological Science, 17,* 1002–1008.

Ghetti, S., Edelstein, R. S., Goodman, G. S., Cordon, I. M., Quas, J. A., Alexander, K. W., et al. (2006). What can subjective forgetting tell us about memory for childhood trauma? *Memory and Cognition, 34,* 1011–1025.

Ghetti, S., Goodman, G. S., Eisen, M. L., Qin, J., & Davis, S. L. (2002). Consistency in children's reports of sexual and physical abuse. *Child Abuse and Neglect, 26,* 977–995.

Goodman, G. S., Ghetti, S., Quas, J. A., Edelstein, R. S., Alexander, K. W., Redlich, A. D., et al. (2003). A prospective study of memory for child sexual abuse: New findings relevant to the repressed-memory controversy. *Psychological Science, 14,* 113–118.

Gould, E., Tanapat, P., McEwen, B. S., Flugge, G., & Fuchs, E. (1998). Proliferation of granule cell precursors in the dentate gyrus of adult monkeys is diminished by stress. *Proceedings of the National Academy of Sciences, USA, 95,* 3168–3171.

Greenhoot, A. F., Bunnell, S. L., Curtis, J. S., & Beyer, A. M. (2008). Trauma and autobiographical memory functioning: Findings from a longitudinal study of family violence. In M. L. Howe, G. S. Goodman, & D. Cicchetti (Eds.), *Stress, trauma, and children's memory development: Neurobiologi-*

*cal, cognitive, clinical, & legal perspectives* (pp. 139–170). Oxford, UK: Oxford University Press.

Greenhoot, A. F., Johnson, R. J., & Legerski, J. P., & McCloskey, L. (2009). Chronic stress and autobiographical memory functioning. In R. Fivush & J. A. Quas (Eds.), *Stress and memory in development: Biological, social, and emotional considerations* (pp. 86–117). Oxford, UK: Oxford University Press.

Greenhoot, A. F., Johnson, R. J., & McCloskey, L. A. (2005). Internal states language in the childhood recollections of adolescents with and without abuse histories. *Journal of Cognition and Development, 6,* 547–570.

Greenhoot, A. F., McCloskey, L., & Glisky, E. (2005). A longitudinal study of adolescents' recollections of family violence. *Applied Cognitive Psychology, 19,* 716–743.

Herman, J. L., & Schatzow, E. (1987). Recovery and verification of memories of childhood sexual trauma. *Psychoanalytic Psychology, 4,* 1–14.

Hoffman-Plotkin, D., & Twentyman, C. T. (1984). A multimodal assessment of behavioral and cognitive deficits in abused and neglected preschoolers. *Child Development, 55,* 794–802.

Horowitz, M. J., Wilner, N., Kaltreider, N., & Alvarez, W. (1980). Signs and symptoms of posttraumatic stress disorder. *Archives of General Psychiatry, 37,* 85–92.

Howe, M. L., Cicchetti, D., Toth, S. L., & Cerrito, B. M. (2004). True and false memories in maltreated children. *Child Development, 75,* 1402–1417.

Howe, M. L., Toth, S. L., & Cicchetti, D. (2006). Memory and developmental psychopathology. In D. Cicchetti & D. Cohen (Eds.), *Developmental psychopathology* (2nd ed., Vol. 2, pp. 629–655). New York: Wiley.

Hudson, J. A. (1990). Constructive processing in children's event memory. *Developmental Psychology, 26,* 180–187.

Johnson, R. J., Greenhoot, A. F., Glisky, E., & McCloskey, L. A. (2005). The relations among abuse, depression, and adolescents' autobiographical memory. *Journal of Clinical Child and Adolescent Psychology, 34,* 235–247.

Kuyken, W., & Brewin, C. R. (1995). Autobiographical memory functioning in depression and reports of early abuse. *Journal of Abnormal Psychology, 104,* 585–591.

Lamb, M. E., Sternberg, K. J., Orbach, Y., Esplin, P. W., Stewart, H., & Mitchell, S. (2003). Age differences in young children's responses to open-ended invitations in the course of forensic interviews. *Journal of Consulting and Clinical Psychology, 71,* 926–934.

Malmquist, C. P. (1986). Children who witness parental murder: Posttraumatic aspects. *Journal of the American Academy of Child Psychiatry, 25,* 320–325.

Matt, G. E., Vasquez, C., & Campbell, W. K. (1992). Mood-congruent recall on affectively toned stimuli: A meta-analytic review. *Clinical Psychology Review, 12,* 227–255.

McGaugh, J. L. (2002). Memory consolidation and the amygdala: A systems perspective. *Trends in Neurosciences, 25,* 456–461.

McNally, R. J., Lasko, N. B., Macklin, M. L., & Pitman, R. K. (1995). Autobiographical memory disturbance in combat-related posttraumatic stress disorder. *Behaviour Research and Therapy, 33,* 619–630.

Merritt, K. A., Ornstein, P. A., & Spicker, B. (1994). Children's memory for a salient medical procedure: Implications for testimony. *Pediatrics, 94,* 17–23.

Morris, G., & Baker-Ward, L. (2007). Fragile but real: Children's capacity to use newly acquired words to convey preverbal memories. *Child Development, 78,* 448–458.

Nadel, L., & Jacobs, W. J. (1998). Traumatic memory is special. *Current Directions in Psychological Science, 7,* 154–157.

Najarian, L. M., Goenjian, A. K., Pelcovitz, D., Mandel, F., & Najarian, B. (1996). Relocation after a disaster: Posttraumatic stress disorder in Armenia after the earthquake. *Journal of the American Academy of Child and Adolescent Psychiatry, 35,* 374–383.

Orbach, Y., Hershkowitz, I., Lamb, M. E., Esplin, P. W., & Horowitz, D. (2000). Assessing the value of structured protocols for forensic interviews of alleged child abuse victims. *Child Abuse and Neglect, 24,* 733–752.

Orbach, Y., Lamb, M. E., Sternberg, K., Williams, J. M. G., & Dawud-Noursi, S. (2001). The effect of being a victim or witness of family violence on the retrieval of autobiographical memories. *Child Abuse and Neglect, 25,* 1427–1437.

Ornstein, P. A., Ceci, S. J., & Loftus, E. F. (1998). Adult recollections of childhood abuse: Cognitive and developmental perspectives. *Psychology, Public Policy, and Law, 4,* 1025–1051.

Park, R. J., Goodyear, I. M., & Teasdale, J. D. (2002). Categoric overgeneral autobiographical memory in adolescents with major depressive disorder. *Psychological Medicine, 32,* 267–276.

Peterson, C., & Whalen, N. (2001). Five years later: Children's memory for medical emergencies. *Applied Cognitive Psychology, 15,* S7–S24.

Pynoos, R. S., & Eth, S. (1984). The child as witness to homicide. *Journal of Social Issues, 40,* 87–108.

Pynoos, R. S., & Nader, K. (1989). Children's memory and proximity to violence. *Journal of the American Academy of Child and Adolescent Psychiatry, 28,* 236–241.

Quas, J. A., Goodman, G. S., Bidrose, S., Pipe, M.-E., Craw, S., & Ablin, D. S. (1999). Emotion and memory: Children's long-term remembering, forgetting, and suggestibility. *Journal of Experimental Child Psychology, 72,* 235–270.

Quas, J. A., Qin, J., Schaaf, J., & Goodman, G. S. (1997). Individual differences in children's and adults' suggestibility and false event memory. *Learning and Individual Differences, 9,* 359–390.

Read, J. D. (1997). Memory issues in the diagnosis of unreported trauma. In

J. D. Read & D. S. Lindsay (Eds.), *Recollections of trauma: Scientific evidence and clinical practice* (pp. 79–100). New York: Plenum Press.

Ross, M. (1989). Relation of implicit theories to the construction of personal histories. *Psychological Review, 96,* 341–357.

Salmon, K., Price, M., & Pereira, J. K. (2002). Factors associated with young children's long-term recall of an invasive medical procedure: A preliminary investigation. *Journal of Developmental and Behavioral Pediatrics, 23,* 347–352.

Sapolsky, R. M., & McEwen, B. S. (1986). Stress, glucocorticoids, and their role in degenerative changes in the aging hippocampus. In T. Crook, R. T. Bartus, S. Ferris, & S. Gershon (Eds.), *Treatment development strategies for Alzheimer's disease* (pp. 151–171). Madison, CT: Mark Powley Associates.

Schooler, J. W., & Eich, E. (2000). Memory for emotional events. In E. Tulving & F. I. M. Craik (Eds.), *The Oxford handbook of memory* (pp. 379–392). New York: Oxford University Press.

Sheingold, K., & Tenney, Y. J. (1982). Memory for a salient childhood event. In U. Neisser (Ed.), *Memory observed* (pp. 201–212). New York: Freeman.

Simcock, G., & Hayne, H. (2002). Breaking the barrier? Children fail to translate their preverbal memories into language. *Psychological Science, 13,* 225–231.

Squire, L. R. (1992). Memory and the hippocampus: A synthesis from findings with rats, monkeys, and humans. *Psychological Review, 99,* 195–231.

Startup, M., Heard, H., Swales, M., Jones, B., Williams, J. M. G., & Jones, R. S. P. (2001). Autobiographical memory and parasuicide in borderline personality disorder. *British Journal of Clinical Psychology, 40,* 113–120.

Stein, M. B., Koverola, C., Hanna, C., Torchia, M. G., & McClarty, B. (1997). Hippocampal volume in women victimized by childhood sexual abuse. *Psychological Medicine, 27,* 951–959.

Sternberg, K. J., Lamb, M. E., & Hershkowitz, I. (1996). Child sexual abuse investigations in Israel. *Criminal Justice and Behavior, 23,* 322–337.

Sugar, M. (1992). Toddlers' traumatic memories. *Infant Mental Health Journal, 13,* 245–251.

Terr, L. C. (1979). Children of Chowchilla: A study of psychic trauma. *Psychoanalytic Study of the Child, 34,* 547–623.

Terr, L. C. (1983). Chowchilla revisited: The effects of psychic trauma four years after a school-bus kidnapping. *American Journal of Psychiatry, 140,* 1543–1550.

Terr, L. (1988). What happens to early memories of trauma? A study of twenty children under age five at the time of documented traumatic events. *Journal of the American Academy of Child and Adolescent Psychiatry, 27,* 96–104.

Terr, L. (1994). *Unchained memories: True stories of traumatic memories, lost and found.* New York: Basic Books.

Usher, J. A., & Neisser, U. (1993). Child amnesia and the beginnings of memory for four early life events. *Journal of Experimental Psychology: General,* *122,* 155–165.

van der Kolk, B. A. (1994). The body keeps the score: Memory and the emerging psychobiology of posttraumatic stress. *Harvard Review of Psychiatry,* *1,* 253–265.

Wessel, I., Meeren, M., Peeters, F., Arntz, A., & Merckelbach, H. (2001). Correlates of autobiographical memory specificity: The role of depression, anxiety and childhood trauma. *Behaviour Research and Therapy, 39,* 409–421.

Widom, C. S., & Morris, S. (1997). Accuracy of adult recollections of childhood victimization: Part 2. Childhood sexual abuse. *Psychological Assessment,* *9,* 34–46.

Widom, C. S., & Shepard, R. L. (1996). Accuracy of adult recollections of childhood victimization: Part I. Childhood physical abuse. *Psychological Assessment, 8,* 412–421.

Williams, J. M. G., Barnhofer, T., Crane, C., Herman, D., Raes, F., Watkins, E., et al. (2007). Autobiographical memory specificity and emotional disorder. *Psychological Bulletin, 133,* 122–148.

Williams, J. M. G., Chan, S., Crane, C., Barnhofer, T., Eade, J., & Healy, H. (2006). Retrieval of autobiographical memories: The mechanisms and consequences of truncated search. *Cognition and Emotion, 20,* 351–382.

Williams, L. M. (1994). Recall of childhood trauma: A prospective study of women's memories for child sexual abuse. *Journal of Consulting and Clinical Psychology, 62,* 1167–1176.

Chapter 4

# Children's Memory in Forensic Contexts
*Suggestibility, False Memory, and Individual Differences*

Iris Blandón-Gitlin
Kathy Pezdek

W hen children come in contact with the legal system as victims or eyewitnesses, one of the challenges they face is the expectation to provide accurate and complete accounts of events. This is especially important in sexual abuse cases in which children's testimony is often the only evidence against the alleged perpetrator. Much of the psychological research prompted by the preschool abuse cases of the 1980s (see Wood, Nathan, Nezworski, & Uhl, Chapter 5, this volume) revealed that children, in particular young children, are especially susceptible to misleading suggestions and memory distortion, which can significantly affect the accuracy of their accounts. More recent research, however, has shown that under many conditions children can be reliable witnesses and provide accounts of events that are accurate and useful to investigators. In this chapter, the current literature on children's memory abilities is reviewed, with a focus on research examining forensically relevant factors that increase or reduce children's suggestibility and memory distortion. We also review recent evidence on individual differences found to be useful in predicting children's witness abilities. We believe that children's experiences in the legal system and the usefulness of their accounts can be greatly enhanced if forensic investigators have an understanding of how social-cognitive factors affect children's memories of autobiographical events.

57

It is important to make a few points before we begin. First, following Quas, Qin, Schaaf, and Goodman's (1997) and Pezdek and Lam's (2007) conceptual distinction, we use the term "suggestibility" to refer to children's susceptibility to suggestions about nonexistent details of witnessed events and the term "false memory" to refer to children's development of memories of entirely new suggested events that never occurred. Second, although for ease we separated the review into factors that reduce or increase children's accuracy, it is important to keep in mind that these factors interact and rarely occur in isolation. For example, age is a factor that is associated with other variables such as knowledge base, source memory, and language ability, which together may affect children's memory and susceptibility to suggestions. Although we review studies that uniquely assessed each of these factors, it is likely that in forensic settings many of these factors interact, and predicting accuracy or suggestibility of individual children may be difficult. Third, because it is beyond the scope of this chapter to review all factors that affect suggestibility and false memories, we present only studies that investigated children's memory using real-world events and procedures that are relevant to issues in the forensic arena.

In a typical suggestibility study, children first experience an event (e.g., a magic show in the lab) and, after a short or long delay, are given suggestions that target events occurred (e.g., the magician gave them a sticker). Accuracy and suggestibility are assessed by analyzing children's responses to free-recall questions/prompts (e.g., "What happened on the day you saw the show?") and to focused nonleading (e.g., "Which trick did you like best?") and misleading/suggestive (e.g., "The magician touched you on your arm, didn't he?") questions. Correct responses to questions determine children's accuracy. Suggestibility is determined by whether children recall suggested details or assent to the occurrence of the target details. In the typical false memory study, children are first asked about true events (e.g., "What happened when you fell off a bicycle?") that parents reported to have occurred, followed by questions about a target false event (e.g., "What happened when you got your hand caught in a mousetrap?"). If children assent to a target suggested false event or actually report details of the false event beyond that conveyed by the interviewer, it is concluded that children have developed a false memory for the event. We next review some of the many factors identified in such studies as influencing children's suggestibility and tendency to develop false memories.

## FACTORS THAT *INCREASE* CHILDREN'S SUGGESTIBILITY AND FALSE MEMORIES

Excellent reviews of many factors that increase children's suggestibility and memory distortion have been reported elsewhere (e.g., Bruck & Ceci, 1999).

Here, we focus on the recent literature on key factors that can increase children's susceptibility to misleading information during forensic investigations: type of interviewing techniques, the experience of stress or negative emotions during recall, and increased delay between event and investigative interviews.

## Interviewing Techniques: Question Type and Props

The types of questions and techniques used in forensic interviews to elicit information from children can be suggestive and increase the likelihood of influencing their accounts. Generally, questions can be classified into open-ended questions (e.g., "What happened on the day you went to his house?") that prompt free recall in children and focused questions that require short (e.g., "On that day, were you on the sofa or bed?") or yes–no (e.g., "Did you go to his house?") responses. Typically, children provide more accurate information with open-ended questions than with focused questions (see Lamb, Orbach, Hershkowitz, Esplin, & Horowitz, 2007). Despite this, the use of focused questions appears to be the norm in forensic interviews around the globe (Lamb et al., 1996; Lamb, Sternberg, & Esplin, 2000; Lamb et al., 2003; see Powell, Fisher, & Wright, 2005, for a review). Furthermore, in sexual abuse investigations, props such as anatomically detailed dolls or their analogue, human figure drawings (two-dimensional drawings of humans with or without clothes), are sometimes used to direct children's attention to specific abuse-related details. The use of focused questions and props in forensic settings may be partly due to the finding that children, particularly young children, sometimes do not provide critical information in free recall.

In theory, open-ended questions allow children to search their memory unconstrained, which can lead to the retrieval of all relevant information. Focused questions, on the other hand, typically trigger the search of single pieces of information that limit the amount retrieved from memory. Moreover, information elicited from open-ended questions tends to be more accurate than information elicited from focused question. This is probably because open-ended questions require the child to extract information from memory, whereas focused questions require the child to recognize from options imposed by the interviewers, which may or may not be correct. In their 2007 field study, Lamb, Orbach, Hershkowitz, Horowitz, and Abbott analyzed interviews of sexual abuse victims and their perpetrators to determine the accuracy of information derived from open-ended versus focused questions. Information provided by the victim and confirmed by the alleged perpetrator was the index of accuracy. Indeed, the findings revealed that details prompted by open-ended questions were more likely to be confirmed by the perpetrator than those from focused questions. Moreover, central details (e.g., references to sexual actions or sexual body parts) were more likely reported by the victim and confirmed by the perpetrator in response to open-ended than focused questions.

However, laboratory studies, in which the accuracy of event details is known with greater certainty than in field studies, have shown that children sometimes omit important information during open-ended questioning. Hutcheson, Baxter, Telfer, and Warden (1995) had two groups of children (5- to 6-year-old and 8- to 9-year-olds) witnessed a staged event at their school. They were later interviewed by professional child interviewers, who used free recall and focused questions. Over 70% of children across age groups who omitted details in response to free-recall questions reported some details when prompted with focused questions. This suggests that children possessed the information in memory but needed specific cues to help them retrieve it.

Retrieval cues in the form of props seem to be important in helping children report critical details of events. Goodman, Quas, Batterman-Faunce, Riddlesberger, and Kuhn (1997) assessed children's memory for a voiding cystourethrogram (VCUG), an invasive medical procedure that involves genital touch and can be painful and embarrassing to children. A few days after undergoing the VCUG, children ages 3–10 were interviewed with open-ended questions (e.g., "I need to know everything that happened when you got the test"), followed by similar queries but accompanied with gender-appropriate anatomically detailed dolls and toy doctor kits for children to demonstrate what occurred during the procedure (e.g., "I want you to show and tell me what happened when you got the medical test"). Following the prop demonstration, focused nonmisleading questions (e.g., "Did the nurse touch you down there?") and misleading questions (e.g., "Didn't they take your socks off after they put the tube in you?") were introduced. Children of all ages reported more information and were more likely to report the critical touch with the props than with open-ended questions. This indicates that children are less likely to report important and potentially embarrassing details unless they are directly prompted. It is vital to note, however, that, although preschoolers in the Goodman et al. (1997) study showed an increase in overall recall when the props were used, this was accompanied by a similar increase in errors. Thus, although props can be helpful in interviewing preschoolers, the risk of inaccuracy can be high. Similar results have been found with human figure drawings, which are often recommended and used by therapists and forensic interviewers (Aldridge et al., 2004).

In sum, the main concern with focused questions and props is that although their use usually elicits an increase in critical information (but see Lamb et al., 2007), there is a risk of triggering children's suggestibility by introducing potentially incorrect information. This is because in forensic settings investigators usually do not know the "ground truth" of alleged acts, and thus using techniques that introduce events believed to have occurred, but that might be false, can potentially contaminate children's accounts.

## Effects of Stress and Emotion

Laboratory and naturalistic studies have shown that stressful or highly emotional events are often remembered better than nonstressful events (see Greenhoot & Bunnell, Chapter 3, this volume). The reasons for this phenomenon may have to do in part with an increased release of stress hormones (e.g., cortisol) during emotional experiences, which assist in memory consolidation (see Cahill & McGaugh, 1998). It can be predicted that with enhanced processing a stronger memory trace forms, which consequently is less malleable and more resistant to forgetting. However, in a review of research on children's and adults' memories of traumatic experiences (e.g., medical procedures, natural disasters, violent events, sexual abuse), Pezdek and Taylor (2002) concluded that cognitive principles that apply to memories for nontraumatic events also apply to memories for traumatic events, and although memory for traumatic experiences are generally correct, they appear to be no more accurate than other memories. They based their conclusion on the finding that, similar to memories of nontraumatic experiences, memories of traumatic events (1) are not impervious to forgetting, (2) show an age-related pattern whereby accuracy and amount of details increases with age, (3) are likely to be accurately remembered in gist but not veridical form, and (4) are susceptible to distortion. It seems clear that traumatic memories are subject to the same laws that govern memory for everyday experiences.

Are children accurate and resistant to suggestion when reporting traumatic experiences in legal settings? The answer to this question is, not always. Especially under the conditions that arise in legal contexts, children may not be accurate at reporting and rejecting misleading information about traumatic events. Quas and Lench (2007) found that arousal at encoding and retrieval of a fear-inducing event differentially affected accuracy in children's reports. Children's arousal (as indexed by heart rate) was recorded once while watching a fearful film and again a week later during an interview by either a supportive (warm and friendly demeanor) or unsupportive (cold and detached demeanor) interviewer. Children who exhibited increased arousal at encoding a week earlier made fewer errors in responses to focused misleading questioning than children who had been in a lower state of arousal during encoding. This suggests that memory was enhanced by a strong emotional reaction to the events in the film. This pattern changed, however, when arousal at retrieval was considered. In the unsupportive interview condition, children who exhibited increased arousal made more errors in response to focused questioning than children who exhibited lower arousal. The association between arousal and memory was not significant in the supportive interview condition. These results suggest that even if a traumatic event is strongly encoded, the accuracy of its retrieval may be compromised when the social context during recall is not optimal.

Quas and Lench's (2007) results directly support findings on the effects of legal involvement and stress on the completeness of children's responses. Being part of certain legal proceedings can be stressful to children; Goodman et al. (1998) reported that pretrial anxiety was higher for children expecting to testify in open court compared with closed-circuit television. In a comprehensive naturalistic study, Goodman, Taub, Jones, and England (1992) monitored 218 children who were involved in legal proceedings stemming from sexual abuse accusations, 55 of whom eventually testified in court. Children who reported greater distress at having to face the defendant were less likely to answer the prosecutor's questions than those who reported lower distress. Thus, the completeness of children's accounts was compromised by the distressful experience.

It is unclear why increased stress at retrieval impairs memory. Malloy, Mitchell, Block, Quas, and Goodman (2007) suggested that children's inability to communicate effectively under high emotional arousal may be due to residual stress from the original event, resulting in focused attention to coping rather than searching memory for relevant information. Alternatively, and more speculatively, increased stress at retrieval may trigger a release of stress hormones that can negatively affect recall. Recent research shows that levels of stress hormones comparable to those that enhance memory consolidation at encoding can also induce impairments at retrieval. de Quervain et al. (2003) reported that adult participants with increased cortisol levels showed impaired cue recall of word pairs learned 24 hours earlier. This impaired recall was also associated with decreased activity in brain regions believed to be important in memory retrieval. Although these are viable explanations for the effect of stress at retrieval, more research is necessary to examine the exact mechanisms and conditions that may mediate this effect. It seems clear, however, that children do experience increased distress in legal settings, which can adversely affect their ability to recall their experiences accurately and in complete form. This condition, however, can be improved by a supportive social context.

## Delay

Information stored in memory is likely to fade after long delays. The greatest loss of information occurs in the period immediately after an event. As with adults, children are susceptible to forgetting after an initial experience but the rate of forgetting is steeper. Flin, Boon, Knox, and Bull (1992) compared forgetting rates of young children, 9- to 10-year-old children, and adults. The target event involved witnessing an argument among adults, which was equally engaging to all age groups. Whereas at the initial interview (1 day after the event) there were no significant differences in overall accuracy among the age groups, at a 5-month interview overall accuracy significantly dropped for children but not for adults. Furthermore, the drop in accuracy was greater for children younger than 9- to 10-years old. The authors concluded that the details of the event were encoded at similar levels by all groups, but the information faded at a greater rate for the children, especially the younger group.

Delay is a relevant factor in forensic settings because children commonly will not provide testimony about criminal acts until months or even years after the original event. In the Goodman et al. (1992) study, some children waited more than 7 months to testify in hearings or in open court. Furthermore, research shows that children who are abused tend to delay disclosure (see Lyon, Chapter 2, this volume). Hershkowitz (2006) reported that, in a sample of approximately 26,000 Israeli children suspected of abuse, 74% delayed disclosures for at least a month after the alleged crime. The effect of delayed disclosure compounded by long intervals in legal proceedings can have an adverse effect on children's memory and their accounts.

Although some studies show that children's memories for salient events can remain accurate over long delays (e.g., Peterson, Parsons, & Dean, 2004), others report that delay increases children's susceptibility to suggestion and reduces accuracy and completeness of their accounts. Burgwyn-Bailes, Baker-Ward, Gordon, and Ornstein (2001) interviewed 3- to 7-year-olds three times (after a few days, at 6 weeks, and at 1 year) following treatment at a plastic surgeon's office for facial lacerations. Interview protocols included various types of questions about events that did or did not occur. To determine one aspect of suggestibility, at each interview, children were asked suggestive questions about absent features of the medical event (e.g., "Did Dr. Hanna put something cold on the hurt place?"). Overall rates of recall were high and did not significantly change over time (78%, 73%, and 72%, respectively); however, assent rates to suggestive questions significantly increased over time (12%, 18%, and 22%, respectively). Because the same protocol was used at each interview, it is possible that repeated testing with the same questions contributed to the highly stable memory trace of both true and suggested events (a topic that is covered in another section). However, because errors were evident even at the first interview, these results also indicate that memory for a highly salient and distressful experience is not immune to suggestibility effects. Furthermore, field studies show that children report significantly less information after a long delay. Lamb et al. (2000) reported that, in a sample of 145 cases of alleged sexual abuse, long delays (5–14 months) were associated with significantly less information reported by children than short delays (less than a month).

An important question is, what happens over long delays when false events have been suggestively planted in children's memory? This question is relevant here because if a child is suggestively questioned during a forensic interview, resulting in the development of a memory for nonexperienced events, it is important to know the likelihood that the false memory will remain after long delays. To determine the long-term stability of false memories, Huffman, Crossman, and Ceci (1997) interviewed a group of children who had participated in a false memory study 2 years earlier (see Ceci, Huffman, Smith, & Loftus, 1994). This reinterviewed group consisted of children who originally assented to having experienced suggested false events (e.g., getting their hand caught in a mousetrap and having to go to the hospital) and had not been convinced that the suggested events were false during debriefing attempts (i.e., children were not fully debriefed). In this second study, children were presented with the same true and false events from the earlier study. The results showed that, whereas the assent rate to true events did not significantly change from Study 1 (80%) to Study 2 (77%), the assent rate to false events from Study 1 (22%) significantly *decreased* in Study 2 (13%). Moreover, further analyses revealed that children were more likely to recant false events than true events. It appears from these results that the rate of survival of memories for suggestively planted events is likely to be low after long delays. It is possible that initial assent rates and errors in these studies were likely due to the demands of the social context rather than real changes in memory (see Brainerd & Poole, 1997, for a review of these issues).

Thus, increased delays between an event and an initial interview are associated with more forgetting and increased suggestibility. Although it is not yet clear what the long-term fate of implanted false memories is, evidence suggests that children's implanted memories are not likely to survive long delays.

## FACTORS THAT *REDUCE* CHILDREN'S SUGGESTIBILITY AND FALSE MEMORIES

In this section, we review relevant literature on factors associated with children's reduced suggestibility and memory distortion and thus increased accuracy: prior event knowledge, repeated experience, multiple nonsuggestive interviews, and source monitoring ability and training.

### Event Knowledge

The type of knowledge base children possess about events is an important factor that has been linked to decreased suggestibility. For example, in Goodman et al. (1997), an association was reported between children's prior knowledge of the VCUG procedure and higher rates of correct responses to suggestive questions. Similarly, Ornstein et al. (2006) found that, controlling for age, prior knowledge about routine doctor's visits was significantly associated with increased recall of a target pediatric examination. Presumably prior knowledge helps children attend to, encode, and integrate relevant details of events, resulting in a well-organized interconnected structure that is easily accessible during retrieval attempts (Ornstein et al., 2006)

The effect of knowledge base on children's memory takes a distinct form when the suggestion involves an entirely new experience. Pezdek and colleagues (Pezdek, Finger, & Hodge, 1997; Pezdek & Hodge, 1999) showed that children are more suggestible if they have schematic representations in memory for the target event. Using information provided by parents, Pezdek and Hodge (1999) asked 19 5- to 7-year-olds and 20 9- to 12-year-olds about true events and suggested that they had also experienced a plausible ("been lost in a mall") and an implausible ("receiving an enema") event. Although across age groups the majority of children (54%) did not report memory for either suggested false event, when they did, it was more likely to occur for the plausible event than the implausible event. Pezdek and colleagues concluded that this effect is due to a lack of event-related knowledge stored in memory for implausible events. When it is suggested to children that an event occurred, they will search in memory for similar episodes of the event. If this search generates related details, then it is likely that the process of constructing a memory of the suggested event will begin. If, on the other hand, the search does not result in activation of related event information, it is likely that the constructive process and resulting false memory will not occur. Thus, because information about implausible events is less likely to exist in memory, memories for suggested implausible events will not be planted. This is an important finding relevant to forensic contexts because an event such as child sexual abuse is reported to be a relatively implausible event for most people. Pezdek and Blandón-Gitlin (2008) reported that the majority of adult participants from the general population (65%) perceived child sexual abuse to be a personally implausible event. Certainly, if the event is plausible for the circumstances of an individual child and the interviewing conditions are highly suggestible, there is an increased risk of planting false events in the child's memory. This problem is further compounded by the fact that in some cases it is difficult to discriminate between accounts of true events and those that are false but familiar to children (see Blandón-Gitlin, Rogers, Pezdek, & Brodie, 2005; Pezdek et al., 2004).

In sum, event knowledge has two distinct effects on children's memory depending on the type of suggestion. Prior knowledge can help children encode and store information about target experiences in a manner that allows them to resist misleading suggestions about an experienced event. However, under some conditions, knowledge about related episodes of a suggested event can increase the likelihood of children developing false memories.

## Repeated Experience

Some criminal acts against children, particularly sexual abuse, rarely occur in isolation. When an experience is repeated, children can be quite accurate and resistant to suggestion. Repetition has been shown to strengthen memories of events. Pezdek and Roe (1995) presented 4- and 10-year-old children with a slide sequence of an event in which four target slides were presented one or two times each. Afterward, a narrative was read to the children that misled them about two target items. On a subsequent recognition memory test, for both age groups, stronger memories (those viewed twice) were more resistant to suggestibility than weaker memories (those viewed once). Powell, Roberts, Ceci, and Hembrooke (1999, Experiment 1) extended these findings to an event that children experienced once or six times over several weeks. They, too, reported that repetition increased memory for the event and resistance to suggestibility. In this study, repetition had a powerful effect of attenuating the detrimental effects of suggestibility, age, and delay on memory. However, if the event was repeatedly experienced with some details varying across repetitions, when children were subsequently asked about specific details of an event that varied across repetitions, the accuracy of their memory was less reliable and they were more vulnerable to suggestive questions. These findings suggest that children's memories of repeated experiences involving fixed details will be strong, and accounts based on those memories are likely to be accurate.

## Multiple Interviews

In forensic settings it is common for children to be repeatedly interviewed and sometimes over long periods of time (Goodman et al., 1992; Malloy, Lyon, & Quas, 2007). For example, Malloy and colleagues (2007) reported that, in a sample of sexual abuse cases from Los Angeles, children were formally interviewed, on average, 4.26 times with a range of 1 to 25 times. Informal interviews with the nonoffending parent, siblings, or therapists averaged 1.65 with a range of 0 to 7. Thus, the frequency of recounting the event was greater than four times in some cases. Consequently, it is important to understand how multiple interviews affect children's memory and suggestibility. The general finding is that repeated interviewing, if suggestive, has a detrimental effect on children's memories. For example, Erdmann, Volbert, and Böhm (2004) found that multiple interviews in which nonexperienced events (e.g., falling off a horse, knocked over by a big wave at the beach) were repeatedly suggested to children led to increases in assent rates over time and resulted in descriptions of false events that could not be distinguished from accounts of true events. However, other research shows that nonsuggestive interviews, like repeated experience, can have a beneficial effect on children's memory.

Potentially, each interview can reactivate the memory of the original event, which can serve to maintain it, reduce the rate of forgetting, decrease suggestibility, and lead to increased recall. This is especially true if an initial interview is conducted shortly after the occurrence of the event. Peterson et al. (2004) interviewed children who had been part of another study assessing memory for a traumatic injury. These children had been interviewed immediately (Interview 1) and 6 months (Interview 2) after the injury. The goal of the Peterson et al. (2004) study was to determine the effects of a delayed suggestive interview on children's recall. Results showed that misleading questions at a 1-year interview (suggestive intervention) had little effect on children's recall during two subsequent interviews conducted 1 week later (Interview 4) and 2 years post-injury (Interview 5). Scores on recall measures were very high—almost at ceiling—even after the misleading interview, which indicates that children's memory for the injury was strong most probably because of repeated interviews with the same interview protocol.

Direct comparisons of delay, repeated interview, age, misleading questions, and interviewer bias on children's reports were made by Quas, Malloy, et al. (2007). In their study, 3- to 5-year-old children played by themselves for 10 minutes in a university's laboratory. This session was followed by a single interview 3 weeks later or three interviews 1 week apart, which included suggestive questions about an interaction with a man. Half of the children in each interview condition were interviewed by a highly biased interviewer who implied that the children had played with a man; the other half were interviewed by a more neutral interviewer who did not imply any interaction. The key comparisons revealed an interesting picture. The worst performance was for children in the *biased single-interview* condition. In memory and suggestibility assessments, this latter group was less accurate than (1) children in the neutral single-interview condition and (2) children in the repeated-interview conditions (biased and neutral). More specifically, despite repeated biased interviews, children in the repeated-interview conditions were more accurate and less likely to falsely report interactions with a man than children who were interviewed once in a biased manner. The age effect was in the predicted direction in most conditions; in general, younger children were less accurate than older children. The researchers concluded that interviewer bias is particularly a problem when children's memories are weak, as was the case in the biased group interviewed for the first time 3 weeks after the event. These results again highlight the importance of an early interview; it can "inoculate" children against the effects of forgetting and bias in subsequent interviews.

Some researchers have not found beneficial effects of multiple interviews, however. The Ornstein et al. (2006) study, in which children's memory for a target pediatric examination was assessed, included delayed interviews at 3 and 6 months after the event. Recall of true information and the ability to deny the occurrence of incorrect details declined over time. Thus, there are conditions under which repeated interviews may not help children's memory. In addition, as previously mentioned, in cases of sexual abuse, children tend to delay disclosure; thus, an initial interview may take place long after the event, which can result in increased vulnerability to suggestion. Therefore, it is possible that in forensic settings the benefit of repeated interviews may not always be realized.

## Source Monitoring Ability and Training

Source monitoring refers to the theoretical cognitive process by which we attribute source to a particular memory (Johnson, Foley, Suengas, & Raye, 1988). Certain characteristics of memory representations (e.g., perceptual detail, vividness, contextual, and semantic information) can allow us to determine whether a particular memory is based on real experience (external source) or is the product of our imagination (internal source). Source monitoring errors can occur when we mistakenly attribute an active memory representation (e.g., image of closing the garage door) to a real experience when, in fact, we only thought about it. In forensic settings, source monitoring ability is important because children are likely to be interviewed multiple times by various individuals who, in some cases, may suggest erroneous details. Children may confuse information they heard earlier with memory for a real experience. This risk is compounded when children are asked to "think really hard" or visualize episodes of the events.

Leichtman, Morse, Dixon, and Spiegel (2000, Experiments 2 and 3) reported significant correlations between performance on suggestibility and source memory tasks. Children ages 3 to 6 who were found to be more vulnerable to suggestion showed decreased ability to identify the sources from which information was obtained (e.g., performed vs. imagined, seen vs. heard). Part of this suggestibility effect is thought to be related to social demand mechanisms, whereby children believe that information from a trusted adult is reliable even when it is not. This suggests that source errors can be partly reduced by training children to make careful judgments about the sources of information stored in memory (Poole & Lindsay, 2002).

Poole and Lindsay (2002) used a source training procedure that can be easily implemented in forensic settings. Children experienced target activities during a session with a man referred to as "Mr. Science." Three months later, parents read a story to children about the session with "Mr. Science," which included information about true and false activities. Soon after this suggestive session, but just before an interview, children assigned to a source training condition were shown three preparation activities by the interviewer that showed differences between performed and talked about actions. For example, in one preparation activity, the interviewer told children that she was going to wipe off the tape recorder, which she proceeded to do. Following this, she told children that sometimes she pushes the button on the recorder to "set the counter," but she did not actually perform this action. Immediately after, children were asked to report, and were given feedback, on which actions she performed and which she only discussed. Analysis of children's recall during a subsequent forensic-style interview showed that, although 3- to 5-year-olds did not benefit from the source training, 6- to 8-year-olds did. For this older group, the error rate in response to focused questions (some of which were suggestive) was half that of the no-training group. Moreover, accurate reports did not decrease with training. This is an important finding because it suggests that a simple procedure in source training can be beneficial in reducing inaccuracy in children's reports.

Although the younger children did not benefit from source training in Poole and Lindsay's (2002) research and other similar studies (Poole & Lindsay, 2001; Leichtman et al., 2000), Thierry and Spence (2002) found that source monitoring training reduced preschoolers' suggestibility. Three- and 4-year-old children saw live and video versions of a science show that included target events. A few days later, before a target interview, children were trained to discriminate between what they had seen live and in the video. Compared with children in a control condition, those in the training condition were more accurate in responding to suggestive questions. This study may have resulted in better training for younger children than in Poole and Lindsay's (2002) research because children had to reach a specified training criterion before they were interviewed, and the interval between the original event and the interview was substantially shorter (3–4 days) than the 3 months in Poole and Lindsay (2002).

Similarly, Bright-Paul, Jarrold, and Wright (2005) found that using age-appropriate source-orienting tasks can substantially reduce preschoolers' suggestibility. Their source-orienting procedure involved verbally or pictorially directing 3- to 7-year-old children to sources of information (film or misleading narrative). The verbal orienting procedure simply asked children whether target information was from the film or narrative, and the pictorial version showed children a card with pictures of a television to represent the film source and a book to represent the narrative source. As expected, suggestibility decreased with age, but the magnitude of the difference between older and younger children was reduced when the picture source-orienting procedure was used.

Together, these studies show that being able to identify the source of information stored in memory can reduce children's suggestibility and inaccuracy in their reports. Older children benefit from relatively easy-source-training procedures, and provided age-appropriate and favorable conditions preschoolers benefit also.

## INDIVIDUAL DIFFERENCES ASSOCIATED WITH SUGGESTIBILITY

An important feature of recent research on social and cognitive factors affecting children's memory is the inclusion of assessments of individual differences, which may be helpful in determining particular children's propensity to suggestibility and false memories. This is important knowledge because in legal settings it is likely that the outcome of a case largely depends on an individual child's report.

In a recent qualitative review of the literature, Bruck and Melnyk (2004) summarized the results of 69 studies that examined the relationship between 17 individual difference factors and suggestibility. They concluded that, although no single factor consistently predicted children's vulnerability to suggestibility, a few factors did show high correlations with suggestibility. In this section, we review five factors found to have a strong association with children's suggestibility and relevant to forensic contexts: age, language ability, inhibitory control, working memory capacity, and attachment styles.

### Age

Intuitively, it can be expected that because of lack of experience, children, compared with adults, are more suggestible and their accounts of events less accurate and detailed. The empirical research presented thus far, along with studies that directly examined developmental trends in memory performance, supports this intuition. In a review of six programs of research on the construction of false events in memory, Pezdek and Hinz (2002) concluded that young children are more suggestible than older children and both of these groups are more suggestible than adults. Pezdek and Hodge (1999) found that, whereas 53% of the younger children developed a false memory for nonexperienced events, only 35% of older children did so, and these percentages differed from the 15% of adults in Pezdek et al. (1997) who developed a memory for a plausible false event.

Some studies have shown, however, that children as young 4 years can be resistant to suggestions about abuse-related events (Rudy & Goodman, 1991) and can free recall as much information in forensic interviews as 8-year-olds (Lamb et al., 2003). Similarly, in a short qualitative review of seven studies assessing children's memories for the VCUG procedure,

Sjöberg and Lindholm (2005) reported that, whereas there were expected age-related differences in commission errors (i.e., recall of nonexistent details) when focused suggestive questions were used, there were no age-related differences in regard to the amount of correct information freely recalled. Results such as these have led some researchers to suggest that age differences may be exaggerated in the literature and that tendencies to emphasize young children's heightened suggestibility may be misguided because older children and adults are also susceptible to suggestion (Bruck & Ceci, 2004). In general, however, most studies show clear developmental trends in suggestibility.

## Language Ability

The ability to use and understand language has been linked to decreased suggestibility in young children. The complexity of language used by adults in suggestive interviews can be confusing for children. For example, Imhoff and Baker-Ward (1999) found that using developmentally appropriate language during interviews (e.g., "Did you pour some blue slimy stuff into a big spoon?") resulted in preschoolers' reduced suggestibility compared with using standard interview language (e.g., "Did you pour some blue slimy stuff into the big measuring spoon?").

Bruck and Melnyk's (2004) review showed that half of 12 studies assessing various aspects of language ability reported an association with suggestibility in preschoolers: Children with advanced language ability were more resistant to misleading information than those with less advanced language ability. Moreover, significant relations between language ability and suggestibility emerged more clearly when comprehensive language tests were used than when a single measure was administered (Bruck & Melnyk, 2004). For example, Clarke-Stewart, Malloy, and Allhusen (2004) assessed 5-year-olds' language skill using various measures (e.g., language comprehension, expressive communication, language with adults) and assessed their correlation to suggestibility. Children participated in a target event followed by an interview that included various types of suggestive questions. The main finding was that higher scores on all language measures were associated with decreased overall suggestibility. Because language ability improves with age, it would be expected that research involving older children would show similar patterns of results.

## Mental Processing Abilities: Inhibitory Control and Working Memory Capacity

These two factors involve the ability to mentally process information effectively. "Inhibitory control" refers to the ability to ignore irrelevant information, and "working memory capacity" refers to the ability to hold information online for efficient processing. These two cognitive processes are related to suggestibility because increased ability on both of these dimensions theoretically allows children to ignore irrelevant or suggestive information (inhibitory control) while keeping track of relevant original event information (working memory capacity; Bruck & Melnyk, 2004). Although Bruck and Melnyk (2004) suggested that results of studies examining the relations of these aspects of mental function and suggestibility are too inconsistent to make definite conclusions, it is likely that the reason for this apparent lack of consistency is due to many factors, including the interview context (Bottoms, Quas, & Davis, 2007), differences in tasks (Roberts & Powell, 2005), and measures of suggestibility (Lee, 2004; Scullin & Bonner, 2006) that have been used within and across studies. This variability in methods can account for the difficulty in interpreting results.

However, recent findings suggest that these aspects of mental functioning account for unique variance in children's suggestibility. Alexander et al. (2002) reported that, after controlling for other important factors, inhibitory control significantly predicted children's suggestibility. Three- to 7-year-olds were tested on their ability to remember a traumatic event (inoculations during a regular checkup), and their cognitive inhibition ability was tested using a Stroop-like task in which children were instructed to respond to conflicting stimuli (say "moon" when a card depicted a sun). After statistically removing the effects of age, socioeconomic level, stress, and parental attachment, children with greater ability to ignore irrelevant information reported fewer incorrect details during free recall and were less likely to make errors when suggestively questioned.

Similarly, Clarke-Stewart et al. (2004) investigated the relations between suggestibility and inhibition in real-life situations by creating a composite measure called "adaptive-inhibitory control," which included experimenter observational data and parents' assessment of (1) children's self-control, (2) ability to follow directions, and (3) functioning in demanding situations. Children with better adaptive-inhibitory control were less likely to succumb to suggestion about nonexperienced harm and body touching than were children with lower inhibitory control. Together, these results suggest that inhibition as assessed with single laboratory tasks or multiple observational measures appears to predict children's suggestibility.

Research also shows that working memory capacity predicts children's suggestibility. Ruffman, Rustin, Garnham, and Parkin (2001) found that, after statistically accounting for age and language ability, children with high working memory capacity were more accurate than those with low working memory capacity in responding to questions about an experienced event. However, this relation may be moderated by contextual factors. In Bottoms et al. (2007), 6- to 7-year-old children determined to have low or high working memory capacity were interviewed about a laboratory experience by either a supportive or an unsupportive interviewer. Across interview conditions, children with low working memory capacity were more suggestible than children with high working memory capacity, confirming earlier findings. In addition, when the interview conditions were considered separately, a large correlation emerged between working memory capacity and suggestibility for children in the nonsupportive interview condition but not for those in the supportive interview condition. Thus, children with low working memory capacity were more suggestible if interviewed in a nonsupportive manner, but the negative effect of low working memory capacity was reduced if the interview was conducted in a supportive manner.

## Maternal Attachment and Quality of Parent–Child Relationship

Goodman and colleagues (e.g., Alexander et al., 2002; Edelstein et al., 2004; Goodman et al., 1997) have proposed an association between mothers' attachment patterns and children's ability to remember distressing events. Mothers who show secure attachments in their relationships with significant others, usually defined by lower levels of anxiety and less discomfort with close relationships, are more likely to discuss negative events that their children may experience. These discussions help children encode and store coherent and elaborate representations of such events. On the contrary, insecurely attached mothers, as defined by higher levels of anxiety and discomfort with close relationships, may transmit more fear and be less comforting to their children in the face of negative experiences. This state can lead to weaker encoding and poorer maintenance of the event memory, rendering children more vulnerable to suggestions.

As indicated in Bruck and Melnyk's (2004) review, children of securely attached mothers were less likely to acquiesce to suggestive questions than children of insecurely attached mothers in five of the six studies. In addition, recent research directly examining the quality of parent–child relationships (e.g., parents' attitudes and behaviors toward their children) shows an association between parents' relationships with their children and suggestibility. Clarke-Stewart et al. (2004) reported that fathers' positive support of their children (e.g., enjoys going to places the child likes) and mothers' healthy attachment styles were related to reduced overall suggestibility in children.

Also, of importance is that children of insecurely attached parents may be protected from suggestibility under some conditions. In the Bottoms et al. (2007) study, there were interactive effects of attachment style and interview condition. Children of insecurely attached parents reported less accurately in the unsupportive condition than in the supportive condition. Children with securely attached parents were not affected by interview condition. Thus, children of insecurely attached parents may be more suggestible in unsupportive forensic interviews. This effect, however, may be reduced if a supportive interview style is adopted.

## CONCLUSION

The quality and quantity of information obtained from children in forensic interviews can be increased by understanding and considering social-cognitive factors that affect children's memory abilities and implementing appropriate evidence-based procedures known to enhance children's ability to provide accurate reports. Forensically relevant factors that increase children's suggestibility and reduce the quality of their reports include (1) focused interview questions and props such as anatomically detailed dolls and human figure drawings, (2) high arousal or stress during retrieval of information, and (3) increased delays between initial experience and interview. When interview protocols include focused questions or props, it is likely that children's memory and their reports will be contaminated, thereby decreasing the reliability of the information. The use of props with young children is especially risky: Although props may help to elicit more correct details, they are equally likely to increase errors. Whenever possible, investigators should avoid these interview techniques and implement protocols such as the one developed by researchers at the National Institute of Child Health and Human Development (NICHD; see Lamb, Orbach, Hershkowitz, Esplin, & Horowitz, 2007, for a review of this procedure; see also Saywitz and Camparo, Chapter 6, this volume). Briefly, the NICHD protocol instructs interviewers to use open-ended questions with children of all ages, and if focused questions must be used to deal with omission of critical information, it is recommended that interviewers follow such questions with open-ended prompts.

Stress or increased arousal experienced during retrieval of events can increase children's suggestibility. Research shows that, although traumatic events can be highly memorable, stress experienced at retrieval impairs children's ability to recall details of events. This stress may be experienced during many legal proceedings, including the unsupportive interview context. The deleterious effect of stress may be reduced by providing a supportive environment in which children can focus more on searching memory for important information rather than on self-regulation. Finally, the longer the delay between an experience and the initial interview, the more likely it is that children will forget the experience and consequently be vulnerable to suggestive influences. Increased delay is especially a problem is sexual abuse cases, where children usually delay disclosure of the negative experience. In these cases in particular, it is important to use investigative techniques that reduce children's suggestibility.

Forensically relevant factors that decrease children's suggestibility and increase the quality of their reports include (1) knowledge base, (2) repeated experience, (3) multiple interviews, and (4) source memory training. Children's knowledge about events may help them resist misleading suggestions and avoid false memories in some cases. Prior or schematic knowledge about events helps to encode new information in a more coherent and well-organized manner that is more resistant to suggestive influences. This can increase the reliability of children's reports. However, under some conditions, prior knowledge may render a child susceptible to false memories. This is when a false event is considered plausible and suggestive interview procedures are employed. However, an important forensic-relevant event, sexual abuse, is perceived to be a personally implausible event by most people in the general population. Thus, it is likely that in the case of sexual abuse the lack of event knowledge reduces children's susceptibility to false memories.

Repeated experience of the same event and multiple nonsuggestive interviews can help children guard against suggestive influences. Repetition serves to keep event memory strong, elaborated, and active over long periods of time. Children's reports under these conditions can be quite reliable. Finally, children's ability to determine whether a particular detail in memory is from suggestions or from actual experience is a cognitive skill that may be influenced by social factors. Thus, it is possible, under some conditions, to train children before providing their accounts to carefully assess whether the to-be-reported information is from interviewer discussions or from actual experiences. This can decrease the detrimental effects of demand characteristics and improve the quality of the information obtained in a forensic interview.

Individual difference factors associated with lower levels of suggestibility include (1) increased age, (2) better language ability, (3) better mental processing abilities, and (4) parents exhibiting healthy attachment styles. Research shows that, although many factors can interact with age to influence levels of suggestibility, the general finding is that younger children are more suggestible than older children and these two groups are more suggestible than adults. Thus, although knowing a child's age is not enough to determine suggestibility, it can be a useful factor to consider when determining appropriateness of interview protocols. Ability to understand language can facilitate young children's resistance to suggestions; children better able to understand questions posed by interviewers are less likely to report erroneous information. Additionally, increased inhibitory control and working memory capacity, aspects of mental processing abilities, can protect children against misleading suggestions. Finally, children whose parents have positive attitudes toward them and who are securely attached are less suggestible than those whose parents do not show these characteristics. Although in forensic settings it may not be feasible to determine a particular child's mental processing capabilities or parents' attachment styles, it is important to note that a supportive interview context can help children overcome potential deficits in these and other domains.

## REFERENCES

Aldridge, J., Lamb, M. E., Sternberg, K. J., Orbach, Y., Esplin, P. W., & Bowler, L. (2004). Using a human figure drawing to elicit information from alleged victims of child sexual abuse. *Journal of Consulting and Clinical Psychology, 72,* 304–316.

Alexander, K. W., Goodman, G. S., Schaaf, J. M., Edelstein, R. S., Quas, J. A., & Shaver, P. R. (2002). The role of attachment and cognitive inhibition in children's memory and suggestibility for a stressful event. *Journal of Experimental Child Psychology, 83,* 262–290.

Blandón-Gitlin, I., Pezdek, K., Rogers, M., & Brodie, L. (2005). Detecting deception in children: An experimental study of the effect of event familiarity on CBCA ratings. *Law and Human Behavior, 29,* 187–197.

Bottoms, B. L., Quas, J. A., & Davis, S. L. (2007). The influence of the interviewer-provided social support on children's suggestibility, memory, and disclosures. In M.-E. Pipe, M. E. Lamb, Y. Orbach, & A. Cederborg (Eds.), *Child sexual abuse: Disclosure, delay, and denial* (pp. 135–157). Mahwah, NJ: Erlbaum.

Brainerd, C. J., & Poole, D. A. (1997). Long-term survival of children's false memories: A review. *Learning and Individual Differences, 9,* 125–151.

Bright-Paul, A., Jarrold, C., & Wright, D. B. (2005). Age-appropriate cues facilitate source-monitoring and reduce suggestibility in 3- to 7-year-olds. *Cognitive Development, 20,* 1–18.

Bruck, M., & Ceci, S. J. (1999). The suggestibility of children's memory. *Annual Review of Psychology, 50,* 419–439.

Bruck, M., & Ceci, S. J. (2004). Forensic developmental psychology: Unveiling four common misconceptions. *Current Directions in Psychological Science, 13,* 229–232.

Bruck, M., & Melnyk, L. (2004). Individual differences in children's suggestibility: A review and synthesis. *Applied Cognitive Psychology, 18,* 947–996.

Burgwyn-Bailes, E., Baker-Ward, L., Gordon, B. N., & Ornstein, P. A. (2001). Children's memory for emergency medical treatment after one year: The impact of individual difference variables on recall and suggestibility. *Applied Cognitive Psychology, 15,* 25–48.

Cahill, L., & McGaugh, J. L. (1998). Mechanisms of emotional arousal and lasting declarative memory. *Trends in Neurosciences, 21,* 294–299.

Ceci, S. J., Huffman, M. L. C., Smith, E., & Loftus, E. F. (1994). Repeatedly thinking about a non-event: Source misattributions among preschoolers. *Consciousness and Cognition, 3,* 388–407.

Clarke-Stewart, K. A., Malloy, L. C., & Allhusen, V. D. (2004). Verbal ability, self-control, and close relationships with parents protect children against misleading suggestions. *Applied Cognitive Psychology, 18,* 1037–1058.

de Quervain, D. J. F., Henke, K., Aerni, A., Treyer, V., McGaugh, J. L., Berthold, T., et al. (2003). Glucocorticoid-induced impairment of declarative memory retrieval is associated with reduced blood flow in the medial temporal lobe. *European Journal of Neuroscience, 17,* 1296–1302.

Edelstein, R. S., Alexander, K. W., Shaver, P. R., Schaaf, J. M., Quas, J. A., Lovas, G. S., et al. (2004). Adult attachment style and parental responsiveness during a stressful event. *Attachment and Human Development, 6,* 31–52.

Erdmann, K., Volbert, R., & Böhm, C. (2004). Children report suggested events even when interviewed in a non-suggestive manner: What are its implications for credibility assessment? *Applied Cognitive Psychology, 18,* 589–611.

Flin, R., Boon, J., Knox, A., & Bull, R. (1992). The effect of a five-month delay on children's and adults' eyewitness memory. *British Journal of Psychology, 83,* 323–336.

Goodman, G. S., Quas, J. A., Batterman-Faunce, J. M., Riddlesberger, M. M., & Kuhn, J. (1997). Children's reactions to and memory for a stressful event: Influences of age, anatomical dolls, knowledge, and parental attachment. *Applied Developmental Science, 1,* 54–75.

Goodman, G. S., Taub, E. P., Jones, D. P. H., & England, P. (1992). Testifying in criminal court: Emotional effects on child sexual assault victims. *Monographs of the Society for Research in Child Development, 57,* 142.

Goodman, G. S., Tobey, A. E., Batterman-Faunce, J. M., Orcutt, H. K., Thomas, S., Shapiro, C., et al. (1998). Face-to-face confrontation: Effects of closed-circuit technology on children's eyewitness testimony and jurors' decisions. *Law and Human Behavior, 22,* 165–203.

Hershkowitz, I. (2006). Delayed disclosure of alleged child abuse victims in Israel. *American Journal of Orthopsychiatry, 76,* 444–450.

Huffman, M. L. C., Crossman, A. M., & Ceci, S. J. (1997). Are false memories permanent? An investigation of the long-term effects of source misattributions. *Consciousness and Cognition, 6,* 482–490.

Hutcheson, G. D., Baxter, J. S., Telfer, K., & Warden, D. (1995). Child witness statement quality: Question type and errors of omission. *Law and Human Behavior, 19,* 631–648.

Imhoff, M. C., & Baker-Ward, L. (1999). Preschoolers' suggestibility: Effects of developmentally appropriate language and interviewer supportiveness. *Journal of Applied Developmental Psychology, 20,* 407–429.

Johnson, M. K., Foley, M. A., Suengas, A. G., & Raye, C. L. (1988). Phenomenal characteristics of memories for perceived and imagined autobiographical events. *Journal of Experimental Psychology: General, 117,* 371–376.

Lamb, M. E., Hershkowitz, I., Sternberg, K. J., Esplin, P. W., Hovav, M., Manor, T., et al. (1996). Effects of investigative utterance types on Israeli children's responses. *International Journal of Behavioral Development, 19,* 627–637.

Lamb, M. E., Orbach, Y., Hershkowitz, I., Esplin, P. W., & Horowitz, D. (2007). A structured forensic interview protocol improves the quality and informativeness of investigative interview with children: A review of research using the NICHD investigative interview protocol. *Child Abuse and Neglect, 31,* 1201–1231.

Lamb, M. E., Orbach, Y., Hershkowitz, I., Horowitz, D., & Abbott, C. B. (2007). Does the type of prompt affect the accuracy of information provided by alleged victims of abuse in forensic interviews? *Applied Cognitive Psychology, 21,* 1117–1130.

Lamb, M. E., Sternberg, K. J., & Esplin, P. W. (2000). Effects of age and delay on the amount of information provided by alleged sex abuse victims in investigative interviews. *Child Development, 71,* 1586–1596.

Lamb, M. E., Sternberg, K. J., Orbach, Y., Esplin, P. W., Stewart, H., & Mitchell, S. (2003). Age differences in young children's responses to open-ended invitations in the course of forensic interviews. *Journal of Consulting and Clinical Psychology, 71,* 926–934.

Lee, K. (2004). Age, neuropsychological, and social cognitive measures as predictors of individual differences in susceptibility to the misinformation effect. *Applied Cognitive Psychology, 18,* 997–1019.

Leichtman, M. D., Morse, M. B., Dixon, A., & Spiegel, R. (2000). Source monitoring and suggestibility: An individual differences approach. In K. P. Roberts & M. Blades (Eds.), *Children's source monitoring* (pp. 257–287). Mahwah, NJ: Erlbaum.

Malloy, L. C., Lyon, T. D., & Quas, J. A. (2007). Filial dependency and recantation of child sexual abuse allegations. *Journal of the American Academy of Child and Adolescent Psychiatry, 46,* 162–170.

Malloy, L. C., Mitchell, E. B., Block, S. D., Quas, J. A., & Goodman, G. S. (2007). Children's eyewitness memory: Balancing children's needs and defendants' rights when seeking the truth. In M. P. Toglia, J. D. Read, D. F. Ross, & R. C. L. Lindsay (Eds.), *The handbook of eyewitness psychology: Vol. 1. Memory for events* (pp. 545–574). Mahwah, NJ: Erlbaum.

Ornstein, P. A., Baker-Ward, L., Gordon, B. N., Pelphrey, K. A., Tyler, C. S., & Gramzow, E. (2006). The influence of prior knowledge and repeated questioning on children's long-term retention of the details of a pediatric examination. *Developmental Psychology, 42,* 332–344.

Peterson, C., Parsons, T., & Dean, M. (2004). Providing misleading and reinstatement information a year after it happened: Effects on long-term memory. *Memory, 12,* 1–13.

Pezdek, K., & Blandón-Gitlin, I. (2008). Planting false memories for childhood sexual abuse only happens to emotionally disturbed people ... Not me or my friends. *Applied Cognitive Psychology, 23,* 162–169.

Pezdek, K., Finger, K., & Hodge, D. (1997). Planting false childhood memories: The role of event plausibility. *Psychological Science, 8,* 437–441.

Pezdek, K., & Hinz, T. (2002). The construction of false events in memory. In H. Wescott, G. Davies, & R. Bull (Eds.), *Children's testimony: A handbook of psychological research and forensic practice* (pp. 99–116). New York: Wiley.

Pezdek, K., & Hodge, D. (1999). Planting false childhood memories in children: The role of event plausibility. *Child Development, 70,* 887–895.

Pezdek, K., & Lam, S. (2007). What research paradigms have cognitive psychologists used to study "false memory," and what are the implications of these choices? *Consciousness and Cognition, 16,* 2–17.

Pezdek, K., Morrow, A., Blandon-Gitlin, I., Goodman, G. S., Quas, J. A., Saywitz, K. J., et al. (2004). Detecting deception in children: Event familiarity affects criterion-based content analysis ratings. *Journal of Applied Psychology, 89,* 119–126.

Pezdek, K., & Roe, C. (1995). The effect of memory trace strength on suggestibility. *Journal of Experimental Child Psychology, 60,* 116–128.

Pezdek, K., & Taylor, J. (2002). Memory for traumatic events in children and adults. In M. L. Eisen, J. A. Quas, & G. S. Goodman (Eds.), *Memory and suggestibility in the forensic interview* (pp. 165–183). Mahwah, NJ: Erlbaum.

Poole, D. A., & Lindsay, D. S. (2001). Children's eyewitness reports after exposure to misinformation from parents. *Journal of Experimental Psychology: Applied, 7,* 27–50.

Poole, D. A., & Lindsay, D. S. (2002). Reducing child witnesses' false reports of misinformation from parents. *Journal of Experimental Child Psychology, 81,* 117–140.

Powell, M. B., Fisher, R. P., & Wright, R. (2005). Investigative interviewing. In N. Brewer & K. Williams (Eds.), *Psychology and law: An empirical perspective* (pp. 11–42). New York: Guilford Press.

Powell, M. B., Roberts, K. P., Ceci, S. J., & Hembrooke, H. (1999). The effects of repeated experience on children's suggestibility. *Developmental Psychology, 35,* 1462–1477.

Quas, J. A., & Lench, H. C. (2007). Arousal at encoding, arousal at retrieval, interviewer support, and children's memory for a mild stressor. *Applied Cognitive Psychology, 21,* 289–305.

Quas, J. A., Malloy, L. C., Melinder, A., Goodman, G. S., D'Mello, M., & Schaaf, J. (2007). Developmental differences in the effects of repeated interviews and interviewer bias on young children's event memory and false reports. *Developmental Psychology, 43,* 823–837.

Quas, J. A., Qin, J., Schaaf, J., & Goodman, G. S. (1997). Individual differences in children's and adults' suggestibility and false event memory. *Learning and Individual Differences, 9,* 359–390.

Roberts, K. P., & Powell, M. B. (2005). The relation between inhibitory control and children's eyewitness memory. *Applied Cognitive Psychology, 19,* 1003–1018.

Rudy, L., & Goodman, G. S. (1991). Effects of participation on children's reports: implications for children's testimony. *Developmental Psychology, 27,* 527–538.

Ruffman, T., Rustin, C., Garnham, W., & Parkin, A. J. (2001). Source monitoring and false memories in children: Relation to certainty and executive functioning. *Journal of Experimental Child Psychology, 80,* 95–111.

Scullin, M. H., & Bonner, K. (2006). Theory of mind, inhibitory control, and preschool-age children's suggestibility in different interviewing contexts. *Journal of Experimental Child Psychology, 93,* 120–138.

Sjöberg, R. L., & Lindholm, T. (2005). A systematic review of age-related errors in children's memories for voiding cysto-urethrograms (VCUG). *European Child and Adolescent Psychiatry, 14,* 104–105.

Thierry, K. L., & Spence, M. J. (2002). Source-monitoring training facilitates preschoolers' eyewitness memory performance. *Developmental Psychology, 38,* 428–437.

Chapter 5

# Child Sexual Abuse Investigations
## Lessons Learned from the McMartin and Other Daycare Cases

JAMES M. WOOD
DEBBIE NATHAN
M. TERESA NEZWORSKI
ELIZABETH UHL

During the 1980s and early 1990s, American newspaper headlines tracked an epidemic of bizarre sexual abuse cases as it spread across the nation. From California to Massachusetts to Florida, hundreds of young children reported being victimized by their teachers and daycare workers, often in orgies involving sex rings or satanic cults (Jenkins, 1998; Nathan & Snedeker, 1995).

Virtually all early media coverage of these so-called daycare abuse cases was uncritical and sensationalistic. Television programs and magazine stories credulously reported electrifying claims that the nation's preschools had been infiltrated by networks of Satan worshipers, essentially witch covens. However, over time, cautionary investigative articles began to appear (Nathan, 1987, 1988; Rabinowitz, 1990). Skepticism deepened even more after jurors acquitted the defendants in the notorious McMartin daycare case in Los Angeles in 1990 and as sociologists and psychologists began to raise serious doubts about the validity of the allegations in similar cases (Ceci & Bruck, 1993; Victor, 1993; see also Bikel, 1991, 1993a, 1993b). By

1995, after defendants in even more cases were acquitted or had their convictions overturned, the daycare abuse panic was mainly over.

Social scientists now generally agree that, although sexual abuse of children is a real and important social problem, the bizarre allegations that fueled the daycare cases of the 1980s were mainly or entirely false (Bottoms & Davis, 1997; Butler, Fukurai, Dimitrius, & Krooth, 2001; de Young, 2004; Jenkins, 1998; La Fontaine, 1998; Victor, 1998). Scholarly interest has come to focus not on whether the allegations were true but instead on two questions that form the topic of this chapter: What contributing factors created these bizarre cases? What practical lessons can be learned from them to guide child abuse investigations in the present?

In some important respects, these cases may seem remote from the routine sexual abuse cases seen by law enforcement and child protection services (CPS) today. Most important, the daycare cases of the 1980s were characterized by epidemics of false allegations by children, whereas the large majority of sexual abuse allegations made by children to police and CPS today are probably true and reliable. In addition, the community hysteria and investigative excesses seen in the 1980s are only rarely encountered today, thanks largely to changes in forensic and interviewing procedures that have been made during the intervening years. However, although the daycare cases of the 1980s are not typical, they can teach a great deal about the problems that can engulf children and communities even today when the necessary factors converge.

## WHAT FUELED THE GREAT DAYCARE ABUSE CASES?

Commentators have identified several contributing factors that fueled the false allegations and daycare abuse cases of the 1980s. Three receive in-depth attention in this chapter: the "satanic panic" that was sweeping across some segments of American society during those years, the suggestive interviews of children by police and child protection investigators, and the "witch hunt" mentality that was ignited in some communities.

### Factor 1: Satanic Panic

It is surprising to realize that the last major witch hunts on North American soil occurred not in Salem, Massachusetts, in 1692 but in communities such as Los Angeles, California, and Maplewood, New Jersey, in the 1980s. During the Middle Ages and well into the modern period, Europe periodically spawned persecutions in which tens of thousands of innocent people were accused of belonging to witch covens and participating in satanic rituals known as "Sabbats" or "Sabbaths," which included human sacrifice, cannibalism, incest, and orgiastic sex (Cohn, 2000). In the 1600s, witch fever infected England's American colonies, giving rise to the Salem trials and other similar episodes (Hill, 1995; Kittredge, 1929). However, by 1750, the witch persecution had burnt itself out, so that two centuries later, in the era of moon landings and nuclear reactors, few observers would have predicted its revival.

The unexpected outbreak of witch fever in late 20th-century America was inaugurated with the 1980 publication of *Michelle Remembers*. This book, by Michelle Smith and her psychiatrist, Lawrence Pazder, told the story of Smith's childhood in Victoria, Canada, where she was purportedly reared in a satanic cult and forced to participate in devil worship, mutilation of corpses, and cannibalistic rites. Although Smith's lurid autobiographical account was exposed as false about a decade after its publication (Allen & Midwinter, 1990; Nathan & Snedeker, 1995), during the intervening years it became a minor best-seller and its portrayal of devil-worshiping sex abusers and "ritual abuse" (a term coined by Pazder) was accepted as true by many influential religious leaders.

*Michelle Remembers* would probably have had little lasting effect had it not appeared at a critical moment in the very beginning of the 1980s when a broad movement of fundamentalist and evangelical Christians was expanding its social and political influence across the United States. Many fundamentalist and conservative leaders of the time believed in satanic conspiracies and saw satanist influences in school textbooks, rock music, and games like Dungeons and Dragons (Jenkins, 1998; Victor, 1993). During the 1980s, the percentage of Americans who believed in the devil increased, and a substantial number of isolated "rumor panics" occurred in which entire communities became electrified by false rumors of local satanic activity, such as the ritualistic murder of animals or the kidnapping of blond teenage girls for sacrifice as virgins (Victor, 1993).

In the context of this broader "satanic panic," certain segments of American society were primed to accept the underlying premise of *Michelle Remembers*: that well-organized cults of devil worshipers had infiltrated Canada and the United States. Some law enforcement trainers, often from conservative Christian backgrounds, set themselves up as experts in satanism and provided workshops to police across the country (Hicks, 1991). When these so-called experts were consulted in prominent sexual abuse cases, children sometimes began to produce allegations involving satanic abuse, thus lending greater credibility to the belief that ritual abuse was a genuine phenomenon.

Many mental health professionals were also swept up in the panic. For example, a substantial number of feminist psychotherapists came to believe in the repressed memories of patients who described having been ritually abused as children (Ofshe & Watters, 1994; Pendergrast, 1996). Similarly, prominent experts on multiple-personality disorder (now known as dissociative identity disorder) claimed that the condition was frequently the result of horrendous childhood abuse by satanic cults (Acocella, 1999).

Only after more than a decade did America's 20th-century witch fever subside. Several factors contributed to its demise. First, as already noted, several criminal prosecutions of alleged satanic abusers collapsed in the early 1990s as defendants were acquitted by juries or released by appellate courts. Second, a growing number of journalists, academics, and members of law enforcement questioned the reality of ritual abuse and the validity of the allegations in prominent daycare cases (e.g., Bikel, 1991, 1993a, 1993b; Ceci & Bruck, 1993; Bottoms & Davis, 1997; Bottoms, Shaver, & Goodman, 1996; Lanning, 1991; Nathan & Snedeker, 1995; Victor, 1993). Third, in several well-publicized lawsuits, mental health professionals were successfully sued for having induced false memories of ritual abuse in their clients (e.g., Bloomberg, 2000).

## Factor 2: Suggestive Interviewing

Because virtually all allegations of organized satanic crime during the past several hundred years have been false, prosecutors of these cases have generally been unable to find reliable legal evidence to convict accused witches in court. For this reason, witch hunters from earlier periods (and modernday satanist hunters) have inevitably depended on types of evidence that, in retrospect, can be recognized as seriously flawed. For instance, in the great European witch hunts, defendants were routinely convicted and burned based on unreliable confessions that had been extracted by torture (Wood, 2005).

In the daycare abuse cases of the 1980s, unreliable evidence came in many different forms, including poorly validated medical tests, coerced confessions, and the testimony of "jailhouse snitches" (Nathan & Snedeker, 1995). However, the crucial evidence in most cases was the testimony of the alleged child victims, which tended to be compelling given the commonly held assumption at the time that "children don't lie about abuse."

When several children testified, as was often true in daycare cases, disbelief in their allegations seemed impossible. Yet as these cases proceeded through the legal system, a substantial number of juries and appeals courts declined to accept the prosecution's claims. They did so not because of an ill-founded distrust of the children's honesty or testimonial competence, but because it became clear that the allegations had been elicited by suggestive and manipulative interviewing techniques. Scientific research over the past 20 years has further confirmed that suggestive interviewing played a crucial role in these cases. In fact, without suggestive interviewing, it is unlikely that any of the major daycare cases of the 1980s would have proceeded to trial. The following sections describe two highly publicized daycare cases from that era and the suggestive interviewing techniques used in them.

## The McMartin Preschool Case

The McMartin Preschool case was the first daycare case in the United States to receive national media attention (for a detailed history, see Butler et al., 2001). In 1983, seven teachers at the McMartin Preschool in the affluent Los Angeles suburb of Manhattan Beach were accused of kidnapping children and flying them to an isolated farm, where children saw animals tortured and were forced to engage in group sex. Charges were eventually dropped against five of the teachers. The remaining two defendants, Peggy McMartin Buckey and her son Raymond Buckey, were tried in the longest criminal case in U.S. history. Peggy Buckey was acquitted on all charges and Raymond on most charges. Jurors failed to reach a decision on the remaining counts against Raymond, and prosecutors eventually dropped all charges in 1990. By then, Raymond had already spent 5 years, and Peggy nearly 2 years, in the Los Angeles County jail because of their inability to raise bail, which was set at more than $1.5 million (Reinhold, 1990). After the trial, jurors publicly criticized interviewers in the case for coaxing children into making allegations against the defendants (Reinhold, 1990; Wilkerson & Rainey, 1990). The McMartin case was later dramatized in *Indictment,* an Emmy award-winning television movie that was highly critical of the prosecutors and interviewers.

The McMartin interviews have been the subject of considerable commentary and scientific research (e.g., Nathan & Snedeker, 1995; Butler et al., 2001; Garven, Wood, & Malpass, 2000; Garven, Wood, Malpass, & Shaw, 1998). This section focuses specifically on a study by Nadja Schreiber and her colleagues (2006) that was carried out in the laboratory of James M. Wood. Schreiber et al. compared interviews from the McMartin case and the Kelly Michaels case (which is described later in this chapter) with a sample of sexual abuse interviews from a CPS agency in the southwestern United States. These CPS interviews were chosen as a standard of comparison because, in an earlier study, they had been shown to be highly similar to CPS interviews collected in another part of the United States (Warren, Garven, Walker, & Goodall, 2000) and could be assumed to be fairly typical of CPS interviews in general.

Schreiber and her colleagues (2006) found that, compared with the CPS interviews, the McMartin interviews were characterized by the use of four highly suggestive techniques. The first of these techniques—Positive Consequences—was defined as (1) giving or promising praise or other rewards to a child or (2) indicating that the child could demonstrate helpfulness, intelligence, or other good qualities by making a statement to the interviewer (more detailed operational definitions can be found in Schreiber et al.). For instance, interviewers in the McMartin case used Positive Consequences by saying things like, "Oh, you're so smart. I knew you'd remember" and "So I bet if you guys put on your thinking caps, you can help remember it. Now let's make a test of your brain and see how good your memories are."

As can be seen, Positive Consequences involves the use of positive reinforcement—praise, rewards, or the promise of praise and rewards—to shape children's behavior. Schreiber and her colleagues (2006) found that this technique was substantially more common in the McMartin interviews than the CPS interviews. Specifically, the researchers divided each interview into numbered exchanges, with each exchange consisting of one turn by the interviewer and one turn by the child, and then counted the number of exchanges in which the interviewer used the suggestive technique. The results of this analysis showed that the Positive Consequences technique was used in 18% of the exchanges in the McMartin interviews but in only 7% of the exchanges in the CPS interviews (a statistically significant difference, considered in this chapter to be $p < .005$).

These percentages can be put in context by realizing that the McMartin interviews tended to be very long (usually more than 1 hour) with an average of 575 exchanges, whereas the typical CPS interview lasted only about 21 minutes with an average of 164 exchanges. Because of the difference in interview length, the Positive Consequences technique was used approximately 103 times (18% of 575 exchanges) in a typical McMartin interview but only 12 times (7% of 164 exchanges) in a CPS interview. Compared with the McMartin interviewers, the CPS interviewers not only used Positive Consequences far less frequently, but they also tended to use the technique in a manner that was relatively innocuous and nonsuggestive, such as complimenting the child during the early rapport-building stage of an interview or thanking a child at the very end of an interview for the child's earlier cooperation.

The second suggestive technique used by the McMartin interviewers—Other People (Schreiber et al. (2006)—involved telling the child that the interviewer had talked with other people regarding the topics of the interview or telling the child what other people had supposedly said. Here is an example from a McMartin interview:

"You see all the kids in this picture? Every single kid in this picture has come here and talked to us. Isn't that amazing? ... These kids came to visit us and we found out they know a lot of yucky old secrets from that old school. And they all came and told us the secrets. And they're helping us figure out this whole puzzle of what used to go on in that place. ..."

As can be seen, the Other People technique pressures a child to conform and go along with what other people have supposedly said. Schreiber and her colleagues (2006) found that CPS interviewers virtually never used this technique (specifically, it occurred in less than 1% of exchanges). In contrast, the McMartin interviewers used this technique in 7% of exchanges, a statistically significant difference. Applying the same arithmetic as previously, the average number of exchanges in which a McMartin interviewer told the child about what other people said was approximately 40 (7% of 575).

The third suggestive technique—Inviting Speculation—involved asking the child to guess, speculate, pretend, or imagine what had happened. Here is an example from a McMartin interview:

INTERVIEWER: Now, I think this is another one of those tricky games. What do you *think*, Rags?

CHILD: Yep.

INTERVIEWER: Yes. Do you *think* some of that yucky touching happened, Rags, when she was tied up and she couldn't get away? Do you *think* some of that touching that—Mr. Ray *might* have done some of that touching? Do you *think* that's *possible*? Where do you *think* he *would have* touched her? Can you use your pointer and show us where he *would have* touched her? [emphasis added]

The technique of Inviting Speculation encourages children to guess, speculate, or pretend rather than simply report what they have observed. Schreiber and her colleagues (2006) found that the McMartin interviewers used the Inviting Speculation technique eight times more frequently than the CPS interviewers did (8% of exchanges vs. 1%), a statistically significant difference. Using the same arithmetic as before, this means that McMartin children were invited to guess or pretend approximately 40 times per interview.

The fourth suggestive technique—Introducing Information—involved introducing new negative, violent, or sexual information into an interview that was not previously mentioned by the child. Here is an example from a McMartin interview:

INTERVIEWER: How about Naked Movie Star? You guys remember that game?

CHILD: No.

INTERVIEWER: Everybody remembered that game. Let's see if we can figure it out.

As can be seen, the technique of Introducing Information involves what
lawyers call "leading" or "suggestive" questioning. Of course, if a child
already feels pressured to make false allegations, Introducing Information
indicates precisely what kind of allegations are expected. It should be noted
that Introducing Information is very broadly defined and can overlap with
other suggestive techniques. For instance, in the example just given, the
interviewer also uses the Other People technique ("Everybody remembered
that game") and Inviting Speculation ("Let's see if we can figure it out").

Schreiber and her colleagues (2006) found that CPS interviewers used
the Introducing Information technique in only about 3% of exchanges.
Because the typical CPS interview contained only 164 exchanges, on average the number of exchanges involving Introducing Information was about
five (3% of 164). In contrast, the McMartin interviewers used Introducing Information in 18% of exchanges, significantly different from the CPS
interviews. Given the greater length of the McMartin interviews, this works
out to more than 100 exchanges per interview. Clearly, the McMartin investigators were injecting many negative, violent, and sexual ideas into the
interviews.

Later in this chapter we discuss how the interviewing techniques used in
the McMartin case affect children's accuracy. However, before doing so, we
briefly discuss the second daycare case studied by Schreiber et al. (2006).

## The Kelly Michaels Case

In 1988, Kelly Michaels, a 26-year-old daycare worker in Maplewood, New
Jersey, was convicted and sentenced to 47 years in prison for sexually abus-
ing 20 preschool children (for a detailed history, see Nathan, 1988; Rabinowitz, 1990). Children alleged that, over a period of 7 months, Michaels
repeatedly raped them with spoons, forks, and Lego blocks; compelled them
to swallow her urine and feces; and forced them to lie naked in the shape of
a satanic pentagram.

Following Michael's conviction, the fairness of her trial was questioned
by investigative articles in the *Village Voice* (Nathan, 1988) and *Harper's
Magazine* (Rabinowitz, 1990). In 1993 Michael's conviction was reversed
by the Appeals Court of New Jersey (*State v Michaels*, 1994), which ruled
that the children who testified against her were interviewed in a manner
so suggestive as to render their statements unreliable (Nathan & Snedeker,
1995).

Taking the same approach as with the McMartin case, Schreiber et al.
(2006) studied interviews from the Michaels case and found that they were

characterized by two suggestive techniques. First, the Michaels interviewers used the Introducing Information technique in 18% of exchanges, which was the same percentage as in the McMartin interviews but substantially higher than the 3% in CPS interviews, a statistically significant difference. Put another way, new negative, sexual, or violent information was introduced 34 times in a typical Michaels interview (18% of 190 exchanges) compared with five times in a typical CPS interview.

The second suggestive technique used by the Michaels interviewers—Negative Consequences (Schreiber et al., 2006)—involved criticizing or disagreeing with a child's statement or otherwise indicating that the child's statement was not fully believed. The following is an example from a Michaels interview:

> INTERVIEWER: Were you ever afraid of Kelly?
>
> CHILD: No.
>
> INTERVIEWER: No?
>
> CHILD: No.
>
> INTERVIEWER: Would you tell me if you were afraid of her?

Like Positive Consequences, Negative Consequences is a form of reinforcement. Whereas Positive Consequences gives the child praise or other rewards for statements, Negative Consequences conveys disapproval or disbelief. Schreiber and her colleagues (2006) found that the Michaels interviewers used Negative Consequences in 15% of exchanges—about 28 times per interview—compared with 4% for CPS interviewers, a statistically significant difference. Put another way, the Michaels interviewers often conveyed disbelief and doubt when children failed to say what the interviewers were expecting.

## Impact of Suggestive Techniques on Children

The foregoing discussion has identified five suggestive techniques that were applied in the McMartin and Michaels cases and in other similar cases not discussed here. This chapter does not present a full scientific review of these techniques and their impact on children because good reviews are already available (Poole & Lamb, 1998; Melnyk, Crossman, & Scullin, 2007; Myers, Saywitz, & Goodman, 1996). However, four points are worth noting not only because they shed light on the daycare cases of the 1980s but because they provide insights relevant to child interviewing practices in the present and future.

1. *All five of the suggestive techniques discussed here have been shown to exert a negative effect on children's accuracy in interviews.* For this rea-

son, all five techniques should be avoided in child sexual abuse interviews (for a summary of relevant research, see Schreiber et al., 2006). A total elimination of suggestive techniques may sometimes be impractical; for instance, even the CPS interviewers studied by Schreiber and her colleagues occasionally used the Introducing Information technique. However, all the techniques should be kept to a minimum, and some, such as Other People or Inviting Speculation, are so rare in ordinary CPS work that their appearance in an interview can be a red flag indicating a seriously flawed interview.

2. *Younger children are especially vulnerable to the negative suggestive effects of Introducing Information.* Of the five suggestive techniques identified here, the most thoroughly researched has been Introducing Information, which is often called "postevent misinformation." Research summarized in the reviews that we have cited indicates that the negative impact of postevent misinformation is age related. Specifically, postevent misinformation (1) can somewhat reduce the accuracy of some witnesses over a wide age range, including adults, (2) has a greater negative impact on children younger than 10 than on older individuals, and (3) has the strongest negative impact on very young children (4 years or younger).

3. *Interviewing techniques that involve reinforcement—that is, Positive Consequences and Negative Consequences—can have an especially powerful and swift suggestive influence on children, including children as old as 7 years.* In the McMartin and Michaels interviews, frequently children initially denied abuse but then were induced to change their stories a few minutes later. Results from a study that examined the effects of McMartin interviewing techniques on a nonabused community sample of children suggest that Positive Consequences and Negative Consequences were probably responsible for the children's swift turnabout. Specifically, Garven et al. (2000) found that when first- and second-graders were questioned using Positive and Negative Consequences in interviews lasting less than 5 minutes, about 50% of children could be induced to make false allegations (based on the McMartin case) that a man had flown them away from their school in a helicopter and taken them to a farm.

Research by Garven et al. (2000) and Finnila, Mahlberg, Santtila, Sandnabba, & Niemi (2003) supports the conclusion that the suggestive impact of the McMartin and Michaels interviews was due mainly to two factors. First, the interviewers *motivated* or *pressured* the children to make accusations by using Positive Consequences and Negative Consequences. Second, the interviewers *obliquely informed* the children what the accusations should be by Introducing Information. Thus, the total suggestive impact on children depended on a combination of both *motivational* and *informational/cognitive* components.

4. *The suggestive influence of Positive Consequences and Negative*

*Consequences often persists over time.* In the McMartin case, some children who were pressured into making false allegations later recanted them. However, other children persisted in their allegations and apparently came to believe, or internalized, them. Research by Garven et al. (2000) sheds light on this phenomenon. After inducing children to make false allegations in an initial interview using reinforcement (Positive and Negative Consequences), the investigators returned about a week later and questioned the children a second time, this time *without* reinforcement. Surprisingly, the children continued to make false allegations at the same rate that they had previously. That is, the effects of the reinforcement from a week before continued to shape the children's answers. The investigators then pointedly asked the children whether their allegations were based on what they had seen personally or if instead they were just describing what they had heard from other children. Even under this pressure, about half the children who had already made false reports insisted that their allegations were based on firsthand observation. For example, approximately 25% of children (about half of the original 50%) insisted that they had, in fact, been flown away from their school to a farm. Such findings are sobering because they suggest that under some circumstances it can be difficult or impossible to "undo" the negative effects of using reinforcement during an interview (although for a study in which suggestive influences were partially reversed following a 2-year period without reinforcement, see Huffman, Crossman, & Ceci, 1997).

## Factor 3: Community Panic and Contamination

Although suggestive child interviews played a central role in the daycare cases of the 1980s, there were also powerful social and emotional forces operating outside the interviewing room to pressure children into make false allegations. The McMartin case illustrates how a rumor panic (or "mass hysteria") can surge through a community and set off a cascade of false accusations.

The first accusations in the McMartin case were made in August 1983 by a woman named Judy Johnson, who alleged that her 3-year-old son and other children had been tied up and sodomized by Raymond Buckey (Nathan & Snedeker, 1995). As later events would show, Johnson was exhibiting the early symptoms of a psychotic illness complicated by alcohol dependence. Over the next 3 years, her condition would steadily worsen and her allegations would grow ever more bizarre, until her death in 1986 from alcohol-induced liver damage. However, when Johnson first raised her allegations, they were accepted at face value by a medical intern and then by police. Soon afterward, in a letter mailed to more than 200 families, police urged parents of former or current McMartin students to question their children about whether they had been fondled or sodomized by Ray Buckey.

Not surprisingly, the letter set off a full-scale panic. Parents began questioning their children, sometimes for several days in a row. When children said nothing had happened, parents often refused to believe the denials and continued to ask questions. When children eventually reported abuse—no matter how strange or self-contradictory their descriptions of what had happened—the allegations were relayed by phone to other parents, who then requestioned their own children.

Within weeks, as allegations multiplied, families began to create an informal network that guaranteed contamination, that is, the sharing of rumors, genuine information, and misinformation. Bizarre new accusations began to surface, including descriptions of satanic rites, and children began to name not only Raymond Buckey as a perpetrator but also his mother and several other women who taught at the school. In the families of the supposed victims, emotions ranged from intense grief over their children's supposed victimization to equally intense rage and threats of violence toward the accused.

In this explosive atmosphere, there was little room for cool appraisals of the evidence. Although many of the children's allegations contradicted each other or were inconsistent with known facts, the inconsistencies were ignored by parents and the law enforcement community. Indeed, the legal authorities and media were also swept up in the panic and contributed to the spread of misinformation. For instance, an assistant district attorney announced to the press that there were "millions of child pornography photographs and films" of the victims, even though, in fact, no such photographs were ever found. Similarly, the press was "plunged into hysteria, sensationalism ... and a 'lynch mob syndrome'" (Shaw, 1990).

More than 20 years later, in 2005, one of the alleged McMartin victims, Kyle Zirpolo, came forward to recant his accusations and explain why he had lied. His account, published in the *Los Angeles Times* (Zirpolo & Nathan, 2005), provided a rare inside picture of the way that the panic and contamination in the McMartin case affected the children. Besides describing the suggestive techniques used by interviewers in the case, Zirpolo told how, with good intentions, his parents pressured him to make accusations against his teachers:

> My parents asked if the teachers took pictures and played games with us. Games like "Naked Movie Star." I remember my mom asking me. She would ask if they sang the song, and I didn't know what she was talking about, so she would sing something like, "Who you are, you're a naked movie star." I'm pretty sure that's the first time I ever heard that: from my mom. After she asked me a hundred times, I probably said yeah, I did play that game.
>
> My parents were very encouraging when I said that things happened. It was almost like saying things happened was going to help get these

people in jail and stop them from what they were trying to do to kids. Also, there were so many kids saying all these things happened that you didn't want to be the one who said nothing did. You wouldn't be believed if you said that. (Zirpolo & Nathan, 2005, pp. I.12–I.13)

As can be seen, Kyle Zirpolo's parents naively resorted to some of the same suggestive techniques discussed earlier in this chapter: Introducing Information, Other People, Positive Consequences, and Negative Consequences. In retrospect, their intense questioning may have been even more problematic than the official investigative interviews because it lasted for weeks and left no record of what was said.

## WHAT PRACTICAL LESSONS CAN BE LEARNED FROM THE DAYCARE ABUSE CASES?

The daycare cases of the 1980s, tainted with witch-hunt fever and the fear of ritual abuse, can seem so strange that it is natural to wonder whether they offer any lessons for the everyday work of law enforcement and child protection agencies. Exotic though they were, however, these cases have proven to be a rich source of insights regarding child witnesses and the investigation of sexual abuse cases. For example, much that has been learned about child suggestibility in the past 25 years was discovered by researchers who set out to understand what went wrong in the McMartin and similar cases. This new knowledge has had an enormous impact on the way child testimony is presently viewed in legal settings.

The remainder of this chapter discusses three other areas in which valuable practical lessons can be learned. The lessons will be framed as recommendations, some of which are already widely accepted, whereas others are offered here for the first time in hope of sparking future discussion.

### Improving Child Forensic Interviews

When prominent daycare prosecutions began to unravel in the early 1990s, many participants in the legal system came to recognize the need for procedures that would minimize suggestive influences in child forensic interviews of children. The following two recommendations are, therefore, widely accepted and frequently adhered to.

### *Recommendation 1*

Child forensic interviewers should receive specialized training. The instructional curriculum should include lessons not only on how to conduct interviews but also on the types of suggestive techniques and the reasons to avoid them. Strong preference should be given to approaches that are based on research and have been empirically tested in peer-reviewed scientific studies, such as the National Institute of Child Health and Human Development (NICHD) interviewing protocol developed by Lamb and his colleagues (Lamb, Orbach, Hershkowitz, Esplin, & Horowitz, 2007; for review, see Saywitz & Camparo, Chapter 6, this volume). Supervisors should regularly monitor interviews to ensure that they are conducted properly. Occasional quality checks of randomly selected interviews by outside qualified experts might also be desirable.

### Recommendation 2

All forensic interviews of children, including but not limited to sexual abuse interviews, should be audiotaped or videotaped, with the tapes retained as evidence. Recording serves two purposes: (1) to create a detailed, objective record of the child's statement and (2) to verify that the interview was conducted in a nonsuggestive manner. To accomplish these purposes, it is essential that *all* investigative interviews be recorded, not just the final interview in the investigative process.

## Identifying Possible Sources of Contamination

In a surprising number of daycare cases in the 1980s, the original false allegations did not freely emerge from children but instead were elicited under pressure by a fearful or even delusional adult (e.g., Judy Johnson). Once a community panic was set in motion, additional false allegations arose as a result of suggestive questioning by parents or therapists, as with Kyle Zirpolo in the McMartin case.

Contamination of children's statements was particularly pervasive in the daycare cases but can also be a problem in some ordinary sexual abuse cases seen by CPS and police. Although fairly uncommon, contamination can have extremely serious consequences, for example when children are unnecessarily removed from their parents on the basis of false allegations or when criminal charges are filed against innocent adults. The authors of this chapter, therefore, offer two recommendations that can help identify contamination of children's statements when it occurs.

### Recommendation 3

When a child makes allegations of abuse or other wrongdoing during a forensic interview, the interviewer should systematically inquire about possible contaminating influences that might have affected the child's statement.

A particularly good example of such an inquiry can be found in the NICHD protocol developed by Lamb et al. (2007, pp. 1229–1230), which includes a section entitled "Information about the Disclosure." Coming near the end of the interview, this section includes several open-ended questions about the disclosure process and possible contamination: "Now I want to understand how other people found out about [the last incident of alleged abuse]. Who was the first person besides you and [the perpetrator] to find out about the [alleged abuse]? Tell me everything about how this [first person] found out ... Tell me everything you talked about."

In addition to the questions about the disclosure process included in the NICHD protocol, we recommend that inquiries be made about other possible sources of contamination. For example, the investigator might inquire, "Have you heard about [the alleged perpetrator] doing bad things to other people? How did you hear? Tell me everything you heard."

## Recommendation 4

Before being interviewed by CPS or police about sexual abuse or other wrongdoing, many children have previously discussed the allegations with a trusted confidante: a parent, caretaker, or friend. We recommend that investigators always conduct an interview with the person we call the "first confidante," that is, the first person with whom the child discussed the allegations (also sometimes called the "outcry witness"). The interview of the first confidante should be conducted early in an investigation, if possible on the same day that the child is first interviewed, and should be audio- or videotaped. In the interview, the investigator should determine, among other things, how the allegations arose and what the child told the confidante.

Most CPS and police investigators already routinely interview the first confidante. Thus, our recommendation involves only two slight modifications to current practice. First, we suggest that this interview always be recorded to ensure that all relevant information is preserved. In our experience, written summaries are often unsatisfactory because they tend to be overly terse and omit valuable information. Second, we suggest that the interview of the first confidante should routinely explore the possibility that the child's statement has been contaminated. Here are some questions that might be helpful for this purpose: "Has the child made any statements to you regarding inappropriate touch or other wrongdoing? When was the most recent time that the child made these statements? How did the subject come up? Please start at the beginning and tell me everything you can remember about the conversation, including what you said and what the child said."

Other helpful lines of questioning might include the following: "Did you ever have prior conversations with the child about inappropriate touching? Please tell me about those conversations, including what you said and what the child said. Have you ever talked with someone else besides this child about inappropriate touching or other wrongdoing by this perpetrator? Before the child told you about the inappropriate touching (or other wrongdoing), did you have suspicions that the child had been victimized? Why?"

## Preventing and Managing Community Panics

The previous recommendations apply to all child forensic interviews. Those that follow, in contrast, are relevant only to cases that have a high potential for setting off a community panic, that is, cases involving multiple alleged perpetrators or multiple victims or in which the alleged perpetrator is a teacher, daycare worker, or someone with extensive contact with children.

Unless managed carefully, such panic-prone cases can sometimes turn into legal and public relations disasters, much like the daycare cases of the 1980s. They have the potential to divide communities into angry factions, tarnish investigators' and prosecutors' reputations, and erode the already-strained budgets of child protection agencies and district attorneys' offices (for a recent example, see Moran, 2008). The following recommendations are intended to help decision makers manage these difficult cases.

### *Recommendation 5*

Panic-prone cases typically begin with an initial allegation from a single child, such as a report of sexual abuse by a teacher. Before widening the scope of the case, for instance, by conducting mass interviews of the child's classmates, investigators should carefully consider an important question: How strong is the evidence that supports the initial allegation of abuse? In cases that later turn into disasters, the initial allegation is typically very weak. For example, the allegation may have come from a very young or mentally disabled child who failed to provide a coherent, detailed description of the abuse. Or the allegation may have been extracted under pressure from a child by an overanxious or even delusional adult. Before launching a wide-reaching investigation that risks setting off a community panic, decision makers need to examine the available evidence with a critical eye and ask themselves whether it is strong enough to justify such a risk.

### *Recommendation 6*

After careful consideration, investigators in a case of this type may decide to press forward and conduct mass interviews of children. For example, if a child has accused a teacher of inappropriate touching at school, a decision may be made to interview all children in the teacher's class one by one to identify other possible victims. The decision to conduct dozens of interviews is a serious one because it may well create a rumor panic among the students in the school and their parents. At present, there is no well-established, "off-the-shelf" protocol for conducting mass interviews of schoolchildren. Therefore, our suggestions are offered tentatively.

First, if mass interviews are considered necessary, we suggest that they be carried out and completed as soon as possible, preferably within 1 or 2 days after the initial allegation is received. Speed is necessary to ensure that the interviews are completed before community panic sets in, with the inevitable cross-contamination among children and their parents.

Second, although speed is necessary, so is adherence to sound interviewing procedures. Specifically, interviewers should be well trained, strictly adhere to standard interviewing procedures, and scrupulously avoid suggestive techniques. All interviews should be conducted individually rather than in groups and should be recorded either on audiotape or videotape. Deviations from good practice should be firmly resisted because of their potential to generate false allegations and fuel community panic.

Third, parents should be notified after the interviewing process has begun (e.g., in a letter sent home from school at the end of the first day of interviewing). However, until all interviews are completed (preferably within the first or second day of interviewing), no information should be released regarding the nature of the allegations or the identity of the alleged perpetrator. Parents should be assured that additional information will be available as soon as interviewing is completed.

## Recommendation 7

At some point, investigators will probably need to provide information to the media and families. However, such a step greatly increases the probability of panic, cross-contamination, and false allegations. For this reason, release of information should generally be delayed until all interviewing of children has been completed.

Information provided to the media and families should be accurate but conservative. For example, information can be provided regarding the name of any charged suspect and the legal charges (such as indecency with a minor). However, it is unwise to provide specific details about the allegations, such as the type of illicit touching or the circumstances under which it occurred. Potentially inflammatory information should also be avoided (such as the claim in the McMartin case that there were pornographic photos). The release of specific details or inflammatory information is undesirable because it can intensify community panic and contaminate the subsequent reports of children in the case.

Releases of information to the media and families should be accompanied by statements that discourage parents from questioning their children, such as the following: "We strongly urge parents *not* to question their children. We have already interviewed children in the school about the case and contacted their parents as appropriate. If you believe that your child needs to be questioned further, please do not do so yourself. Instead, call the following number. We will be glad to discuss your concerns and, if appropriate, arrange for your child to be reinterviewed by a trained professional." Such a statement may not be heeded by all parents, but it can still have a beneficial effect by reducing the amount of amateur interviewing to which children are exposed.

*Recommendation 8*

In panic-prone cases, it is likely that a substantial number of children will eventually be exposed to contaminating information and that a smaller number will be subjected to suggestive questioning by adults. Under these circumstances, the probability of false allegations substantially increases. Thus, when evaluating the allegations made by individual children, decision makers need to take into account any possible effects of contamination. The timing of the allegations is particularly important. Specifically, allegations made *before* there has been media publicity or community panic can generally be viewed with much more confidence than allegations made *after* media publicity or contamination. This is an important reason why we recommend that mass interviews, if deemed necessary, should be carried out very early in the investigative process.

## CONCLUSION

We note that the study of extreme and bizarre events can often teach valuable lessons that can be applied under ordinary circumstances. For example, studies of the Black Plague that ravaged Europe during the late Middle Ages and Renaissance have suggested ways to combat the AIDS epidemic in the 21st century. Similarly, studies focusing on the strange daycare cases of the 1980s can teach us today how to better conduct child interviews and manage community panics. We hope the recommendations offered here are helpful to CPS workers, police, and prosecutors and that they generate discussion, feedback, and new ideas.

# REFERENCES

Acocella, J. (1999). *Creating hysteria: Women and multiple personality disorder.* San Francisco, CA: Jossey-Bass.

Allen, D., & Midwinter, J. (1990, September 30). Michelle remembers: The debunking of a myth. *The Mail on Sunday,* p. 41.

Bikel, O. (Producer). (1991, May 7). Innocence lost. In *Frontline* [Television documentary]. Arlington, VA: Public Broadcasting Service.

Bikel, O. (Producer). (1993a, July 20). Innocence lost: The verdict. Part I. In *Frontline* [Television documentary]. Arlington, VA: Public Broadcasting Service.

Bikel, O. (Producer). (1993b, July 21). Innocence lost: The verdict. Part II. In *Frontline* [Television documentary]. Arlington, VA: Public Broadcasting Service.

Bloomberg, D. (2000). Bennet Braun case settled. *Skeptical Inquirer, 24*(1), 7–8.

Bottoms, B. L., & Davis, S. L. (1997). The creation of satanic ritual abuse. *Journal of Social and Clinical Psychology, 16,* 112–132.

Bottoms, B. L., Shaver, P. R., & Goodman, G. S. (1996). An analysis of ritualistic and religion-related child abuse allegations. *Law and Human Behavior, 20,* 1–34.

Butler, E. W., Fukurai, H., Dimitrius, J.-E., & Krooth, R. (2001). *Anatomy of the McMartin child molestation case.* Lanham, MD: University Press of America.

Ceci, S. J., & Bruck, M. (1993). Suggestibility of the child witness: A historical review and synthesis. *Psychological Bulletin, 113,* 403–439.

Cohn, N. (2000). *Europe's inner demons* (Rev. ed.). Chicago: University of Chicago Press.

De Young, M. (2004). *The day care ritual abuse moral panic.* Jefferson, NC: McFarland.

Finnila, K., Mahlberg, N., Santtila, P., Sandnabba, K., & Niemi, P. (2003). Validity of a test of children's suggestibility for predicting responses to two interview situations differing in their degree of suggestiveness. *Journal of Experimental Child Psychology, 85,* 32–49.

Garven, S., Wood, J. M., & Malpass, R. S. (2000). Allegations of wrongdoing: The effects of reinforcement on children's mundane and fantastic claims. *Journal of Applied Psychology, 85,* 38–49.

Garven, S., Wood, J. M., Malpass, R. S., & Shaw, J. S. (1998). More than suggestion: The effect of interviewing techniques from the McMartin Preschool case. *Journal of Applied Psychology, 83,* 347–359.

Hicks, R. D. (1991). *In pursuit of Satan.* Buffalo, NY: Prometheus.

Hill, F. (1995). *A delusion of Satan.* New York: Doubleday.

Huffman, M. L. C., Crossman, A. M., & Ceci, S. J. (1997). "Are false memories permanent?" An investigation of the long-term effects of source misattributions. *Consciousness and Cognition, 6,* 482–490.

Jenkins, P. (1998). *Moral panic.* New Haven, CT: Yale University Press.

Kittredge, G. L. (1929). *Witchcraft in Old and New England.* Cambridge, MA: Harvard University Press.

La Fontaine, J. (1998). *Speak of the devil.* Cambridge, UK: Cambridge University Press.

Lamb, M. E., Orbach, Y., Hershkowitz, I., Esplin, P. W., & Horowitz, D. (2007). A structured forensic interview protocol improves the quality and informativeness of investigative interviews with children: A review of research using the NICHD Investigative Interview Protocol. *Child Abuse and Neglect, 31,* 1201–1231.

Lanning, K. (1991). Ritual abuse: A law enforcement perspective. *Child Abuse and Neglect, 15,* 171–173.

Melnyk, L., Crossman, A. M., & Scullin, M. H. (2007). The suggestibility of children's memory. In M. P. Toglia, J. D. Read, D. F. Ross, & R. C. L. Lindsay (Eds.), *Handbook of eyewitness psychology: Vol. 1. Memory for events* (pp. 401–427). Mahwah, NJ: Erlbaum.

Moran, G. (2008, January 19). His legal battle draws to close after 5 years. *San Diego Union-Tribune.* Retrieved June 2, 2008, from *www.signonsandiego.com/news/metro/20080119-9999-1m19thad.html.*

Myers, J. E. B., Saywitz, K. J., & Goodman, G. S. (1996). Psychological research on children as witnesses: Practical implications for forensic interviews and courtroom testimony. *Pacific Law Journal, 28,* 3–91.

Nathan, D. (1987, September 29). The making of a modern witch trial. *The Village Voice,* pp. 19–32.

Nathan, D. (1988, August 2). Victimizer or victim? Was Kelly Michaels unjustly convicted? *The Village Voice,* pp. 31–39.

Nathan, D., & Snedeker, M. (1995). *Satan's silence.* New York: Basic Books.

Ofshe, R., & Watters, E. (1994). *Making monsters: False memories, psychotherapy, and sexual hysteria.* New York: Scribners.

Pendergrast, M. (1996). *Victims of memory* (2nd ed.). Hinesburg, VT: Upper Access.

Poole, D. A., & Lamb, M. E. (1998). *Investigative interviews of children: A guide for helping professionals.* Washington, DC: American Psychological Association Press.

Rabinowitz, D. (1990, May). Out of the mouths of babes and into a jail cell. *Harper's Magazine,* 52–63.

Reinhold, R. (1990, January 19). Two acquitted of child molestation in nation's longest criminal trial. *New York Times,* p. A1.

Schreiber, N., Bellah, L. D., Martinez, Y., McLaurin, K. A., Strok, R., Garven, S., et al. (2006). Suggestive interviewing in the McMartin Preschool and Kelly Michaels daycare abuse cases: A case study. *Social Influence, 1,* 16–47.

Shaw, D. (1990, January 19). Where was skepticism in media? *Los Angeles Times,* pp. A1, A20–A21.

Smith, M., & Pazder, L. (1980). *Michelle remembers.* New York: Congdon and Lattes.

State v. Michaels, 625 A.2d. 489 (N. J. Super, 1993), *aff'd* 642 A.2d. 1372 (1994).

Victor, J. S. (1993). *Satanic panic: Creation of a contemporary legend.* Chicago: Open Court.

Victor, J. S. (1998). Moral panics and the social construction of deviant behavior: A theory and application to the case of ritual child abuse. *Sociological Perspectives, 41,* 541–565.

Warren, A. R., Garven, S., Walker, N., & Woodall, C. E. (2000, March). *Setting the record straight: How problematic are "typical" child sexual abuse interviews?* Paper presented at the biennial conference of the American Psychology-Law Society, New Orleans, LA.

Wilkerson, T., & Rainey, J. (1990, January 19). Tapes of children decided the case for most jurors. *Los Angeles Times,* p. A1.

Wood, J. M. (2005). A voice of reason in the midst of the European witch hunts: A review of *Cautio Criminalis, or a Book on Witch Trials. Skeptical Inquirer, 29,* 46–47.

Zirpolo, K., & Nathan, D. (2005, October 30). I'm sorry: A long-delayed apology from one of the accusers in the notorious McMartin Pre-school molestation case. *Los Angeles Times Magazine,* pp. I.10–I.15.

Chapter 6

# Contemporary Child Forensic Interviewing

*Evolving Consensus and Innovation over 25 Years*

Karen J. Saywitz
Lorinda B. Camparo

In 1983, 200 parents in Manhattan Beach, California, received a letter from the chief of police informing them that, Ray Buckey, an employee of their child's current or past preschool, had been arrested the previous day for child molestation. The letter asked the parents to "question your child to see if he or she has been a witness to any crime or if he or she has been a victim." After providing a list of possible criminal acts, the letter stated that "any information from your child regarding having ever observed Ray Buckey to leave a classroom alone with a child during any nap period, or if they have ever observed Ray Buckey tie up a child, is important." Thus began the longest and most expensive trial in U.S. history: the McMartin Preschool abuse trial (for review, see Wood, Nathan, Nezworski, & Uhl, Chapter 5, this volume).

Despite media pronouncements to the contrary, much has been learned about children's abilities and the interview process, and much has changed since the highly publicized McMartin Preschool trial. The egregious interviewing techniques epitomized in this letter to parents, encouraging them to

102

question their children in a suggestive and unchecked manner, are not the norm. In response to such highly publicized cases, early studies focusing on children's memory, suggestibility, and truthfulness were conducted. Methodologies either explicitly or implicitly compared children's performance with adults', feeding the notion that "children are the most dangerous of all witnesses" (see Goodman, 1984, for a historical perspective). Findings that young children did not always perform to adult standards highlighted children's weaknesses as witnesses, inevitably leading to the perception of children as deficient adults.

During the 1980s, it was common during pretrial investigations for child witnesses to be repeatedly interviewed by multiple interviewers from various agencies (e.g., law enforcement, child protection, juvenile law, criminal law, medicine, and mental health), each unaware of the other's activities and with no single agency taking responsibility for coordinating the process. Many interviewers lacked training and sensitivity to children's needs and development. Many were unaware of the dangers of using suggestive interviewing techniques with young children. Children were interviewed in the presence of siblings and parents—fertile ground for cross-contamination and unseen pressures—and interviews occurred in a wide range of uncontrolled settings (e.g., schools, hospitals, courthouses, police stations, homes, cars, and cafeterias), lacking safeguards and objectivity necessary to minimize potential for false accusations.

In contrast, today's forensic interview is more likely to take place in one of the nation's more than 600 accredited children's advocacy centers (CACs) with a child interview specialist or in the context of a multidisciplinary team (MDT) or child unit. A large body of relevant scientific research on child witness capabilities and limitations now exists (Cronch, Viljoen, & Hansen, 2006; Goodman & Melinder, 2007; Perona, Bottoms, & Sorenson, 2006) highlighting the need for a developmental perspective and identifying the conditions under which children of different age groups are more or less reliable, complete, and suggestible. In addition, to inform professional training and decision making, there are now a burgeoning number of field studies of actual child witnesses to complement the highly controlled, laboratory-based analogue studies.

In this chapter, we identify and discuss improvements in child forensic interviewing over the last two decades. First, we discuss research-derived best-practice recommendations promulgated by professional and governmental organizations and describe several interview protocols designed to accommodate children's developmental levels and avoid contamination. Next, we describe advances in the infrastructure of forensic child interviewing over the same period. We end with a discussion of the next steps for moving beyond "getting the facts" by adopting a holistic approach to research and practice.

# RESEARCH-DERIVED INTERVIEW
# TECHNIQUES AND PROTOCOLS

One of the advances in the past 25 years is the emerging consensus on general principles of child forensic interviewing, coalescing around a group of
research-based questioning techniques to either use or avoid. We summarize
these general recommendations here, yet readers should know that there is
still debate and mixed findings to untangle on the finer points of interviewing. Many books and special issues of journals are devoted to the discussion
(e.g., Eisen, Quas, & Goodman, 2002; Faller, 2007; Pipe, Lamb, Orbach,
& Cederborg, 2007; Westcott, Davies, & Bull, 2002). In addition, there are
gaps in the literature where existing findings shed little light on important
issues that practitioners must decide in real time every day in the field. As
discussed later, a more holistic approach to research and practice is necessary
to create a database from which competing priorities may be balanced.

## Defining the Problem

Wood and Garven (2000) distinguished two ways in which interviews may
go astray: improper interviewing and clumsy interviewing. They state that
improper interviewing involves the use of interviewing techniques that
should be avoided (e.g., suggestiveness, reinforcement for disclosure, inviting the child to speculate or "pretend") because their use could lead to false
allegations. In contrast, clumsy interviewing involves not using those skills
and techniques commonly recommended in the literature, a problem Wood
and Garven believe is unlikely to lead to false allegations. To reduce both
improper and clumsy interviewing, research indicates that, in addition to
training interviewers in developmentally appropriate interview techniques
and protocols and developing specific selection criteria for interviewers
(e.g., personal warmth, demonstrated ability to work with children, formal
training in counseling or interviewing, ability to incorporate feedback, and
a master's degree or advanced training as an undergraduate), ongoing supervision and feedback are necessary and effective (e.g., Cronch et al., 2006;
Lamb, Sternberg, Orbach, Esplin, & Mitchell, 2002).

## General Guidelines for a Developmental Perspective

There is remarkable consensus among clinicians and researchers on a wide
range of techniques and general guidelines for interviewing children in a
forensic setting from a developmental perspective (e.g., Ceci, Crossman, Scullin, Gilstrap, & Huffman, 2002; Cronch et al., 2006; Faller, 2007; Lamb et
al., 2003; London, 2001; Poole & Lamb, 1998; Saywitz & Camparo, 1998;
Saywitz, Goodman, & Lyon, 2002; Sternberg, Lamb, Davies, & Westcott,

2001; Wakefield, 2006; Wood & Garven, 2000). These general guidelines include:

1. Adapt the interview to the child's developmental level.
2. Take time to establish trust and rapport with children through non-suggestive means.
3. Videotape the interview when possible for supervision, feedback, and accountability.
4. Provide an age-appropriate, private environment with minimal distractions.
5. Promote a supportive, welcoming, nonthreatening atmosphere.
6. Prior to the substantive interview, provide an opportunity for children to practice telling about events, responding to open-ended questions, and using evidence-based memory and communication strategies that have been shown not to lead to false reporting.
7. Set ground rules and provide explicit instructions, such as:
   a. Instruct the child to tell only what really happened and everything he or she can remember, even the small details, from the beginning to the end.
   b. Instruct the child to ask for clarification if he or she does not understand a question.
   c. Instruct the child to say "I don't know" or "I don't remember" if he or she does not know the answer to a question or cannot recall a detail or event.
   d. Remind the child that the interviewer was not present at the alleged incident and instruct the child to correct the interviewer if the interviewer says something that is wrong.
   e. Instruct the child to tell the truth and not to pretend or make up anything.
8. Remain objective and neutral to the veracity of the allegations. Explore alternative hypotheses and explanations. Keep biases in check.
9. Avoid suggestive techniques that mislead, introduce bias, reinforce interviewer expectations, apply peer pressure, stereotype the accused as a bad person who did bad things, or invite children to pretend and speculate.
10. Use open-ended questions that require multiword responses whenever possible. Invite children to elaborate in their own words (e.g., "What happened next? Tell me more about that.").
11. Use "Wh" questions as follow-ups to elicit details about aspects of the alleged incident that the child has already disclosed (what, where, who, when, etc.). This may take the form of rewording yes–no or multiple-choice questions (e.g., "Did John hit you?" becomes "What did he do with his hands?").

12. Avoid utterances that are coercive (e.g., "You cannot play until after you tell me what happened with John"), tags that ask for verification (e.g., "He hurt you, didn't he? Isn't that true?"), negative terms (e.g., "Didn't he hurt you?"), suppositional questions (e.g., "When he hurt you, was he happy or mad?"), and multiple-choice questions (e.g., "Was Mary, Jane, or someone else in the house?") whenever possible. If necessary, ask option-posing questions after the child has had an opportunity to respond to open-ended questions or to describe the alleged incident in his or her own words. Use yes–no questions thoughtfully and cautiously.
13. When the interview is over, take time for closure, prepare the child for the next stage of the process, thank the child for his or her effort, and invite questions.

These recommendations enjoy high levels of consensus, although they vary in degree of empirical support. In both research and practice literatures, there is consensus on a phased approach to interviewing, including an initial preparatory phase, a second phase of information gathering, and a third phase of closure. The initial phase can include introductions, rapport development, a practice interview, instructions, a developmental assessment, and, depending on the local laws, a competency assessment, promise to tell the truth, or some type of truth–lie discussion (e.g., Lyon & Saywitz, 1999). The second phase often contains an invitation for a free-recall description of what happened followed by more specific questioning. A final phase is recommended to allow children time for recomposure if upset, to identify potential stressors that could result from outcome of interview and the need for anticipatory coping strategies, and to address children's questions, but there is little to no empirical research to guide these practices.

Recommendations regarding social support are based on a substantial amount of empirical evidence suggesting that when it is not tied to specific content, it can help children overcome resistance and improve performance, without contaminating their accounts of nonabusive events, even after a 1-year delay (see Bottoms, Quas, & Davis, 2007, for review). In contrast, research on rapport development is scant, despite the fact that it is uniformly recommended. Typically, studies include cursory initial interchanges that are not tested independently. We know little about how children decide whom to trust and whom not to trust (Cashmore, 2002) or about the conditions under which techniques designed to overcome resistance or anxiety or to build trust might have positive, negative, or no effects on memory and disclosure. Evidence for a developmental approach and a child-friendly setting with minimal distraction is strong. For example, studies highlight that questions must be matched to the child's level of language acquisition and cognitive development (e.g., Saywitz, 2002; Saywitz & Camparo, 1998; Saywitz, Snyder, & Nathanson, 1999).

Practice tasks and instructions enjoy much empirical support from both field and laboratory studies. For example, ground rules listed previously have shown positive effects on amount recalled without increasing errors (e.g., McCauley & Fisher, 1995; Mulder & Vrij, 1996; Saywitz, Snyder, & Lamphear, 1996; Saywitz, et al., 1999; Sternberg, Lamb, Esplin, & Baradaran, 1999). Practice exercises involving answering open-ended questions showed positive effects in the field on amount of information reported (Sternberg, Lamb, Hershkowitz, Yudilevitch, Orbach, Espilin, et al., 1997) and in the lab on accuracy of recall (Roberts, Lamb, & Sternberg, 2004; Saywitz, Geiselman, & Bornstein, 1992). Experimental studies manipulating the effects of a priori interviewer knowledge and suggestive questioning clearly support the need for interviewer objectivity (e.g., Bruck, Ceci, & Hembrooke, 1998).

One area in which there is overwhelming consensus is for the use of open-ended questions in place of directive, option-posing, leading, or suggestive utterances (e.g., Cronch et al., 2006; Lamb & Fauchier, 2001; Lamb et al., 2003; London, 2001; Sternberg et al., 1996; Wood & Garven, 2000). Analogue and field studies demonstrate consistently that open-ended invitations elicit longer, more detailed, more accurate, and less self-contradictory responses from older children and adolescents than do the other types of interviewer utterances. However, research also suggests that nonleading specific questions and cued invitations (e.g., "You mentioned that he touched you … tell me more about that") are most effective for children younger than 12 (e.g., Cronch et al., 2006).

Despite high consensus for the efficacy of these "guidelines" in best practice, studies of interviews conducted in multiple countries have found that interviewers often do not use these techniques (e.g., Lamb, Orbach, Hershkowitz, Esplin, & Horowitz, 2007; Warren et al., 1999). In fact, Lamb and Fauchier (2001) found that only about 6% of the total number of prompts by forensic interviewers were open-ended invitations, and even when interviewers receive intensive training, demonstrate understanding of the underlying conceptual issues, and are able to explain the rationale for appropriate techniques, they still often do not use them (Orbach et al., 2000). Consequently, a variety of child forensic interview protocols specifically designed to incorporate the aforementioned guidelines have been developed over the past 20 years.

## Putting Guidelines into Practice: Research-Derived Protocols

Protocols that have received recent attention include the Step-Wise Interview (Yuille, 2002), the Cognitive Interview (CI; Geiselman et al., 1984;

McCauley & Fisher, 1995; Saywitz et al., 1992), the National Institute of Child Health and Human Development (NICHD) investigative interview (Orbach et al., 2000; Sternberg et al., 1999), the Narrative Elaboration (NE) procedure (Camparo, Wagner, & Saywitz, 2001; Saywitz & Snyder, 1996), and Finding Words, a forensic interview training program (Vieth, 2006; Walters, Holmes, Bauer, & Vieth, 2003).

## The Step-Wise Interview

The Step-Wise Interview (Yuille, 2002) involves a series of seven steps that have been modified over the years to include the general guidelines listed earlier. These steps include (1) introductions; (2) rapport development and assessment of the child's development, memory skills, and language; (3) a statement stressing the need for the child to tell the truth; (4) raising the topic of concern using language such as "Do you know why we're talking today?" if the child has already disclosed; (5) disclosure, which involves (a) an uninterrupted free narrative, (b) open questions (e.g., "Do you remember more?," "Who?," "What?," "When?," or "Where?"), and (c) optional specific questions that do not include multiple-choice questions and never include information that the interviewer obtained from another source; (6) clarification, during which the interviewer clarifies problems and inconsistencies in the child's report and in sexual abuse cases queries sexual knowledge that is inappropriate for the child's age; and (7) conclusion, during which the interviewer thanks the child, asks the child if he or she has any questions, and tells the child what will happen next. Although the efficacy of the Step-Wise Interview as a whole has not been tested rigorously, several components have been, and there is ample overlap with consensus recommendations (but see Lindberg, Chapman, Samsock, Thomas, & Lindberg, 2003).

## The Narrative Elaboration Procedure

The NE procedure (Saywitz & Snyder, 1996) incorporates many of the general guidelines listed earlier; however, the NE procedure is unique in that it teaches children strategies for reporting the kinds of information and level of detail important in a forensic interview, using four "reminder cards" (and/or verbal prompts depending on children's ages) as external cues to cue forensically relevant categories of information (i.e., participants, settings, actions, emotional states, and conversations), with each card consisting of a generic line drawing representing its category (e.g., people card, talking/feeling card; Saywitz & Snyder, 1996; Saywitz et al., 1996).

Described as both a procedure for preparing children to be questioned and a format for interviewing them, the original procedure was streamlined by Camparo et al. (2001), consisting of four main components: (1) *preparation for interview*, including rationale for and introduction to the strategy for organizing and reporting recall into the four categories represented by the reminder cards, introduction to the reminder cards, practice using the strategy with feedback and modeling, and reinstruction immediately prior to interview; (2) *free recall*; (3) *cued recall*, which involves presenting the child with each of the four reminder cards individually and asking, "Does this card remind you to tell something else? ... to tell about the people there?" and/or using verbal prompts for each category (e.g., "Who was there? What are their names? What did the people look like? What did the people say?); and (4) *specific follow-up questions*.

Analogue studies comparing NE with standard protocols (i.e., free-recall prompt followed by specific questions) have found that school-age children recalled 53% more information with NE than in the standard interview condition, with no group differences in inaccuracies. In some studies, improvements ranged from 65 to 85% depending on comparison groups. Positive effects have been found by varied research teams in different countries testing more than 800 children using short and long delays of up to 9 months (Brown & Pipe, 2003b). NE has been adapted for preschoolers (Dorado & Saywitz, 2001) and children with learning disabilities (Nathanson, Crank, Saywitz, & Ruegg, 2007). Several components have been tested independently (Bowen & Howie, 2002; Brown & Pipe, 2003b; Dorado & Saywitz, 2001; Elischberger & Roebers, 2001; Saywitz et al., 1996). In addition, research examining school-age children's reports of a fictitious event using the NE procedure in comparison to a standard interview yielded no group differences in the amount of false information reported about the fictitious event (Camparo et al., 2001), and NE has been found to reduce the effect of lower IQ scores on children's ability to report details (Brown & Pipe, 2003a).

## The Cognitive Interview

The CI was developed by Geiselman and Fisher (Geiselman et al., 1984) for adult witnesses. CI employs memory-jogging strategies based on two principles: First, memories are composed of multiple features, and retrieval of any given memory is based on feature overlap between the memory and the memory cues; second, any particular memory may be retrieved via a variety of paths so that if one path is not successful, another path may be so. The four primary interview techniques are (1) mentally reconstructing the environmental and personal context in existence at the time of the event; (2) reporting everything, even partial information; (3) recounting the sequence of events in a variety of orders; and (4) reporting the events from a variety of perspectives.

In a series of laboratory and field studies, the CI elicited up to 35% more accurate details from adults without increased inaccuracies. The original protocol was not as effective for children, so the instructions and wording were revised to make them more developmentally appropriate (McCauley & Fisher, 1995; Saywitz et al., 1992). Saywitz et al. found that this version elicited 45% more accurate details when children were provided with an opportunity to practice the techniques before substantive questioning. Moreover, there were no group differences in the number of inaccurate details recalled. Subsequently, components have been studied independently (e.g., Brown & Pipe, 2003b; Milne & Bull, 2002), and although some studies have found increased inaccuracies, there is debate as to whether researchers used appropriate control conditions in those studies (see Fisher, 1996, for discussion).

## The NICHD Investigative Interview

One protocol that has been examined extensively in the field is the NICHD investigative interview (Orbach et al., 2000; Sternberg et al., 1999). Typically, field research cannot directly examine the completeness and accuracy of children's responses because researchers often cannot know what actually occurred during alleged sexual abuse crimes; therefore, this body of research determines the efficacy of the interview protocol indirectly. It does so by examining the proportion of details elicited from children as well as interviewers' use of techniques that have been found in laboratory research to elicit more complete and accurate responses from children (i.e., proportion of open-ended invitations and option-posing, directive, leading, and suggestive utterances).

The NICHD protocol uses four strategies that have received widespread support in laboratory research (Orbach et al., 2000). First, the interviewer creates an interview environment that is supportive and free from distractions. Second, the interviewer empowers the child through a series of preinterview reminders and instructions similar to those described in the general guidelines mentioned earlier in this chapter. Third, similar to the NE and CI protocols, during the presubstantive phase of the interview, the interviewer provides the child with an opportunity to practice providing complete and detailed narratives and reinforces the child's efforts. Fourth, during the substantive phase of the interview, especially in interviews in which the child may be recounting multiple incidents, the interviewer instructs the child to recount only specific events, particularly the first and last events in a series, to reduce the likelihood that the child will recount "generic" or "script" information (Orbach et al., 2000).

Extensive examination of the NICHD protocol in more than 40,000 field interviews has found that its use improves the quality of investigative child forensic interviews (see Lamb et al., 2007, for review). Although NICHD interviews do not elicit more details across the entire interview from 4- to 13-year-old alleged sex abuse victims than standard interview protocols (Orbach et al., 2000), when forensic interviewers use recommended procedures, NICHD interviews contain at least three times more open-ended prompts overall and half as many suggestive and option-posing utterances than standard interviews. This finding is particularly important in that, as discussed previously, option-posing, directive, leading, and suggestive utterances are associated with greater inaccuracy in laboratory studies of children's reports (e.g., Goodman & Reed, 1986; Hershkowitz, Orbach, Lamb, Sternberg, & Horowitz, 2002; Lamb et al., 2007; Orbach et al., 2000; Sternberg, Lamb, Orbach, Esplin, & Mitchell, 2001; Quas et al., 2007; Waterman, Blades, & Spencer, 2001). In addition, field studies of the NICHD protocol have found that nearly 50% of information provided by children as young as 4 years came in response to free-recall, open-ended invitations and more than 80% of the initial disclosures of sexual abuse provided by preschoolers were in response to free-recall, open-ended invitations (Lamb et al., 2007).

## Finding Words

Another approach to incorporating professionally approved guidelines is Finding Words, a forensic interview training program developed in 1998 by the American Prosecutors Research Institute (APRI) at the National Center for Prosecution of Child Abuse in partnership with CornerHouse, an Interagency Child Abuse Evaluation and Training Center in Minneapolis, Minnesota (Vieth, 2006; Walters et al., 2003). Finding Words is a 5-day training program for multidisciplinary teams composed of prosecutors, law enforcement officers, child protection workers, and forensic interviewers. This training program was designed by "frontline child abuse professionals" to train future child forensic interviewers in conducting interviews in the field.

Finding Words uses CornerHouse's RATAC protocol for questioning children, which is a semistructured and developmentally sensitive protocol that can be used for victims and witnesses of all forms of abuse, neglect, or other violent crimes. RATAC stands for different stages of the protocol: Rapport, Anatomy identification, Touch inquiry, Abuse scenario, and Closure (Walters et al., 2003). Similar to the Step-Wise Interview, it draws heavily on the areas of consensus in the literature outlined in the previous section, but some techniques have not been tested independently, and there is little to no empirical testing of the protocol as a whole.

Finding Words is based on several core beliefs (Walters et al., 2003): (1) Forensic interview training is most effective when teams receive instruction;

(2) forensic interviewers should use protocols that are based on research and are defensible in court; (3) trainees should be taught a range of knowledge and skills; (4) trainees must read pertinent research themselves; (5) trainees must demonstrate their skills and be critiqued by their peers and by professional interviewers; and (6) trainees must be able to defend basic interview concepts in court. The curriculum for Finding Words consists of readings; lectures; training exercises that include practice interviews with children and adults that are videotaped, critiqued, and subjected to feedback from peers and professionals; and a final essay exam, resulting in certification.

High demand for Finding Words has resulted in the Half a Nation by 2010 Project devised by APRI and CornerHouse. This project involves an intense 3-week certification process for individual states, which can then run the course on their own to meet the needs of their own child abuse professionals. A search of the literature failed to reveal systematic assessment of the effectiveness and durability of the training program.

# IMPROVEMENTS IN CONTEXT
# AND INFRASTRUCTURE

Over the last 25 years, efforts to reform the interview process were not limited to research-driven improvements in questioning techniques. Policymakers and practitioners set out to create a context and an infrastructure that facilitate rather than undermine children's abilities and that reduce stress on families. The next section highlights some core components of community response to child abuse allegations that have advanced the context and infrastructure of forensic interviewing over the last 25 years.

## Child Advocacy Centers

In the United States, a nationwide trend toward coordinated, cross-discipline, child-friendly interviews by highly trained specialists commenced in the 1980s. To this end, communities began (1) to promote interagency cooperation in response to allegations of child abuse; (2) to reduce system-induced stress on children; (3) to provide the greatest number of services to children and families in one location; and (4) to provide competent, objective, forensically defensible interviewing. Community-based child witness/child advocacy centers grew from a handful of pilot projects in the mid-1980s to well over 600 accredited centers across the country today.

The hallmark of these child-friendly centers is the fact that they colocate legal, social service, and medical personnel in one facility where the child has contact with a single highly skilled interviewer who gathers sufficient information for multiple agencies to make a variety of decisions. Often other professionals watch from behind a one-way mirror or via closed-circuit television. Centers maintain policies and safeguards necessary for videotaping and confidentiality/privacy. Videotapes are often used to limit the dependence of further decision making on reinterviewing children. Centers typically house a pediatrician to examine injuries as well as legal representatives from juvenile and criminal justice systems. Staff members are trained to identify mental health needs and refer or provide services. Victim/witness support and advocacy are often available. Case-tracking systems ensure that cases do not fall through the cracks. Cross-agency advisory committees continually revise protocols and policies to accommodate statutory reforms and new research findings.

The effectiveness of these centers has not been tested rigorously. A few quasi-experimental evaluations have compared the center model with standard community services (e.g., Cross, Jones, Walsh, Simone, & Kolko, 2007; Kolbo & Strong, 1997). Findings suggest that children interviewed at such centers are more likely to receive medical examinations and referrals to needed mental health services. Parents' satisfaction is higher, and centers are more successful in promoting interagency collaboration. One study found investigations in communities with CACs to be 36% less expensive than those in communities without centers (Formby, Shadoin, Shao, Magnuson, & Overman, 2006). However, the impact of the centers on prosecution outcomes, false allegations, children's disclosure rates, and stress reduction is not yet clear.

## Multidisciplinary Team Approach

Failure to respond to reports of child abuse in a timely and appropriate manner because of a lack of communication and coordination across investigating agencies has been blamed for the deaths of many children at the hands of caretakers after being the subject of multiple reports of abuse to authorities (Ells, 2000). In response to these tragedies, policymakers across the globe have promoted interagency teamwork (Cross et al., 2007; Kolbo & Strong, 1997). Teams are based in hospitals, prosecutors' offices, or child protection agencies; are not necessarily part of a CAC; and do not have special interview facilities, but they use available resources to try to accomplish many of the same goals (Ells, 2000). In the United States, all 50 states have initiatives promoting MDTs.

Compared with the United States, smaller countries like New Zealand, with a population of 4 million, have been far more aggressive in their reforms, in that they have overhauled their entire infrastructure to implement MDTs with national interagency protocols, a specialization of forensic interviewers, a single national training program and interview format, and a national peer review process (Wilson, 2007). Training is jointly funded and

coordinated by police and social services departments. Pretrial interviews
are videotaped and conducted according to joint guidelines. Ongoing supervision and feedback maintain interview quality.

Although there is little outcome research on the effectiveness of the
MDT approach, it would be fair to say that it is considered "best practice"
(American Bar Association [ABA] Criminal Justice Task Force on Child
Witnesses, 2002; Ells, 2000; Jones, Cross, Walsh, & Simone, 2005; Kolbo
& Strong, 1997). MDTs are often credited with decreasing fragmentation in
service delivery, reducing the number of interviews and secondary stress to
children from the system, and increasing accuracy of assessment and predic-
tion of risk (ABA, 2002).

Results of available studies are mixed. For example, some researchers
found that the MDT approach was related to fewer interviews per child
(e.g., California Attorney General's Office, 1994; Henry, 1997; Jaudes &
Martone, 1992); greater professional and family satisfaction (e.g., Finkelhor
& Williams, 1988); increased likelihood of substantiating allegations and
filing charges (Jaudes & Martone, 1992); and higher levels of victim corroboration, perpetrator confessions, and conviction rates (Tjaden & Anhalt,
1994). Other researchers found no effects (Hicks, Stolfi, Ormond, & Pascoe, 2003; Steele, Norris, & Komula, 1994). However, MDTs vary widely
in configuration, function, composition, training, and attendant legislation.
Studies are often unable to control for significant preexisting factors (e.g.,
demography of catchment areas, characteristics of children served, such as
age and type/severity of abuse). According to Jones et al.'s (2005) review of
the literature, in aggregate, results indicate no evidence of negative effects
and tend to suggest that MDTs improve the overall quality of investigations
and promote the well-being and safety of children.

## Separation of Forensic and Clinical Interviews

Another important change in the context of contemporary interviewing is
the trend toward maintaining clear boundaries between the role, methods,
and goals of the forensic and clinical interviewer. The forensic interviewer is
considered a fact finder, objectively gathering details of legal relevance and
documenting children's statements verbatim, if possible. He or she is supportive but remains neutral to the veracity of the information provided and
refrains from a relationship that could unduly influence children's reports.
In contrast, the goals of the clinical interview are diagnosis, treatment planning, and symptom reduction. A basic aim of a therapeutic conversation is
to effect change. The child's behaviors and perceptions are central. There is
no obligation to determine the reliability of the child as a historian; hence,
there is less demand to pursue alternative hypotheses. The therapist seeks
to establish a therapeutic alliance with warmth and empathy. He or she

might take the role of advocate, educator, role model, or coach (Deblinger & Heflin, 1996).

Both the research and clinical literatures now make clear the value of differentiating between forensic interviews and clinical efforts (see Saywitz, Esplin, & Romanoff, 2007, for discussion). Most professional organizations recommend that forensic interviews be conducted separately from therapeutic efforts in separate sessions by different professionals, often with limited sharing of information between the two (American Academy of Child and Adolescent Psychiatry [AACAP], 1998; American Professional Society on the Abuse of Children [APSAC], 1997; American Psychological Association [APA], 1998). They underscore the potential for blurred boundaries to result in distortion or false allegation or to jeopardize the child's credibility and the treatment itself. For example, if in the course of treatment a child reveals forensically relevant information and the therapist responds with detailed questioning and is then called to testify, he or she may be required to answer questions regarding the entire treatment, not only the forensic event, revealing information provided in confidence. This can violate the child's trust and undermine the therapeutic alliance. In contrast, if the child had been referred to a forensic interviewer while continuing in therapy with the original therapist, the interviewer could testify to the forensic event with little consequence to the treatment.

## Procedural and Statutory Reforms

Over the last two decades, many statutory and procedural innovations in the legal system have been introduced worldwide to accommodate the needs and limitations of child witnesses (e.g., court schools; alternatives to live, in-court testimony like closed-circuit television or videotaped depositions for vulnerable children; closing the courtroom to spectators; or allowing support persons to be present during questioning). A review of the growing literature on the effects of innovative reforms would be beyond the scope of this chapter (see Goodman et al., Chapter 8, this volume, for review). In general, existing studies seem to indicate that progressive reforms are underutilized (Goodman, Quas, Bulkley, & Shapiro, 1999).

One contemporary trend, however, is particularly germane: the trend toward vertical prosecution. Vertical prosecution refers to the notion that, whenever possible, the same prosecutor handles all aspects of a case involving a child victim/witness. Vertical prosecution is considered best practice and is thought to increase the attorney's familiarity with the child and the case, rapport between child and attorney, ability to gather more compelling evidence, and coordination among investigating agencies (e.g., ABA, 2002; Williams, 2006). Again, research on effectiveness is limited. One survey found that vertical prosecution was associated with an increase in guilty pleas (Goodman et al., 1999). However, there is no centralized database to examine its effects. Available studies comparing smaller jurisdictions tend to provide a distorted view of the population of children being questioned by focusing on the very small number of cases (9%) that result in a trial (Cross, Whitcomb, & DeVos, 1995). More information is needed to understand the implications for interviewing children when cases are declined for prosecution, are plea bargained, or result in guilty pleas. Cross et al. (1995) proposed a new paradigm for understanding prosecution based on the entire distribution of outcomes, not just highly visible, controversial cases of sexual abuse.

## NEXT STEPS IN RESEARCH AND PRACTICE: A HOLISTIC APPROACH

Over time, distinct subsystems have evolved along separate paths to address the needs of justice, child protection, and trauma recovery (e.g., legal, social service, mental health, and medical systems). Although the structure in its entirety is fragmented, the interaction among subsystems is considerable and increasing (Finkelhor, Cross, & Cantor, 2005). Clearly, forensic interviews are embedded in an infrastructure replete with competing priorities and cross-purposes. Everyday decision making in the field requires a balance of competing objectives that need to be prioritized in real time.

Similarly, distinct research domains have evolved separately as well. Over the last 25 years, there has been little connection between progress in child witness research and clinical treatment outcome studies. The latter have made notable strides in the development of (1) effective treatments for posttraumatic symptoms and (2) innovative prevention and early intervention programs to deter maltreatment and mental health disorders, especially in high-risk populations. This divergence of subsystems and research domains has been exacerbated by the adversarial nature of the legal system that tends to polarize forensic and clinical researchers and practitioners.

However, many of the advances described in this chapter support a more holistic approach to research and practice, including the promulgation of guidelines from professional organizations (e.g., AACAP, 1998; American Academy of Pediatrics, 2005; ABA, 2002; APA, 1998; APSAC, 1997; World Health Organization, 2006), the proliferation of child-friendly centers, and the use of multidisciplinary teams. This approach to research and practice would treat children holistically, not merely as witnesses or victims of crime. It would respect the fact that interviews are embedded in a larger multisystemic infrastructure and would promote greater cross-pollination across forensic and clinical domains to produce new research questions and paradigms that neither field could develop in isolation. Next are a number of illustrations of the kinds of items to be found on a more holistic research agenda.

## Broader Conceptualization of the Information-Gathering Process

There are a number of reasons for a more holistic approach. First, forensic interviews are not conducted in isolation, as the bulk of past experimental methodologies suggest. Children are involved in multiple systems simultaneously. There are (1) questions by parents, neighbors, or teachers; (2) social service interviews regarding risk assessment and placement; (3) medical interviews regarding cause and treatment of injuries; (4) clinical interviews regarding diagnosis and treatment of mental health problems; and (5) civil legal interviews regarding personal injury or custody disputes. There are myriad opportunities for genuine disclosure outside formal forensic interviews as well as opportunities for suggestion, coaching, or misinterpretation. This scenario calls for a broader conceptualization of the information-gathering process, the contexts in which it unfolds, and the circumstances under which forensic guidelines are called into play.

## Moving Beyond "Getting the Facts"

Second, existing research and guidelines focus almost exclusively on "getting the facts" from children who are alleged "victims" of "sexual abuse." A more holistic approach would acknowledge that children's voices are heard on a wide range of issues where legal decisions are pending. Methods are needed to elicit information about more than memories, including preferences, attitudes, fears, feeling states, expectations, and opinions. For example, increasing numbers of children are interviewed to make decisions about deporting immigrant parents who are not citizens but whose children were born in the new country. Clearly, these cases highlight cultural and linguistic factors not yet addressed by the literature. Interviews in custody disputes focus on children's preferences; victim impact statements permit children to express their views concerning the personal consequences of victimization. Although some of the research thus far is applicable to a range of circumstances, available findings are far from sufficient.

## Meeting Mental Health Needs without Tainting Reports

Third, children are often referred for ongoing therapy while still involved in protracted legal cases both when interviews are inconclusive (to monitor risk factors or treat symptoms when the cause is unclear) and when there are clear substantiated disclosures (treatment of posttraumatic symptoms). This presents an opportunity for additional forensically relevant information to emerge as a trusting relationship develops over time with a therapist and children test the waters with partial or vague disclosures. Unfortunately, these circumstances also increase the potential for contamination, inconsistencies, and misunderstandings because therapeutic techniques were not designed to preserve reliability of children's reports. A more holistic research agenda would consider what kinds of therapeutic interventions could be implemented during this extended phase of information gathering to create an opportunity for clarity to emerge while meeting children's mental health needs without jeopardizing their reports or credibility.

If children are not referred for mental health services because of concerns over contamination, their mental health needs remain unidentified and unmet. Moreover, childhood abuse is a significant risk factor for adult psychiatric disorders and adolescent problems of substance abuse, promiscuity, depression, and delinquency. Withholding effective treatments for fear of contamination creates a dilemma. Yet the knowledge base necessary to balance competing priorities does not yet exist (Saywitz et al., 2007).

Even when questionable therapies are excluded from the discussion (e.g., hypnosis, memory-recovery techniques) and only efficacious evidence-based treatments, well accepted in the field, are considered, there remains a dilemma. Some of the most efficacious treatments involve discussion of the facts of the case. For example, in well-controlled, multisite treatment outcome studies with sexually abused children, trauma-focused cognitive-behavioral therapy outperforms other therapies with which it has been compared (e.g., Cohen, Deblinger, Mannarino, & Steer, 2004; see Saywitz, Mannarino, Berliner, & Cohen, 2000, for a review). This intervention uses techniques for reducing posttraumatic symptoms (e.g., graduated exposure and systematic desensitization) that involve discussion of the child's memories, attributions, and perceptions of the traumatic event. Although there is no evidence that such discussions must be conducted in a suggestive manner to be effective, relevant research to create guidelines for therapists is scant.

A holistic agenda would establish efficacy for both forensic and therapeutic objectives, addressing the following questions: Can interventions efficacious for treating depression or anxiety, symptoms common in abused children, be unpackaged and components tested with regard to their effects on both children's reports and therapeutic outcome? Which techniques require discussion and remembering of the facts of the case to be effective? Is repeated discussion of memories in and of itself contaminating? Can discussions be conducted in ways that are unbiased, nonleading, and still effective therapeutically? What guidelines could be imported from the available knowledge base on child witnesses to help therapists avoid contamination without impairing symptom reduction? A more holistic research agenda would begin to address these questions.

## Alternative Models for "Nondisclosing" Children

Fourth, even after the most ideal of interviews, a subgroup of children will fail to provide unambiguous, straightforward information, making it difficult to substantiate or reject suspicions of abuse (see Lyon, Chapter 2, this volume). Some were not abused, but their statements are so contradictory that they fail to dispel adult concerns. Others are genuinely abused but are afraid or unable to articulate their experiences clearly. In other cases, there is physical or medical evidence or imitation of adult sexual behavior despite no disclosure of abuse. Although it is difficult to estimate the size of this group, available estimates range from 10 to 24% (e.g., Department of Health and Human Services, 2004; Herman, 2005; Wilson, 2007). However, most experimental methodologies assume motivated, cooperative participants, and most existing protocols are designed for children who have already made at least a partial disclosure of abuse (but see Pipe et al., 2007).

As mentioned earlier, one direction for future research would be to test how clinical techniques designed to overcome resistance or reduce anxiety affect recall, disclosure of genuine abuse, false allegation, and false denial. For example, Saywitz and Moan-Hardie (1994) examined the effects of clinical techniques (i.e., normalization and cognitive-behavioral positive self-statements) on 100 7-year-olds' suggestibility. They found that the children who received the clinical techniques before the interview made fewer errors in response to misleading questions about past classroom activities. Saywitz et al. (2007) speculate about the efficacy of various clinical techniques (e.g., empathy, self-soothing strategies, relaxation, emotional expression skills training, and coping skills training) for promoting disclosure of genuine abuse and reducing symptoms without tainting children's reports.

A holistic agenda also addresses the need to establish alternative pathways when forensic interviews are inconclusive but abuse is still suspected. In New Zealand, when forensic (evidential) interviews fail to result in a clear allegation but a high level of risk remains (e.g., sexually transmitted disease, children giving partial unclear allegations in contact with known offenders, children with persistent sexualized behaviors, offender confessions), interviewers move to a "diagnostic," or exploratory, format. The entire process is videotaped, and the diagnostic interview may take up to three sessions with a more flexible structure covering a wider range of topics. This approach is not a panacea because guidelines for diagnostic interviews are not clear, but the national infrastructure explicitly acknowledges the need for alternative pathways in such cases.

## Opportunities for Prevention, Early Identification, and Early Intervention

Fifth, children referred for interviews constitute a high-risk population who would benefit from access to prevention, early identification, and early intervention efforts. Often these are children living in high-risk situations, alternating between foster care and reunification with biological families, as parents struggle with addiction, poverty, homelessness, adolescence, divorce, and domestic and community violence. This population displays high rates of emotional, cognitive, and behavioral problems (e.g., posttraumatic stress disorder, anxiety, depression, aggressivity, suicidal ideation) that interfere with functioning in ways that place them at greater risk for abuse and interfere with determining whether abuse occurred. A holistic research agenda considers how to promote prevention of child maltreatment and increased access to mental health care as children progress through the legal system. New psychometric instruments may be needed to identify early warning signs at forensic interviews, given that attorneys often object to available screening tools because they contain items that may undermine witness credibility when exposed in court (e.g., difficulties with reality testing and judgment). Alternatively, a holistic approach might seek to develop ways to link child witnesses and their families with programs that promote well-being and prevention (e.g., evidence-based positive parenting training), programs that have been tested and adapted to be mindful of the impact on children's statements. Studies might require an integration of intervention outcome paradigms, analogue studies of recall, and partnerships across disciplines. For example, in Arizona evidence-based prevention programs for divorcing families are now implemented through courts to prevent mental health problems from developing (e.g., Tein, Sandler, MacKinnon, & Wolchik, 2004).

## Special Techniques for Special Populations

Last, special approaches may be both necessary and beneficial for reluctant/resistant children, developmentally delayed children, and children with emotional and behavioral problems. Although clinically derived methods may not be necessary in a majority of cases, our research trajectory should not ignore this sizable group. For example, there is growing evidence to suggest that such children with learning disabilities benefit from special interview techniques that provide them with memory enhancement strategies. They provide more complete reports of past events without increased errors and demonstrate greater resistance to misleading questions using CI and NE protocols in comparison to standard techniques (Milne & Bull, 1996; Nathanson et al., 2007).

## CONCLUSION

Important strides have been made in the field of contemporary forensic child interviewing over the past 25 years. In this chapter, we have reviewed many advances in questioning technique and infrastructure. However, new paradigms will be necessary to create a knowledge base that informs how to

(1) elicit reliable and sufficient information from children to make a wider range of decisions beyond prosecution of abuse, (2) meet children's mental health needs without tainting their reports, (3) prioritize actions when forensic and clinical goals conflict, (4) promote children's well-being and optimal development, and (5) implement prevention and early intervention programs for abuse and mental health problems.

## REFERENCES

American Academy of Child and Adolescent Psychiatry. (1998). Practice parameters for the assessment and treatment of children and adolescents with posttraumatic stress disorder. *Journal of American Academy of Child and Adolescent Psychiatry, 37*, 4S–26S.

American Academy of Pediatrics. (2005). The evaluation of sexual abuse in children. *Pediatrics, 116*, 506–512.

American Bar Association Criminal Justice Task Force on Child Witnesses. (2002). *The child witness in criminal cases.* Washington, DC: American Bar Association.

American Professional Society on the Abuse of Children. (1997). *Guidelines for psychosocial evaluation of suspected sexual abuse in young children.* Chicago: Author.

American Psychological Association. (1998). *Professional, ethical, and legal issues concerning interpersonal violence, maltreatment, and related trauma.* Washington, DC: Author.

Bottoms, B. L., Quas, J. A., & Davis, S. L. (2007). The influence of interviewer-provided social support on children's suggestibility, memory, and disclosures. In M.-E. Pipe, M. E. Lamb, Y. Orbach, & A.-C. Cederborg (Eds.), *Child sexual abuse: Disclosure, delay, and denial* (pp. 135–158). Mahwah, NJ: Erlbaum.

Bowen, C. J., & Howie, P. M. (2002). Context and cue cards in young children's testimony: A comparison of brief narrative elaboration and context reinstatement. *Journal of Applied Psychology, 87*, 1077–1085.

Brown, D., & Pipe, M.-E. (2003a). Individual differences in children's event memory reports and the narrative elaboration technique. *Journal of Applied Psychology, 88*, 195–206.

Brown, D., & Pipe, M.-E. (2003b). Variations on a technique: Enhancing children's recall using narrative elaboration training. *Applied Cognitive Psychology, 17*, 377–399.

Bruck, M., Ceci, S. J., & Hembrooke, H. (1998). Reliability and credibility of young children's reports. *American Psychologist, 53*, 136–151.

California Attorney General's Office. (1994). *Child victim witness investigative pilot projects: Research and evaluation final report.* Washington, DC: Author.

Camparo, L. B., Wagner, J. T., & Saywitz, K. J. (2001). Interviewing children about real and fictitious events: Revisiting the narrative elaboration procedure. *Law and Human Behavior, 25,* 63–80.

Cashmore, J. (2002). Promoting the participation of children and young people in care. *Child Abuse and Neglect, 26,* 837–847.

Ceci, S. J., Crossman, A. M., Scullin, M. H., Gilstrap, L., & Huffman, M. L. C. (2002). Children's suggestibility research: Implications for the courtroom and the forensic interview. In H. Westcott, G. Davies, & R. Bull (Eds.), *Children's testimony: A handbook of psychological research and forensic practice* (pp. 117–132). New York: Wiley.

Cohen, J. A., Deblinger, E., Mannarino, A. P., & Steer, R. (2004). A multisite, randomized controlled trial for children with sexual abuse-related PTSD symptoms. *Journal of Child and Adolescent Psychiatry, 43,* 393–402.

Cronch, L. E., Viljoen, J. L., & Hansen, D. J. (2006). Forensic interviewing in child sexual abuse cases: Current techniques and future directions. *Aggression and Violent Behavior, 11,* 195–207.

Cross, T. P., Jones, L. M., Walsh, W. A., Simone, M., & Kolko, D. (2007). Child forensic interviewing in children's advocacy centers: Empirical data on a practice model. *Child Abuse and Neglect, 31,* 1031–1052.

Cross, T. P., Whitcomb, D., & DeVos, E. (1995). Criminal justice outcomes of prosecution of child sexual abuse: A case flow analysis. *Child Abuse and Neglect, 19,* 1431–1442.

Deblinger, E., & Heflin, A. H. (1996). *Treating sexually abused children and their nonoffending parents.* Thousand Oaks, CA: Sage.

Department of Health and Human Services. (2002). *Child maltreatment 2002.* Washington, DC: Department of Health and Human Services. Retrieved March 6, 2009, from *www.acf.hhs.gov/programs/cb/stats_research/index. htm#can.*

Dorado, J., & Saywitz, K. J. (2001). Interviewing preschoolers from low and middle income communities: A test of the narrative elaboration recall improvement technique. *Journal of Clinical Child Psychology, 30,* 566–578.

Eisen, M. L., Quas, J. A., & Goodman, G. S. (2002). *Memory and suggestibility in the forensic interview.* Mahwah, NJ: Erlbaum.

Elischberger, H. B., & Roebers, C. M. (2001). Improving young children's free narratives about an observed event: The effects of nonspecific verbal prompts. *International Journal of Behavioral Development, 25,* 160–166.

Ells, M. (2000). *Forming a multidisciplinary team to investigate child abuse.* Washington, DC: U.S. Department of Justice.

Faller, K. C. (2007). *Interviewing children about sexual abuse: Controversies and best practice.* New York: Oxford University Press.

Finkelhor, D., Cross, T. P., & Cantor, E. N. (2005). The justice system for juvenile victims: A comprehensive model of case flow. *Trauma, Violence and Abuse, 6,* 1–20.

Finkelhor, D., & Williams, L. M. (1988). *Nursery crimes: Sexual abuse in day care.* Newbury Park, CA: Sage.

Fisher, R. P. (1996). Misconceptions in design and analysis of research with the cognitive interview. *Psycoloquy, 7*(35). Retrieved January 25, 2008, from *www.cogsci.ecs.soton.as.uk/ cgi/psyc/newpsy?7.35.*

Formby, J. P., Shadoin, A. L., Shao, L., Magnuson, S. N., & Overman, L. B. (2006). *Cost-benefit analysis of community responses to child maltreatment: A comparison of communities with and without child advocacy centers.* (Research Report No. 06-3). Huntsville, AL: National Children's Advocacy Center.

Geiselman, R. E., Fisher, R. P., Firstenberg, I., Hutton, L. A., Sullivan, S., Avetissian, I., et al. (1984). Enhancement of eyewitness memory: An empirical evaluation of the cognitive interview. *Journal of Police Science and Administration, 12,* 74–80.

Goodman, G. S. (1984). Children's testimony in historical perspective. *Journal of Social Issues, 40,* 9–31.

Goodman, G. S., & Melinder, A. (2007). Child witness research and forensic interviews of young children: A review. *Legal and Criminological Psychology, 12,* 1–19.

Goodman, G. S., Quas, J. A., Bulkley, J., & Shapiro, C. (1999). Innovation for child witnesses: A national survey. *Psychology, Public Policy, and Law, 5,* 255–281.

Goodman, G. S., & Reed, R. S. (1986). Age differences in eyewitness testimony. *Law and Human Behavior, 10,* 317–332.

Henry, J. (1997). System intervention trauma to child sexual abuse victims following disclosure. *Journal of Interpersonal Violence, 12,* 35–49.

Herman, S. (2005). Improving decision making in forensic child sexual abuse evaluations. *Law and Human Behavior, 29,* 87–120.

Hershkowitz, I., Orbach, Y., Lamb, M. E., Sternberg, K. J., & Horowitz, D. (2002). A comparison of mental and physical context reinstatement in forensic interviews with alleged victims of sexual abuse. *Applied Cognitive Psychology, 16,* 429–441.

Hicks, R. D., Stolfi, A., Ormond, M., & Pascoe, J. (2003, May). *Evaluation services provided by a children advocacy center.* Paper presented at the meeting of the Pediatric Academic Society, Seattle, WA.

Jaudes, P., & Martone, M. (1992). Interdisciplinary evaluations of alleged sexual abuse cases. *Pediatrics, 89,* 1164–1168.

Jones, L. M., Cross, T. P., Walsh, W. A., & Simone, M. (2005). Criminal investigations of child abuse: The research behind "best practices." *Trauma, Violence and Abuse, 6,* 254–268.

Kolbo, J. R., & Strong, E. (1997). Multidisciplinary team approaches to the investigation and resolution of child abuse and neglect: A national survey. *Child Maltreatment, 2,* 61–72.

Lamb, M. E., & Fauchier, A. (2001). The effects of question type on self-contradictions by children in the course of forensic interviews. *Applied Cognitive Psychology, 15,* 483–491.

Lamb, M. E., Orbach, Y., Hershkowitz, I., Esplin, P. W., & Horowitz, D. (2007). A structured interview protocol improves the quality and informativeness of investigative interviews with children: A review of research using the NICHD investigative interview protocol. *Child Abuse and Neglect, 31,* 1201–1231.

Lamb, M. E., Sternberg, K. J., Orbach, Y., Esplin, P. W., & Mitchell, S. (2002). Is ongoing feedback necessary to maintain the quality of investigative interviews with allegedly abused children? *Applied Developmental Science, 6,* 35–41.

Lamb, M. E., Sternberg, K. J., Orbach, Y., Esplin, P. W., Stewart, H., & Mitchell, S. (2003). Age differences in young children's responses to open-ended invitations in the course of forensic interviews. *Journal of Consulting and Clinical Psychology, 71,* 926–934.

Lindberg, M. A., Chapman, M. T., Samsock, D., Thomas, S. W., & Lindberg, A. W. (2003). Comparisons of three different investigative interview techniques with young children. *Journal of Genetic Psychology, 164,* 5–28.

London, K. (2001). Investigative interviews of children: A review of psychological research and implications for police practices. *Police Quarterly, 4,* 123–144.

Lyon, T. D., & Saywitz, K. J. (1999). Young maltreated children's competence to take the oath. *Applied Developmental Science, 3,* 16–27.

McCauley, M. R., & Fisher, R. P. (1995). Facilitating children's eyewitness recall with the revised cognitive interview. *Journal of Applied Psychology, 80,* 510–516.

Milne, R., & Bull, R. (1996). Interviewing children with mild learning disability with the cognitive interview. *Issues in Criminal and Legal Psychology, 26,* 44–51.

Milne, R., & Bull, R. (2002). Back to basics: A componential analysis of the original cognitive interview mnemonics with three age groups. *Applied Cognitive Psychology, 16,* 743–753.

Mulder, M., & Vrij, A. (1996). Explaining conversation rules to children: An intervention study to facilitate children's accurate responses. *Child Abuse and Neglect, 10,* 623–631.

Nathanson, R., Crank, J. N., Saywitz, K. J., & Ruegg, E. (2007). Enhancing the oral narratives of children with learning disabilities. *Reading and Writing Quarterly, 23,* 315–331.

Orbach, Y., Hershkowitz, I., Lamb, M. E., Sternberg, K. J., Esplin, P. W., & Horowitz, D. (2000). Assessing the value of structured protocols for forensic interviews of alleged child abuse victims. *Child Abuse and Neglect, 24,* 733–752.

Perona, A. R., Bottoms, B. L., & Sorenson, E. (2006). Research-based guidelines for child forensic interviews. *Journal of Aggression, Maltreatment and Trauma, 12,* 81–130.

Pipe, M.-E., Lamb, M.-E., Orbach, Y., & Cederborg, A.-C. (2007). *Child sexual abuse: Disclosure, delay, and denial.* Mahwah, NJ: Erlbaum.

Poole, D. A., & Lamb, M. E. (1998). *Investigative interviews of children: A guide for helping professionals.* Washington, DC: American Psychological Association.

Quas, J. A., Malloy, L. C., Melinder, A., Goodman, G. S., D'Mello, M., & Schaaf, J. (2007). Developmental differences in the effects of repeated interviews and interviewer bias on young children's event memory and false reports. *Developmental Psychology, 43,* 823–837.

Roberts, K. P., Lamb, M. E., & Sternberg, K. J. (2004). The effects of rapport building style on children's reports of a staged event. *Applied Cognitive Psychology, 18,* 189–202.

Saywitz, K. J. (2002). Developmental underpinnings of children's testimony. In H. Westcott, G. Davies, & R. Bull (Eds.), *Children's testimony: A handbook of psychological research and forensic practice* (pp. 3–20). New York: Wiley.

Saywitz, K. J., & Camparo, L. B. (1998). Interviewing child witnesses: A developmental perspective. *Child Abuse and Neglect, 22,* 825–843.

Saywitz, K. J., Esplin, P. W., & Romanoff, S. L. (2007). A holistic approach to interviewing and treating children in the legal system. In M.-E. Pipe, M. E., Lamb, Y. Orbach, & A.-C. Cederborg (Eds.), *Child sexual abuse: Disclosure, delay, and denial* (pp. 219–250). Mahwah, NJ: Erlbaum.

Saywitz, K. J., Geiselman, R. E., & Bornstein, G. K. (1992). Effects of cognitive interviewing and practice on children's recall performance. *Journal of Applied Psychology, 77,* 744–756.

Saywitz, K. J., Goodman, G. S., & Lyon, T. D. (2002). Interviewing children in and out of court: Current research and practice implications. In J. E. B. Myers, L. Berliner, J. N. Briere, C. T. Hendrix, T. A. Reid, & C. Jenny (Eds.), *APSAC handbook of child maltreatment* (2nd ed., pp. 349–378). Newbury Park, CA: Sage.

Saywitz, K. J., Mannarino, A. P., Berliner, L., & Cohen, J. A. (2000). Treatment for sexually abused children and adolescents. *American Psychologist, 55,* 1040–1049.

Saywitz, K. J., & Moan-Hardie, S. (1994). Reducing the potential for distortion of childhood memories. *Consciousness and Cognition, 3,* 257–293.

Saywitz, K. J., & Snyder, L. (1996). Narrative elaboration: Test of a new procedure for interviewing children. *Journal of Consulting and Clinical Psychology, 64,* 1347–1357.

Saywitz, K. J., Snyder, L., & Lamphear, V. (1996). Helping children tell what happened: Follow-up study of the narrative elaboration procedure. *Child Maltreatment, 1,* 200–212.

Saywitz, K. J., Snyder, L., & Nathanson, R. (1999). Facilitating the communicative competence of the child witness. *Applied Developmental Science, 3,* 58–68.

Steele, P., Norris, M., & Komula, K. (1994). *Evaluation of the children's safe house of Albuquerque.* Albuquerque: University of New Mexico, Youth Resource and Analysis Center.

Sternberg, K. J., Lamb, M. E., Davies, G. M., & Westcott, H. L. (2001). The memorandum of good practice: Theory versus application. *Child Abuse and Neglect, 25,* 669–681.

Sternberg, K. J., Lamb, M. E., Esplin, P. W., & Baradaran, L. P. (1999). Using a scripted protocol in investigative interviews: A pilot study. *Applied Developmental Science, 3,* 70–76.

Sternberg, K. L., Lamb, M. E., Hershkowitz, I., Esplin, P. W., Redlich, A., & Sunshine, N. (1996). The relation between investigative utterance types and the informativeness of child witnesses. *Journal of Applied Developmental Psychology, 17,* 439–451.

Sternberg, K. L., Lamb, M. E., Hershkowitz, I., Yudilevitch, L., Orbach, Y., Esplin, P. W., et al. (1997). Effects of introductory style on children's abilities to describe experiences of sexual abuse. *Child Abuse and Negelct, 21,* 1133–1146.

Sternberg, K. J., Lamb, M. E., Orbach, Y., Esplin, P. W., & Mitchell, S. (2001). Use of a structured investigative protocol enhances young children's responses to free-recall prompts in the course of forensic interviews. *Journal of Applied Psychology, 86,* 997–1005.

Tein, J. Y., Sandler, I. N., MacKinnon, D. P., & Wolchik, S. A. (2004). How did it work? Who did it work for? Mediation in the context of a moderated prevention effect for children of divorce. *Journal of Consulting and Clinical Psychology, 72,* 617–624.

Tjaden, P. G., & Anhalt, J. (1994). *The impact of joint law enforcement-child protective services investigations in child maltreatment cases.* Denver, CO: Center for Policy Research.

Vieth, V. I. (2006). Unto the third generation: A call to end child abuse in the United States within 120 years. *Journal of Aggression, Maltreatment and Trauma, 12,* 5–54.

Wakefield, H. (2006). Guidelines on investigatory interviewing of children: What is the consensus in the scientific community? *American Journal of Forensic Psychology, 24,* 57–74.

Walters, S., Holmes, L., Bauer, G., & Vieth, V. (2003). *Finding words: Half a nation by 2010: Interviewing children and preparing for court.* Alexandria, VA: American Prosecutors Research Institute.

Warren, M. A. R., Woodall, C. E., Thomas, M., Nunno, M., Keeney, J. M., Larson, S. M., et al. (1999). Assessing the effectiveness of a training program for interviewing child witnesses. *Applied Developmental Science, 3,* 128–135.

Waterman, A. H., Blades, M., & Spencer, C. (2001). Interviewing children and adults: The effect of question format on the tendency to speculate. *Applied Cognitive Psychology, 15,* 521–531.

Westcott, H. L., Davies, G. M., & Bull, R. (2002). *Children's testimony: A handbook of psychological research and forensic practice.* New York: Wiley.

Williams, D. (2006). Children first: National model for vertical prosecution of cases involving murdered and physically abused children. *Journal of Aggression, Maltreatment and Trauma, 12,* 131–148.

Wilson, K. (2007). Forensic interviewing in New Zealand. In M.-E. Pipe, M. E. Lamb, Y. Orbach, & A.-C. Cederborg (Eds.), *Child sexual abuse: Disclosure, delay, and denial* (pp. 265–280). Mahwah, NJ: Erlbaum.

Wood, J. M., & Garven, S. (2000). How sexual abuse interviews go astray: Implications for prosecutors, police, and child protection services. *Child Maltreatment, 5,* 109–118.

World Health Organization. (2006). *Preventing child maltreatment: A guide to taking action and generating evidence.* Geneva, Switzerland: Author.

Yuille, J. C. (2002). *The step-wise interview: Guidelines for interviewing.* Available from J. Yuille, Department of Psychology, University of British Columbia, 2136 W. Mall, Vancouver, BC, Canada V6T 1Z4.

# Chapter 7

# Child Victims
# in Dependency Court

Jodi A. Quas
Alexia Cooper
Lindsay Wandrey

For several decades, there has been considerable scientific, legal, and public interest in children's involvement in the criminal justice system. This interest has focused on a range of critical issues, including children's eyewitness capabilities, consequences of criminal court participation on children's well-being, juvenile defendants' competencies, trying juvenile defendants as adults, and jurors' perceptions of child victims and defendants. Yet another large group of children with considerable legal contact is worthy of similar attention: children involved in the dependency division of juvenile court (often known as dependency court) because of maltreatment.

Specifically, approximately 1 million children each year experience maltreatment that is substantiated, or deemed true, by social services (U.S. Department of Health and Human Services [DHHS], 2008a). For many of these children, formal dependency cases are filed. The stakes in these cases are quite high. They always involve some sort of interference with the parent–child relationship, which may include requirements that the parents receive services to improve their parenting, temporary removal of the child from the parents' custody, termination of the parents' rights, and adoption of the child. Many children who have contact with the dependency system also experience later legal involvement, for example, as a result of delinquent behaviors or adult criminal activity (e.g., Herrera & McCloskey, 2001; Lansford et al., 2007; Siegel & Williams, 2003; Smith & Thornberry,

1995; Widom & Maxfield, 2001). Given these factors, it is imperative to understand children's experiences in dependency court, including how those experiences affect children's well-being, so that, to the extent possible, negative consequences are reduced.

In this chapter, we review existing knowledge concerning children's reactions to dependency court involvement. We begin with a brief overview of the purpose of dependency courts and the general process followed when children take part. We then describe three topics that have been the focus of empirical research concerning children in dependency court: (1) children's understanding of the dependency system, (2) children's experiences during dependency proceedings, and (3) the consequences of dependency court intervention, particularly out-of-home placement, on children. Throughout, we provide suggestions regarding methods of facilitating children's legal participation and areas in need of continued research.

## DEPENDENCY COURT PURPOSE AND PROCESS

In 1899 in Illinois, the first juvenile court was established with the explicit goal of regulating the treatment and control of maltreated and delinquent children. By the early part of the 20th century, virtually all states had established similar juvenile courts (Lenroot & Lundberg, 1925). One part of the juvenile court is the dependency division, which works in conjunction with broader state and federal welfare agencies to promote the well-being of maltreated children and ensure their safety. The specific purpose of dependency court is to evaluate maltreatment allegations and determine how best to intervene on children's behalf. Thus, for example, dependency proceedings may be held to decide whether children should be placed outside the home for their protection, what types of services should be given to children, and what parents must do for children to return home (i.e., reunification). Proceedings are also held to evaluate the progression of the case and, if needed, render decisions about placement for children should parents fail to improve their parenting by the end of the reunification period (see Edwards, 2007).

The progression of a dependency case is rarely simple or brief. Once an allegation of maltreatment is made, an investigation is conducted by social services, sometimes with law enforcement involved. If the authorities conclude on the basis of the investigation that the maltreatment is likely to have occurred and that the child is at risk for additional harm, intervention is necessary. In many and perhaps the less severe cases, voluntary supervision will occur. However, in more serious cases or cases in which the parents are uncooperative, a dependency petition is usually filed. If the child faces imminent risk without removal, the child will be placed in foster care or with relatives. At the initial hearing, the court determines whether there is a reasonable basis for the allegations and reviews the appropriateness of the child's placement pending trial. Subsequent hearings further evaluate the allegation, the family situation, and the child's continued well-being. These hearings include a trial at which the veracity of the allegations is assessed and hearings to determine the most appropriate placement and to monitor that placement, to evaluate the parents' progress in treatment and their compliance with court orders, and to implement plans for establishing the child's permanent living situation (e.g., reunification, termination of parental rights, adoption, long-term foster care).

Given the complexity of dependency cases, plus the range of hearings that may take place, it is not surprising that cases' lengths vary considerably. Certainly some are resolved quickly, for instance, because the allegations were unfounded or not severe, or the parents responded quickly and appropriately. However, most cases last for years (e.g., Bishop et al., 2000; Johnson & Wagner, 2005; Malloy, Lyon, & Quas, 2007; White, Albers, & Bitonti, 1996). For example, Bishop et al. (2000) reported that, in a Boston sample of maltreated children, the dependency cases lasted, on average, 5 years. Also, despite statutory time lines that typically allow up to 12 or 18 months for reunification, the average length of time a child remains in nonparental living situations is approximately 28 months (DHHS, 2008b).

In summary, the dependency system is charged with protecting children who have been exposed to maltreatment. The system renders decisions about where children should reside, the conditions that must be met for children to be removed from and returned to parental custody, services to be delivered, requirements for parents or guardians with regard to children's care, and interventions to facilitate children's development. Numerous individuals and professionals are involved and cases often last for years, despite mandates to move to permanency plans after much shorter periods. As we review next, several of these features of the dependency system may profoundly affect children, both initially and over time.

## CHILDREN'S REACTIONS TO DEPENDENCY COURT INVOLVEMENT

In light of the number of children who become involved in the dependency court and the potential significance of their experiences during this process, it is important to determine how children react to such involvement. A small body of research has begun to examine children in dependency court. Here we review this research and relevant studies of child victims in criminal court and defendants in juvenile court, focusing on (1) children's legal understanding, (2) children's participation in dependency proceedings, and (3) out-of-home placement.

## Children's Legal Understanding

During a dependency case, children may interact with a range of legal professionals, including social workers, investigators, court-appointed special advocates, guardian *ad litems,* foster parents, attorneys, and judges. Many professionals are advised to inform children about the nature of legal proceedings, what is happening in the case, and the decisions being made (Khoury, 2006). It is unclear, however, whether children actually understand that information, which may be incomplete, contradictory to that provided by other professionals, or too complex for children to understand (e.g., Eltringham & Aldridge, 2000; Perry et al., 1995). Any lack of understanding on the part of children may serve to exacerbate the distress that children already experience as a result of the maltreatment (e.g., Carlson, Cicchetti, Barnett, & Braunwald, 1989; Putnam, 2003; see Myers et al., 2002) and initial legal intervention (Johnson, Yoken, & Voss, 1995; *Nicholson v. Williams et al.,* 2002; Shlonsky & Friend, 2007).

A large body of research has examined children's understanding of the legal system, focusing on community samples' knowledge of criminal terms, juvenile defendants' understanding of the juvenile justice system and their rights within that system, and child victim/witnesses' understanding of criminal court (e.g., Cauffman & Steinberg, 2000; Flin, Stevenson, & Davies, 1989; Grisso et al., 2003; Melton, 1980; Ruck, Keating, Abramovitch, & Koegl, 1998; Saywitz, Jaenicke, & Camparo, 1990; Viljoen, Zapf, & Roesch, 2007). Far fewer studies have investigated legal understanding among maltreated children involved in dependency proceedings (e.g., Block, Oran, Oran, Baumrind, & Goodman, in press; Quas, Wallin, Horwitz, Davis, & Lyon, 2009), although results are fairly similar across the different samples and legal contexts.

Perhaps the most consistent finding is that concerning age: With age, children's legal understanding improves (e.g., Cauffman & Steinberg, 2000; Cooper, 1997; Grisso et al., 2003). For instance, Quas, Wallin, Horwitz, Davis, and Lyon (2009) interviewed 4- to 15-year-olds awaiting dependency hearings because of exposure to maltreatment. Children were first asked to define legal terms (e.g., lawyer), including those unique to the dependency system (e.g., foster care). Next, children listened to a story about a boy removed from home because of maltreatment and answered questions about their understanding of the story. Clear age-related improvements emerged. For instance, when defining terms, few of the youngest children provided detailed, correct responses (e.g., such as police "protect people, arrest you for breaking the laws" and a lawyer "defends your case"). Some others provided correct but skeletal responses (e.g., answering that a social worker "asks you how you're doing in school" or a lawyer "talks to people"), but many failed to provide any correct information. Although the number of older children who provided detailed, accurate responses increased, none of the oldest children obtained a perfect score on the definitions (or initial story questions). It was only in response to closed-ended questions about the story that the oldest children demonstrated high levels of accuracy, a finding consistent with previous research indicating that children appear more knowledgeable (e.g., about their understanding of lies) when asked recognition rather than recall questions (e.g., Lyon & Saywitz, 1999).

A second consistent finding is that neither contact with the legal system nor more extensive involvement predicts enhanced knowledge (e.g., Freshwater & Aldridge, 1994; Grisso, 1981; Peterson-Badali, Abramovitch, & Duda, 1997; Quas et al., 2009; Saywitz et al., 1990). In other words, contrary to what one might expect, contact with the legal system does not improve children's understanding of that system. Saywitz et al. (1990), for instance, asked a community sample of 5- to 11-year-olds to define legal terms (e.g., jury, lawyer). Children were classified into one of three legal experience groups based on parental report: (1) no prior contact, (2) family member who worked in the legal system/child had visited court, or (3) child had participated in a legal case (e.g., witness in personal injury case). The three groups' definition accuracy did not significantly vary. Cashmore and Bussey (1990) also reported no differences in understanding of legal officials' roles (e.g., what a lawyer does) among first-time adolescent defendants, adolescent repeat offenders, and demographically similar adolescents with no prior legal experiences. Finally, Cooper, Quas, Wallin, Davis, and Lyon (2008) compared legal understanding between 4- to 14-year-olds with and without direct experience in the dependency system. No differences in general knowledge emerged, although children with dependency court experience were more accurate in defining terms specific to that system (e.g., foster care).

The results described thus far concerned children's general understanding of various legal terms and professionals. Yet maltreated children are expected to have at least a minimal knowledge of their situation so that they can help their legal representative by providing relevant information. Given evidence from community and maltreated samples indicating that children's general knowledge often fails to predict their understanding of case-specific information (Quas et al., 2009; Warren-Luebecker, Tate, Hinton, & Ozbek, 1989), it is imperative to determine how much children actually understand about their own case.

The few studies that have been conducted reveal considerable deficits. Block et al. (in press) interviewed 7- to 10-year-old maltreated children at the courthouse immediately after they had attended a dependency hearing (for approximately 50% of the children, the hearing corresponded to the initial detention hearing held subsequent to their emergency removal, whereas the remaining hearings focused on evaluating ongoing cases).

When asked why they had to go to court, 65% of the children responded either that they didn't know or that it was because they had "been bad." Only 24% said that it was to keep them safe or to talk to the judge. Quas et al. (2009) asked 4- to 15-year-old maltreated children immediately after their dependency hearings (e.g., trials, placement review proceedings) ended what had happened. Older children were more accurate than younger children, although many of the oldest children still had difficulty answering. For instance, among children age 12 and older, 33% correctly described the judge's decision (50% others provided an incomplete but correct response and 17% provided no correct information). Across age, one-third of the total sample provided no correct information about the judge's decision, and among these, half of the children were actually inaccurate.

Two other studies revealed similar limitations in maltreated children's understanding, specifically in regard to their removal from home and placement in foster care. Johnson et al. (1995) interviewed 11- to 14-year-olds living in foster care between 6 months and 2 years about their removal. A majority of the children reported correctly that they had been removed because of abuse or neglect, although nearly half of these children seemed confused about the circumstances surrounding their placement in foster care. Murphy (1998) interviewed 10- to 17-year-old children living in foster care about their experiences and compared children's responses with information in their case files. When asked why they were living in foster care, only 28% were accurate (most simply replied, "I don't know"). When asked about the court's plans for their future, only 54% were accurate. Of interest, children who had been involved in a previous dependency case were less knowledgeable of the court's plans for their future than children who had not been involved in a prior case. Also, number of placements was negatively related to children's understanding. Of course, when the courts do not have clear plans for the children's future, children would not be able to articulate what those plans are. The court's plans may also be more ambiguous for children who have experienced repeated maltreatment or for whom the court has difficulty finding a permanent placement. However, these negative associations between prior dependency experience and understanding are similar to those obtained in studies of legal experience and legal knowledge in community and juvenile delinquent samples (e.g., Grisso, 1981; Saywitz, 1989) and thus represent a worthy topic of continued investigation.

In summary, children's understanding improves with age, both in general and in relation to their own case, although even older children have significant limitations in their knowledge. Also, experience with the legal system does not appear to help children better understand the legal system, key personnel involved, or their placement in foster care. The implication that naturally falls from these trends is straightforward: Maltreated children need considerable help in understanding how the legal system works, the function of legal personnel with whom they interact, and why specific decisions (e.g., placement) are made. This assistance needs to be age appropriate and provided to older and younger children. Moreover, this assistance must be given even to children who already have endured legal involvement.

## Children's Participation in Dependency Proceedings

Most states afford children the right to participate in dependency proceedings. This includes attending hearings in the case, voicing their opinions to influence legal decisions, being notified of decisions, and testifying in the hearings. Despite being afforded the right to participate, however, evidence indicates that children rarely actually do participate or at least rarely feel as though they do (e.g., Arad-Davidzon & Benbenishty, 2008; Johnson et al., 1995). For instance, children may not meet regularly with their legal representative, may not be informed of recommendations made to the courts, may not know what actions their caregivers need to take to resolve the case, and may not know what the court's plans are for their placement (Arad-Davidzon & Benbenishty, 2008). Some jurisdictions have taken steps to increase children's involvement. Michigan, for example, requires youth older than 11 to be notified of review, permanency, and termination of parental rights hearings. In Los Angeles County, children ages 4 years and older are required to attend at least some of their hearings, whether or not they testify. Lancaster County, Nebraska, has adopted a similar model, as has New York for children ages 10 and older (Khoury, 2006). Finally, in Kansas, the courts are directed to hear testimony of youth 14 years or older in dependency cases if the youth requests it and is of sound intellect (K.S.A., 38-1570a). Of interest, however, is whether such participation is helpful or harmful to children.

### Children's Attendance in Dependency Proceedings

One area of controversy concerning children's direct participation involves having children attend their hearings (Khoury, 2006). It is not particularly common and instead primarily occurs only in jurisdictions that have specific mandates in place (e.g., Los Angeles County), and with these mandates sometimes existing only for children above a certain age.

On the one hand, there are several reasons why attendance is believed to be beneficial (see Khoury, 2006). First, children want to be involved (e.g., Cashmore, 2002; Home at Last, 2006; Jenkins, 2008; Johnson et al., 1995). In Cashmore's (2002) review of studies conducted in the United Kingdom, North America, Australia, and New Zealand, children in foster care consistently expressed the desire to be active participants in the decision-making process in their cases and did not believe they were given enough opportunities to do so. Second, some legal professionals assume that attendance is helpful (Jenkins, 2008; Khoury, 2006; Krinksy & Rodriquez, 2006). They contend that, by being involved, children should be more comfortable with their legal representatives and more helpful in providing relevant information, both of which should facilitate the case's progression and children's continued participation. Third, studies of perceptions of justice consistently indicate that individuals feel more positive about legal decisions, even those that are not in the individuals' favor, when they are directly involved in and knowledgeable about the process (Tyler, 1990; Tyler & Huo, 2002; Lind & Tyler, 1988; Tyler, Boeckmann, Smith, & Huo, 1997). Similar links between perceptions of fairness and involvement in the process have emerged in children in response to hypothetical scenarios (Gold, Darley, Hilton, & Zanna, 1984; Hicks & Lawrence, 2004) and in adults involved in criminal cases because of victimization in childhood (e.g., Quas et al., 2005). Although such links have not been examined in maltreated children in dependency cases, they may also exist. As Khoury (2006) notes in regard to maltreated children's participation, "Youth have the opportunity to understand the process by seeing firsthand the court proceedings" (p. 15).

On the other hand, however, concerns have been raised that attendance may result in adverse consequences to children. These concerns primarily focus on whether, as a result of attending dependency hearings, children experience high levels of distress. For instance, children may feel positive that the abuse ended but, upon seeing their parent, feel guilty about their family's situation or about their own allegations. Children may also be distressed because of the graphic nature of the discussions or perhaps because they are not able to interact freely with their parents in the courtroom environment (Block et al., in press; see Khoury, 2006, for further discussion). Each of these factors suggest that attendance may not be advantageous.

Research has not systematically examined how attending dependency proceedings affect children. However, a few studies have some relevant data. For example, although it is assumed that attendance leads to increased legal understanding in maltreated children, studies by Quas et al. (2009) and Block et al. (in press) suggest that even children who attend their dependency hearings are not fully aware of their situation. That is, Quas et al. found that even some younger adolescents did not understand the decisions made in hearings that they had just attended. Moreover, both Quas et al. and Block et al. identified a subset of children who did not know why they were in court (e.g., they thought it was because they had been bad). Certainly, it is possible that these children's understanding is still greater than that of children who never attended (which was not directly compared in the studies), but these data suggest that attendance, in isolation, may not be adequate in helping children fully understand their dependency case. Instead, children's attendance may need to be coupled with greater contact between children and their legal representative or other professionals both before and after proceedings, more opportunities for children to ask questions, and perhaps longer hearings so that the judge and others have time to answer children's questions (Khoury, 2006).

Despite attendance possibly not increasing children's understanding, attendance does not appear to cause unduly high levels of stress in children (Block et al., in press; Quas et al., 2009). For instance, Quas et al. (2009) asked maltreated children, immediately before attending a dependency hearing, how they felt about their upcoming hearing and about what the judge might decide. Afterward, the children were asked how they had felt during the hearing and about the decision. Their mean ratings, according to a 5-point faces scale (1 = *large frown*, 5 = *large smile*), ranged from 3.10 to 3.79, suggesting that children, on average, felt neutral or mildly positive before and after their hearings. Observer ratings confirmed that children were not, on average, highly distressed while attending their hearings.

Of importance, in the aforementioned studies, because children were not randomly assigned to "present" versus "not present" hearing conditions, the question of whether attendance per se, either in terms of knowledge or distress, is beneficial has not yet been addressed directly. Thus, it is unknown whether children who attend hearings know more about their case than they would if they had not attended the hearing at all or whether children are less distressed generally as a result of attending their hearings, again compared with if they had not attended. Overall, given debates about whether children should participate, further research is needed to examine the effects of attendance as well as other case characteristics on children's knowledge and distress.

## Testifying in Dependency Hearings

Controversy also exists concerning whether children should take the stand during legal proceedings. Several studies have examined the consequences on child victim/witnesses of testifying in criminal cases, with this research focusing virtually exclusively on testifying in cases involving alleged child sexual abuse. Findings reveal that testifying is associated with poorer psychological functioning, both in the short and long term, when children testify multiple times, when children lack caregiver support during their cases, when the cases lack other corroborative evidence, and when children testify in particularly severe cases (Goodman et al., 1992; Quas et al., 2005; Tedesco & Schnell, 1987; Whitcomb, 1992). Several of these factors (e.g., lack of caregiver support) may be especially common in dependency cases, given that these cases inevitably involve acts of wrongdoing perpetrated by parental caregivers, raising concerns about whether testifying in dependency cases may also result in adverse consequences.

In one of the only studies to investigate testifying in dependency cases, Runyan, Everson, Edelsohn, Hunter, and Coulter (1988) interviewed 79 victims of sexual abuse, ages 6 to 17, shortly after the abuse was reported to the authorities and again 5 months later. At the 5-month interview, 45% of the allegations had resulted in dependency cases being filed, and 12 children had testified in dependency proceedings. Compared with children who had not testified, those who testified had higher levels of anxiety at the initial interview but lower anxiety at follow-up. Runyan et al. (1988) speculated that the testifiers' improvement was due to them having the opportunity to express their feelings and tell their story in court. However, other factors may also have contributed. For instance, 63% of the children had been removed from the home. If a greater number of testifiers had been removed from an unsupportive or coercive caregiver, their anxiety may have decreased as a result of their removal rather than as a result of testifying. Also, the cases for children who had already testified may have been resolved more quickly, and case length has been related to behavioral adjustment in child victims in criminal cases (e.g., Goodman et al., 1992). In general, given that so few children testified, that these children differed from nontestifiers initially, and that it was simply not possible to control for other factors that may affect children's functioning, further studies are needed to continue to assess the relations between testifying in dependency cases and children's psychological well-being.

## Summary

Although allowing children to be present during their hearings does not guarantee that they will be informed and knowledgeable, attendance represents a potential first step in enhancing children's experiences in dependency court, so long as that attendance is coupled with increased explanation, psychological support, and guidance to children regarding what is happening. With this input, children may gain a better understanding of their own role in the case and their and others' responsibilities with regard to case resolution. Also, attendance does not appear to lead to uniformly high levels of distress among maltreated children, although it will be important to assess whether certain hearings are especially distressing and whether children's attendance at such hearings should be avoided. Finally, the consequences of testifying in dependency cases are not clear. Further research controlling for potential confounds is needed. Overall, insofar as children participate and possibly testify in dependency cases, care must be taken to ensure that they understand what is happening and receive adequate support during and afterward.

## Out-of-Home Placement

A third crucial area of interest regarding children's reactions to dependency court concerns the effects on children of removal from home and out-of-home placement (i.e., foster care), the most salient legal intervention that can result from a dependency case filing. Out-of-home placements occur in about 22% of all substantiated cases, with this percentage exceeding 40% in some states (DHHS, 2008a). Annually, approximately 500,000 children in the United States are living in formal out-of-home placements (DHHS, 2008b). This number has increased over the past two decades, not only in the United States but in other countries as well (e.g., Australia; Australian Institute of Health and Welfare, 2008). Removal may occur immediately after an allegation is filed or after a case has been ongoing. When and for how long removal occurs depends on the court's evaluation of the allegations, parents' behaviors, and children's needs.

The purpose of out-of-home placement is to promote the well-being of the child by providing a safe, temporary home until permanent arrangements can be made (Adoption and Safe Familes Act of 1997; Pecora & Maluccio, 2000). A large body of research has examined the consequences of out-of-home placement on children (e.g., Berliner & Conte, 1995; Buehler, Orme, Post, & Patterson, 2000; Connell, Katz, Saunders, & Tebes, 2006; Henry, 1997; Newton, Litrownik, & Landsverk, 2000; Widom, 1991). Given space limitations, it is not possible to review this entire literature. Instead, we highlight key findings and review the complexities associated with studying the consequences of out-of-home placement. We focus first on studies comparing children who experience out-of-home placement and those who have not and then on studies of predictors of functioning among children who have been removed.

### Children Who Have versus Have Not Experienced Out-of-Home Placement

Numerous questions have been raised regarding whether removing maltreated children from home causes more harm to already victimized children. Several studies indeed report adverse outcomes (e.g., behavior and mental health problems, substance abuse, criminal behavior, poor physical health, low educational attainment) among individuals who are or were living in foster care settings (e.g., Blome, 1997; Fantuzzo & Perlman, 2007; Lawrence, Carlson, & Egeland, 2006; Weinberg, Weinberg, & Shea, 1997; Clausen, Landsverk, Ganger, Chadwick, & Litrownik, 1998; McIntyre & Kessler, 1986; Pilowsky, 1995; Pottick, Warner, & Yoder, 2005). However, other studies suggest that when other risk factors that commonly co-occur with maltreatment (e.g., family poverty, parental drug use, parent or child mental health problems) are controlled, out-of-home placement per se is not related to greater problems (Runyan & Gould, 1985; Buehler et al., 2000). In fact, a few studies suggest that, over time, removal and placement in foster care may actually be beneficial to children (Fanshel & Shinn, 1978; Horwitz, Balestracci, & Simms, 2001; Taussig, 2002), for instance, because they are no longer exposed to negative or violent home environments.

Several studies nicely demonstrate not only the conflicting findings but also the challenges associated with trying to identify causal links between out-of-home placement and various outcomes. Lawrence et al. (2006) compared behavioral adjustment among (1) maltreated children living in foster care, (2) maltreated children not placed in foster care, and (3) children who did not experience maltreatment or foster care but were matched on other risk factors (e.g., poverty, young maternal age, low parental education). The foster care children exhibited more behavior problems than the two other groups immediately following their release from foster care. Of course, the initial reasons why those children were placed in out-of-home care while others were not may also have contributed to the former's problems. For example, the foster care children may have experienced more severe abuse or may not have had a parental support figure to assist in their care following their removal, both of which could contribute to greater problems regardless of their placement per se.

Buehler et al. (2000) compared adults with at least 6 months of prior foster care experience with two comparison groups of adults drawn from the 1988 National Survey of Families and Households: (1) adults randomly selected to mirror the general population (community sample) and (2) adults without prior foster care experience but who matched the foster care sample on gender, race, current age, parental level of education, and whether they had lived with a stepparent (matched sample). Robust differences emerged between the foster care and community sample. The former had more adjustment difficulties, poorer education, lower socioeconomic well-being, greater marital problems, and lower happiness. Only one difference, however, was evident between the foster care and matched sample. The foster care sample had lower socioeconomic well-being. Thus, the negative outcomes in the former foster care adults were more a function of characteristics common in high-risk samples than the experience of out-of-home placement.

Courtney and Dworsky (2006) interviewed former foster care youth who had aged out of care (i.e., had been emancipated from state custody because of their transition to adulthood) 1 year previously. One-third had mental health (e.g., depression) or drug (e.g., alcohol or substance use) problems, and many had failed to complete high school. Yet a large minority of these adolescents had returned to live with a biological parent after being released from the state's care. Thus, their postemancipation environment (e.g., being back in a violent home or with parents who use drugs) could have contributed to some of the evident problems. Moreover, other analyses indicated that adolescents who had resided in foster homes longer had also remained in school for longer periods. Taussig, Clyman, and Landsverk (2001) reported somewhat similar results. Among children who had been removed from home, those who were later reunited with their biological parents evinced a greater number of behavioral problems than those who remained in out-of-home care. Thus, once children experience maltreatment and are removed, remaining in foster care may actually be better than returning home, at least for some children.

Studies concerning the links between out-of-home placement and later risk for delinquency and crime are similarly mixed. Runyan and Gould (1985) failed to find differences in later criminal behavior between maltreated children placed in foster care and maltreated children who remained in the home. Widom (1989, 1991) found that maltreated children relative to nonmaltreated children were at increased risk for later criminality. However, foster care per se did not further increase children's risk. Instead, it was only when children were placed in foster care because of a combination of abuse/neglect and delinquent behavior that their risk for later criminality increased (Widom, 1991). Ryan and Testa (2005) found somewhat different results. In a longitudinal study tracking children from birth to age 18, delinquency rates were higher in maltreatment victims than nonvictims, similar to findings in Widom (1989, 1991). Further, when only the maltreated children were considered, delinquency rates were higher in those who had been placed in foster care than in those with no placement experience, controlling for age, race, gender, and type of maltreatment. Nonetheless, without additional information regarding why certain children were placed in foster care, it is not possible to draw definitive conclusions about causal directions from Ryan and Testa's findings.

## Functioning among Children Who Experienced Out-of-Home Placement

Rather than attempting to address the daunting and perhaps overly simplistic question of whether removing children from home is good or bad, some researchers have focused on identifying those factors that moderate or mediate specific outcomes among children who have been removed. Assuming it is inevitable that some children will be removed, insight into which specific experiences increase or decrease children's adjustment to that removal is critical to intervention efforts.

Two factors that have received considerable attention include the number and types of placements children experience. First, across studies of foster care and children's functioning, increases in the number of placements are fairly consistently associated with poorer mental health, poorer academic performance, and increased delinquency (e.g., Cooper, Peterson, & Meier, 1987; Courtney & Barth, 1996; Newton et al., 2000; Ryan & Testa, 2005). Frequent placement changes can prevent children from forming long-term bonds with caregivers (Bowlby, 1973) and require that children repeatedly establish new relationships with unfamiliar adults (Cooper et al., 1987). Children must also learn new routines, make new friends, and change schools, all of which create instability in children's home, relationships, and education (Weinberg et al., 1997).

To understand the reasons for the evident negative effects of multiple placements, it is imperative to understand why certain children experience multiple placements in the first place. These reasons (rather than placement changes per se) may directly affect children's functioning. According to a meta-analysis of predictors of "placement failure," defined by such terms as placement instability, placement moves, and multiple transitions, children with adjustment problems (which often arise as a result of maltreatment) had more difficulty remaining in a single home, leading to increased likelihood of multiple placements (Oosterman, Schuengel, Slot, Bullens, & Doreleijers, 2007). Older children were also more likely to experience placement failure than younger children, although the effect size was small. It is often easier to find foster family placements for younger than older children, the latter of whom are more often placed in group homes (which also predicted placement failure). Critically, Oosterman et al. (2007) did not investigate whether the identified predictors of placement failure actually explained the aforementioned associations between placement frequency and adverse outcomes. Thus, causal inferences cannot be drawn, and placement changes may be both a cause and a consequence of other risk factors. Multivariate studies are needed to identify the complex number of factors that contribute both to changes in children's placement and their well-being (see Pinderhughes, Harden, & Guyer, 2007).

Second, as mentioned, when children are removed from home because of maltreatment, they may experience one of several types of placement: with relatives in what is typically referred to as kinship care, with an unrelated family who is licensed to take care of foster children, in a group home, or in an institutional facility. The likelihood of being placed in one versus another situation varies based on several characteristics of children, their maltreatment experiences, and their family situation. For instance, African American children are more likely to be placed in kinship care than foster care with a nonrelative. Also, neglected children are more likely to end up in kinship care, whereas abused children are more likely to end up in nonrelative care (Benedict, Zuravin, & Stallings, 1996; Ehrle & Geen, 2002). Clearly, it is not possible to evaluate effects of different placement experiences without taking into account differences in the populations of children most likely to experience one type of care or another. Moreover, in the United States, it is not possible to randomly assign children to different placement contexts, which would allow for causal inference. Of note, a novel international collaboration between the United States and Romania—the Bucharest Early Intervention Project—is a large study in which children are randomly assigned to either foster or institutional care (e.g., see Nelson, Zeanah, & Fox, 2007; Zeanah et al., 2003). Although the results will not enable clear differentiation between kinship versus nonrelative foster care, they will provide much-needed insight into how specific facets of out-of-home care, namely institutional versus foster care, affect children's development.

With the exception of the Bucharest Early Intervention Project, most attention concerning foster care placement has focused on the question of whether it is best for children to be placed with kin rather than unfamiliar foster families (e.g., Berrick, 2000; Broad, 2004; Valentine & Gray, 2006). Children in kinship care likely know their new caretaker, which should make the transition less traumatic than placement with unfamiliar adults (Broad & Skinner, 2005; Green, 2004; Rowe, Hundleby, & Garnett, 1989). Courtney and Needell (1997) found no differences in case outcome between children placed in kinship versus a foster care environment; both groups of children were similarly likely to be adopted or reunited with their family. However, a significantly larger percentage of cases involving children in kinship (83%) relative to foster (67%) care reached a final disposition within 4 years of the cases being filed. Also, Wulczyn, Hislop, and Harden (2002) found that infants placed in kinship care were less likely to reenter foster care but had longer stays in care. Yet other evidence indicates that children in kinship care do not receive the level and quality of service or as much monetary compensation from the child welfare system as children in foster care (Berrick, Barth, & Needell, 1994; Ehlre & Geen, 2002; Gebel, 1996). Overall, the divergent findings indicate that neither being placed with relatives nor being placed with nonrelatives is automatically better for children. Instead, relations between placement and outcomes vary across children depending on their age, type of care they receive, type of maltreatment they endured, and a number of other factors that have the potential to affect children's functioning during and after their removal from home.

## Summary

Research that has examined functioning in children currently or formerly living in out-of-home placement environments has not yielded consistent findings concerning whether removal is related to increased or decreased problems. Preexisting conditions, child characteristics, type of home environment, and services the children and families receive all play key roles in how children adjust to placement, and continued research is needed to clarify the roles of these different factors in conjunction with removal on children's functioning.

## CONCLUSION

A large number of children come into contact with the dependency division of juvenile court as a result of exposure to maltreatment. These children's legal experiences are significant, and the court's decisions affect children's lives in profound ways for many years. The court decides with whom children shall live and for how long, whether and how often children can have contact with their parents, and what services are to be provided to children and families. It is imperative to identify how children understand and cope with dependency court, how best to intervene and facilitate children's functioning once they become involved, and how to help children after their involvement has ended, either because they returned home or they were emancipated out of the system. Such knowledge will serve to benefit some of the most vulnerable children in our society.

## REFERENCES

Adoption and Safe Families Act of 1997, Public Law No. 105-89 (1997).

Arad-Davidzon, B., & Benbenishty, R. (2008). The role of workers' attitudes and parent and child wishes in child protection workers' assessments and recommendations regarding removal and reunification. *Children and Youth Services Review, 30,* 107–121.

Australian Institute of Health and Welfare. (2008). *Child protection in Australia 2006–07.* (Child Welfare Series no. 43). Canberra: Author.

Benedict, M., Zuravin, S., & Stallings, R. (1996). Adult functioning of children who lived with kin versus non-relative family foster homes. *Child Welfare, 75,* 529–549.

Berliner, L., & Conte, J. (1995). The effects of disclosure and intervention on sexually abused children. *Child Abuse and Neglect, 19,* 371–384.

Berrick, J. D. (2000). What works in kinship care. In M. P. Kluger, G. Alexander, & P. A. Curtis (Eds.), *What works in child welfare* (pp. 139–147). Washington, DC: CWLA Press.

Berrick, J. D., Barth, R. P., & Needell, B. (1994). A comparison of kinship foster homes and foster family homes: Implications for kinship foster care as family preservation. *Children and Youth Services Review, 16,* 33–64.

Bishop, S. J., Murphy, J. M., Hicks, R., Quinn, D., Lewis, P. J., Grace, M., et al. (2000). What progress has been made in meeting the needs of seriously maltreated children? The course of 200 cases through the Boston Juvenile Court. *Child Abuse and Neglect, 24,* 599–610.

Block, S., Oran, D., Oran, H., Baumrind, N., & Goodman, G. S. (in press). Abused and neglected children in court: Knowledge and attitudes. *Child Abuse and Neglect.*

Blome, W. (1997). What happens to foster kids: Educational experiences of a random sample of foster care youth and a matched group of non-foster care youth. *Child and Adolescent Social Work Journal, 14,* 41–53.

Bowlby, J. (1973). *Attachment and loss: Vol. 2. Separation—anxiety and anger.* London: Penguin.

Broad, B. (2004). Kinship care for children in the UK: Messages from research, lessons for policy and practice. *European Journal of Social Work, 7,* 211–227.

Broad, B., & Skinner, A. (2005). *Relative benefits: Placing children in kinship care.* London: British Association for Adoption and Fostering.

Buehler, C., Orme, J. G., Post, J., & Patterson, D. A. (2000). The long-term correlates of family foster care. *Children and Youth Service Review, 22,* 595–625.

Carlson, V., Cicchetti, D., Barnett, D., & Braunwald, K. (1989). Disorganized/ disoriented attachment relationships in maltreated infants. *Developmental Psychology, 25,* 525–531.

Cashmore, J. (2002). Promoting the participation of children and young people in care. *Child Abuse and Neglect, 26,* 837–847.

Cashmore, J., & Bussey K. (1990). Children's conceptions of the witness role. In J. R. Spencer, G. Nicholson, R. H. Flin, & R. Bull (Eds.), *Children's evidence in legal proceedings: An international perspective* (pp. 177–188). Cambridge, UK: J.R. Spencer.

Cauffman, E. E., & Steinberg, L. (2000). Researching adolescents' judgment and culpability. In T. Grisso & R. G. Schwartz (Eds.), *Youth on trial: A developmental perspective on juvenile justice* (pp. 325–344). Chicago: University of Chicago Press.

Clausen, J. M., Landsverk, J. A., Ganger, W., Chadwick, D., & Litrownik, A. (1998). Mental health problems of children in foster care. *Journal of Child and Family Studies, 7,* 283–296.

Connell, C. M., Katz, K. H., Saunders, L., & Tebes, J. K. (2006). Leaving foster care: The influence of child and case characteristics on foster care exit rates. *Children and Youth Services Review, 28,* 780–798.

Cooper, A., Quas, J. A., Wallin, A. R., Davis, E. L., & Lyon, T. D. (2008, March). *Maltreated and nonmaltreated children's knowledge and understanding of the juvenile court system.* Paper presented at American Psychology–Law Society conference, Jacksonville, FL.

Cooper, C. S., Peterson, N. L., & Meier, J. H. (1987). Variables associated with disrupted placement in a select sample of abused and neglected children. *Child Abuse and Neglect, 11,* 75–86.

Cooper, D. K. (1997). Juveniles' understanding of trial-related information: Are they competent defendants? *Behavioral Sciences and the Law, 15,* 167–180.

Courtney, M. E., & Barth, R. P. (1996). Pathways of older adolescents out of foster care: Implications for independent living services. *Social Work, 41,* 75–84.

Courtney, M. E., & Dworsky, A. (2006). Early outcomes for young adults transitioning from out-of-home care in the USA. *Child and Family Social Work, 11,* 209–219.

Courtney, M., & Needell, B. (1997). Outcomes of kinship care: Lessons from California. In J. Berrick, R. Barth, & N. Gilbert (Eds.), *Child welfare research review* (Vol. 2, pp. 130–150). New York: Columbia University Press.

Edwards, L. P. (2007). Achieving timely permanency in child protection courts: The importance of frontloading the court process. *Juvenile and Family Court Journal, 58*(2), 1–38.

Eltringham, S., & Aldridge, J. (2000). The extent of children's knowledge of court as estimated by guardians ad litem. *Child Abuse Review, 9,* 275–286.

Ehlre, J., & Geen, R. (2002). Kin and non-kin foster care: Findings from a national survey. *Children and Youth Services Review, 24,* 15–35.

Fanshel, D., & Shinn, E. B. (1978). *Children in foster care: A longitudinal investigation.* New York: Columbia University Press.

Fantuzzo, J., & Perlman, S. (2007). The unique impact of out-of-home placement and the mediating effects of child maltreatment and homelessness on early school success. *Children and Youth Services Review, 29,* 941–960.

Flin, R. H., Stevenson, Y., & Davies, G. M. (1989). Children's knowledge of court proceedings. *British Journal of Psychology, 80,* 285–297.

Freshwater, K., & Aldridge, J. (1994). The knowledge and fears about court of child witnesses, schoolchildren and adults. *Child Abuse Review, 3,* 183–195.

Gebel, T. J. (1996). Kinship care and nonrelative family foster care: A comparison of caregiver attributes and attitudes. *Child Welfare, 75,* 5–18.

Goodman, G. S., Taub, E. P., Jones, D. P. H., England, P., Port, L. K., Rudy, L., et al. (1992). Testifying in criminal court. *Monographs of the Society for Research in Child Development, 57*(5, Serial No. 229).

Gold, L. J., Darley, J. M., Hilton, J. L., & Zanna, M. P. (1984). Children's perceptions of procedural justice. *Child Development, 55,* 1752–1759.

Green, R. (2004). The evolution of kinship care policy and practice. *Children, Families, and Foster Care, 14,* 130–149.

Grisso, T. (1981). *Juveniles waiver of rights: Legal and psychological competence.* New York: Plenum Press.

Grisso, T., Steinberg, L., Woolard, J. L., Cauffman, E. E., Scott, E. S., Graham, S., et al. (2003). Juveniles' competence to stand trial: A comparison of adolescents' and adults' capacities as trial defendants. *Law and Human Behavior, 27,* 333–363.

Henry, J. (1997). System intervention trauma to child sexual abuse victims following disclosure. *Journal of Interpersonal Violence, 12,* 499–512.

Herrera, V. M., & McCloskey, L. A. (2001). Gender differences in the risk for delinquency among youth exposed to family violence. *Child Abuse and Neglect, 25,* 1037–1051.

Hicks, A. J., & Lawrence, J. A. (2004). Procedural safeguards for young offenders: Views of legal professionals and adolescents. *Australian and New Zealand Journal of Criminology, 37,* 401–417.

Home at Last. (2006). *My voice, my life, my future: Foster youth participation in court: A national survey.* Monterey Park, CA: The Pew Commission.

Horwitz, S. M., Balestracci, K. M. B., & Simms, M. D. (2001). Foster care placement improves children's functioning. *Archives of Pediatrics and Adolescent Medicine, 155,* 1255–1260.

Jenkins, J. (2008). Listen to me! Empowering youth and courts through increased youth participation in dependency hearings. *Family Court Review, 46,* 163–179.

Johnson, K., & Wagner, D. (2005). Evaluation of Michigan's foster care case management system. *Research on Social Work Practice, 15,* 372–380.

Johnson, P. R., Yoken, C., & Voss, R. (1995). Family foster care placement: The child's perspective. *Child Welfare, 74,* 959–976.

Khoury, A. (2006, December). Seen and heard: Involving children in dependency court. *ABA Child Law Practice, 25,* 145–155.

Krinsky, M., & Rodriquez, J. (2006). Giving a voice to the voiceless: Enhancing youth participation in court proceedings. *Nevada Law Journal, 6,* 1302–1308.

Lansford, J. E., Miller-Johnson, S., Berlin, L. J., Dodge, K. A., Bates, J. E., & Pettit, G. S. (2007). Early physical abuse and later violent delinquency: A prospective longitudinal study. *Child Maltreatment, 12,* 233–45.

Lawrence, C. R., Carlson, E. A., & Egeland, B. (2006). The impact of foster care on the development of behavior problems. *Development and Psychopathology, 18,* 57–76.

Lenroot, K., & Lundberg, E. (1925). *Juvenile courts at work* (U.S. Children's Bureau Report No. 141). Washington, DC: U.S. Printing Office.

Lind, E. A., & Tyler, T. R. (1988). *The social psychology of procedural justice.* New York: Plenum Press.

Lyon, T. D., & Saywitz, K. J. (1999). Young maltreated children's competence to take the oath. *Applied Developmental Science, 3,* 16–27.

Malloy, L. C., Lyon, T. D., & Quas, J. A. (2007). Filial dependency and recantation of child sexual abuse allegations. *Journal of the American Academy of Child and Adolescent Psychiatry, 46,* 162–170.

McIntyre, A., & Kessler, T. (1986). Psychological disorders among foster children. *Journal of Clinical Child Psychology, 15,* 297–303.

Melton, G. B. (1980). Children's concepts of their rights. *Journal of Clinical Child Psychology, 9,* 186–190.

Murphy, K. C. (1998). *Foster care from the child's perspective: Knowledge and attitudes about foster care and their relationship with developmental functioning and the foster care environment.* Unpublished doctoral dissertation, University of Kansas.

Myers, J. E. B., Berliner, L., Brier, J., Hendrix, C. T., Jenny, C., & Reid, T. A. (2002). *The APSAC handbook on child maltreatment* (2nd ed.). Thousand Oaks, CA: Sage.

Nelson, C. A., Zeanah, C. H., & Fox, N. A. (2007). The effects of early deprivation on brain-behavioral development: The Bucharest Early Intervention Project. In D. Romer & E. Walker (Eds.), *Adolescent psychopathology and the developing brain: Integrating brain and prevention science* (pp. 197–215). New York: Oxford University Press.

Newton, R. R., Litrownik, A. J., & Landsverk, J. A. (2000). Children and youth in foster care: Disentangling the relationship between problem behaviors and number of placements. *Child Abuse and Neglect, 24,* 1363–1374.

Nicholson v. Williams et al., No. 00-CV-2229. U.S. Dist. Court (E.D. New York, 2002).

Oosterman, M., Schuengel, C., Slot, N. W., Bullens, R. A. R., & Doreleijers, T. A. H. (2007). Disruptions in foster care: A review and meta-analysis. *Children and Youth Services Review, 29,* 53–76.

Pecora, P. J., & Maluccio, A. N. (2000). What works in family foster care. In M. P. Kluger, G. Alexander, & P. A. Curtis (Eds.), *What works in child welfare* (pp. 139–147). Washington, DC: CWLA Press.

Perry, N. W., McAuliff, B. D., Tam, P., Claycomb, L., Dostal, C., & Flanagan, C. (1995). When lawyers question children: Is justice served? *Law and Human Behavior, 19,* 609–629.

Peterson-Badali, M., Abramovitch, R., & Duda, J. (1997). Young children's legal knowledge and reasoning ability. *Canadian Journal of Criminology, 39,* 145–170.

Pilowsky, D. (1995). Psychopathology among children placed in family foster care. *Psychiatric Services, 46,* 906–910.

Pinderhughes, E. E., Harden, B. J., & Guyer, A. E. (2007). Children in foster care. In L. Aber, S. J. Bishop-Josef, S. M. Jones, K. T McLearn, & D. A. Phillips (Eds.), *Child development and social policy: Knowledge for action* (pp. 201–216). Washington, DC: American Psychological Association.

Pottick, K. J., Warner, L. A., & Yoder, K. A. (2005). Youths living away from families in the U.S. mental health system: Opportunities for targeted intervention. *Journal of Behavioral Health Services and Research, 32,* 264–281.

Putnam, F. (2003). Ten-year research update review: Child sexual abuse. *Journal of the American Academy of Child and Adolescent Psychiatry, 42,* 269–278.

Quas, J. A., Goodman, G. S., Ghetti, S., Alexander, K. W., Edelstein, R., Redlich, A. D., et al. (2005). Childhood sexual assault victims: Long-term outcomes after testifying in criminal court. *Monographs of the Society for Research in Child Development, 70,* 1–145.

Quas, J. A., Wallin, A. R., Horwitz, B., Davis, E., & Lyon, T. D. (2009). Maltreated children's understanding of and emotional reactions to dependency court involvement. *Behavioral Sciences and the Law, 27,* 97–117.

Rowe, J., Hundleby, M., & Garnett, L. (1989). *Child care now—A survey of placement patterns.* London: BAAF.

Ruck, M. D., Keating, D. P., Abramovitch, R., & Koegl, C. J. (1998). Adolescents' and children's knowledge about rights: Some evidence for how young people view rights in their own lives. *Journal of Adolescence, 21,* 275–289.

Runyan, D. K., Everson, M. D., Edelsohn, G. A., Hunter, W. M., & Coulter, M. L. (1988). Impact of legal intervention on sexually abused children. *Journal of Pediatrics, 113,* 647–653.

Runyan, D. K., & Gould, C. L. (1985). Foster care for child maltreatment: Impact on delinquent behavior. *Pediatrics, 75,* 562–568.

Ryan, J. P., & Testa, M. F. (2005). Child maltreatment and juvenile delinquency: Investigating the role of placement and placement instability. *Children and Youth Services Review, 27,* 227–249.

Saywitz, K. J. (1989). Children's conceptions of the legal system: Court is a place to play basketball. In S. J. Ceci, D. F. Ross, & M. P. Toglia (Eds.), *Perspectives on children's testimony* (pp. 131–157). New York: Springer-Verlag.

Saywitz, K. J., Jaenicke, C., & Camparo, L. B. (1990). Children's understanding of legal terminology. *Law and Human Behavior, 14,* 523–535.

Shlonsky, A., & Friend, C. (2007). Double jeopardy: Risk assessment in the context of child maltreatment and domestic violence. *Brief Treatment and Crisis Intervention, 4,* 249–252.

Siegel, J. A., & Williams, J. A. (2003). The relationship between child sexual abuse and female delinquency and crime: A prospective study. *Journal of Research in Crime and Delinquency, 40,* 71–94.

Smith, C., & Thornberry, T. P. (1995). The relationship between childhood maltreatment and adolescent involvement in delinquency. *Criminology, 33,* 451–481.

Taussig, H. N. (2002). Risk behaviors in maltreated youth placed in foster care: A longitudinal study of protective and vulnerability factors. *Child Abuse and Neglect, 26,* 1179–1199.

Taussig, H. N., Clyman, R. B., & Landsverk, J. A. (2001). Children who return home from foster care: A 6-year prospective study of behavioral health outcomes in adolescence. *Pediatrics, 108,* E10.

Tedesco, J. F., & Schnell, S. V. (1987). Children's reactions to sex abuse investigation and litigation. *Child Abuse and Neglect, 11,* 267–272.

Tyler, T. R. (1990). *Why people obey the law.* New Haven, CT: Yale University Press.

Tyler, T. R., Boeckmann, R. J., Smith, H. J., & Huo, Y. J. (1997). *Social justice in a diverse society.* Boulder, CO: Westview Press.

Tyler, T. R., & Huo, Y. J. (2002). *Trust in the law: Encouraging public cooperation with the police and courts.* New York: Russell Sage.

U.S. Department of Health and Human Services, Administration on Children,

Youth, and Families. (2008a). *Child maltreatment 2006*. Washington, DC: U.S. Government Printing Office.

U.S. Department of Health and Human Services, Administration on Children, Youth, and Families. (2008b). *The AFCARS report: Preliminary FY 2006 estimates as of January 2008 (14)*. Washington, DC: U.S. Department of Health and Human Services.

Valentine, B., & Gray, M. (2006). Keeping them home: Aboriginal out-of-home care in Australia. *Families in Society, 87*, 537–545.

Viljoen, J. L., Zapf, P. A., & Roesch, R. (2007). Adjudicative competence and comprehension of *Miranda* rights in adolescent defendants: A comparison of legal standards. *Behavioral Sciences and the Law, 25*, 1–19.

Warren-Leubecker, A., Tate, C., Hinton, I., & Ozbek, N. (1989). What do children know about the legal system and when do they know it? In S. J. Ceci, D. F. Ross, & M. P. Toglia (Eds.), *Perspectives on children's testimony* (pp. 131–157). New York: Springer-Verlag.

Weinberg, L. A., Weinberg, C., & Shea, N. M. (1997). Advocacy's role in identifying dysfunctions in agencies serving abused and neglected children. *Child Maltreatment, 2*, 212–225.

Whitcomb, D. (1992). *When the victim is a child* (2nd ed.). Washington, DC: National Institute of Justice.

White, M., Albers, E., & Bitonti, C. (1996). Factors in length of foster care: Worker activities and parent-child visitation. *Journal of Sociology and Social Welfare, 23*, 75–84.

Widom, C. S. (1989). Child abuse, neglect, and violent criminal behavior. *Criminology, 27*, 251–271.

Widom, C. (1991). Avoidance of criminality in abused and neglected children. *Psychiatry, 54*, 162–174.

Widom, C. S., & Maxfield, M. G. (2001). *An update on the "cycle of violence."* National Institute of Justice: Research in brief. Retrieved January 24, 2008, from *www.ncjrs.gov/pdffiles1/nij/184894.pdf*.

Wulczyn, F., Hislop, K. B., & Harden, B. J. (2002). The placement of infants in foster care. *Infant Mental Health Journal, 23*, 454–475.

Zeanah, C. H., Nelson, C. A., Fox, N. A., Smyke, A. T., Marshall, P., Parker, S. W., et al. (2003). Designing research to study the effects of institutionalization on brain and behavioral development: The Bucharest Early Intervention Project. *Development and Psychopathology, 15*, 885–907.

# Chapter 8

# Child Witnesses
# in Criminal Court

NATALIE R. TROXEL
CHRISTIN M. OGLE
INGRID M. CORDON
MICHAEL J. LAWLER
GAIL S. GOODMAN

Children become involved in criminal court typically after witnessing or experiencing unlawful events. For example, witnessing domestic violence, suffering child physical abuse, or being kidnapped can bring children into the criminal justice system. However, the most likely reason for children to enter the courtroom doors is because they have allegedly experienced child sexual abuse. Increased interest in children's testimony has resulted in a growing body of research concerning the outcomes for children who testify in criminal court and the procedures that can reduce potential distress and trauma for child witnesses as a result of criminal court involvement (see Davies, in press; Hall & Sales, 2008; Quas & Goodman, 2008).

The main goal of this chapter is to review scientific literature relevant to the topic of child witnesses in criminal court. We first briefly outline the series of steps that unfolds for children who become involved in the U.S. criminal court process and describe several methodological issues that scientists confront when studying children's reactions to this complex sequence of events. Second, we discuss child witnesses' fears and anxieties as well as the attitudinal and emotional outcomes that can follow from children's legal involvement. Third, we analyze practices developed to aid child witnesses.

150

Finally, we discuss gaps in the current literature and make recommendations for future research.

## PROCEDURAL STEPS
## AND METHODOLOGICAL ISSUES

When a child experiences or witnesses a crime in the United States, a series of steps typically unfolds if the case goes to trial and the child is to be a witness:

1. A call to police or child protective services is made. A police officer or social worker then interviews the child.
2. A detective is assigned to the case. The detective will likely also interview the child.
3. If the case is accepted for prosecution, the prosecutor will interview the child several months after the case was reported to authorities.
4. A victim advocate (e.g., a social worker who works with the courts) may be assigned to help explain the legal system to the child and family and to guide them through the criminal court process.
5. The child may testify in depositions and/or preliminary hearings.
6. A trial date is set, although the trial date may be postponed one or more times, each time possibly requiring the child to emotionally prepare to testify and wait at the courthouse for hours.
7. The child may be called as a witness in the trial; if so, he or she would generally be treated like an adult witness (e.g., face the defendant, submit to cross-examination).
8. If the defendant is found guilty, the child might be encouraged to testify at the sentencing hearing.
9. Especially in child abuse prosecutions, at the same time as the criminal case is winding its way through to trial, the child may also be involved in a juvenile court dependency case to determine whether the child should be removed from home.

However, at any point in the process, the criminal charges may be dropped or a plea bargain arranged, and the child's involvement in the prosecution might thus end and a trial never be held. Alternatively, if a conviction is appealed, the legal case could start all over again.

Given this complex legal process, how can researchers conduct valid scientific studies of children's reactions to legal involvement and their needs as victims and witnesses? There are many methodological challenges, although we mention only a few here. First, lack of random assignment to groups (e.g., open court vs. closed-circuit television

[CCTV] testimony) typically precludes causal inference about the effects of criminal court on children. For example, if one was studying the outcomes of testifying in court and found that children who testified had more mental health problems than those who did not testify, it would be problematic to attribute the cause of such problems to testifying per se because other factors might have influenced ("confounded") the results. Although researchers try to statistically control confounding variables, for instance in quasi-experimental designs, there may be important variables that are not measured.

A second crucial methodological issue concerns the representativeness of samples. It is often difficult to convince prosecutors or courts to permit researchers to approach crime-exposed children for research participation. Even when permission is gained, convincing caretakers of the value of research can be challenging. When limited access to certain types of cases ensues (e.g., child victims of incest; Goodman et al., 1992), restrictions to the generalizability of research findings can result. A third methodological issue concerns the potential that data will be subpoenaed, making it problematic to include certain questions in the study and creating ethical dilemmas.

These are just a subset of the methodological challenges researchers face when they enter the courtroom (see also Quas, Cooper, & Wandrey, Chapter 7, this volume; Quas & Goodman, 2008). Despite these difficulties, scientists have forged ahead to examine children's experiences and reactions to criminal court involvement. Many replicable findings have emerged from these efforts. Although there is more to learn, overall, valuable and important information has been gained.

## OUTCOMES FOR CHILDREN FOLLOWING INVOLVEMENT IN THE LEGAL SYSTEM

Participation in the legal system can be anxiety provoking and have emotional and attitudinal effects on children. Many fear that court involvement is generally a negative experience for children, although there may actually be some beneficial outcomes as well. Next, we summarize research on child witnesses' fears and anxieties about criminal court. We then review studies of attitudinal and emotional outcomes for child witnesses, particularly for children who are asked to testify in criminal cases.

### Fears and Anxieties

Criminal court testimony is associated with fear and anxiety for a substantial subset of children (Goodman et al., 1992; Quas & Goodman, 2008;

Spencer & Flin, 1993). Several factors identified as potential contributors to these reactions include (1) the adversarial and formal nature of criminal courts; (2) direct-examination and, even more so, cross-examination procedures; (3) facing the defendant; and (4) children's general lack of knowledge about the legal system. We discuss each of these in turn.

The adversarial, formal, and possibly even hostile court environment during a hearing and especially a trial is a source of child witnesses' fear and distress (e.g., Brennan & Brennan, 1988). Such reactions can be heightened when children are afraid that their anxiety or discomfort may negatively affect the trial (Sas, Hurley, Austin, & Wolfe, 1991). In a study conducted by Goodman et al. (1992), a majority of children said it was upsetting or frightening to testify in court, and most parents reported that testifying had been a negative experience for their children. In general, children report being more afraid of crying and answering questions in front of a room full of strangers and adults than in a near-empty classroom (Saywitz & Nathanson, 1993). Even children as old as 17 indicate that taking the witness stand in a formal courtroom is one of their biggest fears when involved in a legal case (Sas et al., 1991).

Anticipation of specific experiences inside the formal courtroom (e.g., being yelled at, feeling embarrassed) can increase children's anxiety (Berliner & Conte, 1995), as can the reality of testifying. Direct examination typically involves describing the crime. Discussing highly personal or traumatic events may cause embarrassment and discomfort (e.g., Herman & Hirschman, 1981) and may force children to relive traumatic events in a retraumatizing context (Brennan & Brennan, 1988; Ghetti, Alexander, & Goodman, 2002; Goodman et al., 1992). Cross-examination is designed to discredit the witness. Two common fears expressed by child witnesses related to cross-examination are (1) being accused of lying in court and (2) being badgered while they testify (Sas et al., 1991).

Some research has focused on children's reactions to the defendant's presence in the courtroom (e.g., facing the defendant). Sas, Wolfe, and Gowdey (1996), Goodman et al. (1992), and Brannon (1994) all cited "facing the defendant" as one of the primary causes of fear and anxiety to child witnesses. This may be particularly evident in cases in which the defendant is important to the children's lives (e.g., a family member; Quas, Goodman, & Jones, 2003) or when the defendant has threatened the child or has a known history of violence (Goodman et al., 1992). The possibility that the defendant would be declared "not guilty" is also a common fear of child witnesses (Sas et al., 1991; see Spencer & Flin, 1993, for review).

Although courtrooms can be anxiety provoking even for adults, children's anxiety is likely exacerbated by a poor understanding of the linguistic terms and concepts used and of the role each person plays (e.g., Flin, Stevenson, & Davies, 1989; Gal & Windman, 2003; Goodman et al., 1998;

Saywitz & Nathanson, 1993). Even in an experimental analogue context of testifying in a mock court, and with age statistically controlled, children's poor understanding of legal terms was related to increased anxiety (Goodman et al., 1998).

Overall, an appreciation of children's anxieties is important so that interventions can be devised to reduce children's fears. At present, some children leave the courtroom with a number of their worst fears realized. In contrast, many other children are relieved that the ordeal was not as bad as they had anticipated (Goodman et al., 1992).

## Attitudinal Outcomes

Negative attitudes (e.g., disillusionment with the legal system) have been documented among children involved in the legal system. Lack of information and long, drawn-out prosecutions contribute to negative attitudes (Ben-Arieh & Windman, 2007; Goodman et al., 1992). Most of the relevant studies have, however, focused on attitudes in relation to children's testimony. Tedesco and Schnell (1987), for example, found that compared with children who did not testify in criminal cases, those who testified in such cases rated the legal system as less helpful. In Goodman et al.'s (1992) study, children rated the effects of not testifying as more positive than the effects of testifying.

Nevertheless, there is also scientific evidence suggesting that many children need their day in court. In the long term, children who testify actually view the legal system as more fair than children who do not take the stand. Quas et al. (2005) conducted a long-term follow-up of the children who were originally questioned by Goodman et al. (1992). The child victims were reinterviewed approximately 12 years after their legal participation. These former child victims, now older adolescents and young adults, rated the legal system as less fair if they had *not* testified than if they had taken the stand in childhood. Thus, although testifying can be stressful for children, in the long term, testifying may foster positive attitudes toward the legal system.

## Emotional Outcomes

In addition to the possible attitudinal outcomes of participating in the legal system, child witnesses may experience emotional sequelae. These emotional effects can take the form of internalizing (e.g., depression, headaches) and externalizing (e.g., aggression, delinquency) behavioral problems (Goodman et al., 1992). In Goodman et al.'s study, children's emotional well-being was assessed using Achenbach's Child Behavioral Checklist (CBCL). Internalizing and externalizing problems generally decreased over the course of the prosecution. However, children who testified showed less improvement in mental health than those who did not testify. That is, nontestifiers improved relative to their level of behavioral problems at intake, whereas testifiers did not. Testifiers were still within the clinical range on their total CBCL scores, and their internalizing and externalizing subscale scores hovered near the clinical cutoff. By the time the prosecution closed, children's internalizing and externalizing problem scores dropped on average compared with their scores at intake, indicating that the children's mental health was improving. There were no significant differences between testifiers and nontestifiers on externalizing behavioral problem scores. However, testifiers were still doing more poorly in general in terms of internalizing behavior problems than nontestifiers. Thus, overall, testifying was associated with less improvement in the children's emotional well-being.

In further analyses of the Goodman et al. (1992) data, it became clear that children were at particular risk of emotional problems if they had testified multiple times. This finding is similar to those of Henry (1997) and Whitcomb et al. (1991), who reported that the number of times children testified and the harshness of questioning were the best predictors of trauma and stress scores. Quas et al.'s (2005) follow-up of the child victims from the Goodman et al. study showed that child victims who testified multiple times in more severe sexual abuse cases (e.g., prolonged incest) showed more emotional problems later as older adolescents and young adults compared with the other child victims studied. Other predictors of emotional risk include lack of maternal support, lack of corroborative evidence, and emotional problems evident during the initial assessment (Goodman et al., 1992; Whitcomb et al., 1991).

Children's behavioral problems after involvement in the legal system are quite troubling to parents of child victims and to professionals who work with children. However, it is difficult to determine whether behavioral problems that arise postlegal involvement are due to testifying per se or to other factors (e.g., family disruption).

Moreover, some researchers have found, or at least proposed, that testifying or otherwise being involved in court may actually be beneficial or cathartic for child victims (Berliner & Barbieri, 1984; Goodman et al., 1992). Testifying may make children feel less victimized and more in control rather than revictimized and further traumatized (Brennan & Brennan, 1988). Berliner and Barbieri (1984) argued that testifying in court gives children a more powerful role in the case and can ease the effects of victimization by giving child victims a voice in court. Goodman et al. (1992) noted that when children are invited to give testimony, it could be a sign that their claims are being taken seriously, and if the defendant is found guilty, children may feel that their statements helped bring about justice. By extension, if children are not permitted to testify, they may feel disenfranchised or helpless, especially if the defendant is not convicted or receives a lenient sentence (Quas et al., 2005), possibly increasing feelings of victimization. Moreover, as indicated earlier, there is growing evidence that involvement in the legal system per se is not emotionally harmful to child victims but rather that testifying multiple times is associated with adverse outcomes.

Runyan, Everson, Edlesohn, Hunter, and Coulter (1988) and Lipovsky et al. (1992; see also Lipovsky, 1994) reported nonsignificant effects of court involvement, likely reflecting a lack of behavioral disturbance resulting directly from legal participation. Quas et al. (2005), in their long-term follow-up of children involved in criminal court prosecutions, found that, overall, there were no detectable differences in behavioral adjustment and trauma-related psychopathology between children who had testified once and those who had not testified. However, there were considerable differences in mental health and adjustment between child victims who were involved in the legal system and the control group of nonabused children who were never involved in the legal system, with the former evincing a greater level of emotional disturbance, but possibly from the abuse itself.

In conclusion, testifying in court is not necessarily harmful to children. Testifying multiple times, however, predicts greater adverse outcomes. In any case, the issue is not so much whether or not children should testify in court; rather, the issue is how best to accommodate children who must be involved. Findings of studies to date largely concern children's reactions to traditional adversary procedures. As criminal investigations and courts change, so might children's reactions. Fortunately, the criminal justice system has evolved to better respond to children's needs, as described next.

## PRACTICES TO AID CHILDREN IN THE LEGAL SYSTEM

Recognition of the distress children may experience in criminal prosecutions has led to the creation of interventions to reduce secondary trauma (Hall & Sales, 2008). Legal interventions and protective measures that alleviate children's emotional distress throughout a trial serve to promote the well-being of child victims and may enable children to provide more reliable testimony (Malloy, Mitchell, Block, Quas, & Goodman, 2006; Zajac & Hayne, 2003). These interventions include, but are not limited to, the use of child advocacy centers (CACs), victim advocates, hearsay testimony, and CCTV.

### Child Advocacy Centers (CACs)

The CAC multidisciplinary approach to child forensic interviews is designed to reduce secondary victimization in children by (1) facilitating collaboration between relevant agencies (e.g., child protective services, law enforcement, prosecution, mental health, and medicine), (2) providing child-sensitive interview settings, and (3) limiting the number of interviews a child victim must undergo. In principle, CACs can thereby reduce the trauma associated with the investigative process. An additional core component of the CAC model is the coordination of specialized therapeutic services to the child and family, including victim support and advocacy (Connell, 2009; Jackson, 2004; Newman, Dannenfelser, & Pendleton, 2005).

Evaluations of the efficacy of the CAC model relative to traditional methods of investigative interviewing in which agencies work independently reveal that CACs decrease the delay between law enforcement report and indictment date (Walsh, Lippert, Cross, Maurice, & Davison, 2008; Wolfteich & Loggins, 2007), increase the receipt of medical examinations (Smith, Witte, & Fricker-Elhai, 2006; Walsh, Cross, Jones, Simone, & Kolko, 2007), improve prosecution rates (e.g., Smith et al., 2006), improve the experience of nonoffending parents during child sexual abuse investigations (Jones, Cross, Walsh, & Simone, 2007), and decrease the level of fear experienced by children during interviews (Jones et al., 2007). Data are accumulating that CACs are likely to be helpful to children and families who enter the criminal justice system.

## Victim Advocates and Court Preparation Programs

A victim advocate is an individual appointed (e.g., by the prosecutor's office) to pursue the rights entitled to the child victim and to assist children in overcoming the anxiety and trauma associated with testifying in court. According to Wolfteich and Loggins (2007), victim advocates typically provide emotional support to the child before and during court proceedings. In addition, advocates often help prepare children for court by educating them about court procedures and their role as witnesses, providing them with case scheduling information, and giving child witnesses a tour of the courthouse. After the court has reached a decision, the victim advocate meets with children and their families to answer questions about the verdict and facilitates the delivery of services available in the greater community (McAuliff, Chapter 12, this volume).

Research on court preparation programs is relevant to the potential for victim advocates to have a positive impact on child victims. For example, recipients of a child witness court preparation program that included individually tailored court preparation better understood legal procedures and terminology than child witnesses who received the standard court preparation services (Sas et al., 1996). In addition, the stress reduction component of the program, which involved deep-breathing exercises, deep muscle relaxation, and cognitive restructuring and empowerment, significantly reduced generalized and abuse-related fears compared with the standard court preparation services offered to the control group.

Other studies have documented the benefits to child victims of a supportive adult in the courtroom (e.g., Goodman et al., 1992). Sas et al. (1996) reported that the presence of a support person, typically the mother, during the trial proceedings was the most influential factor for child witnesses in relieving their distress. To the extent that a victim advocate can serve as a support person for child witnesses, the presence of a victim advocate in the courtroom may become increasingly influential in reducing the adverse outcomes of testifying in court.

Additional research is needed to examine the impact of victim advocates and court preparation programs on both short- and long-term outcomes for children who testify in criminal cases. Specifically, comparison studies of children with and without victim advocates may elucidate which factors increase the well-being of children in the courtroom and decrease their experience of additional trauma. Using research from the adult victim literature as a model (e.g., Campbell, 2006), important indices to evaluate may include the quantity of services received by children and families and the amount of system-induced trauma symptomology, such as self-blame and depression, experienced by children with and without support from victim advocates. Furthermore, research on different types of court preparation programs could lead to identification of particularly effective ways to optimize children's legal involvement.

## Out-of-Court Statements and Closed-Circuit Television (CCTV)

To help alleviate potential trauma for child witnesses, statements made outside of the courtroom (e.g., via videotaped forensic interviews or CCTV testimony) are at times accepted in court cases involving child victims. Hearsay testimony allows children's out-of-court statements (e.g., to their mothers) to be entered as evidence into trial on behalf of child victims. In addition, forensic interviews with child witnesses may be videotaped and presented as hearsay evidence to the court. CCTV allows the child to give evidence outside the courtroom by means of a camera; the child's image is then relayed to the courtroom for viewing while the child undergoes direct and cross-examination.

In several countries, use of hearsay and/or CCTV has become standard practice in child sexual abuse cases. For example, in the United Kingdom, the admittance of videotaped interviews as evidence in place of live direct examination at trial by child victims has become acceptable practice and is generally viewed favorably because of the perception that it reduces stress for child witnesses (Davies, Wilson, Mitchell, & Milsom, 1995). Based on similar reasoning, CCTV is then regularly utilized with child witnesses in place of live cross-examination in court (Davies, in press).

In contrast, in the United States, use of hearsay evidence and CCTV is controversial largely because criminal defendants have rights under the Sixth and Fourteenth Amendments of the U.S. Constitution to confront their accusers during criminal trials and to due process, respectively (Hall & Sales, 2008). Related concerns center on several assumptions about the value and significance of witness confrontation. These assumptions include that (1) the stress of testifying on the stand facing the accused improves the accuracy of witness testimony; (2) the jury's ability to detect deception is impeded unless the witness testifies live in court; and (3) the introduction of out-of-court statements may negatively bias the jury's perception of the defendant and adversely affect case outcomes. Researchers have examined several of these issues, mostly in mock trial studies (e.g., Goodman et al., 1998, 2006; Landstrom, Granhag, & Hartwig, 2005; Ross, Lindsay, & Marsil, 1999; Warren, Nunez, Keeney, Buck, & Smith, 2002; but see Myers, Redlich, Goodman, Prizmich, & Imwinkelreid, 1999), shedding light on the delicate balance between protecting child witnesses and protecting the rights of the accused.

## Hearsay Evidence

Hearsay evidence is defined as "a statement, other than one made by the declarant while testifying at the trial or hearing, offered in evidence to prove the truth of the matter asserted" (Federal Rules of Evidence 801(c)). Testimony given outside the courtroom may not meet the court's "indicia of reliability" because such evidence cannot be subject to full cross-examination (Goodman et al., 2006). On that basis, in a recent U.S. Supreme Court decision (*Crawford v. Washington,* 2004), the admissibility of out-of-court "testimonial" statements (e.g., statements made to law enforcement) was challenged, resulting in the likely need for children to appear live in court for videotaped forensic interviews to be admitted. Nevertheless, there are numerous exceptions to hearsay rules that result in children's out-of-court statements being heard at trial (Myers et al., 1999).

In regard to hearsay, the possibility that testifying live facing the accused can contribute to children's accuracy needs to be balanced by consideration of the adverse effects of intimidation on children's testimony and the long delays to trial, which can weaken children's memory, increase their suggestibility, and delay emotional recovery from the crime. Nevertheless, when hearsay is entered by way of an adult testifying in place of a child, there is the risk that the adult may misstate children's words and distort the questions asked (e.g., Lamb, Orbach, Sternberg, Hershkowitz, & Horowitz, 2004). This problem is lessened when a videotaped forensic interview is introduced as hearsay.

Regarding the concern that the jury's ability to detect deception is impeded unless the witness testifies live, research to date (albeit limited) does not support this assumption. Adults' ability to distinguish between truthful and deceptive adults (e.g., Malone & DePaulo, 2001; Vrij & Baxter, 1999) and children (e.g., Edelstein, Luten, Ekman, & Goodman, 2006; Orcutt, Goodman, Tobey, Batterman-Faunce, & Thomas, 2001; Talwar, Kang, Nicholas, & Lindsay, 2006; Vrij, Akehurst, Brown, & Mann, 2006) is often not much better than chance. Moreover, a 2006 meta-analysis by Aamodt and Custer indicated that most legal professionals (e.g., judges, police officers) were no more accurate at detecting deception than were untrained individuals. More directly on point, in comparing live testimony, videotaped testimony, and adult hearsay testimony, Goodman et al. (2006) found that mock jurors had difficulty discerning accurate from deceptive child statements regardless of testimony format. As to whether the introduction of out-of-court statements negatively biases jurors against the defendant, Goodman et al. (2006) found that mock jurors were less convinced of the defendant's guilt after hearing hearsay than after hearing live testimony from child witnesses.

In addition, Goodman et al.'s (2006) study revealed that observing the child witness live was associated with higher perceived credibility and higher sympathy toward the child. Nevertheless, and somewhat ironically, adults who appear in court to repeat children's statements secondhand are viewed as more accurate and truthful than are children who give firsthand accounts (Warren et al., 2002). In that regard, the effectiveness of hearsay testimony may depend on the perceived credibility or prestige (e.g., a doctor) of a witness (Ross et al., 1999). Further research is needed to better assess the role of hearsay testimony on trial outcomes as well as on the short- and long-term impact on the emotional health of child witnesses.

## Closed-Circuit Television

Despite its frequent use in the United Kingdom, CCTV is rarely utilized for child victims in U.S. courtrooms. This is so notwithstanding the fact that, in a U.S. Supreme Court ruling, the constitutionality of CCTV in child sexual abuse trials was verified if, on a case-by-case basis, a judge ruled that the child would be so traumatized by live testimony as not to be able to reasonably communicate (*Maryland v. Craig,* 1990). Goodman and colleagues (1998) examined the effects of CCTV on children's testimony and mock jurors' perceptions of child witnesses. Their findings indicated that older children (8- to 9-year-olds) generally provided more accurate reports than did younger children (5- to 6-year-olds) regardless of confrontational condition (i.e., CCTV or open court), but that CCTV was associated with reduced suggestibility for younger children. Other studies suggest no significant differences in children's overall completeness or believability as a function of confrontational condition (Clifford, Davies, Westcott, & Garratt, 1992; Westcott, Davies, & Clifford, 1991; but see Landstrom, 2008). Overall, the extant literature does not provide support for the common assumption that face-to-face confrontation increases child witness accuracy compared with testimony given via CCTV. Indeed, face-to-face confrontation in some cases may decrease, rather than facilitate, children's ability (and willingness) to provide complete and accurate testimony.

It has been argued that CCTV, like videotaped forensic interviews, might interfere with jurors' abilities to detect deception and thus hamper the fact-finding process. In general, research does not support this assumption. Given adults' poor accuracy in detecting deception overall, it seems unlikely that watching children testify via CCTV would interfere with jurors' ability to assess truthfulness. Indeed, that was the finding of a study by Orcutt and colleagues (2001), in which they examined the influence of CCTV on jurors' ability to detect deception in children's testimony. Overall, the study indicated that jurors were no better at detecting deception when children testified in open court than when they testified via CCTV.

It has also been argued that protective measures such as CCTV can increase the defendant's appearance of guilt (violating the legal presumption of innocence), thereby increasing the risk of a wrongful conviction. Research examining adults' perceptions of children's testimony and trial fairness as a function of confrontational setting (i.e., traditional court setting vs. CCTV) has not revealed significant differences in the way jurors perceive the defendant, the fairness of the trial, or the outcome of the verdict as a function of confrontational setting (Goodman et al., 1998; Lindsay, Ross, Lea, & Carr, 1995; Orcutt et al., 2001; Swim, Borgidia, & McCoy, 1993). However, one negative effect of CCTV concerns the lowered emotional impact of children's testimony (Cashmore, 1992; Davies & Noon, 1991). Although the impact is reduced even more when children's statements are presented via videotaped interviews compared with via CCTV (Landstrom, 2008), children's testimony still loses some of its emotional impact when delivered via CCTV compared to when given in open court, a finding that is more favorable to the defense than to the prosecution. Moreover, Orcutt et al. (2001) found that children testifying via CCTV were seen as less accurate, less believable, less consistent, less confident, less attractive, and less intelligent than children who testified in open court.

## Summary

Overall, children who testify live are seen more positively than children who testify via CCTV, with the latter rated more positively than those whose statements are viewed on videotape (Landstrom, 2008). It is no wonder, therefore, that prosecutors are reluctant to utilize CCTV (Goodman, Quas,

Bulkley, & Shapiro, 1999) and typically, at least in child sexual abuse trials in the United States, have children testify live in court in addition to introducing hearsay evidence when possible (Myers et al., 1999).

## CONCLUSION

Research on children in criminal court has led to new insights into the effects of legal involvement on children. Both experimental research and field studies have been conducted, leading to several consistent findings: (1) Legal involvement is often, but not always, a stressful event for children, (2) the number of interviews completed is a predictor of emotional outcomes for child witnesses, and (3) there are legal aids (e.g., support persons, CCTV) that can make child witnesses' legal involvement less stressful. Future research is needed, however, on a number of pressing issues.

First, studies have not sufficiently identified the specific effects of a defendant's presence or absence in the courtroom on children's ability to testify or on their well-being. When children testify via CCTV, for example, there are other modifications made (e.g., lack of courtroom context, lack of an audience) compared with when children testify live in court face-to-face with the accused. Researchers need to systematically investigate precisely how a defendant's presence affects children.

Second, although Quas et al. (2005) conducted a follow-up study of children who had participated in criminal court prosecutions, such research is rare. Further research on the long-term outcomes for child victims who testify in court is essential. Moreover, because of changes in the interviewing process (e.g., the establishment of CACs in many jurisdictions), the nature of the legal experience may have significantly changed for children, thus necessitating further research.

Third, children become involved in criminal court proceedings not only as victims of child sexual abuse but also as victims or bystander witnesses of other crimes such as domestic violence, murder, and assault. Studies on such children's legal experiences are needed.

In conclusion, research on children in criminal court promotes a scientific understanding of the effects on child victims of current legal practices. It also directs us toward ways to improve the legal system for child victims, for criminal defendants, and for justice.

## REFERENCES

Aamodt, M. G., & Custer, H. (2006). Who can best catch a liar? A meta-analysis of individual differences in detecting deception. *The Forensic Examiner*, *15*, 6–11.

Ben-Arieh, A., & Windman, V. (2007). Secondary victimization of children in Israel and the child's perspective. *Annual Review of Victimology, 14,* 321–336.

Berliner, L., & Barbieri, M. K. (1984). The testimony of the child victim of sexual assault. *Journal of Social Issues, 40,* 125–137.

Berliner, L., & Conte, J. (1995). The effects of disclosure and intervention on sexually abused children. *Child Abuse and Neglect, 19,* 371–384.

Brannon, L. (1994). The trauma of testifying in court for child victims of sexual assault v. the accused's right to confrontation. *Law and Psychology Review, 18,* 439–460.

Brennan, M., & Brennan, R. E. (1988). *Strange language: Child victims under cross examination* (3rd ed.). Wagga Wagga, NSW: Riverina Murray Institute of Higher Education.

Campbell, R. (2006). Rape survivors' experiences with the legal and medical systems: Do rape victim advocates make a difference? *Violence Against Women, 12,* 30–45.

Cashmore, J. (1992). *The use of closed circuit television for child witnesses in the Australian Capital Territory.* Sydney: Australian Law Reform Commission.

Clifford, B., Davies, G. M., Westcott, H. L., & Garratt, K. (1992). *Video technology and the child witness. Final report to the Police Foundation.* London: University of East London.

Connell, M. (2009). The child advocacy center model. In K. Kuehnle & M. Connell (Eds.), *The evaluation of child sexual abuse allegations: A comprehensive guide to assessment and testimony* (pp. 423–450). New York: Wiley.

Crawford v. Washington, 541 U.S., 36 (2004).

Davies, G. M. (in press). Safeguarding vulnerable and intimidated witnesses in the courtroom: Are the "special measures" working? In J. Adler & J. Gray (Eds.), *Forensic psychology: Concepts, debates and practice* (2nd ed.). Cullompton, Devon, UK: Willan.

Davies, G. M., Wilson, C., Mitchell, R., & Milsom, J. (1995). *Videotaping children's evidence: An evaluation.* London: Home Office.

Edelstein, R. S., Luten, T. L., Ekman, P., & Goodman, G. S. (2006). Detecting lies in children and adults. *Law and Human Behavior, 30,* 1–10.

Flin, R. H., Stevenson, Y., & Davies, G. M. (1989). Children's knowledge of court proceedings. *British Journal of Psychology, 80,* 285–297.

Gal, T., & Windman, V. (2003). Child victims in Israel: Varieties of difficulties, few solutions. *Social Security, 63,* 210–235.

Ghetti, S., Alexander, K. W., & Goodman, G. S. (2002). Legal involvement in child sexual abuse cases: Consequences and interventions. *International Journal of Law and Psychiatry, 25,* 235–251.

Goodman, G. S., Myers, J. E. B., Qin, J., Quas, J. A., Castelli, P., Redlich, A. D., et al. (2006). Hearsay versus children's testimony: Effects of truthful and deceptive statements on jurors' decisions. *Law and Human Behavior, 30,* 363–401.

Goodman, G. S., Quas, J. A., Bulkley, J., & Shapiro, C. (1999). Innovations for child witnesses: A national survey. *Psychology, Public Policy, and Law, 5,* 255–281.

Goodman, G. S., Taub, E. P., Jones, D. P. H., England, P., Port, L. K., Rudy, L., et al. (1992). Testifying in criminal court: Emotional effects on child sexual assault victims. *Monographs of the Society for Research in Child Development, 57* (Serial No. 229).

Goodman, G. S., Tobey, A. E., Batterman-Faunce, J. M., Orcutt, H. K., Thomas, S., Shapiro, C., et al. (1998). Face-to-face confrontation: Effects of closed-circuit technology on children's eyewitness testimony and jurors' decisions. *Law and Human Behavior, 22,* 165–203.

Hall, S., & Sales, B. D. (2008). *Courtroom modifications for child witnesses: Law and science in forensic evaluations.* Washington, DC: American Psychological Assocation.

Henry, J. (1997). System intervention trauma to child sexual abuse victims following disclosure. *Journal of Interpersonal Violence, 12,* 499–512.

Herman, J., & Hirschman, S. L. (1981). *Father-daughter incest.* Cambridge, MA: Harvard University Press.

Jackson, S. L. (2004). A USA national survey of program services provided by child advocacy centers. *Child Abuse and Neglect, 28,* 411–421.

Jones, L. M., Cross, T. P., Walsh, W. A., & Simone, M. (2007). Do children's advocacy centers improve families' experiences of child sexual abuse investigations? *Child Abuse and Neglect, 31,* 1069–1085.

Lamb, M. E., Orbach, Y., Sternberg, K. J., Hershkowitz, I., & Horowitz, D. (2004). Accuracy of investigators' verbatim notes of their forensic interviews with alleged child abuse victims. *Law and Human Behavior, 24,* 699–708.

Landstrom, S. (2008). *CCTV, live, and videotapes: How presentation mode affects the evaluation of witnesses.* Unpublished doctoral dissertation, University of Gotenborg, Sweden.

Landstrom, S., Granhag, P. A., & Hartwig, M. (2005). Witnesses appearing live versus on video: Effects on observers' perception, veracity assessments, and memory. *Applied Cognitive Psychology, 19,* 913–933.

Lindsay, R. C. L., Ross, D. F., Lea, J. A., & Carr, C. (1995). What's fair when a child testifies? *Journal of Applied Social Psychology, 25,* 870–888.

Lipovsky, J. A. (1994). The impact of court on children: Research findings and practical recommendations. *Journal of Interpersonal Violence, 9,* 238–257.

Lipovsky, J. A., Tidwell, R. P., Crisp, J., Kilpatrick, D. G., Saunders, F. F., & Dawson, V. L. (1992). Child witnesses in criminal court: Descriptive information from three southern states. *Law and Human Behavior, 16,* 635–650.

Malloy, L. C., Mitchell, E. B., Block, S. D., Quas, J. A., & Goodman, G. S. (2006). Children's eyewitness memory: Balancing children's needs and defendants' rights when seeking the truth. In M. P. Toglia, J. D. Read, D. F. Ross, & R. C. L. Lindsay (Eds.). *Handbook of eyewitness psychology: Volume 1. Memory for events* (pp. 545–574). Mahwah, NJ: Erlbaum.

Malone, B. E., & DePaulo, B. M. (2001). Measuring sensitivity to deception. In J. A. Hall & F. J. Bernieri (Eds.), *Interpersonal sensitivity* (pp. 103–124). Mahwah, NJ: Erlbaum.

Maryland v. Craig, 47 CrL 2258 U.S. SupCt (1990).

Myers, J. E. B., Redlich, A. D., Goodman, G. S., Prizmich, L. P., & Imwinkelreid, E. (1999). Jurors' perceptions of hearsay in child sexual abuse cases. *Psychology, Public Policy, and Law, 5,* 388–419.

Newman, B. S., Dannenfelser, P. L., & Pendleton, D. (2005). Child abuse investigations: Reasons for using child advocacy centers and suggestions for improvement. *Child and Adolescent Social Work Journal, 22,* 165–180.

Orcutt, H. K., Goodman, G. S., Tobey, A. E., Batterman-Faunce, J. M., & Thomas, S. (2001). Detecting deception in children's testimony: Factfinders' abilities to reach the truth in open court and closed-circuit trials. *Law and Human Behavior, 25,* 339–372.

Quas, J. A., & Goodman, G. S. (2008). *Child victims in criminal court cases: Emotional and attitudinal outcomes.* Manuscript submitted for publication.

Quas, J. A., Goodman, G. S., Ghetti, S., Alexander, K. W., Edelstein, R. S., Redlich, A. D., et al. (2005). Childhood victims of sexual assault: Long-term outcomes after testifying in criminal court. *Monographs of the Society for Research in Child Development, 70.* (Serial No. 280).

Quas, J. A., Goodman, G. S., & Jones, D. P. H. (2003). Predictors of attributions of self-blame and internalizing behavior problems in sexually abused children. *Journal of Child Psychology and Psychiatry, 44,* 723–736.

Ross, D. F., Lindsay, R. C. L., & Marsil, D. F. (1999). The impact of hearsay testimony on conviction rates in trials of child sexual abuse: Toward balancing the rights of defendants and child witnesses. *Psychology, Public Policy, and Law, 5,* 439–455.

Runyan, D. K., Everson, M. D., Edelsohn, G. A., Hunter, W. M., & Coulter, M. L. (1988). Impact of intervention on sexually abused children. *Journal of Pediatrics, 113,* 647–653.

Sas, L. D., Hurley, P., Austin, G., & Wolfe, D. (1991). *Reducing the system-induced trauma for child sexual abuse victims through court preparation, assessment, and follow-up.* London, Ontario, Canada: London Family Court Clinic.

Sas, L. D., Wolfe, D. A., & Gowdey, K. (1996). Children in the courts in Canada. *Criminal Justice and Behavior, 23,* 338–357.

Saywitz, K. J., & Nathanson, R. (1993). Children's testimony and their perceptions of stress in and out of the courtroom. *Child Abuse and Neglect, 17,* 613–622.

Smith, D. W., Witte, T. H., & Fricker-Elhai, A. E. (2006). Service outcomes in physical and sexual abuse cases: A comparison of child advocacy center-based and standard services. *Child Maltreatment, 11,* 354–360.

Spencer, J., & Flin, R. H. (1993). *The evidence of children* (2nd ed.). London: Blackstone.

Swim, J. K., Borgida, E., & McCoy, K. (1993). Videotaped versus in-court witness testimony: Does protecting the child witness jeopardize due process? *Journal of Applied Social Psychology, 23,* 603–631.

Talwar, V., Kang, L., Nicholas, B., & Lindsay, R. C. L. (2006). Adults' judgments of children's coached reports. *Law and Human Behavior, 30,* 561–570.

Tedesco, J., & Schnell, S. (1987). Children's reactions to sex abuse investigation and litigation. *Child Abuse and Neglect, 11,* 267–272.

Vrij, A., & Baxter, M. (1999). Accuracy and confidence in detecting truths and lies in elaborations and denials: Truth bias, lie bias and individual differences. *Expert Evidence, 7,* 25–36.

Vrij, A., Akehurst, A., Brown, L., & Mann, S. (2006). Detecting lies in young children, adolescents and adults. *Applied Cognitive Psychology, 20,* 1225–1237.

Walsh, W. A., Cross, T. P., Jones, L. M., Simone, M., & Kolko, D. J. (2007). Which sexual abuse victims receive medical examination? The impact of children's advocacy centers. *Child Abuse and Neglect, 31,* 1053–1068.

Walsh, W. A., Lippert, T., Cross, T. P., Maurice, D. M., & Davison, K. S. (2008). How long to prosecute child sexual abuse for a community using a children's advocacy center and two comparison communities? *Child Maltreatment, 13,* 3–13.

Warren, A. R., Nunez, N., Keeney, J. M., Buck, J. A., & Smith, B. (2002). The believability of children and their interviewers' hearsay testimony: When less is more. *Journal of Applied Psychology, 87,* 846–857.

Westcott, H. V., Davies, G. M., & Clifford, B. (1991). Adults' perceptions of children's videotaped truthful and deceptive statements. *Children and Society, 5,* 123–135.

Whitcomb, D., Runyan, D. K., De Vos, E., Hunter, W. M., Cross, T. P., Everson, M. D., et al. (1991). *Child victim as witness research and development program* (Report to the Office of Juvenile Justice and Delinquency Prevention). Washington, DC: U.S. Department of Justice.

Wolfteich, P., & Loggins, B. (2007). Evaluation of the children's advocacy center model: Efficiency, legal and revictimization outcomes. *Child and Adolescent Social Work Journal, 24,* 333–352.

Zajac, R., & Hayne, H. (2003). The effect of cross-examination on the accuracy of children's reports. *Journal of Experimental Psychology: Applied, 10,* 187–195.

## Chapter 9

# Expert Psychological Testimony in Child Sexual Abuse Trials

JOHN E. B. MYERS

This book provides in-depth analysis of psychological research on children as victims, witnesses, and offenders. In addition to the theoretical importance of psychological research, advances in experimental and clinical knowledge have immediate, on-the-ground implications for the legal system. To name a few, psychology contributes to improved techniques for interviewing children. Psychology deepens our understanding of the short- and long-term effects of sexual abuse. Research affords us a greater appreciation of the impact on children of testifying in court and of techniques to prepare children for the courtroom. Psychological research sheds light on why some children sexually abuse other children and which young offenders are at risk of reoffending.

The results of psychological research and clinical experience find their way into court through expert testimony. Testimony from psychologists and other mental health professionals plays a central role in many litigated cases of child sexual abuse. Yet, just as the courtroom is unfamiliar territory for children, most mental health professionals have limited experience testifying. With that in mind, the goal of this chapter is to familiarize readers with the principles governing expert testimony in child sexual abuse litigation. I begin with an introduction to the legal rules governing expert testimony. From there, I discuss screening tools used by judges to assess the validity and reliability of expert testimony. I end the chapter with a description of common uses of psychological expertise in child sexual abuse cases.

# RULES GOVERNING EXPERT TESTIMONY

In the United States, every state and the federal government has laws called rules or codes of evidence that govern expert testimony. The Federal Rules of Evidence apply only in federal court. Yet the Federal Rules have been extremely influential, and today most states have adopted the Federal Rules of Evidence for use in state court. Even states that do not have the Federal Rules (e.g., California, New York State) have evidence rules similar to the Federal Rules of Evidence. Because the Federal Rules are influential nationwide, the following discussion is couched in the language of the Federal Rules of Evidence.

## Assistance for the Jury

The rules of evidence allow expert testimony when an expert is needed to help the jury understand scientific, technical, or clinical issues. In many cases, there is no jury, and the judge fills the fact-finding role assigned to jurors. This chapter refers to the jury, but bear in mind that in some cases, particularly noncriminal cases in family and juvenile court, there is no jury.

The issue on which expert testimony is offered does not have to be entirely beyond the ken of the jury. Expert testimony often adds depth and clarity to subjects that are somewhat familiar to jurors. On the other hand, if the jury is adequately equipped to decide the issue without assistance, expert testimony is inadmissible. As issues become more complex, assistance for the jury is required. Thus, expert testimony is admissible to explain the results of psychological tests, the intricacies of psychiatric diagnosis, the likelihood a sex offender will recidivate, proper and improper techniques for interviewing children, and more.

## Qualification to Testify as an Expert

Before a professional may testify as an expert, the judge must be convinced that the professional possesses sufficient education, training, and experience to assist the jury. Typically, the attorney offering the professional's testimony asks questions highlighting the professional's qualifications. The opposing attorney has the right to voir dire the professional, that is, to ask questions designed to convince the judge that the professional is not qualified to provide expert testimony. When the professional is clearly qualified, there usually is no voir dire.

## Direct Examination: Form of Expert Testimony; Reasonable Certainty

Once the judge approves the professional as an expert witness, testimony begins with direct examination. During direct examination, the attorney offering the expert asks questions to elicit the expert's testimony. The expert's direct testimony typically takes one or more of the following forms: an opinion, an answer to a hypothetical question, or a lecture providing technical or clinical information to the jury.

An opinion is the most common form of expert testimony. Thus, an expert might opine that an interviewer used too many suggestive questions while questioning a child. An expert might describe the psychological examination of a convicted sex offender and opine on the risk the offender will recidivate.

An expert offering opinion testimony must be reasonably confident that the opinion is correct. Judges and lawyers use the term "reasonable certainty" to describe the required level of confidence. Unfortunately, reasonable certainty is not well defined in law. It is clear that expert witnesses may not speculate or guess. It is equally clear that experts do not have to be 100% certain that their opinion is correct. Thus, reasonable certainty lies at some poorly defined location between speculation and complete certainty, closer to the latter than the former. A helpful way to analyze the certainty of opinion testimony is to ask the following questions: In formulating the opinion, did the expert consider all relevant facts? Does the expert have adequate understanding of pertinent clinical and scientific principles? Did the expert use methods of assessment that are appropriate, reliable, and valid? Are the expert's assumptions and conclusions reasonable? The California Supreme Court observed, "Like a house built on sand, the expert's opinion is no better than the facts on which it is based" (*People v. Gardeley,* 1996, p. 816).

The concept of reasonable certainty for expert testimony should not be confused with the burden of proof. The burden of proof is the level of certainty by which the jury must be persuaded by evidence presented by the party shouldering the burden of proof. Three burdens of proof are used in the United States: (1) proof beyond a reasonable doubt, (2) preponderance of the evidence, and (3) clear and convincing evidence. The burden of proof beyond a reasonable doubt is used in criminal cases and is the highest and most difficult burden to meet. The prosecutor must prove the defendant guilty beyond a reasonable doubt. Most civil litigation uses the less exacting preponderance of the evidence standard. Under the preponderance standard, the party with the burden of proof need only convince the jury that it is more likely than not that the party is entitled to win. The third burden of proof, clear and convincing evidence, is reserved for a small number of civil cases where the stakes are particularly high, including termination of parental rights and involuntary psychiatric hospitalization of the mentally ill. Burdens of proof are complex legal concepts that are not reducible to simple percentages. Yet a measure of insight is afforded by comparing proof beyond a reasonable doubt to 95% certainty, preponderance of evidence to 51% certainty, and clear and convincing evidence to 75% certainty.

Expert witnesses must be reasonably certain of their opinions, but the degree of certainty needed for expert testimony does *not* vary with the type of litigation. Thus, experts do not have to be more certain of their opinions in a criminal case, where the burden of proof is highest, than in a civil case. Regardless of the type of litigation—criminal or civil—experts should take all necessary steps to ensure the correctness of the opinion.

Occasionally, attorneys ask experts whether they are certain of their opinions beyond a reasonable doubt or by a preponderance of the evidence. An accurate response to such a question is:

"Counsel, when I reach an opinion, I do not employ the legal concepts of burden of proof. Burdens of proof are legal constructs, and are not used in psychology. Instead, I use clinical and scientific principles to reach my opinion. In reaching my opinion in this case, I took all the steps I could to ensure that my opinion is correct. I am reasonably certain of my opinion, and by reasonably certain I mean I am confident my opinion is correct."

As mentioned, the most common form of expert testimony is the opinion to a reasonable degree of certainty. Less often, the expert answers a hypothetical question posed by the attorney. The attorney describes a hypothetical set of facts that parallel the facts of the case on trial. Then the expert is asked for an opinion, to a reasonable degree of certainty, about the hypothetical facts. The jury applies the expert's opinion about the *hypothetical* facts to the *actual* facts of the case on trial.

Many attorneys conducting direct examination of expert witnesses avoid hypothetical questions. The hypothetical question can seem stilted and artificial, leaving the jury to wonder, "Why is the lawyer asking about a hypothetical case? Why doesn't the lawyer ask about *this* case?" The rules of evidence allow experts to opine about the facts of the case on trial, and many attorneys prefer the direct approach over the circuitous route of the hypothetical question.

Experts are more likely to encounter hypothetical questions during cross-examination than direct examination. The cross-examiner may try to weaken the expert's opinion by asking about a hypothetical set of facts that differs from the set of facts described by the expert. The cross-examiner then asks, "If the hypothetical facts I have suggested to you turn out to be true, would that change your opinion?" Chadwick (1990) observes that it is "common to encounter hypothetical questions based on hypotheses that are extremely unlikely, and the witness may need to point out the unlikelihood" (p. 967). When a cross-examiner asks a hypothetical question containing new facts, the answer might be:

"If the facts were as you suggest, my opinion could change, yes. Of course, the facts you suggest were not the facts of the case I examined."

The third form of expert testimony is a lecture that gives the jury technical, clinical, or scientific information it needs to properly evaluate the evidence in the case. With this form of expert testimony, the expert does not render an opinion, and the expert's testimony is limited to educating the jury. This form of expert testimony is sometimes used in child sexual abuse cases when the defense attorney argues that because a child delayed reporting, made inconsistent statements, or recanted, the child cannot be believed. When the defense attacks the child's credibility this way, judges often allow an expert witness to help the jury understand that it is not uncommon for sexually abused children to delay reporting, provide partial or piecemeal disclosures, and recant. Equipped with this information, the jury is in a better position to evaluate the child's credibility.

## Cross-Examination and Impeachment of Expert Witnesses

Direct examination is followed by cross-examination. When cross-examination is complete, the attorney who asked the expert to testify may conduct redirect examination to clarify issues that were raised on cross-examination.

### Positive and Negative Cross-Examination

Cross-examination can be broken down into two types: positive and negative. With positive cross-examination, the cross-examining attorney does not attack the expert. Rather, the attorney questions the expert in a positive, even friendly, way, seeking agreement from the expert on certain facts or inferences that may be helpful to the attorney's client. With negative cross-examination, by contrast, the attorney seeks to undermine (impeach) the expert's testimony. A cross-examining attorney who plans to employ both types of cross-examination typically begins with positive questioning in the hope of eliciting favorable testimony from the expert. Negative cross-examination is postponed until positive cross-examination proves ineffective.

### Preparation: Mastering the Facts

The skilled cross-examiner is a master of the facts of the case and shapes questions to manipulate the facts to favor the cross-examiner's client. To avoid manipulation, the expert witness must know the facts of the case as well as or better than the cross-examiner. An expert who fumbles with the facts loses credibility in the eyes of the jury.

## Maintaining Professional Demeanor

The experienced expert refuses to be cajoled, dragged, or tricked into verbal sparring with the cross-examiner. The professional is at all times just that—professional. Given the aggression of some cross-examiners—aggression that is sometimes laced with error, insinuation, and even personal attack—it can be difficult to maintain a calm, professional demeanor on the witness stand. Yet, remember that the jury is looking to you for objective guidance and wisdom. The jury wants a strong expert but not someone who takes off the gloves and fights it out with the cross-examiner. This does not mean, of course, that the expert cannot use pointed responses during cross-examination. The expert should express confidence when challenged and should not vacillate or equivocate in the face of attack. On the other hand, the expert should concede weak points and acknowledge conflicting evidence.

## Asking for Clarification

We encourage child witnesses to say "I don't know" when they are asked questions they don't understand. As adults, we should take a dose of our own medicine. The expert should not answer a question unless the question is fully understood. When in doubt, ask the attorney to clarify. Such a request does not show weakness. After all, if you don't understand a question, it is very likely the jury doesn't either. When a cross-examiner's question is two or three questions in one, the other attorney may object that the question is "compound." Absent an objection, it is proper for the expert to ask the cross-examiner which of the several questions the attorney would like answered.

## Leading Questions during Cross-Examination

From the lawyer's perspective, the key to successful cross-examination is controlling the witness's answers to questions. With the goal of witness control in mind, the cross-examining attorney asks often highly leading questions. Unlike the attorney conducting direct examination, who generally stays away from leading questions, the cross-examiner has free reign to ask all the leading questions the examiner desires. Indeed, some experienced cross-examiners almost always ask leading questions during cross-examination. The cross-examiner seeks to control the expert with leading questions that require short, specific answers, preferably limited to "yes" or "no."

The cross-examiner keeps the expert hemmed in with leading questions and seldom asks "why" or "how" something happened. "Why" and "how" questions relinquish control to the expert, which is precisely what the cross-examiner does not want.

When an expert attempts to explain an answer to a leading question, the cross-examiner may interrupt and say, "Please just answer yes or no." If the expert persists, the cross-examiner may ask the judge to admonish the expert to limit answers to the questions asked. Experts are understandably frustrated when an attorney thwarts efforts at clarification, and it is sometimes proper to say, "Counsel, it is not possible for me to answer with a simple yes or no. May I explain myself?" Chadwick (1990) advises: "When a question is posed in a strictly 'yes or no' fashion, but the correct answer is 'maybe,' the witness should find a way to express the true answer. A direct appeal to the judge may be helpful in some cases" (p. 967). Judges sometimes permit witnesses to amplify their opinion during cross-examination. And remember, after cross-examination there is redirect examination, affording the expert an opportunity to clarify matters that were left unclear during cross-examination.

## Undermining the Expert's Facts, Inferences, or Conclusions

One of the most effective cross-examination techniques with expert witnesses is to get the expert to agree to the facts, inferences, and conclusions that support the expert's opinion and then to dispute one or more of those facts, inferences, or conclusions. Consider a case in which a psychologist testifies that a teenage sex offender is likely to abuse other children. The cross-examiner begins by committing the expert to the facts and assumptions underlying the opinion. The attorney might say:

> "So, doctor, your opinion is based exclusively on your interview with the subject, your review of the file, and on the results of psychological tests, is that correct? And there is nothing else you relied on to form your opinion. Is that correct?"

The cross-examiner commits the expert to a specific set of facts and assumptions so that when the attorney disputes those facts or assumptions, the expert's opinion cannot be justified on some other basis.

Once the cross-examiner pins down the basis of the expert's opinion, the examiner attacks the opinion by disputing one or more of the facts, inferences, or conclusions that support it. The attorney might ask whether the expert's opinion would change if certain facts were different (a hypothetical question). The attorney might press the expert to acknowledge alternative explanations for the expert's conclusion. The attorney might ask the psychologist whether experts could come to different conclusions based on the same facts.

Rather than attack the expert's facts, inferences, and conclusions during cross-examination, the attorney may limit cross-examination to pinning the expert down to a limited set of facts, inferences, and conclusions and then, when the expert has left the witness stand, offer another expert to contradict the data supporting the expert's testimony.

## Learned Treatises

The cross-examiner may seek to undermine the expert's testimony by confronting the expert with books or articles (called learned treatises) that contradict the expert. The rules on impeachment with learned treatises vary from state to state. There is agreement on one thing, however. When an expert is confronted with a sentence or a paragraph selected by an attorney from an article or chapter, the expert has the right to put the selected passage in context by reading surrounding material. The expert might say to the cross-examining attorney:

> "Counsel, I cannot comment on the sentence you have selected unless I first read the entire article. If you will permit me to read the article, I'll be happy to comment on the sentence that interests you."

## Impeaching the Expert Who Violates Ethical Standards

A potentially damaging area of cross-examination involves the use of ethical standards to impeach an expert witness. There are few things that undermine an expert's credibility more rapidly than a suggestion that the expert violated the ethical standards of the expert's profession. The skilled cross-examiner is familiar with the applicable ethical standards and looks for opportunities to use them against the expert. As part of pretrial preparation, discuss applicable ethical guidelines with the attorney who asked you to testify. It may be advisable to provide the attorney a copy of the ethical standards for your profession.

## JUDGE'S RESPONSIBILITY AS GATEKEEPER OF EXPERT TESTIMONY BASED ON SCIENTIFIC PRINCIPLES

As explained previously, the judge presiding over a trial determines whether a professional has sufficient education, training, and experience to testify as an expert witness. The judge also determines whether the expert's testimony will assist the jury. When expert testimony is based on scientific principles, especially principles that are novel, the judge has a third responsibility. The judge determines whether the science underlying proposed expert testimony is sufficiently valid and reliable to justify use in court. The judge is the "gate-keeper" to ensure that invalid, unreliable "junk science" does not find its way into court. As an aside, judges understand the difference between valid-ity and reliability. Yet judges generally use the term "reliability" to cover both.

When one of the attorneys or the judge has serious reservations about the reliability of proposed expert testimony, the judge may hold a hearing to determine whether the science underlying the testimony is sufficiently reliable. Such hearings are called *Frye* or *Daubert* hearings, named after two famous cases: *Frye v. United States* (1923) and *Daubert v. Merrell Dow Pharmaceuticals, Inc.* (1993).

*Frye* was decided in 1923 by the Court of Appeals for the District of Columbia and dealt with a precursor of the modern polygraph. The court fashioned a legal test to evaluate the reliability of novel scientific principles underlying expert testimony. The court ruled that expert testimony based on novel scientific principles cannot be admitted in court until the principles are generally accepted as reliable by the scientific community, that is, until the principles pass the admittedly fuzzy line that separates novelty from general acceptance. This test for novel scientific evidence is known as the "general acceptance" test or simply *Frye*.

During a *Frye* hearing, expert testimony is offered concerning the reliability (i.e., general acceptance) of the disputed scientific principle. If the judge finds general acceptance, then the proposed expert testimony is allowed. On the other hand, if the judge finds that the principles underlying the proposed expert testimony are not generally accepted as reliable, the judge excludes the expert testimony.

For most of the 20th century, *Frye* was the dominant test in the United States for evaluating the admissibility of novel scientific evidence. Over the years, however, particularly in the 1980s, *Frye* was criticized by judges and scholars. The basic criticism was that *Frye*'s requirement of general accep-tance had the undesirable effect of excluding scientific evidence that had yet to achieve general acceptance but that nevertheless was sufficiently reliable for use in court. Criticism of *Frye* culminated in the U.S. Supreme Court's 1993 decision in *Daubert v. Merrell Dow Pharaceuticals, Inc.* In *Daubert*, the Supreme Court rejected *Frye* and replaced it with a new test for scientific evidence.

Under *Daubert*, the trial judge is the gatekeeper for *all* scientific evi-dence, not just novel scientific evidence. As was the case with *Frye*, under *Daubert* an attorney may object that expert testimony is based on unreliable scientific principles and request a hearing, now called a *Daubert* hearing.

Unlike *Frye*, where the only issue at the hearing was general acceptance by the scientific community, the judge conducting a *Daubert* hearing considers all evidence that sheds light on reliability.

In *Daubert* the Supreme Court wrote that judges conducting *Daubert* hearings should consider the following factors. First, has the scientific principle underlying the proposed expert testimony been subjected to testing under the scientific method? Second, has the principle been subjected to peer review and publication? Third, is there an established error rate when the principle is used? Fourth, are there standards that govern proper use of the principle? Finally, borrowing from *Frye*, is the principle generally accepted as reliable in the scientific community? A scientific principle that has yet to achieve general acceptance may nevertheless be sufficiently reliable under *Daubert* for use in court.

*Daubert* dealt with expert testimony based squarely on science. Following *Daubert,* there was uncertainty as to whether *Daubert* applied to expert testimony that combines science and professional judgment and interpretation. Thus, does *Daubert* apply to expert testimony from engineers, physicians, and mental health professionals who combine scientific knowledge with professional or clinical judgment? In 1999 the Supreme Court answered in the affirmative with its decision in *Kumho Tire Company, Ltd. v. Carmichael*. In *Kumho*, the Supreme Court ruled: "*Daubert*'s general holding—setting forth the trial judge's gatekeeping obligation—applies not only to testimony based on scientific knowledge, but also to testimony based on technical and other specialized knowledge" (p. 141). In *Kuhmo* the Court reiterated that the trial judge considers all evidence shedding light on the reliability of expert testimony.

The Supreme Court's rulings in *Daubert* and *Kuhmo* are only binding on federal courts and do not compel states to abandon *Frye*. As of 2009, a majority of states had jettisoned *Frye* in favor of *Daubert*. States retaining *Frye* include California, Florida, Illinois, New Mexico, and Washington.

In the vast majority of child abuse and neglect cases involving expert testimony, there is no *Frye* or *Daubert* hearing. The expert gets on the witness stand, is qualified, testifies, is cross-examined, and that is the end of it. *Frye* or *Daubert* hearings arise only in the exceptional case where an attorney believes expert testimony offered by the opponent is based on demonstrably unreliable scientific, technical, or clinical principles. In such exceptional cases, the attorney requests a *Frye* or *Daubert* hearing in an effort to exclude the expert testimony.

A few states (e.g., California and Florida) have the odd rule that *Frye/Daubert* hearings do not apply to expert testimony in the form of opinion. The thinking behind this rule is that jurors are not likely to be misled or overimpressed by opinion testimony. Jurors, so the theory goes, can evaluate the worth of opinion, especially with the aid of skillful cross-examination.

By contrast, jurors may be awestruck or blindsided by machines, devices, and techniques that profess to be based on science and that purport to yield definitive answers to complex questions. Jurors, and cross-examining lawyers for that matter, are not equipped to peer into "little black 'scientific' boxes" to determine whether they yield valid and reliable data. Out of concern that jurors will be too impressed by little black boxes, California and Florida courts limit *Frye/Daubert* hearings to expert testimony based on novel scientific machines, devices, and techniques.

The problem with the approach used in California and Florida is that opinion testimony can be just as misleading, inaccurate, obtuse, invalid, and unreliable—just as likely to blindside the jury—as anything emerging from the scientific version of the little black box. Moreover, there is little reason to believe that cross-examining attorneys are better at dissecting opinion testimony than expert testimony based on devices or techniques. If the primary concern is protecting juries from "junk science," the best approach is to apply *Frye/Daubert* hearings to any expert testimony that is of dubious validity or reliability, whether in the form of opinion or a little black box.

## EXPERT PSYCHOLOGICAL TESTIMONY IN CHILD SEXUAL ABUSE LITIGATION: TESTIMONY FOCUSED ON THE OFFENDER

Mental health professionals provide expert testimony on a range of issues regarding the individual accused of sexual abuse.

### Competence to Stand Trial; Insanity

In rare cases, questions arise about the mental competence of a defendant—adolescent or adult—to stand trial. When this occurs, psychologists or psychiatrists evaluate the defendant and testify regarding the defendant's comprehension of the proceedings and capacity to assist the defense attorney. Rarer than questions of competence to stand trial are questions about a defendant who seeks to escape responsibility by raising the insanity defense. Here, too, psychological evaluation and testimony play key roles.

### Expert Testimony That the Defendant Does Not Fit the Profile of a "Typical" Sex Offender

Appellate courts in some states permit defendants accused of child sexual abuse to offer expert testimony that the defendant does not fit the psychological profile of a pedophile or sex offender (e.g., California: *People v. Stoll*, 1989; Utah: *State v. Miller*, 1985; Wisconsin: *State v. Walters*, 2004).

Such testimony is controversial in view of the consensus in the literature that there is no profile of a typical sex offender. Becker and Murphy (1998) wrote, "There is clear evidence in the sex offender treatment field that there is no specific profile of a sexual offender" (p. 123). The Association for the Treatment of Sexual Abusers (ATSA) (2005) adds: "Members recognize, and when providing expert testimony, acknowledge, that there is no known psychological or physiological test, profile, evaluation procedure, or combination of such tools that prove or disprove whether an individual has committed a specific sexual act" (p. 10). A number of courts reject profile testimony offered by the accused (e.g., Louisiana: *State v. Hughes*, 2003; Michigan: *People v. Dobek*, 2007).

## Sentencing

When a defendant is convicted of sexual abuse, the judge decides the appropriate sentence, which may include prison, probation, a fine, or some combination thereof. At sentencing, mental health professionals can assist the judge by evaluating the defendant's amenability to treatment and general mental functioning.

Changing the focus from adult court to juvenile court, the past quarter-century witnessed a shift in juvenile justice policy toward a more punitive response to delinquency (see Reppucci, Michel, & Kostelnik, Chapter 15, and Tolan & Titus, Chapter 16, this volume). Yet, despite this shift, juvenile court judges, the attorneys who work in juvenile court, and the probation officers who are so key to its success continue to believe that most teenagers who break the law can be helped. This is true for teens who sexually abuse younger children and who are adjudicated delinquent in juvenile court for this offense. Mental health professionals make an enormous contribution to the future of these youngsters when they help juvenile court professionals understand the differences between adult sex offenders and youth with sexual behavior problems. In particular, mental health professionals help judges understand that most teenagers who engage in sexually inappropriate conduct outgrow the behavior and are not destined to become adult sex offenders. As Caldwell reports, "The majority of juvenile sexual offenders do not sexually offend as adults" (2007, p. 112).

## Civil Commitment of "Dangerous Sexual Predators"

During the late 20th century, a substantial number of state legislatures resurrected laws from midcentury that allow involuntary psychiatric hospitalization of convicted sex offenders who pose an ongoing risk to children (Myers, 2006). Under the new laws, when an offender's prison sentence is about to expire, a prosecutor files a petition seeking the involuntary civil commitment of the offender. Mental health professionals provide expert testimony during commitment proceedings. Typically, risk assessment testimony combines clinical judgment and actuarial tools. ATSA (2005) reports, "Actuarial risk assessment methods are generally more accurate than clinical judgment alone in predicting the likelihood of sexual offending over a long-term period" (p. 49). Courts are receptive to actuarial tools such as the Static-99 and the Minnesota Sex Offender Screening Tool (e.g., *Commitment of J. M. B.*, 2009; *Commitment of R. S.*, 2002; *Darren M.*, 2006; *Detention of Thorell*, 2003; *Murrell v. State*, 2007; *People v. Castillo*, 2009).

There is some disagreement among courts as to whether risk assessment testimony based on actuarial tools is subject to analysis under *Frye/ Daubert* (Farrell, 2006). Generally, when the *Frye/Daubert* approach is applied, judges rule that actuarial assessment is sufficiently reliable for use in court (*Commitment of R.S.*, 2002).

## EXPERT TESTIMONY FOCUSED ON CHILD VICTIMS

This final section canvasses the most common uses of psychological expert testimony focused on the child victim of sexual abuse.

### Testimonial Competence: A Child's Competence to Testify

For a child to testify, the judge must be persuaded that the child possesses the ability to remember salient events, is able to communicate, understands the difference between truth and lies, and apprehends the duty to tell the truth (Myers, 2005). Children as young as 4 possess the necessary moral and cognitive capacities to meet these requirements (Lyon, 2000; Lyon & Saywitz, 1999).

Expert testimony is seldom necessary to help the judge evaluate a child's testimonial competence. In rare cases, when there are significant questions about a child's competence, the judge seeks guidance from a mental health professional, perhaps the child's therapist. In other cases, a psychologist is appointed by the judge to evaluate the child's capacity to testify. To repeat, however, expert testimony is rarely needed to assess children's testimonial competence.

## ACCOMMODATING CHILD WITNESSES

The judge has authority to make testifying less stressful for young witnesses. In civil cases in family and juvenile court, the judge's authority to accommodate child witnesses is broad indeed. In criminal cases, by contrast, the defendant has constitutional rights that limit but do not eliminate the judge's authority to accommodate young witnesses. Thus, the judge presiding over a criminal trial may allow a child to take a comfort item to the witness stand. The judge may permit a trusted adult to be present in court and to sit near the child if necessary. The judge may give the child frequent breaks during testimony. The judge can prohibit lawyers from asking questions the child does not understand. Now and then expert testimony is presented to help the judge decide on accommodations for children.

The defendant in a criminal case has a constitutional right to face-to-face confrontation with the prosecution's witnesses, including the child. Although the right to confrontation is important, it is not without limit. In *Maryland v. Craig* (1990), the U.S. Supreme Court ruled that a defendant's right to confront a child witness may be curtailed on a showing that face-to-face confrontation could so seriously traumatize the youngster as to restrict the child from reasonably communicating. Such a showing is usually made with expert testimony from mental health professionals. If the judge is convinced, the child may testify outside the physical presence of the defendant, typically via closed-circuit television (Hall & Sales, 2008) (see Goodman, Chapter 8, this volume, for review).

## Expert Testimony in Juvenile Court to Prove Psychological Damage

In juvenile court proceedings to protect a child, mental health testimony may be offered to prove that the child suffered psychological harm as a result of abuse or neglect. As noted by Melton, Petrila, Poythress, and Slobogin, "Perhaps least controversial, testimony by a mental health professional may be sought when the child protection statute requires proof of harm as an element of abuse or neglect" (2007, p. 515).

## Expert Testimony to Rehabilitate a Child's Credibility

In criminal cases, the defense attorney sometimes attacks the child's credibility by pointing out that the child delayed reporting, was inconsistent, or recanted. Legally, this attack on a child's credibility is legitimate. Following such an assault, however, the question arises, Should the prosecutor be permitted to offer expert testimony to help the jury understand that many children who are sexually abused delay reporting, are inconsistent, or recant? As explained earlier, judges generally answer in the affirmative. By attacking the child's credibility, the defense opens the door to expert testimony designed to rehabilitate the child in the eyes of the jury. Such rehabilitative expert testimony is not controversial and is not subject to analysis under *Frye* or *Daubert*.

## Expert Testimony Attacking the Interviewer

Increasingly in child sexual abuse prosecutions, defense attorneys attack the way forensic interviews of the child were conducted (Myers, 2005). It is in this arena that expert testimony on suggestibility, memory, and proper interviewing take center stage. Judges are generally receptive to such testimony. Thus, judges typically allow expert testimony describing general principles of proper and improper interviewing. As well, judges usually allow an expert to apply these principles to the interviews in the case on trial and to critique the interview's strengths and weaknesses. Most judges, however, do not permit the expert to go the final step and offer an opinion that defective interviewing rendered the child unreliable (*State v. Wigg*, 2005). Judges feel that the latter testimony treads too closely to a forbidden opinion on the child's credibility, which is ultimately up to the jury to decide.

## Expert Psychological Testimony That a Child Was Sexually Abused

The most controversial form of expert mental health testimony in child sexual abuse litigation is testimony offered to prove that the child was abused. Such testimony takes several forms. The expert might state, "In my opinion, to a reasonable degree of certainty, the child was sexually abused." Alternatively, the expert might say, "The child's symptoms and behaviors are consistent with sexual abuse." Finally, the expert might opine, "The child demonstrates developmentally unusual sexual knowledge." Whatever form the testimony takes, the purpose is the same: to prove sexual abuse.

There is controversy in the psychological literature over expert mental health testimony offered to prove sexual abuse. Gary Melton is perhaps the most outspoken critic of such testimony. Melton argues that mental health professionals have no special skill at differentiating abused from nonabused children. Melton and his colleagues (2007) wrote:

> There is no reason to believe that clinicians' skill in determining whether a child has been abused is the product of specialized knowledge. Because testimony as an expert involves an implicit representation that the opinions presented are grounded in specialized knowledge, a mental health professional should decline on ethical grounds to offer an opinion about whether a child told the truth or has been abused. By the same token, under the rules of evidence, such an opinion should never be admitted. (p. 516)

Melton not only believes that mental health professionals lack the knowledge required to differentiate abused from nonabused children, but he argues too that mental health testimony that a child was sexually abused is little more than an opinion that the child was telling the truth. Melton reasons that a professional's decision about sexual abuse rests largely on the child's description of abuse and the professional's assessment of the child's credibility. Thus, expert testimony that a child was abused is little more than a thinly disguised statement that the child was telling the truth. Courts agree that expert witnesses are not permitted to testify that someone, including a child, was telling the truth. Melton and Limber (1989) conclude, therefore, that "under no circumstances should a court admit the opinion of an expert about whether a particular child has been abused" (p. 1230).

Herman (2005) agrees with Melton that mental health professionals are not adept at distinguishing abused from nonabused children. Herman writes, "There is a widespread (but not universal) consensus among experts in the field that decisions by clinicians to either substantiate or not substantiate uncorroborated sexual abuse allegations currently lack a firm scientific foundation and that such opinions may be based on little more than a clinician's subjective opinion or hunch that abuse did or did not occur" (p. 90). (See also Herman, 2009). Faust, Bridges, and Ahern (2009) add that psychological evaluations for child sexual abuse "rest mainly on unverified methods or conjecture that almost certainly at times increase, rather than decrease error" (p. 4).

Melton, Herman, and Faust, Bridges, and Ahern make a strong case against mental health testimony offered to prove child sexual abuse. Yet they do not speak for all professionals with expertise on child sexual abuse. Sgroi, Porter, and Blick (1983) wrote, "Most cases can be validated by investigative interviewing and by assessing the credibility and the history of sexual abuse elicited from the child" (p. 72). Faller (2002) observed that "the majority opinion is that interviewers can form conclusions about the likelihood of sexual abuse" (p. 254). The legal system, not to mention clinical assessment, would benefit from research on whether mental health professionals can validly and reliably determine whether children have been sexually abused.

Turning from the psychological literature to the courts, it should be noted at the outset that judges presiding over civil matters (juvenile court protective and family court proceedings) are often more receptive to psychological expertise than judges trying criminal cases, especially criminal cases in which there is a jury. Judges worry that jurors may be "too impressed" with expert testimony and that jurors are poorly equipped to critique the reliability of expert opinion. As the Tennessee Supreme Court put it, "Expert scientific testimony solicits the danger of undue prejudice or confusing the issues or misleading the jury because of its aura of special reliability and trustworthiness" (*State v. Ballard*, 1993, p. 561). In juvenile, protective, and family court trials, there typically is no jury, and the judge has the experience needed to give expert testimony its due. Not surprisingly then, most of the court decisions discussing mental health expert testimony offered to prove sexual abuse are criminal appeals.

A substantial number of appellate courts, in line with Melton and Herman, reject most or all mental health expert testimony that a particular child was sexually abused (e.g., *State v. Churchill*, 2003). The Massachusetts Supreme Court ruled, for example, that "the expert may not directly opine on whether the alleged victim was in fact subject to sexual abuse" (*Commonwealth v. Federico*, 1997, p. 1039). By contrast, a small number of appellate court decisions approve expert mental health testimony that a child was sexually abused (e.g., *State v. Hester*, 1988).

Some appellate courts, again in line with Melton, hold that expert testimony that a child was sexually abused comes too close to an opinion that the child was telling the truth. In *State v. Haseltine* (1984), for example, the 16-year-old victim testified and described repeated sexual intercourse with her father. A psychiatrist testified for the prosecutor that the child was an incest victim. The Wisconsin Court of Appeals ruled that such testimony amounted to an impermissible opinion that the child was telling the truth. Similarly, the North Carolina Supreme Court ruled in *State v. Stancil* (2002), "In a sexual offense prosecution involving a child victim, the trial court should not admit expert opinion that sexual abuse has in fact occurred because, absent physical evidence supporting a diagnosis of sexual abuse, such testimony is an impermissible opinion regarding the victim's credibility" (p. 789).

Appellate court decisions in most states allow expert testimony that a child demonstrates symptoms and behavior consistent with sexual abuse (e.g., *State v. Kallin*, 1994). Unfortunately, few of these decisions demonstrate an awareness of the impact of base rates on determining whether psychological symptoms or behaviors have a tendency to prove sexual abuse. With symptoms and behaviors that are seen in nonabused as well as abused children (e.g., regression, sleep disturbance, hypervigilance), the probative value of a particular symptom or behavior is dependent on the base rate of the symptom or behavior in nonabused as well as abused children. (For discussion of base rates, see Bridges, Faust, & Ahern, 2009; Faust, Bridges, & Ahern, 2009; Koehler, 2003; Melton et al., 2007; Myers, 2005; Wood & Wright, 1995.)

An occasional appellate decision comes to grips with base rates. In *State v. Cressey* (1993), for example, the New Hampshire Supreme Court evaluated expert testimony that children exhibited symptoms consistent with sexual abuse. The court wrote:

Our first concern is that the evaluations of the children deal almost exclusively in vague psychological profiles and symptoms, and unquantifiable evaluation results. ... Many of the symptoms considered to be indicators of sexual abuse, such as nightmares, forgetfulness, and overeating, could just as easily be the result of some other problem, or simply may be appearing in the natural course of the children's development. ... Many of the factors considered by Dr. B_____, while they may accurately indicate that the children's mental health may be suffering to some degree, do not necessitate a finding that the children have been sexually abused. (pp. 700–701)

The Tennessee Supreme Court was equally perceptive in *State v. Ballard* (1993), in which the court wrote:

We are also troubled by the accuracy and reliability of expert testimony involving the emotional and psychological characteristics of sexually abused children. ... A dysfunctional behavioral profile may be brought on by any number of stressful experiences, albeit, including sexual abuse. However, the list of symptoms described by Dr. L_____ is too generic. The same symptoms may be exhibited by many children who are merely distressed by the turbulence of growing up. (p. 562)

The insights of the New Hampshire and Tennessee courts are the exception. Few court decisions allude to base rates, and it is likely that in the hurly-burly of child abuse trials, the importance of base rates often goes unnoticed. If this concern is well founded, it raises questions about the validity of expert testimony that a child's symptoms and behavior are consistent with sexual abuse. Unfortunately, there is no way of knowing how often base rates are noticed and addressed in court because there is no research on point.

## CONCLUSION

Sexual abuse is often difficult to prove. In *Pennsylvania v. Ritchie* (1987), the U.S. Supreme Court wrote, "Child abuse is one of the most difficult crimes to detect and prosecute, in large part because there often are no witnesses except the victim" (p. 60). In the same vein, the New York Court of Appeals wrote, "Abuse is difficult to detect because the acts are predominantly nonviolent and usually occur in secret rendering the child the only witness" (*In re Nicole V.,* 1987, p. 915). The California Supreme Court added: "There are particular difficulties with proving child sexual abuse: the frequent lack of physical evidence, the limited verbal and cognitive abilities of child victims, the fact that children are often unable or unwilling to act as witnesses because of the intimidation of the courtroom setting and the reluctance to testify against their parents" (*In re Cindy L.,* 1997, p. 28).

Unlike physical abuse, where injuries often provide powerful evidence, medical evidence is lacking in most sexual abuse cases (Dubowitz, 2007). Typically, the child's testimony is the most important evidence. When children are prepared for the courtroom, most testify effectively. Yet testifying is not easy, and some children are too young, too traumatized, or too frightened to testify effectively or at all.

With sexual abuse so difficult to prove, expert testimony from mental health professionals plays an important role in court. Mental health professionals assist the legal system on the broad array of issues described in this chapter, each of which is vital to the search for truth.

## REFERENCES

Association for the Treatment of Sexual Abusers. (2005). Practice Standards and Guidelines for Members of the Association for the Treatment of Sexual Abusers. Beaverton, OR: ASTA.

Becker, J. V., & Murphy, W. D. (1998). What we know and do not know about assessing and treating sex offenders. *Psychology, Public Policy and Law, 4,* 116–137.

Bridges, A. J., Faust, D., & Ahern, D. C. (2009). Methods for the identification of sexually abused children: Reframing the clinician's task and recognizing disparity with research on indicators. In K. Kuehnle and M. Connell (Eds.), *The evaluation of child sexual abuse allegations* (pp. 21–48). New York: Wiley.

Caldwell, M. F. (2007). Sexual offense adjudication and sexual recidivism among juvenile offenders. *Sexual Abuse, 19,* 107–113.

Chadwick, D. L. (1990). Preparation for court testimony in child abuse cases. *Pediatric Clinics of North America, 37,* 955–970.

Commitment of J.M.B., 964 A.2d 752 (N.J. 2009).

Commitment of R.S., 801 A.2d 219 (N.J. 2002).

Commonwealth v. Federico, 683 N.E.2d 1035 (Mass. 1997).

Darren M., 856 N.E.2d 624 (Ill. Ct. App. 2006).

Daubert v. Merrell Dow Pharmaceuticals, Inc., 509 U.S. 579 (1993).

Detention of Thorell, 72 P.3d 708 (Wash. 2003).

Dubowitz, H. (2007). Healing hymenal injuries: Implications for child health care professionals. *Pediatrics, 119,* 997–999.

Faller, K. C. (2002). *Understanding and assessing child sexual maltreatment* (2nd ed.). Thousand Oaks, CA: Sage.

Farrell, T. B. (2006). Admissibility of actuarial risk assessment testimony in proceedings to commit sex offenders. *American Law Reports, 20,* 607.

Faust, D., Bridges, A. J., & Ahern, D. C. (2009). Methods for the identification of sexually abused children: Issues and needed features for abuse indicators: In K. Kuehnle and M. Connell (Eds.), *The evaluation of child sexual abuse allegations* (pp. 3–19). New York: Wiley.

Frye v. United States, 293 F. 1013 (D.C. 1923).

Hall, S. R., & Sales, B. D. (2008). Courtroom modifications for child witnesses: Law and science in forensic evaluations. Washington, DC: American Psychological Association.

Herman, S. (2005). Improving decision making in forensic child sexual abuse evaluations. *Law and Human Behavior, 29,* 87–120.

Herman, S. (2009) Forensic child sexual abuse evaluations: Accuracy, ethics, and admissibility. In K. Kuehnle and M. Connell (Eds.), *The evaluation of child sexual abuse allegations* (pp. 247–266). New York: Wiley.

In re Cindy L., 17 Cal. 4th 15 (1997).

In re Nicole V., 518 N.E.2d 914 (NY 1987).

Koehler, J. J. (2003). The normative status of base rates at trial. In J. Castellan, Jr. (Ed.), *Individual and group decision making: Current issues* (pp. 137–149). Hillsdale, NJ: Erlbaum.

Kuhmo Tire Company, Ltd. v. Carmichael, 526 U.S. 137 (1999).

Lyon, T. D. (2000). Child witnesses and the oath: Empirical evidence. *University of Southern California Law Review, 73,* 1017–1074.

Lyon, T. D., & Saywitz, K. J. (1999). Young children's competence to take the oath. *Applied Developmental Science, 3,* 16–27.

Maryland v. Craig, 497 U.S. 836 (1990).

Melton, G. B., Petrila, J., Poythress, N. G., & Slobogin, C. (2007). *Psychological evaluations for the courts: A handbook for mental health professionals and lawyers.* (3rd ed.). New York: Guilford Press.

Melton, G. B., & Limber, S. (1989). Psychologists' involvement in cases of child maltreatment. *American Psychologist, 44,* 1225–1233.

Murrell v. State, 2007 WL 465932 (Mo. 2007).

Myers, J. E. B. (2006). *Child protection in America: Past, present, and future.* New York: Oxford University Press.

Myers, J. E. B. (2005). *Myers on evidence in child, domestic, and elder abuse cases.* New York: Aspen Law and Business.

Pennsylvania v. Ritchie, 480 U.S. 39 (1987).

People v. Castillo, 170 Cal. App. 4th 1156 (2009).

People v. Dobek, 732 N.W.2d 546 (Mich. Ct. App. 2007).

People v. Gardeley, 14 Cal. 4th 605 (1996).

People v. Stoll, 783 P.2d 698 (Cal. 1989).

Sgroi, S. M., Porter, F. S., & Blick, L. C. (1983). Validation of child sexual abuse. In S. M. Sgroi (Ed.), *Handbook of clinical intervention in child sexual abuse* (pp. 39–79). Lexington, MA: Lexington Books.

State v. Ballard, 855 S.W.2d 557 (Tenn. 1993).

State v. Churchill, 98 S.W. 3d 536 (Mo. 2003).

State v. Haseltine, 352 N.W.2d 673 (Wis. Ct. App. 1984).

State v. Hester, 760 P.2d 27 (Idaho 1988).

State v. Hughes, 841 So.2d 718 (La. 2003).
State v. Kallin, 877 P.2d 138 (Utah 1994).
State v. Miller, 709 P.2d 350 (Utah 1985).
State v. Stancil, 559 S.E.2d 788 (N.C. 2002).
State v. Walters, 675 N.W.2d 778 (Wis. 2004).
State v. Wigg, 889 A.2d 233 (Vt 2005).
Wood, J. M., & Wright, L. (1995). Evaluation of children's sexual behaviors and incorporation of base rates judgments in sexual abuse. *Child Abuse and Neglect, 19,* 1263–1273.

# Chapter 10

# Jurors' Perceptions of Children's Eyewitness Testimony

JONATHAN M. GOLDING
EMILY E. DUNLAP
EMILY C. HODELL

It has been more than two decades since Goodman, Golding, and Haith (1984) published their classic article investigating jurors' perceptions of children's eyewitness testimony. Since then, there has been a great deal of research on this topic. Much of the research on children as eyewitnesses has expanded from Goodman et al.'s (1984) original focus on children as bystander witnesses to victims/witnesses in cases of sexual assault. This shift in research focus was motivated by the fact that when children are called to testify they are often doing so as victims of sexual assault (Goodman, Quas, Bulkley, & Shapiro, 1999). In fact, child sexual abuse accounts for the majority of sexual abuse cases handled by the judicial system (Bottoms, Golding, Stevenson, Wiley, & Yozwiak, 2007), even though it only makes up about 10% of the approximately 1 million child maltreatment cases substantiated every year (Jones & Finkelhor, 2001; U.S. Department of Health and Human Services, Administration on Children, Youth and Families, 2005). Because child sexual abuse cases often lack physical evidence and corroborating witnesses, understanding jurors' perceptions is critical because of the increased reliance on the child victim's testimony (Myers, 1998). This chapter reviews the literature on the perception of children as witnesses in court and examines some of the critical factors that impact these perceptions.

## METHODOLOGICAL ISSUES

The mock juror paradigm has been the most popular method used by empirical scientists to investigate perceptions of children in court (see Bornstein, 1999). This simulation methodology presents summarized child sexual abuse court cases (using plausible details often based on facts from actual court cases) to participants who play the role of mock jurors. The cases are generally designed to present an equal amount of evidence for the prosecution and defense as a way to determine the effect of a manipulated variable. Presentation of the cases typically occurs in a variety of ways, from short trial scenarios to more elaborate videotaped simulated trials. Mock jurors, usually jury-eligible undergraduates receiving course credit or community members paid for their time, are asked to render a verdict and give other judgments (e.g., perceived credibility of the defendant, alleged victim, and other witnesses). Typically, researchers measure individual judgments; however, in some studies mock jurors deliberate before rendering verdicts (i.e., a mock jury study).

Despite its popularity, the simulation methodology has been criticized. A full examination of all criticisms is beyond the scope of the present chapter (see Kerr & Bray, 2005; Weiten & Diamond, 1979, for reviews), but the major point of contention is that simulations are viewed as too unrealistic compared with actual trials. Several points are typically raised to support this position. First, critics point out that a trial simulation does not have a real-world consequence—no one will be sent to prison based on the results of an experiment (see Bornstein & McCabe, 2005, for a review)—therefore, participants in a role-playing simulation may not process information in the same manner as an actual juror. Second, the materials in simulations are viewed as too brief compared with real trials (Read, Connolly, & Welsh, 2006) and sometimes do not include important aspects of a trial (e.g., jury instructions, cross-examination of witnesses). Written trial summaries have the added disadvantage of not being able to capture important visual aspects of a trial such as the demeanor of trial participants (Weiten & Diamond, 1979). Third, the use of undergraduates as mock jurors has been criticized because these individuals are not representative of actual jurors and rarely serve as jurors in actual trials (Bornstein, 1999; Diamond, 1997). Fourth, critics argue that, unlike actual jury trials, most simulation studies involve individual judgments; there are no deliberations and no group decisions (e.g., Weiten & Diamond, 1979). This is considered problematic because group discussion may correct misunderstandings for any particular juror and may lead to a better grasp of the information presented at trial than does individual-level processing (Diamond, 1997).

These methodological criticisms have concerned journal reviewers and grant advisory panels as they (and others) have come to question whether simulation results generalize to actual cases (see Kerr & Bray, 2005). In fact, Read et al. (2006) used an archival data methodology to investigate the correspondence between outcomes of mock juror research and actual trials. Archival data have the benefit of high ecological validity because they use information from actual court cases, such as verdict and specific elements of each trial (e.g., repressed memory testimony, involvement in therapy, length of delay, age of complainant, presence of expert, and frequency of abuse). Their examination of criminal trials in Canada between 1980 and 2002 involving delayed allegations of child sexual abuse found that only two (age of complainant and presence of an expert) of six variables that had been related to decisions in mock juror research predicted verdicts in actual trials. They stated that "whether this outcome is seen as providing support for continued use of the mock juror paradigm is, of course, a matter of opinion. At a minimum, the results do question the presumed link between archival and mock juror studies and may motivate similar comparisons to be drawn between mock jury research and actual trials on a variety of other psycholegal topics" (p. 280).

Although the aforementioned criticisms are important to consider, many argue that it is still valuable to conduct simulation research (Bray & Kerr, 1979; Diamond, 1997; Kerr & Bray, 2005; Lieberman & Sales, 2000; Weiten & Diamond, 1979). Nonetheless, it must be clear that a jury simulation study is just that, a "simulation," and does not mirror exactly what occurs in an actual courtroom (Bornstein & McCabe, 2005). Thus, with regard to the initial criticism concerning real-world consequences, participants appear to take their role as a mock juror quite seriously (see Kerr & Bray, 2005). This is especially evident when examining deliberation data in studies investigating children in court (e.g., Golding, Bradshaw, Dunlap, & Hodell, 2007; Goodman et al., 1984). In addition, Bornstein and McCabe (2005) reviewed five studies that directly tested the issue of whether a decision had an actual consequence or not and found no clear support for the impact of consequentiality.

With regard to the criticism of using an unrealistic context (materials and participants), the materials used in simulation research offer the appropriate control necessary for manipulating variables while keeping all other factors constant. It is this control that allows researchers to better understand the impact of the variables in question (i.e., establish causal relationships) and examine specific psychological theories (see Golding, Warren, & Ross, 1997; Lieberman & Sales, 2000). The ability to control variables is extremely difficult in actual jury cases because each case is unique. As for using different types of materials in simulation research, Bornstein (1999) found that in only three of 11 studies from *Law and Human Behavior* in a 20-year period (1977–1997) did varying the medium of presentation result in different outcomes, and these differences were equivocal. Bornstein

(1999) also investigated the use of undergraduate students as participants. In the same 20-year period, he examined 26 studies from *Law and Human Behavior* that involved a variety of crimes and found that only five instances in which a direct comparison of a student sample differed from a nonstudent sample. In addition, Bornstein (1999) described other studies involving an experimental replication of a result using a different sample and found that these studies led to very few sample differences.

Although the use of individual judgments has been criticized, there are several reasons why such judgments may prove useful. First, the collection of a large amount of data from many participants can serve to maximize generalizability (Bottoms et al., 2007). Second, there is some research suggesting that jury verdicts are often representative of individual jurors' verdicts before deliberation (Kalven & Zeisel, 1966; MacCoun & Kerr, 1988; but see Sandys & Dillehay, 1995). Third, the collection of individual data followed by research involving group judgments may be a preferred research strategy, especially when investigating new areas of study (e.g., Golding, Sego, Sanchez, & Hasemann, 1995). It should be noted, however, that the transition to group studies might not be moving as quickly as some would like (Bornstein, 1999). One must keep in mind that mock jury studies are substantially more time consuming and expensive to conduct than studies involving individual mock jurors (Bray & Kerr, 1979; Golding, Bradshaw, Dunlap, & Hodell, 2007; Weiten & Diamond, 1979). A mock jury study requires (1) having a certain number of individuals participate at the same time; (2) time-consuming scoring and analyses of deliberation data; and (3) many more participants (i.e., the verdict rendered by a six-member mock jury results in a single data point, whereas the verdicts rendered by six individual mock jurors lead to six data points).

Finally, although there is support for the use of archival data (e.g., Diamond, 1997; Kerr & Bray, 2005), it is important to note the limitations. First, researchers are restricted to investigating variables that the courts recorded. For example, Read et al. (2006) did not have information on the gender composition of juries, a factor that has been shown to impact mock jurors' perceptions of child witnesses (Bottoms et al., 2007). Second, archival data typically only include the dependent variable of verdict. However, understanding how children are perceived in court at a theoretical level requires measuring other variables (e.g., witness credibility). Third, actual trials have a bias toward conviction (see Read et al., 2006). Therefore, archival studies may not be able to provide an adequate model of how certain variables predict verdicts in cases involving children. Fourth, the data available through archival analyses may not be complete. Read et al. (2006) noted that data may be missing and not all cases dealing with a particular issue may be in the database. Finally, actual court cases will always have the problem of confounded variables (i.e., lack of control; Bornstein & McCabe, 2005).

The preceding discussion makes clear that no one method is best when investigating the perception of children in court, and it is best to use methodological diversity (Kerr & Bray, 2005). This strategy acknowledges that no study is free from compromises; simulation studies gain control at the cost of realism, and field studies gain realism at the cost of control (Bray & Kerr, 1979). To this end, the present chapter uses data from studies utilizing all types of methodologies to focus on 11 factors that may impact perceptions of child witnesses: (1) juror gender, (2) victim and defendant gender, (3) defendant criminal history, (4) victim and defendant race, (5) victim age, (6) victim intelligence, (7) victim demeanor, (8) delayed reporting, (9) type of abuse, (10) courtroom accommodations, and (11) experts. (For more in-depth coverage of these factors, see Bottoms et al., 2007.)

## JUROR GENDER

The impact of juror gender on perceptions of children in court is one of the most consistent effects found in the mock juror literature. Many studies indicate that women are more likely than men to show a pro-victim/pro-prosecution bias in their judgments, especially in child sexual abuse cases. These pro-victim judgments often include a higher number of guilty verdicts and greater believability in the child (Quas, Bottoms, Haegerich, & Nysse-Carris, 2002; Redlich, Myers, Goodman, & Qin, 2002; Ross et al., 1994; see Bottoms et al., 2007, and Schutte & Hosch, 1997, for reviews). In addition, these gender differences have been found in unique types of child witness cases such as those involving parricide (Haegerich & Bottoms, 2000), satanic ritual abuse (Bottoms, Diviak, & Davis, 1997), and recovered memories (Golding et al., 1995).

Although this juror gender effect has typically been shown in the context of individual judgments, some research has investigated juror gender in the context of group deliberation. For example, Golding, Bradshaw, Dunlap, and Hodell (2007) manipulated the number of men and women on a mock jury so that there was a woman majority or a nonwoman majority (i.e., juries with more men than women and juries with an equal number of men and women). Mock jurors heard a fictional child sexual abuse case with a 6-year-old victim. Before deliberations, women were more pro-prosecution in their verdict choices and victim believability ratings than men. During deliberations, women generated about equal numbers of pro-prosecution and pro-defense statements, whereas men made more pro-defense statements than pro-prosecution statements. Also, when votes were taken during deliberations, woman-majority jurors who initially voted not guilty changed their final vote to guilty more often than did mock jurors on non-woman-majority juries and vice versa. Finally, woman-majority mock juries convicted most often. These findings show that predeliberation gender differences led to unique jury deliberation strategies and voting patterns.

The large differences between men and women mock jurors in perceiving child witnesses have been interpreted in several ways. First, because women are more often targets of victimization, they may be more likely to sympathize with the alleged victim more than men (Bottoms, 1993). Second, because women are typically more nurturing than men (Feingold, 1994), they may be more inclined to protect defenseless people, such as children. Third, Bottoms (1993) suggested that the gender difference might be the result of traits such as empathy for children and attitudes relevant to child victims (e.g., attitudes toward child sexual abuse, children's general believability). Finally, the internalization of societal gender roles, which demand women to be more caring, empathic, and child oriented than men, may partially mediate the gender effect (e.g., Gilligan, 1982).

## VICTIM AND DEFENDANT GENDER

Mock jurors are aware of the differing frequency with which men and women abuse boys versus girls (Golding, Bradshaw, & Hodell, 2007). When asked to rate the likelihood of occurrence of the sexual abuse of a child (with all genders crossed), participants identified the man perpetrator/girl victim condition as the most frequent, followed by the man perpetrator/boy victim, woman perpetrator/boy victim, and finally the woman perpetrator/girl victim conditions. Thus, mock jurors correctly identified men as the primary perpetrators and girls as the most frequent victims of child sexual assault (Donnelly & Kenyon, 1996; Finkelhor, Hotaling, Lewis, & Smith, 1990). Despite the knowledge that these cases occur with varying frequency, the effects of victim gender on mock juror judgments are equivocal. Some research has found little to no effect of victim gender (e.g., Bottoms & Goodman, 1994; Golding, Bradshaw, & Hodell, 2007), whereas other studies indicate a possible bias, with mock jurors finding allegations of abuse made by girls more believable than allegations by boys (Haegerich & Bottoms, 2000). However, the alleged perpetrator in Haegerich and Bottoms' (2000) case was the father of the child, which regardless of the gender of the child, possibly introduced biases against homosexual child sexual abuse (Bornstein, Kaplan, & Perry, 2007; Quas et al., 2002; Wiley & Bottoms, 2009). As for defendant gender, some research indicates that mock jurors perceive men as more likely to perpetrate sexual abuse on children: A mock juror study of a child sexual abuse trial revealed higher conviction rates when the defendant was a man versus a woman (McCoy & Gray, 2007). Quas et al. (2002) similarly discovered a general leniency toward women defendants versus men defendants in a child sexual abuse case.

## DEFENDANT CRIMINAL HISTORY

Information about the defendant's criminal history can be an effective component of determining the overall dangerousness of the defendant. Typically, information about the defendant's criminal history is used by prosecutors to determine whether and what kinds of plea negotiations are available and to determine appropriate punishment. However, under certain circumstances, this information may be presented to jurors during trial to establish evidence of the defendant's enduring sexual preference. Although it is possible that the presentation of the defendant's criminal history may prejudice jurors against the defendant, in some circumstances this type of evidence is admissible when it is relevant to the present case (Federal Rules of Evidence 404b). Presentation of the defendant's criminal history can be highly effective in swaying jurors toward conviction in child sexual abuse cases (see Devine, Clayton, Dunford, Seying, & Pryce, 2001, for a review). In particular, if the defendant's past crimes are similar to the current crime in question, criminal history can be used to establish a precedent of behavior that is predictive of future criminal act and to discredit the defendant's testimony. Prosecutors find this evidence particularly useful in child sexual abuse cases because other demonstrative evidence may be lacking as a result of the secrecy of sexual abuse (Myers, 1998). Bottoms and Goodman (1994) found that mock jurors who received the defendant's criminal history and other negative character evidence gave higher ratings of victim credibility and defendant guilt than mock jurors who were not presented with the negative information.

## VICTIM AND DEFENDANT RACE

Given the widely documented examples of racial stereotypes affecting various legal contexts (e.g., Devine, 1989; Weinberg & Williams, 1988; Wilson, 1996), it is interesting that the issue of race has rarely been examined with regard to the perception of child witnesses in court. What makes this a significant omission is that children of all races and ethnicities may be victims of abuse and are all likely to testify. For example, research has shown that African American children and Hispanic children are sexually abused as often as Caucasian children (Epstein & Bottoms, 1998; Finkelhor & Baron, 1986).

Stereotypes regarding race may play a role in juror perceptions. For example, Bottoms, Davis, and Epstein (2004) found that African American and Hispanic girl victims were judged as more responsible than Caucasian girl victims for their sexual abuse by a Caucasian teacher; however, there were no race effects for guilt or credibility judgments. Additionally, in a second experiment reported in that study, mock jurors assigned more guilt to defendants in cases involving victims and defendants of the same race relative to cases involving different races (Bottoms et al., 2004). Bottoms et al. attributed this finding to laypeople's general belief that different-race child sexual abuse is less common and thus less plausible than same-race abuse. Stereotypes such as this about same- versus different-race abuse may, unfortunately, lead to differential belief in the occurrence of the abuse by jurors.

## VICTIM AGE

Generally, adults perceive children as less accurate in memory reports than adults (Goodman et al., 1984; Goodman, Golding, Helgeson, Haith, & Michelli, 1987; Newcombe & Bransgrove, 2007), even when their actual accuracy is controlled for (Leippe, Manion, & Romanczyk, 1992). Although young children are generally perceived as honest, their cognitive ability to remember and report details of an event is often questioned (Bottoms & Goodman, 1994).

Research exploring perceptions of child sexual abuse victims has found that young children are often perceived as more credible than older children (i.e., > 12 years) or adults (Myers, Redlich, Goodman, Prizmich, & Imwinkelried, 1999; Nightingale, 1993). For example, Nightingale (1993) showed an inverse relationship between age and credibility: As a child sexual abuse victim's age increased, perceived credibility decreased. In child sexual abuse cases, very young children are thought to be perceived as more believable because of sexual naïveté; that is, children at very young ages likely have little to no sexual knowledge and, therefore, are perceived as credible witnesses in child sexual abuse cases (Bottoms & Goodman, 1994; Castelli, Goodman, & Ghetti, 2005). As the age of the child increases, sexual naïveté decreases, increasing the plausibility that the child fabricated the abuse (Bottoms & Goodman, 1994).

## VICTIM INTELLIGENCE

Recent research has examined a subset of children who have received little attention from the criminal justice system: children with intellectual disabilities (Bottoms, Nysse-Carris, Harris, & Tyda, 2003). Unfortunately, these children are especially likely to be sexually abused (Westcott & Jones, 1999). Bottoms et al. (2003) first examined perceptions of intellectually disabled children in court. It was predicted that these children would be perceived as even more credible than children of average intelligence because, like younger children, they would be deemed trustworthy and honest and lacking in the level of cognitive competence necessary for fabricating false charges. Undergraduate participants read a case summary and were then presented with videotaped excerpts from an actual trial in which a 16-year-old sexual assault victim was portrayed as "mildly mentally retarded" or "having average intelligence." Conviction rates were higher when the victim was described as "mildly mentally retarded" versus described as having average intelligence.

Another study by Yozwiak (2003) used a different sample (community members) and a different design than Bottoms et al. (2003) in which victim age (6 or 15 years) and diagnosis (mild mental retardation, severe mental retardation, or no diagnosis of mental retardation) were varied. Like Bottoms et al. (2003), Yozwiak (2003) showed that participants tended to attribute less responsibility for the incident of sexual abuse to the children with diagnoses of mental retardation. However, Yozwiak (2003) found that diagnosis did not significantly affect conviction rates. Yozwiak (2003) noted that the absence of this effect might be due to the medium of presentation. Because participants only read a trial scenario in which the description of the child's testimony did not vary as a function of diagnosis, the impact of the diagnosis variable might have been masked. It is also possible that the Bottoms et al. (2003) and Yozwiak (2003) studies are examples of when the use of different samples (undergraduates vs. community members) leads to differences in the impact of the variable of interest.

## VICTIM DEMEANOR

During trials, jurors assess not only the content of the child's testimony but also the demeanor or "outward behavior" of the child witness (Miller & Burgoon, 1982). This behavior can include facial expressions, voice intonation, and displays of emotion (e.g., crying). The importance of demeanor in court is noted in the "confrontation clause" in the Sixth Amendment of the U.S. Constitution that grants the accused a face-to-face confrontation with his or her accuser in court, allowing the accused and trier of fact to view the witness's demeanor. Moreover, it is generally accepted that the demeanor of a witness is critical to judging his or her credibility (Blumenthal, 1993).

Research has shown that trial judgments are significantly impacted by the demeanor of children who testify in court, especially in child sexual abuse trials. Goodman et al. (1992) reported that 65% of the children who testified in actual child sexual abuse cases experienced some type of distress, with many of these children becoming teary during their testimony. Myers et al. (1999) found that actual jurors' verdicts were correlated with the degree to which jurors perceived the child's facial expressions, gestures and movements, eye contact, nervousness, and manner of speaking to be important. Of these jurors, 16% indicated that crying was the most important emotion displayed by the child.

In laboratory studies, the investigation of demeanor in cases involving child witnesses has been rare; most research involving child witnesses does not describe the demeanor of the children or any witness. However, Kovera, Gresham, Borgida, Gray, and Regan (1997) showed undergraduates a trial video in which an 8-year-old girl accused her stepfather of sexual assault. The alleged victim appeared either prepared and calm or unprepared and emotional. In addition, there was either no expert testimony or an expert who described common symptoms displayed by victims of sexual abuse and specifically discussed the ways in which these symptoms matched those of a typical child sexual abuse victim. The results showed that if the child appeared emotional, expert testimony related to this demeanor led to higher conviction rates than if there was no expert. It appears that the expert's testimony sensitized jurors to how a victim of child sexual abuse may act.

Other studies have not included expert witnesses to explain the victim's demeanor but have focused on the behavior itself. In a study by Regan and Baker (1998, Experiment 2), participants read a written description of a trial in which the child was either calm or crying. Conviction rates were higher when the child was crying versus when the child was calm. In addition, the child in the crying condition was judged more honest, credible, accurate, and reliable. Golding, Fryman, Marsil, and Yozwiak (2003) extended these results by including levels of crying: calm, teary, or hysterically crying. Participants were more likely to convict the defendant when the child was teary than when either calm or hysterical.

## DELAYED REPORTING

In cases of abuse, it is possible that a victim will not immediately disclose the criminal activity (see Pipe, Lamb, Orbach, & Cederborg, 2007). This delay in disclosure may occur over a relatively short amount of time (e.g., several interviews) or across a number of years. Regardless, the impact of the delayed reporting can affect jurors' perceptions. The effect of a short-term delay was examined in a study by Yozwiak, Golding, and Marsil (2004). A case summary involving the alleged sexual assault of a 6-year-old girl was presented to community members. The independent variable was whether the child provided full and complete disclosure of the details of the incident during two interviews or whether she provided incomplete details during a first interview but included additional details of the event during a subsequent interview. Complete disclosure led to more guilty verdicts and greater believability than when the disclosure occurred only during the second interview. Although mock jurors were more likely to believe the child when the memory reporting was complete and consistent versus inconsistently reporting, children's actual memory reporting tends to be more similar to the latter (Fivush, 1993; Quas, Davis, Goodman, & Myers, 2007). When reporting an event of body touching, Quas et al. (2007) found that during repeated questioning following a relatively short delay (1–3 weeks), children who had experienced benign body touching were generally not forthcoming, answering questions inaccurately and inconsistently. In contrast, children who did not experience body touching and children who were told to lie about the touching reliably and accurately reported their memories. Unfortunately, Yozwiak et al.'s (2004) study reveals that mock jurors may be unlikely to believe a child who less reliably presents his or her memories, when research suggests children truthfully reporting memories do so in an inconsistent manner (see Fivush, 1993; Quas et al., 2007).

Long-term delays in reporting may involve an allegation of repressed memory (i.e., a memory of child sexual abuse forgotten for many years and later recalled as an adult). Loftus, Weingardt, and Hoffman (1993) first examined courtroom perceptions of this type of delayed reporting, and found that mock jurors were more skeptical of victims who claimed to have repressed their memories before recovering and reporting them compared with victims who claimed that they always remembered their abuse but kept it a secret. Golding et al. (1995; see also Golding, Sego, & Sanchez, 1999) extended this research by including a condition in which a child reported the abuse immediately. The results were somewhat counter to Loftus et al.'s (1993) in that there was no difference in believability of the alleged victims who claimed to have repressed versus kept secret the memory. Still, both of the delay conditions led to lower victim believability than the condition in which the child testified immediately (but see Bottoms et al., 1997). Despite these findings, Read et al.'s (2006) archival study, described earlier, found that only age of complainant and presence of an expert predicted verdicts in delayed disclosure cases.

## PHYSICAL ABUSE

Only a few studies have examined the perception of children in court in cases of child physical abuse. As stated earlier, this is likely due to children testifying less often in these cases (Bottoms et al., 2007). An early study by Dukes and Kean (1989) investigated perceptions of child psychological abuse, physical abuse, and neglect in court. In addition to the type of abuse, the researchers manipulated the degree to which the victim precipitated the abuse (e.g., the child threw a dish of ice cream during a birthday party, which triggered the parent's abusive response) and the age of the child (3 or 10 years). Among the results, it was found that physical abuse was perceived as equally serious for both very young and older victims, psychological abuse was perceived as more serious for the older victim, and neglect was perceived as more serious for the younger victim. Precipitation and type of abuse also interacted, with precipitation leading to the child being viewed as more at fault in a case of psychological or physical abuse. In another study conducted by Muller, Caldwell, and Hunter (1993), undergraduates read scenarios describing an interaction between a parent and an 8-year-old child that resulted in the parent harming the child (e.g., hitting the child with a plastic baseball bat). The results showed that men were more likely than women to blame the child (see also Golding, Hodell, & Dunlap, 2007) for the abuse and that the greatest blame was ascribed to high-provocative (verbally aggressive and insolent) children. Finally, Golding, Hodell, and Dunlap (2006) had participants read a fictional criminal trial summary of a parricide (i.e., killing of one's parents) case in which either child sexual or physical abuse was alleged by the defendant. Overall, the type of abuse did not impact the type of verdict; participants rendered relatively more manslaughter convictions than murder convictions or not guilty verdicts (see also Haegerich & Bottoms, 2000).

## COURTROOM ACCOMMODATIONS

Motivated by the need to protect children from the potentially stressful experience of in-court testimony (see Bottoms, Reppucci, Tweed, & Nysse-Carris, 2002), various evidentiary and procedural innovations have been introduced by the judicial system to help facilitate children's accurate testimony, especially in child sexual abuse cases. These procedural innovations seek to protect the welfare of children by allowing for additional supportive and protective accommodations, such as the presence of a supportive adult or a protective shield that forms a barrier between the child and the defendant in court (for more discussion, see Bussey, Chapter 11, and Goodman, Chapter 8, this volume).

Other innovations allow jurors to hear the child's story through alternative evidentiary forms, like the presentation of the child's testimony via closed-circuit television (CCTV) from another room in the courthouse. Although there is some indication that children are more resistant to suggestion and provide less incorrect information when testifying via CCTV (Doherty-Sneddon & McAuley, 2000), mock juror research involving this accommodation is equivocal (see McAuliff & Kovera, 2002). For example, in Goodman et al.'s (1998) elaborate mock trial involving 5- to 6-year-old and 8- to 9-year-old alleged child sexual abuse victims, children who testified via CCTV were viewed as less credible despite a higher rate of accuracy than those children who testified live in court. In contrast, Orcutt, Goodman, Tobey, Batterman-Faunce, and Thomas (2001) found that, following deliberations, mock jurors were no less likely to determine the truth when children testified via CCTV versus live.

Evaluations of jurors' perceptions of hearsay testimony (i.e., testimony in place of a child sexual abuse victim's in-court testimony) have also yielded mixed results. Although hearsay testimony is typically not allowed in the American court system because of Sixth Amendment Confrontation Clause issues, there are special exceptions available in cases of child sexual abuse (see Buck, 2006, but see *Crawford v. Washington*, 2005). Special exceptions are allowed because child sexual abuse victims are considered to be at high risk of being incapable of giving in-court testimony either because they may be too young to provide a sworn statement or because the act of testifying in court may cause additional trauma. In such cases, hearsay testimony allows jurors to hear the child's story from an adult in whom the child confided details of the abuse during a previous conversation or interview.

Myers et al. (1999) evaluated how actual jurors reacted to hearsay in child sexual abuse cases and found that in terms of overall credibility there were no significant differences between a child victim and an adult hearsay witness. However, jurors rated the hearsay witness as more confident, accurate, and consistent and less suggestible than the child witness. More controlled laboratory experiments have also concluded that mock jurors are impacted by hearsay testimony to a considerable degree. For example, like Myers et al. (1999), Golding, Sanchez, and Sego (1997) showed that hearsay testimony in a child sexual abuse case is believed as much as that of a child victim. In addition, Golding et al. (1997) found that hearsay testimony affected trial outcome variables in similar ways as child witness testimony (see also Ross, Lindsay, & Marsil, 1999).

## EXPERTS

A number of studies have examined the use of experts in cases involving child witnesses, especially in child sexual abuse cases (see Kovera & Borgida, 1996, for a review of sexual abuse trials). In general, research on experts has focused on testimony presented as part of the prosecution's case (i.e., in support of the child victim). For example, Gabora, Spanos, and Joab (1993) investigated the effect of expert testimony about general psychological issues relating to child sexual abuse, such as delayed reporting. When an expert testified about these issues, mock jurors were more supportive of the prosecution case (i.e., less accepting of misconceptions regarding child sexual abuse) and more likely to convict the defendant than mock jurors who heard no expert testimony. In a study by Kovera, Levy, Borgida, and Penrod (1994), an expert testified that she believed a child witness was credible based on (1) the content of therapy sessions with the child; (2) her opinion that the child's behaviors and emotions matched a "syndrome" of characteristics typical of child sexual abuse victims; or (3) the child's use of an anatomically detailed doll during an interview. Again, the presence of any expert's testimony led to increased conviction rates compared with no expert testimony.

Only a few studies have examined cases in which expert testimony has been presented by both the prosecution and the defense. In one of these studies, Stewart, Whiteside, and Golding (2000) examined expert testimony in a repressed-memory child sexual abuse case. In Experiment 1, there were two expert conditions involving repressed memories of child sexual abuse: (1) Experts for the prosecution and defense testified about general memory processes and repression and (2) experts for the prosecution and defense discussed the memory techniques (visualization and hypnosis) used by the plaintiff's psychotherapist. Neither expert condition led to more decisions for the prosecution compared with conditions in which there was no expert testimony: a child testifying immediately or an adult testifying (with or without a claim of repression) about alleged abuse that occurred years earlier. In Experiment 2, only the prosecution and defense experts describing memory techniques were included to examine why the impact of the experts was negligible in Experiment 1. The impact of each expert was examined after the direct- and cross-examination of each witness. Results showed that each expert had an impact on jurors during direct examination, but the influence of each expert was effectively countered during cross-examination.

Other research involving experts for both the prosecution and the defense, however, has shown greater impact of expert testimony. For example, Golding, Stewart, Yozwiak, Djadali, and Sanchez (2000) investigated the impact of presence or absence of DNA evidence on judgments involving a 6-year-old girl accusing her neighbor of rape. When DNA evidence was presented, both a prosecution expert and a defense expert testified concerning the nature of the DNA evidence and the accuracy of matching DNA samples. Despite a defense expert's refutation, the DNA evidence increased both jurors' positive perceptions of the child's credibility and the likelihood of conviction. Thus, the nature of the evidence discussed by an expert for one side can greatly affect the perceptions of mock jurors.

## CONCLUSION

This review highlights the impact of specific variables on the perception of children in court. The value of this understanding cannot be overstated, because, as noted by Bottoms et al. (2007, p. 534), "understanding how people perceive child victims and make decisions in child sexual abuse cases is important if courtrooms are to be places of fairness and justice." In this way, the research findings presently reviewed can better inform the police, prosecutors, and defense attorneys about the nature of the evidence that jurors take into consideration. However, it is always important to keep in mind that, although mock jury research reveals trends across many experimental participants, the judgments of a particular juror cannot be predicted.

It is important to continue investigating the factors discussed in the present review as well as other important variables (e.g., types of crimes in which children are witnesses, defendant age, the relationship between the victim and abuser) that have only been minimally examined or not investigated at all in the past. As stated earlier, this research should employ methodological diversity (Kerr & Bray, 2005), including both simulation studies as well as field-based research that is more ecologically valid and may allow for greater generalizability. Also, this research should attempt to include jury deliberation research as a way to increase understanding of the group processes that occur within a jury in cases with children as witnesses. Continued research investigating perceptions of children as eyewitnesses will also be important in public policy as policymakers seek to formulate legislation that balances the well-being of children in the courtroom with the rights of the accused.

## REFERENCES

Blumenthal, J. A. (1993). A wipe of the hands, a lick of the lips: The validity of demeanor evidence in assessing witness credibility. *Nebraska Law Review, 72*, 1157–1204.

Bornstein, B. H. (1999). The ecological validity of jury simulations: Is the jury still out? *Law and Human Behavior, 23*, 75–91.

Bornstein, B. H., Kaplan, D. L., & Perry, A. R. (2007). Child abuse in the eyes of the beholder: Lay perceptions of child sexual and physical abuse. *Child Abuse and Neglect, 31*, 375–391.

Bornstein, B. H., & McCabe, S. G. (2005). Jurors of the absurd? The role of consequentiality in jury simulation research. *Florida State University Law Review, 32,* 443–467.

Bottoms, B. L. (1993). Individual differences in perceptions of child sexual assault victims. In G. S. Goodman & B. L. Bottoms (Eds.), *Child victims, child witnesses: Understanding and improving testimony* (pp. 229–261). New York: Guilford Press.

Bottoms, B. L., Davis, S. L., & Epstein, M. A. (2004). Effects of victim and defendant race on jurors' decisions in child sexual abuse cases. *Journal of Applied Social Psychology, 34,* 1–33.

Bottoms, B. L., Diviak, K. R., & Davis, S. L. (1997). Jurors' reactions to ritual abuse allegations. *Child Abuse and Neglect, 21,* 845–859.

Bottoms, B. L., Golding, J. M., Stevenson, M. C., Wiley, T. R. A., & Yozwiak, J. A. (2007). A review of factors affecting jurors' decisions in child sexual abuse cases. In J. D. Read, D. Ross, M. Toglia, & R. C. Lindsay (Eds.), *The psychology of eyewitness memory* (pp. 509–543). Mahwah, NJ: Erlbaum.

Bottoms, B. L., & Goodman, G. S. (1994). Perceptions of children's credibility in sexual assault cases. *Journal of Applied Social Psychology, 24,* 702–732.

Bottoms, B. L., Nysse-Carris, K. L., Harris, T., & Tyda, K. (2003). Juror's perceptions of adolescent sexual abuse victims who have intellectual disabilities. *Law and Human Behavior, 27,* 205–227.

Bottoms, B. L., Reppucci, N. D., Tweed, J., & Nysse-Carris, K. (2002). Children, psychology, and law: Reflections on past and future contributions to science and policy. In J. R. P. Ogloff & R. Roesch (Eds.), *Taking psychology and law into the twenty-first century* (pp. 61–117). Kluwer Academic/ Plenum.

Bray, R. M., & Kerr, N. L. (1979). Use of the simulation method in the study of jury behavior: Some methodological considerations. *Law and Human Behavior, 3,* 107–119.

Buck, J. (2006). Hearsay testimony in child sexual abuse cases. In S. M. Sturt (Ed.), *New developments in child abuse* (pp. 73–93). New York: Nova Science.

Castelli, P., Goodman, G., & Ghetti, S. (2005). Effects of interview style and witness age on perceptions of children's credibility in sexual abuse cases. *Journal of Applied Social Psychology, 35,* 297–319.

Crawford v. Washington, 541 U.S. 36 (2004).

Devine, P. G. (1989). Stereotypes and prejudice: Their automatic and controlled components. *Journal of Personality and Social Psychology, 56,* 5–18.

Devine, D. J., Clayton, L. D., Dunford, B. B., Seying, R., & Pryce, J. (2001). Jury decision making: 45 years of empirical research on deliberating groups. *Psychology, Public Policy, and Law, 7*(3), 622–727.

Diamond, S. S. (1997). Illuminations and shadows from jury simulations. *Law and Human Behavior, 21,* 561–571.

Doherty-Sneddon, G., & McAuley, S. (2000). Influence of video mediation on adult-child interviews: Implications for the use of the live link with child witnesses. *Applied Cognitive Psychology, 14,* 379–392.

Donnelly, D. A., & Kenyon, S. (1996). "Honey, we don't do men": Gender stereotypes and the provision of services to sexually assaulted males. *Journal of Interpersonal Violence, 11,* 441–448.

Dukes, R. L., & Kean, R. B. (1989). An experimental study of gender and situation in the perception and reportage of child abuse. *Child Abuse and Neglect, 13,* 351–360.

Epstein, M. A., & Bottoms, B. L. (1998). Memories of childhood sexual abuse: A survey of young adults. *Child Abuse and Neglect, 22,* 1217–1238.

Feingold, A. (1994). Gender differences in personality: A meta-analysis. *Psychological Bulletin, 116,* 429–456.

Finkelhor, D., & Baron, L. (1986). Risk factors for child sexual abuse. *Journal of Interpersonal Violence, 1,* 43–71.

Finkelhor, D., Hotaling, G., Lewis, I. A., & Smith, C. (1990). Sexual abuse in a national sample of adult men and women: Prevalence, characteristics, and risk responsibility. *Child Abuse and Neglect, 14,* 19–28.

Fivush, R. (1993). Developmental perspectives on autobiographical recall. In G. S. Goodman & B. L. Bottoms (Eds.), *Child victims, child witnesses: Understanding and improving testimony* (pp. 1–24). New York: Guilford Press.

Gabora, N. J., Spanos, N. P., & Joab, A. (1993). The effects of complainant age and expert psychological testimony in a simulated child sexual abuse trial. *Law and Human Behavior, 17,* 103–119.

Gilligan, C. (1982). *In a different voice: Psychological theory and women's development.* Cambridge, MA: Harvard University Press.

Golding, J. M., Bradshaw, G. S., Dunlap, E. E., & Hodell, E. C. (2007). The impact of mock jury gender composition on deliberations and conviction rates in a child sexual assault trial. *Child Maltreatment, 12,* 182–190.

Golding, J. M., Bradshaw, G. S., & Hodell, E. C. (2007). *Juror gender: An effect of the courtroom or predetermined?* Unpublished manuscript.

Golding, J. M., Fryman, H. M., Marsil, D. F., & Yozwiak, J. A. (2003). Big girls don't cry: The effect of child witness demeanor on juror decisions in a child sexual abuse trial. *Child Abuse and Neglect, 27,* 1311–1321.

Golding, J. M., Hodell, E. C., & Dunlap, E. E. (2006). *The perception of abused children who kill their parents: Parricide in the courtroom.* Unpublished manuscript.

Golding, J. M., Hodell, E. C., & Dunlap, E. E. (2007). *Perceptions of physical child abuse in the courtroom.* Unpublished manuscript.

Golding, J. M., Sanchez, R. P., & Sego, S. A. (1997). The believability of hearsay testimony in a child sexual assault trial. *Law and Human Behavior, 21,* 299–325.

Golding, J. M., Sego, S. A., & Sanchez, R. P. (1999). Brief research report: Age factors affecting the believability of repressed memories of child sexual assault. *Law and Human Behavior, 23,* 257–268.

Golding, J. M., Sego, S. A., Sanchez, R. P., & Hasemann, D. (1995). The believ-ability of repressed memories. *Law and Human Behavior, 19,* 569–592.

Golding, J. M., Stewart, T. L., Yozwiak, J. A., Djadali, Y., & Sanchez, R. P. (2000). The impact of DNA evidence in a child sexual assault trial. *Child Maltreatment, 5,* 373–383.

Golding, J. M., Warren, A. R., & Ross, D. F. (1997). On legal validity, internal validity, and ecological validity: Comment on Wasby and Brody. *Law and Human Behavior, 21,* 693–695.

Goodman, G. S., Golding, J. M., & Haith, M. M. (1984). Jurors' reactions to child witnesses. *Journal of Social Issues, 40,* 139–156.

Goodman, G. S., Golding, J. M., Helgeson, V. S., Haith, M. M., & Michelli, J. (1987). When a child takes the stand: Jurors' perceptions of children's eyewitness testimony. *Law and Human Behavior, 11,* 27–40.

Goodman, G. S., Quas, J. A., Bulkley, J., & Shapiro, C. (1999). Innovations for child witnesses: A national survey. *Psychology, Public Policy, and Law, 5,* 255–281.

Goodman, G. S., Taub, E. P., Jones, D. P. H., England, P., Port, L. K., Rudy, L., et al. (1992). Testifying in criminal court. *Monographs of the Society for Research in Child Development, 57,* 1–159.

Goodman, G. S., Tobey, A. E., Batterman-Faunce, J. M., Orcutt, H. K., Thomas, S., Shapiro, C., et al. (1998). Face-to-face confrontation: Effects of closed-circuit technology on children's eyewitness testimony and jurors' decisions. *Law and Human Behavior, 22,* 165–203.

Haegerich, T. M., & Bottoms, B. L. (2000). Empathy and jurors' decisions in patricide trials involving child sexual assault allegations. *Law and Human Behavior, 24,* 421–448.

Jones, L. M., & Finkelhor, D. (2001). *The decline in child sexual abuse cases.* Washington, DC: U.S. Department of Justice Programs, Office of Justice Programs, Office of Juvenile Justice and Delinquency Programs.

Kalven, H., & Zeisel, H. (1966). *The American jury.* Boston: Little, Brown.

Kerr, N. L., & Bray, R. M. (2005). Simulation, realism, and the study of the jury. In N. Brewer & K. D. Williams (Eds.), *Psychology and law: An empirical perspective* (pp. 322–364). New York: Guilford Press.

Kovera, M. B., & Borgida, E. (1996). Children on the witness stand: The use of expert testimony and other procedural innovations in U. S. child sexual abuse trials. In B. L. Bottoms & G. S. Goodman (Eds.), *International per-spectives on child abuse and children's testimony: Psychological research and law* (pp. 201–220). Thousand Oaks, CA: Sage.

Kovera, M. B., Gresham, A. W., Borgida, E., Gray, E., & Regan, P. C. (1997). Does expert testimony inform or influence juror decision-making? A social cognitive analysis. *Journal of Applied Psychology, 82,* 178–191.

Kovera, M. B., Levy, R. J., Borgida, E., & Penrod, S. D. (1994). Expert wit-nesses in child sexual abuse cases: Effects of expert testimony and cross-examination. *Law and Human Behavior, 18,* 653–674.

Leippe, M., Manion, A., & Romanczyk, A. (1992). Eyewitness persuasion: How and how well do fact finders judge the accuracy of adults' and children's memory reports? *Journal of Personality and Social Psychology, 63,* 181–197.

Lieberman, J. D., & Sales, B. D. (2000). Jury instructions: Past, present, and future. *Psychology, Public Policy, and Law, 6,* 587–590.

Loftus, E. F., Weingardt, K., & Hoffman, H. (1993). Sleeping memories on trial: Reactions to memories that were previously repressed. *Expert Evidence, 2,* 51–59.

MacCoun, R. J., & Kerr, N. L. (1988). Asymmetric influence in mock jury deliberation: Jurors' bias for leniency. *Journal of Personality and Social Psychology, 54,* 21–33.

McAuliff, B. D., & Kovera, M. B. (2002). The status of evidentiary and procedural innovations in child abuse proceedings. In B. L. Bottoms, M. B. Kovera, & B. D. McAuliff (Eds.), *Children, social science, and the law* (pp. 412–445). New York: Cambridge University Press.

McCoy, M. L., & Gray, J. M. (2007). The impact of defendant gender and relationship to victim on juror decisions in a child sexual abuse case. *Journal of Applied Social Psychology, 37,* 1578–1593.

Miller, G. R., & Burgoon, J. K. (1982). Factors affecting assessments of witness credibility. In N. L. Kerr & R. M. Bray (Eds.), *The psychology of the courtroom* (pp. 169–194). New York: Academic Press.

Muller, R. T., Caldwell, R. A., & Hunter, J. E. (1993). Child provocativeness and gender as factors contributing to the blaming of victims of physical child abuse. *Child Abuse and Neglect, 17,* 249–260.

Myers, J. E. B. (1998). *Legal issues in child abuse and neglect* (2nd ed.). Thousand Oaks, CA: Sage.

Myers, J. E. B., Redlich, A. D., Goodman, G. S., Prizmich, L. P., & Imwinkelried, E. (1999). Jurors' perceptions of hearsay in child sexual abuse cases. *Psychology, Public Policy, and Law, 5,* 388–419.

Newcombe, P. A., & Bransgrove, J. (2007). Perceptions of witness credibility: Variations across age. *Journal of Applied Developmental Psychology, 28,* 318–331.

Nightingale, N. (1993). Juror reactions to child victim witnesses: Factors affecting trial outcome. *Law and Human Behavior, 17,* 679–694.

Orcutt, H. K., Goodman, G. S., Tobey, A. E., Batterman-Faunce, J. M., & Thomas, S. (2001). Detecting deception in children's testimony: Fact finders' abilities to reach the truth in open court and close-circuit trials. *Law and Human Behavior, 25*(4), 339–372.

Pipe, M.-E., Lamb, M.-E., Orbach, Y., & Cederborg, A.-C. (2007). *Child sexual abuse: Disclosure, delay, and denial.* Mahwah, NJ: Erlbaum.

Quas, J. A., Bottoms, B. L., Haegerich, T. M., & Nysse-Carris, K. L. (2002). Effects of victim, defendant and juror gender on decisions in child sexual assault cases. *Journal of Applied Social Psychology, 32,* 1993–2021.

Quas, J. A., Davis, E. L., Goodman, G. S., & Myers, J. E. B. (2007). Repeated questions, deception, and children's true and false reports of body touch. *Child Maltreatment, 12*, 60–67.

Read, J. D., Connolly, D. A., & Welsh, A. (2006). An archival analysis of actual cases of historic child sexual abuse: A comparison of jury and bench trials. *Law and Human Behavior, 30*, 259–285.

Redlich, A. D., Myers, J. E. B., Goodman, G. S., & Qin, J. (2002). A comparison of two forms of hearsay in child sexual abuse cases. *Child Maltreatment, 7*, 312–328.

Regan, P. C., & Baker, S. J. (1998). The impact of child witness demeanor on perceived credibility and trial outcome in sexual abuse cases. *Journal of Family Violence, 13*, 187–195.

Ross, D. F., Hopkins, S., Hanson, E., Lindsay, R. C. L., Eslinger, T., & Hazen, K. (1994). The impact of protective shields and videotape testimony on conviction rates in trials of child sexual abuse. *Law and Human Behavior, 18*, 553–566.

Ross, D. F., Lindsay, R. C. L., & Marsil, D. F. (1999). The impact of hearsay testimony on conviction rates in trials of child sexual abuse: Toward balancing the rights of defendants and child witnesses. *Psychology, Public Policy and Law, 5*, 439–455.

Sandys, M., & Dillehay, R. C. (1995). First-ballot votes, predeliberation dispositions, and final verdicts in jury trials. *Law and Human Behavior, 19*, 175–195.

Schutte, J. W., & Hosch, H. M. (1997). Gender differences in sexual assault verdicts: A meta-analysis. *Journal of Social Behavior and Personality, 12*, 759–772.

Stewart, T. L., Whiteside, S., & Golding, J. M. (2000). The effectiveness of expert witnesses in civil trials involving repressed memories of sexual assault. *American Journal of Forensic Psychology, 18*, 27–62.

U.S. Department of Health and Human Services, Administration on Children, Youth and Families. (2005). *Child maltreatment*. Washington, DC: U.S. Government Printing Office.

Weinberg, M. S., & Williams, C. J. (1988). Black sexuality: A test of two theories. *Journal of Sex Research, 25*, 197–218.

Weiten, W., & Diamond, S. S. (1979). A critical review of the jury simulation paradigm: The case of defendant characteristics. *Law and Human Behavior, 3*, 71–93.

Westcott, H. L., & Jones, D. P. H. (1999). Annotation: The abuse of disabled children. *Journal of Child Psychology and Psychiatry and Allied Disciplines, 40*, 497–506.

Wiley, T. R., & Bottoms, B. L. (2009). Effects of defendant sexual orientation on jurors' perceptions of child sexual assault. *Law and Human Behavior, 33*, 46–60.

Wilson, T. C. (1996). Cohort and prejudice: Whites' attitudes toward blacks, Hispanics, Jews, and Asians. *Public Opinion Quarterly, 60*, 253–274.

Yozwiak, J. A. (2003). The testimony of a child witness with mental retardation in a sexual abuse case: To believe or not to believe? *Dissertation Abstracts International: Section B. The Physical Sciences and Engineering, 63,* 10B.

Yozwiak, J. A., Golding, J. M., & Marsil, D. F. (2004). The impact of type of out-of-court disclosure in a child sexual assault trial. *Child Maltreatment, 9,* 325–334.

# Chapter 11

# An International Perspective on Child Witnesses

KAY BUSSEY

As witnesses and victims of crime, children have provided testimony in courts of law for more than a century. Although research has been conducted on child witnesses since the early 1900s, it is only over the past 30 years that a systematic research agenda has been established. The scope of topics researched, both in the field and the laboratory, are evident from earlier chapters, and the findings are increasingly being used to guide legal reforms. This chapter examines, from an international perspective, evidentiary and procedural innovations that have been implemented to accommodate child witnesses. It is important to examine reforms from such a perspective because legal reforms not only are influenced by evidence-based research but are also dependent on the evidentiary rules relating to children's testimony in specific jurisdictions. In some jurisdictions such as Israel and Holland, for example, children simply do not testify in court, and there is no need to adopt innovative procedures to accommodate them as witnesses.

It is not possible to cover all the evidentiary and procedural innovations that have been introduced in recent years to accommodate child witnesses. Therefore, in this chapter, I present only those innovations that have been most crucial in giving children a voice in legal proceedings while aiming to reduce their stress and to increase the accuracy and completeness of their testimony without diminishing the rights of the defendant for a fair trial. These include the initial pretrial interview, testimonial competence, and modes of evidence presentation. Before examining these innovations, I briefly discuss the different legal systems and cultural values pertaining to child witnesses, why reforms are needed, and the route to children becoming child witnesses.

## LEGAL SYSTEMS AND CULTURAL INFLUENCES

There are many impediments to children serving effectively as witnesses. Some are universal and others result from particular requirements relating to child witnesses in specific jurisdictions. Universal issues include how to obtain sufficient information from children, particularly from young children, without using leading or suggestive questions; how children should present their evidence; how to appraise children's evidence; and how to balance children's rights to a voice in the legal system with defendants' rights to a fair trial. The extent to which each of these issues takes primacy varies across legal systems depending on the demands and constraints of the particular legal system and the extent to which the jurisdiction is committed to legal reform to accommodate child witnesses.

One of the greatest sources of variability in legal systems internationally is the philosophy underpinning their operation. There are three main types of law: common law, civil law, and religious law. Broadly speaking, countries with a British heritage operate under common law, entailing an adversarial approach, while European countries such as France and Germany and those with a European heritage operate under civil law, entailing an inquisitorial approach. In civil-law countries, the need for innovation has not been as pressing because children rarely testify in court and, therefore, do not have to face the accused. Typically, in these countries, judges rather than attorneys play an important part in interrogating witnesses. Of course, the issues of obtaining reliable evidence from children and judging its credibility remain. However, the added overlay of obtaining this information and deciding its credibility in an open courtroom that is challenging for children is not of major concern in many civil-law jurisdictions. Among common-law countries (e.g., Australia, Canada, England, New Zealand, Republic of Ireland, Scotland, South Africa, and the United States), there is considerable variability in the way in which the criminal justice system operates and the ease with which reform is possible. Legal systems in the various jurisdictions have evolved so that South Africa, for example, has incorporated aspects of both common and civil law (Hoyano & Keenan, 2007).

In the United States, which follows a common-law approach, cultural values emphasize the rights of the individual. These are paramount and protected in the Constitution. The right of the accused to confront the accuser, particularly during cross-examination, has made legal reform to accommodate child witnesses more difficult than in other common-law countries. Consistent with the strong beliefs in the presumption of innocence of the accused, much of the research in the United States has, therefore, focused on the possible contamination of children's evidence by interviewers asking suggestive questions (see Ceci & Bruck, 1995). These concerns provided the basis for overturning the initial guilty verdicts in a number of high-profile cases in the 1990s (e.g., *State v. Michaels*, 1994). Constitutional protection of the accused is not as strong in most other common-law countries; therefore, there has been more emphasis on striking a balance between the rights of child witnesses and the rights of the accused. In these jurisdictions, a major focus has been on the intimidating and alien practices of an adult-oriented adversarial system. A lack of effective voice by children in this system has also led to the acquittal of defendants in high-profile cases in the 1990s (e.g., "Mr. Bubbles" in Australia). To address these concerns, there has been an increasing trend in recent reforms to permit children not to be present in the courtroom and not to face the accused. Legislative changes have permitted children's prerecorded evidence to be tendered to the court as their evidence-in-chief, or they are able to give their evidence out of the courtroom via closed-circuit television (CCTV).

## THE CASE FOR LEGAL REFORM IN COMMON-LAW COUNTRIES

Children testify in courts as witnesses to a variety of incidents ranging from car accidents, school shootings, domestic violence, and abuse. Since the late 1970s, accompanying a dramatic rise in reports of child sexual abuse, this category of child witnesses has proved to be the major challenge. Accordingly, the main focus of this chapter is on child witnesses who testify about their own alleged sexual abuse. Of course, many of the issues addressed are relevant to other classes of child witnesses.

Increased reporting of child abuse, often as a result of mandatory reporting mechanisms, led to greater numbers of victims who could potentially testify in court. However, many were prevented from doing so because they were not deemed competent to testify. Subsequently, the liberalization of competency requirements in most common-law countries enabled many young children to testify in court. Problems with their testimony surfaced. In such an intimidating environment, children frequently provided too little information for the prosecution to succeed. The completeness and quality of their testimony were found wanting. Further, many children did not want to appear in court for fear of facing the accused (Flin, Davies, & Tarrant, 1988; Goodman et al., 1992; Sas, 1992).

Goodman et al.'s (1992) landmark study showed that the more frightened children were about having to face the accused, the less able they were to answer the prosecutor's questions. Other factors, including multiple testimony, proved to be traumatic for children; the more distress they experienced in the courtroom, the worse their adjustment some 12 years later (Quas et al., 2005). Long delays between the child's complaint and their court appearance, coupled with complex, often hostile cross-examination contributed to children's distress when testifying and their ability to provide complete and reliable information. It has been widely acknowledged that children's successful performance as witnesses is marred by the manner in which the court operates, and this impacts on the delivery of justice to child witnesses (Goodman et al., 1998; Oates & Tong, 1987; Sas, 1992; Tobey, Goodman, Batterman-Faunce, Orcutt, & Sachsenmaier, 1995).

These findings heightened concern about children testifying in criminal courts, the province of adults, which are ill-equipped to handle child witnesses. Historically, the focus has been on protecting the rights of the accused adult rather than enabling children to participate optimally as witnesses in court within their developmental capabilities. The lack of regard for children's special needs in justice systems was formally acknowledged by the United Nations' (U.N.) Convention on the Rights of the Child (1989). This charter challenged legal systems throughout the world to focus on the rights of child witnesses without negating the rights of the accused. It is noteworthy that all countries except the United States and Somalia are signatories to this Convention. In the United States, the rights of the accused, enshrined in the Constitution, remain paramount; therefore, many of the innovations adopted in common-law jurisdictions have been implemented only under a strict set of conditions or not used at all for fear that their use would spark an appeal (Marsil, Montoya, Ross, & Graham, 2002).

## BECOMING A CHILD WITNESS

### Disclosure

The issue of disclosure is most relevant to child sexual abuse victims. Child sexual abuse differs from other forms of childhood victimization in that there is usually no witness apart from the victim and the accused and often no physical evidence. Therefore, children must tell someone about it or someone who suspects abuse questions the child about it. Children are often reluctant to acknowledge their victimization, particularly sexual abuse, for fear of reprisal from the perpetrator, embarrassment, or lack of power within the system (Hershkowitz, Lanes, & Lamb, 2007; Lawson & Chaffin, 1992; Palmer, Brown, Rae-Grant, & Loughlin, 1999). Although there is increasing societal acceptance that sexual abuse occurs, there remains skepticism about the veracity of such allegations because of children's often delayed and reluctant disclosure (London, Bruck, Ceci, & Shuman, 2005).

To underscore the importance of disclosing abuse so that it can be stopped and the child supported, many jurisdictions have enacted legislative requirements for the mandatory reporting of all forms of suspected child abuse, not just sexual abuse. The main aim is to override reservations and recriminations that may result from such reporting. Although Canada and all the Australian states except Western Australia have followed the lead of the United States where mandatory reporting has been in force since 1967 (Hutchison, 1993), New Zealand has not yet done so, and England and Wales are only now in the process of introducing a mandatory reporting system (Munro & Parton, 2007). Despite the importance of mandatory reporting for heightening societal awareness of protecting children, its benefits remain controversial. The lack of absolute indicators of abuse leads professionals who fear sanctions for not reporting abuse to sometimes overreport and overload the system with unnecessary investigations (Ainsworth, 2002; Harries & Clare, 2002).

In most Western countries, whether or not mandatory reporting is in operation, there are systems in place to report, manage, and prosecute child abuse allegations. This is not the case in many other countries in the world. Although child sexual abuse is universally decried, its prevalence is sometimes downplayed. Widespread societal recognition and condemnation of child sexual abuse emerged in the United States after the seminal report of Kempe, Silverman, Steele, Droegmueller, and Silver (1962). In contrast, other countries, such as Ireland, South Africa, and sub-Saharan Africa, have only recently begun to acknowledge the extent of child sexual abuse and to investigate its prevalence (Lalor, 2004; Levett, 1989; McGee, Garavan, deBarra, Byrne, & Conroy, 2002). As noted previously, although most countries are signatories to the U.N. Convention on the Rights of the Child (1989), some of the most populous countries such as India, China, and Indonesia, either from lack of commitment or lack of resources, have no mandatory reporting requirement and no official system for reporting abuse (Hesketh, Hong, & Lynch, 2000).

Perceptions of abuse vary culturally. In most Asian countries, there is little acknowledgment of the existence of familial sexual abuse (Hesketh & Lynch, 1996). In Chinese culture, for example, there is a belief that the unity and reputation of the family should be sustained even if there is a cost to the individual (O'Brian & Lau, 1995); maintaining face through the reputation of the family is essential for the preservation of the family unit (Qiao & Chan, 2005). Apart from the reluctance to acknowledge intrafamilial child sexual abuse, Chinese adults believe that child sexual abuse involves physical force and injury (Chen, Dunne, & Han, 2007). Widespread educational campaigns are required to highlight the serious nature of child sexual abuse and to educate people that it is an important form of child maltreatment. Even in Australia, where there is considerable public awareness of child sexual abuse and rigorous prosecution of such cases, cultural sensitivities have largely precluded investigating and prosecuting child sexual abuse cases in the Aboriginal community, where the rates of child sexual abuse are significantly higher than in the rest of the Australian population. In a poignant and disturbing review of the neglect of dealing with the child sexual abuse of Aboriginal children in the Northern Territory (Australia), it was noted that although many in the Aboriginal community were keen to address the issue of child sexual abuse, there was widespread confusion about what it actually was (Board of Inquiry into the Protection of Aboriginal Children from Sexual Abuse, 2007).

Even in jurisdictions where child sexual abuse allegations are investigated, there is no guarantee that children will be involved in legal proceedings. There has been resistance to accept children as witnesses in the legal system in most jurisdictions in the world, and if they are accepted, there are many barriers to them performing their testimonial role. Before children can testify in court, they need to provide sufficient detail about the alleged abuse for the prosecution to proceed. Therefore, once a report of abuse has been made or suspicion of abuse has been raised, the initial interview with the child is crucial.

## Pretrial Interviewing

The pretrial interview, particularly for cases involving child sexual abuse where the child's evidence is crucial, is used to establish whether the child can provide sufficient information for the trial to proceed. Most common-law jurisdictions have adopted legislation permitting electronic recording of interviews to reduce the stress that children experience from undergoing multiple interviews, often involving the same questions. This not only is traumatic for children but can reduce the reliability of information they report.

Electronic pretrial interviewing has enabled greater scrutiny of the quality of interviews, thereby establishing a need for consistency in interviewing practices. In the past, a number of high-profile cases have alerted the community and professionals to how justice is not served when children are subjected to flawed interviewing practices that have contaminated their evidence (Bruck & Ceci, 1995). Not only have interviewers used closed and leading questions, but they have sometimes pressured children into alleging abuse. Extensive research shows that the use of such interviewing techniques reduces the reliability of children's reports (Ceci & Bruck, 1995; Goodman & Melinder, 2007; Melnyk, Crossman, & Scullin, 2007). It has been consistently shown that information reported during free narrative and in response to open-ended questions is more accurate and more detailed than information reported in response to closed, option posing and leading questions (Sternberg, Lamb, Orbach, Esplin, & Mitchell, 2001). However, most interviewers ask too few open-ended questions.

To promote better interviewing practices, professional interviewing guidelines have been established in many jurisdictions. For example, Britain's Home Office, in the guidelines *Memorandum of Good Practice* (1992) and *Achieving Best Evidence in Criminal Proceedings* (2001), recommends that interviews follow a stepwise approach: rapport building followed by establishing ground rules; truth and lie assessment; a narrative phase; a questioning phase involving the presentation of open-ended questions first, followed by specific questions; and finally a closure phase, which involves recapping the child's account and acknowledging his or her contribution (Davies & Westcott, 1999; Hoyano & Keenan, 2007).

To monitor and increase the quality of interviews, many jurisdictions have established specialist interview teams. In the state of New South Wales (Australia), for example, as in Britain, children are interviewed by two members of a joint investigatory response team, one of whom is a police officer and the other a welfare worker. Their interviewing practices draw on many of the recommendations of the Home Office's (1992) *Memorandum of Good Practice*. However, as in other jurisdictions, interviews frequently include leading, closed, and option-posing questions even after they have received training in using open-ended questions (Davies, Wilson, Mitchell, & Milsom, 1995; Davies & Wilson, 1997; Warren, Woodall, & Thomas, 1999). To enable interviewers to use appropriate questions, the structure of the interview needs to be considered. A range of interview protocols have been developed for this purpose.

One of the most researched protocols is the cognitive interview, developed for use with adult bystander witnesses (Fisher & Geiselman, 1992). It, too, follows a staged approach but with the addition of context reinstatement whereby children are required to visually recreate the scene about which they are reporting to increase retrieval cues and enhance their recall of the event. Although context reinstatement increases the amount of information children report, other memory-retrieval procedures involving reverse-order recall and changing perspective are problematic for young children (Memon, Wark, Bull, & Koehnken, 1997). In addition, the lack of specific procedures for avoiding option-posing and leading questions often means that interviewers do not obtain sufficient detail from young children for the prosecution to proceed. Extensive training is required to master these techniques. Other interview protocols focus more explicitly on the questioning strategies available to interviewers so that they start with open-ended questions and progress to more specific ones. This funnel approach characterizes the stepwise interview, which has mainly been used in Canada (Yuille, Hunger, Joffe, & Zaparniuk, 1993). Field studies have shown that interviewers using this procedure were effective in eliciting information from children

(Yuille et al., 1993); however, its efficacy for increasing the amount of accurate information has not been established.

By far, the most extensively researched protocol is the National Institute of Child Health and Human Development (NICHD) protocol (Orbach et al., 2000; Sternberg et al., 2001). This scripted interview protocol focuses on questioning strategies. Similar to the stepwise interview, the interview starts with more general questions and proceeds to specific ones, with the recommendation that open-ended questions are preferred, that specific questions are to be used sparingly; and that closed-questions, option-posing, and leading questions, in particular, are to be avoided. The NICHD protocol provides more standardized wording of prompts for interviewers to draw on in specific interviews than do other interview protocols. Extensive field tests using this protocol in Israel and the United States with children who have already disclosed abuse show that children do provide more information in response to open-ended questions. Further, intensive training sessions in the use of the NICHD protocol with accompanying comprehensive feedback has revealed this interview protocol to be effective in increasing interviewers' use of open-ended questions (Sternberg, Lamb, Esplin, & Baradaran, 1999; Sternberg et al., 2001). However, whether these procedures can be effectively taught in the field without high-cost intensive training is yet to be demonstrated.

More uniformity in interviewing methods and interviewer training based on research evidence will be important for improving the quality of investigative interviews and thereby serving justice better (see Powell, 2002). At this stage, most jurisdictions have not yet adopted any one interview protocol exclusively.

## Child Witness Competence

Concerns about children's competence to testify came to the fore during the late 1970s when increasing numbers of children were required to testify about their alleged abuse. Their competence was challenged on a number of grounds, including their understanding of the oath, their memory capacity, and their reporting ability. Significant reform to enable young child witnesses to testify has involved substantial modifications to the requirements for providing evidence and judicial warnings about the adequacy of children's testimony.

## Competence to Provide Sworn Testimony and Corroboration Rules

In many jurisdictions, competency requirements made it impossible for young children to testify. Until 1990 in New South Wales, if children did not understand the religious connotations of the oath, and that there would be divine retribution for providing false testimony, they were deemed ineligible to testify (Shrimpton, Oates, & Hayes, 1996). Britain, however, began modifying competency requirements in 1933 (Children and Young Persons Act) by permitting children to give unsworn evidence, although a conviction could only be obtained if the unsworn evidence could be corroborated. There was a mandatory requirement for the judge to warn the jury about convicting on the basis of the child's unsworn statement. Because in child sexual abuse cases there are usually no other witnesses or other forms of evidence, children's unsworn testimony did little to advance the prosecution's case. Therefore, to enable prosecutions to proceed, issuing this warning was made discretionary some 60 years later (Criminal Justice and Public Order Act; Home Office, 1994). This has meant that sworn and unsworn testimonies are treated equivalently, thereby providing less reason for juries to dismiss the unsworn evidence provided by children. It is noteworthy that children whose unsworn evidence is accepted as if it were sworn would not incur the same criminal sanctions for lying as adults and children who had reached the age of criminal responsibility.

To provide unsworn testimony, it remained a requirement that children had to understand abstract concepts such as truth and the duty to tell the truth to be eligible to testify. There was controversy, however, about children's capabilities to understand such concepts (see *R v. Wright and Ormond*, 1990). Subsequent research, using developmentally appropriate assessment materials, has shown that children as young as 4 years can differentiate between a lie and a truth and can appreciate the importance of telling the truth (Bussey, 1992; Bussey & Grimbeek, 2000; Lyon & Saywitz, 1999). Consequently, Britain and most other common-law jurisdictions have adopted legislation with a presumption that children are competent to testify unless it is shown otherwise. In England, the Youth Justice Criminal Evidence Act (Home Office, 1999) proclaimed that it was not necessary to assess children's knowledge of lies and truths or their understanding of the duty to speak the truth for them to be able to testify in court. The presumption was that all children, regardless of age, were competent to testify as witnesses unless they could not understand the questions and answer them in a comprehensible manner. It was up to the jury to decide whether the child was telling the truth or not. Only in exceptional circumstances was a child's competency to be considered. Currently, when a child's evidence-in-chief is tendered via videotape, the judge watches the videotape and decides whether the child is capable of understanding questions and responding intelligibly to them. If, in the judge's view, they do not meet this requirement, the video evidence can be excluded in the interests of justice.

A similar progression of relaxing competency requirements and corroboration rules has followed in most, but not all, common-law jurisdictions.

Until recently, in Canada, for example, it was still essential for children to undergo formal competence testing whereby they were asked questions about truth, lying, and promises. On the basis of research findings from a group of Canadian scholars (Bala, Lee, Lindsay, & Talwar, 2000) and the trend in other common-law jurisdictions, the competency requirement was abolished in 2005 (Canada Evidence Act ss16, Bill C-2). This legislation requires all witnesses younger than 14 years to testify by promising to tell the truth, not under the oath or affirmation, and no assessment is undertaken of whether they understand the promise to tell the truth. Evidence obtained in this manner is accorded the same weight as if it were obtained under oath or affirmation.

Have these modifications to the competence requirements led to improvements in the outcomes for child witnesses? The major aims of the competence requirements were to act as a gatekeeper for children who had little or no knowledge of lying and truthfulness. It was assumed that once children developed a conceptual understanding of lying and truth telling, they would be more likely to provide truthful and accurate testimony. Whether a strict competence requirement serves justice by increasing the accuracy and truthfulness of children's testimony has not been established in any field studies. This is not surprising because of the lack of evidence against which to verify children's testimony. Laboratory studies, however, have shed some light on this issue. Overall, they reveal little support for the view that children's ability to answer competence questions relating to their knowledge of lies or truths is predictive of the accuracy of the information they provide (Goodman, Aman, & Hirschman, 1987) or the truthfulness of their reports (Talwar, Lee, Bala, & Lindsay, 2002). One consequence of the liberalization of the competence requirement has been the prosecution of more cases. Further research, however, is required to establish whether such liberalization has increased false convictions or has had any impact on the conviction rate.

## MODES OF EVIDENCE PRESENTATION

### Technological Innovations

The impetus for the use of technological innovations in many common-law countries was provided by the controversial recommendations of the Home Office Report of the advisory group on video evidence (1989) in England. Two main principles guided these recommendations. The first was that child witnesses should participate in the proceedings as soon as possible after the complaint to maximize their recollections and to enable them to seek therapy to deal with their negative experiences. The second principle aimed at enabling children to give evidence in a nonthreatening, more child-friendly environment than a criminal court, not facing the accused. This led initially to the adoption of CCTV (closed-circuit television) or Live Link, as it is known in Britain, so that children did not have to face the accused and did not have to appear in the courtroom. The report also recommended the videotaping of investigative interviews for use as evidence-in-chief. The most controversial recommendation, however, was for the pretrial videotaping of cross-examination. Legislation permitting the use of CCTV and videotaping of the initial interview to be used as evidence-in-chief was enacted in Australia, Canada, England, New Zealand, Scotland, and Wales during the 1990s. Most countries have been slow to adopt the recommendation of pretrial videotaping of the cross-examination. However, it has been adopted in Western Australia and is currently being considered for adoption in Britain (Office for Criminal Justice Reform, 2007).

## Closed-Circuit Television

The main aim of enabling children to testify via CCTV was to reduce their reluctance to testify in court because they feared facing the accused and to reduce their emotional stress from testifying before the accused, thereby increasing their ability to answer questions posed by legal personnel (Flin et al., 1988; Goodman et al., 1992; Sas, 1992). Although the rules governing its use vary across jurisdictions and are subject to ongoing reform, children mostly give their testimony via CCTV in a location away from the courtroom and the defendant. They are usually located in a room adjoining the court with a support person; all other legal personnel and the defendant can view the CCTV via monitors in the courtroom. In England and Wales, although its use is only permitted through application to the judge, the presumption is in favor of its use. In Canada, however, it needs to be shown that a child witness would be highly traumatized by testifying live (Bala et al., 2000). In other jurisdictions, such as New South Wales, CCTV can be used if the child so chooses and the judge deems that its use serves the interests of justice (Cashmore, 1992).

A number of field studies conducted across different jurisdictions have evaluated the efficacy of children presenting their evidence via CCTV. The findings from Australia, England, and Scotland reveal that the adoption of this innovative technological procedure has not impacted on guilty verdicts or guilty pleas (Cashmore, 1991; Davies & Noon, 1991). This is taken as evidence that this innovation does not unfairly prejudice or undermine the presumption of innocence of the defendant. But does it better serve justice? This is impossible to tell because there is no way to assess whether defendants found guilty were guilty and whether those acquitted were innocent.

Of the other indices that are used to assess the efficacy of CCTV, the most robust finding is that children are more willing to testify via CCTV than in open court and that they experience less stress when testifying via CCTV (Cashmore, 1992; Cashmore & Trimboli, 2005; Davies & Noon, 1991; Murray, 1995). The impact on the accuracy and completeness of children's testimony is more equivocal. Because there is no record of the event about which children are testifying, accuracy is inferred from the consistency of children's reports and their ability to resist misleading questions. To the extent that children are less stressed when they testify via CCTV and are not afraid to speak the truth because they do not have to face the accused, it could be expected that children would provide more reliable and truthful testimony. Ratings by court personnel and adults observing children in court lend some support to this in that children have been less likely to succumb to leading questions when giving evidence, both under direct and cross-examination, and they have been shown to provide less inconsistent information about the central elements of their testimony when testifying via CCTV (Davies & Noon, 1991). The findings from a Scottish study, however, showed the reverse (Murray, 1995). That is, the amount of detail children provided and their ability to resist leading questions were judged superior when they testified in the open court.

A downside of children testifying via CCTV is the belief held by attorneys that it diminishes the impact of children's testimony compared with open-court testimony (Cashmore & Trimboli, 2005; Davies & Noon, 1991). To overcome this, some jurisdictions have begun using large plasma screens on the walls of the courtroom. This solution, however, has increased the concern of some child witnesses that they are under the scrutiny of the accused. To overcome this concern, it has been proposed that the accused be denied access to the monitor. This highlights the difficult task of balancing the interests of the accused and the child witness so that justice is served.

As with most field evaluations, not all variables in the studies reported previously could be controlled, and most involved a small number of participants. There was extensive variation among children included in the studies in terms of the severity of their abuse, relationship with the accused, quality of the questioning procedures used in court, and degree of parental support. All these factors could have influenced the findings as much as the type of innovative procedure that children used to present their testimony. Furthermore, in most of the evaluations of children testifying via CCTV, children were not randomly allocated to the innovative procedure versus the open court.

To complement the field research, experimental research in which it is possible to manipulate variables and to randomly allocate children to different conditions in the research design has been conducted. These studies, of course, lack the ecological validity of field studies and are often not conducted with children who have been victimized. In a controlled assessment of the effect of testifying via CCTV on children, Goodman et al. (1998) replicated many of the findings of the field studies. In contrast to the field study by Murray (1995), but consistent with others (Cashmore & Trimboli, 2005; Davies & Noon, 1991), younger children who testified in a mock open court made more errors in response to leading questions than did children who testified via CCTV. Those children who testified via CCTV provided more answers to direct questions. However, the accuracy of children's free recall of events was not influenced by whether they testified in an open mock court or via CCTV. Children who expected to testify in open court showed higher stress levels than those who expected to testify via CCTV. As with the field studies, the effect of how the children testified did not impact the verdict. Jurors' ability to discern the accuracy of children's testimony was not attenuated by the child testifying via CCTV. Rather, their discernment of accuracy was less than perfect regardless of how the child testified. This finding replicates Ross et al.'s. (1994) study in which mock jurors watched a videotape of a trial showing the child testifying in open court, in open court behind a protective screen out of sight of the defendant, or via remote CCTV. Guilty verdicts and trial fairness did not differ across the testimonial conditions.

Overall, most studies have not found greater effects on guilt determination of the defendant dependent on the presentation mode of the evidence. Jurors in mock trials have judged children as less stressed when they testified via CCTV than in open court; judges and court personnel in field settings also judged children as less stressed when they testified via CCTV. However, judges and legal personnel in field settings believed that their testimony had less impact when they testified via CCTV, despite their testimony presumably being more accurate because they succumbed to fewer leading questions. Ultimately, any procedure that attenuates stress and heightens the accuracy of child witness testimony has the potential to better serve justice.

## Videotaped Testimony

The main aims of videotaped testimony are to enable children to give evidence prior to court, to reduce the stress of giving evidence in court, to increase the quality and completeness of their evidence, and to reduce the delay between reporting their abuse and giving evidence in court. This should increase the accuracy of the child's evidence because there is substantial research showing that children's memory for events diminishes over time (Goodman & Melinder, 2007). It has the added advantage of not requiring children to give their evidence multiple times, which as already indicated, many children find stressful. The countries that legislated for the use of CCTV during the 1990s also legislated for the electronic recording of children's investigative interviews and for their use as evidence-in-chief. However, not all common-law countries have embraced its use. In the United States, as discussed in Chapter 8 by Goodman and her colleagues, in the landmark decision of *Crawford v. Washington* (2004), the U.S. Supreme Court again upheld the accused's rights to confrontation by declaring that testimonial hearsay, which is usually the status of prerecorded interviews, does not enable the rights of the accused to be preserved in accordance with the Confrontation Clause of the Sixth Amendment. Therefore, this decision makes the use of the pretrial interview as evidence-in-chief difficult in the United States (Malloy, Mitchell, Block, Quas, & Goodman, 2007).

In Britain, the legislation regarding videotaped testimony enables judges to exclude all or part of the interview that has not been conducted appropriately. Its use is, therefore, subject to the discretion of the presiding judge (Davies et al., 1995). In most Australian states, there is a presumption in favor of the child giving evidence-in-chief in the form of videotaped testimony. In most jurisdictions, however, it is a requirement that the child be available for cross-examination either live in court, with or without a screen, or via CCTV. Judges must warn the jury about not drawing any adverse conclusions about the accused or the witness when the child's evidence is presented electronically.

Field evaluations of this innovation conducted in Australia and Britain revealed that its use did not impact the verdict of the case. However, children appeared less stressed when their evidence was obtained by an out-of-court interview than in person or via CCTV (Davies et al., 1995; McConachy, 2002). In Australia, attorneys and prosecuting lawyers believed that the quality of the videotaped evidence was superior to that obtained during court cases as the evidence was taken closer in time to the complaint, the interviews were conducted by specialist interviewers, and the child's statement was clearer. In Britain, however, judges' views about the adequacy of the interview were mixed; the prosecution lawyers believed the videotaped evidence had less impact, and the defense lawyers did not believe that they complied with the rules of evidence. Surprisingly, in Australia defense lawyers preferred it because they were aware of the evidence before reaching court. From the children's perspectives, most preferred the use of the prerecording rather than having to repeat their evidence in court; however, some children found it upsetting to have to watch the recording again (Cashmore & Trimboli, 2005; McConachy, 2002).

Despite the generally positive evaluations of videotaped testimony, its use is not without problems. In McConachy's (2002) study, for example, electronic recordings of children's testimony were not always used because of the poor-quality interviewing. The most frequently stated reason for not using the interview in court was its quality. Interviews were peppered with leading and suggestive questions and were found to be too lengthy, providing additional information that was not evidentially relevant. In England

and Wales, despite interviewers following the *Memorandum of Good Practice* (Home Office, 1992), many interviews involved an excessive number of closed questions and some leading questions (Davies et al., 1995).

Interview guidelines were updated further in Britain (*Achieving Best Evidence in Criminal Proceedings*; Home Office, 2001) to recommend that two interviewers conduct the interview, with one taking the primary lead and the other filling in any gaps. Usually one is a police officer and the other a professional child interviewer. Not only has this joint investigative interviewing procedure been adopted in Britain and other common-law jurisdictions such as New South Wales, as noted earlier, but a similar approach is used by the children's advocacy centers (CACs) in the United States (Cross, Jones, Walsh, Simone, & Kolko, 2007). Still, many interviews are lengthy and difficult to follow because young children do not readily construct a narrative that is coherent to others (Westcott & Kynan, 2004). Although coherence is not such an issue when the interview is used for investigative purposes, it becomes problematic when it is used as evidence-in-chief and jurors and judges are required to appraise it. To address these problems, it has been suggested that investigative interviews undergo editing before being tendered as evidence. Another option is the use of separate investigative and evidentiary interviews. However, this would lead to children retelling their narrative, thereby negating a major reason for using videotaped testimony. The challenge, therefore, is to develop investigative interview protocols that are more appropriate for obtaining information to be used as evidence-in-chief.

The use of videotaped testimony as evidence-in-chief has done little to overcome the difficulties that children encounter during cross-examination. By forgoing direct examination, children need to be cross-examined "cold," either live or via CCTV. This is quite a challenging task for many children. One solution to this harks back to the original recommendation of the Pigot Report for the pretrial recording of the cross-examination. This solution has been adopted for some time in Western Australia, and pilot data suggest that conviction rates have not attenuated (Eastwood & Patton, 2002). However, it does not address the main obstacle faced during cross-examination: the complex, grammatically confusing, credibility-challenging leading and closed questions typically used by the defense lawyers.

There is a growing body of research showing that cross-examination leads to the reporting of unreliable evidence by children (Brennan & Brennan, 1988; Zajac, Gross, & Hayne, 2003). In Australia, Britain, and New Zealand, it has been shown that defense lawyers ask a higher proportion of confusing, complex, and leading questions than prosecution lawyers (Davies & Seymour, 1997, 1998; Zajac et al., 2003). In response to these questions, children provide inconsistent information and change aspects of their evidence provided under direct examination (Zajac et al., 2003). Far from achieving the goal of establishing the truth, cross-examination renders children's testimony unreliable. Consistent with field studies that have highlighted the inconsistencies in children's testimony resulting from confusing cross-examination, Zajac and Hayne (2003) have shown in an experimentally controlled study that 5- and 6-year-olds, subject to complex, ambiguous, and repeated leading and closed questions, changed their responses to earlier questions, even when they were accurate. Although 9- and 10-year-olds were less influenced by the cross-examination questioning style than younger children, it still reduced the accuracy of their reports (Zajac & Hayne, 2006). These striking findings are not unexpected. A wealth of research shows that children provide unreliable evidence in response to suggestive questions (see Goodman & Melinder, 2007). There is no reason to believe that children's vulnerability to suggestion would pertain only to direct, and not to cross-examination. If defense attorneys cannot be trained to ask more developmentally appropriate questions during cross-examination, an alternate solution is to involve trained child interviewers in the cross-examination process. In England and Wales, the use of intermediaries to help children interpret the defense attorney's questions has been proposed in a recent consultation report (Office for Criminal Justice Reforms, 2007). Such a solution would bring the common-law and some civil-law approaches closer together in that others would talk for the child. This is quite a different approach than one that empowers the child to participate in modified proceedings, which remove the confrontational and confusing aspects of cross-examination. In Israel, youth investigators typically testify on behalf of child victims, thereby avoiding the traumatic effects on children of testifying in court. However, because the youth investigators' evidence is hearsay, it needs to be corroborated and this is rarely possible. Therefore, the lack of corroborating evidence and denying judges the opportunity to observe the demeanor of the witness have contributed to the low conviction rates of alleged perpetrators in Israel (Sternberg, Lamb, & Hershkowitz, 1996). This poor outcome has led to a rethinking of the child's role in criminal proceedings and the need for the child to be more involved in the proceedings (Cordon, Goodman & Anderson, 2003).

## CONCLUSIONS AND FUTURE DIRECTIONS FOR EVIDENTIARY AND PROCEDURAL REFORMS

Five key conclusions emerge from the review of evidentiary and procedural innovations presented in this chapter. First, although these innovations have gone partway to redressing some of the problems that children experience in delivering their testimony in court, more needs to be done. Permitting children to testify out of court via CCTV has reduced the stress that children experience and arguably has also increased the accuracy and completeness of their testimony. However, it remains a challenging task to increase the detail and accuracy of information obtained from children during the investigative interview prior to their court experience. The introduction of electronic recording of investigative interviews has laid bare the need for high-quality interviewing to obtain truthful, accurate, and complete accounts relating to children's complaints. This problem exists regardless of the legal system in place. These same interviewing challenges are faced in civil-law countries such as the Netherlands, which rely on the inquisitional system where the child is usually not involved in the actual court proceedings (Lambers-Winkelman & Buffing, 1996).

Second, changing laws does not guarantee their effective implementation. Many innovations have been compromised by the lack of training provided to the personnel required to use them. In some jurisdictions, the judiciary members were unfamiliar with the changed procedures, and the technology was often faulty. The use of prerecorded testimony is highly reliant on well-trained interviewers using a validated interview protocol. At the heart of the matter is the need to obtain high-quality testimony from children. Until interviewers and all those who interact with children in court, including defense lawyers, are better trained in communicating with children, justice will not be delivered to children and their voice will be muted.

Third, there is a lack of quality data to evaluate the effectiveness of the innovative procedures. Field studies are necessary to evaluate the efficacy of the innovations and problems with their implementation. More cooperation from legislatures to conduct rigorous, well-designed studies with measures from all participants will assist in decision making about the adoption of innovative procedures. Although hampered by ethical constraints, it is also crucial that laboratory research continues to complement field research.

Fourth, cross-examination remains one of the greatest challenges facing children who testify in criminal courts. There is no systematic order in which the questioning occurs, and the same questions are asked several times in different ways. This leads children to believe that they have answered incorrectly in the first instance. Defense attorneys undermine the reliability of children's evidence through the use of discredited questioning involving leading questions, which prosecution attorneys and interviewers have been barred from using for some time. Truth is not achieved by the use of confusing and leading questions. This approach only serves to increase the unreliability of children's testimony. Although children may be less likely to succumb to leading questions when cross-examined via CCTV, it is incumbent on the fact finders to establish more developmentally appropriate ways to test the veracity of children's evidence than through leading questions, complex language, and credibility-challenging comments.

Fifth, the perspective provided in this chapter is based on reforms and research relating to child witnesses that have been undertaken in common-law jurisdictions in the Western industrialized world. Most of the world's population does not live in the West. There is an urgent need for Western scholars to familiarize themselves with the workings of the legal and social systems throughout the world so that there can be a better exchange of ideas across cultures. In many countries, particularly in Asia and Africa, where children's rights are often forgotten amid the daily battle for survival, there are no formal channels for reporting child abuse, and children are abused with no redress from the legal system. Therefore, before these countries can address issues relating to children's participation in their legal systems, it is first necessary to put in place systems for reporting child abuse and prosecuting perpetrators. When this is achieved, the important task of appropriately accommodating child witnesses in the different legal systems that exist internationally can begin in earnest.

In conclusion, it is important to note that many of the innovations that have had the greatest impact on child witnesses in common-law countries have been sparingly used in the United States because of their potential to undermine the rights of the accused. Eliminating the need for children to confront the accused by permitting them to testify via CCTV or by tendering their pretrial interview as evidence-in-chief has reduced children's reluctance to proceed with criminal proceedings and reduced the stress of their participation in such proceedings. These innovations have enabled children's voices to be heard in court although they are not physically present. Despite these accommodations, guilty pleas and guilty verdicts have not been impacted. If children are less stressed when they testify, then arguably their testimony should be more detailed and accurate, which should lead to more convictions if indeed the accused was guilty. However, children are still being undermined during cross-examination. Until innovative and less confrontational ways to cross-examine children are found, conviction rates and guilty pleas are unlikely to change. These changes will not come easily, particularly in the United States, where hostile and confrontational cross-examination is believed to be necessary to preserve the defendant's rights. These beliefs are increasingly at odds with the research evidence showing that such questioning procedures do not serve the truth-seeking function of the court. Not only does there need to be a balance between the rights of child witnesses and defendants, but both rights need to be balanced within the truth-seeking function of the court. Only then will justice be served for all.

## ACKNOWLEDGMENTS

I thank Elizabeth Grimbeek for her insightful comments on this chapter and the Australian Research Council for a grant that, in part, supported the preparation of this chapter.

## REFERENCES

Ainsworth, F. (2002). Mandatory reporting of child abuse and neglect: Does it really make a difference? *Child and Family Social Work, 7,* 57–64.

Bala, N., Lee, K., Lindsay, R. C. L., & Talwar, V. (2000). A legal and psychological critique of the present approach to the assessment of the competence of child witnesses. *Osgoode Hall Law Journal, 38,* 409–452.

Board of Inquiry into the Protection of Aboriginal Children from Sexual Abuse. (2007). *Little children are sacred.* Darwin: Northern Territory Government of Australia.

Brennan, M., & Brennan, R. E. (1988). *Strange language: Child victims under cross-examination* (3rd ed). Wagga Wagga, NSW: Charles Sturt University.

Bruck, M., & Ceci, S. J. (1995). Amicus brief for the case of *State of New Jersey v. Michaels.* Presented by Committee of Concerned Social Scientists. *Psychology, Public Policy and Law, 1,* 272–322.

Bussey, K. (1992). Lying and truthfulness: Children's definitions, standards, and evaluative reactions. *Child Development, 63,* 129–137.

Bussey, K., & Grimbeek, E. J. (2000). Children's conceptions of lying and truth-telling: Implications for child witnesses. *Legal and Criminological Psychology, 5,* 187–199.

Canada Evidence Act ss16, 16.1, as amended by 53-54 Elizabeth II, 2004-2005 Bill C-2.

Cashmore, J. (1991). Problems and solutions in lawyer-child communication. *Criminal Law Journal, 15,* 193–202.

Cashmore, J. (1992). *The use of closed-circuit television for child witnesses in the ACT.* Sydney, NSW: Australian Law Reform Commission.

Cashmore, J., & Trimboli, L. (2005). *An evaluation of the NSW Child Sexual Assault Specialist Jurisdiction Pilot.* Sydney, NSW: Bureau of Crime Statistics and Research.

Ceci, S. J., & Bruck, M. (1995). *Jeopardy in the courtroom: A scientific analysis of children's testimony.* Washington, DC: American Psychological Association.

Chen, J., Dunne, M. P., & Han, P. (2007). Prevention of child sexual abuse in China: Knowledge, attitudes, and communication practices of parents of elementary school children. *Child Abuse and Neglect, 31,* 747–755.

Children and Young Persons Act 1933 414 s.1.

Cordon, I . M., Goodman, G. S., & Anderson, S. J. (2003). Children in court.

In P. J. van Koppen & S. Penrod (Eds.). *Adversarial versus inquisitorial justice: Psychological perspectives on criminal justice systems* (pp. 167–189). New York: Plenum Publishers.

Crawford v. Washington, 541 U.S. 36; 124 S. Ct. 1354 (2004).

Cross, T. P., Jones, L. M., Walsh, W. A., Simone, M., & Kolko, D. J. (2007). Child forensic interviewing in children's advocacy centers: Empirical data on a practice model. *Child Abuse and Neglect, 31,* 1031–1052.

Davies, E., & Seymour, F. W. (1998). Questioning child complainants of sexual abuse: Analysis of criminal court transcripts in New Zealand. *Psychiatry, Psychology and Law, 47,* 47–61.

Davies, G. M., & Noon, E. (1991). *An evaluation of the live link for child witnesses.* London: Home Office.

Davies, G. M., & Westcott, H. L. (1999). *Interviewing children under the Memorandum of Good Practice: A research review.* London: Home Office.

Davies, G., & Wilson, C. (1997). Implementation of the memorandum: An overview. In H. Westcott & J. Jones (Eds.), *Perspectives on the memorandum: Policy, practice and research in investigative interviewing* (pp. 1–12). Aldershot, UK: Arena.

Davies, G., Wilson, C., Mitchell, R., & Milsom, J. (1995). *Videotaping children's evidence: An evaluation.* London: Home Office.

Eastwood, C., & Patton, W. (2002). *The experiences of child complaints of sexual abuse in the criminal justice system.* Report to the Criminology Research Council, Canberra.

Fisher, R. P., & Geiselman, R. E. (1992). *Memory-enhancing techniques for investigative interviewing: The cognitive interview.* Springfield, IL: Charles C Thomas.

Flin, R. H., Davies, G. M., & Tarrant, A. (1988). *The child witness* (Final report to the Scottish Home and Health Department, Edinburgh). Edinburgh: Scottish Home and Health Department.

Goodman, G. S., Aman, C., & Hirschman, J. (1987). Child sexual and physical abuse: Children's testimony. In S. J. Ceci, M. P. Toglia, & D. P. Ross (Eds.), *Children's eyewitness memory* (pp. 1–23). New York: Springer-Verlag.

Goodman, G. S., & Melinder, A. (2007). Child witness research and forensic interviews of young children: A review. *Legal and Criminological Psychology, 12,* 1–19.

Goodman, G. S., Taub, E. P., Jones, D. P. H., England, P., Port, L. K., Rudy, L., et al. (1992). Testifying in criminal court: Emotional effects on child sexual assault victims. *Monographs of the Society for Research in Child Development, 57*(Serial No. 229).

Goodman, G. S., Tobey, A. E., Batterman-Faunce, J. M., Orcutt, H. K., Thomas, S., Shapiro, C., et al. (1998). Face-to-face confrontation: Effects of closed-circuit technology on children's eyewitness testimony and jurors' decisions. *Law and Human Behavior, 22,* 165–203.

Harries, M., & Clare, M. (2002). *Mandatory reporting of child abuse: Evidence and options; Report for the Western Australian Child Protection Council;*

*Discipline of Social Work and Social Policy.* Perth: University of Western Australia.

Hershkowitz, I., Lanes, O., & Lamb, M. E. (2007). Exploring the disclosure of child sexual abuse with alleged victims and their parents. *Child Abuse and Neglect, 31,* 111–123.

Hesketh, T., Hong, Z. S., & Lynch, M. A. (2000). Child abuse in China: The views and experiences of child health professionals. *Child Abuse and Neglect, 24,* 867–872.

Hesketh, T., & Lynch, M. A. (1996). Child abuse and neglect in China: What the papers say. *Child Abuse Review, 5,* 346–355.

Home Office. (1989). *Report of the advisory group on video evidence.* (Chairman Judge Thomas Pigot QC). London: Author.

Home Office. (1992). *Memorandum of good practice on video recorded interviews with child witnesses for criminal proceedings.* London: Author with Department of Health.

Home Office. (1994). *Criminal Justice and Public Order Act.* London: Author.

Home Office. (1999). *Youth Justice and Criminal Evidence Act.* London: Author.

Home Office. (2000). *Achieving best evidence in criminal proceedings: Guidance for vulnerable or intimidated witnesses, including children.* (2001). London: Author. Retrieved January 29, 2009, from *www.homeoffice.gov.uk/documents/ach-bect-evidence/guidance-for-witnesses?view=Binary.*

Hoyano, L., & Keenan, C. (2007). *Child abuse: Law and policy across boundaries.* Oxford: Oxford University Press.

Hutchison, E. (1993). Mandatory reporting laws: Child protection case findings gone awry. *Social Work, 38,* 56–62.

Kempe, C. H., Silverman, F. N., Steele, B. F., Droegmueller, W., & Silver, H. K. (1962). The battered child syndrome. *Journal of the American Medical Association, 181,* 17–24.

Lalor, K. (2004). Child sexual abuse in sub-Saharan Africa: A literature review. *Child Abuse and Neglect, 28,* 439–460.

Lambers-Winkelman, F., & Buffing, F. (1996). Children's testimony in the Netherlands: A study of statement validity analysis. In B. L. Bottoms & G. S. Goodman (Eds.), *International perspectives on child abuse and children's testimony: Psychological research and law* (pp. 45–61). Thousand Oaks: Sage.

Lawson, L., & Chaffin, M. (1992). False negatives in sexual abuse disclosure interviews: Incidence and influence of caretaker's belief in abuse in cases of accidental abuse discovery by diagnosis of STD. *Journal of Interpersonal Violence, 7,* 532–542.

Levett, A. (1989). A study of childhood sexual abuse among South African university women students. *South African Journal of Psychology, 19,* 122–129.

London, K., Bruck, M., Ceci, S. J., & Shuman, D. W. (2005). Disclosure of child sexual abuse: What does the research tell us about the ways that children tell? *Psychology, Public Policy, and the Law, 11,* 194–226.

Lyon, T. D., & Saywitz, K. J. (1999). Young maltreated children's competence to take the oath. *Applied Developmental Science, 3,* 16–27.

Malloy, L. C., Mitchell, E. B., Block, S. D., Quas, J. A., & Goodman, G. S. (2007). Children's eyewitness memory: Balancing children's needs and defendants' rights when seeking the truth. In M. P. Toglia, J. D. Read, D. F. Ross, & R. C. L. Lindsay (Eds.), *Handbook of eyewitness psychology: Vol. 1. Memory for events* (pp. 545–574). Mahwah, NJ: Earlbaum.

Marsil, D. F., Montoya, J., Ross, D., & Graham, L. (2002). Child witness policy: Law interfacing with social science. *Law and Contemporary Problems, 65,* 209–241.

McConachy, D. (2002). *Evaluation of the electronic recording of children's evidence.* Sydney: Attorney-General's Department.

McGee, H., Garavan, R., de Barra, M., Byrne, J., & Conroy, R. (2002). *The SAVI Report: Sexual abuse and violence in Ireland—A national study of Irish experiences, beliefs and attitudes concerning sexual violence.* Dublin: Liffey Press & Dublin Rape Crisis Centre.

Melnyk, L., Crossman, A. M., & Scullin, M. H. (2007). The suggestibility of children's memory. In M. P. Toglia, J. D. Read, D. F. Ross, & R. C. L. Lindsay (Eds.), *The handbook of eyewitness psychology: Vol.1. Memory for events* (pp. 401–427). Mahway, NJ: Erlbaum.

Memon, A., Wark, L., Bull, R., & Koehnken, G. (1997). Isolating the effects of the cognitive interview techniques. *British Journal of Psychology, 88,* 179–197.

Munro, E., & Parton, N. (2007). How far is England in the process of introducing a mandatory reporting system? *Child Abuse Review, 16,* 5–16.

Murray, K. (1995). *Live television link: An evaluation of its use by child witnesses in Scottish criminal trials.* Edinburgh: Scottish Office, Central Research Unit.

Oates, R. K., & Tong, L. (1987). Sexual abuse of children: An area with room for professional reforms. *Medical Journal of Australia, 147,* 544–548.

O'Brian, C., & Lau, L. S. W. (1995). Defining child abuse in Hong Kong. *Child Abuse Review, 4,* 38–46.

Office for Criminal Justice Reform. (2007). *Improving the criminal trial process for young witnesses: A consultation paper.* London: Author.

Orbach, Y., Hershkowitz, I., Lamb, M. E., Sternberg, K. J., Esplin, P. W., & Horowitz, D. (2000). Assessing the value of structured protocols for forensic interviews of alleged child abuse victims. *Child Abuse and Neglect, 24,* 733–752.

Palmer, S. E., Brown, R. A., Rae-Grant, N. I., & Loughlin, M. J. (1999). Responding to children's disclosure of familial abuse: What survivors tell us. *Child Welfare, 78,* 259–282.

Powell, M. B. (2002). Specialist training in investigative and evidential interviewing: Is it having any effect on the behaviour of professionals in the field? *Psychiatry, Psychology and Law, 9,* 44–55.

Qiao, D. P., & Chan, Y. C. (2005). Child abuse in China: A yet-to-be-acknowledged "social problem" in the Chinese Mainland. *Child and Family Social Work, 10,* 21–27.

Quas, J. A., Goodman, G. S., Ghetti, S., Alexander, K. W., Edelstein, R. S., Redlich, A. P., et al. (2005). Childhood sexual assault victims: Long-term consequences after testifying in criminal court. *Monographs of the Society for Research in Child Development, 70*(Serial No. 280).

Ross, D. F., Hopkins, S., Hanson, E., Lindsay, S., Hazen, K., & Eslinger, T. (1994). The impact of protective shields and videotape testimony on conviction rates in a simulated trial of child sexual abuse. *Law and Human Behavior, 18,* 553–566.

R v Wright and Ormond (1990) 90 Cr App R 91 (CA) 94–95.

Sas, L. D. (1992). Empowering child witnesses for sexual abuse prosecution. In H. Dent & R. H. Flin (Eds.), *Children as witnesses* (pp. 181–199). Chichester, UK: Wiley.

Shrimpton, S., Oates, K., & Hayes, S. (1996). The child witness and legal reforms in Australia. In B. L. Bottoms & G. S. Goodman (Eds.), *International perspectives on child abuse and children's testimony: Psychological research and law* (pp. 132–144). Thousand Oaks, CA: Sage.

State v. Michaels, 642 A.2d 1372, 1376 (N.J. 1994).

Sternberg, K. J., Lamb, M. E., Esplin, P. W., & Baradaran, L. P. (1999). Using a scripted protocol in investigative interviews: A pilot study. *Applied Developmental Science, 3,* 70–76.

Sternberg, K. J., Lamb, M. E., & Hershkowitz, I. (1996). Child sexual abuse investigations in Israel: Evaluating innovative practices. In B. L. Bottoms & G. S. Goodman (Eds.), *International perspectives on child abuse and children's testimony: Psychological research and law* (pp. 62–76). Thousand Oaks, CA: Sage.

Sternberg, K. J., Lamb, M. E., Orbach, Y., Esplin, P. W., & Mitchell, S. (2001). Use of a structured investigative protocol enhances young children's responses to free recall prompts in the course of forensic interviews. *Journal of Applied Psychology, 86,* 997–1005.

Talwar, V., Lee, K., Bala, N., & Lindsay, R. C. L. (2002). Children's conceptual knowledge of lying and its relation to their actual behaviors: Implications for court competence examinations. *Law and Human Behavior, 26,* 395–415.

Tobey, A. E., Goodman, G. S., Batterman-Faunce, J. M., Orcutt, H. K., & Sachsenmaier, T. (1995). Balancing the rights of children and defendants: Effects of closed-circuit television on children's accuracy and juror's perceptions. In M. S. Zaragoza, J. R. Graham, G. C. N. Hall, R. Hirschman, & Y. S. Ben-Porath (Eds.), *Memory and testimony in the child witness* (pp. 214–39). Thousand Oaks, CA: Sage.

United Nations. (1989). *Convention on the Rights of the Child.* New York: Author.

Warren, A. R., Woodall, C. E., & Thomas, M. (1999). Assessing the effectiveness of a training program for interviewing child witnesses. *Applied Developmental Science, 3,* 128–135.

Westcott, H. L., & Kynan, S. (2004). The application of a 'story-telling' framework to investigative interviews for suspected child sexual abuse. *Legal and Criminological Psychology, 9,* 37–56.

Yuille, J. C., Hunter, R., Joffe, R., & Zaparniuk, J. (1993). Interviewing children in sexual abuse cases. In G. S. Goodman & B. L. Bottoms (Eds.), *Child victims, child witnesses: Understanding and improving testimony* (pp. 95–115). New York: Guilford Press.

Zajac, R., Gross, J., & Hayne, H. (2003). Asked and answered: Questioning children in the courtroom. *Psychiatry, Psychology and Law, 10,* 199–209.

Zajac, R., & Hayne, H. (2003). I don't think that's what really happened: The effect of cross-examination on the accuracy of children's reports. *Journal of Experimental Psychology: Applied, 9,* 187–195.

Zajac, R., & Hayne, H. (2006). The negative effect of cross-examination style questioning on children's accuracy: Older children are not immune. *Applied Cognitive Psychology, 20,* 3–16.

Chapter 12

# Child Victim and Witness Research Comes of Age
## Implications for Social Scientists, Practitioners, and the Law

BRADLEY D. McAULIFF

Child maltreatment remains a pervasive problem in the United States. In 2007 alone, an estimated 794,000 children were victims of child abuse or neglect, resulting in a victimization rate of 10.6 per 1,000 children (U.S. Department of Health and Human Services, 2009). Intervening on children's behalf is a complex process, often involving different agencies (child protective services, law enforcement), systems (dependency court, criminal court), and outcomes (removing child from home, incarcerating perpetrator). The efficacy of this process hinges largely on the active and effective participation of child victims. Children's participation must be *active* in the sense that they are willing to report and discuss maltreatment. In most cases, the only witness to crimes against children is the victim, so if a child does not disclose abuse or refuses to discuss disclosed abuse, maltreatment will likely continue unabated. At the same time, children's participation must be *effective* in that the information they report is accurate. False or distorted allegations of maltreatment misdirect society's resources away from true victimization, undermine the credibility of actual victims, and implicate innocent individuals.

Sixteen years after the publication of the seminal *Child Victims, Child Witnesses: Understanding and Improving Testimony* (Goodman & Bottoms, 1993), this volume revisits and updates the issues central to children's active and effective participation in legal proceedings: disclosure, interviewing, memory, testimony, and juror decision making. My goal in writing this commentary is to move beyond the microlevel of analysis presented in each chapter in this volume to the macro by identifying common themes within and across chapters. Only then can we truly begin to understand recent developments in child victim research and their implications for social scientists, practitioners, and the law.

## DISCLOSURE, MEMORY, AND INTERVIEWING

A fitting place to begin is Lyon's chapter (Chapter 2) on abuse disclosure, which highlights the critical role that methodology plays in how social scientists interpret data and draw conclusions. He presents a compelling argument that estimates of disclosure inevitably are biased by reluctance to disclose. Clinical samples of children who have disclosed abuse and population surveys of adult respondents known to have been abused concomitantly overestimate the likelihood that abuse victims will disclose abuse because they rely on nonrepresentative samples of child sexual abuse victims (namely, those who disclose abuse). These individuals also may be at increased risk for exposure to misinformation because abuse disclosure is prompted or followed by questions from someone—a parent, law enforcement officer, or therapist—who does not know what actually occurred. Lyon argues for the use of more general population surveys, which in and of themselves are not entirely free from bias but are desirable in that they do not systematically exclude previous nondisclosers and do reduce the extent to which misinformation may taint true allegations or create false ones. Data from general population surveys indicate that many children and adults (anywhere from 13 to 60%, according to Lyon) had never disclosed abuse.

These data are relevant to both researchers and practitioners. From a methodological perspective, we are reminded that sampling is inextricably intertwined with the validity and generalizability of our results. Individuals who disclose abuse are a unique slice of the general abuse victim population. Estimates of disclosure based solely on these individuals will be biased and nonrepresentative of abuse victims in general, as will any other information derived from these limited samples such as victim/perpetrator characteristics, abuse sequelae, and treatment efficacy. Continued development and incorporation of more objective measures, such as medical records or photos/videos taken during the abuse (see Dickinson, Del Russo, & D'Urso, 2008), may help overcome some bias inherent in surveys and self-report studies. Moreover, population surveys aimed at measuring abuse via perpetrators' reports may provide a much-needed comparison point for data from victims who report being abused. The fact that adults, as well as children, are reluctant to disclose also calls into question the adequacy of state statutes that only extend the time period for filing criminal charges in sexual offense cases (e.g., until the minor reaches the age of majority or for a longer period of time after the crime) instead of completely removing the limitations altogether. With respect to practitioners, Lyon himself says it best when he notes, "It is obviously wrongheaded to assume that denial is an indicator that abuse occurred, but it is just as wrong to assume that denials conclusively rule out abuse." Practitioners and social scientists must continue to work together in developing questioning methods that overcome reluctance to disclose true abuse without encouraging false reports.

Greenhoot and Bunnell's chapter (Chapter 3) moves from victims' initial reluctance to disclose abuse to their ability to remember and recount abuse accurately. The authors provide an excellent synthesis of an extremely complex body of theory and research related to children's memory for stressful events. Much of that research was sparked by the satanic ritual daycare abuse allegations of the 1980s and the following decade to determine whether memory for traumatic experiences involves special mechanisms that operate in fundamentally different ways from those involved in the memory of nontraumatic experiences. Recent cognitive and developmental research calls into question whether traumatic events are "repressed" or "dissociated" from regular memory, as suggested by the early work of Freud and other clinicians. Instead, there appears to be considerable overlap in the processes involved in traumatic and nontraumatic memories even though maltreatment appears to be associated with some atypical patterns of memory functioning. For example, individuals with abuse histories have difficulty recollecting episodic details in their memories for personal experiences and individuals who experience trauma-induced PTSD may suffer more global memory problems.

Undoubtedly, we have benefited from the increased theoretical and methodological sophistication of research on children's traumatic memories. In particular, these studies emphasize the importance of collecting data from control or comparison groups. Without this reference point, the data are descriptive but virtually meaningless. It is only by comparing the memories of children versus adults, maltreated versus nonmaltreated individuals, single versus repeated traumatic episodes, and prospective versus retrospective accounts that we can begin to pinpoint truly how trauma and memory intersect. Yet, even with this increasingly sophisticated research, we see that much of the take-home message remains the same: Children, like adults, usually are able to remember details of single and ongoing traumatic events quite well, but at the same time these memories are vulnerable to distortion and forgetting depending on a variety of individual and situational factors. Law enforcement and legal professionals must be mindful of the emerging consensus that traumatic memories do not involve special mechanisms that repress or dissociate extremely stressful events. Realistically, we can expect victims to forget the *details* of events over time, especially in cases of chronic maltreatment, but police and attorneys must be cautious when working with individuals who claim to have forgotten *entire episodes* of severely abusive events. Such memories may be more indicative of highly suggestive interviewing and therapy work than of actual abuse (see Loftus & Davis, 2006).

Blandón-Gitlin and Pezdek (Chapter 4) focus on the individual and situational factors that influence children's reports in forensic contexts. They synthesize more than 20 years of research to identify forensically relevant factors that have been shown to affect children's suggestibility and accuracy. Certain situational factors known to increase suggestibility and decrease the quality of their reports include focused interview questions and the use of props or anatomically detailed dolls, high arousal or stress during memory retrieval, and long delays between the event and subsequent interview. Other situational factors have been shown to decrease suggestibility and enhance accuracy such as prior knowledge base, repeated experience, multiple interviews, and source monitor training. More recent research has begun to explore individual differences associated with resistance and susceptibility to misleading information. Increased age, superior language ability, more sophisticated mental processing abilities, and parents with healthy attachment styles all have been associated with decreased memory suggestibility.

The lessons to be learned here for forensic interviewers and attorneys at first appear to be simple and straightforward: Avoid factors that increase suggestibility and maximize factors that decrease suggestibility. Unfortunately, as we all know, life is rarely so clear-cut, and children's memory is no exception. We have learned, for example, that children's responses to open-ended prompts, although accurate, are often incomplete compared with their responses to more direct, focused questions. Yet what we gain in quantity with direct questions we often lose in terms of accuracy if direct questions introduce suggestive or misleading information. Prior event knowledge also may have mixed effects on children's suggestibility depending on the plausibility of the suggested information. Plausible events for children such as getting lost in a mall are, by definition, more likely to have occurred than implausible events; therefore, when a plausible suggestion is provided, witnesses search their memories and are more likely to find details related to the plausible suggestion. According to Pezdek and her colleagues (1997, 1999), this initiates the construction of a false memory. In stark contrast, implausible events are less likely to have occurred, and as a result witnesses often come up empty-handed when searching their memories for details related to an implausible suggestion. What does this mean in the context of forensic interviews? Essentially, it is unlikely that forensic interviewing will create false memories in a child for whom sexual abuse is an implausible event. One final challenge we face with children's suggestibility is that, although some variables are under the interviewer's control (question type, use of props, multiple interviews), other situational (length of delay between event and interview, repeated experience) and individual (age, language ability, and mental processing ability) variables are not. In this sense, children come into the system as they are. We know, for example, that children are often reluctant to disclose abuse. Once a child discloses, we can expedite the system's handling of the case (and many states do); however, predisclosure delays are often long and the opportunity for suggestive questioning is great. Recognizing these uncontrollable factors should help mitigate their negative effects on child witness memory.

The last two chapters in this section deal with child abuse investigations and contemporary forensic interviewing. Wood, Nathan, Nezworski, and Uhl (Chapter 5) stress that there are vital lessons to be learned from the outrageous daycare cases of the 1980s and 1990s. Systematic comparisons between children's interviews in two of the most notorious daycare cases (*McMartin* and *Michaels*) and those regularly conducted by Child Protective Services have shed much-needed light on suggestive questioning techniques and their devastating effects on children's reports. On the basis of those findings, we know that certain practices such as promising rewards, relaying other witnesses' reports, inviting speculation, and introducing new information should be avoided when questioning children. To improve the quality of forensic interviews, Wood and colleagues recommend that interviewers receive specialized training, audio- or videotape their interviews, explore potential sources of contamination for children's reports, and interview the first person with whom the child discussed the alleged abuse ("first confidante" or "outcry witness").

The need for specialized training is certain, but we must ensure that curricula are updated on a regular basis to reflect recent developments in our empirically based understanding of children's memory and suggestibility. Training, much like the research it draws upon, must be an ongoing process subject to constant revision and improvement. Audiotaping or video recording all forensic interviews of children is essential to creating an objective record of the child's statements and interviewer's questions; however, we must keep two things in mind. First, audio or visual records of an interview are only as good as the interview itself. Sloppy or improper questioning provides the defense attorney solid grounds to object to the interview's admissibility at trial or, if admitted, provides the defense attorney ample ammunition to attack the interviewer (and child victim) on cross-examination. Second, when forensic interviews are videotaped, camera operators must be sure that the child, interviewer, and any one else present in the room all appear on film. Basic research on what social psychologists have termed the "fundamental attribution error" (Jones & Harris, 1967) suggests that when determining causes for a person's behavior, we tend to overestimate internal or dispositional factors and underestimate the power of the situation. This tendency can be influenced by perceptual focus; that is, using a camera angle that includes all of the actors present can increase observers' awareness of the situational factors that impinge on the child's behavior (Storms, 1973). This may be particularly significant in cases in which children appear nervous or distracted; attributing the cause of this behavior to the individual child ("She is lying") versus the situation ("It must be very intimidating to answer such personal questions in front of strangers") can lead to dramatically different outcomes (for related research on videotaped confessions, see Lassiter et al., 2005).

Wood and colleagues' third and fourth recommendations—identifying and interviewing sources of potential contamination—are spot-on. In my experience as a legal consultant and expert witness, I have found that most forensic interviews of children by trained professionals are conducted relatively well with very few egregious errors. Instead, exposure to potentially contaminating information or the pressure to allege abuse often arises at home from siblings, neighbors, or parents long before the child is ever interviewed in a formal forensic context. For these reasons, background work is necessary to identify potential threats to the accuracy of children's reports.

Saywitz and Camparo (Chapter 6) echo many of the same sentiments as Wood et al., but their scope of analysis extends beyond the daycare cases, and they rely on a more holistic approach to frame their recommendations. The authors argue that, although advances in questioning techniques and infrastructure related to forensic interviews are plentiful, new paradigms are needed to ensure that we (1) broaden our conceptualization of the information-gathering process to better reflect the multiple systems that child victims are involved in simultaneously; (2) move beyond "getting the facts" to ensure that children's voices are heard on a wider range of legal issues; (3) meet child victims' mental health needs through appropriate therapy and counseling without tainting the quality of their reports; (4) promote children's well-being and optimal development; and (5) implement prevention and early intervention programs for abuse and mental health problems.

Although this chapter is abundantly rich with insight and practical applications, I focus on two points in particular. Saywitz and Camparo's recommendation that we need to reconceptualize the information-gathering process with child victims is nothing short of revolutionary and, in my opinion, transcends the issue of interviewing alone. Our piecemeal approach to children's victimization and legal involvement, although necessary to some degree, has meant that we have often failed as researchers and practitioners to see the forest for the trees. From the moment a child alleges or is questioned about maltreatment, every event that follows is, like dominoes, unavoidably linked to what came before and what follows. Interviews influence children's accuracy. Perceived accuracy affects whether charges are filed. Children's testimonial behavior influences jurors' verdicts. Case outcomes influence children's short- and long-term well-being. We must remind ourselves that the forensic- and mental health-related issues that accompany child maltreatment are not independent; they intersect and affect one another throughout this entire process. Ignoring this reality and, more important, failing to act on it undermine our efforts to serve child victims effectively.

Saywitz and Camparo also discuss the need for future research to tease apart the various elements of rapport-building protocols to determine their individual effects on children's memory and disclosure. I agree and would go a step further by saying that researchers need to better differentiate rapport from support in their research designs. As defined by *American Heritage Dictionary,* rapport is "a relationship, especially one of mutual trust or affinity" and support is the act of "aiding the cause, policy, or interests of." In this sense, rapport is interactive (something that is built or shared between two people), whereas support is more transitive and unidirectional (something that is provided by one person to another). Some studies that have examined the effects of interviewers' supportive behaviors (e.g., smiling, maintaining eye contact, using a warm voice tone, using relaxed and open body posture; Almerigogna, Ost, Bull, & Akehurst, 2007; Carter, Bottoms, & Levine, 1996) also have included behaviors designed to facilitate rapport (e.g., having the interviewer introduce him- or herself at the beginning of the interview). When "supported" children in these studies are more resistant to misleading information than control children, two questions arise: (1) What is driving the observed effects: support or rapport? (2) If support is the answer, are all the supportive behaviors required or only some or one?

More recent research has begun to break down interviews into more isolated behaviors, for example, "smiling" for supportive and "fidgeting" for nonsupportive (Almerigogna, Ost, Akehurst, & Fluck, 2008). Children questioned by the smiling interviewer in that study were more accurate and less likely to falsely report having been touched than those interviewed by the fidgeting interviewer. With respect to rapport, research by Roberts, Lamb, and Sternberg (2004) compared procedures designed to establish rapport with alleged victims using either open-ended questions (e.g., "Tell me about yourself") or direct, focused questions (e.g., "How old are you?") and found that children in the open-ended rapport-building condition were more accurate than children in the direct rapport-building condition after both short and long delays. Additional studies such as these are needed to identify specific elements of supportive interviewing and rapport building that either alone or in concert work to reduce children's suggestibility and increase their accuracy.

## CHILDREN IN COURT

Quas, Cooper, and Wandrey's chapter on child victims in dependency court (Chapter 7) represents a welcome addition to the existing literature on children's involvement in the legal system. As the authors point out, the paucity of research on this topic is quite surprising given the critical role that dependency courts play in protecting children's well-being and rendering judgments that directly influence children and their families. These characteristics, in conjunction with the significant number of children who become involved in legal proceedings after Child Protective Services has substantiated abuse or neglect (18,100 in 2006; U.S. Department of Health and Human Services, 2008), demonstrate the urgent need to learn more about children's experiences in dependency court as well as in criminal court.

What does this nascent body of research tell us? Much like children in criminal court, children in dependency court do not sufficiently understand key legal concepts and the nature of decisions being rendered in their cases (Quas, Wallin, Horwitz, Davis, & Lyon, 2009). Children's legal knowledge has been shown to improve with age (Flin, Stevenson, & Davies, 1989), yet prior contact or involvement with the legal system does not predict (or in some cases is negatively related to) children's understanding of that system (Freshwater & Aldridge, 1994; Saywitz, Jaenicke, & Camparo, 1990). Although important in their own right, these findings are directly relevant to the arguments Quas et al. review in favor of children's increased involvement in dependency proceedings. One cannot deny that some children desire to participate more actively in their cases and that doing so may lead to more positive outcomes in terms of both case resolution and psychological adjustment. At the same time, however, one must question the extent to which the observed deficits in children's legal knowledge and understanding of their cases might attenuate these positive outcomes or perhaps in some cases even exacerbate negative outcomes. Is it realistic to expect a child who does not sufficiently comprehend key legal terminology or the purpose and possible outcome of his or her case to participate in a meaningful and constructive way? I am inclined to think not, unless such involvement is accompanied by efforts to educate children better about the legal system generally and their cases specifically. These efforts may include pretrial preparation programs or support persons who provide children the information they lack.

Troxel, Ogle, Cordon, Lawler, and Goodman (Chapter 8) take us from dependency court to criminal court by examining the effects of children's participation in criminal cases and recent efforts to accommodate children's testimony without infringing on defendants' constitutional rights. The authors review research indicating that being involved in criminal proceedings often, but not always, is associated with negative psychological outcomes. Not surprisingly, children are fearful and intimidated by certain aspects of testifying in court such as cross-examination by opposing counsel and facing the defendant in open court. However, the increased stress associated with children's courtroom testimony appears to dissipate over time, and at least one longitudinal study suggests that children who did not testify were no more maladjusted than those who did testify approximately 12 years earlier (Quas, Goodman, et al., 2005).

Several evidentiary and procedural innovations have been introduced in the United States (as reviewed by Troxel et al.) and abroad (as reviewed by Bussey in Chapter 11) to help facilitate children's testimony in criminal cases. Such innovations include, but are not limited to, the use of hearsay exceptions, videotaped testimony, and closed-circuit television (CCTV). Despite the admirable goals of these efforts to reduce children's stress and increase their accuracy, much of the legislation permitting these innovations was enacted in the late 1980s before a solid body of empirical research had taken shape. In this sense, legislators advocating for child victims put the cart before the horse and in doing so placed social scientists in the precarious position of having to defend the use of such procedures before knowing exactly how they affected children and defendants. Consider, for example, the use of CCTV. In 1990, the U.S. Supreme Court heard the case of *Maryland v. Craig,* in which the defendant argued that broadcasting a child witness's testimony from outside the courtroom via one-way CCTV violated his Sixth Amendment right to confrontation. The American Psychological Association filed an amicus curiae, or "friend of the court," brief concluding in part that child sexual abuse victims may be particularly vulnerable to distress in the legal system, especially when forced to confront the defendant in open court. The brief cited a handful of studies, many of which had not been subjected to the rigors of peer review and did not directly address the legal issues raised in the *Craig* case.

Why is this specific example and our general "cart-before-the-horse" tendency troubling? Because subsequent research by Goodman and colleagues (1998) revealed that CCTV use reduces children's stress and suggestibility without unfair prejudice against the defendant yet also decreases children's perceived credibility in the eyes of jurors. One reason for this unanticipated and undesirable effect may be that CCTV mutes the emotional impact of children's testimony by eliminating many of the verbal and nonverbal features that jurors expect victims of sexual abuse to display while testifying. Attorneys in a study by Kovera, Gresham, Borgida, Gray, and Regan (1997) indicated that prepared child witnesses tend to be confident, maintain eye contact, and keep their emotions under control. If these behaviors generalize to other accommodations, it would appear that they are directly at odds with how jurors expect child sexual abuse victims to behave. To investigate this possibility, McAuliff, Maurice, Neal, and Diaz (2008) measured jurors' expectancies for children's testimonial behavior and then systematically confirmed or violated these expectancies in the child's simulated sexual abuse testimony. They observed that when the child's nonverbal behavior violated jurors' expectancies (i.e., she did not cry, was not nervous, and maintained eye contact), jurors perceived the child witness to be less credible than when she confirmed these expectancies. Thus, it is possible that introducing the use of innovative procedures with children, although effective at reducing stress and suggestibility, may undermine their credibility at trial. Should this be the case, attorneys may wish to reserve the use of such innovations for instances of extreme abuse or when the child victim cannot otherwise testify.

It is also clear that social scientists need to expand the scope of their research to include innovations that are used more frequently than CCTV or hearsay exceptions. Surveys indicate that U.S. attorneys are reluctant to use CCTV with children for fear of harming the case or providing grounds for a defense challenge or appeal (Goodman, Quas, Bulkley, & Shapiro, 1999; Hafemeister, 1996). The use of hearsay exceptions, although more common than CCTV and equally well studied, may become a less viable alternative for child witnesses because of a recent landmark decision by the U.S. Supreme Court in *Crawford v. Washington* (2004). In *Crawford*, the Court held that "testimonial" hearsay is inadmissible at trial unless the defendant has the opportunity to cross-examine the victim, regardless of the quality of the statement. Some courts have held that children's statements during a forensic interview constitute testimonial hearsay (e.g., *State v. Kennedy*, 2007; *Williams v. State*, 2007) and thus require children to appear in court for cross-examination for their statements to be admitted at trial.

My students and I have initiated one such program of research in our laboratory to examine the use and perception of support persons in cases involving child victims. We have learned from a national survey of victim-witness assistants (VWAs) that support person use is quite common with children of all ages, particularly in cases involving child abuse and adult domestic violence and to a much lesser degree in divorce and custody cases. Prosecution-based VWAs and parents/guardians typically serve as support persons and tend to provide more informational (e.g., referrals to community resources, courtroom visit/orientation, procedural information) than emotional (e.g., comforting the child, accompanying child to hearings) support to children (McAuliff, Nicholson, Amarilio, & Ravanshenas, 2008). In a separate but related study, we simply varied the presence versus absence of a support person who sat next to the child during her simulated courtroom testimony and found that jurors perceived the child to be less trustworthy when she was accompanied by a support person than when she testified alone (Nefas, Neal, Maurice, & McAuliff, 2008). Thus, we are once again reminded of the unforeseen dangers of implementing innovative procedures with child victims when actual (versus anticipated) effects are unknown.

## EXPERT TESTIMONY

Myers provides an excellent road map for how psychological research and clinical experience find their way into court through expert testimony in child sexual abuse cases. Perhaps one of the most valuable lessons to be learned from this chapter is to understand the evidentiary framework within which experts who wish to testify and attorneys who seek their testimony must operate. Judges' determinations regarding the admissibility of expert evidence are based on legal precedent (*Daubert v. Merrell Dow Pharmaceuticals, Inc.,* 1993; *Frye v. United States,* 1923) and evidentiary standards involving the relevance, probativeness, and helpfulness of the expert's testimony.

With this framework in mind, we can see the value of expert testimony on specific issues related to defendants accused of sexual abuse (competence to stand trial, sexual offender profiles, sentencing) and child victims (testimonial competence, interview quality, need for accommodation). At the same time, however, we must not overlook the potential value of more general social framework testimony to assist jurors' decision making in cases involving child sexual abuse. Social framework testimony relies on general conclusions from a body of social scientific research that are presented in court to aid in the determination of factual issues in a specific case (Monahan & Walker, 1991). One type of social framework testimony relevant to child sexual abuse cases is testimony describing findings from the witness suggestibility literature. Some courts have ruled that such testimony is inadmissible because it fails to exceed jurors' common understanding and, therefore, cannot improve their decision making (*People v. Johnston,* 2000; *Wright v. State,* 1998). However, recent research suggests that jurors do not necessarily "know what isn't so" about child witnesses (Quas, Thompson, & Clarke-Stewart, 2005) and that expert testimony can, in fact, tell jurors something "they don't already know" about witness suggestibility (McAuliff & Kovera, 2007) and the negative effects of yes–no questions on the accuracy of children's reports (Laimon & Poole, 2008).

For example, McAuliff and Kovera (2007) found that laypeople do not sufficiently understand certain factors that influence witness suggestibility, such as age, interviewer authority, and event detail centrality. Those researchers asked jurors, college students, and experts to estimate the effects of misleading information on witnesses of different ages across various witnessing conditions. Compared with experts, laypeople underestimated the size of suggestibility differences between preschoolers versus older children and adults. Both jurors and college students lacked knowledge about how event detail centrality (central vs. peripheral), level of witness participation in the to-be-remembered event (actively participated vs. observed), and source prestige (high- vs. low-authority interviewer) can moderate the effects of misleading information on witness accuracy. Of particular interest, laypeople reported that they were largely unfamiliar with witness suggestibility research and that expert testimony on that topic would be helpful to them. Similar deficits in suggestibility-related knowledge were observed by Quas et al. (2005) and Laimon and Poole (2008) as well. Taken together, these findings should help attorneys argue successfully against objections to witness suggestibility expert testimony on the grounds that it will be unhelpful.

Demonstrating that jurors do not sufficiently understand witness suggestibility or some other topic relevant to child sexual abuse cases is only half the battle. Attorneys and experts must also ensure that the proffered testimony "is sufficiently tied to the facts of the case that it will aid the jury in resolving a factual dispute" (*Daubert v. Merrell Dow Pharmaceuticals, Inc.*, 1993, pp. 2795–2796). This requirement can best be described as one of "fit" between the expert's research and the facts of the case in which the expert wishes to testify (Lyon, 2002). Here, once again, we can realize the value of social framework testimony. By relying on a large body of scientific work to draw conclusions, an expert increases the likelihood that his or her testimony will fit the facts of a specific case. Referring once again to our witness suggestibility example, any attorney would be hard-pressed to argue that certain factors such as age, interviewer authority, repeated questioning, or the use of yes–no questions are not present in a case involving child sexual abuse allegations. The challenge remains for experts and attorneys to work together in drafting motions that highlight the specific nexus between the relevant research and case facts. Moreover, getting jurors to connect the two during trial may require the use of more concrete forms of testimony such as the use of hypothetical scenarios that mirror the case facts and allow the expert to offer an opinion based on the relevant research (see Kovera et al., 1997).

Experts and attorneys must also be careful not to overlook the probative versus prejudicial balance test when arguing for testimony in court. Essentially, the probative value of proffered evidence cannot be substantially outweighed by its potential to unfairly prejudice, confuse, or mislead the jury (Federal Rules of Evidence [FRE], Rule 403). One way social scientists in the eyewitness identification literature (e.g., Cutler, Penrod, & Dexter, 1989) have addressed this issue is to examine whether expert testimony on certain factors known to influence eyewitness accuracy *sensitizes* jurors to the presence or absence of those factors in the witnessing conditions of the particular case. This essentially speaks to the probativeness of the expert testimony or its ability to establish other facts (namely, that certain factors present in the case may have influenced the witness's memory). Alternatively, the expert testimony may create *skepticism,* in which case jurors disregard all eyewitness testimony, or *optimism,* in which case jurors accept all eyewitness testimony irrespective of its relation to the specific factors present or absent in the witnessing conditions of the case. Skepticism or optimism effects would support objections that the expert testimony unfairly prejudices, confuses, or misleads jurors.

We have conducted related work in our lab to determine whether expert testimony educates and sensitizes jurors to factors influencing witness suggestibility (McAuliff, Ainsworth, & Nicholson, 2008). Jury-eligible citizens read a sexual abuse trial in which expert testimony (none, standard, hypothetical, or repetitive), interview suggestiveness (high, low), and victim age (5, 10, or 15 years) varied. In the high interview suggestiveness condition, the victim was questioned by an authoritative source about peripheral event details; in the low interview suggestiveness condition, she was not. Expert testimony educated jurors about differences in witness suggestibility related to age, interviewer authority, and event detail centrality. However, this knowledge did not influence other trial-related judgments, even when the expert supplemented his testimony by discussing the suggestibility of a hypothetical child interviewed in conditions that were identical to the actual case jurors were deciding. In other words, even though expert testimony on witness suggestibility was not prejudicial, neither was it particularly helpful in enabling jurors to render appropriate trial-related decisions.

## JUROR DECISION MAKING

All of the issues relevant to children's active and effective participation in legal proceedings discussed thus far culminate in several extremely difficult questions that jurors must decide: Is the child victim telling the truth? Can the child accurately recall what happened? Is the defendant guilty of child sexual abuse? Golding, Dunlap, and Hodell (Chapter 10) provide an integral review of the empirical literature on the various factors that influence jurors' perceptions of child victim testimony. One of the most consistent findings to emerge can be summed up in two simple words: Gender matters! Time and time again, researchers have observed that women are more likely than men to show a pro-victim/pro-prosecution bias in their judgments, particularly in child sexual abuse cases. This bias is evinced by more guilty verdicts and enhanced believability of child witnesses for women versus men jurors. Golding, Bradshaw, Dunlap, and Hodell's (2007) experiment examining the effects of mock jury gender composition on deliberations and conviction rates in a sexual abuse case is extremely telling: Woman-majority juries convicted most often, and men on woman-majority juries changed their individual verdicts to guilty more often than men on men-majority juries.

What implications do these findings have for researchers and legal professionals? Researchers should include gender as an independent variable when examining juror decision making in child sexual abuse trial simulations. Moreover, the verdict shifts that occurred during jury deliberations in Golding et al.'s (2007) study suggest that incorporating jury deliberations into experimental research is a must if we wish to understand fully the myriad factors that influence jurors' decisions in child sexual abuse cases.

With respect to legal practice, these results beg the question of whether prosecutors and defense attorneys should use their peremptory ("freebie" or unjustified) challenges to strike jurors from the venire based on their gender. In principle, the answer is "no," but in practice the answer may be less clear. In 1994 the U.S. Supreme Court heard the case of *J.E.B v. Alabama,* which presented the legal question of whether the Equal Protection Clause of the Constitution forbids intentional discrimination on the basis of gender in peremptory challenges. The Court answered in the affirmative, emphasizing that "equal opportunity to participate in the fair administration of justice is fundamental to our democratic system ... When persons are excluded from participation in our democratic processes solely because of race or gender, this promise of equality dims, and the integrity of our judicial system is jeopardized" (pp. 145–146). In light of this ruling, attorneys should not use peremptory challenges to remove jurors from the venire solely on the basis of gender. Recent research by Norton, Sommers, and Brauner (2007), however, indicates that individuals do, in fact, rely on gender when making peremptory challenge decisions and often provide gender-neutral explanations to justify their decisions. Even worse, explicit warnings against using gender to strike potential jurors failed to attenuate the gender bias and actually led individuals to provide even more elaborate justifications for their decisions. Attorneys must resist this temptation and challenge their adversaries who appear to be using gender to strike jurors during jury selection in cases involving child victims. Similarly, judges must be aware of this strategy and realize that it may be operating even when attorneys provide gender-neutral justifications for their strikes.

Golding et al. also discuss prosecuting attorneys' use of a defendant's criminal history in child sexual abuse cases. Historically, the American judicial system has barred the introduction of prior misconduct to prove a defendant's guilt, character, or propensity to commit a crime, even though such evidence was sometimes admitted for other narrow purposes such as proof of motive, opportunity, or intent (Waltz & Park, 1999). The rationale behind excluding such evidence was that a defendant should be tried on the merits of the case at hand and not on prior behavior. In 1975, this common-law rule was codified in FRE Rule 404(b). Nearly 20 years after this rule was enacted, Congress passed the Violent Crime Control and Law Enforcement Act of 1994, which included controversial FRE Rules 413 and 414. In stark contrast to the common-law tradition and Rule 404(b), the new rules declared that evidence of a defendant's prior misconduct (including that for which the defendant was neither charged nor convicted) was admissible in criminal cases involving sexual assault and child molestation. To be admitted, a trial judge must rule that a jury could reasonably find by a "preponderance of the evidence" (more likely than not) that the defendant committed the alleged prior act. Opponents of the new rules argued that introducing alleged prior misconduct would compromise defendants' presumed innocence and would be extremely prejudicial given people's visceral, punitive reactions to sexual crimes. Supporters, including David Karp (1994), who authored the new rules, cited the probative versus prejudicial balance test of FRE Rule 403 as a safeguard for defendants' rights.

Although the FRE bind federal courts only, several states have turned to Rules 413 and 414 when drafting similar legislation. For example, in 1995 California amended its evidence code by adding Section 1108 to permit the admission of a defendant's alleged prior sexual misconduct in criminal proceedings involving sexual offenses. Section 1108 received a great deal of publicity in the Michael Jackson trial (*State of California v. Michael Jackson*, 2004) when the judge admitted testimony from several witnesses who claimed they saw Jackson engage in inappropriate physical contact with young boys years earlier. In 1997, Arizona codified a similar exception (Rule 404c) to its evidence rule that had previously prohibited the use of relevant character evidence in sexual misconduct cases.

It is critical to question the role psychological science can play in providing empirical answers to questions raised by Rules 413 and 414. What effects, if any, does the admission of prior misconduct have on jurors' decisions in child sexual abuses cases? Work by Bottoms and Goodman (1994) revealed that mock jurors who received the defendant's criminal history and other negative character evidence provided higher ratings of victim credibility and defendant guilt than those who did not receive this information. Should these findings replicate in other studies, we must begin to explore what legal safeguards can be implemented to minimize or eliminate these effects. Empirical studies of how variations in the legal status of the defendant's prior misconduct (i.e., alleged, charged, or convicted) affect jurors' decisions also would be instructive.

## BEYOND THE STATES

Bussey's Chapter 11 is international in scope and serves as a fitting reminder that social scientists in the United States must be careful to avoid an ethnocentric or "adversarial system only" bias when examining child victims. Undeniably, children's status in legal proceedings is limited by jurisdiction-specific rules and practices; however, the need to better understand child victims and advocate on their behalves is not. Social scientists must develop research agendas that target specific reform at the jurisdictional level while being mindful of more general research on the cognitive, social, and developmental factors that influence children's capabilities in legal settings. This ever-expanding body of knowledge draws on the collective efforts of the international scientific community. The same can be said for legislators, judges, and attorneys: There is much to be learned by examining how other jurisdictions (both within the United States and abroad) have confronted the challenges that child victims and witnesses pose for traditional legal process. These lessons will prove fruitful not only in how laws are created and refined but in whether they are implemented effectively as well. After all, even the most perfectly crafted, scientifically informed legislation is impotent if law enforcement and legal personnel are unaware it exists or do not understand how it affects their routine interactions with children. Specialized training and continuing education almost certainly will be required to bridge this gap between law and practice.

Bussey also argues that efforts to advance legal reform for child victims cannot be limited to countries with laws and systems already firmly in place. Without a doubt, there is great room for improvement in the common-law jurisdictions of the West and the civil-law jurisdictions of Europe; however, other countries such as Asia and Africa are deficient in more fundamental ways that must not be overlooked by the global community. Crimes against children cannot be redressed properly if adequate channels and mechanisms for the reporting of maltreatment do not exist. For children in such unfortunate circumstances, frankly much, if not all, of the scholarly wisdom contained in this book is irrelevant because they do not have an established path to justice. Social scientists, legal professionals, and practitioners must work together with these countries in a culturally sensitive way to help ensure that such paths are created and that children are given a voice to speak out against the crimes they endure. Bussey's acknowledgment of this problem represents a crucial first step in this process, and now journal editors and conference organizers must continue the movement by creating opportunities for increased collaboration between scientific and legal communities worldwide.

## CONCLUSION

It is clear that recent developments in child victim research have yielded a wealth of new insight regarding disclosure, interviewing, memory, testimony, and juror decision making. Armed with this knowledge, social scientists and legal professionals must continue to work together to ensure that children are able to participate actively and effectively in maltreatment proceedings. This process is inherently arduous and in all likelihood definitive answers and simple solutions will continue to elude us. Yet we must not let adversity steer us from our course. With renewed spirits, steadfast dedication, and continued research, we can make the difference in maltreated children's lives that they so desperately need and deserve.

## REFERENCES

Almerigogna, J., Ost, J., Bull, R., & Akehurst, L. (2007). A state of high anxiety: How non-supportive interviewers can increase the suggestibility of child witnesses. *Applied Cognitive Psychology, 21,* 963–974.

Almerigogna, J., Ost, J., Akehurst, L., & Fluck, M. (2008). How interviewers' nonverbal behaviors can affect children's perceptions and suggestibility. *Journal of Experimental Child Psychology, 100,* 17–39.

Bottoms, B. L., & Goodman, G. S. (1994). Perceptions of children's credibility in sexual assault cases. *Journal of Applied Social Psychology, 24,* 702–732.

Carter, C. A., Bottoms, B. L., & Levine, M. (1996). Linguistic and socioemotional influences on the accuracy of children's reports. *Law and Human Behavior, 20,* 335–358.

Crawford v. Washington, 124 S.Ct. 1354 (2004).

Cutler, B. L., Penrod, S. D., & Dexter, H. R. (1989). The eyewitness, the expert psychologist, and the jury. *Law and Human Behavior, 13,* 311–322.

Daubert v. Merrell Dow Pharmaceuticals, Inc., 113 S.Ct. 2786 (1993).

Dickinson, J. J., Del Russo, J. A., & D'Urso, A. (2008, March). *Children's disclosure of sex abuse: A new approach to answering elusive questions.* Paper presented at the annual meeting of the American Psychology-Law Society, Jacksonville, FL.

Flin, R. H., Stevenson, Y., & Davies, G. M. (1989). Children's knowledge of court proceedings. *British Journal of Psychology, 80,* 285–297.

Freshwater, K., & Aldridge, J. (1994). The knowledge and fears about court of child witnesses, school children, and adults. *Child Abuse Review, 3,* 183–195.

Frye v. United States, 293 F. 1013 (1923).

Golding, J. M., Bradshaw, G. S., Dunlap, E. E., & Hodell, E. C. (2007). The impact of mock jury gender composition on deliberations and conviction rates in a child sexual assault trial. *Child Maltreatment, 12,* 182–190.

Goodman, G. S., & Bottoms, B. L. (Eds.). (1993). *Child victims, child witnesses: Understanding and improving testimony.* New York: Guilford Press.

Goodman, G. S., Quas, J. A., Bulkley, J., & Shapiro, C. (1999). Innovations for child witnesses: A national survey. *Psychology, Public Policy, and Law, 5,* 255–281.

Goodman, G. S., Tobey, A. E., Batterman-Faunce, J. M., Orcutt, H. K., Thomas, S., Shapiro, C., et al. (1998). Face-to-face confrontation: Effects of closed-circuit technology on children's eyewitness testimony and jurors' decisions. *Law and Human Behavior, 22,* 165–203.

Hafemeister, T. L. (1996). Protecting child witnesses: Judicial efforts to minimize trauma and reduce evidentiary barriers. *Violence and Victims, 11,* 71–91.

J.E.B v. Alabama, 511 U.S. 127 (1994).

Jones, E. E., & Harris, V. A. (1967). The attribution of attitudes. *Journal of Experimental Social Psychology, 3,* 1–24.

Karp, D. J. (1994). Symposium on the admission of prior offense evidence in sexual assault cases: Evidence of propensity and probability in sex offense and other cases. *Chicago-Kent Law Review, 70,* 15–34.

Kovera, M. B., Gresham, A. W., Borgida, E., Gray, E., & Regan, P. C. (1997). Does expert psychological testimony inform or influence juror decision making? A social cognitive analysis. *Journal of Applied Psychology, 82,* 178–191.

Laimon, R. L., & Poole, D. A. (2008). Adults usually believe young children: The influence of eliciting questions and suggestibility presentations on perceptions of children's disclosures. *Law and Human Behavior, 32,* 489–501.

Lassiter, G. D., Munhall, P. J., Berger, I. P., Weiland, P., Handley, I. M., & Geers, A. L. (2005). Attributional complexity and the camera perspective bias in videotaped confessions. *Basic and Applied Social Psychology, 27,* 27–35.

Loftus, E. F., & Davis, D. (2006). Recovered memories. *Annual Review of Clinical Psychology, 2,* 469–498.

Lyon, T. D. (2002). Expert testimony of the suggestibility of children: Does it fit? In B. L. Bottoms, M. B. Kovera, & B. D. McAuliff (Eds.), *Children, social science, and the law* (pp. 378–411). New York: Cambridge University Press.

Maryland v. Craig, 497 U.S. 836 (1990).

McAuliff, B. D., Ainsworth, A., & Nicholson, E. (2008, March). "You can lead a horse to water, but … " Expert testimony, witness suggestibility, and juror decisions. In J. A. Buck & K. London (Chairs), *Expert testimony relating to child witnesses: When does it have probative value for jurors?* Symposium conducted at the meeting of the American Psychology-Law Society, Jacksonville, FL.

McAuliff, B. D., & Kovera, M. B. (2007). Estimating the effects of misleading information on witness accuracy: Can experts tell jurors something they don't already know? *Applied Cognitive Psychology, 21,* 849–870.

McAuliff, B. D., Maurice, K. A., Neal, E. S., & Diaz, A. (2008, March). *"She should have been more upset . . . ": Expectancy violation theory and jurors' perceptions of child victims.* Paper presented at the annual meeting of the American Psychology-Law Society, Jacksonville, FL.

McAuliff, B. D., Nicholson, E., Amarilio, D., & Ravanshenas, D. (2008). *Supporting children in U.S. legal proceedings: Descriptive data from a national survey of victim/witness assistants.* Manuscript submitted for publication.

Monahan, J., & Walker, L. (1991). Judicial use of social science research. *Law and Human Behavior, 15,* 571–584.

Nefas, C., Neal, E. S., Maurice, K. A., & McAuliff, B. D. (2008, March). *Support person use and child victim testimony: Believe it or not.* Paper presented at the annual meeting of the American Psychology-Law Society, Jacksonville, FL.

Norton, M. I., Sommers, S. R., & Brauner, S. (2007). Bias in jury selection: Justifying prohibited in peremptory challenges. *Journal of Behavioral Decision Making, 20,* 467–479.

People v. Timothy Johnston, 273 A.D.2d 514 (3rd Dept, 2000).

Pezdek, K., Finger, K., & Hodge, D. (1997) Planting false childhood memories: The role of event plausibility. *Psychological Science, 8,* 437–441.

Pezdek, K., & Hodge, D. (1999). Planting false childhood memories in children: The role of event plausibility. *Child Development, 70,* 887–895.

Quas, J. A., Goodman, G. S., Ghetti, S., Alexander, K. W., Edelstein, R. S., Redlich, A. D., et al. (2005). Childhood sexual assault victims: Long-term outcomes after testifying in criminal court. *Monograph of the Society for Research in Child Development, 70*(Serial No. 280).

Quas, J. A., Thompson, W. C., & Clarke-Stewart, K. A. (2005). Do jurors "know" what isn't so about child witnesses? *Law and Human Behavior, 29,* 425–456.

Quas, J. A., Wallin, A. R., Horwitz, B., Davis, E. L., & Lyon, T. D. (2009). Maltreated children's understanding of and emotional reactions to dependency court involvement. *Behavioral Sciences and the Law, 27,* 97–117.

Roberts, K. P., Lamb, M. E., & Sternberg, K. J. (2004). The effects of rapport-building style on children's reports of a staged event. *Applied Cognitive Psychology, 18,* 189–202.

Saywitz, K. J., Jaenicke, C., & Camparo, L. B. (1990). Children's knowledge of legal terminology. *Law and Human Behavior, 14,* 523–535.

State of California v. Michael Jackson, Superior Court No. 1133603 (2004).

State v. Kennedy, 957 So.2d 757, 2005-1981 (La. 2007).

Storms, M. D. (1973). Videotape and the attribution process: Reversing actors' and observers' points of view. *Journal of Personality and Social Psychology, 27,* 165–175.

U.S. Department of Health and Human Services. (2009). *Child maltreatment 2007*. Washington, DC: U.S. Government Printing Office.

Waltz, J. R., & Park, R. C. (1999). *Evidence: Cases and materials* (9th ed.). New York: Foundation Press.

Williams v. State, 970 So.2d 727 (Miss. App. Sep 4, 2007).

Wright v. State, 233 Ga. App. 358 (1998).

# PART II

## CHILDREN AS OFFENDERS

# Chapter 13

# How Victims Become Offenders

CATHY SPATZ WIDOM
HELEN W. WILSON

Child maltreatment represents a serious social problem confronting our society. During fiscal year 2005, approximately 3.6 million cases of suspected child abuse or neglect were investigated in the United States, and 899,000 children were determined to be victims of abuse or neglect (U.S. Department of Health and Human Services, 2007). The same report estimated that 1,460 children died from a child maltreatment-related cause (U.S. Department of Health and Human Services, 2007). Although the accuracy of these estimates of the extent of child abuse and neglect and the criteria for defining various forms of maltreatment continue to be debated (Feerick, Knutson, Trickett, & Flanzer, 2006), it is clear that large numbers of children are victims of maltreatment. Moreover, knowledge about the effects of child abuse and neglect is mounting and underscores the significance of this social problem.

One of the most common assumptions in the scholarly and popular literature refers to a "cycle of violence," whereby abused children become abusers and victims of violence become violent victimizers. This theory may have first been articulated by Curtis (1963) in a brief clinical note entitled "Violence Breeds Violence—Perhaps?," expressing concern that abused and neglected children would "become tomorrow's murderers and perpetrators of other crimes of violence, if they survive" (p. 386). Since then, numerous studies have sought to answer the question, What happens to victims of child abuse and neglect if they survive?

Through the 1980s, writers concluded that evidence for the cycle of violence had not really "passed scientific muster" (Garbarino & Gilliam, 1980). In 1989, Widom wrote that conclusions about the strength of the cycle of violence needed to be tempered by the dearth of convincing empirical evidence and methodological problems limiting confidence in the link between child maltreatment and subsequent violent behavior (Widom, 1989b). The most significant of these methodological limitations were the reliance on cross-sectional designs, ambiguous definitions of abuse and neglect, and lack of control or comparison groups of nonabused and non-neglected children. Since that time, however, researchers have attempted to address many of the limitations inherent in earlier work. The relationship between childhood victimization and juvenile offending is now well recognized in the fields of child development, mental health, and criminal justice. This chapter presents the current state of knowledge about the relationship between childhood victimization and juvenile offending and examines some of the potential mechanisms whereby abused and neglected children develop from child victims into child and adolescent offenders.

## FROM CHILD VICTIM TO CHILD OFFENDER: EMPIRICAL EVIDENCE

Six large prospective investigations in different parts of the United States have now documented a relationship between childhood abuse and neglect and juvenile delinquency. The first study was conducted in a metropolitan county in the Midwest using cases of child maltreatment that came to the attention of the courts from 1967 through 1971. Children (ages 0–11 years) with substantiated cases of childhood abuse or neglect were matched with a control group of children of the same age, sex, race, and approximate social class (Widom, 1989a), and both groups were followed up approximately 25 years later through examination of official criminal records (Maxfield & Widom, 1996; Widom, 1989a). Findings indicated that child abuse and neglect increased the risk of arrest as a juvenile by 55% and increased the risk of committing a violent crime as a juvenile by 96%.

The Midwest study (Maxfield & Widom, 1996; Widom, 1989a) also found that child abuse and neglect were associated with earlier onset of juvenile crime. Abused and neglected children were first arrested about a year earlier than those in the comparison group and were more likely to become recidivists and chronic offenders. As shown in Figure 13.1, the abused and neglected children diverged from their matched peers at a very young age (as early as 8–9 years) and continued to have a higher prevalence of crime in adulthood.

A second investigation of this relationship involved a cohort of youth

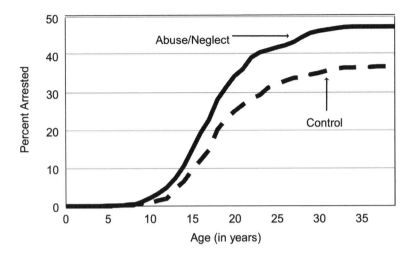

**FIGURE 13.1.** Percentage of individuals ever arrested for nontraffic offenses by age in the abuse and neglect and control groups. From Widom (2006). Reprinted with permission from the author.

recruited from public schools in Rochester, New York. As part of the Rochester Youth Development Study, a longitudinal study of the causes and correlates of crime and delinquency, Smith and Thornberry (1995) collected records of child abuse and neglect (through age 12) from the county Department of Social Services. These investigators extended prior research by comparing official arrest records with youths' self-reports of delinquency. Compared with those without records of maltreatment, the abused and neglected children were more likely to have arrest records, had more arrests, and reported more frequent delinquent activity at approximately age 17.

Mecklenburg County, North Carolina, was the site of the third study addressing the child maltreatment—delinquency connection. Zingraff, Leiter, Myers, and Johnsen (1993) recruited children with substantiated cases of abuse and neglect and two comparison samples: a general school sample and an impoverished sample recruited through the county Department of Social Services. Similar to the findings described earlier in this chapter, results of this study indicated that maltreated children had more arrests for delinquency (at approximately age 15) than both comparison samples. Compared with the school sample (but not the impoverished sample), the maltreated youth also had a higher rate of arrests for violence. However, these relationships were diminished, although not eliminated, when the authors controlled for demographic and family structure variables.

The fourth study (English, Widom, & Brandford, 2002), designed as a replication and extension of Widom's original Midwest study, was based on a cohort of abused and neglected children in the Northwest region of the United States. This study represents a different time period (1980–1985) and includes different ethnic backgrounds (Native Americans in addition to European Americans and African Americans) than the Midwest study. Substantiated cases of child abuse and neglect from court dependency records were selected from court records in a large urban area of Washington State. A matched control group of children was identified on the basis of age, race/ethnicity, gender, and approximate family social class. The dependent children in this study represent a subset of abused and neglected children, whose cases were substantiated and for whom there was sufficient evidence to remove them from home. Abused and neglected children were 4.8 times more likely than matched controls to be arrested for any juvenile crime and 11 times more likely to be arrested for a violent crime as a juvenile than the matched controls.

In the fifth study, Stouthamer-Loeber, Loeber, Homish, and Wei (2001) described findings from the Pittsburgh Youth Study, in which researchers collected substantiated child maltreatment records of a large sample of boys recruited from public schools in Pittsburgh. Using these data, they created matched cohorts of maltreated and nonmaltreated youths and compared their rates of arrest and self-reported delinquency through approximately age 19. Consistent with the results of earlier studies conducted in other regions of the country, youths with substantiated records of maltreatment were more likely than those in the comparison group to have juvenile arrest records and to self-report delinquent and violent behavior.

Finally, analyses of data from a two-site longitudinal study also confirm a relationship between childhood victimization and juvenile delinquency. The Child Development Project (Dodge, Bates, & Pettit, 1990) recruited children entering kindergarten in Tennessee and Indiana and has followed them to age 21. In the context of a detailed initial interview about disciplinary strategies, mothers responded to questions about physical abuse of their children (e.g., had the child ever been hit severely enough by an adult to require medical attention?). On the basis of this information, the researchers classified 69 children (12%) as having experienced early physical abuse. This study differs in an important way from the studies described earlier because these cases of abuse did not necessarily come to the attention of authorities or reach the threshold of legal definitions of child abuse. Nonetheless, the findings were generally consistent with those of studies based on documented cases of maltreatment. Youths who experienced physical abuse in the first 5 years of their lives were more likely than the comparison group to be arrested as juveniles for violent and nonviolent offenses (Lansford et al., 2007). Interestingly, however, they were not more likely to report delinquent acts.

## To What Extent Does the Relationship between Child Abuse and Neglect and Later Offending Apply to Girls as Well as Boys?

Although rates of delinquency are higher for boys than girls (U.S. Department of Justice, Federal Bureau of Investigation, 2007), child abuse and neglect appear to increase risk for juvenile crime among *both* girls and boys. In the Midwest study (Maxfield & Widom, 1996), abused and neglected girls were almost twice as likely as girls without histories of abuse and neglect to be arrested as juveniles (20.0% vs. 11.4%), twice as likely to be arrested as adults (28.5% vs. 15.9%), and 2.4 times more likely to be arrested for a violent crime (8.2% vs. 3.6%). Figure 13.2 shows rates of juvenile arrests for abused and neglected and control girls and boys. Contrary to the notion that female offenders are not serious or chronic or career criminals, findings from the Midwest study have also revealed a subset of abused and neglected girls (approximately 8% vs. 18% of abused and neglected boys) who develop antisocial and delinquent lifestyles that persist into adulthood and who become chronic persistent offenders with serious criminal careers (Widom, Nagin, & Lambert, 1998). See also Garbarino, Levene, Walsh, and Coupet, Chapter 17, this volume.

Thus, despite differences in gender of the child, geographic region, time period, age, definition of child maltreatment, and assessment technique, these six prospective investigations provide evidence that childhood mal-

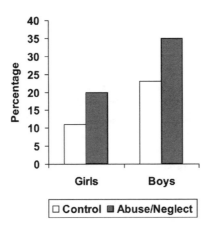

FIGURE 13.2. Percentage of girls and boys in the Midwest study of abuse and neglect and control groups with juvenile arrest records. For both girls and boys, the difference between the abuse and neglect and control groups is significant ($p < .001$). Data from Maxfield and Widom (1996).

treatment increases later risk for delinquency and violence. Replication of this relationship across a number of well-designed studies supports the generalizability of results and increases confidence in them. Indeed, conclusions from research are strengthened through replication because the limitations of any one study may impact the interpretation of findings (Taubes, 2007). Although the randomized controlled trial is considered the gold standard for understanding health-related risk and preventive factors (Taubes, 2007), it is obviously not possible to randomly assign children to maltreatment or control groups. Thus, the fact that these different studies involving comparisons of matched groups of maltreated and nonmaltreated children reveal similar findings provides strong evidence of this relationship. Of importance, these six studies also reveal that the relationship between childhood maltreatment and criminal behavior is not inevitable or deterministic. Many abused and neglected children do not become delinquent or violent youths.

## FROM CHILD VICTIM TO CHILD OFFENDER: POTENTIAL DEVELOPMENTAL MECHANISMS

Many theories have been put forth to explain the potential mechanisms whereby childhood victims become criminal offenders later in life. These theories range from more traditional criminological or psychological theories to more recent models drawing on social information processing or the literature on children's responses to traumatic events. In the following section, we review a number of prominent and frequently cited theories describing how victimized children may grow up to become juvenile and adult offenders.

Social learning theory suggests that children acquire behaviors through modeling and reinforcement contingencies in the context of social interactions (Bandura, 1973). Children learn behavior, at least in part, by imitating other people's behavior, and observed behavior is particularly salient when the model is someone of high status, such as a parent. Thus, physical aggression within a family provides a powerful model for children to learn aggressive behaviors and gives the message that such behavior is appropriate (Bandura, 1973). As suggested by White and Straus (1981), physical punishment "lays the groundwork for the normative legitimacy of all types of violence." In addition to modeling aggressive behaviors, family members reinforce or punish children's aggressive behavior through their reactions, which serve to either perpetuate the behavior or extinguish it. For example, a neglectful parent who pays more attention to a child when she is aggressive, even if that attention is hostile, rewards the behavior through increased responsiveness, thereby increasing the likelihood that it will recur in the future.

Several studies have found that aggressive parents tend to produce aggressive children (Bandura & Walters, 1959; Egeland & Sroufe, 1981). Furthermore, research on exposure to family violence or media violence provides some support for the notion that observing violence leads to increased aggression and violence (Friedrich-Cofer & Huston, 1986; Wolfe, Jaffe, Wilson, & Zak, 1985). In their coercion model, Patterson, Reid, and Dishion (1992) have expanded on social learning theory to suggest that coercive interactions between parents and children foster aggressive behavior in children, which leads to coercive interactions with peers and association with deviant and aggressive peers. In this trajectory, peer interactions provide further social modeling and reinforcement of aggressive behavior initially learned at home.

According to a strict interpretation of the cycle of violence theory (Widom, 1989b), or the notion that children who experience violent victimization will become perpetrators of violence when they grow up, one would expect physically abused children to have the highest risk of arrest for violent criminal behavior relative to other forms of child abuse or neglect. Empirical research provides some support for this hypothesis. Specifically, both the Midwest (Maxfield & Widom, 1996; Widom, 1989a) and Northwest (English et al., 2002) studies described previously found that physical abuse (i.e., being the victim of violence as a child) was associated with high risk of subsequent arrests for violence. However, neglected children also exhibited increased rates of arrests for violence compared with controls, and the degree of increased risk was very similar to that of the physically abused children (English et al., 2002; Maxfield & Widom, 1996; Widom, 1989b). Maxfield and Widom (1996) reported that 21% of physically abused children and 20% of neglected children had arrests for violent crime compared with 14% of matched controls. In the Northwest study, rates of arrests for violent crimes were approximately 30% for physically abused children and 31% for neglected children. Although these findings support a cycle of violence (experiencing violence as a child leads to increased risk of committing violence), they also call attention to the fact that childhood neglect may lead to violent behavior. Thus, theories other than social learning are needed to explain the mechanisms leading child victims to become offenders.

One theory that may be particularly relevant to understanding how neglected children may turn to delinquency, crime, and violence is found in the writings of Abraham Maslow. According to Maslow's hierarchy of needs (Maslow, 1943), certain basic needs must be met before individuals can attain "self-actualization," or an optimal level of psychological functioning. The most basic needs are physiological (e.g., food, water, sleep) and safety (e.g., security of one's own body, health, and family). After those needs are met, love and belonging and then self-esteem can be achieved. More advanced psychological functions such as coping, problem solving, and moral reasoning require that these needs be met. Childhood neglect is defined as lack of enough food, clothing, shelter, or medical attention to provide a healthy and secure environment for the developing child. Physical and sexual abuse can also interfere with a child's sense of safety as well as development of connections with others and self-esteem. According to Maslow (1968), "Only a child who feels safe dares to grow forward healthily" (p. 49). In other words, children who do not have their most basic needs met may be disadvantaged in terms of psychological and emotional development.

Bowlby's (1969) attachment theory has played an important role in attempts to understand the development of aggressive and criminal behavior from abusive childhoods. Bowlby's theory was influenced by case studies of 44 clinic-referred youths with histories of theft and a comparison group of clinic-referred youths without histories of theft (Bowlby, 1944). On the basis of his interviews with the children, caretakers, and teachers, Bowlby concluded that the large majority of juvenile thieves, particularly those classified as "affectionless characters," had "suffered the complete emotional loss of their mother or foster-mother during infancy and early childhood" (p. 6). These observations led to his emphasis on the early caretaker–child relationship and the belief that deprivations in this relationship can lead to antisocial characteristics.

According to Bowlby (1969), attachment refers to the early bond that an infant develops with a caretaker and is the basis for an "internal working model" of the world that functions as a framework for subsequent interactions with the interpersonal environment, including other caretakers, school, peers, romantic partners, and the community at large. According to attachment theory, abuse, inconsistency, or rejection from a primary caretaker can lead children to develop insecure and/or avoidant attachment and a negative internal working model. Such children are then prone to interpret neutral, or even friendly, behavior as hostile and to respond with inappropriate aggression. Similarly, Ainsworth (1989) describes the development of a hostile worldview in children with disrupted attachment relationships. Unresponsive or inconsistent parenting during infancy may also lead to antisocial behavior by interfering with the development of emotion regulation capacities needed to cope with stressful or stimulating situations (Keenan & Shaw, 2003). Some research has found high rates of attachment problems (e.g., dismissive attachment style, unresolved with respect to trauma/abuse or loss) in groups of incarcerated or psychiatrically hospitalized criminal offenders (Frodi, Dernevik, Sepa, Philipson, & Bragesjo, 2001; van Ijzendoorn et al., 1997). Attachment problems have also been associated with conduct disorder and antisocial personality traits in psychiatrically hospitalized adolescents (Rosenstein & Horowitz, 1996). However, Wekerle and Wolfe (1998) did not find that attachment was related to adolescent relationship violence, beyond increased risk associated with childhood maltreatment.

In another attempt to explain the cycle of violence, Dodge et al. (1990) have suggested that severe physical harm during early childhood (before age 5) leads to chronic aggression by bringing about the development of biased and deficient social information-processing patterns. Lending empirical support to this hypothesis, Dodge et al. (1990) found that 4-year-old children whose mothers reported ever having used physically harmful discipline evidenced deviant patterns of processing social information at age 5. These social information processing patterns were, in turn, associated with aggressive behavior. Relative to other children, physically harmed children were significantly less attentive to relevant social cues, more likely to attribute hostile intent to others' actions, and less likely to generate effective solutions to problems. Such children might then interpret a harmless action, such as an unintentional bump from another child, as an attack and respond aggressively.

Childhood victimization may also impact the development of a child's self-concept, attitudes, or attributional style, which influence how she or he will respond to situations later in life. The clinical literature has identified low self-esteem as one of the most common sequelae of childhood victimization (Kazdin, Moser, Colbus, & Bell, 1985; Kim & Cicchetti, 2006). Lowered self-esteem may result directly from the experience of victimization or from the child's belief that he or she is somehow responsible for or deserving of the abuse or neglect. However, low self-esteem may also be indirectly related to abuse and neglect as a byproduct of lowered cognitive functioning, poor social and interpersonal skills, and antisocial and, ultimately, violent behavior.

Abuse or neglect may lead children to develop maladaptive styles of coping. For example, early maltreatment might give rise to impulsive or risk-taking behaviors that are related to deficiencies in problem-solving skills, poor school performance, or inadequate occupational functioning. Adaptations or coping styles that may be functional at one point in development (e.g., running away from home, emotional distancing, avoiding an abusive parent) may later compromise an individual's ability to draw on and respond to the environment in a healthy and flexible way. Empirical evidence regarding maladaptive forms of coping among abused and neglected children is not extensive (Spaccarelli, 1994). Running away and substance abuse are perhaps the maladaptive coping strategies that have received the most attention as outcomes of childhood maltreatment.

Interviews with homeless and runaway youths have found that many children left home in response to abusive or neglectful home environments (Simons & Whitbeck, 1991; Yoder, Whitbeck, & Hoyt, 2001). In one prospective study that followed up on maltreated children, victims of childhood abuse and neglect were more likely to run away from home than nonmaltreated comparison children (Kaufman & Widom, 1999). Moreover, some evidence suggests that childhood sexual abuse increases the likelihood that homeless youths become involved in criminal behaviors, such as theft or prostitution (Chen, Tyler, Whitbeck, & Hoyt, 2004). Although running away may be an effective way of removing oneself from an abusive home, it places the child at risk for exposure to other forms of victimization and a street culture that promotes crime and violence.

Numerous studies have also reported associations between childhood maltreatment and drug abuse in adolescence or adulthood (Brown & Anderson, 1991; Dembo et al., 1990; Moran, Vuchinich, & Hall, 2004). Abused and neglected youths may initiate drug use as a way of emotional or psychological escape from an abusive environment (Downs, Miller, & Testa, 1991; Lindberg & Distad, 1985; Yamaguchi & Kandel, 1984); to enhance self-esteem (Dembo et al., 1989); as part of a general pattern of self-destructive behavior associated with low self-worth, poor self-concept, and self-blame (Lindberg & Distad, 1985); to relieve symptoms of depression (Kazdin et al., 1985); to obtain peer support and reduce feelings of loneliness and isolation (Singer, Petchers, & Hussey, 1989); or to self-medicate (Downs et al., 1991; Lindberg & Distad, 1985; Singer et al., 1989). Substance use and abuse may also develop in conjunction with participation in delinquent and criminal subcultures, because substance abuse and criminal behavior frequently coexist (White, 1997). These problematic behaviors often occur together as part of a generalized "deviance syndrome" (Donovan & Jessor, 1985) or because similar traits (e.g., impulsivity, lack of control, emotional instability, and negative affect) are associated with both delinquency and substance abuse (White & Labouvie, 1994).

However, the relationship between child maltreatment and drug use or abuse may be more complex than a simple linear relationship. Evidence from one prospective longitudinal study (Widom, Weiler, & Cottler, 1999) found no increase in risk of drug abuse diagnoses in a group of abused and neglected children assessed in young adulthood (approximately 29 years). When these same individuals were followed into middle adulthood (approximately 40 years), Widom, Marmorstein, and White (2006) determined that abused and neglected women were more likely to report past year use of illicit drugs (marijuana, cocaine, and heroin) compared with control women. Other findings from this prospective study indicate that abused and neglected women who use alcohol or drugs as a coping strategy are at increased risk for alcohol problems (Schuck & Widom, 2001).

Experiences of early childhood victimization may also lead to physiological changes that relate to the development of antisocial and violent behavior. Exposure to stress during critical developmental periods may alter neurological systems related to stress response, affect regulation, memory, social and emotional development, and cognition (De Bellis, 2001; De Bellis et al., 1999; Glaser, 2000), and alterations of normal brain chemistry may give rise to aggressive behavior (Eichelman, 1990). The brain's stress–response system involves the catecholamine system (e.g., epinephrine, norepinephrine), the sympathetic nervous system (SNS), and the limbic–hypothalamic–pituitary–adrenal (LHPA) axis. Animal studies have shown that traumatic stress activates the catecholamine system and the SNS, which stimulate a biological fight-or-flight response (i.e., increased heart rate, blood pressure, metabolic rate, and alertness) and activation of the LHPA axis (De Bellis, 2001, 2005; Glaser, 2000). As part of the LHPA reaction, the pituitary gland secretes adrenocorticotropic hormone (ACTH), which in turn triggers the adrenal gland to produce and release cortisol. Cortisol triggers a negative feedback loop that suppresses LHPA activity and restores the brain to homeostasis (and basal cortisol level). Studies have found that maltreated children evidence elevated levels of catecholamines, cortisol, and ACTH (De Bellis, 2001; De Bellis et al., 1999). Thus, it is hypothesized that trauma may "prime" the stress–response system, resulting in overreactivity to stressors. Hyperarousal and oversensitivity to stress might lead to aggressive behavior. Alterations of the biological stress–response systems also appear to have a global and adverse impact on neurological development (De Bellis, 2001; Glaser, 2000), which may be responsible for many behavioral problems that result from childhood maltreatment (De Bellis, 2005).

Further complicating this picture, the brain appears to compensate for elevated LHPA activity through enhanced negative feedback, resulting in reduced response to stimulation of the LHPA axis and desensitization to stress (De Bellis et al., 1994). Desensitization may result in a maladaptive response to stress (Glaser, 2000) and traits such as callousness, lack of empathy, lack of remorse or guilt, nonresponsiveness to conditioning by punishment (characteristic of psychopaths), and an increased need for external stimulation. These characteristics make adaptive socialization difficult and increase the potential for crime and violence.

Childhood victimization may also be related to violent behavior in part through its effect on neurotransmitter systems, such as serotonin, which is related to impulse control and reduction of aggression (De Bellis, 2005; Lewis, 1992). Studies with nonhuman primates have found that rearing experiences may be associated with changes in central nervous system neurotransmitter activity. For example, rhesus monkeys who were rejected by their mothers in the first 6 months of life had lower levels of the serotonin metabolite 5-HIAA (Maestripieri, McCormack, Lindell, Higley, & Sanchez, 2006). Although the extent to which one can generalize from this research with nonhuman primates to humans is questionable, the striking similarities between the concepts operationalized in the nonhuman primate literature (stress, anxiety, and rearing conditions of neglect) and in the child development literature (Crittendon & Ainsworth, 1989) invite serious consideration.

Several recent studies of gene × environment interactions have revealed that a functional polymorphism in the promoter region of the monoamine oxidase A (MAOA) gene can moderate the impact of childhood maltreatment on antisocial behavior in adulthood and adolescence. Two studies have examined the role of variants in the gene for MAOA transcription in conjunction with the environment (childhood adversity) to predict antisocial behavior (Caspi et al., 2002) and conduct disorder (Foley et al., 2004). Caspi et al. (2002) studied 442 New Zealand Caucasian boys who had been followed from birth to age 26 and found "initial evidence that a functional polymorphism in the MAOA genotype moderates the impact of early childhood maltreatment on the development of antisocial behavior in males" (p. 853). Maltreatment was defined as a composite index including prospective information about maternal rejection, repeated loss of a primary caregiver, harsh discipline, and retrospective self-reports of physical and sexual abuse. High levels of MAOA appeared to protect boys exposed to childhood adversities from developing antisocial or aggressive behaviors. Foley et al. (2004) studied a sample of Caucasian twin boys (ages 8–17; mean age, 12) to examine whether childhood adversity and MAOA level interacted to predict risk for conduct disorder. Childhood adversity was defined as exposure to parental neglect (parent self-report) and interparental violence and inconsistent discipline (child report). Findings from this study indicated that low MAOA increased risk for conduct disorder only in the presence of childhood adversity. Replication of these methods with a sample of adults with documented records of childhood abuse and neglect found that high MAOA activity served a protective function only for whites (Widom & Brzustowicz, 2006). These studies suggest that genetic predisposition may make some individuals more vulnerable to the effects of childhood adversity and may serve as a protective factor for others. In either case, these findings make clear that genes do not play a deterministic role (a main effect in statistical terms) but rather interact with environmental experiences in leading to antisocial behavior.

The systems or community response to childhood abuse and neglect may also buffer or exacerbate its impact on the developing child. Contact with the police and child welfare workers can itself be frightening, confusing, and even traumatic for children and may add to the sense of chaos that maltreated children are already experiencing. Although often necessary for ensuring a child's safety and well-being, removal from the home and caretakers further disrupts processes related to attachment, development of basic security, and reliance on caretakers. Thus, it is important that the professionals who respond to cases of childhood abuse and neglect keep these issues in mind and make efforts to lessen, rather than exacerbate, the impact of maltreatment experiences. In addition, some authors have suggested that the juvenile justice system might disproportionately label and adjudicate victims of childhood maltreatment as juvenile delinquents, thereby inflating the number of maltreated children with delinquent records (Smith, Berkman, & Fraser, 1980). Thus, delinquency may appear to be an outcome of childhood abuse and neglect because many of the behavioral "symptoms" of childhood maltreatment (e.g., aggression, disruptive behavior) are officially defined as delinquent (Garbarino & Plantz, 1986).

## DO MECHANISMS LEADING FROM CHILD VICTIMIZATION TO JUVENILE OFFENDING DIFFER FOR GIRLS AND BOYS?

Knowledge of how criminal behavior develops in girls, and whether it differs significantly from that of boys, is limited because most longitudinal studies of delinquent behavior have not included girls or have not had sufficiently large samples of seriously delinquent girls (Giordano, Cernkovich, & Rudolph, 2002). Although the mechanisms we have described in this chapter likely apply to both boys and girls who are victims of childhood abuse and neglect, research suggests that pathways from victimization to crime may also differ for girls and boys (Giordano et al., 2002). For example, childhood abuse and other forms of trauma are more often reported by delinquent females than their male counterparts (Chesney-Lind & Shelden, 1998; Gavazzi & Yarcheck, 2006). In a sample of 500 juvenile offenders, Funk (1999) found that different models were needed to predict reoffending in girls and boys. In particular, histories of child abuse and running away from home, recorded in case files, predicted reoffending among girls but not boys. Maxfield and Widom's (1996) prospective findings indicate a stronger relationship between abuse and neglect and violent offending for women than for men.

One reason why girls and boys may have different pathways to delinquency relates to gender differences in socialization. Girls traditionally are closely supervised, which limits their opportunities and settings for delinquent activity (Triplett & Myers, 1995). In addition, social sanctions typically discourage girls' antisocial behavior. As Steffensmeier and Broidy (2001) point out, risk-taking behavior among girls is generally discouraged, whereas it is often encouraged and even rewarded among boys. Moreover, closer monitoring of girls results in more closely monitored female peer networks, making it less likely for girls' friends to be involved in (and influence) delinquent activity (Giordano, Cernkovich, & Pugh, 1986). Although these mechanisms of social control may serve a protective function, reducing delinquent behavior among girls and women in general, the situation for abused and neglected girls is typically quite different. Almost by definition, neglected children in particular, and very likely abused children as well, are not reared in environments providing traditional social controls.

In addition, interpersonal relationships are particularly strong influences on girls' development, decision making, and behavior (Gilligan, 1982; Jordan, Kaplan, Miller, Stiver, & Surrey, 1991). Thus, disruptions in family relationships may have a more potent effect on girls than boys and "can reduce self esteem and intensify social isolation, thereby increasing females' likelihood to rebel and engage in delinquent behaviors" (Funk, 1999, p. 48). In addition, the centrality of relationships for girls may increase their risk for being derailed into delinquency and crime through relationships with delinquent friends and relatives (Funk, 1999; Widom, 2000). Abused and neglected children followed up into young adulthood are more likely than nonmaltreated individuals to report that a parent or sibling was arrested (Widom, 1998), and Cloninger and Guze (1973) reported high rates of psychopathology among the families of female delinquents and felons. The work of Robins (1966) indicates that antisocial women and men often engage in assortative mating. If behavioral preferences are a function of the networks in which a person is embedded (Smith-Lovin & McPherson, 1993), then it would not be surprising that abused and neglected girls and women engage in deviant or criminal behaviors because their networks offer models or support for such behavior. Moreover, if girls' moral decision making places a high priority on maintaining relationships, they may be more likely to engage in illegal, delinquent activities with peers, romantic partners, or family members (Funk, 1999).

## CONCLUSION

Evidence from several prospective longitudinal studies demonstrates quite clearly that childhood abuse and neglect are important risk factors for subsequent crime and violence. We have discussed several mechanisms through which abused and neglected children may grow up to become offenders. The implications of this work are that victims of childhood abuse and neglect are in need of early assessment and intervention to prevent or reduce the likely cascading of negative consequences and, ultimately, increased risk for the development of aggressive and antisocial behavior. However, more research is needed to understand mechanisms leading from victimization to offending and protective factors that may prevent children from developing aggressive and delinquent behavior. Although childhood abuse and neglect increase risk for delinquency, many victims do not become involved in such behavior. Thus, it is important that policymakers and practitioners recognize the link between childhood maltreatment and juvenile delinquency but also avoid perpetuating a damaging self-fulfilling prophecy.

# REFERENCES

Ainsworth, M. D. (1989). Attachments beyond infancy. *American Psychologist, 44,* 709–716.

Bandura, A. (1973). *Aggression: A social learning analysis.* Englewood Cliffs, NJ: Prentice Hall.

Bandura, A., & Walters, R. H. (1959). *Adolescent aggression.* New York: Ronald.

Bowlby, J. (1944). Forty-four juvenile thieves: Their characters and home-life. *International Journal of Psychoanalysis, 25,* 107–128.

Bowlby, J. (1969). *Attachment and loss, Volume I. Attachment.* New York: Basic Books.

Brown, G. R., & Anderson, B. (1991). Psychiatric morbidity in adult inpatients with childhood histories of sexual and physical abuse. *American Journal of Psychiatry, 148,* 55–61.

Caspi, A., McClay, J., Moffit, T. E., Mill, J., Martin, J., & Craig, I. A., et al. (2002). Role of genotype in cycle of violence in maltreated children. *Science, 297,* 851–854.

Chen, X., Tyler, K. A., Whitbeck, L. B., & Hoyt, D. R. (2004). Early sexual abuse, street adversity, and drug use among female homeless and runaway adolescents in the midwest. *Journal of Drug Issues, 34,* 1–22.

Chesney-Lind, M., & Shelden, R. H. (1998). *Girls, delinquency, and juvenile justice* (2nd ed.). Pacific Grove, CA: Brooks/Cole.

Cloninger, C. R., & Guze, S. B. (1973). Psychiatric illness in the families of female criminals: A study of 288 first-degree relatives. *British Journal of Psychiatry, 122,* 697–703.

Crittendon, P. M., & Ainsworth, M. D. S. (1989). Child maltreatment and attachment theory. In D. Cicchetti & V. Carlson (Eds.), *Child maltreatment* (pp. 432–463). New York: Cambridge University Press.

Curtis, G. C. (1963). Violence breeds violence—perhaps? *American Journal of Psychiatry, 120,* 386–387.

De Bellis, M. D. (2001). Developmental traumatology: The psychobiological development of maltreated children and its implications for research, treatment, and policy. *Development and Psychopathology, 13,* 539–564.

De Bellis, M. D. (2005). The psychobiology of neglect. *Child Maltreatment, 10,* 150–172.

De Bellis, M. D., Baum, A. S., Birmaher, B., Keshavan, M. S., Eccard, C. H., Boring, A. M., et al. (1999). Developmental traumatology: Part I. Biological stress systems. *Biological Psychiatry, 45,* 1259–1270.

De Bellis, M. D., Chrousos, G. P., Dorn, L. D., Burke, L., Helners, K., Kling, M. A., et al. (1994). Hypothalamic-pituitary-adrenal axis dysregulation in sexually abused girls. *Journal of Clinical Endocrinology and Metabolism, 78,* 249–255.

Dembo, R., Williams, L., La Voie, L., Berry, E., Getreu, A., Kern, J., et al. (1990). Physical abuse, sexual victimization and marijuana/hashish and cocaine use over time: A structural analysis among a cohort of high risk youths. *Journal of Prison and Jail Health, 9,* 13–43.

Dembo, R., Williams, L., La Voie, L., Berry, E., Getreu, A., Wish, E., et al. (1989). Physical abuse, sexual victimization, and illicit drug use: Replication of a structural analysis among a new sample of high-risk youths. *Violence and Victims, 4,* 121–137.

Dodge, K. A., Bates, J. E., & Pettit, G. S. (1990). Mechanisms in the cycle of violence. *Science, 250,* 1678–1683.

Donovan, J. E., & Jessor, R. (1985). Structure of problem behavior in adolescence and young adulthood. *Journal of Consulting and Clinical Psychology, 53,* 890–904.

Downs, W. R., Miller, B. A., & Testa, M. (1991, November). *The impact of childhood victimization experiences on women's drug use.* Paper presented at the annual meeting of the American Society of Criminology, San Francisco.

Egeland, B., & Sroufe, L. A. (1981). Developmental sequelae of maltreatment in infancy. In R. Rizley & D. Cicchetti (Eds.), *Developmental perspectives on child maltreatment: New directions for child development* (pp. 77–92). San Francisco: Jossey-Bass.

Eichelman, B. (1990). Neurochemical and psychopharmacologic aspects of aggressive behavior. *Annual Review of Medicine, 41, 149–158.*

English, D. J., Widom, C. S., & Brandford, C. (2002). *Childhood victimization and delinquency, adult criminality, and violent criminal behavior: A replication and extension.* Rockville, MD: National Institute of Justice.

Feerick, M. M., Knutson, J. F., Trickett, P. K., & Flanzer, S. M. (Eds.). (2006). *Child abuse and neglect: Definitions, classifications, and a framework for research.* Baltimore, MD: Paul H. Brookes.

Foley, D. L., Eaves, L. J., Wormley, B., Silberg, J. L., Maes, H. M., Kuhn, J., et al. (2004). Childhood adversity, monoamine oxidase A genotype, and risk for conduct disorder. *Archives of General Psychiatry, 61,* 738–744.

Friedrich-Cofer, L., & Huston, A. C. (1986). Television violence and aggression: The debate continues. *Psychological Bulletin, 100,* 364–371.

Frodi, A., Dernevik, M., Sepa, A., Philipson, J., & Bragesjo, M. (2001). Current attachment representations of incarcerated offenders varying in degree of psychopathy. *Attachment and Human Development, 3,* 269–283.

Funk, S. J. (1999). Risk assessment for juveniles on probation: A focus on gender. *Criminal Justice and Behavior, 26,* 44–68.

Garbarino, J., & Gilliam, G. (1980). *Understanding abusive families.* Lexington, MA: Lexington Books.

Garbarino, J., & Plantz, M. (1986). Part I. Review of the literature. In E. Gray, J. Garbarino, & M. Plantz (Eds.), *Child abuse: Prelude to delinquency?* (pp. 5–18). Washington, DC: U.S. Department of Justice, Office of Juvenile Justice and Delinquency Prevention.

Gavazzi, S. M., & Yarcheck, C. M. (2006). Global risk indicators and the role of gender in a juvenile detention sample. *Criminal Justice and Behavior, 33,* 597–612.

Gilligan, C. (1982). *In a different voice: Psychological theory and women's development.* Cambridge, MA: Harvard University Press.

Giordano, P. C., Cernkovich, S. A., & Pugh, M. D. (1986). Friendships and delinquency. *American Journal of Sociology, 91,* 1170–1202.

Giordano, P. C., Cernkovich, S. A., & Rudolph, J. L. (2002). Gender, crime, and desistance: Toward a theory of cognitive transformation. *American Journal of Sociology, 107,* 990–1064.

Glaser, D. (2000). Child abuse and neglect and the brain—A review. *Journal of Child Psychology and Psychiatry and Allied Disciplines, 41,* 97–116.

Jordan, J. V., Kaplan, A. G., Miller, J. B., Stiver, I. P., & Surrey, J. L. (1991). *Women's growth in connection: Writings from the Stone Center.* New York: Guilford Press.

Kaufman, J. G., & Widom, C. S. (1999). Childhood victimization, running away, and delinquency. *Journal of Research in Crime and Delinquency, 36,* 347–370.

Kazdin, A. E., Moser, J., Colbus, D., & Bell, R. (1985). Depressive symptoms among physically abused and psychiatrically disturbed children. *Journal of Abnormal Psychology, 94,* 298–307.

Keenan, K., & Shaw, D. S. (2003). Starting at the beginning: Exploring the etiology of antisocial behavior in the first years of life. In B. B. Lahey, T. E. Moffitt, & A. Caspi (Eds.), *Causes of conduct disorder and juvenile delinquency* (pp. 153–181). New York: Guilford Press.

Kim, J., & Cicchetti, D. (2006). Longitudinal trajectories of self-system processes and depressive symptoms among maltreated and nonmaltreated children. *Child Development, 77,* 624–639.

Lansford, J. E., Miller-Johnson, S., Berlin, L. J., Dodge, K. A., Bates, J. E., & Pettit, G. S. (2007). Early physical abuse and later violent delinquency: A prospective longitudinal study. *Child Maltreatment, 12,* 233–245.

Lewis, D. O. (1992). From abuse to violence: Psychophysiological consequences of maltreatment. *Journal of the American Academy of Child and Adolescent Psychiatry, 31,* 383–391.

Lindberg, F. H., & Distad, L. S. (1985). Survival responses to incest: Adolescents in crisis. *Child Abuse and Neglect, 9,* 521–526.

Maestripieri, D., McCormack, K., Lindell, S. G., Higley, J. D., & Sanchez, M. M. (2006). Influence of parenting style on the offspring's behaviour and CSF monoamine metabolite levels in crossfostered and noncrossfostered female rhesus macaques. *Behavioural Brain Research, 175,* 90–95.

Maslow, A. H. (1943). A theory of human motivation. *Psychological Review, 50,* 370–396.

Maslow, A. H. (1968). *Toward a psychology of being.* New York: Van Nostrand.

Maxfield, M. G., & Widom, C. S. (1996). The cycle of violence: Revisited six years later. *Archives of Pediatric and Adolescent Medicine, 150,* 390–395.

Moran, P. B., Vuchinich, S., & Hall, N. K. (2004). Associations between types of maltreatment and substance use during adolescence. *Child Abuse and Neglect, 28*(5), 565–574.

Patterson, G. R., Reid, J. B., & Dishion, T. J. (1992). *Antisocial boys: A social interactional approach* (Vol. 4). Eugene, OR: Castalia.

Robins, L. N. (1966). *Deviant children grown up: A sociological and psychiatric study of sociopathic personality.* Baltimore, MD: Williams & Wilkins.

Rosenstein, D. S., & Horowitz, H. A. (1996). Adolescent attachment and psychopathology. *Journal of Consulting and Clinical Psychology, 64,* 244–253.

Schuck, A., & Widom, C. S. (2001). Childhood victimization and alcohol symptoms in females: Causal inferences and hypothesized mediators. *Child Abuse and Neglect, 25,* 1069–1092.

Simons, R. L., & Whitbeck, L. B. (1991). Sexual abuse as a precursor to prostitution and victimization among adolescent and adult homeless women. *Journal of Family Issues, 12,* 361–379.

Singer, M., Petchers, M., & Hussey, D. (1989). The relationship between sexual abuse and substance abuse among psychiatrically hospitalized adolescents. *Child Abuse and Neglect, 13,* 319–325.

Smith, C., & Thornberry, T. P. (1995). The relationship between childhood maltreatment and adolescent involvement in delinquency. *Criminology, 33,* 451–481.

Smith, C. P., Berkman, D. J., & Fraser, W. M. (1980). *A preliminary national assessment of child abuse and neglect and the juvenile justice system: The shadows of distress.* Washington, DC: Office of Juvenile Justice and Delinquency Prevention.

Smith-Lovin, L., & McPherson, J. M. (1993). You are who you know: A network approach to gender. In P. England (Ed.), *Theory on gender/feminism on theory* (pp. 223–254). New York: Aldine de Gruyter.

Spaccarelli, S. (1994). Stress, appraisal, and coping in child sexual abuse: A theoretical and empirical review. *Psychological Bulletin, 116,* 340–362.

Steffensmeier, D., & Broidy, L. (2001). Explaining female offending. In L. Goodstein (Ed.), *Women, crime and criminal justices: Contemporary issues* (pp. 111–134). Los Angeles, CA: Roxbury Press.

Stouthamer-Loeber, M., Loeber, R., Homish, D. L., & Wei, E. (2001). Maltreatment of boys and the development of disruptive and delinquent behavior. *Development and Psychopathology, 13,* 941–955.

Taubes, G. (2007, September 16). Do we really know what makes us healthy? *New York Times Magazine.* Retrieved January 30, 2009, from *www.nytimes.com/2007/09/16/magazine/16epidemiology-t.html?_r=1&scp=1&sq=Taubes:%20do%20we%20really%20know%20 what%20makes%20us%20health?%20&st=cse.*

Triplett, R., & Myers, L. B. (1995). Evaluating contextual patterns of delinquency: Gender-based differences. *Justice Quarterly, 12,* 59–84.

U.S. Department of Health and Human Services. (2007). *Child maltreatment 2005*. Washington, DC: U.S. Government Printing Office.

U.S. Department of Justice, Federal Bureau of Investigation. (2007). *Crime in the United States, 2006*. Washington, DC: U.S. Government Printing Office.

van Ijzendoorn, M. H., Feldbrugge, J. T. T. M., Derks, F. C. H., de Ruiter, C., Verhagen, M. F. M., Philipse, M. W. G., et al. (1997). Attachment representations of personality-disordered criminal offenders. *American Journal of Orthopsychiatry, 67*, 449–459.

Wekerle, C., & Wolfe, D. A. (1998). The role of child maltreatment and attachment style in adolescent relationship violence. *Development and Psychopathology, 10*, 571–586.

White, H. R. (1997). Alcohol, illicit drugs, and violence. In D. Stoff, J. Brieling, & J. D. Maser (Eds.), *Handbook of antisocial behavior* (pp. 511–523). New York: Wiley.

White, H. R., & Labouvie, E. W. (1994). Generality versus specificity of problem behavior: Psychological and functional differences. *Journal of Drug Issues, 24*(1-2), 55–74.

White, S. O., & Straus, M. A. (1981). The implications of family violence for rehabilitation strategies. In S. E. Martin, L. B. Sechrest, & R. Redner (Eds.), *New directions in the rehabilitation of criminal offenders* (pp. 255–288). Washington, DC: National Academies Press.

Widom, C. S. (1989a). The cycle of violence. *Science, 244*, 160–166.

Widom, C. S. (1989b). Does violence beget violence? A critical examination of the literature. *Psychological Bulletin, 106*, 3–28.

Widom, C. S. (1998). Childhood victimization: Early adversity and subsequent psychopathology. In B. P. Dohrenwend (Ed.), *Adversity, stress, and psychopathology* (pp. 81–95). New York: Oxford University Press.

Widom, C. S. (2000). Childhood victimization and the derailment of girls and women to the criminal justice system. In *Research on women and girls in the justice system* (pp. 27–36). Washington, DC: U.S. Department of Justice, Office of Justice Programs, National Institute of Justice.

Widom, C. S. (2006, January). *Child abuse and neglect and delinquency*. Paper presented at the Office of Juvenile Justice and Delinquency Prevention National Conference Workshop, Washington, DC.

Widom, C. S., & Brzustowicz, L. M. (2006). MAOA and the "cycle of violence": Childhood abuse and neglect, MAOA genotype, and risk for violent and antisocial behavior. *Biological Psychiatry, 60*, 684–689.

Widom, C. S., Marmorstein, N. R., & White, H. R. (2006). Childhood victimization and illicit drug use in middle adulthood. *Psychology of Addictive Behaviors, 20*, 394–403.

Widom, C. S., Nagin, D., & Lambert, L. (1998). *Does childhood victimization alter developmental trajectories of criminal careers?* Washington, DC: American Society of Criminology.

Widom, C. S., Weiler, B. L., & Cottler, L. B. (1999). Childhood victimization and drug abuse: A comparison of prospective and retrospective findings. *Journal of Consulting and Clinical Psychology, 67,* 867–880.

Wolfe, D. A., Jaffe, P., Wilson, S. K., & Zak, L. (1985). Children of battered women: The relation of child behavior to family violence and maternal stress. *Journal of Consulting and Clinical Psychology, 53,* 657–665.

Yamaguchi, K., & Kandel, D. B. (1984). Patterns of drug use from adolescence to early adulthood: III. Predictors of progression. *American Journal of Public Health, 74,* 673–681.

Yoder, K. A., Whitbeck, L. B., & Hoyt, D. R. (2001). Event history analysis of antecedents to running away from home and being on the street. *American Behavioral Scientist, 45,* 51–65.

Zingraff, M. T., Leiter, J., Myers, K. A., & Johnsen, M. C. (1993). Child maltreatment and youthful problem behavior. *Criminology, 31,* 173–202.

Chapter 14

# Police Interrogation and False Confessions
## The Inherent Risk of Youth

ALLISON D. REDLICH
SAUL M. KASSIN

The notion of the juvenile "superpredator" was first introduced by Princeton University Professor John DiIulio in the mid-1990s (Bennett, DiIulio, & Walters, 1996; DiIulio, 1996). Superpredators were considered an especially violent breed of juvenile offenders who acted impulsively and without remorse (see Stevenson, Najdowski, Bottoms, & Haegerich, Chapter 18, this volume). One of the earliest cases to lend itself to this notion was the Central Park Jogger case. In April 1989, a female investment banker was jogging in Central Park and was brutally attacked, raped, and left to die. Within hours, five teenage boys (age 14–16 years) who had been "wilding" in the park were apprehended and subjected to intense, lengthy interrogations by police and prosecutors. The boys eventually confessed (after interrogations lasting 14–30 hours), providing compelling details, statements of regret, and promises not to do it again. Based on these confessions, all five boys were tried and convicted of the crime, each spending between 5 and 11.5 years in prison. At the time, and for several years thereafter, the media highlighted the seemingly increased depravity and ruthlessness of youthful offenders (Hancock, 2003; Pizarro, Chermak, & Gruenewald, 2007). The five boys were likened to a pack of wolves, and Donald Trump spent $85,000 on full-page newspaper ads calling for their execution (Hancock, 2003).

In 2002, however, Matias Reyes, a serial rapist and murderer, came forward from prison and said that he was the Central Park Jogger rapist and that he had acted alone. As it turned out, Reyes's confession was consistent with the evidence (his DNA matched semen found at the scene) and he provided details that were not known even to police investigators, details that were later verified. In addition, after the five boys had confessed in 1989, all had immediately retracted their statements and continued to assert their innocence through their trials and convictions. DNA tests of the semen recovered from the victim excluded all of the defendants as the rapists, a result that led the prosecutor to argue successfully at trial that the boys were guilty by virtue of their confessions, even if one or more other culprits had escaped. Thirteen years later, after a thorough reinvestigation, the Manhattan district attorney's office joined a defense motion to vacate all five convictions (*New York v. Wise et al.*, 2002).

Today, the Central Park Jogger case is infamous for producing five false confessions from a single investigation. The case no longer stands for the depravity of juveniles but rather for their susceptibility to interrogative influence. Indeed, youth is a well-known and often-cited risk factor for false confession (Drizin & Leo, 2004; Gross, Jacoby, Matheson, Montgomery, & Patil, 2005; Owen-Kostelnik, Reppucci, & Meyer, 2006; Redlich, 2007). In the present chapter, we discuss the evidence for this increased susceptibility to false confessions. Our particular focus is on adolescents because, compared with their preteen counterparts, they are more likely to encounter police as crime suspects. Indeed, it is safe to assume that the disparities between adolescents and adults can be extended to, if not magnified in, younger children.

In this chapter, we describe the processes of police interrogation and the problem of false confessions. We then pose four questions: (1) How are adolescents different from adults? (2) Do these differences affect their capabilities during interrogation? (3) Do the police interrogate adolescents differently than adults? (4) Why aren't adolescents interrogated differently than adults? In answering these questions, we review the extant literature on juveniles, police interrogations, and the inherent risk their youthful status poses. Finally, we discuss policy implications and potential reforms to reduce the likelihood of juvenile false confessions.

## THE PROCESS OF POLICE INTERROGATION

Over the past decade, scientific knowledge about the processes and outcomes of police interrogation has increased tremendously (see Gudjonsson, 2003; Kassin & Gudjonsson, 2004; Leo, 2008). Police interviews and interrogations have been studied from a number of vantage points and methodologies, including individual (e.g., Gudjonsson & MacKeith, 1990) and aggregated (e.g., Drizin & Leo, 2004; Leo & Ofshe, 1998) case studies, laboratory experiments (e.g., Kassin & Norwick, 2004; Russano, Meissner, Narchet, & Kassin, 2005), self-report questionnaires of juveniles and adults (e.g., Gudjonsson, Sigurdsson, Asgeirsdottir, & Sigfusdottir, 2006; Sigurdsson & Gudjonsson, 1996), and surveys of police (e.g., Kassin et al., 2007; Meyer & Reppucci, 2007). Across these differing forms of data collection and analysis, a convergent picture emerges of police interrogation as a guilt-presumptive, psychologically manipulative process designed to elicit an admission of guilt followed by a full narrative confession. The most well-known approach is the Reid technique (Inbau, Reid, Buckley, & Jayne, 2001). It is also clear that the types of techniques described as egregious in child victim-witness interviews (Wood, Nathan, Nezworski, & Uhl, Chapter 5, this volume) typify and define police interrogation.

Often, when police have identified a suspect, they bring him or her to the police station for questioning. Prior to the interrogation, the police will conduct a nonaccusatorial interview during which they ask a series of behavior-provoking questions, observe the suspect's verbal and nonverbal behavior, and attempt to determine whether the suspect is telling the truth or lying. In the Reid technique, this approach begins with the behavioral analysis interview (BAI), a series of presumably diagnostic questions such as "What do you think should happen to the person who committed this crime?" Using a behavioral symptom analysis, the interviewer then seeks to distinguish between innocent and guilty suspects by observing such nonverbal behaviors as slouching, diminished eye contact, frozen posture, and other behaviors that are developmentally typical of youth. The use of the BAI for making judgments of truth and deception is quite important to interrogation: If a suspect is judged to be deceptive, interrogation will ensue; if the suspect is judged to be truthful, he or she will be released.

However, research does not support the use of the BAI as a diagnostic tool. A large and consistent literature demonstrates that individuals cannot reliably tell when others are being deceptive and that people, on average, perform at chance levels (Bond & DePaulo, 2006; Vrij, 2008). When police officers are tested in controlled studies, they, too, fare no better than chance, although they are often found to be highly confident in their abilities and biased toward judgments of deception (Kassin & Fong, 1999; Kassin, Meissner, & Norwick, 2005; Meissner & Kassin, 2002). Vrij, Mann, and Fisher (2006) examined the validity of the BAI in a laboratory study by randomly assigning participants to a truth-telling or a deceptive condition. In both conditions, participants had to convince interviewers that they did not take money out of a wallet (and be able to receive money if they were successfully convincing). In the truth-telling condition, participants did not take the money; in the deceptive condition, participants were instructed to take money out of the wallet and then convince the interviewer they did not (i.e., lie). In all cases, the interviewer was a uniformed male police officer, who conducted a BAI interview, which was subsequently coded according to Inbau et al.'s (2001) guidelines. The results showed that some of the behaviors that are supposed to be characteristic of liars (such as shifting posture and evasive answers) were actually correlated with truth telling.

For suspects judged to be deceptive, a waiver of *Miranda* rights to silence and to an attorney must be obtained before police can legally proceed with the interrogation (*Miranda v. Arizona,* 1966). At this stage, the suspect must waive these constitutionally afforded rights voluntarily, knowingly, and intelligently. In the more than 40 years since the *Miranda* ruling, the courts have increasingly and quite narrowly insisted on unequivocal or unambiguous invocations. For example, in the case of *People v. Ricky Mitchell* (2004), a 15-year-old boy was arrested for armed robbery. Before placing the suspect in a lineup, the police called his mother and invited her to attend. The mother could not attend but told the police that her son had a lawyer and offered to provide that lawyer's phone number. The police, who already knew the boy had a lawyer, did not call and proceeded with the lineup. Mitchell was identified by two eyewitnesses and convicted. Upon appeal, his conviction was affirmed because the court ruled that the mother did not unequivocally invoke the right to counsel on her son's behalf.

Although the process by which police attempt to obtain a suspect's waiver of his or her *Miranda* rights has not been systematically studied, Leo (1996) described from his own observations of live and videotaped interrogations that police often portray the process as a mere formality rather than a protection of rights and have developed techniques that enhance the likelihood of waivers (e.g., nodding their heads while reading the *Miranda* warning, thereby inducing agreement with signing away rights). Further, Rogers, Harrison, Shuman, Sewell, and Hazelwood (2007) examined the reading comprehensibility of 560 *Miranda* warnings taken from different jurisdictions within the United States and found that comprehensibility levels ranged from second-grade to postgraduate levels. Further, whereas some components of the waiver, such as the rights to remain silence and that anything said could be held against you, tended to be presented in a comprehensible form (i.e., sixth-grade or lower reading level) in the majority of jurisdictions, other components were not. For example, the right to free legal services required a 10th-grade reading level or above in almost two-thirds of the jurisdictions studied.

If suspects waive their *Miranda* rights, interrogation can proceed in the absence of a lawyer. By all accounts, current-day interrogations rely on psychological tactics to obtain self-incriminating statements (e.g., Davis & O'Donohue, 2004; Gudjonsson, 2003; Kassin & Gudjonsson, 2004; see Inbau et al., 2001). The Reid technique of interrogation is a nine-step process, culminating in a written confession. As part of this approach, interrogators isolate suspects, confront them with accusations of guilt, present false evidence of guilt, interrupt denials, and utilize motivational "themes" that minimize the crime by offering moral justification and face-saving excuses (e.g., committing a robbery to feed one's family). In addition to these minimization tactics, interrogators may also use "maximization" tactics. These techniques attempt to scare or intimidate suspects by exaggerating the strength of the evidence or the magnitude of the charges (see Kassin & McNall, 1991). Ultimately, the interrogator poses an "alternative question" that offers the suspect a choice between two guilty options to elicit an initial admission.

Inbau et al. (2001) claim that the techniques used for adult suspects are just as applicable for juvenile suspects. In general, there is little discrimination between adults and juveniles in the training book. However, the authors do offer minimization themes exclusively for use with juveniles, including citing strategies that would work particularly well given their impulsive tendencies, inability to resist temptations, and excitability. For example, Inbau et al. recommend using the fact that a juvenile was neglected by his or her alcoholic parents as a morally acceptable excuse for the criminal behavior. Inbau et al. also offer advice on how to manage the presence of parents, which includes ignoring them and relegating their role to that of observers.

In principle, the Reid interrogation abides by the following standard: "The basic guideline in all cases should be that nothing shall be said or done that is apt to make an innocent person confess" (Inbau et al., 2001, p. 521). This standard is explicitly stated as applying equally to juveniles and adults. However, it is unclear whether police (or the courts) are aware of or understand what statements and actions lead innocents to confess (see Kassin, 2005). Basic psychology research, archival false confession cases, and laboratory and field studies have identified certain legal and commonly used techniques, often involving trickery and deception, which can induce false confessions (e.g., Drizin & Leo, 2004; Kassin & Kiechel, 1996; Redlich & Goodman, 2003). In large part, the problem is that the same interrogation tactics that secure true confessions from the guilty can induce false confessions from the innocent. Lacking a reliable means of distinguishing between offenders and innocents, police use guilt-presumptive social influence techniques that increase the risk of false confessions (Kassin, 2005).

## THE PROBLEM OF FALSE CONFESSIONS

The United States is currently undergoing an "age of innocence," although one quite different than that written about by Edith Wharton (1920). Because of advances in DNA technology and a renewed interest or belief in miscarriages of justice, the number of identified wrongful convictions has skyrocketed in the past decade. At the time of this writing, the Innocence Project of the Benjamin N. Cardozo Law School has officially exonerated 238 innocents, many of whom spent decades in prison. In approximately one in four of these exonerations, false confessions/admissions were contributing factors.

Both situational and dispositional characteristics have been identified by empirical means as contributing factors to false confessions (for reviews, see Gudjonsson, 2003; Kassin, 2008; Kassin & Gudjonsson, 2004; Lassiter, 2004; Leo, 2008). Among the situational factors that have been implicated are excessive lengths of custody and interrogation time as well as some of the common interrogation ploys discussed previously: namely, guilt-presumptive posture of the interrogator, the presentation of false evidence, and minimization of the seriousness or immorality of the crime.

Turning to the dispositional characteristics of the suspect, the two most commonly cited risk factors for false confession are youth (see Drizin & Colgan, 2004; Owen-Kostelnik et al., 2006; Redlich, Silverman, Chen, & Steiner, 2004; Scott-Hayward, 2007) and mental impairment, which often combines intellectual deficiencies and mental illness (Redlich, 2007; Redlich & Drizin, 2007). Both populations are overrepresented among identified false confessors. For example, of the 125 proven-false confessors studied by Drizin and Leo (2004), 35% were younger than 18 years and 62% were younger than 25 years (see also Gross et al., 2005). To further complicate matters, a majority of justice-involved youth have one or more mental health problems (e.g., Teplin, Abram, McClelland, Dulcan, & Mericle, 2002; Redlich, 2007) as well as intellectual disabilities (Quinn, Rutherford, Leone, Osher, & Poirier, 2005). According to Closson and Rogers (2007), 20 to 70% of youth in juvenile detention settings have learning disabilities compared with 5% in the general population.

In addition to youth and mental impairment, dispositional risk factors include compliant and suggestible personalities, immaturity and impulsivity, a lack of criminal justice experience, substance use problems, chronic stress, fatigue, and cultural upbringing (Gudjonsson, 2003). Gudjonsson, Sigurdsson, Asgeirsdottir, and Sigfusdottir (2007) reported that multiple past victimizations (such as having been bullied or experienced violence at home) predicted increases in self-reported false confession among Icelandic youth. Previous sexual abuse, as an individual factor, also significantly distinguished false confessors from nonfalse confessors: 31% of the youth claiming false confession reported having been sexually abused compared with only 9% of youth who did not claim false confession. In essence, many of the factors that can increase the risk of false confession are also characteristics that define adolescence, such as immaturity, impulsivity, and a lack of experience, and are associated with delinquency and hence an increased likelihood of police contact, such as substance use, prior victimizations, and intellectual difficulties.

When the voluntariness or veracity of confessions is questioned, the courts use a totality of circumstances approach for adults and juveniles alike. As stated in *Fare v. Michael C.* (1979), a U.S. Supreme Court case dealing with a juvenile's *Miranda* waiver, the totality of circumstances "includes evaluation of the juvenile's age, experience, education, background, and intelligence, and into whether he has the capacity to understand the warnings given him, the nature of his Fifth Amendment rights, and the consequences of waiving those rights" (p. 725). However, in a more recent Supreme Court case, *Yarborough v. Alvarado* (2004), on the question of whether juveniles can reasonably surmise if they are in police custody (thus necessitating the *Miranda* warning), the Court disagreed that age and inexperience with law enforcement were relevant factors to consider. In the following sections, we review similarities and differences between adolescents and adults, both broadly and specifically in interrogation settings. We address several factors that often arise when the totality of circumstances are examined in individual cases.

## ARE ADOLESCENTS DIFFERENT FROM ADULTS?

For more than 100 years, developmental psychologists have known that adolescents differ from adults in profound ways (Parke, Ornstein, Reiser, & Waxler, 1994). Hence, entire textbooks and scholarly journals are devoted to the study of adolescents and their development (Lerner & Steinberg, 2004; Steinberg, 2008). Similarly, the U.S. legal system clearly differentiates between juveniles and adults. All states require individuals to be 21 years old to purchase alcohol; most states require individuals to be at least 18 before they can marry, vote, or serve on a jury. The U.S. Supreme Court made note of these state laws in *Roper v. Simmons* (2005), when it abolished the death penalty for defendants younger than 18 years.

Adolescence is a period marked by changes in biological, cognitive, social, and emotional development. According to Steinberg (2005), and as reviewed in detail by Reppucci, Michel, and Kostelnik (Chapter 15, this volume), early adolescence marks the onset of puberty, heightening emotional arousability, sensation seeking, and reward orientation; midadolescence is a period of increased vulnerability to risk taking and problems in affect and behavior; and late adolescence is a period during which the frontal lobes continue to mature, facilitating regulatory competence and executive functioning. Adolescence is also a time when the influence of peers becomes especially important. More recently, the concept of "emerging adulthood" has been proposed, which is a distinct period of growth between the ages of 18 and 25 years (Arnett, 2000). It is characterized as a period of transition and identity exploration; thus, although the legal system generally recognizes individuals as adults by age 18 (age 16 in some states), adulthood (and all the qualities defining adulthood) may be several years off from a developmental perspective.

Recent functional magnetic resonance imaging studies have revealed that the typical adolescent's brain is qualitatively different from the adult's. There is evidence that the limbic (socioemotional) system and prefrontal cortex (planning and cognitive control) continue to develop well into the early 20s of young adulthood (Steinberg, 2005, 2007), including the processes of synaptic pruning and myelination. Hence, adolescence can be described as a period when the socioemotional and cognitive control centers of the brain compete, with the socioemotional network gaining prominence (Steinberg, 2007).

In regard to adolescent suggestibility, the empirical evidence is limited. To be sure, clear and consistent research shows that age and suggestibility are negatively related (Bruck & Melnyck, 2004). However, the age at which this relation plateaus is less clear. Singh and Gudjonsson (1992) define interrogative suggestibility as "the tendency of an individual's account of events to be altered by misleading information and interpersonal pressure within interviews" (p. 155). Using the Gudjonsson Suggestibility Scale, Richardson, Gudjonsson, and Kelly (1995) compared the interrogative suggestibility of adolescents and adults and found that the two groups did not differ significantly in their memory scores or the number of times they yielded (or succumbed) to leading or misleading questions, but adolescents were significantly more likely to shift, or change their answers after receiving negative feedback (see also Warren, Hulse-Trotter, & Tubbs, 1991). These results suggest that whereas teens and adults do not differ in the cognitive-based component of suggestibility (i.e., memorial abilities), teens are more malleable when it comes to the social component of suggestibility (i.e., influence from examiners).

## ARE ADOLESCENTS DIFFERENT FROM ADULTS WITHIN INTERROGATION SETTINGS?

Many and varied capabilities can affect behavior in the interrogation room, including, but not limited to, decision making, perspective taking, maturity of judgment, and a knowledge and appreciation of legal processes (Cauffman & Steinberg, 2000; Modecki, 2008; Steinberg & Scott, 2003). In this section, we focus on research directly relevant to juveniles and interrogation, such as their comprehension of *Miranda* rights (see also Reppucci et al., Chapter 15, this volume) and the tendency to confess, even if inno-cent. It is reasonable to expect that those who do not fully comprehend the purpose and nature of interrogation, the importance of their rights, or the legal system more generally may be at increased risk for making false self-incriminating statements (Owen-Kostelnik et al., 2006; Redlich et al., 2004; Scott-Hayward, 2007).

Since Grisso's (1981) seminal research on *Miranda* comprehension, it has been evident that juveniles aged 14 years and younger do not pos-sess an adequate understanding and appreciation of their *Miranda* rights to the same degree as older teens and adults (Peterson-Badali & Koegl, 1998; Redlich, Silverman, & Steiner, 2003). Specifically, although 16- and 17-year-olds may achieve an adult-like understanding of what it means "to remain silent" or that something will "be held against you," it is less clear whether these older teens will voluntarily cede their rights in the face of authority figures using psychologically oriented social influence tactics. Research on adult waivers suggests that 75 to 80% of suspects waive their rights and talk to the police (e.g., Leo, 1996). Among juveniles, the rates are even higher, typically greater than 90% (Grisso & Pomicter, 1977; Viljoen, Klaver, & Roesch, 2005; but see Feld, 2006a).

Research on juveniles' legal competence has produced a similar pic-ture in regard to age. Grisso and colleagues (2003) interviewed close to 1,400 preteens, teens, and young adults in the community and in jail with regard to their adjudicative competence abilities (ability to confer with their lawyer and to make decisions; see Bonnie, 1992). Minors aged 15 and younger, regardless of their community/detention status, were more likely to be impaired on measures of competence than were older teens and young adults. Moreover, when presented with hypothetical interrogation scenar-ios, these younger juveniles were the most likely to choose "confess" rather than "remain silent" or "deny offense" options (see also Goldstein, Condie, Kalbeitzer, Osman, & Geier, 2003).

Of importance, some states require parents/guardians to be present during (or at least notified of) the interrogation of juvenile suspects, largely because of deficits in competence to waive *Miranda* rights. However, it is unclear whether parents will indeed be beneficial and act in their child's best interest. Woolard and colleagues (2008) examined the behavior of juveniles and their caretakers. Her results suggest that in the child–caretaker dyads she surveyed, about 25% of the caretakers exhibited impaired *Miranda* comprehension and 31% had both an impaired child and an impaired care-taker.

In a laboratory study that measured actual behavior, Redlich and Good-man (2003) found a significant, negative relation between age and likelihood of false confession. Specifically, using the ALT-key paradigm developed by Kassin and Kiechel (1996), 12- to 13-year-olds, 15- to 16-year-olds, and young adults were accused of crashing a computer and were asked to sign a statement taking responsibility for this "crime." The "crime" was hitting the ALT key after explicitly being told not to because doing so would crash the computer. With increasing age, compliance with signing the statement significantly decreased. Of importance, half of the juvenile participants signed the statement without comment or question in comparison to only one-third of the young adults. In addition, individual differences in suggestibility were positively correlated with false confession. Although it is difficult to recreate ethical and valid interrogation-like scenarios in the laboratory, especially when including juveniles, more laboratory and field research needs to be conducted. In the meantime, the robust findings from research on the capabilities and limitations of adolescents generally, and in interrogation specifically, serve as a secure base from which to extrapolate and to conclude that children and adolescents are distinguishable from adults in interrogation settings.

## ARE ADOLESCENTS INTERROGATED DIFFERENTLY FROM ADULTS?

Direct observation of actual interrogations has been difficult for researchers. Nonetheless, accumulating evidence suggests that adolescents and adults are similarly interrogated, regardless of their age, using the police interrogation tactics described earlier. Indeed, police interrogation training manuals, such as Inbau et al. (2001), are explicit that the same techniques can be used on juveniles and adults alike. In this section, we review evidence from self-report surveys of police and field and case studies.

### Police Officer Surveys

Kassin and colleagues (2007) conducted a survey of 631 police investigators from the United States and Canada. Although their focus was not on the interrogation of juvenile suspects, Kassin et al. (2007) confirmed that police officers frequently use Reid technique-like tactics, even when not formally trained. Also, police acknowledged that false confessions occur, an estimated 4.78% of the time when outliers in the distribution were excluded (original responses were skewed, so outliers were omitted to normalize the data; respondents were not asked to provide whether false confessions were from juveniles or adults).

More relevant to the focus of the present chapter is Meyer and Reppucci's (2007) survey of 332 Baltimore County, Maryland, law enforcement investigators about their juvenile interrogation practices and beliefs about child and adolescent development. Several notable findings emerged. First, police officers acknowledged that developmental differences exist among children (13 years and younger), youth (14–17 years), and adults (18 years and older); for example, that children and youths are more impulsive and more influenced by authority than adults. However, these developmental distinctions were acknowledged only outside of interrogation contexts. For example, whereas police agreed that children and youth generally are more suggestible than adults, when police rated the suggestibility of child and youth suspects during interrogation, significant differences between perceptions of minors and adults did not emerge. Second, despite recognizing in general terms that there are behavioral differences between children and youth compared with adults (e.g., that children are less likely to make eye contact and more likely to slouch), this awareness did not translate into differences in their own interrogation practices. More specifically, there were no significant differences in reports of interrogation practices for children, youth, or adults. Hence, police reported using the same techniques of deception detection, repeated questions, minimization, and deceit with the same frequency regardless of the suspect's age. Indeed, when asked directly whether juveniles and adults are or should be interrogated with the same techniques, on average, respondents slightly agreed (scale of 1 = *strongly disagree* to 6 = *strongly agree*; "Are Interrogated": $M = 3.77$, $SD = 1.15$; "Should be Interrogated": $M = 3.87$, $SD = 1.11$). Finally, police respondents did not acknowledge that the use of suggestive or repeated questions had differential effects by age on the likelihood of obtaining inaccurate, or false, answers. Although these results are based on findings from only one police jurisdiction, they are consistent with additional data from nearly 2,000 law enforcement professionals from police agencies nationwide (Reppucci, Meyer, & Kostelnik, 2007).

## Field and Case Studies

In the mid-1970s, Grisso and Pomicter (1977) accessed a random sample of juvenile court records for a 3-year period in St. Louis County, Missouri. Across 491 juveniles (aged 6–17 years) totaling 707 felony referrals, police questioning occurred 65 to 75% of the time, and in those cases 90% of juveniles waived their rights and talked to the police. Nearly all of the juveniles who chose not to waive their rights were aged 15 or older. Attorneys were almost never present, and the presence of a parent or a court officer had no influence on the invocation of rights. Although these data are informative, they are now more than 30 years old. More recently, Viljoen and colleagues (2005) interviewed 152 defendants aged 11 to 17 years. Of those aged 14 years or younger, only 8% asserted their right to silence and none requested to have a lawyer present (see also Redlich et al., 2004).

In contrast, in England, "appropriate adults" (e.g., family members, social workers) are required in the interrogations of juveniles and other vulnerable persons. Medford, Gudjonsson, and Pearse (2003) compared a sample of English adults and juveniles who had appropriate adults present at police questioning. An interesting pattern emerged: The majority of *juvenile* suspects (78%) had laypersons fulfilling the role of the appropriate adult, and overall 62% *waived* their right to legal representation. In contrast, the majority of *adult* suspects (69%) with appropriate adults present (58% of all adults) had professionals fulfilling that role. Adults with appropriate adults present waived their rights only 34% of the time. In contrast, adults without appropriate adults present waived their right to legal counsel 48% of the time.

In a recent observational study, Feld (2006a, 2006b) obtained transcripts of interrogations involving 16- to 18-year-old felony suspects in Ramsey County, Minnesota. Although Feld did not similarly obtain or code a comparable sample of adult interrogations, he concluded on the basis of other research on adult samples that police interrogated the juveniles "in much the same way as they did adults" (2006b, p. 304). Feld found that 80% of the juveniles waived their rights and that 70% had partially or fully confessed. Moreover, Feld reported that the police used both maximization (e.g., 70% confronted suspects with evidence; 49% accused suspects of lying; and 28% used techniques designed to heighten anxiety) and minimization (e.g., 50% presented scenarios or themes; 33% appealed to the suspect's honor; see also Redlich et al., 2004) techniques. It is important to note that although Feld's findings are interesting, they were derived from a nonrandom selection of cases, drawn from a single county, and without a comparable adult sample.

## Summary

There is converging evidence from interrogation training manuals, surveys of law enforcement, and field and case studies that the police do not distinguish between teen and adult suspects in interrogation practices. As stated in Redlich et al. (2004), "There is no contrary evidence in refute of this claim" (p. 122). Fours years later, we still cannot find evidence that police interrogate juvenile suspects differently than adults, despite clear and compelling developmental differences between them.

We have raised three questions and have provided a scientific basis for the propositions that (1) adolescents are developmentally different than adults, (2) these differences correspond to impaired decision making and behavior in interrogation settings, and (3) despite these differences, adolescents and adults are interrogated in the same manner. We must now ask, Why aren't different interrogation tactics used on adolescents and adults?

## WHY AREN'T CHILDREN AND ADULTS INTERROGATED DIFFERENTLY?

Meyer and Reppucci's (2007) survey research suggests that police are conceptually aware of the developmental differences between teens and adults, but they do not moderate their practice accordingly. Although we do not have a definitive answer as to why, we can only surmise that police officers, and perhaps people in general, believe that juveniles who commit crimes are qualitatively different than those who do not. As one police officer put it, "The juveniles I interrogate aren't kids, they're monsters" (Owen-Kostelnik et al., 2006, p. 298). Yet studies that have compared delinquent youth with nondelinquent youth have found either no qualitative differences between the two groups (Modecki, 2008) or, when differences are found, delinquents are more vulnerable, not more sophisticated. For example, in comparison to their peers, delinquent youth are often less intelligent and have more learning disabilities (Grisso et al., 2003) and mental health and substance use problems (Teplin et al., 2002; Redlich, 2007), all of which are associated with an increased risk of false confession. Although the 1990s concept of the juvenile superpredator has been generally discredited (Pizzaro, Chermak, & Gruenewald, 2007), a failure to recognize that juveniles can be vulnerable to manipulation by professional interrogators remains.

## POLICY RECOMMENDATIONS

Policy recommendations regarding the interrogation of juveniles are not new. More than 25 years ago, Grisso (1981) recommended the adoption of a per se rule requiring attorneys to be present during the questioning of youth. Yet today only a handful of states have such rules (Huang, 2001). Many other reforms have been advocated, including the electronic recording of interrogations (Drizin & Reich, 2004; Sullivan, 2005); requiring the presence of an "appropriate adult," such as a parent or victim-witness advocate; training police officers to question youths in developmentally appropriate ways (Owen-Kostelnik et al., 2006); and allowing for the increased presence of expert testimony in disputed confession cases involving juveniles (Redlich & Meissner, 2009).

Potentially most effective is a wholesale reform of interrogation practices with suspects, as seen in the United Kingdom and Australia and as planned in Belgium, Norway, and New Zealand (Bull, 2007). In response to a rash of problematic false-confession cases, England and Wales adopted a new ethos of interrogation beginning with the Police and Criminal Evidence (PACE) Act in 1984. PACE prompted a switch from the highly adversarial approach characterized by the Reid technique to investigative interviewing, an approach that emphasizes planning and preparation, training and supervision, and evaluation after the interview is over. In this model, the primary goal of questioning is to seek the truth, not necessarily to obtain a confession. The PACE model has been implemented for all interrogations regardless of suspect age.

A similar approach has been recommended and implemented when interviewing children who are alleged to be witnesses to crimes, either as victims or as bystanders (American Professional Society on the Abuse of Children, 2002; Poole & Lamb, 1998; see also Saywitz & Camparo, Chapter 6, this volume). Indeed, many commonalities exist between the problems previously identified in the interviewing of youth alleged to be victims and those currently identified in the interrogation of youth alleged to be perpetrators (see Redlich et al., 2004). In Israel, specially trained officers are thus responsible for interviewing youth, regardless of their status as victim, witness, or suspect.

Researchers at the National Institute of Child Health and Human Development (NICHD) developed a protocol for actual investigators to use when interviewing alleged child victims and witnesses (for a brief review, see Saywitz & Camparo, Chapter 6, this volume), with much of the research occurring in Israel. The protocol relies on the use of invitational, open-ended questions rather than leading and suggestive questions, on the grounds that invitational questions produce more information. Using a variation of the NICHD protocol, Hershkowitz, Horowitz, Lamb, Orbach, and Sternberg (2004) examined how the use of invitations, directive, option posing, and suggestive utterances influenced the statements, including confessions, of Israeli juveniles suspected of sexual crimes. As far as we could discern, there were two primary variations from the original NICHD protocol. First, in interviews of alleged victims, interviewers make an effort "to entrain narrative response style in the pre-substantive portion of the interview" and then "switch focus to substantive issues in a non-suggestive fashion" (p. 426). When using this protocol with suspects, these strategies were not used. Second, via pilot work, Hershkowitz and colleagues determined that the use of more directive and suggestive prompts (in comparison to initial open-ended prompts) were needed when interviewing suspects. However, as in victim interviews, interviewers of suspects were encouraged to ask for open-ended elaboration whenever possible.

The youthful suspects ($n$ = 72) ranged in age from 9 to 14 years. Although suspect age did not influence the use of question type, confessors were asked significantly more invitation, directive, and option-posing questions than nonconfessors (deniers). However, youth who denied and youth who admitted to the offense were asked a similar number of suggestive questions. Of particular note, more information was provided by suspects in response to open-ended than suggestive questioning, regardless of whether they confessed or denied involvement.

The results of the Hershkowitz et al. (2004) study, although largely cor-relational in nature, provide initial support that interrogations of juveniles (or adults) need not be suggestive to succeed and that the use of open-ended questions can educe information. In conjunction with the investigative inter-viewing methods successfully used in Europe and Australia, these results indicate that it is possible to obtain information, even self-incriminating information, from suspects without the use of confrontation, false evidence, minimization, and confirmation-seeking questions.

## CONCLUSION

By most accounts, juveniles are at increased risk of false confession when contemporary interrogation techniques are used. Although this susceptibil-ity has been recognized for decades (see *Haley v. Ohio,* 1948; *Gallegos v. Colorado,* 1962), interrogators continue in practice to adopt a one-size-fits-all approach. There appears to be one consideration that supersedes all others: the presupposition of guilt. When suspects are believed to be guilty, considerations of age, developmental maturity, intelligence, mental health, suggestibility, and other dispositional sources of vulnerability are set aside. It is clear, however, that the commission of a crime does little to alter one's youth, maturity, or vulnerability to influence. It is with this understanding, along with the undisputed fact that some suspects are innocent, that U.S. police interrogation practices must undergo reform.

## REFERENCES

American Professional Society on the Abuse of Children. (2002). *Practice guidelines: Investigative interviewing in cases of alleged child abuse.* Chicago: Author.

Arnett, J. J. (2000). Emerging adulthood: A theory of development from the late teens through the twenties. *American Psychologist, 55,* 469–480.

Bennett, W. J., DiIulio, J. J., & Walters, J. P. (1996). *Body count: Moral poverty and how to win America's war against crime and drugs.* New York: Simon & Schuster.

Bond, C. F., & DePaulo, B. M. (2006). Accuracy of deception judgments. *Personality and Social Psychology Bulletin, 10,* 214–234.

Bonnie, R. (1992). The competence of criminal defendants: A theoretical refor-mulation. *Behavioral Sciences and the Law, 10,* 291–316.

Bruck, M., & Melnyk, L. (2004). Individual differences in children's suggestibil-ity: A review and synthesis. *Applied Cognitive Psychology, 18,* 947–996.

Bull, R. (2007, September). *What really happens in police interviews with suspects?* Paper presented at Interrogations and Confessions: A Conference Exploring Research, Practice and Policy, El Paso, TX.

Cauffman, E. E., & Steinberg, L. (2000). (Im)maturity of judgment in adolescence: Why adolescents may be less culpable than adults. *Behavioral Sciences and the Law, 18,* 1–21.

Closson, M., & Rogers, K. M. (2007). Educational needs of youth in the juvenile justice system. In C. L. Kessler & L. Kraus (Eds.), *The mental health needs of young offenders: Forging paths through reintegration and rehabilitation* (pp. 229–240). Cambridge, UK: Cambridge University Press.

Davis, D., & O'Donohue, W. (2004). The road to perdition: "Extreme influence" tactics in the interrogation room. In W. O'Donohue & E. Levensky (Eds.), *Handbook of forensic psychology* (pp. 897–996). New York: Elsevier/Academic Press.

DiIulio, J. J., Jr.(1996, Spring). My black crime problem and ours. *City Journal, 6.* Retrieved January 30, 2009, from *www.city-journal.org/html/6_2_my_black.html.*

Drizin, S. A., & Colgan, B. (2004). Tales from the juvenile confession front: A guide to how standard police interrogation tactics can produce coerced and false confessions from juvenile suspects. In G. D. Lassiter (Ed.), *Interrogations, confessions, and entrapment* (pp. 127–162). New York: Kluwer Academic/Plenum.

Drizin, S. A., & Leo, R. A. (2004). The problem of false confessions in the post-DNA world. *North Carolina Law Review, 82,* 891–1008.

Drizin, S. A., & Reich, M. J. (2004). Heeding the lessons of history: The need for mandatory recording of police interrogations to accurately assess the reliability and voluntariness of confessions. *Drake Law Review, 52,* 619–646.

Fare v. Michael C., 442 U.S. 707 (1979).

Feld, B. (2006a). Juveniles' competence to exercise *Miranda* rights: An empirical study of policy and practice. *Minnesota Law Review, 91,* 26–100.

Feld, B. (2006b). Police interrogation of juveniles: An empirical study of policy and practice. *Journal of Criminal Law and Criminology, 97,* 219–316.

Gallegos v. Colorado, 370 U.S. 49 (1962).

Goldstein, N. E. S., Condie, L., Kalbeitzer, R., Osman, D., & Geier, J. L. (2003). Juvenile offenders' *Miranda* rights comprehension and self-reported likelihood of offering false confessions. *Assessment, 10,* 359–369.

Grisso, T. (1981). *Juvenile's waiver of rights: Legal and psychological competence.* New York: Plenum Press.

Grisso, T., & Pomicter, C. (1977). Interrogation of juveniles: An empirical study of procedures, safeguards, and rights waiver. *Law and Human Behavior, 1,* 321–342.

Grisso, T., Steinberg, L., Woolard, J. L., Cauffman, E. E., Scott, E. S., Graham, S., et al. (2003). Juveniles' competence to stand trial: A comparison of adolescents' and adults' capacities as trial defendants. *Law and Human Behavior, 27,* 333–363.

Gross, S. R., Jacoby, K., Matheson, D. J., Montgomery, N., & Patil, S. (2005). Exonerations in the United States 1989 through 2003. *Journal of Criminal Law and Criminology, 95*, 523–560.

Gudjonsson, G. H. (2003). *The psychology of interrogations and confessions.* Chichester, UK: Wiley.

Gudjonsson, G. H., & MacKeith, J. A. C. (1990). A proven case of false confession: Psychological aspects of the coerced-compliant type. *Medicine, Science, and the Law, 30*, 329–335.

Gudjonsson, G. H., Sigurdsson, J. F., Asgeirsdottir, B. B., & Sigfusdottir, I. D. (2006). Custodial interrogation, false confession, and individual differences: A national study among Icelandic youth. *Personality and Individual Differences, 41*, 49–59.

Gudjonsson, G. H., Sigurdsson, J. F., Asgeirsdottir, B. B., & Sigfusdottir, I. D. (2007). Custodial interrogation: What are the background factors associated with claims of false confession to the police? *Journal of Forensic Psychiatry and Psychology, 18*, 266–275.

Haley v. Ohio, 332 U.S. 596 (1948).

Hancock, L. (2003, January/February). Wolf pack: The press and the Central Park jogger. *Columbia Journalism Review*, pp. 1–11.

Hershkowitz, I., Horowitz, D., Lamb, M. E., Orbach, Y., & Sternberg, K. J. (2004). Interviewing youthful suspects in alleged sex crimes: A descriptive analysis. *Child Abuse and Neglect, 28*, 423–438.

Huang, D. T. (2001). "Less unequal footing": State courts' per se rules for juvenile waivers during interrogations and the case for their implementation. *Cornell Law Review, 86*, 437–477.

Inbau, F. E., Reid, J. E., Buckley, J. P., & Jayne, B. C. (2001). *Criminal interrogation and confessions* (4th ed.). Gaithersburg, MD: Aspen.

Kassin, S. M. (2005). On the psychology of confessions: Does innocence put innocents at risk? *American Psychologist, 60*, 215–228.

Kassin, S. M. (2008). False confessions: Causes, consequences, implications for reform. *Current Directions in Psychological Science, 17*, 249–253.

Kassin, S. M., & Fong, C. T. (1999). "I'm innocent!" Effects of training on judgments of truth and deception in the interrogation room. *Law and Human Behavior, 27*, 499–516.

Kassin, S. M., & Gudjonsson, G. H. (2004). The psychology of confessions: A review of the literature and issues. *Psychological Science in the Public Interest, 5*, 33–67.

Kassin, S. M., & Kiechel, K. L. (1996). The social psychology of false confessions: Compliance, internalization, and confabulation. *Psychological Science, 7*, 125–128.

Kassin, S. M., Leo, R. A., Meissner, C. A., Richman, K. D., Colwell, L. H., Leach, A.-M., et al. (2007). Police interviewing and interrogation: A self-report survey of police practices and beliefs. *Law and Human Behavior, 31*, 381–400.

Kassin, S. M., & McNall, K. (1991). Police interrogations and confessions:

Communicating promises and threats by pragmatic implication. *Law and Human Behavior, 15,* 233–251.

Kassin, S. M., Meissner, C. A., & Norwick, R. J. (2005). "I'd know a false confession if I saw one": A comparative study of college students and police investigators. *Law and Human Behavior, 29,* 211–227.

Kassin, S. M., & Norwick, R. J. (2004). Why people waive their *Miranda* rights: The power of innocence. *Law and Human Behavior, 28,* 211–221.

Lassiter, G. D. (Ed.). (2004). *Interrogations, confessions, and entrapment.* New York: Kluwer Academic.

Leo, R. A. (1996). Miranda's revenge: Police interrogation as a confidence game. *Law and Society Review, 30,* 259–288.

Leo, R. A. (2008). *Police interrogation and American justice.* Cambridge, MA: Harvard University Press.

Leo, R. A., & Ofshe, R. J. (1998). The consequences of false confessions: Deprivations of liberty and miscarriages of justice in the age of psychological interrogation. *Journal of Criminal Law and Criminology, 88,* 429–496.

Lerner, R. M., & Steinberg, L. (2004). *Handbook of adolescent psychology.* Hoboken, NJ: Wiley.

Medford, S., Gudjonsson, G. H., & Pearse, J. (2003). The efficacy of the appropriate adult safeguard during police interviewing. *Legal and Criminological Psychology, 8,* 253–266.

Meissner, C. A., & Kassin, S. M. (2002). "He's guilty!" Investigator bias in judgments of truth and deception. *Law and Human Behavior, 26,* 469–480.

Meyer, J. R., & Reppucci, N. D. (2007). Police practices and perceptions regarding juvenile interrogation and interrogative suggestibility. *Behavioral Sciences and the Law, 25,* 1–24.

Miranda v. Arizona, 384 U.S. 436 (1966).

Modecki, K. L. (2008). Addressing gaps in the maturity of judgment literature: Age differences and delinquency. *Law and Human Behavior, 32,* 78–91.

New York v. Wise, Richardson, McCray, Salaam, & Santana. Affirmation in Response to Motion to Vacate Judgment of Conviction, Indictment No. 4762/89 (December 5, 2002).

Owen-Kostelnik, J., Reppucci, N. D., & Meyer, J. R. (2006). Testimony and interrogation of minors: Assumptions about maturity and morality. *American Psychologist, 61,* 286–304.

Parke, R. D., Ornstein, P. A., Reiser, J. J., & Waxler, C. (1994). *A century of developmental psychology.* Washington, DC: American Psychological Association.

People v. Ricky Mitchell, 18 NY Court of Appeals (2004).

Peterson-Badali, M., & Koegl, C. J., (1998). Young people's knowledge of the Young Offenders Act and the youth justice system. *Canadian Journal of Criminology, 40,* 127–152.

Pizzaro, J. M., Chermak, S. M., & Gruenewald, J. A. (2007). Juvenile "superpredators" in the news: A comparison of adult and juvenile homicides. *Journal of Criminal Justice and Popular Culture, 14,* 84–111.

Poole, D. A., & Lamb, M. E. (1998). *Investigative interviews of children: A guide for helping professionals.* Washington, DC: American Psychological Association.

Quinn, M. M., Rutherford, R. B., Leone, P. E., Osher, D. M., & Poirier, J. M. (2005). Youth with disabilities in juvenile corrections: A national survey. *Exceptional Children, 71,* 339–345.

Redlich, A. D. (2007). Double jeopardy in the interrogation room: Young age and mental illness. *American Psychologist, 62,* 609–611.

Redlich, A. D., & Drizin, S. A. (2007). Police interrogation of youth. In C. L. Kessler & L. Kraus (Eds.), *The mental health needs of young offenders: Forging paths through reintegration and rehabilitation* (pp. 61–78). Cambridge, UK: Cambridge University Press.

Redlich, A. D., & Goodman, G. S. (2003). Taking responsibility for an act not committed: The influence of age and suggestibility. *Law and Human Behavior, 27,* 141–156.

Redlich, A. D., & Meissner, C. A. (2009). Techniques and controversies on the interrogation of suspects: The artful practice versus the scientific study. In J. L. Skeem, K. S. Douglas, & S. O. Lilienfeld (Eds.), *Psychological science in the courtroom: Consensus and controversy* (pp. 124–148). New York: Guilford Press.

Redlich, A. D., Silverman, M., Chen, J., & Steiner, H. (2004). The police interrogation of children and adolescents. In G. D. Lassiter (Ed.), *Interrogations, confessions, and entrapment* (pp. 107–126). New York: Kluwer Academic/Plenum.

Redlich, A. D., Silverman, M., & Steiner, H. (2003). Factors affecting preadjudicative and adjudicative competence in juveniles and young adults. *Behavioral Sciences and the Law, 21,* 1–17.

Reppucci, N. D., Meyer, J. R., & Kostelnik, J. O. (September, 2007). *Police interrogation of juveniles: Results of a national survey of police.* Paper presented at Interrogations and Confessions: A Conference Exploring Research, Practice and Policy, El Paso, TX.

Richardson, G., Gudjonsson, G. H., & Kelly, T. P. (1995). Interrogative suggestibility in an adolescent forensic population. *Journal of Adolescence, 18,* 211–216.

Rogers, R., Harrison, K. S., Shuman, D. W., Sewell, K. W., & Hazelwood, L. L. (2007). An analysis of *Miranda* warnings and waivers: Comprehension and coverage. *Law and Human Behavior, 31,* 177–192.

Roper v. Simmons, 543 U.S. 551 (2005).

Russano, M. B., Meissner, C. A., Narchet, F. M., & Kassin, S. M. (2005). Investigating true and false confessions within a novel experimental paradigm. *Psychological Science, 16,* 481–486.

Scott-Hayward, C. S. (2007). Explaining juvenile false confessions: Adolescent development and police interrogation. *Law and Psychology Review, 31,* 53–74.

Sigurdsson, J. F., & Gudjonsson, G. H. (1996). The psychological characteristics of false confessors: A study among Icelandic prison inmates and juvenile offenders. *Personality and Individual Differences, 20,* 321–329.

Singh, K. K., & Gudjonsson, G. H. (1992). Interrogative suggestibility among adolescent boys and its relationship with intelligence, memory, and cognitive set. *Journal of Adolescence, 15,* 155–161.

Steinberg, L. (2005). Cognitive and affective development in adolescence. *Trends in Cognitive Sciences, 9,* 69–74.

Steinberg, L. (2007). Risk taking in adolescence: New perspectives from brain and behavioral science. *Current Directions in Psychological Science, 16,* 55–59.

Steinberg, L. (2008). *Adolescence* (8th ed.). New York: McGraw-Hill.

Steinberg, L., & Scott, E. S. (2003). Less guilty by reason of adolescence: Developmental immaturity, diminished responsibility, and the juvenile death penalty. *American Psychologist, 58,* 1009–1018.

Sullivan, T. P. (2005). Electronic recording of custodial interrogations: Everybody wins. *Journal of Criminal Law and Criminology, 95,* 1127–1144.

Teplin, L. A., Abram, K. M., McClelland, G. M., Dulcan, M. K., & Mericle, A. A. (2002). Psychiatric disorders in youth in juvenile detention. *Archives of General Psychiatry, 59,* 1133–1143.

Viljoen, J. L., Klaver, J., & Roesch, R. (2005). Legal decisions of preadolescent and adolescent defendants: Predictors of confessions, pleas, communication with attorneys, and appeals. *Law and Human Behavior, 29,* 253–277.

Vrij, A. (2008). *Detecting lies and deceit: Pitfalls and opportunities.* Chichester, UK: Wiley.

Vrij, A., Mann, S., & Fisher, R. P. (2006). An empirical test of the behaviour analysis interview. *Law and Human Behavior, 30,* 329–345.

Warren, A., Hulse-Trotter, K., & Tubbs, E. (1991). Inducing resistance to suggestibility in children. *Law and Human Behavior, 15,* 273–285.

Wharton, E. (1920). *The age of innocence.* New York: D. Appleton and Company.

Woolard, J. L., Cleary, H. M. D., Harvell, S. A. S., & Chen, R. (2008). Examining adolescents' and their parents' conceptual and practical knowledge of police interrogation: A family dyad approach. *Journal of Youth and Adolescence, 37,* 685–698.

Yarborough v. Alvarado, 541 U.S. 652 (2004).

Chapter 15

# Challenging Juvenile Transfer

*Faulty Assumptions*
*and Misguided Policies*

N. Dickon Reppucci
Jaime L. Michel
Jessica O. Kostelnik

Over the last 20 years, the number of juvenile offenders transferred from the juvenile court and tried in adult criminal court has increased drastically. Various sociopolitical and historical forces have confounded the initial rehabilitative philosophy of the juvenile court; the focus has shifted from recognizing needs associated with developmental immaturity to punishing deeds (Reppucci, 1999). Inherent in this shift are changing conceptions regarding the developmental maturity of youthful offenders. In our opinion, the "waiver" of youth to the adult system is a misguided and reactionary crime control measure that exposes adolescents to the more adversarial and punishment-oriented adult criminal system where a consideration of developmental maturity is not required. This chapter briefly outlines the history, appropriateness, and consequences of this increasing trend toward the "waiver" of adolescents to the adult court. In particular, it explores how psychology informs the transfer debate regarding (1) the developmental maturity of youthful offenders in the preadjudicative and adjudicative contexts and (2) how policymakers should consider developmental maturity in their response to youthful offenders.

## HISTORY OF TRANSFER LAWS

The juvenile justice system was originally designed with the intent of providing rehabilitation for delinquent youth. The first juvenile court, established in 1899 by progressive reformers in Chicago, operated under the assumption that the appropriate response to "delinquent" youth was to take the youth's immaturity and malleability into account. Progressive social reformers criticized the lack of consistent interventions in the lives of delinquent youth who were at risk of being placed in adult courts and jails or arbitrarily released without any plan for remediation (Manfredi, 1998). Individualized justice was the guiding principle, and informal proceedings were designed to serve as a forum in which to assess the needs of these youth and develop appropriate interventions. Reformers believed it was incumbent on the state to act in a paternalistic manner toward such youth and to curb them from their "wayward" paths by focusing on their personal characteristics and needs as opposed to the nature of the offense (Mack, 1909).

Since its inception, the juvenile court has exercised the option to transfer certain youth to the adult/criminal court, predominantly on a case-by-case basis, in the form of judicial discretion. Transfer was a "minor current" running through earlier juvenile courts because its practice was initially geared toward older adolescents and recidivists, who were perceived as a threat to younger adolescents residing in reform school settings (Tanenhaus, 2000). Eventually, the practice was used as a safety valve by which judges could transfer those youth deemed nonamenable to treatment or a threat to public safety. The practice of transfer took a legal center stage in *Kent v. the United States* (1966) as the Supreme Court formally recognized the severity of the waiver of jurisdiction from juvenile to criminal court. The Supreme Court determined that waiver to the adult criminal court for adjudication must be preceded by an investigation and judicial hearing in which a judge had to weigh specific criteria in order to establish the necessity of transfer. These criteria included the nature and severity of the offense, prior delinquent history, sophistication of the minor, the potential threat the minor poses to the community, the amenability of the juvenile to rehabilitation, and the availability and accessibility of rehabilitative services within the juvenile court jurisdiction. In a review of the Supreme Court's holding and the litigation strategy in *Kent*, Manfredi (1998) noted that procedural issues were prioritized over equally important conceptual clarification of the transfer criteria laid out in Kent, such as "amenability to treatment" and "sophistication of the minor." Only recently have researchers begun to clarify the factors underlying these psychological constructs and how psychologists and juvenile judges weigh them (Brannen et al., 2006; Salekin, Rogers, & Ustad, 2001; Salekin, Yff, Neumann, Leistico, & Zalot, 2002).

In 1967, the landmark Supreme Court case *In re Gault* instigated the due process revolution in the juvenile courts. *Gault* did not directly address the issue of transfer; however, critics interpret *Gault* as unintentionally setting the stage for the more punitive transfer polices of the 1990s (Feld, 1999; Manfredi, 1998). Before *Gault,* constitutional rights to due process were perceived as unnecessary as juvenile courts operated in a nonadversarial and informal manner. However, these informal court proceedings and the notion of individualized justice came under fire in the 1960s as juvenile courts were criticized as being susceptible to arbitrary judicial decision making, creating vast disparities in consequences received by juvenile offenders (Feld, 1999). In *Gault,* the Supreme Court ruled that juveniles have a constitutional right to due process and should be afforded the procedural protections of the rights (1) against self-incrimination, (2) to counsel, (3) to cross-examine witnesses, and (4) to notification of the charges against them. Justice Fortas, writing for the majority, stated that he did not foresee the introduction of these procedural protections into juvenile courts as an impediment to their rehabilitative mission (*In re Gault,* 1967). In hindsight, this assessment seems faulty in that the constitutional domestication of the juvenile courts appears to have had the unintended consequence of legitimizing punitive juvenile justice reforms, most notably by increasing the number of youth transferred and tried in adult criminal courts (Feld, 1999). Thus, although youth were granted more adult-like due process rights, they soon became more subject to adult-like punishments.

The punitive legislative reforms appear to have been in response to a much-publicized increase in adolescent violence, particularly adolescent homicide, which began in the mid-1980s (Blumstein, 1995). Exaggerated perceptions of this increase in violence (Males, 1996) elicited a response that labeled these violent youth as "qualitatively different" from youth of an earlier era. Prophetic claims of a "new breed" of adolescents in future generations engendered fear in the public, and crime control advocates demanded stricter accountability administered by the punishment-oriented adult criminal courts rather than the presumed leniency of the rehabilitation-oriented juvenile courts (Meyer, Reppucci, & Owen, 2006; Zimring, 1998). Between 1985 and 1994, there was a 71% increase in the number of adolescents transferred to the adult court, as the annual number of transfer cases grew from 7,200 in 1985 to 12,300 in 1994 (Butts, 1997). This increase was aided by a flurry of legislative activity that ensued between 1992 and 1997, in which 47 states and the District of Columbia "got tough" on adolescent crime by expanding the punitive nature of existing laws and writing new ones that dictate the criminal prosecution and sentencing of juvenile offenders (Snyder & Sickmund, 1999).

These new laws shifted the emphasis away from the juvenile court model of individualized justice, using offender-based criteria on a case-by-case basis to make the transfer decision to a criminal court model based solely on the alleged crime committed. In most states, the age at which youth are eligible for transfer was lowered from 16 to 14 years or younger, and the range of eligible offenses for transfer was widened (Snyder & Sickmund, 1999). Initially, waiver had been determined through a judicial hearing. Although judicial waiver is still widely used, the discretion of judges has been curtailed as reforms have led many states to endorse additional mechanisms for transfer. By the end of 1997, 28 states had included automatic or statutory waiver in their legislative statutes, whereby some youth, depending on the offense, could be automatically transferred and prosecuted in the adult system. Also, 15 states enacted legislation referred to as prosecutorial discretion or direct file, which enabled prosecutors to file charges directly against an adolescent offender in adult criminal court (Snyder & Sickmund, 1999). Both automatic and prosecutorial waiver laws bypassed judicial hearings in which a more comprehensive investigation of the offense, and particularly of the offender, could be obtained. Blended sentencing was also implemented in 20 states by 1997, allowing either juvenile or adult courts to impose both a juvenile and an adult sentence, with the adult sentence coming into effect after the juvenile jurisdiction ended, usually at age 21 (Redding & Howell, 2000). Zimring (1998) noted that the symbolism of creating and increasing the use of new modes of transfer served to resolve the conundrum of treating adolescents as adults. Recategorizing these adolescents as adults relieved the states' obligation of paternal protection, as is reflected in the rationale: "Old enough to do the crime, old enough to do the time."

## DEVELOPMENTAL MATURITY OF JUVENILE OFFENDERS

Through a developmental lens, psychologists entered the public discourse on transfer in the mid-1990s by challenging the presumption that the recategorization of youth as adult defendants did not, by definition, negate the developmental immaturity of adolescents (Scott & Grisso, 1998). By reconfiguring previous developmental models of decision making, a new research agenda was formed to explore the inherent difficulties in presuming adolescents' adjudicative competence in the more adversarial venue of adult criminal court proceedings and in the preadjudicative context of adolescents' comprehension of *Miranda* warnings. Simultaneously, scholars fleshed out the nature of the developmental construct of "psychosocial immaturity" and noted its relevance to these competencies as well as to the concept of culpability. Theory and research in these areas have played an important role in highlighting the developmental differences between juveniles and adults, differences that had largely been neglected within the public discourse on transfer policies.

## Cognitive Constructs and Decision Making

Historically, paternalistic policies regarding medical decision making have relied on intuitive models of developmental maturity to deem adolescents incompetent to make important decisions in medical and legal contexts. Supreme Court decisions, such as *Parham v. J.R.* (1979) and *Bellotti v. Baird* (1979), used the developmental immaturity of adolescents as a rationale to limit adolescents' ability to make their own decisions about medical procedures without parental consent. This perspective was challenged in the wake of the debate regarding adolescents' access to abortion. Advocates of adolescent self-determination used an informed consent framework to support a minor's capacity to "knowingly, voluntarily, and intelligently" make a medical decision regarding abortion (Interdivisional Committee on Adolescent Abortion, 1987). The informed consent framework of understanding adolescent decision making was based on theories and research (e.g., Melton, 1987; Weithorn & Campbell, 1982) that posit that adolescents and adults do not necessarily differ developmentally on cognitive constructs relevant to decision making such as understanding, reasoning, and appreciation.

## Psychosocial Maturity and Decision Making

Critical of the cognitive orientation of the informed consent framework and its applicability to youth in the juvenile justice system, other researchers sought to expand this framework to include the influence of psychosocial factors on adolescent decision making (Scott, Reppucci, & Woolard, 1995; Steinberg & Cauffman, 1996). This newly constructed "judgment" framework takes the following psychosocial factors into consideration: (1) conformity and compliance with peers and authority figures; (2) risk assessment and perception; and (3) temporal perspective and calculation of long-term consequences (Scott et al., 1995). It is this judgment framework that has served as the theoretical model for more recent research on adjudicative competence, preadjudicative competence, and culpability, reviewed next.

## Developmental Maturity in the Context of Criminal Adjudication

### Adjudicative Competence

Developmental maturity and its impact on the adjudicative competence of adolescents in the adult criminal system have recently been given more consideration in the discourse on transfer. Adult incompetence has generally been attributed to mental illness or mental retardation. *Dusky v. United States* (1960) required that adult defendants be found competent to stand trial by a standard that takes into account a defendant's ability to have both a factual and rational understanding of the legal proceedings as well as an ability to communicate effectively with counsel. Adolescents subject to "get-tough" transfer policies run the risk of being adjudicated in an adult criminal system where their developmental immaturity may impede their ability to participate fully in criminal proceedings. Thus, constitutional issues of fundamental fairness are at stake because incompetent transferred youth are more vulnerable to the full penalties imposed on them by the adult courts (Scott & Grisso, 2005). The current wave of theory and research on adjudicative competence in adolescents explores primarily the role of developmental immaturity (Bonnie & Grisso, 2000; Grisso et al., 2003; Scott & Grisso, 2005; Viljoen, Zapf, & Roesch, 2007).

Bonnie and Grisso (2000) explain two important concepts linked to the *Dusky* criteria that are critical for conceptualizing adjudicative competence. The first is "competence to assist counsel," which includes the capacity to communicate with counsel on one's own behalf, to understand the charges and the purpose of criminal court proceedings, and to appreciate one's own role as a defendant in these proceedings. A second fundamental concept is "decisional competence," which includes the capacity of a defendant to understand and appreciate the significance of the important decisions that must be made during the adjudication process and to be able to engage rationally in that decision-making process. They conclude that failing to attend to developmental differences relevant to decision making "may result in unfair jeopardy for youths whose developmental incapacities impair their ability to participate in their defense" (p. 88).

Regarding decisional competence, within the attorney–juvenile client relationship, Schmidt, Reppucci, and Woolard (2003) compared 203 juveniles and 110 adults detained pretrial and used a hypothetical attorney–client vignette to examine how psychosocial factors are reflected in decision-making processes and linked to decision outcomes and effective participation within the attorney–client relationship. Their results demonstrated age-related differences in decision outcomes. For example, adolescents were more likely to suggest refusing to talk to their attorney than adults. In addition, several developmental judgment factors were implicated as potentially influential in the decision-making processes of adolescents. For example, adolescents compared with adults were more likely to focus on short-term rather than long-term consequences.

Grisso et al. (2003) conducted the most comprehensive study of the influence of developmental maturity on the adjudicative competence of adolescents. These investigators used a large sample of juveniles in both detention and community settings in multiple geographic regions in the United States. The researchers administered a standardized measure to evaluate participants' capacity to understand, reason about, and appreciate critical aspects related to their capacities to serve as trial defendants. In addition, decisional competence was assessed by measuring the psychosocial influences on adolescent decision making in the adjudicative context. Their findings suggest that adolescents 15 years old and younger were significantly more impaired than 16- and 17-year-old adolescents and young adults in abilities related to competence to stand trial. Adolescents aged 11 to 13 years old showed the most significant impairments. In fact, 33% of the 11- to 13-year-olds and 20% of the 14- to 15-year-olds were "as impaired in capacities relevant to adjudicative competence as are seriously mentally ill adults who would likely be considered incompetent to stand trial by clinicians who perform evaluations for courts" (p. 356). Adolescents with lower IQs showed significant impairment in competency abilities. This finding is relevant because of the disproportionate number of adolescents in juvenile justice populations who have low IQ scores (Moeller, 2001). Regarding the psychosocial characteristics of decision making, youth 15 years old and younger were significantly more likely than older youth to make decisions that represented "compliance with authorities" and to choose options associated with higher risks. Those youth aged 14 years and younger were significantly less likely to consider the long-term consequences of their choices.

In reference to transfer laws that have lowered the age of youth eligible for transfer to 14 years or younger, these findings challenge the assumption that the commission of a specific crime automatically implies that an adolescent is as competent as an adult to proceed in the highly adversarial adjudicative criminal process. As a result, Grisso et al. (2003) proposed a "two-tier" system of adjudicative competence whereby competency standards, specifically regarding incompetence as a result of developmental immaturity, should be set at a lower level in the juvenile courts than in adult courts so that juvenile courts may serve as appropriate alternatives for youth who may demonstrate developmental incompetence in the adult criminal system. Such a system would eliminate transfer to adult courts for many youth because they would be considered developmentally incompetent per se in adult court but not in the juvenile court system.

Building on Grisso et al.'s (2003) research, Viljoen et al. (2007) applied different adjudicative standards to a sample of 152 juvenile defendants between the ages of 11 and 17 years. They compared an adult standard of competence using measures that assessed understanding, appreciation, and communication with an adolescent standard of competence that used only basic understanding and communication. Over half of the defendants younger than 15 were significantly impaired on adult standards of incompetence, but only 26% of youth 15 and younger were found impaired when an adolescent standard was applied. These findings offer strong support for integrating competency evaluations and using developmental maturity as a criterion in transfer proceedings to ensure that adolescents' rights to fundamental fairness are upheld. Viljoen et al. (2007) note that numerous professional and financial resources would need to be expended to accommodate competency evaluations for youth who have been transferred, and that another possible solution would be to adjudicate these youth in juvenile courts with a lower competency standard, providing that the penalties are not as severe as those they could receive in the adult courts. Many states and jurisdictions have not yet formalized policies regarding adolescent adjudicative competence; however, there are state appellate courts that have held that a lower standard of competence should be accepted in juvenile courts (*In re Carey*, 2000; *Ohio v. Settles*, 1998).

It is worth noting that in adult courts, if a defendant is found incompetent to stand trial because of mental disorder, an attempt may be made to *restore* the defendant to competence and then, once restored, to take that person to trial. It has been suggested that the same idea be applied to youth; however, if a youth is developmentally incompetent to begin with, it is problematic to assume that competence can be restored in an individual who was never previously competent. Viljoen and Grisso (2007) suggest that the term "remediation" rather than "restoration" more aptly describes psychoeducational interventions used to facilitate competence in adolescence precisely because this term does not assume prior competence. They discuss the challenges of remediating competence in adolescent defendants and conclude that competence based on developmental immaturity in youth may not be so easily remediated. In light of the unique problems that developmental immaturity poses for remediating competence, they suggest the need for more research that adequately investigates strategies for the remediation of the legal capacities of incompetent youth. Viljoen and Grisso cautiously recommend training attorneys in adolescent development so as to enable them to develop better working relationships with their juvenile clients in order to facilitate effective "legal instruction." A more preferred alternative is the adjudication of incompetent youth in juvenile as opposed to criminal court. In spite of valiant efforts to explore remediation interventions for incompetent youth because of developmental immaturity, the question remains as to whether or not it is fair to try a youth for a crime committed when the youth was not, nor ever had been, competent.

## Preadjudicative Competence

Research and theory on the influence of developmental maturity on adjudicative competence are often inextricably linked with both theory and research on adolescents' comprehension of *Miranda* rights. It is important to understand that comprehension of *Miranda* rights occurs at an earlier preadjudicative stage when a youth is first arrested and faced with the possibility of an interrogation. *Miranda v. Arizona* (1966) required that adult criminal suspects, upon arrest, be informed of their "right to remain silent" and their "right to request counsel" as a fundamental part of their rights to due process. Adolescents were granted these same due process rights in *Gault* (*In re Gault*, 1967). The significance of a waiver of *Miranda* rights is that a confession on the part of a suspect is often the critical evidence in the fact-finding stage of criminal proceedings. Given that the interrogation process often occurs in a highly adversarial and manipulative setting, adolescents may be more vulnerable than adults in this legal context and fail to understand and appreciate the significance of their *Miranda* rights as an important procedural safeguard (Owen-Kostelnik, Reppucci, & Meyer, 2006; for more discussion, see Redlich & Kassin, Chapter 14, this volume). Although in *Haley v. Ohio* (1948) and *Gallegos v. Colorado* (1962) the Supreme Court upheld the fact that minors are not mature (competent) enough to withstand the pressures of a police interrogation without the presence of a lawyer or another concerned adult, the Court reexamined the issue in *Fare v. Michael C.* (1979) and endorsed a "totality of circumstances" versus a "per se" approach in assessing whether a juvenile's waiver of *Miranda* rights was made "knowingly, voluntarily and intelligently." What this means is that during criminal proceedings a judge may evaluate the defendant's capacities to waive *Miranda* rights by analyzing the entire circumstances of the interrogation to elicit a confession instead of finding it unacceptable for all minors.

Grisso (1980) questioned the legitimacy of the totality approach in an influential study exploring adolescents' capacities not only to understand *Miranda* warnings but also to appreciate their significance in deciding whether or not to waive these rights. A large adolescent sample was drawn from a detention facility, a juvenile correctional facility, and a boys' town residential program, and adult samples consisted of ex-offenders living in a halfway house and nonoffenders drawn from local custodial and maintenance crews. Standardized measures were created to assess the ability of participants to understand the words and phrases used in *Miranda* warnings and to assess their understanding of the function and significance of *Miranda*'s critical procedural safeguards. Adolescents younger than 15 were significantly less likely to meet the adult norm for comprehension and appreciation of *Miranda* rights compared with adults. Moreover, as a class, 15- and 16-year-olds with an IQ below 80 did not meet the adult standard of comprehension, nor was their comprehension comparable to same-age peers. In light of these findings, Grisso warned that adolescents, particularly those 15 years old and younger, may not adequately comprehend their *Miranda* rights at a level such that they can competently waive them.

More recent research, often conducted in conjunction with adjudicative competence studies, has continued to question the capacity of adolescents to comprehend and appreciate the significance of *Miranda* warnings. Viljoen et al. (2007) found that more than half of adolescents 15 years old and younger had limited abilities in their understanding and appreciation of *Miranda* warnings, although significantly more of these youth were able to comprehend *Miranda* warnings when a lower "adolescent standard" of understanding was used. Viljoen et al. (2007) found that adolescent defendants aged 15 years old and younger were more likely than older defendants to waive their right to an attorney and make a confession. Broadening the scope of *Miranda* comprehension to explore its relationship to self-reports of offering a false confession, Goldstein, Condie, Kalbeitzer, Osman, and Geier (2003) used age, IQ, and *Miranda* comprehension as predictor variables. These investigators reported that, in their sample of 57 adolescent males in a postdispositional juvenile facility, comprehension of *Miranda* rights was negatively correlated with self-reports of offering a false confession. Age was the most significant predictor of the likelihood of offering a false confession. When controlling for IQ and comprehension of *Miranda* rights, adolescents aged 13 through 15 years were significantly more likely than adolescents aged 16 through 18 years to report that they would make a false confession. Goldstein et al. (2003) make policy recommendations identical to Grisso's (1980), specifically, that a per se approach should replace the current totality of circumstances and an interested adult, preferably an attorney, should be present during any interrogation.

## Culpability

At the heart of the punitive transfer reform policies is the assumption that adolescents who commit serious crimes are equally as culpable as adults and deserving of the same punishment. This is in direct opposition to the underlying assumptions of the juvenile justice system, which applies a lower standard of culpability or blameworthiness to adolescent offenders because of their immaturity (Scott & Grisso, 1998). This lower standard of culpability relates to the legal principle of proportionality, which requires that punishment be determined by the level of responsibility assigned to the criminal actor (Zimring, 2000). For example, the juvenile justice system has traditionally perceived adolescents as less culpable and, therefore, deserving of a lesser punishment. The Supreme Court has echoed this principle of proportionality as it relates to lesser culpability in *Thompson v. Oklahoma* (1988), holding that adolescents younger than age 16, because of their immaturity, are subject to "reduced culpability." Writing for the majority, Justice Stevens determined that "inexperience, less education, and less intelligence make the teenager less able to evaluate the consequences of his or her conduct while at the same time he or she is much more apt to be motivated by mere emotion or peer pressure than is an adult." More recently, in *Roper v. Simmons*

(2005), the Court held that it was unconstitutional to apply the death penalty to juveniles younger than 18 years and cited "scientific and sociological studies" for the proposition that "it would be misguided to equate the failings of a minor with those of an adult." Although it appears that it is only in the most extreme (i.e., death penalty) cases that public support has been garnered for diminished responsibility for adolescents, the tide may be turning in regard to the public discourse on the transfer debate. Several recent public polls (e.g., Moon, Sundt, Cullen & Wright, 2000; Roberts, 2004) and an extensive empirical investigation of a diverse and representative community sample of approximately 800 participants (Scott, Reppucci, Antonishak, & DeGennaro, 2006) have indicated that rehabilitation plus appropriate punishment should be the goal for juvenile offenders. Scott et al. (2006) found that the offender's age was a significant predictor of participants' perceptions of culpability, psychosocial maturity, and preference for transferring a minor who had committed a serious offense (armed robbery) to the adult/criminal court. These findings, in conjunction with the *Roper v. Simmons* decision, may be a harbinger of change regarding the public's perception of the immaturity of adolescents and the need for a lower standard of culpability for adolescents.

The legal concepts of proportionality and diminished responsibility in which immaturity mitigates adolescent criminal behavior is in alignment with the psychological judgment model that emphasizes the significance of psychosocial factors (peer influence, temperance, impulsivity, and risk perception) on adolescent antisocial decision making (Scott et al., 1995; Steinberg & Cauffman, 1996). In an effort to provide empirical support for this developmental model of adolescent decision making, Cauffman and Steinberg (2000) compared a large community sample of adolescents and adults, ranging in age from 12 to 48 years, on assessments of psychosocial maturity and responses to hypothetical dilemmas about antisocial behaviors. Age was a significant predictor of antisocial decision making, with older participants exhibiting more responsible decision making than younger participants. The authors noted that the most dramatic increase in development of more responsible decision making seemed to occur between the ages of 16 and 19 years, with fewer marked differences after age 19. Psychosocial maturity, particularly in the realm of temperance (i.e., the ability to regulate impulsive and risky behavior) and perspective (i.e., the ability to evaluate the different perspectives in a given situation and place them in a larger context), was an even stronger predictor of antisocial decision making than age. Given the influence of psychosocial maturity, above and beyond age, the authors warn that "bright line distinctions" based on age alone may be inaccurate in that they do not take into account the level of variability in psychosocial maturity possible at various ages. Although hesitant to take a definitive stance on the appropriate age to transfer adolescents, Steinberg and Cauffman do suggest that their findings question offense-based policies that do not take into account the variability of psychosocial maturity in offenders and the role it plays in adolescents' involvement in antisocial behavior.

Fried and Reppucci (2002) also studied the influence of temporal perspective, peer influence, and risk perception in criminal decision making by asking adolescents from a community agency that works with delinquent youth, an alternative high school, and a juvenile detention center to imagine that they are participants in a fictitious video vignette portraying an incident in which poor judgment ultimately results in a crime with grave consequences. Results suggested that risk preference increases with age; however, for temporal perspective and susceptibility to peer influence and for risk assessment and a measure of criminal responsibility, adolescents at the youngest and oldest ends of the age continuum indicated more mature levels of development than those in the middle of the continuum. This U-shaped function has been found in other studies of decision making and psychosocial maturity (Cauffman & Steinberg, 2000). Specifically, the least mature responses were from the 15- to 16-year-olds, which corresponds roughly with the age at which a sharp increase in the frequency of delinquent acts tends to occur (Moffitt, 1993). Age was also related to perceptions of culpability, with younger adolescents thinking that youth were less deserving of transfer to adult court and expecting less harsh punishment. The investigators concluded that, although culpability is an elusive concept, modest support exists for the hypothesis that some developmental differences may influence decision making and the exercise of judgment in criminal situations.

Modecki (2008) expanded on the Cauffman and Steinberg (2000) study by including a sample of adjudicated delinquent youth and self-report measures of delinquent/criminal behavior. Adolescents aged 14 to 17 years displayed significantly less responsibility and perspective in their decision-making responses to hypothetical dilemmas regarding antisocial behavior than did older adolescents and adults. There were no differences in maturity of judgment between youth adjudicated delinquent and those who were not adjudicated delinquent. However, maturity of judgment did predict self-reported measures of delinquency more so than age, gender, race, education level, socioeconomic status, and antisocial decision making. Similar to Cauffman and Steinberg (2000), these findings lend support to the relationship among adolescence, maturity of judgment, and antisocial decision making.

These empirical findings, taken in conjunction with the results of the public opinion studies previously mentioned, appear to indicate that public support for transfer of younger adolescents may have shifted from that which was present in the 1990s, when the age for transfer of youth was lowered from 16 to 14 and younger in the majority of states.

# CONSEQUENCES OF TRANSFER

Until recently, the transfer debate has omitted an examination of (1) the consequences of transfer for adolescents and (2) the possible iatrogenic effects of the policy on public safety. Regarding the consequences for transferred youth, research indicates that adolescents detained in adult jails and sentenced to adult penitentiaries are a "vulnerable population" facing conditions that potentially threaten their physical safety and mental health (Woolard, Odgers, Lanza-Kaduce, & Daglis, 2005). Youth younger than age 18 incarcerated in adult jails have higher rates of suicide compared with all other inmates and with youth in the general population and are significantly more at risk for sexual assault than adult inmates (Campaign for Youth Justice, 2007; Schiraldi & Zeidenberg, 1997).

Scott and Grisso (1998) reviewed studies demonstrating that adolescents charged with serious offenses in adult court are convicted at about the same rate as adults convicted of the same crimes and, when convicted, receive sentences of similar severity. Others have found that criminal courts imprison youths more often and with longer sentences than do juvenile courts (McNulty, 1996; Rudman, Hartstone, Fagan, & Moore, 1986). Such findings clearly suggest that the concept of lesser culpability for youth is not being realized by the current system for transferred youth.

Utilitarian arguments claim that community safety is preserved by the deterrent effects of transfer policies and that these benefits to society outweigh the costs to individual adolescents. Yet these claims are not supported by empirical research. For example, Fagan (1996) compared adolescents processed in the juvenile justice system in New Jersey with a same-age cohort from neighboring communities in New York, where all youth 16 years old and older are adjudicated in the adult criminal system. This cross-jurisdictional design avoided the dangers of comparing youth within a single jurisdiction, where multiple offense and offender criteria can influence the transfer decision, differentiating those youth in the adult system from those in the juvenile system. For youth sentenced in the adult court, Fagan found higher incarceration rates and significantly higher recidivism rates. Lanza-Kaduce, Frazier, Lane, and Bishop (2002) replicated Fagan's findings in a study that compared pairs of Florida adolescents matched on several offense- and offender-based criteria and who were either retained in the juvenile system or transferred to the adult system. They found that the subsequent offenses committed by transferred adolescents were more likely to escalate in severity than those committed by adolescents retained in the juvenile justice system. The Fagan (1996) and Lanza-Kaduce et al. (2002) investigations are two of the most comprehensive and widely cited studies on transfer and recidivism by social scientists and advocates for legal policy change. This is in part due to stringent research designs that avoid a selection bias in comparing recidivism rates of those youth who were adjudicated in criminal court with those of youth adjudicated in juvenile court. Their high visibility is also due to their controversial findings that challenge the fundamental assumptions regarding the utility and efficacy of transfer policies. Both studies were cited in a systematic review of the empirical research on the deterrent effects of transfer policies conducted by the Center for Disease Control-appointed Task Force on Community Preventive Services (McGowan et al., 2007). The Task Force report has entered the public debate on transfer, using empirical research to discredit claims that transfer policies make communities safer. The studies reviewed (Barnoski, 2003; Fagan, 1996; Lanza-Kaduce et al., 2002; Myers, 2001; Podkopacz & Feld, 1996; Winner, Lanza-Kaduce, Bishop, & Frazier, 1997) in this report all concluded that transferring adolescents increases, rather than decreases, youth violence.

## CONCLUSION

The empirical evidence regarding the influence of developmental maturity on adolescents' preadjudicative and adjudicative competence and on diminished culpability challenges the underlying assumptions of the current policies on transfer and calls into question constitutional issues of fundamental fairness when subjecting developmentally immature youth to adult criminal proceedings. In addition, although political considerations, namely the claim that lowering the age of transfer will preserve the public safety and, therefore, should trump considerations of developmental maturity, have made transfer a popular policy, empirical findings suggest these transfer policies have had an adverse effect on both adolescents and public safety.

Decision makers should lift the veil of fear and ignorance that has resulted in these misguided juvenile justice policies and should heed the current social science research on adolescence and developmental maturity that clearly suggests that adolescents younger than 16 years should not be treated as adults. Although the question of 16- and 17-year-olds' developmental maturity is less clear, the research on recidivism calls into question the efficacy and utility of transfer for this age group also. In addition, given the impact of psychosocial factors on developmental maturity in adolescents' antisocial decision making and their legal capacities, a return to judicial waiver as the appropriate mechanism for transfer is warranted. Judicial waiver necessitates a transfer hearing in which the alleged perpetrator has legal representation and the judiciary has the discretion to make the transfer determination upon a full investigation of the characteristics of the offender and the alleged offense. Only in such a venue can an adolescent be justly evaluated as to the necessity and the appropriateness of transfer. The mechanisms of automatic transfer and prosecutorial discretion are solely offense based and deny the opportunity for a full investigation of the characteristics of the offender, including the recognition of the offender's mental capacities and developmental maturity. Prosecutorial discretion as a mode of transfer should be eliminated, and automatic transfer should, at minimum, be greatly restricted as to eligible crimes and youth aged 16 and older.

In summary, we advocate for reduced usage of, and fewer mechanisms for, transfer, with a return to a standard of judicial waiver. In conjunction with this process, we recommend the additional requirement that a full evaluation of a juvenile's competence to stand trial in an adult court occurs as part of the transfer hearing during which the juvenile has an unwaivable right to legal representation. These modifications reflect an understanding and recognition that adolescents are not adults, even if they are accused of committing heinous crimes.

## REFERENCES

Barnoski, R. (2003). *Changes in Washington State's jurisdiction of juvenile offenders: Examining the impact.* Olympia, WA: State Institute for Public Policy.

Bellotti v. Baird, 443 U.S. 622 (1979).

Blumstein, A. (1995, August). Violence by young people: Why the deadly nexus? *National Institute of Justice Journal*, pp. 2–9. Retrieved February 1, 2009, from *www.ncjrs.gov/pdffiles/nijj_229.pdf.*

Bonnie, R. J., & Grisso T. (2000). Adjudicative competence and youthful offenders. In T. Grisso & R. G. Schwartz (Eds.), *Youth on trial: A developmental perspective on juvenile justice* (pp. 73–104). Chicago: University of Chicago Press.

Brannen, D. N., Salekin, R. T., Zapf, P. A., Salekin, K. L., Kubak, F. A., & DeCoster, J. (2006). Transfer to adult court: A national study of how juvenile court judges weigh pertinent *Kent* criteria. *Psychology, Public Policy, and Law, 12,* 332–355.

Butts, J. A. (February, 1997). *Delinquency cases waived to criminal court, 1985–1994.* Washington, DC: U.S. Department of Justice, Office of Justice Programs, Office of Juvenile Justice and Delinquency Prevention.

Campaign for Youth Justice. (2007, November). *Jailing juveniles: The dangers of incarcerating youth in adult jails in America.* Washington, DC: Campaign for Youth Justice.

Cauffman, E. E., & Steinberg, L. (2000). (Im)maturity of judgment in adolescence: Why adolescents may be less culpable than adults. *Behavioral Sciences and the Law, 18,* 741–760.

Dusky v. United States, 362 U.S. 402 (1960).

Fagan, J. A. (1996). The comparative advantage of juvenile versus criminal court sanctions on recidivism among adolescent felony offenders. *Law & Policy, 18*, 77–113.

Fare v. Michael C., 442 U.S. 707 (1979).

Feld, B. C. (1999). *Bad kids: Race and the transformation of the juvenile court.* New York: Oxford University Press.

Fried, C. S., & Reppucci, N. D. (2001). Criminal decision making: The development of adolescent judgment, criminal responsibility, and culpability. *Law and Human Behavior, 25*, 45–61.

Gallegos v. Colorado, 370 U.S. 49, 54 (1962).

Goldstein, N. E. S., Condie, L. O., Kalbeitzer, R., Osman, D., & Geier, J. L. (2003). Juvenile offenders' *Miranda* rights comprehension and self-reported likelihood of offering false confessions. *Assessment, 10*, 359–369.

Grisso, T. (1980). Juveniles' capacities to waive *Miranda* rights: An empirical analysis. *California Law Review, 68*, 1134–1166.

Grisso, T., Steinberg, L., Woolard, J. L., Cauffman, E. E., Scott, E. S., Graham, S., et al. (2003). Juveniles' competence to stand trial: A comparison of adolescents' and adults' capacities as trial defendants. *Law and Human Behavior, 27*, 333–364.

Haley v. Ohio, 332 U.S. 596, 601 (1948).

In re Carey, No. 219592, 2000 Mich App. LEXIS 124 (241 Mich. App. 222 2000).

In re Gault, 387 U.S. 1 (1967).

Interdivisional Committee on Adolescent Abortion. (1987). Adolescent abortion: Psychological and legal issues. *American Psychologist, 42*, 73–78.

Kent v. the United States, 383 U.S. 541 (1966).

Lanza-Kaduce, L., Frazier, C. E., Lane, J., & Bishop, D. M. (2002). *Juvenile transfer to criminal court study: Final report.* Tallahassee, FL: Department of Juvenile Justice.

Mack, J. (1909). The juvenile court. *Harvard Law Review, 23*, 104–122.

Manfredi, C. P. (1998). *The Supreme Court and juvenile justice.* Lawrence: University Press of Kansas.

McGowan, A., Hahn, R., Liberman, A., Crosby, A., Fullilove, M., Johnson, R., et al. (2007). Effects on violence of laws and policies facilitating the transfer of juveniles from the juvenile justice system to the adult justice system: A systematic review. *American Journal of Preventive Medicine, 3*, 7–28.

McNulty, E. W. (1996). The transfer of juvenile offenders to adult court: Panacea or problem? *Law and Policy, 18*, 61–76.

Melton, G. B. (Ed.). (1987). *Reforming the law: Impact of child development research.* New York: Guilford Press.

Meyer, J. R., Reppucci, N. D., & Owen, J. A. (2006). Criminalizing childhood: The shifting boundaries of responsibility in the justice and school systems. In K. Freeark & W. S. Davidson, II (Eds.), *The crisis in youth mental health: Critical issues and effective programs* (Vol. 3, pp. 219–248). Westport, CT: Praeger.

Myers, D. L. (2001). *Excluding violent youths from juvenile court: The effectiveness of legislative waiver*. New York: LFB Scholarly.

Miranda v. Arizona, 384 U.S. 436 (1966).

Modecki, K. L. (2008). Addressing gaps in maturity of judgment literature: Age differences and delinquency. *Law and Human Behavior, 32*, 78–91.

Moeller, T. G. (2001). *Youth aggression and violence: A psychological approach*, Mahwah, NJ: Erlbaum.

Moffitt, T. E. (1993). Adolescent-limited and life course persistent antisocial behavior: A developmental taxonomy. *Psychological Bulletin, 100*, 674–700.

Moon, M. M., Sundt, J., Cullen, F. T., & Wright, J. P. (2000). Is child saving dead? Public support for juveniles' rehabilitation. *Crime and Delinquency, 46*, 38–60.

Ohio v. Settles, No. 13-97-50, 1998 Ohio App. LEXIS 4973 (Ohio App. 3d. 1998).

Owen-Kostelnik, J., Reppucci, N. D., & Meyer, J. R. (2006). Testimony and interrogation of minors: Assumptions about maturity and morality. *American Psychologist, 61*, 286–304.

Parham v. J. R., 422 U.S. 584 (1979).

Podkopacz, M. R., & Feld, B. C. (1996). The end of the line: An empirical study of judicial waiver. *Journal of Criminal Law and Criminology, 86*, 449–492.

Redding, R. E., & Howell, J. C. (2000). Blended sentencing in American juvenile courts. In J. A. Fagan & F. E. Zimring (Eds.), *The changing borders of juvenile justice* (pp. 145–180). Chicago: University of Chicago Press.

Reppucci, N. D. (1999). Adolescent development and juvenile justice. *American Journal of Community Psychology, 27*, 307–326.

Roberts, J. V. (2004). Public opinion and youth justice. In M. Tonry & A. M. Doob (Eds.), *Youth crime and youth justice: Comparative and cross-national perspectives* (Vol. 31, pp. 495–542). Chicago: University of Chicago Press.

Roper v. Simmons, 543 U.S. 551 (2005).

Rudman, C., Hartstone, E., Fagan, J. A., & Moore, M. (1986). Violent youth in adult court: Process and punishment. *Crime and Delinquency, 36*, 75–96.

Salekin, R. T., Rogers, R., & Ustad, K. L. (2001). Juvenile waiver to adult criminal courts: Prototypes for dangerousness, sophistication-maturity, and amenability to treatment. *Psychology, Public Policy, and Law, 7*, 381–408.

Salekin, R. T., Yff, R. M. A, Neumann, C. S., Leistico, A. R., & Zalot, A. A. (2002). Juvenile transfer to adult courts: A look at the prototypes for dangerousness, sophistication-maturity, and amenability to treatment through a legal lens. *Psychology, Public Policy, and Law, 8*, 373–410.

Schiraldi, V., & Zeidenberg, J. (1997). *The risks juveniles face when they are incarcerated with adults*. Washington, DC: The Justice Policy Institute.

Schmidt, M., Reppucci, N. D., & Woolard, J. L. (2003). Effectiveness of participation as a defendant: The attorney-juvenile client relationship. *Behavioral Sciences and the Law, 21,* 175–198.

Scott, E. S., & Grisso, T. (1998). The evolution of adolescence: A developmental perspective on juvenile justice reform. *Journal of Criminal Law and Criminology, 88,* 137–184.

Scott, E. S., & Grisso, T. (2005). Developmental incompetence, due process and juvenile justice policy. *North Carolina Law Review, 83,* 793–845.

Scott, E. S., Reppucci, N. D., Antonishak, J., & DeGennaro, J. T. (2006). Public attitudes about the culpability and punishment of young offenders. *Behavioral Sciences and the Law, 24,* 815–832.

Scott, E. S., Reppucci, N. D., & Woolard, J. L. (1995). Evaluating adolescent decision making in legal contexts. *Law and Human Behavior, 19,* 224–244.

Snyder, H. N., & Sickmund, M. (1999). *Juvenile offenders and victims: 1999 national report.* Washington, DC: U.S. Department of Justice, Office of Justice Programs, Office of Juvenile Justice and Delinquency Prevention.

Steinberg, L., & Cauffman, E. E. (1996). Maturity of judgment: Psychosocial factors in adolescent decision making. *Law and Human Behavior, 20,* 249–273.

Tanenhaus, D. S. (2000). The evolution of transfer out of the juvenile court. In J. A. Fagan & F. E. Zimring (Eds.), *The changing borders of juvenile justice* (pp. 13–35). Chicago: University of Chicago Press.

Thompson v. Oklahoma, 487 U.S. 815 (1998).

Viljoen, J. L., & Grisso, T. (2007). Prospects for remediating juveniles' adjudicative incompetence. *Psychology, Public Policy, and Law, 13,* 87–114.

Viljoen, J. L., Zapf, P. A., & Roesch, R. (2007). Adjudicative competence and comprehension of *Miranda* rights in adolescent defendants: A comparison of legal standards. *Behavioral Sciences and the Law, 25,* 1–19.

Weithorn, L. A., & Campbell, S. A. (1982). The competency of children to make informed treatment decisions. *Child Development, 53,* 1589–1598.

Winner, L., Lanza-Kaduce, L., Bishop, D. M., & Frazier, C. E. (1997). The transfer of juveniles to criminal court: Reexamining recidivism over the long term. *Crime and Delinquency, 43,* 548–563.

Woolard, J. L., Odgers, C., Lanza-Kaduce, L., & Daglis, H. (2005). Juveniles within adult correctional settings: Legal pathways and developmental considerations. *International Journal of Forensic Mental Health, 4,* 1–18.

Zimring, F. E. (1998). *American youth violence.* New York: Oxford University Press.

Zimring, F. E. (2000). Penal proportionality for the young offender: Notes on immaturity, capacity, and diminished responsibility. In T. Grisso & R. G. Schwartz (Eds.), *Youth on trial: A developmental perspective on juvenile justice* (pp. 271–290). Chicago: University of Chicago Press.

Chapter 16

# Therapeutic Jurisprudence
# in Juvenile Justice

PATRICK H. TOLAN
JENNIFER ANNE TITUS

Since its inception in 1899, juvenile justice has been charged with the dual responsibilities of remediating, through therapeutic intervention, normal child development gone awry and disciplining youth (Tanenhaus, 2004). Juvenile court, distinct from adult corrections, recognizes the unique psychological and social conditions of juveniles and is founded on the assumption that children should be given an opportunity to correct their mistakes (Laub, 2002). Whereas establishing legal responsibility (or "guilt") is not overlooked in juvenile courts, it is balanced with a focus on rehabilitation of youth.

Although the emphasis on these two societal responsibilities—sanction and rehabilitation—has shifted over the court's history, the dual focus has remained. To aid while ensuring accountability is thus at the core of juvenile justice. Attempting to synthesize these often competing goals has been and remains the vexing charge of the court (Feld, 1990). This integrative mission is often referred to as "therapeutic jurisprudence." Therapeutic jurisprudence refers to the study of the law as a potentially therapeutic agent: how legal rules, legal procedures, and legal actors impact psychological well-being (Wexler & Winick, 1996). In this chapter, we focus on the relation between the therapeutic and criminal justice in the juvenile court. In particular, we examine scientific and mental health issues that have influenced the court's practices and policy, focusing on some key issues of current empirical understanding and influential jurisprudence perspectives.

# LINKING CHILD DEVELOPMENT, MENTAL HEALTH, AND CRIMINAL BEHAVIOR

The first juvenile court, established in Cook County, Illinois, in 1899, arose from a philosophy of deep humanitarian concern exemplified by Jane Addams at Hull House and her followers (Beuttler, 2004). That humanitarian concern was also grounded in a faith in scientific knowledge as the most reliable and informative approach to understanding criminal behavior in childhood (Tanenhaus, 2004). In line with this movement was the establishment in 1909 of the first "child guidance" clinic, whose key focus was to better understand the link between behavioral or psychological pathology and criminal behavior. The Juvenile Psychopathic Institute (later renamed the Institute for Juvenile Research [IJR]) examined pathology in context— what was typical, expectable, or needed for children to develop as effective citizens (Healy, 1915). The intent was to study the causes of juvenile delinquency, learning disabilities, and mental illness and to establish interventions and preventive measures to remediate these problems. The work at IJR would establish a tradition of connecting biological, psychological, and sociological factors and solidifying our understanding of pathology by first establishing what is typical or healthy (Tanenhaus, 2004). Today, scientific study and methodical formulation of personal reasons for criminal behavior remain at the center of therapeutic jurisprudence and in the organization of the juvenile court.

This initial recognition that the best guidance for juvenile justice was to be gained from scientific study of child development remains a central, if not always fully recognized, organizing principle. Three areas of study have had enduring importance to juvenile justice. The first is establishing the typical developmental patterns and course across childhood and adolescence. A second area is understanding the personal, familial, and environmental characteristics that contribute to delinquency. In particular, there is an abiding interest in differentiating delinquency that marks the early stages of an enduring and serious career of criminal behavior from youthful behavior caused by immature judgment and limited understanding (Tolan & Gorman-Smith, 1998). A third area is to identify promising methods for preventing, diverting, curtailing, and controlling delinquent behavior (Guerra, Kim, & Boxer, 2008). In this chapter, we examine recent key findings in these three areas and discuss their implications for therapeutic jurisprudence within juvenile justice.

## Normal Development and Juvenile Justice

A founding premise of the juvenile court was an acknowledgment that youth do not have fully formed personalities and that this immaturity warrants different standards of judging responsibility for criminal acts. Therefore, one of the major concerns of the court was to attune court procedures, expectations, and case management to this reality and to rely on psychological and child development research in determining appropriate treatment and punishment (Steinberg & Scott, 2003). A review of the history of the court's approach to delinquency shows an ongoing incorporation of psychological, sociological, and biological knowledge, albeit not always quickly or with the needed sophistication (Tanenhaus, 2004).

During the 1990s, findings from initial longitudinal and cohort studies produced evidence that serious and repetitive delinquency was concentrated in a small portion of the population (about 6% of males; Loeber & Hay, 1997). Although rare in early adolescence, criminal involvement of some sort was more common by midadolescence. Prevalence of criminal involvement peaked in late adolescence, with most juveniles curtailing their criminal behavior as they left adolescence (Blumstein, Cohen, Roth, & Visher, 1986).

As time passed, study results began to suggest that adolescents should be evaluated differently from adults because they lack the adult capacity for judgment, intent, and responsibility. Neuroscience has documented what behavioral researchers had long theorized about the importance of adolescence as a time of cognitive, moral, and social maturing and about the distinction of adolescence from adulthood (Siegel, 1999). Recently, with the advent of brain-imaging techniques, it has become apparent that substantial change occurs over time in the areas of the brain thought to be the center of judgment and moral decision making (Steinberg & Scott, 2003). In particular, a set of studies has shown that significant development in the regions of the brain responsible for processes of long-term planning, regulation of emotion, impulse control, and the evaluation of risk and reward continues through the end of adolescence (Spear, 2000; Yakovlev & Lecours, 1967). Moreover, other research suggests that brain development in adolescents is related to immature cognitive decision-making processes that are susceptible to stress (Dolcos & McCarthy, 2006). These studies suggest that adolescents are typically still developing decision-making and social judgment faculties and that, in times of stress, these faculties are more diminished in adolescents than in adults. In addition to having less ability to judge what wrong behavior is in the first place, adolescents may be more susceptible to peer pressure than adults. In fact, one of the best predictors of delinquency is the extent of friends' involvement in delinquency (Tolan, Gorman-Smith, & Henry, 2003).

These studies show an important step forward in integrating scientific knowledge of normative development with juvenile justice processes. Although providing some basic direction, these studies only set the stage for more careful work on how developmental needs and capabilities can be

316     CHILDREN AS OFFENDERS

addressed and related to responsibility for self-control and social responsibility.

## Identifying Risk Predictors and Patterns

In addition to an ongoing interest in understanding development, juvenile court jurisprudence has maintained an interest in scientific understanding of what causes and predicts delinquency and how delinquent behavior predicts later and serious criminal activity (Tolan & Gorman-Smith, 1998). The past 20 years have seen a surge of interest in the predictors of delinquency and what might differentiate patterns of criminal involvement (Loeber & Farrington, 1998). Spurred by longitudinal studies that apply developmental understanding to delinquency and its precursors and consequences, these studies have substantially altered how delinquency is viewed and the operating principles of most courts, and they have increased the sophistication of the therapeutic and legal processing aspects of the juvenile justice system (Grisso & Schwartz, 2000).

Beginning with a series of longitudinal studies in the late 1980s that identified the key role of age of onset (i.e., first involvement in delinquency) in predicting seriousness and chronicity of delinquency (cf. Moffitt, 1993, for review), researchers created a sophisticated developmental model of delinquency risk (Loeber & Farrington, 1998). This model differentiated the nearly universal involvement of adolescents in some delinquent behavior, which was typically of limited seriousness and extent and lasted only through adolescence, from its rarer instance as a continuation of childhood aggression well into adulthood (Tolan, 1987). Termed "adolescent-limited" and "life-course persistent" patterns, respectively (Moffitt, 1993), these patterns had different antecedents and merited different levels of concern for public safety. Accordingly, psychologists argued that they should also benefit from different interventions (Tolan & Guerra, 1994a). Age of onset emerged as a key differentiating characteristic of these two patterns, but other factors, such as impulsive behavior, poor social judgment, and prior experiences of child abuse (see also Widom & Wilson, Chapter 13, this volume), were also important, at least into late adolescence (Tolan & Gorman-Smith, 2003).

A large body of longitudinal research in the 1990s mapped the development of delinquency risk, the validity of the adolescent-limited and life course-persistent patterns, and the long-term consequences of involvement in criminal acts (see Loeber & Farrington, 1998, for a compendium of some of the key findings). A well-coordinated research effort led to a rapid exchange of information and a clearer articulation of the role of important predictors, such as parenting practices, involvement with delinquent peers and susceptibility to their influence, and the variations in risk by gender and ecological context (Lipsey & Wilson, 1998). As the components of multivariate–multilevel models emerged with substantial consistency across studies, and with significant continuities and distinctions across populations, ecological and social forces, disposition planning, and intervention, many courts began to incorporate a developmental perspective and emphasize its key features. These features included a focus on cognitive skills, effective parenting practices, and the link between peer and school factors and family relationships, as well as opportunities for bonding to school (Hawkins et al., 2003; Tolan & Guerra, 1994b). Research and policy also emphasized a developmental-ecological perspective that related variations in prevalence of delinquency across populations and different patterns of criminal involvement to understanding of risk and to individual differences within a given population. It became evident that even the strongest predictors of delinquency had modest capability to predict delinquency engagement and that persistence in delinquency depended on many microsystem influences. For example, even though early involvement is one of the best predictors of seriousness of violence, most who start early will not, in fact, continue involvement past adolescence (Loeber & Farrington, 1998). Also, the likelihood of involvement continuing and the seriousness are affected by peer influences and vary by neighborhood condition (Tolan et al., 2003). These multiple influences, in turn, lead to an emphasis on ecological conditions, including access to services and normal developmental supports in case management, interventions, and policies (Tolan, Guerra, & Kendall, 1995).

Another major implication of the research was its identification of meaningful subgroups or developmental patterns during adolescence that influence delinquency. The accumulation of large, longitudinal data sets with similar measures advanced the field beyond just showing relations between variables to permitting a focus on how youth clustered into identifiable patterns of delinquency. These patterns, in turn, helped clarify multiple courses within normal and problematic development during adolescence (Elliott & Tolan, 1999; Nagin & Tremblay, 2001). As expected, early onset of delinquency remained the best indicator for serious and chronic involvement. It was also clear that serious and chronic offenders were primarily those whose elevated aggression appeared early in development (Tremblay, 2000). However, even among this early aggression group and even among those within that early aggressive group with comparatively elevated levels of other risk factors, the risk is low for becoming a serious, chronic, or violent offender in adolescence or adulthood (Tolan & Gorman-Smith, 1998). Also, population studies showed that individuals were rarely serious, chronic, *and* violent offenders. Rather, most chronic offenders were seldom serious or violent offenders, and few violent offenders repeated their violent offenses (Snyder, 1998). In addition, as researchers refined their methods for tracking developmental patterns over time, it became evident that most of those thought to be on the road to life course delinquency were not and a substantial portion of those with later-onset delinquency did not stop after adolescence (Nagin, Farrington, & Moffitt, 1995). Although this information, at first glance, calls into question the life course delinquency and adolescent-limited delinquency labels, careful evaluation suggests that, rather than undercutting this basic distinction, elaborations of the patterns or subgroupings within patterns are probably distinguishable, even if not yet well identified or well understood (Tolan, 2007). For example, longitudinal research suggests that within each overall pattern two to three subpatterns can be identified (Brame, Nagin, & Tremblay, 2001; Schaeffer, Petras, Ialongo, Poduska, & Kellam, 2003).

## How Related Are Delinquency and Mental Illness?

The extensive investigations of the past 20 years have identified common mental health features as correlates of delinquency, and many of the predictors of delinquency are implicated in risk for various forms of mental illness (Grisso, 2007). However, the link between these two is still not well understood or firmly determined. A key question for both the therapeutic and public safety responsibilities of the court is resolving this relation between delinquency and adolescent mental health.

A set of studies has shown that prevalence rates of mental health problems among those in juvenile detention centers are as much as two to three times higher than in the general population (Teplin, Abram, McClelland, Dulcan, & Mericle, 2002). This high rate holds even when diagnoses that coincide with criminal behavior (such as conduct disorders, antisocial personality, substance abuse disorders) are separated from the calculations. These findings validate the call by Cocozza (1992) to make identification and treatment of mental health disorders a central consideration in juvenile justice.

However, the implications of these findings for preventive and remediative interventions are less clear. Few studies examine mental health issues carefully. Whereas research has found a substantial incidence of certain mental health symptoms (e.g., depression symptoms, anxiety, and trauma), these findings are often limited in specificity. Although finding correlations that are statistically significant and substantial enough to support a mental health focus, research does not differentiate symptoms that might characterize the exigencies of delinquency apart from symptoms of mental illness. Several studies have shown that the co-occurrence of both attention-deficit disorder and conduct problems increases risk for delinquency and for persistent delinquency (Moffitt & Caspi, 2001). Yet studies are inconsistent in identifying the role of internalizing problems, such as depression and anxiety, in delinquency risk (Hirschfield, Maschi, White, Traub, & Loeber,

2006). The role may depend on the type of delinquency and whether mental health disorders predict delinquency or exacerbate youths' involvement and its consequences (Grisso, 2007). For example, whereas anxiety and depression may not predict delinquency well, they may, when substantial, exacerbate risk resulting from other influences (Grant, Compas, Thurm, McMahon, & Gipson, 2004).

A further problem is one of overrepresentation of at-risk populations in detention samples. Youth in detention include not only those involved in serious delinquent behaviors but also those with fewer resources to help them stay out of detention and those who more often face racial and ethnic discrimination. Both of these characteristics could contribute to the elevated rates of mental health problems identified in detention studies. A community study suggests elevated rates of diagnosable mental illness among delinquents and an independent contribution of these to later delinquency, even controlling for other potential confounds (Copeland, Miller-Johnson, Keeler, Angold, & Costello, 2007). However, as in other studies, the elevated rates are most common when the youth has both substance abuse issues and a conduct disorder.

Thus, the accumulated studies suggest that mental health problems are common among those involved in delinquency and correlate with key features, such as the seriousness of the offense. However, it is unclear whether the co-occurrence of disorders other than those that have delinquency as defining features exacerbates susceptibility and continuation of delinquency. Moreover, the patchwork of studies, although yielding some clues, does not offer a coordinated understanding of the role of mental disorders in delinquency risk. The most consistent finding is that delinquents (particularly serious delinquents) have an elevated rate of mental health problems, suggesting that integration and attention to mental health needs is of first priority, before focusing on interventions meant to affect behavior and the psychological influences on behavior (Cocozza, 1992). Many interventions have been shown to reduce delinquency either through prevention or treatment (Lipsey & Wilson, 1998). However, most do not include direct attention to mental disorders. Fortunately, many include attention to risk factors at least related to the level of symptomology and impairment for most mental disorders (e.g., cognitive functioning, parenting skills, family involvement). In addition, because these same factors have been theorized as causal for some mental health problems, it may be that many of these impart mental health benefits in addition to curtailing delinquency risk.

## Establishing Effective Interventions and Court Procedures

In the past two decades, the field of delinquency intervention has moved from one with minimal empirical grounding to one with a range of sound science. Most delinquency interventions focus on promoting protective factors, such as better family relationships, improved parental monitoring and disciplinary practices, and social-cognitive features associated with reducing aggression and delinquency (Guerra, Williams, Tolan, & Modecki, 2007; Lipsey & Wilson, 1998). Effective interventions range from nurse visitations with mothers at childbirth to intensive, multisystemic, family-focused interventions that help the family manage rules and emotions while advocating for educational and child welfare needs. Stringent reviews have identified a set of promising programs (Mihalic, Fagan, Irwin, Ballard, & Elliott, 2004). Similarly, meta-analytic techniques have identified intervention approaches, rather than programs, that have significant impacts on delinquency (Lipsey & Wilson, 1998). Together, these findings suggest that programs focusing on parenting and family relationships and those that improve cognitive processes in managing interpersonal conflicts and social situations are the most promising (Sukhodolsky & Ruchkin, 2006). For example, with proper delivery, multisystemic therapy can cut recidivism for serious offenses by one-third or more (Sheidow, Henggeler, & Schoenwald, 2003). Similarly, a meta-analysis of 12 randomized trials showed that, 1 year after intervention, recidivism rates for delinquent youths receiving cognitive-behavioral interventions were 10% less than for those who received normal processing and programming (Armelius & Andreassen, 2007).

These findings are further supported by cost–benefit analyses. These same programs lead to substantial cost savings from reduced incarceration, less restrictive placements, and other avoided social program and special education costs (Aos, Lieb, Mayfield, Miller, & Pennucci, 2004). These analyses do not include the economic and social benefits that would likely accrue when youth are more readily engaged in and more able to be productive contributors to society rather than expensive consumers of care and criminal justice resources (Butts & Mears, 2001).

More recently, intervention studies have expanded beyond programs to examine how case management procedures, identification and diversion of youth, and judicial decision making affect outcomes (Mulvey, Schubert, & Chung, 2007). These studies are finding that screening, identification, and case formulation can promote a better fit of interventions to needs as well as improve impact on delinquency outcomes. One of the initial findings shows that many juvenile justice systems are not systematically organized, leaving room for idiosyncratic decision making and limited mapping of response to the current knowledge base (Cuellar, McReynolds, & Wasserman, 2006). Also, coordination is low across systems involved with helping those at risk for or engaged in delinquency (Tolan & Gorman-Smith, 2003).

One of the key questions of the last decade was whether incapacitation or incarceration for an extended period of time was more effective than direct therapeutic interventions aimed at family and other key developmental influences (Cuellar et al., 2006; Grisso, 2007). Although this is a difficult matter to study, there is some evidence that both have positive effects (Hamilton, Sullivan, Veysey, & Grillo, 2007). However, overall, enforcement and incapacitation have very limited benefits for adolescents (Lipsey & Wilson, 1998). A few studies have compared similarly charged youth provided intervention in a residential setting versus the same approach provided within the community. For example, cognitive-behavioral programs provided in community-based settings led to lower rearrest rates than the same programs for youth with the same level of offending exposed to the program in a residential/corrections setting (Lipsey & Wilson, 1998). These studies reveal that community-based interventions have a greater and longer-lasting impact than interventions implemented in a residential setting on youth behavior (Caldwell, Vitacco, & Van Rybroek, 2006; Tolan & Gorman-Smith, 1997). Among the advantages of community-based approaches are more continuity of services and closer connection to home and school (Chung, Schubert, & Mulvey, 2007). This translates to greater community safety and greater savings to society, because such services are much less costly (Sherman et al., 1997). With effective nonresidential interventions available for families with delinquent youths (e.g., functional family therapy; Sexton & Alexander, 2000), for youths with substantial criminal involvement (Curtis, Ronan, & Borduin, 2004), and for youths also involved with the foster care system (e.g., multidimensional treatment foster care; Eddy, Whaley, & Chamberlain, 2004), there is a basis for favoring community-based treatment over institutional efforts for almost all delinquents (Woolfenden, Williams, & Peat, 2001). For example, Aos, Phipps, Barnoski, and Lieb (2001) estimate a long-term taxpayer cost savings of $21,836 to $87,622 per youth for community-based multidimensional treatment foster care compared with incarceration.

In addition to identifying programs that reduce delinquency involvement and recidivism, research has identified several approaches that relate to increased risk and recidivism. Most of these approaches fall into three categories: (1) insight-oriented psychotherapy (Tolan & Guerra, 1994b); (2) small groups for at-risk delinquent youths (Dishion, McCord, & Poulin, 1999); and (3) scare or punish tactics. The latter "boot camps" and "scared-straight" programs consistently show negative effects in high-quality evaluations. Some studies further suggest that incarceration increases recidivism for young adolescents (MacKenzie, 2000).

## RECONCILING RESPONSIBILITY AND THERAPEUTIC INTERESTS

The increasing level of policy analysis, the growing access to quality data that can identify subgroup variations, and the increasing size and quality of the empirical research base help to define a more rational policy that tempers the rhetoric about public safety and promotes child needs and strong development (Tolan, 2007). There is growing recognition that taking responsibility for one's behavior is a developmental task of great importance, and that juvenile proceedings that emphasize responsibility are not necessarily problematic. This recognition once again reflects the core missions of the juvenile court and therapeutic jurisprudence. Some examples of what is to come from this grounded understanding are already emerging.

## Specialized Courts for Mentally Ill and Substance-Abusing Youth

Although many teens are transferred from the juvenile court to the criminal court for punishment, others are transferred to specialized courts for treatment and rehabilitation. In recent years, the number of juvenile drug courts and mental health courts has significantly increased in response to high rates of mental disorders among youth in the juvenile justice system (Teplin et al., 2002). Both juvenile drug courts and mental health courts are based on the premise that young offenders with serious mental illnesses and substance use disorders require specialized services. These courts attempt to integrate care and responsibility with approaches to reduce recidivism. This integrative and specialized focus is one approach that exemplifies therapeutic jurisprudence (Hora, Schma, & Rosenthal, 1999; Winick, 2003).

Juvenile drug courts aim to reduce substance use and criminal behavior by providing offenders with services and treatment in the community. One of the defining features of juvenile drug courts is collaboration among the juvenile justice system, the mental health system, the school system, and community agencies. In juvenile drug courts, services are not just for the youths themselves; these courts also provide services to the families of young offenders to promote parental monitoring and guidance (Cooper, 2001).

Although the more developed literature on adult drug courts suggests they are effective in reducing both cost and recidivism (Government Accountability Office, 2005), to date, there have been few rigorous evaluations of juvenile drug courts (Belenko & Dembo, 2003). A 2006 randomized controlled trial showed that drug court was more effective than family court in reducing substance use and criminal behavior over a 1-year period (Henggeler, Halliday-Boykins, Cunningham, Randall, & Shapiro, 2006). However, the reductions in self-reported criminal behavior did not translate into reductions in recidivism or incarceration, as documented by official records. Perhaps, as the authors point out, this inconsistency was due to the more intense monitoring and surveillance of youth in the drug court than youth in family court. Thus, juvenile drug courts remain a promising approach in need of further study.

Another approach is mental health courts, whose recent popularity is tied to legislation in 2000 that earmarked federal funding for such courts

(Erickson, Campbell, & Lamberti, 2006). This approach borrowed heavily from the drug court model. In fact, opponents have criticized the mental health court movement for lacking a theoretical basis of its own and lacking a common model (Steadman, Davidson, & Brown, 2001). Whereas juvenile drug courts target youth with substance use disorders, whose symptoms by definition are also classified as delinquent behaviors, juvenile mental health courts do not necessarily target youth whose mental health symptoms are classified as delinquent behaviors. As a consequence, the logic of the drug court—that treatment can lead to a decline in delinquent behavior—does not readily translate to the mental health court unless there is a causal connection between mental illness and delinquent behavior (Wolff, 2002).

It is difficult to identify any evaluations of juvenile mental health courts in the literature, possibly because of a lack of a common definition of what constitutes a mental health court (Wolff & Pogorzelski, 2005). Beyond the lack of proven effectiveness are a number of common criticisms of specialized mental health courts. These criticisms include (1) the possibility of coercive treatment for mental illnesses (Erickson et al., 2006); (2) overlooking the real problem of severely limited resources for community-based services (Steadman et al., 2001); (3) potential collateral consequences for youth (e.g., stigmatization, negative impact on future contacts with the juvenile and criminal justice systems, loss of confidentiality, and impediment to employment, to name a few; Harris, Seltzer, & Carter, 2004); and (4) the risk of "net widening" (because youth must be arrested to receive necessary mental health treatment, police may be unintentionally encouraged to arrest more juveniles to get them help; Harris et al., 2004). Critics of specialized mental health courts argue that, instead of using the justice system as an entry point to mental health treatment, what is needed is to reform the fragmented mental health system and to place more emphasis on preventive approaches (Bernstein & Seltzer, 2003).

It is clear that the rapid growth of specialized juvenile courts in recent years preceded evidence of their effectiveness. Whereas research provides limited support for the effectiveness of drug courts, the evidence for mental health courts remains uncertain, largely because this new approach requires evaluation. Although rigorous research is needed, evaluation efforts may be complicated by the interconnected nature of these programs. In other words, it may be difficult to separate the effects of the courts from the effects of the community-based service providers to whom they refer offenders (Erickson et al., 2006; Wolff & Pogorzelski, 2005).

## The Promise of Restorative Justice

Restorative justice is a promising approach that attempts to balance the treatment and punishment functions of the juvenile justice system while dealing with adolescents in a developmentally appropriate manner. Repair-

ing harm done to victims and community, instilling consequences for criminal behavior, and reintegrating offenders into the community are the main
goals of restorative justice (Bazemore & Umbreit, 1995; McGarrell, 2001).
Juvenile justice programs based on restorative justice principles, such as
victim–offender mediation and family group conferencing, bring together
victims, offenders, and community members (including supporters of both
the victim and the offender) to discuss the crime and its consequences and to
develop a restorative or reparation agreement. The agreement details how
the offender can make amends for the crime. Agreements often include an
apology and requirements for restitution to the victim or community service. Sometimes youth are required to improve school attendance, complete
homework, or perform chores at home or school (McGarrell, 2001). Objectives for offenders include gaining an understanding of the consequences
of crime for victims, experiencing feelings of remorse, recognizing that
they have been sanctioned, developing empathy with victims, repaying victims, and completing community service and other reparative requirements
(Bazemore & Umbreit, 1995).

Although restorative justice participants consistently report high levels
of satisfaction and feelings of inclusion, respect, and procedural fairness
(McCold & Wachtel, 1998; McGarrell, 2001), it is difficult to summarize
the findings on the programs' effectiveness. Several recent meta-analyses
and quasi-experimental studies show that the programs reduce recidivism,
particularly among girls and offenders with fewer than two prior offenses
but also among juveniles with prior records and violent offenses (Bergseth
& Bouffard, 2007; Rodriguez, 2007). Even so, these results should be interpreted cautiously given that many of the meta-analyses included studies with
methodological shortcomings, such as varying outcome definitions, selection biases, short follow-up time periods, and inappropriate comparison
group strategies. To date, only a select few evaluations of restorative justice programs have used rigorous evaluation methods such as randomized
experimental study designs. The results of these studies tend to support the
effectiveness of the program in reducing recidivism among young, first-time
offenders (McCold & Wachtel, 1998; McGarrell, 2001). Again, the results
of subgroup analyses suggest that the interventions may be more effective
for girls than for boys (McGarrell & Hipple, 2007).

The promise of restorative justice programs is that they provide developmentally appropriate services for juveniles by involving family members
in the treatment process (Sullivan, Veysey, Hamilton, & Grillo, 2007). They
give juveniles an opportunity to learn from their past mistakes by supporting them as they face consequences and make amends for their delinquent
behavior. In this manner, by promoting both rehabilitation and accountability, these programs have the potential to resolve the tension between
treatment and punishment. A restructured juvenile justice system based on

restorative justice philosophy might serve to balance the long-competing goals of treatment and punishment in a developmentally appropriate way. However, the inconclusive evaluation results leave many unanswered questions of if and how the programs might function to deter delinquent behavior (McGarrell & Hipple, 2007). The need for stronger evidence is not the only reason to be cautious about promoting broader implementation of these programs. The possibility for differential treatment of offenders is one of the greatest threats to restorative justice programs (Rodriguez, 2007). Restorative justice processes place considerable emphasis on involving the community. However, community members might be inclined to respond punitively to certain types of offenders (e.g., boys, minorities). Under such circumstances, restorative justice practices could become a means to perpetuate discrimination and prejudice. Therefore, it is of the utmost importance to cautiously implement and critically evaluate restorative justice programs to guard against differential treatment. Finally, when restorative justice practices are implemented, restorative justice goals are often viewed as secondary to goals of punishment and treatment. Restorative justice programs may not be effective and may even cause harm if they are implemented outside a system based on restorative values, goals, and policies (Bazemore & Umbreit, 1995).

## Teen Courts

Another recent development in juvenile jurisprudence is the teen court. The number of teen court programs in the United States has increased by more than 1,200%, from 78 courts in 1994 to more than 1,100 courts in 2006 (National Youth Court Center, 2006). Teen court sentences reflect restorative justice principles in that they aim to promote accountability, reparation, and reengagement (Forgays & DeMilio, 2005). Although restorative justice philosophies provide the basis for the teen court model, teen courts place less emphasis on victim involvement and more emphasis on the role of peers in reinforcing social norms (Hanish & Tolan, 2001).

The defining feature of the teen court is the prominent role of young people in handling cases, starting with the intake process and ending with sentencing. Adults typically play supervisory roles, overseeing the work of young volunteers. Another key feature of teen courts is the system of graduated sanctions; every guilty youth receives a sanction, even those who have committed relatively minor offenses. Teen court sanctions often include community service, victim apology letters, written essays, teen court jury duty, drug/alcohol classes, and restitution (Nissen, Butts, Merrigan, & Kraft, 2006).

This approach puts into action cognitive-behavioral features of social learning, norms, and problem solving associated with lower risk of delinquency (Guerra et al., 2008; Hanish & Tolan, 2001). In addition, it taps into the important role of peers. Because adolescents are expected to be more responsive to sanctions from their own peers, teen involvement in sanctioning may lead to greater adherence and impact than sanctioning from adult authority figures (Forgays & DeMilio, 2005). Furthermore, accountability, timeliness, cost savings, and community cohesion are thought to be four potential benefits of teen courts (Nissen et al., 2006). In addition, although much of the early research on teen courts was characterized by inadequate study designs or produced inconclusive results, recent evaluation studies have shown that teen courts can be more effective than typical juvenile courts at reducing recidivism for first-time offenders (Butts, Buck, & Coggeshall, 2002), second-time offenders (Forgays & DeMilio, 2005), and even third-time offenders (Dick, Geertsen, & Jones, 2003).

## CONCLUSION

This chapter shows the critical steps taken in building a foundation of knowledge that can help the juvenile court in its second century better integrate its initial responsibility to provide public safety with the concern for adolescents' developmental needs and mental health. The last 20 years have seen significant advances in the number of quality studies, the sophistication of the questions and analyses in those studies, and policy and practice preferences for empirically based findings (Migdole & Robbins, 2007).

However, considerable challenges remain, including gaps in knowledge, limited robustness of some findings, patchwork efforts in many key areas, and skepticism about the validity of the findings among some policymakers and segments of the public. Also, moving forward may rest as much on considering how therapeutic jurisprudence should look or function as it does on testing specific principles, hypotheses, or programs.

A review of the court and its movement toward a more effective form and purpose (Grisso, 2007) suggests that care in reframing issues and approaches is essential. There is evidence of overinterpretation, overextension, and oversimplification of research when translating it into operations or when characterizing the robustness of the findings. There is also potential to foreclose innovations that could play important roles in establishing effective and appropriate therapeutic jurisprudence. Instead, present knowledge should be used to guide practice and at the same time encourage further vigorous study. As additional findings are produced, they should be incorporated to adjust what is considered best practice, appropriate limitations of various preferred interventions, and the level of confidence that can be accorded the empirical basis for a given action. There is also risk of undercutting needed support for and attention to child and adolescent mental health in other systems if too much is made of the benefits of therapeutic jurisprudence and mental health attention within the juvenile justice system (Tolan & Dodge, 2005). The juvenile justice system should not be engaged quickly in trying to address mental health needs of youth. Most youth are better served through primary care systems such as health care, community agencies, and schools.

There is clearly need for more research that translates these basic findings into stronger and clearer operational guidance, guidance that is more centrally based in the typical systems of services related to juvenile justice (Sukhodolsky & Ruchkin, 2006). Similarly, there is a need to identify the funding, perspective, and operational issues that may limit links across systems or may mitigate against the use of therapeutic methods in juvenile justice settings (Desai et al., 2006). Funding efforts that may promote more community-based care should be studied, including efforts that increase incentives to use evidence-based interventions (Knitzer & Cooper, 2006). The testing of systems of care that integrate mental health and other developmental care, with due consideration of how juvenile justice accountability can be developmentally appropriate, is also needed. These efforts can provide additional building blocks in the construction of a system that better expresses the need for therapeutic jurisprudence (Butts & Mears, 2001).

## REFERENCES

Aos, S., Lieb, R., Mayfield, J., Miller, M., & Pennucci, A. (2004). *Benefits and costs of prevention and early intervention programs for youth: Technical appendix* (No. 04-07-3901). Olympia: Washington State Institute for Public Policy.

Aos, S., Phipps, P., Barnoski, R., & Lieb, R. (2001). *The comparative costs and benefits of programs to reduce crime version 4.0* (No. 01-05-1201). Olympia: Washington State Institute for Public Policy.

Armelius, B. A., & Andreassen, T. H. (2007). Cognitive-behavioral treatment for antisocial behavior in youth in residential treatment. *Cochrane Database of Systematic Reviews* (4), CD005650.

Bazemore, G., & Umbreit, M. (1995). Rethinking the sanctioning function in juvenile-court—Retributive or restorative responses to youth crime. *Crime and Delinquency, 41*(3), 296–316.

Belenko, S., & Dembo, R. (2003). Treating adolescent substance abuse problems in the juvenile drug court. *International Journal of Law and Psychiatry, 26*(1), 87–110.

Bergseth, K. J., & Bouffard, J. A. (2007). The long-term impact of restorative justice programming for juvenile offenders. *Journal of Criminal Justice, 35*(4), 433–451.

Bernstein, R., & Seltzer, T. (2003). Criminalization of people with mental illnesses: The role of mental health courts in system reform. *University of the District of Columbia Law Review, 7,* 143–162.

Beuttler, F. W. (2004). *For the welfare of every child: A brief history of the Institute for Juvenile Research, 1909–2004.* Chicago: University of Illinois at Chicago.

Blumstein, A., Cohen, J. A., Roth, J. A., & Visher, C. (1986). *Criminal careers and "career criminals."* Washington, DC: National Academies Press.

Brame, B., Nagin, D. S., & Tremblay, R. E. (2001). Developmental trajectories of physical aggression from school entry to late adolescence. *Journal of Child Psychology and Psychiatry, 42*(4), 503–512.

Butts, J. A., Buck, J., & Coggeshall, M. (2002). *The impact of teen court on young offenders.* Washington, DC: The Urban Institute.

Butts, J. A., & Mears, D. P. (2001). Reviving juvenile justice in a get-tough era. *Youth and Society, 33*(2), 169–198.

Caldwell, M. F., Vitacco, M., & Van Rybroek, G. J. (2006). Are violent delinquents worth treating? A cost-benefit analysis. *Journal of Research in Crime and Delinquency, 43*(2), 148–168.

Chung, H. L., Schubert, C. A., & Mulvey, E. P. (2007). An empirical portrait of community reentry among serious juvenile offenders in two metropolitan cities. *Criminal Justice and Behavior, 34*(11), 1402–1425.

Cocozza, J. (1992). *Responding to the mental health needs of youth in the juvenile justice system.* Seattle, WA: National Coalition for the Mentally Ill in the Criminal Justice System.

Cooper, C. S. (2001). *Juvenile drug court programs.* Washington, DC: Office of Justice Programs, Office of Juvenile Justice and Delinquency Prevention.

Copeland, W. E., Miller-Johnson, S., Keeler, G., Angold, A., & Costello, E. J. (2007). Childhood psychiatric disorders and young adult crime: A prospective, population-based study. *American Journal of Psychiatry, 164*(11), 1668–1675.

Cuellar, A. E., McReynolds, L. S., & Wasserman, G. A. (2006). A cure for crime: Can mental health treatment diversion reduce crime among youth? *Journal of Policy Analysis and Management, 25*(1), 197–214.

Curtis, N. M., Ronan, K. R., & Borduin, C. M. (2004). Multisystemic treatment: A meta-analysis of outcome studies. *Journal of Family Psychology, 18*(3), 411–419.

Desai, R. A., Goulet, J. L., Robbins, J., Chapman, J. F., Migdole, S. J., & Hoge, M. A. (2006). Mental health care in juvenile detention facilities: A review. *Journal of the American Academy of Psychiatry and the Law, 34*(2), 204–214.

Dick, A. J., Geertsen, R., & Jones, R. M. (2003). Self-reported delinquency among teen court participants. *Journal for Juvenile Justice and Detention Services, 18*(1), 33–49.

Dishion, T. J., McCord, J., & Poulin, F. (1999). When interventions harm: Peer groups and problem behavior. *American Psychologist, 54,* 755–764.

Dolcos, F., & McCarthy, G. (2006). Brain systems mediating cognitive interference by emotional distraction. *Journal of Neuroscience, 26,* 2072–2079.

Eddy, J. M., Whaley, R. B., & Chamberlain, P. (2004). The prevention of violent behavior by chronic and serious male juvenile offenders: A 2-year follow-up of a randomized clinical trial. *Journal of Emotional and Behavioral Disorders, 12,* 2–8.

Elliott, D., & Tolan, P. H. (1999). Youth, violence prevention, intervention, and social policy: An overview. In D. Flannery & R. Hoff (Eds.), *Youth violence: Prevention, intervention, and social policy* (pp. 3–46). Washington, DC: American Psychiatric Press.

Erickson, S. K., Campbell, A., & Lamberti, J. S. (2006). Variations in mental health courts: Challenges, opportunities, and a call for caution. *Community Mental Health Journal, 42*(4), 335–344.

Feld, B. (1990). The punitive juvenile court and the quality of procedural justice: Disjunctions between rhetoric and reality. *Crime and Delinquency, 36,* 443–464.

Forgays, D. K., & DeMilio, L. (2005). Is teen court effective for repeat offenders? A test of the restorative justice approach. *International Journal of Offender Therapy and Comparative Criminology, 49*(1), 107–118.

Government Accountability Office. (2005). *Adult drug courts: Evidence indicates recidivism reductions and mixed results for other outcomes* (No. GAO-05-219). Washington, DC: U.S. Government Accountability Office.

Grant, K. E., Compas, B. E., Thurm, A. E., McMahon, S. D., & Gipson, P. Y. (2004). Stressors and child and adolescent psychopathology: Measurement issues and prospective effects. *Journal of Clinical Child and Adolescent Psychology, 33*(2), 412–425.

Grisso, T. (2007). Progress and perils in the juvenile justice and mental health movement. *Journal of the American Academy of Psychiatry and the Law, 35*(2), 158–167.

Grisso, T., & Schwartz, R. G. (Eds.). (2000). *Youth on trial: A developmental perspective on juvenile justice.* Chicago: University of Chicago Press.

Guerra, N. G., Kim, T. E., & Boxer, P. (2008). What works: Best practices with juvenile offenders. In R. D. Hoge, N. G. Guerra, & P. Boxer (Eds.), *Treating the juvenile offender* (pp. 79–102). New York: Guilford Press.

Guerra, N. G., Williams, K. R., Tolan, P. H., & Modecki, K. L. (2007). Theoretical and research advances in understanding the causes of juvenile offending. In R. D. Hoge, N. G. Guerra, & P. Boxer (Eds.), *Treating the juvenile offender* (pp. 33–53). New York: Guilford Press.

Hamilton, Z. K., Sullivan, C. J., Veysey, B. M., & Grillo, M. (2007). Diverting multi-problem youth from juvenile justice: Investigating the importance of community influence on placement and recidivism. *Behavioral Sciences and the Law, 25*(1), 137–158.

Hanish, L., & Tolan, P. (2001). Antisocial behaviors in children and adolescents: Expanding the cognitive model. In W. J. Lyddon & J. V. Jones (Eds.),

*Empirically supported cognitive therapies* (pp. 182–199). New York: Springer.

Harris, E., Seltzer, T., & Carter, L. (2004). *The role of specialty mental health courts in meeting the needs of juvenile offenders.* Retrieved January 14, 2008, from *www.bazelon.org/issues/criminalization/publications/mentalhealthcourts/juvenilemhcourts.htm.*

Hawkins, J. D., Smith, B. H., Hill, K. G., Kosterman, R., Catalano, R. F., & Abbott, R. D. (2003). Understanding and preventing crime and violence: Findings from the Seattle Social Development Project. In T. P. Thornberry & M. D. Krohn (Eds.), *Taking stock of delinquency: An overview of findings from contemporary longitudinal studies* (pp. 255–312). New York: Kluwer.

Healy, W. (1915). *The individual delinquent: A text-book of diagnosis and prognosis for all concerned in understanding offenders.* Boston: Little, Brown.

Henggeler, S. W., Halliday-Boykins, C. A., Cunningham, P. B., Randall, J., & Shapiro, S. B. (2006). Juvenile drug court: Enhancing outcomes by integrating evidence-based treatments. *Journal of Consulting and Clinical Psychology, 74*(1), 42–54.

Hirschfield, P., Maschi, T., White, H. R., Traub, L. G., & Loeber, R. (2006). Mental health and juvenile arrests: Criminality, criminalization, or compassion? *Criminology, 44*(3), 593–630.

Hora, P. F., Schma, W. G., & Rosenthal, J. T. A. (1999). Therapeutic jurisprudence and the drug treatment court movement: Revolutionizing the criminal justice system's response to drug abuse and crime in America. *Notre Dame Law Review, 74*(2), 439–538.

Knitzer, J., & Cooper, J. (2006). Beyond integration: Challenges for children's mental health. *Health Affairs, 25*(3), 670–679.

Laub, J. H. (2002). A century of delinquency research and theory. In M. K. Rosenheim, F. E. Zimring, D. S. Tanenhaus, & B. Dohrn (Eds.), *A century of juvenile justice* (pp. 179–205). Chicago: University of Chicago Press.

Lipsey, M. W., & Wilson, D. B. (1998). Effective intervention for serious juvenile offenders: A synthesis of research. In R. Loeber & D. P. Farrington (Eds.), *Serious and violent juvenile offenders: Risk factors and successful interventions* (pp. 313–345). Thousand Oaks, CA: Sage.

Loeber, R., & Farrington, D. P. (1998). *Serious and violent juvenile offenders: Risk factors and successful interventions.* Thousand Oaks, CA: Sage.

Loeber, R., & Hay, D. (1997). Key issues in the development of aggression and violence from childhood to early adulthood. *Annual Review of Psychology, 48,* 371–410.

MacKenzie, D. (2000). Evidence-based corrections: Identifying what works. *Crime and Delinquency, 46*(4), 457–471.

McCold, P., & Wachtel, B. (1998). *Restorative policing experiment: Bethlehem, Pennsylvania Police Family Conferencing Project.* Washington, DC: Department of Justice, National Institute of Justice.

McGarrell, E. F. (2001). *Restorative justice conferences as an early response to young offenders.* Washington, DC: U.S. Department of Justice, Office of Justice Programs.

McGarrell, E. F., & Hipple, N. K. (2007). Family group conferencing and re-offending among first-time juvenile offenders: The Indianapolis experiment. *Justice Quarterly, 24*(2), 221–246.

Migdole, S. J., & Robbins, J. P. (2007). Commentary: The role of mental health services in preadjudicated juvenile detention centers. *Journal of the American Academy of Psychiatry and the Law, 35*(2), 168–171.

Mihalic, S., Fagan, A. A., Irwin, K., Ballard, D., & Elliott, D. (2004). *Blueprints for violence prevention.* Washington, DC: Office of Juvenile Justice and Delinquency Prevention.

Moffitt, T. E. (1993). Adolescent-limited and life-course-persistent antisocial behavior: A developmental taxonomy. *Psychological Review, 100*(4), 674–701.

Moffitt, T. E., & Caspi, A. (2001). Childhood predictors differentiate life-course persistent and adolescence-limited antisocial pathways among males and females. *Developmental Psychopathology, 13,* 355–375.

Mulvey, E. P., Schubert, C. A., & Chung, H. L. (2007). Service use after court involvement in a sample of serious adolescent offenders. *Children and Youth Services Review, 29*(4), 518–544.

Nagin, D. S., Farrington, D. P., & Moffitt, T. E. (1995). Life-course trajectories of different types of offenders. *Criminology, 33*(1), 111–139.

Nagin, D. S., & Tremblay, R. E. (2001). Parental and early childhood predictors of persistent physical aggression in boys from kindergarten to high school. *Archives of General Psychiatry, 58,* 389–394.

National Youth Court Center. (2006). *National program directory and national resources 2006–2007.* Retrieved January 14, 2008, from *www.youthcourt. net/content/view/74.*

Nissen, L. B., Butts, J. A., Merrigan, D., & Kraft, M. K. (2006). The RWJF Reclaiming Futures Initiative: Improving substance abuse interventions for justice-involved youths. *Juvenile and Family Court Journal, 57*(4), 39–51.

Rodriguez, N. (2007). Restorative justice at work: Examining the impact of restorative justice resolutions on juvenile recidivism. *Crime and Delinquency, 53*(3), 355–379.

Schaeffer, C. M., Petras, H., Ialongo, N., Poduska, J., & Kellam, S. (2003). Modeling growth in boys' aggressive behavior across elementary school: Links to later criminal involvement, conduct disorder, and antisocial personality disorder. *Developmental Psychology, 39*(6), 1020–1035.

Sexton, T. L., & Alexander, J. F. (2000). *Functional family therapy.* Washington, DC: U.S. Department of Justice.

Sheidow, A. J., Henggeler, S. W., & Schoenwald, S. K. (2003). Multisystemic therapy. In T. L. Sexton, G. R. Weeks, & M. S. Robbins (Eds.), *Handbook of family therapy* (pp. 303–322). New York: Brunner-Routledge.

Sherman, L. W., Gottfredson, D. C., MacKenzie, D., Eck, J., Reuter, P., & Bushway, S. (1997). *Preventing crime: What works, what doesn't, what's prom-*

*ising.* College Park: University of Maryland, Department of Criminology and Criminal Justice.

Siegel, D. J. (2001). *The developing mind: How relationships and the brain interact to shape who we are.* New York: Guilford Press.

Snyder, H. N. (1998). Serious, violent, and chronic juvenile offenders—An assessment of the extent of and trends in officially recognized serious criminal behavior in a delinquent population. In R. Loeber & D. P. Farrington (Eds.), *Serious and violent juvenile offenders: Risk factors and successful interventions* (pp. 428–444). Thousand Oaks, CA: Sage.

Spear, L. P. (2000). The adolescent brain and age-related behavioral manifestations. *Neuroscience and Biobehavioral Reviews, 24*(4), 417–463.

Steadman, H. J., Davidson, S., & Brown, C. (2001). Mental health courts: Their promise and unanswered questions. *Psychiatric Services, 52*(4), 457–458.

Steinberg, L., & Scott, E. S. (2003). Less guilty by reason of adolescence: Developmental immaturity, diminished responsibility, and the juvenile death penalty. *American Psychologist, 58*(12), 1009–1018.

Sukhodolsky, D. G., & Ruchkin, V. (2006). Evidence-based psychosocial treatments in the juvenile justice system. *Child and Adolescent Psychiatric Clinics of North America, 15*(2), 501–516.

Sullivan, C. J., Veysey, B. M., Hamilton, Z. K., & Grillo, M. (2007). Reducing out-of-community placement and recidivism—Diversion of delinquent youth with mental health and substance use problems from the justice system. *International Journal of Offender Therapy and Comparative Criminology, 51*(5), 555–577.

Tanenhaus, D. S. (2004). *Juvenile justice in the making.* New York: Oxford University Press.

Teplin, L. A., Abram, K. M., McClelland, G. M., Dulcan, M. K., & Mericle, A. A. (2002). Psychiatric disorders in youth in juvenile detention. *Archives of General Psychiatry, 59*(12), 1133–1143.

Tolan, P. H. (1987). Implications of age of onset for delinquency risk. *Journal of Abnormal Child Psychology, 5*(1), 47–65.

Tolan, P. H. (2007). Understanding violence. In D. Flannery (Ed.), *Cambridge handbook of violence research* (pp. 5–18). New York: Cambridge University Press.

Tolan, P. H., & Dodge, K. A. (2005). Children's mental health as a primary care and concern: A system for comprehensive support and service. *American Psychologist, 60,* 601–614.

Tolan, P. H., & Gorman-Smith, D. (1997). Treatment of juvenile delinquency: Between punishment and therapy. In D. Stoff, J. Breiling, & J. Maser (Eds.), *Handbook of antisocial behavior* (pp. 405–415). New York: Wiley.

Tolan, P. H., & Gorman-Smith, D. (1998). Development of serious, violent and chronic offenders. In R. Loeber & D. P. Farrington (Eds.), *Never too early, never too late: Serious, violent and chronic juvenile offenders* (pp. 68–85). Beverly Hills, CA: Sage.

Tolan, P. H., & Gorman-Smith, D. (2003). What violence prevention can tell us about developmental psychopathology. *Development and Psychopathology, 14,* 713–729.

Tolan, P. H., Gorman-Smith, D., & Henry, D. (2003). The developmental ecology of urban male's youth violence. *Developmental Psychology, 39*(2), 274–291.

Tolan, P. H., & Guerra, N. G. (1994a). Prevention of delinquency: Current status and issues. *Applied and Preventive Psychology, 3,* 215–273.

Tolan, P. H., & Guerra, N. G. (1994b). *What works in reducing adolescent violence: An empirical review of the field.* Boulder: University of Colorado, Center for the Study and Prevention of Youth Violence.

Tolan, P. H., Guerra, N. G., & Kendall, P. C. (1995). A developmental-ecological perspective on antisocial behavior in children and adolescents: Toward a unified risk and intervention framework. *Journal of Consulting and Clinical Psychology, 63*(4), 579–584.

Tremblay, R. E. (2000). The development of aggressive behavior during childhood: What have we learned in the past century? *International Journal of Behavioral Development, 24,* 129–141.

Wexler, D. B., & Winick, B. J. (Eds.). (1996). *Law in a therapeutic key: Developments in therapeutic jurisprudence (Carolina Academic Press Studies in Law and Psychology).* Durham, NC: Carolina Academic Press.

Winick, B. J. (2003). Therapeutic jurisprudence and problem solving courts. *Fordham Urban Law Journal, 30,* 1055–1090.

Wolff, N. (2002). Courts as therapeutic agents: Thinking past the novelty of mental health courts. *Journal of the American Academy of Psychiatry and the Law, 30,* 431–437.

Wolff, N., & Pogorzelski, W. (2005). Measuring the effectiveness of mental health courts. *Psychology, Public Policy, and Law, 11*(4), 539–569.

Woolfenden, S. R., Williams, K., & Peat, J. (2001). Family and parenting interventions in children and adolescents with conduct disorder and delinquency aged 10–17. *Cochrane Database of Systematic Reviews* (2), CD003015.

Yakovlev, P., & Lecours, A. R. (1967). The myelination cycles of regional maturation of the brain. In A. Minkowski (Ed.), *Regional brain development in early life* (pp. 3–70). Oxford, UK: Blackwell Science.

# Chapter 17

# Girl Offenders
## *Special Issues*

JAMES GARBARINO
KATHRYN LEVENE
MARGARET WALSH
SACHA M. COUPET

Girls constitute the fastest growing segment of the juvenile justice population, creating something of a "gendered nature" to issues related to juvenile justice over the last decade (Taylor-Thompson, 2006). Evidence for the narrowing gender gap in juvenile justice is highlighted in Chen and Giles's 2003 review of male–female offense charges. Canadian data from 1983 to 2000 (Statistics Canada, 2002) provide evidence of the gender-convergence rates for the majority of the 20 offenses assessed under the criminal code (e.g., manslaughter, breaking and entering, property crimes, theft). At the same time, there is a divergence of opinion on how to understand such increases (Austin, 1993). Are they primarily the result of changes in policies and practices of child welfare agencies, schools, police, and the juvenile legal system (Zahn, 2007) that lead to changes in reports, or do they represent a genuine upward spiraling in girl offending in relation to boy offending (Garbarino, 2006)? What is clear is that a growing number of girls are entering the juvenile justice system who deserve and require our attention.

Reservations have been expressed about the existence of an "early-starter model" that identifies the subgroup of aggressive young girls who are likely to become engaged in juvenile offending (e.g., Silverthorne & Frick, 1999). A growing body of research suggests that there is a small but important group of girls who do display early conduct problems (Capaldi, Kim, &

Shortt, 2004; Serbin & Karp, 2004; Walsh, Yuile, Pepler, Jiang, & Levene, 2004; Yuile, 2007). In this chapter, we examine the early developmental pathway that appears to lead to future girl offending, expecting that this perspective will enhance our understanding of early risk factors and support effective prevention and intervention initiatives. To begin, we review theory and research regarding early risk factors. Next, within the context of research findings emerging from a gender-sensitive clinical program, we review key early risk factors, in particular, childhood exposure to abuse. In closing, we reflect on long-term outcomes for untreated girls with an early aggressive history, including a discussion of the inadequate response of the juvenile justice system in spite of legislated requirements for gender-sensitive programming (Juvenile Justice and Delinquency Prevention Appropriations Authorization, 1992).

## DEVELOPMENTAL PATHWAYS FOR AGGRESSION AND DELINQUENCY

Virtually all children express aggression in infancy and early childhood, so the real issue is not "how do children become aggressive?" but rather "why do some children continue to be aggressive and thus become violent teenagers?" The foundations for children who become delinquent are set in childhood, when they did not succeed in learning nonviolent strategies for meeting their needs in constructive ways to respond to emotions like anger, frustration, and shame. Negative modeling combined with other accumulated risk factors (e.g., trauma, school failure) may instigate high levels of negative emotional responses and behaviors. Research reveals two principal processes that control the developmental pathway for aggression in childhood (Tolan & Guerra, 1998): The ideas a child learns about aggression (cognitive structuring) and the experiences a child has in situations where aggression is modeled and reinforced (behavioral rehearsal). Some children receive consistent messages that reduce the legitimacy of aggression ("Don't hit"), while others receive messages that legitimatize aggression ("Fight back when attacked" and "Aggression is successful"). Similarly, some children observe parents, siblings, and peers resolving conflict nonaggressively while others witness abusive and high-conflict models. Just mapping patterns of cognitive structuring and behavioral rehearsal goes a long way toward understanding why some children arrive at adolescence with a high level of aggressive behavior and others do not.

Girls and boys most at risk for bringing a pattern of serious childhood aggression into adolescence are those who have developed early, chronic patterns of problem behaviors and violating the rights of others, kids who might be described as meeting the criteria for what mental health professionals call "conduct disorder." Research shows that patterns of aggression start to become stable and predictable by the time a child is 8 years old (Loeber, Farrington, & Petechuk, 2003). For girls, there is some evidence of onset at age 7 (Walsh et al., 2004). Unless we do something to intervene, children identified as aggressive at this age are in danger of entrenching similar life patterns. All children are not equally vulnerable to moving down this developmental pathway. The most common pathway to this pattern of aggression at age 8 is for temperamentally vulnerable children to be the victims of abuse and, as a result, to develop a negative pattern of relating to the world in general (see Widom & Wilson, Chapter 13, this volume, for discussion).

Abuse, a far-reaching concept that incorporates witnessing and experiencing neglect as well as physical, sexual, and psychological abuse, plays a key role in what is likely to be a problem-ridden developmental process. The odds that a child will develop conduct disorder reflect the intersection of being abused and having lower levels of social information processing (Garbarino, 1999). The negative pattern that can result from this intersection has four parts: (1) being hypervigilant and hypersensitive to negatives and interpreting ambiguous situations in the social environment as negative; (2) being oblivious to positive social information (such as smiles); (3) having very limited ideas of alternatives to physical aggression as a social tactic and developing a tendency to respond aggressively when frustrated; and (4) drawing the conclusion that aggression is successful in the world. According to research by Dodge, Pettit, and Bates (1977), this negative pattern is the most potent link between a child being the victim of maltreatment and developing a pattern of chronic bad behavior and aggression. They found that being abused produces a sevenfold increase in the odds of developing conduct disorder. Young girls who have experienced abuse (e.g., sexual, physical, witnessing) are particularly vulnerable, and they exhibit a higher level of aggressive behaviors than boys who have experienced similar abuse (Cummings, Pepler, & Moore, 1999; O'Keefe, 1994). There is strong evidence that more than 60% of girl delinquents have been abused (Corrado, Odgers, & Cohen, 2000).

## The Ecology of Aggression and Delinquency

As noted by Garbarino (1995), troubled girls and boys are especially susceptible to "social toxicity," the presence of social and cultural "poisons" in the environment. Just as asthmatic children are most affected by air pollution, so are "psychologically asthmatic" children most affected by social toxicity. The glorification of violence on television, in movies, and in video games is part of this social toxicity, and it affects aggressive kids more than others. The same is true for the size of high schools. Academically marginal students are particularly affected in a negative way by being enrolled in big schools (i.e., those with more than 500 students in grades 9 to 12). The availability of drugs and guns contribute to this toxic environment. Over the past 25 years, the percentage of children and youth with mental health and developmental adjustment problems severe and chronic enough to warrant professional intervention has doubled, according to the research of psychologist Tom Achenbach (Achenbach & Howell, 1993). The spreading problem of youth violence is related to these larger developments.

## Pathways to Girl Delinquency

Traditionally, boys have engaged in more physical aggression than girls (Garbarino, 2006). Girls were taught that "girls don't hit" and were generally excluded from situations where they could practice being physically aggressive, whereas boys were taught that "boys do hit—it's just a matter of learning who, when, and where to hit" and were welcomed into situations, most notably competitive sports, where physical aggression is normal. Shifts in these same processes also help explain why the gap between boys and girls is narrowing, because girls are increasingly told and shown that "girls do hit" and have opportunities to participate in activities such as competitive sports where they can practice being physically aggressive. The ratio of girls' to boys' participation in high school sports, for example, has changed over the past 30 years from 1:32 to 1:1.5 (Garbarino, 2006).

The social construction of how girls behave has also changed dramatically over the past 30 years, as suggested in the impact, for example, of the aggressive marketing targeted at preteen girls. Research into the effects of televised violence on aggressive childhood in the 1960s indicated that girls were immune to the effect; it now has the same effects on girls as on boys (Garbarino, 2006). Advancing along an early developmental pathway, young girls are now increasingly challenged by confusing expectations and models. Such confusion is reflected in the broad continuum of "model" girls, ranging from outmoded stereotypes of "proper" behavior to depictions of highly sexualized and aggressive modern girls. In the face of such contradictory messages, it is challenging, especially for girls already aligned with aggressive and antisocial responses to their environment, to find ways to develop resilient and healthy identities. Their perilous early experiences may already have marginalized and robbed them of learning opportunities that serve as the foundation for healthy development.

## IDENTIFYING AND MANAGING EARLY RISKS

To further unravel key factors that influence the development of girlhood aggression, findings from studies of a special program for behaviorally troubled young girls and their families are reviewed next.

## SNAP® (Stop Now And Plan) Programming

For more than 20 years, Child Development Institute, located in Toronto, has conducted clinic-based, cognitive-behavioral programs for conduct problem children (6- to 11-year-olds) and their families. These programs are based on SNAP, a self-control and problem-solving approach to building healthy and effective ways of interacting; the first such program was the evidenced-based SNAP Outreach Program (SNAP ORP) introduced in 1985 (Augimeri, Jiang, Koegl, & Carey, 2006). An empirically validated program, it consists of structured, 12-session, concurrent child and parent groups; treatment is also tailored to individual needs and includes adjunct services (e.g., school consultation, family counseling). In the early 1990s, we became increasingly aware of the absence of sustained and proven violence prevention programming for young girls. To address this void and provide a gender-sensitive alternative to primarily male-oriented programs for children exhibiting conduct problems, the SNAP Girls Connection (SNAP GC) was introduced in 1996 (Levene, 1997). Using a framework similar to the SNAP ORP, this feminist-informed intervention addresses the spectrum of challenges these girls experience across the key domains in which they interact: home, school, and community. This program has evolved into a well-developed, evidence-based (Pepler et al., 2008), and replicated (Lipman et al., 2008) model intervention. The need for the program has been substantiated by the number of referrals and admissions (more than 500 girls and families) and the girls' clinical profiles, which indicate that they are exhibiting aggressive behaviors significantly more elevated than those displayed by other girls their age and by their male counterparts (Walsh & Levene, 2006). Key SNAP GC goals are to increase acquisition of protective skills (e.g., build healthy relationships, coping abilities), diminish the impact of existing risk factors (e.g., abuse history, lack of family and community supports), and enhance effective parenting skills.

To improve the capacity of clinicians to evaluate and respond to each referred girl's level of risk for future delinquency, the SNAP team created a risk assessment tool: Early Assessment Risk List for Girls (EARL-21G; Levene et al., 2001). This tool is used to identify the presence and severity of risks in three domains: family, child, and responsivity (Table 17.1). The content of each of the 21 risk constructs was chosen because gender differences had been noted in those domains from both clinical experience and research literature (e.g., early sexualized interactions; Caspi, Lynam, Moffitt, & Silva, 1993). At the clinical level, this focused identification of risks guides clinicians in their treatment planning to provide each girl and family with the intensity of service likely to have optimal results. As described next, program evaluation research on SNAP GC has highlighted the robust influence of certain risk factors on treatment outcome (Walsh et al., 2004; Yuile, 2007) and fostered program development.

**TABLE 17.1. Items in the Early Assessment Risk List for Girls**

| Family (F) items | Child (C) items | Responsivity (R) items |
| --- | --- | --- |
| Household circumstances | Developmental problems | Family responsivity |
| Caregiver continuity | Onset of behavioral difficulties | Child responsivity |
| Supports | Abuse/neglect/trauma | |
| Stressors | Hyperactivity/impulsivity/ attention deficits | |
| Parenting style | Likeability | |
| Caregiver–daughter interaction | Peer socialization | |
| Antisocial values and conduct | Academic performance | |
| | Neighborhood | |
| | Sexual development | |
| | Antisocial attitude | |
| | Antisocial behavior | |
| | Coping ability | |

Evaluations of the SNAP GC have included qualitative (Levene, Madsen, & Pepler, 2005), retrospective file audit (Walsh, Pepler, & Levene, 2002), and prospective randomized controlled (Pepler et al., 2007; Yuile, Walsh, Jiang, Pepler, & Levene, 2007) studies. These studies have made it possible to examine the nature of and interactions among the EARL-21G risk factors and to identify key factors that appear to contribute to girlhood aggression (Walsh et al., 2004; Yuile, 2007). This research has provided support for the saliency of abuse as a factor that has a profound impact on the development of girlhood aggression and future delinquency. The abuse/neglect/trauma (ANT) risk factor of the EARL 21-G has emerged as a prominent predictor, for girls participating in the SNAP GC, of the severity of behavior problems and immediate response to intervention. For the purposes of this chapter, we focus on this factor and examine the complex cluster of interacting risk factors.

## Profile of Admission Indicators of Family and Child Risk

A review of SNAP GC admission data from 1996 to 2001 (Pepler et al., 2008; Walsh et al., 2004; Yuile, 2007) indicates that referred girls (*mean age = 9 years*) and their families were primarily of European Canadian or Caribbean Canadian ethnicity. They were largely poor, mother-led, single-parent families in which maternal mental and physical illnesses were prevalent. Mother–daughter interactions were fraught with high conflict as well as inconsistent and punitive parenting practices. Abuse and trauma were pervasive issues for both mothers and girls. Notably, a majority of the girls had witnessed violence in their homes. Almost half of the families had been involved with child welfare services because of concerns about the girls' experience of neglect and physical, emotional, verbal, and sexual abuse. Healthy girlhood development had also been compromised by verbal and physical delays, attention difficulties, academic deficits, and serious externalizing (e.g., vandalism, physical aggression, bullying, theft) and internalizing (e.g., depression, anxiety, suicidal thinking, self-harm) symptoms. Criminal involvement across the extended family and overall lack of supportive relationships distinguished the most troubled families.

## Risk Levels Associated with Initial Conduct Problems and Positive Change

A scientific evaluation of the SNAP GC program revealed significant results with regard to decreases in girlhood aggression, increases in parenting effectiveness, and increases in girls' prosocial behaviors (Pepler et al., 2008; Walsh et al., 2002). There was, however, a subset of girls (48%) who had been initially assessed as having experienced elevated levels of abuse (on the ANT domain) and who showed significantly less immediate improvement than girls who had been rated at a less serious level[1] on this factor. This subset of girls displayed elevated behavior problems at admission and continued to remain in or near the clinical range (score $\geq 70$) for conduct disorder, despite making some improvement, during the long-term follow-up period. However, these improvements were not found to be statistically significant. Girls rated as having experienced high levels of risk in the ANT domain had a significantly increased probability of having co-occurring multiple risks across the family and child domains. Girls with confirmed histories of abuse were more likely to come from financially disadvantaged families who lived in crowded homes, were socially isolated, faced unemployment, had a maternal history of abuse, had low parental education attainment, and experienced teen pregnancy. Having multiple caregivers, placement in foster care, strained mother–daughter relationships, family members involved in criminal activity, substance abuse, and domestic violence also characterized their histories. In comparison to their peers who did not have chronicled abuse histories, these girls had had very early onset of behavioral problems (before the age of 7 years) and exhibited poor peer relations and age-inappropriate sexual behavior (i.e., sexualized language, mimicking sexual acts). The severity of their behavior problems was evidenced as well by their level of direct police contact. Although direct police referrals are relatively rare for young girls[2] referred to SNAP GC, the seven admitted girls who had had such contact all had confirmed histories of abuse.

Such a constellation of multiple risks is likely, without intervention, to have a profound impact on girls' development and future life course. For this subgroup of young girls participating in the SNAP GC, their immediate response to intervention may be viewed as reflecting the nature of the pre-dominant risk factors to which they had been exposed, their elevated overall pretreatment levels of conduct problems, and their prior contact with the law. In the following case history, the nature and interactions of heightened risks as well as buffering factors are illustrated.

> Sara and her mother, Jean, had a close relationship. Since they lived in a high-crime neighborhood, they tended to be isolated from their community. Jean's extended family provided them with a social life. Many of the family members, including Jean, abused alcohol. The strong and caring mother–daughter relationship often suffered when Jean was drinking as she tended to neglect and be verbally abusive with Sara. At school Sara did well academically but often exhibited poorly developed social and coping skills with peers. On a few occasions she was sus-pended from school for swearing at and threatening classmates.
>
> On a holiday with the extended family, 9-year-old Sara reported that an uncle had sexually assaulted her when she and her cousins had been left unsupervised. The uncle denied the allegations and was sup-ported by the rest of the family. Jean successfully laid charges against her brother and as a result was excluded from her family. Jean accessed appropriate services for herself and her daughter but Sara refused to participate or discuss the abuse. While simultaneously trying to engage supportively with Sara, Jean was struggling to deal with her own abuse problems. Feeling guilty about not having protected her daughter, Jean tended to "give in" to Sara's demands and refusals. In turn, Sara became increasingly rude and aggressive with her mother. At school, problems with classmates escalated, her academic progress was stalled, and she began to display sexualized language and behaviors. The school referred the family to the SNAP GC program.
>
> Outcomes of their active and regular participation in the SNAP core group programs were promising in that Sara began to display some improved emotional and behavioral regulation skills at home and school. Jean implemented more effective parenting skills and joined a community support group. They participated in continuing SNAP GC services that supported their growing reconnection and shared learning about physical and sexual health as well as Sara's academic progress and peer relationships. Eventually Sara began to do reparative work to address the sexual abuse. Follow-up research indicates that this family is experiencing significant positive changes.

This case example illustrates the impact of exposure to sexual abuse, verbal abuse, neglect, trauma, and co-occurring risk factors (e.g., isolation, dangerous neighborhood, scarcity of positive supports, family history of alcohol abuse) early in a girl's life. This constellation of risks had profound negative effects on Sara's ability to regulate effectively her emotions, and she struggled with feelings of hostility, anger, and shame. In terms of strengths and buffers, this example suggests the powerful role of a caring and ultimately resilient mother–daughter relationship and the ability to acquire, through intervention, healthy and effective ways of interacting, coping with challenges, and growing. Sara's academic strengths provided a continuous source of success and she formed friendships with peers also invested in school. To date, she has made fundamental positive choices, which have protected her from entering a juvenile justice pathway. Her positive gains are further reinforced by her ongoing participation in SNAP GC, including acting as a peer mentor with girls entering the program. This role gives her an extended opportunity to practice, reinforce, and model her SNAP skills.

## DISCUSSION

Identifying and understanding interactions between early risk factors that contribute to the vulnerability of young girls to delinquent trajectories provide support for the concept of an "early-starter model." A difference was found in the immediate treatment effects for a small subgroup of high-risk girls whose profiles exhibited a different pattern than the low- to moderate-risk girls. Abuse was found to play a key role in the problem-ridden lives of these particularly troubled young girls; high levels of risk in the ANT domain significantly increased the likelihood of a girl's having several, co-occurring risks in other risk domains. Although these high-risk girls were still elevated in problem behavior in comparison to their lower risk counterparts, it was encouraging to find that girls in this highly vulnerable subgroup did display some positive changes over time. These delayed findings may be explained by the multifaceted nature of the program and the access that the girls and their families had to additional treatment components that address unique risks and needs and their elevated clinical risk levels at admission to the SNAP GC program. Research findings have helped chart the early developmental pathway for girls most at risk for a delinquent trajectory and support the view that there is a group of vulnerable young girls who exhibit early patterns of elevated behavior problems. These speak to the need for effective and enhanced interventions to address specific issues in the lives of particularly vulnerable young girls that have, for far too long, been neglected.

With regard to intervention enhancement and public education, the issue of meaningfulness also merits our attention. We believe that at the core of the youth violence problem is a spiritual crisis. Human beings are not simply animals with complicated brains. Rather, we are spiritual beings having a physical experience. This recognition directs our attention to the multiple spiritual crises in the lives of violent adolescents. They often have a sense of meaninglessness, in which they are cut off from a sense of life having a higher purpose. By the same token, they often have difficulty envision-ing themselves in the future. This terminal thinking undermines their moti-vation to contribute to their community and to invest their time and energy in schooling and healthy lifestyles. Finally, they often have lost confidence in the ability and motivation of the adults in their world to protect and care for them. This leads them to adopt the orientation of "juvenile vigilantism." For example, a teenager may reason, "If I join a gang I am 50% safe; if I don't join a gang I am 0% safe."

The point is that adults do not enter into the equation. On the one hand, nonpunitive, love-oriented religion institutionalizes spirituality and func-tions as a buffer against social pathology, according to research reviewed by psychologist Andrew Weaver (see, e.g., Weaver, Revilla, & Koenig, 2002). On the other hand, the culture in which we live undermines spirituality and exacerbates social problems. One way to deal with these issues is to have schools join with community leaders to embrace the national character education campaign, as developed, for example, by psychologist Thomas Lickona (see, e.g., Lickona, 1991). Character education offers all positive elements within a community a focal point for their actions. It provides a framework in which to pursue an agenda that nourishes spirituality (without invoking constitutionally insoluble issues of church and state). However, at present, this analysis stands largely outside of or at least parallel to the way the children's mental health, education, and legal/justice systems respond to aggressive girls. Dealing with girl delinquency will require both a broadly based prevention perspective on community life and a conscious focusing of attention on dealing humanely and effectively with troubled aggressive girls in childhood lest they fall in line to proceed down the pathway to youth violence.

## LONG-TERM OUTCOMES

About one-third of children with conduct disorder will eventually become violent, delinquent youth, and about 90% will go on to demonstrate some serious problems in adulthood (Garbarino, 1999). In juvenile prisons, typi-cally about 80% will have followed this negative pathway (Garbarino, 1999). Although boys clearly outnumber girls in this grim picture, girls with an early aggressive history are, without effective intervention, increasingly at risk for engaging in delinquent offenses. As well, these girls are at risk of early school dropout, poor employment prospects, serious mental and phys-ical health problems, and early parenthood and at increased risk for abuse and neglect of their offspring (Moffitt, Caspi, Rutter, & Silva, 2001; Wood-ward & Fergusson, 1999). They are especially vulnerable to affiliations with antisocial peers and partners, to self-limitation as a result of exposure to antisocial patterns (Caspi, Lynam, Moffitt, & Silva, 1993), as well as to further abuse, exploitation, and negative influence (Levene et al., 2001). For some girls, profound early relationship deficits become entrenched and fuel subsequent highly problematic partner relationships (Ehrensaft, 2005).

## JUVENILE JUSTICE SYSTEM

When at-risk girls enter adolescence and engage in antisocial behaviors, the problems they face grow exponentially. The rapid growth of girl delinquency has not been met with corresponding gender-sensitive responses across the legal decision-making process. Although there has been a documented rise in the arrest of girls for violent offenses over the past two decades, girls are still far less likely than boys to be arrested for serious violent crimes and are, instead, more likely than boys to be arrested for minor property offenses and status offenses. Girls are disproportionately charged with status offenses, such as running away, violating curfew, incorrigibility, and truancy, which would not constitute a criminal offense were the activity in question committed by an adult. As observed by Poulin (1996), "Gender bias still operates to bring girls into the system for conduct that would not result in juvenile charges against a boy and to treat girls more harshly for some conduct and more leniently for other behavior" (p. 545). The disparate treatment of girl and boy offenders raises the question of whether the law functions as a form of social control, responsive to gender-based perceptions of appropriate behavior and leaving girls with less room for deviation from socially accepted behavioral norms.

Girls committing violent offenses are not spared from a gender-biased response. Critics (Zahn, 2007; Taylor-Thompson, 2006; Barnickol, 2000) point to instances of disproportionate response to similar types of behavior that strongly support the belief that aggression is less tolerated when displayed by girls and, therefore, more likely to be punished severely. Girls may encounter gender bias in the system at the initial stage of contact not only because of a lowered threshold for antisocial behaviors among girls but also because of a failure to contextualize girl offending appropriately within the scope of responsive or adaptive behaviors, of which girls are more likely than boys to avail themselves (Garbarino, 2006). Law enforcement authorities, attentive to the offending conduct itself, may overlook significant underlying precipitants. There is a high incidence of physical, sexual, or psychological abuse among girls in the delinquency system and, in failing to take into account risk factors most prevalent among girls, the focus of attention is on the deviant juvenile rather than a holistic view. Taylor-Thompson (2006) noted: "In many instances what appears to be self-destructive, delinquent behavior by girls—running away from home or engaging in prostitution— may in fact be understandable responses to traumatizing home environments" (p. 1137). Add the interaction of race and gender and there is an even more skewed portrait of offending among girls, with the greatest increase in arrest rates and greatest incidence of secure confinement occurring among African American girls (Taylor-Thompson, 2006). Perhaps because of systemic racial bias, "girls of color tend to benefit least from opportunities for diversion from or lenient treatment within the system," with cases dismissed at significantly lower rates than their white peers (Taylor-Thompson, 2006, p. 1137). In a pattern that mirrors the plight of young minority boys, girls of color are not only disproportionately represented in the juvenile justice population but they also tend to receive the most severe sentences (Taylor-Thompson, 2006). Like girl offending, the underlying causes of racial disproportionality are, as yet, poorly understood.

Girls who find themselves in trouble with the law are unlikely to find appropriate gender-specific therapeutic interventions, because such services have been designed to suit the needs of the overwhelming majority of boy offenders. The absence of gender-specific treatment and prevention models persists despite a 1992 amendment to the Juvenile Justice and Delinquency Prevention Act supporting their development.

## CONCLUSION

There is disagreement about whether the reported rise in girl aggressive delinquency is the result of policy changes and practices or reflects actual increases in behavior. We favor the latter explanation. In any case, it is important to examine the complex early factors that contribute to girl delinquency because more girls are involved in the social systems created to deal with aggressive delinquency. It is essential that we, as a society, not only recognize that these vulnerable young girls exist but understand the unique risks that are present in their lives and respond with early and effective gender-sensitive prevention, treatment, and youth legal interventions. The environment in which young girls develop has been changing at an accelerated rate, and this needs to be reflected in how our communities respond to and support them. An understanding of the pathways to aggressive delinquency shared by girls and boys as well as an appreciation for the special gendered issues facing girls is essential for creating and sustaining well-informed approaches that will help troubled and aggressive girls move toward safe and healthy life pathways.

## NOTES

1. "High risk" indicates confirmed abuse/neglect/trauma, and lesser levels include unconfirmed allegations and/or no evidence.
2. In Canada, the age of legal responsibility is 12 years. Police may work with

schools or other institutions to encourage parents to seek services for the girls rather than making a direct referral.

## REFERENCES

Achenbach, T. M., & Howell, C. T. (1993). Are American children's problems getting worse? A thirteen year comparison. *Journal of the American Academy of Child and Adolescent Psychiatry, 32,* 1145–1154.

Augimeri, L. K., Jiang, D., Koegl, C. J., & Carey, J. (2006). *Differential effects of the SNAP Under 12 Outreach Project (ORP) associated with client risk & treatment intensity.* Ottawa, Ontario: Centre of Excellence for Child and Youth Mental Health at CHEO.

Austin, R. L. (1993). Recent trends in official male and female crime rates: The convergence controversy. *Journal of Criminal Justice, 21,* 447–66.

Barnickol, L. A. (2000). The disparate treatment of males and females within the juvenile justice system. *Journal of Law and Policy, 2,* 429–457.

Capaldi, D. M., Kim, H. K., & Shortt, J. W. (2004). Women's involvement in aggression in young adult romantic relationships: A developmental systems model. In M. Putallaz & K. L. Bierman (Eds.), *Aggression, antisocial behavior, and violence among girls: A developmental perspective* (pp. 223–241). New York: Guilford Press.

Caspi, A., Lynam, D., Moffitt, T. E., & Silva, P. A. (1993). Unraveling girls' delinquencies: Biological, dispositional, and contextual contributions to adolescent misbehavior. *Developmental Psychology, 29,* 19–30.

Chen, J.-Y. J., & Giles, D. E. A. (2003). *Gender convergence in crime: Evidence from Canadian adult offence charge data.* Victoria, British Columbia: University of Victoria, Department of Economics.

Corrado, R., Odgers, C., & Cohen, I. M. (2000). The incarceration of female young offenders: Protection from whom? *Canadian Journal of Criminology, 4,* 189–207.

Cummings, J. G., Pepler, D. J., & Moore, T. E. (1999). Behavior problems in children exposed to wife abuse: Gender differences. *Journal of Family Violence, 14,* 133–156.

Dodge K., Pettit, G., & Bates, J. (1977). How the experience of early physical abuse leads children to become chronically aggressive. In C. Cicchetti & S. Toth (Eds.), *Development psychopathology: Developmental perspectives on trauma:* Vol. 9. *Theory, research, and intervention* (pp. 341–381). Washington, DC: American Psychological Association.

Ehrensaft, M. K. (2005). Interpersonal relationships and sex differences in the development of conduct problems. *Clinical Child and Family Psychology Review, 8,* 39–63.

Garbarino, J. (1995). *Raising children in a socially toxic environment.* San Francisco: Jossey-Bass.

Garbarino, J. (1999). *Lost boys: Why our sons turn violent and how we can save them.* New York: Free Press.

Garbarino, J. (2006). *See Jane hit: Why girls are growing more violent and what we can do about it.* New York: Penguin.

Juvenile Justice and Delinquency Prevention Appropriations Authorization. (1992). Public Law 102-586, §1, 106 Stat. 4982.

Levene, K. (1997). The Earlscourt Girls Connection: A model for intervention. *Canada's Children, 4,* 14–17.

Levene, K., Augimeri, L. K., Pepler, D. J., Walsh, M. M., Webster, C. D., & Koegl, C. J. (2001). *Early Assessment Risk List for Girls EARL-21G Version 1—Consultation edition.* Toronto, Ontario: Earlscourt Child and Family Center.

Levene, K.., Madsen, K. C., & Pepler, D. J. (2005). Girls growing up angry: A qualitative study. In D. J. Pepler, K. C. Madsen, K. Levene, & C. Webster (Eds.), *The development and treatment of girlhood aggression* (pp. 169–190). Hillsdale, NJ: Erlbaum.

Lickona, T. (1991). *Educating for character: How our schools can teach respect and responsibility.* New York: Bantam.

Lipman, E. L., Kenny, M., Sniderman, C., O'Grady, S., Augimeri, L. K., Khayutin, S., et al. (2008). Evaluation of a community-based program for young boys at risk for antisocial behaviour: Results and issues. *Journal of the Canadian Academy of Child and Adolescent Psychiatry, 17,* 12–19.

Loeber, R., Farrington, D. P. & Petechuk, D. (2003). Child delinquency: Early intervention and prevention. Bulletin. Washington, DC: U.S. Department of Justice, Office of Justice Programs, Office of Juvenile Justice and Delinquency Prevention.

Moffitt, T. E., Caspi, A., Rutter, M., & Silva, P. A. (2001). *Sex differences in antisocial behaviour: Conduct disorder, delinquency, and violence in the Dunedin Longitudinal Study.* Cambridge, UK: Cambridge University Press.

O'Keefe, M. (1994). Linking marital violence, mother-child/father-child aggression, and child behavior problems. *Journal of Family Violence, 9,* 63–78.

Pepler, D. J., Jiang, D., Walsh, M. M., Yuile, A., Vaughan, A., & Levene, K. (2007, November). *Intervening with aggressive girls: Effectiveness of the SNAP ™ Girls Connection.* Paper presented at the annual meeting of the American Society for Criminology Conference, Atlanta.

Pepler, D., Walsh, M., Yuile, A., Levene, K., Webber, J., Vaughan, A., et al. (2008). *Bridging the gender gap: Understanding and treating girls' aggression.* Manuscript in preparation.

Poulin, A. B. (1996). Female delinquent: Defining their place in the justice system, Wisconsin. *Law Review* (3), 541–575.

Serbin, L. A., & Karp, J. (2004). The intergenerational transfer of psychosocial risk: Mediators of vulnerability and resilience. *Annual Review of Psychology, 55,* 333–363.

Silverthorn, P., & Frick, R. (1999). Developmental pathways to antisocial

CHILDREN AS OFFENDERS

348

behavior: The delayed-onset pathway in girls. *Development and Psychopathology, 11,* 101–126.

Statistics Canada. (2002). *CANSIM databank.* Ottawa, Ontario: Statistics Canada.

Taylor-Thompson, K. (2006). Girl talk: Examining racial and gender lines in juvenile justice. *Nevada Law Journal, 6,* 1137–1164.

Tolan, P. H., & Guerra, N. G. (1998). *What works in reducing adolescent violence: An empirical review of the field.* Chicago: University of Chicago Press.

Walsh, M. M., & Levene, K. (2006). *Gender differences in admission criteria for SNAP model programs.* Unpublished raw data.

Walsh, M. M., Pepler, D. J., & Levene, K. (2002). A model intervention for girls with disruptive behavior problems: The Earlscourt Girls Connection. *Canadian Journal of Counseling, 36,* 297–311.

Walsh, M. M., Yuile, A., Pepler, D. J., Jiang, D., & Levene, K. (2004). *Risk profiles and treatment outcomes for aggressive girls: An evaluation using the Early Assessment Risk List for Girls (EARL 21-G).* Paper presented at the 12th Annual Meeting of the Society for Prevention Research, Quebec City, Quebec.

Weaver, A. J., Revilla, L. A., & Koenig, H. G. (2002). *Counseling families across the stages of life: A handbook for pastors and other helping professionals.* Nashville, TN: Abingdon Press.

Woodward, L. J., & Fergusson, D. M. (1999). Early conduct problems and later risk of teenage pregnancy in girls. *Development and Psychopathology, 11,* 127–141.

Yuile, A. (2007). *Developmental pathways of aggressive girls: A gender-sensitive approach to risk assessment, intervention, and follow-up.* Unpublished doctoral dissertation, York University, Toronto, Ontario.

Yuile, A., Walsh, M. M., Jiang, D., Pepler, D. J., & Levene, K. (2007). *Risk factors and intervention outcomes for aggressive girls in the SNAP™ Girls Connection: A prospective replication.* Manuscript in preparation.

Zahn, M. A. (2007). The causes of girls' delinquency and their program implications. *Family Court Review, 45,* 456–465.

# Chapter 18

# Understanding Adults' Perceptions of Juvenile Offenders

MARGARET C. STEVENSON
CYNTHIA J. NAJDOWSKI
BETTE L. BOTTOMS
TAMARA M. HAEGERICH

Although arrests for violent juvenile crime have decreased 31% since 1995 (Snyder, 2006), societal perceptions of the incidence and seriousness of juvenile crime rose in the 1990s. A resulting "get-tough" attitude motivated legislative changes designed to stem the tide of juvenile crime. Among them, juvenile waiver statutes facilitate the transfer of juveniles from protective juvenile court into adult criminal court (for discussion, see Reppucci, Michel, & Kostelnik, Chapter 15, and Slobogin, Chapter 20, this volume). In 2004, for example, there were more than 2 million arrests of juveniles in the United States. Of those cases eligible for processing in the juvenile justice system, 7% were referred directly to criminal court (Snyder, 2006).

In adult criminal court, cases involving juveniles can be decided by jurors rather than by family or juvenile court judges. It is, therefore, important to understand adults' perceptions of juvenile defendants and the factors that influence jurors' decisions in criminal cases involving juveniles. This research has value for research psychologists interested in legal decision making and for professionals within the legal system who seek to understand how jurors react to juveniles accused of crimes and how they reach their verdicts in cases involving juveniles. In this chapter, we consider three broad categories of factors that affect perceptions of juveniles: (1) juror individual difference factors, including jurors' gender and stereotypes about juveniles; (2) courtroom and trial factors, including attorneys' attempts to induce jurors' empathy for and stereotypes about juvenile defendants and jury deliberation as a potential moderator of such tactics; and (3) juvenile individual difference factors, including gender, race, history of maltreatment, intellectual disability, and tendency to confess.

Generally, the research we review is conducted with methods much like those described by Golding, Dunlap, and Hodell (Chapter 10, this volume) in their review of factors affecting jurors' perceptions of child witnesses. Specifically, within a mock trial paradigm, adult participants assume the role of jurors and consider a criminal case involving a juvenile defendant. The details of cases are often based on facts from actual cases and presented via summarized written scenarios or trial transcripts that are sometimes accompanied by pictures or videotaped excerpts from simulated or actual trials. Mock jurors are asked to render a verdict and provide other judgments such as ratings of their confidence in the verdict, perceived credibility of witnesses, perceived responsibility of the alleged offender, and so on. Researchers typically collect mock jurors' individual verdict preferences, but in some studies jurors also deliberate before rendering verdicts.

Although researchers attempt to conduct these studies with as much realism as practically feasible, the studies we review vary in the extent to which they approximate the actual circumstances of trials. As discussed thoroughly by Golding and colleagues (Chapter 10, this volume), there is a trade-off in mock trial research between using methods that are high in ecological validity versus methods that allow for precise experimental control (i.e., the ability to draw cause-and-effect conclusions about the influence of independent variables). Mock trial methodology allows researchers to have the control necessary for varying certain factors (e.g., defendant age or gender) while keeping all other factors constant, which would be impossible if studying actual trials. Artificiality of methods should be taken into account when generalizing from laboratory studies to actual legal situations (Diamond, 1997; Weiten & Diamond, 1979), so researchers should always strive for the most realism possible.

## JUROR FACTORS

Individual jurors differ from one another in many ways. Courts intuitively understand this and use the process of voir dire in an attempt to identify juror individual differences that are thought to present a risk to fair decision making. What individual differences influence the outcomes of criminal trials involving juvenile offenders?

## Juror Gender

Women jurors are generally more pro-child victim (i.e., more pro-prosecution) than are men in cases involving child sexual and physical abuse (see Bottoms, Golding, Stevenson, Wiley, & Wozniak, 2007, for a review). Considering that these gender differences are driven in part by gender differences in empathy for children and positive attitudes toward children generally (Bottoms, 1993), one would expect similar gender differences in jurors' perceptions of juvenile offenders. But perhaps not, given that gender differences in child victim/witness cases are also driven in part by women's stronger negative reactions to the specific crime of child sexual abuse (Bottoms, 1993).

In fact, some studies have found that women are more positively disposed toward juvenile defendants than are men. For example, in a study by Haegerich and Bottoms (2000), a juvenile offender was tried for patricide alleged to have been in self-defense after years of child sexual abuse. Women mock jurors rendered fewer guilt judgments and rated the defendant as more credible than did men. In addition, the gender of the juvenile defendant was varied experimentally, and although men jurors felt more sympathy and empathy toward a boy than a girl defendant, women jurors were equally sympathetic and empathic regardless of defendant gender. This might be evidence of a general gender difference in reactions to juvenile defendants, or it might reflect gender differences in response to the "embedded" crime of the defendant's alleged child sexual abuse, especially given that more women than men believed that the defendant had been sexually abused.

Still other studies suggest that women are more pro-juvenile defendant than men, even in the absence of child sexual abuse. Stalans and Henry (1994) found that men were more likely than women to favor the harsh disposition of waiving a juvenile's case to adult court and to favor longer sentences. (Although judges usually make sentencing decisions in noncapital cases, jurors are charged with this task in some states; King, 1999.) Women also favored less severe sentences for juveniles than did men in a study by Crosby, Britner, Jodl, and Portwood (1995). Redlich and colleagues' research revealed that, compared with men, women considered (1) a juvenile defendant as less likely to have committed a crime (Redlich, Ghetti, & Quas, 2008), (2) a juvenile defendant as having less understanding of criminal interrogation situations (Redlich, Quas, & Ghetti, 2008), and (3) interrogations of juveniles as less fair and the police who conduct them as more manipulative (Redlich, Ghetti, et al., 2008).

Not all research on reactions to juvenile crime reveals such a pro-juvenile defendant bias for women compared with men, however. For example, Stevenson and Bottoms (in press) found no pervasive juror gender differences in mock jurors' reactions toward a juvenile accused of murder. Juror gender did, however, play some role in judgments: Men, but not women, were influenced by the race of the juvenile defendant, as we discuss later.

## Jurors' Stereotypes about Juvenile Offenders

Levesque (1996) reported that community members overwhelmingly endorse a "get-tough" or "just-deserts" approach to juvenile crime. Other surveys, however, demonstrate a preference for rehabilitating rather than punishing juvenile offenders (Moon, Sundt, Cullen, & Wright, 2000; Sundt, Cullen, Applegate, & Turner, 1998). In fact, a 2006 survey revealed that Pennsylvania community members prefer allocating money toward rehabilitating juveniles who commit serious violent crimes than toward longer incarceration costs (Nagin, Piquero, Scott, & Steinberg, 2006).

In samples of college students and community members, Haegerich and Bottoms (2004) identified two different stereotypes held about juvenile offenders: (1) relatively innocuous "wayward youths" or (2) cold and calculating "superpredators." The wayward youth stereotype portrays juvenile offenders as having fallen prey to criminal behavior because of their inadequate peer and familial support systems, impoverished living environment, insufficient educational opportunities, and decreased understanding of the negative consequences and seriousness of their actions. In contrast, the superpredator stereotype holds that juvenile offenders lack morals and are violent by nature, commit crime with premeditation, understand the severity and consequences of their actions, and manipulate the justice system to avoid accountability for their actions. Further, people who endorse the wayward youth stereotype believe that juvenile offenders are immature adolescents who can and should be rehabilitated rather than punished, whereas people who endorse the superpredator stereotype believe that juvenile offenders are mature, cold, cruel, and not amenable to rehabilitation. Haegerich and Bottoms found that, although most people are aware of both stereotypes, people endorse them to varying degrees. Surprisingly, given media and legislative attention to the supposed rise in juvenile crime and to specific cases of severe crimes committed by juveniles, laypeople in that study were, on average, more likely to perceive juvenile offenders as wayward youths than as superpredators. Even so, participants overestimated the amount and severity of juvenile crime. Further, endorsement of juvenile offender stereotypes translates into biased juror decisions. Several months after completing measures of their endorsement of the superpredator versus wayward youth stereotypes study, participants assumed the role of juror in an ostensibly unrelated mock trial and read a detailed trial transcript describing a juvenile being tried for murder in adult criminal court. Mock jurors who endorsed the superpredator stereotype rendered more severe case judgments (e.g., more guilty verdicts, lengthier sentences) than did those who endorsed the wayward youth stereotype.

## COURTROOM AND TRIAL FACTORS: ATTORNEYS' TACTICS AND JURY DELIBERATION

To what extent do attorneys' actions and trial processes influence case decisions when juveniles are on trial? Next, we review research that addresses this question.

### Attorneys' Tactics: Empathy Induction and Stereotype Activation

When juvenile offenders are transferred to adult criminal court, defense and prosecuting attorneys play an important role in determining how their cases are presented. Consider the jury that is exposed to defense attorneys who are adept at creating a very compelling empathic atmosphere toward a juvenile offender or who ask jurors to place themselves in the shoes of the defendant, as trial lawyers have instinctively done for years (Archer, Foushee, Davis, & Aderman, 1979). Empathy is a multidimensional construct, referring to the ability to take another person's perspective both cognitively and emotionally (Davis, 1994). When individuals have empathy for perpetrators of negative behavior, they are less likely to attribute responsibility for the behavior to the perpetrators (Sulzer & Burglass, 1968). Trial attorneys have intuitively suspected this for years. To illustrate, in a handbook for attorneys, Hamlin (1985) writes, "The ability to actually experience, internally, what is at issue, to empathize and put themselves in another person's place, is something of which jurors are not consciously aware. Yet this process is human and universal, and it is a powerful inner voice in decision-making" (p. 315).

Haegerich and Bottoms (2000) investigated the impact of attorney-induced empathy on mock jurors' verdicts in a case involving a teenager being tried as an adult for patricide. The juvenile defendant claimed the murder was in self-defense because of the father's long-standing sexual abuse. Empathy for the victim/defendant was manipulated in the written case transcript via the defense attorney's opening and closing statements to the jury. For half of the mock jurors (those who were in the empathy condition), the attorney made an impassioned plea asking them to take the perspective of the child defendant and to think of how they would be thinking and feeling if they were the defendant. Compared with jurors who received no such empathy-inducing instructions, jurors primed with empathy were less likely to render guilty verdicts in the trial, considered the defendant to be less responsible for the murder, and were more likely to accept the defendant's claim of child sexual abuse as a mitigating factor in the killing. Compared with men, women mock jurors were more lenient toward the juvenile defendant overall and were more affected by the empathy induction.

Earlier, we described research that identified preexisting stereotypes that people hold about juvenile offenders (i.e., the superpredator and wayward youth stereotypes). Haegerich and Bottoms (2004) examined whether those stereotypes could be activated in mock jurors more strongly than usual by attorneys in their opening and closing trial statements. In their study, a detailed trial transcript described a case in which a juvenile offender was being tried as an adult for a robbery/murder. In one condition of the study, the prosecutor argued that the defendant was a superpredator who could not be rehabilitated. In the other condition, the defense attorney argued that the defendant was a wayward youth who could be rehabilitated. There was also a control condition in which neither stereotype was activated. Attorney arguments influenced case judgments in the expected direction: Mock jurors exposed to the superpredator stereotype rendered more guilty verdicts and favored lengthier sentences than did jurors who were exposed to the wayward youth stereotype or jurors in the control condition. Jurors exposed to the wayward youth stereotype were more lenient in their judgments than those exposed to the superpredator stereotype.

In summary, our research suggests that attorneys can shape jurors' reactions to juvenile offenders tried in adult court. This is particularly interesting because, in these studies as in actual trials, jurors were specifically instructed that attorneys' opening statements and closing arguments are not evidence and should not be given undue weight in decision making. Despite this admonition, jurors' legal decisions were affected by the attorneys' statements, a finding consistent with psychological research demonstrating that individuals can be fully aware of input from the environment but not aware of its influence on their thoughts and behaviors (e.g., Fiske & Taylor, 1991). Future research should test whether the biasing influence of attorneys' statements could be diminished by modifying courtroom procedures, such as modifying jury instructions to explicitly warn about the potential for attorneys' statements to affect decision making.

## Jury Deliberation

After jurors individually hear and interpret evidence presented during a trial, they may reach individual conclusions about the guilt or innocence of the juvenile offender, but then they face a second task: deliberating with others to reach a consensus verdict. In their previously mentioned study, Haegerich and Bottoms (2004) examined whether group deliberation changed the impact of the attorney's attempt to activate mock jurors' superpredator and wayward youth stereotypes. Psychological theory and a few empirical studies on this topic indicate a number of different possibilities. Some studies have found that jury verdicts often simply reflect the collection of individual jurors' verdicts before deliberation (e.g., Sandys & Dillehay, 1995; see Devine, Clayton, Dunford, Seying, & Pryce, 2001, for a review). In fact, after their classic study of actual juries in Chicago, Kalven and Zeisel (1966) concluded that the "deliberation process might be likened to what the developer does for an exposed film: it brings out the picture, but the outcome is pre-determined" (p. 489).

Postdeliberation decisions, however, do not always mirror predeliberation decisions (e.g., Bray & Noble, 1978; Davis, Spitzer, Nagao, & Stasser, 1978). As noted by Haegerich and Bottoms (2004), jurors' predeliberation stereotypes could be maximized as a result of social pressure among jurors to conform and also because of personal acceptance of attitudes based on group consensus (Moscovici & Zavalloni, 1969). In contrast, minimization could occur as a result of jurors attempting to control their biased cognitions and avoid applying a stereotype. These self-presentational and normative goals (i.e., not wanting to appear biased in front of other jurors) are theorized to be stronger in group deliberation than during solitary decision making (e.g., Devine, 1989). Finally, deliberation might have no impact on the extent to which jurors' stereotypes influence decisions, but jurors might exhibit a general leniency bias. That is, prior research suggests an overall trend for jurors' judgments to be more lenient after deliberation than before deliberation because deliberation highlights the legal standard of reasonable doubt, and in group discussion it is easier to raise a doubt in the mind of a fellow juror than to quash all doubts (MacCoun & Kerr, 1988).

Haegerich and Bottoms (2004) found that mock jurors' postdeliberation judgments were neither maximized nor minimized compared with predeliberation judgments, nor was there consistent evidence of a general leniency bias. Jury verdicts simply reflected the average of individual juror verdicts rendered before deliberation. These results speak to a continuing debate in the field of psychology and law: whether mock jury research conducted without deliberation is valid (Diamond, 1997). Although other studies have produced different results, Haegerich and Bottoms' findings are consistent with the argument that regardless of whether studies examine juror or jury judgments, the results are generally similar (e.g., MacCoun & Kerr, 1988; Sandys & Dillehay, 1995; see Devine et al., 2001, for a review).

## JUVENILE DEFENDANT CHARACTERISTICS

Research has also begun to address a third broad category of factors that vary in cases involving juvenile defendants: characteristics of the youth him- or herself.

## Gender

Although most juvenile offenders whose cases are formally handled within the juvenile justice system are boys, girls, too, are involved in delinquent and criminal activity before reaching adulthood, as discussed in detail by Garbarino, Levene, Walsh, and Coupet (Chapter 17, this volume). Given that girls commit less crime and less violent crime than boys (Snyder, 2006) and that girls and women are stereotyped as less aggressive than boys and men generally (Deaux & Lewis, 1984), it is reasonable to expect that jurors would be more lenient in cases involving girl than boy defendants. Alternatively, Nunez, Dahl, and Hess (2005) theorized that girls who commit violent crimes might be perceived as particularly aggressive and deviant because they are violating gender norms.

It is tempting to draw from research on the impact of child gender on jurors' perceptions of child sexual abuse victims to understand whether and how gender will influence juror judgments in criminal cases. Yet this is difficult for two reasons. First, that literature is mixed. When victim/witnesses are very young, jurors do not generally differentiate between boy and girl victims (e.g., Bottoms & Goodman, 1994; Crowley, O'Callaghan, & Ball, 1994). When victim/witnesses are teenagers, jurors sometimes favor girl victims but not always (e.g., Clark & Nunez-Nightingale, 1997; Quas, Bottoms, Haegerich, & Nysse-Carris, 2002; for a review, see Bottoms et al., 2007). Second, jurors' reactions to children in such cases are complicated by their beliefs about the nature of child sexual abuse and the sexual victimization of boys versus girls, factors not at issue in many juvenile crime cases.

To date, there have been only a few direct tests of the influence of juvenile gender on jurors' perceptions. One such study is the previously mentioned Haegerich and Bottoms (2000) study, in which a teenager allegedly murdered his/her father in self-defense because of the father's sexual abuse. No key case judgments were affected by defendant gender. Mock jurors were, however, more likely to believe the girl defendant's self-defense claim of sexual abuse than the boy's, and jurors were more likely to attribute the boy's killing of the father to the boy being a bad person, whereas the girl was perceived as less likely to have killed because of such an inherent disposition. In Nunez, Dahl, Tang, and Jensen's (2007) study, there were no main effects of juvenile offender gender on mock jurors' case judgments when the juvenile was accused of murder. Yet the researchers found that age, abuse history, and victim type predicted case judgments for girls (i.e., older, nonabused girls who murdered their neighbors were more likely to be recommended to juvenile court than younger, abused girls who murdered their fathers), but these variables only predicted judgments for boy offenders in a complex, interactive manner. Thus, defendant gender may have few direct effects of consequence, but more research is needed to examine unique mediators and moderators that affect judgments separately for boy and girl offenders, especially for crimes that do not involve claims of child abuse.

## Race

Numerous studies have shown that African American adult offenders receive harsher treatment than white adult offenders (e.g., Lynch & Haney, 2000; Pfeifer & Ogloff, 1991; Ugwuegbu, 1979; for a meta-analytic review, see Sweeney & Haney, 1992). These findings are consistent with established theories of stereotyping and racism, especially aversive racism (Gaertner & Dovidio, 1986), which suggest that deep-rooted, anti-black stereotypes cause whites to devalue blacks and subsequently treat black defendants more severely than white defendants.

There is also some evidence of racial bias in the treatment of juvenile offenders. Compared with whites, black juvenile offenders are overrepresented in the juvenile justice system relative to their total population: In 2002, although only 16% of the total U.S. population younger than 18 was black, black youth made up 43% of all juvenile arrests (Snyder, 2004). Even after controlling for offense severity and prior offenses, black juveniles are more likely than white juveniles to be detained, transferred to adult court, and receive lengthy sentences (Engen, Steen, & Bridges, 2002; Wordes, Bynum, & Corley, 1994). Thus, it should come as no surprise that older black juvenile offenders, relative to younger black and nonminority juveniles, are more likely to anticipate unfair treatment by the courts (Woolard, Harvell, & Graham, 2008).

Two studies have addressed jurors' perceptions of minority juvenile offenders. Scott, Reppucci, Antonishak, and DeGennaro (2006) showed community members (1) a video clip of a convenience store armed robbery involving a masked perpetrator and (2) a separate picture of a juvenile defendant portrayed as either white or black and as either 12 or 15 years old. The younger defendant was judged less culpable and sentenced more leniently than the older defendant, but race had no significant effect. Although race simply might not affect jurors' decisions in such cases, it is more likely that a different methodology is necessary to find its effects. Specifically, the sole focus in Scott et al.'s study was the defendant's photograph. In real trials and many mock juror studies, the defendant is usually not the *sole* element of focus, but rather other witnesses and attorneys are focal points as well throughout the course of the trial (e.g., Lynch & Haney, 2000). In the context of a psychology experiment, the photo of the black youth might have raised participants' suspicion, increased their awareness of race, heightened their motivation to avoid racial prejudice, and, in turn, caused participants to overcompensate for preexisting prejudice by treating the black and white defendants similarly. In keeping with theories of aversive and modern racism, Sommers and Ellsworth (2001) argue that this will be the outcome when race is overly salient in such studies. Further, participants in Scott and colleagues' study were told to assume the defendant's guilt. Racism is most likely to manifest in cases in which the evidence is more ambiguous. Participants might not have relied on race as a peripheral cue shaping their judgments because there was no ambiguity as to the defendant's guilt.

Stevenson and Bottoms (in press) varied defendant and victim race (black or white) in an ambiguous simulation of a robbery/murder trial and examined non-black mock jurors' (college students') reactions to all resulting racial combinations. Men, but not women, voted guilty more often when the juvenile defendant was portrayed as black than as white. Men also rendered fewer judgments of guilt when the victim was black than white. This is consistent with Dovidio, Smith, Donnella, and Gaertner's (1997) finding that men (but not women) recommended the death penalty more often when an adult defendant was black versus white. It also fits with research findings that men, on average, tend to score higher on measures of explicit racism than women do (for a review, see Ekehammar, Akrami, & Araya, 2003). Perhaps women's experience with sexism leads to a subsequent greater tendency to empathize with victims of discrimination (Carter, 1990; Mills, McGrath, Sobkoviak, Stupec, & Welsch, 1995). Thus, this study provides some evidence for racial bias in the treatment of juvenile offenders, at least among men jurors. It is even possible that this study underestimates the role of race because of its undergraduate participant sample. That is, Sommers and Ellsworth (2001) argue that on a college campus, where diversity and equal rights are typically emphasized as normative values, racism is likely to be particularly salient and, arguably, more aversive to undergraduates than to older community members, who might not be as regularly exposed to such liberal values. In fact, Stevenson and Bottoms drew their sample from the University of Illinois at Chicago, one of the most diverse institutions in the nation. Racial bias might be even more pervasive in a community sample, as was the case in a study of perceptions of adult offenders conducted by Sommers and Ellsworth.

## Abuse History

The link between child maltreatment and juvenile delinquency is so well documented (e.g., Smith & Thornberry, 1995; Widom & Maxfield, 2001; Widom & Wilson, Chapter 13, this volume) that Grisso (2002) expressed concern that clinicians testifying in court as expert witnesses might incorrectly use the link between child abuse and juvenile delinquency as evidence that abused juveniles will reoffend and should, therefore, be treated more punitively than their nonabused counterparts. How does a history of child abuse influence jurors' perceptions of juvenile offenders? There have been at least three studies in which mock jurors considered cases involving a juvenile offender who was portrayed as formerly abused or not. Mock jurors generally used the juvenile defendant's abuse history as a mitigating factor, leading to less severe case decisions such as fewer transfers to adult court (Nunez et al., 2005; Nunez et al., 2007; Stalans & Henry, 1994). These effects were typically strongest, however, when the juvenile was accused of murdering the perpetrator of the abuse (an abusive parent as opposed to a nonabusive neighbor), so self-defense considerations might have contributed to the lenient decisions.

We are currently engaged in two new lines of related research. In the first (Najdowski, Bottoms, & Vargas, 2009), we asked mock jurors to read about a 16-year-old girl who had either no known abuse or a history of neglect and physical and sexual abuse at the hands of her father. Participants read four vignettes describing the juvenile as unambiguously guilty of shoplifting, selling drugs near a school, murder committed in self-defense against her abusive father, and aggravated assault/murder of a peer. In the self-defense murder case, but not in the other three cases, the abused juvenile was considered less responsible for the crime, less "bad," and more amenable to rehabilitation than the nonabused juvenile. The only significant effect of abuse in any of the other three cases was one effect in aggravated assault/murder case that involved no self-defense. In that case, mock jurors perceived the abused juvenile as less amenable to rehabilitation than the nonabused juvenile, a finding consistent with Grisso's (2002) fear that abuse history might be interpreted as a predictor for future crime and, in turn, used against juveniles in sentencing.

Thus, our study and those reviewed previously suggest that effects of abuse history appear tied to its use as a reason for self-defense rather than jurors harboring a general sympathy for juveniles who just happen to have been abused as children. Our second line of work, however, illustrates at least one crime situation in which jurors are influenced by an adult defendant's history of child maltreatment. Specifically, we (Stevenson, 2009; Stevenson et al., 2008) coded in detail mock jurors' comments during deliberations in the sentencing phase of a capital murder trial. The adult defendant was convicted of a robbery/murder and portrayed as having been physically abused throughout his childhood. Results suggest that mock jurors are less likely to use the evidence of child abuse as a mitigating factor than defense attorneys might hope. In fact, jurors are more likely to argue against other jurors' attempts to discuss abuse in a mitigating manner, and they sometimes even use child abuse as an aggravator, arguing that the defendant is "damaged goods" and not capable of rehabilitation and, thus, more fit for the death penalty than life in prison. This type of "backfire" effect has also been observed in research examining jurors' use of supposedly mitigating evidence about a defendant's alcoholism and mental illness (Barnett, Brodsky, & Price, 2007; Brodsky, Adams, & Tupling, 2007). Of course, in this study, the defendant was an adult rather than a juvenile, but we believe the

results are relevant in trying to understand the impact of abuse information on jurors' perceptions of juvenile offenders. Future research should test
other potential moderators of the mitigating effect of child abuse on jurors'
case judgments of juvenile offenders. For example, perhaps strong endorsement of the superpredator stereotype prevents jurors from using child abuse
as a mitigating factor, while endorsement of the wayward youth stereotype
promotes it.

## Intellectual Disability

An unfortunate reality is that intellectually disabled (i.e., mentally retarded)
juveniles are disproportionately represented in delinquent populations compared with nondelinquent populations (Kazdin, 2000). The high rate of
delinquency among disabled juveniles may be a consequence of diminished
decision-making and psychosocial capacities, deficits that characterize most
juveniles (see Reppucci et al., Chapter 15, this volume; Steinberg & Scott,
2003) and are likely exacerbated by intellectual disability. In fact, acknowledging that impairments in these domains diminish legal culpability, the
U.S. Supreme Court ruled that capital punishment is unconstitutional for all
juveniles and intellectually disabled adults (*Atkins v. Virginia*, 2002; *Roper
v. Simmons*, 2005). Yet diminished culpability is not considered by courts
in other situations. For example, many disabled juveniles continue to be
waived to adult criminal court from juvenile court. In fact, only seven states
explicitly consider intellectual disability when evaluating a waiver decision
(Griffin, Torbet, & Szymanski, 1998). Therefore, it is important to determine whether jurors' perceptions of juveniles' intellectual disability influence their judgments.

In the first research to examine jurors' perceptions of intellectually disabled children in a courtroom context, Bottoms, Nysse-Carris, Harris, and
Tyda (2003) found that mock jurors rendered more favorable judgments
if a child sexual abuse victim was described as "mildly mentally retarded"
compared with "of average intelligence." Gibbons, Gibbons, and Kassin's
(1981) research revealed that mock jurors reported favorable attitudes
toward disabled adult defendants (e.g., they agreed that disabled adults
should be handled in special courts or facilities). Also, jurors used disability
as a mitigating factor for more severe crimes, but they used it as an aggravating factor for less severe crimes. Jurors may find it less plausible that a
disabled adult could commit more severe crimes, which involve cognitive
sophistication.

To examine whether intellectual disability would affect perceptions of
juvenile offenders, we varied the disability status of the juvenile defendant in
the study of abuse history described previously (Najdowski, Bottoms, & Vargas, 2009). Specifically, we portrayed the juvenile as either "developmentally
delayed, functioning in the mild range of mental retardation" or "of average

intelligence." Overall, participants perceived an unambiguously guilty juvenile as less "bad" and less responsible when she was portrayed as disabled rather than nondisabled. In contrast, follow-up research in which a juvenile defendant's guilt or innocence was relatively ambiguous revealed that jurors were less likely to convict a disabled juvenile only when she was accused of a fairly nonserious offense (i.e., a drug offense). This was not the case when she was accused of more serious offenses (i.e., assault, murder) (Najdowski, Bottoms, & Vargas, 2009; Najdowski, Bottoms, Vargas, & Cummens, 2009). These results contrast with Gibbons and colleagues' (1981) findings regarding perceptions of disabled adult offenders, and suggest that jurors may not distinguish between disabled and nondisabled juveniles when deciding how likely it is that they committed serious crimes such as murder.

## Confessions

As discussed in detail by Redlich and Kassin (Chapter 14, this volume; see also Woolard et al., 2008), given their diminished capacities, juvenile crime suspects are likely to be at substantial risk for confessing, falsely or not, especially under coercive interview circumstances. For instance, 67% of a sample of boy offenders stated that they were more likely than not to falsely confess under certain hypothetical circumstances (Goldstein, Condie, Kalbeitzer, Osman, & Geier, 2003; see also Drizin & Leo, 2004; Redlich & Kassin, Chapter 14, this volume). Jurors are strongly biased to perceive adult confessions as true (Kassin & Gudjonsson, 2004). Redlich, Ghetti, and Quas (2008) have provided preliminary evidence that this effect extends to cases involving juvenile defendants. In their mock trial study, jurors were twice as likely to believe that a boy was involved in a crime when he confessed and recanted compared with when he never admitted involvement.

In contrast to voluntary confessions, coerced false confessions occur when suspects are induced through police interrogation tactics to confess to a crime they did not commit (Redlich & Kassin, Chapter 14, this volume). Mock jurors convict adults who confess under coercion just as often as those who confess voluntarily (for review, see Kassin & Gudjonsson, 2004). Redlich, Quas, and Ghetti (2008) found results consistent with this in a study examining jurors' perceptions of a juvenile accused of murdering a toddler. Even though the juvenile denied allegations more than 40 times before eventually admitting guilt, mock jurors' guilt verdicts were not influenced by perceptions of the voluntariness (of lack thereof) of her confession. They were, however, less likely to vote guilty if they thought the juvenile did not understand the interrogation or that the police were unfair.

We extended this body of research by examining mock jurors' reactions to a juvenile who was portrayed confessing voluntarily, under coercion, or not at all in a second study in which we again portrayed a juvenile defendant as either intellectually disabled or not (Najdowski, Bottoms, & Vargas,

2009). Intellectually disabled juveniles may be especially prone to false confessions because of comprehension and reasoning impairments (e.g., Goldstein, Kalbeitzer, Zelle, & Romaine, 2006) and vulnerability to even subtle psychological influence, persuasion, deception, and coercion (Gudjonsson & Henry, 2003). In our study, the 16-year-old girl either (1) maintained her innocence during police questioning (no confession), (2) immediately confessed but later recanted (voluntary confession), or (3) confessed under coercion but later recanted (coerced confession). When the juvenile was portrayed as intellectually disabled, mock jurors perceived the juvenile who confessed voluntarily as significantly more guilty and responsible than a juvenile who confessed under coercion or never confessed, with jurors reacting to the latter two conditions similarly. However, jurors still perceived the nondisabled juvenile as significantly more guilty and responsible if she had confessed under coercion versus never confessing. These results suggest that jurors may not recognize the increased vulnerability of juveniles unless they are also intellectually disabled, a condition that highlights their suggestibility. However, preliminary results of new research suggest that, under more ecologically valid circumstances including videotaped testimony of an actual juvenile offender and actual jury instructions, jurors are sensitive to the social–psychological circumstances of juveniles' confessions and discount both disabled and nondisabled juveniles' coerced confessions (Najdowski, Bottoms, Vargas, & Cummens, 2009). Future research should examine what conditions are necessary and sufficient to make suggestibility salient to jurors when evaluating juvenile defendants' confessions.

## CONCLUSION

We have summarized a growing body of research, much of it from our own laboratory, addressing many factors that influence jurors' perceptions of juvenile offenders. Juror, juvenile defendant, and trial factors can all influence trial outcomes in ways that may or may not lead to fair trials. Identifying such factors is necessary before pursuing interventions aimed at increasing fairness in trials, such as voir dire strategies, jury instruction reform, and expert witness testimony. Clearly, much more research is needed. For example, we have shown that crime type and case-related factors (e.g., abuse history, intellectual disability, and presence of confession evidence) sometimes have an important influence on jurors' perceptions. Consider sex offenses: In many states, laws require public registration of adult sex offenders (i.e., public access—often via the Internet—to information about the offender, such as name, date of birth, address, place of employment, photograph). These laws are being applied to juveniles. We have investigated support for these laws (Salerno, et al., in press). Although support is high for applying these laws to juveniles in the abstract, support decreases when people are asked about specific types of nonserious offenses that juveniles have been charged with in many states (e.g., child pornography for looking at naked pictures of an underage girlfriend, or "sexting"; Stockinger, 2009).

Future research should also explore the perceptions of other key legal players such as juvenile court intake workers, probation officers, and judges. For example, whereas jurors sometimes use child abuse as a mitigating factor, juvenile court officials actually perceive maltreated juvenile offenders, compared to nonmaltreated juvenile offenders, as less likely to be rehabilitated and as more deserving of incarceration or transfer to adult court (Grisso, Tomkins, & Casey, 1988; Salekin, Yff, Neumann, Leistico, & Zalot, 2002), perhaps because child abuse is often confounded with a host of other factors such as an unsupportive and chaotic family environment, behavioral and mental health problems, and school problems, all of which predict punitive juvenile dispositions (Clarke & Koch, 1980; Fenwick, 1982; Grisso et al., 1988; Horowitz & Wasserman, 1980; for a review, see Stevenson, in press). Even so, although juvenile probation officials are more likely to recommend secure residential placement and expect difficulty in supervision for an abused than a nonabused juvenile, they are also more likely to recommend psychological services and "go the extra mile" in their supervision of abused juveniles (Vidal & Skeem, 2007).

In conclusion, it is increasingly important to understand factors that influence perceptions of juveniles, in light of their vulnerability and of current societal trends of increasing the severity of legal processes and outcomes for young offenders. Continued efforts to conduct scientifically sound research with ecologically valid techniques will ensure that future research on these issues will yield generalizable results of importance to law and policy.

## ACKNOWLEDGMENTS

We thank Kathleen Acuesta, Matt Badanek, Danielle Brandstetter, Erika Chang, Jessica Dilley, Kara Doering, Michaela Drury, Laura Dutzi, Sandy Estrada, Koren Ganas, Amber Glow, Saba Khan, Michael Keaveny, Lauren Kasprzyk, Anthony Marino, Jodie Pasternak, Michelle Prestige, Kelly Ricketts, Joanna Slusarczyk, Lisa Tockman, Orlando Torres, Maria Vargas, Sonja Veile, Lachelle White, and Lauren Whitehair for valuable research assistance, and Alison Perona for legal consultation on several of the studies described in this chapter.

## REFERENCES

Archer, R. L., Foushee, H. C., Davis, M. H., & Aderman, D. (1979). Emotional empathy in a courtroom simulation: A person-situation interaction. *Journal of Applied Social Psychology, 9,* 275–291.

Atkins v. Virginia, 536 U.S. 304 (2002).

Barnett, M. E., Brodsky, S. L., & Price, J. R. (2007). Differential impact of miti-gating evidence in capital case sentencing. *Journal of Forensic Psychology Practice, 7,* 39–45.

Bottoms, B. L. (1993). Individual differences in perceptions of child sexual assault victims. In G. S. Goodman & B. L. Bottoms (Eds.), *Child victims, child witnesses: Understanding and improving testimony* (pp. 229–261). New York: Guilford Press.

Bottoms, B. L., Golding, J. M., Stevenson, M. C., Wiley, T. R. A., & Wozniak, J. (2007). A review of factors affecting jurors' decisions in child sexual abuse cases. In J. D. Read, D. Ross, M. Toglia, & R. C. L. Lindsay (Eds.), *The psychology of eyewitness memory* (pp. 509–545). Hillsdale, NJ: Erlbaum.

Bottoms, B. L., & Goodman, G. S. (1994). Perceptions of children's credibility in sexual assault cases. *Journal of Applied Social Psychology, 24,* 702–732.

Bottoms, B. L., Nysse-Carris, K. L., Harris, T., & Tyda, K. (2003). Jurors' per-ceptions of adolescent sexual assault victims who have intellectual disabili-ties. *Law and Human Behavior, 27,* 205–227.

Bray, R. M., & Noble, A. M. (1978). Authoritarianism and decisions of mock juries: Evidence of jury bias and group polarization. *Journal of Personality and Social Psychology, 36,* 1424–1430.

Brodsky, S. L., Adams, D., & Tupling, J. E. (2007, August). The backfire effect of substance abuse: When a mitigating factor becomes aggravating. In S. L. Brodsky (Chair), *Mitigation evidence and testimony in capital trial sen-tencing.* Symposium conducted at the 115th Annual Convention of the American Psychological Association, San Francisco, CA.

Carter, R. T. (1990). The relationship between racism and racial identity among White Americans: An exploratory investigation. *Journal of Counseling and Development, 69,* 46–50.

Clark, H. L., & Nightingale, N. N. (1997). When jurors consider recovered memory cases: Effects of victim and juror gender. *Journal of Offender Rehabilitation, 25,* 87–104.

Clarke, S. H., & Koch, G. G. (1980). Juvenile court: Therapy or crime control, and do lawyers make a difference? *Law and Society Review, 14,* 263–308.

Crosby, C. A., Britner, P. A., Jodl, K. M., & Portwood, S. G. (1995). The juve-nile death penalty and the eighth amendment. *Law and Human Behavior, 19,* 245–261.

Crowley, M. J., O'Callaghan, M., & Ball, P. J. (1994). The juridical impact of psychological expert testimony in a simulated child sexual abuse trial. *Law and Human Behavior, 18,* 89–105.

Davis, M. H. (1994). *Empathy.* Madison, WI: Brown & Benchmark.

Davis, J. H., Spitzer, C. E., Nagao, D. H., & Stasser, G. (1978). Bias in social decisions by individuals and groups: An example from mock juries. In H. Brandstatter, J. H. Davis, & H. Schuler (Eds.), *Dynamics of group deci-sions* (pp. 33–52). Beverly Hills, CA: Sage.

Deaux, K., & Lewis, L. (1984). Structure of gender stereotypes: Interrelation-ships among components and gender label. *Journal of Personality and Social Psychology, 46,* 991–1004.

Devine, D. J., Clayton, L. D., Dunford, B. B., Seying, R., & Pryce, J. (2001). Jury decision making: 45 years of empirical research on deliberating groups. *Psychology, Public Policy, and Law, 7,* 622–727.

Devine, P. G. (1989). Stereotypes and prejudice: Their automatic and controlled components. *Journal of Personality and Social Psychology, 56,* 5–18.

Diamond, S. S. (1997). Illuminations and shadows from jury simulations. *Law and Human Behavior, 21,* 561–571.

Dovidio, J. F., Smith, J. K., Donnella, A. G., & Gaertner, S. L. (1997). Racial attitudes and the death penalty. *Journal of Applied Social Psychology, 27,* 1468–1487.

Drizin, S. A., & Leo, R. A. (2004). The problem of false confessions in the post-DNA world. *North Carolina Law Review, 82,* 891–1007.

Ekehammar, B., Akrami, N., & Araya, T. (2003). Gender differences in implicit prejudice. *Personality and Individual Differences, 34,* 1509–1523.

Engen, R. L., Steen, S., & Bridges, G. S. (2002). Racial disparities in the punishment of youth: A theoretical and empirical assessment of the literature. *Social Problems, 49,* 194–220.

Fenwick, C. R. (1982). Juvenile court intake decision making: The importance of family affiliation. *Journal of Criminal Justice, 10,* 443–453.

Fiske, S. T., & Taylor, S. E. (1991). *Social cognition* (2nd ed.). New York: McGraw-Hill.

Gaertner, S. L., & Dovidio, J. F. (1986). The aversive form of racism. In J. F. Dovidio & S. L. Gaertner (Eds.), *Prejudice, discrimination, and racism* (pp. 61–90). Orlando, FL: Academic Press.

Gibbons, F. X., Gibbons, B. N., & Kassin, S. M. (1981). Reactions to the criminal behavior of intellectually disabled and nondisabled offenders. *American Journal of Mental Deficiency, 86,* 235–242.

Goldstein, N. E. S., Condie, L. O., Kalbeitzer, R., Osman, D., & Geier, J. L. (2003). Juvenile offenders' *Miranda* rights comprehension and self-reported likelihood of offering false confession. *Assessment, 10,* 359–369.

Goldstein, N. E. S., Kalbeitzer, R., Zelle, H., & Romaine, C. R. (2006, March). *The Totality of Circumstances Test and juveniles' Miranda rights comprehension: Going beyond the factors of age and IQ.* Paper presented at the annual meeting of the American Psychology-Law Society, St. Petersburg, FL.

Griffin, P., Torbet, P., & Szymanski, L. (1998). *Trying juveniles as adults in criminal court: An analysis of state transfer provisions.* Washington, DC: U.S. Department of Justice.

Grisso, T. (2002). Using what we know about child maltreatment and delinquency. *Children's Services: Social Policy, Research, and Practice, 5,* 299–305.

Grisso, T., Tomkins, A., & Casey, P. (1988). Psychosocial concepts in juvenile law. *Law and Human Behavior, 12,* 403–437.

Gudjonsson, G. H., & Henry, L. A. (2003). Child and adult witnesses with learning disabilities: The importance of suggestibility. *Legal and Criminological Psychology, 8,* 241–252.

Haegerich, T. M., & Bottoms, B. L. (2000). Empathy and jurors' decisions in patricide trials involving child sexual assault allegations. *Law and Human Behavior, 24,* 421–448.

Haegerich, T. M., & Bottoms, B. L. (2004, March). *Effect of jurors' stereotypes of juvenile offenders on pre- and post-deliberation case judgments.* Paper presented at the biennial meeting of the American Psychology-Law Society, Scottsdale, AZ.

Hamlin, S. (1985). *What makes juries listen: A communications expert looks at the trial.* Englewood Cliffs, NJ: Prentice Hall.

Horwitz, A., & Wasserman, M. (1980). Formal rationality, substantive justice, and discrimination: A study of a juvenile court. *Law and Human Behavior, 4,* 103–115.

Kalven, H., & Zeisel, H. (1966). *The American jury.* Boston: Little, Brown.

Kassin, S. M., & Gudjonsson, G. H. (2004). The psychology of confessions: A review of the literature and issues. *Psychological Science in the Public Interest, 5,* 33–67.

Kazdin, A. E. (2000). Adolescent development, mental disorders, and decision making of delinquent youths. In T. Grisso & R. G. Schwartz (Eds.), *Youth on trial: A developmental perspective on juvenile justice* (pp. 33–65). Chicago: University of Chicago Press.

King, N. J. (1999). The American criminal jury. *Law and Contemporary Problems, 62,* 41–67.

Levesque, R. J. R. (1996). Is there still a place for violent youth in juvenile justice? *Aggression and Violent Behavior, 1,* 69–79.

Lynch, M., & Haney, C. (2000). Discrimination and instructional comprehension: Guided discretion, racial bias, and the death penalty. *Law and Human Behavior, 24,* 337–358.

MacCoun, R. J., & Kerr, N. L. (1988). Asymmetric influence in mock jury deliberation: Jurors' bias for leniency. *Journal of Personality and Social Psychology, 54,* 21–33.

Mills, J. K., McGrath, D., Sobkoviak, P., Stupec, S., & Welsch, S. (1995). Differences in expressed racial prejudice and acceptance of others. *Journal of Psychology, 129,* 357–359.

Moon, M. M., Sundt, J. L., Cullen, F. T., & Wright, J. P. (2000). Is child saving dead? Public support for juvenile rehabilitation. *Crime and Delinquency, 46,* 38–60.

Moscovici, S., & Zavalloni, M. (1969). The group as a polarizer of attitudes. *Journal of Personality and Social Psychology, 12,* 125–135.

Najdowski, C. J., Bottoms, B. L., & Vargas, M. C. (2009). Jurors' perceptions of juvenile defendants: The influence of intellectual disability, abuse history, and confession evidence. *Behavioral Sciences and the Law, 27.* Advance online publication. Retrieved April 24, 2009, doi: 10.1002/bsl.873.

Najdowski, C. J., Bottoms, B. L., Vargas, M. C., & Cummens, M. L. (2009, March). *Understanding jurors' perceptions of juvenile defendants: Effects of intellectual disability and confession evidence.* Presentation at the annual meeting of the American Psychology–Law Society, San Antonio, TX.

Nagin, D. S., Piquero, A. R., Scott, E. S., & Steinberg, L. (2006). Public preferences for rehabilitation versus incarceration of juvenile offenders: Evidence from a contingent valuation survey. *Criminology and Public Policy, 5,* 627–652.

Nunez, N., Dahl, M. J., & Hess, C. (2005, March). *Juror perceptions of juveniles who commit murder: Are female defendants at a disadvantage?* Paper presented at the annual meeting of the American Psychology-Law Society, La Jolla, CA.

Nunez, N., Dahl, M. J., Tang, C. M., & Jensen, B. L. (2007). Trial venue decisions in juvenile cases: Mitigating and extralegal factors matter. *Legal and Criminological Psychology, 12,* 21–39.

Pfeifer, J. E., & Ogloff, J. R. P. (1991). Ambiguity and guilt determinations: A modern racism perspective. *Journal of Applied Social Psychology, 21,* 1713–1725.

Quas, J. A., Bottoms, B. L., Haegerich, T. M., & Nysse-Carris, K. L. (2002). Effects of victim, defendant and juror gender on decisions in child sexual assault cases. *Journal of Applied Social Psychology, 32,* 1993–2021.

Redlich, A. D., Ghetti, S., & Quas, J. A. (2008). Perceptions of children during a police interview: A comparison of alleged victims and suspects. *Journal of Applied Social Psychology, 38,* 705–735.

Redlich, A. D., Quas, J. A., & Ghetti, S. (2008). Perceptions of children during a police interrogation: Guilt, confessions, and interview fairness. *Psychology, Crime, and Law, 14,* 201–223.

Roper v. Simmons, 543 U.S. 551 (2005).

Salekin, R. T., Yff, R. M. A., Neumann, C. S., Leistico, A. R., & Zalot, A. A. (2002). Juvenile transfer to adult courts: A look at the prototypes for dangerousness, sophistication-maturity, and amenability to treatment through a legal lens. *Psychology, Public Policy, and Law, 8,* 373–410.

Salerno, J. M., Stevenson, M. C., Wiley, T. R. A., Najdowski, C. J., Bottoms, B. L., & Schmillen, R. A. (in press). Public attitudes toward applying sex offender registration laws to juvenile offenders. In J. M. Lampinen & K. Sexton-Radek (Eds.), *Protecting children from violence: Evidence based interventions.* New York: Psychology Press.

Sandys, M., & Dillehay, R. C. (1995). First-ballot votes, predeliberation dispositions, and final verdicts in jury trials. *Law and Human Behavior, 19,* 175–195.

Scott, E. S., Reppucci, N. D., Antonishak, J., & DeGennaro, J. T. (2006). Public attitudes about the culpability and punishment of young offenders. *Behavioral Sciences and the Law, 24,* 815–832.

Smith, C., & Thornberry, T. P. (1995). The relationship between childhood maltreatment and adolescent involvement in delinquency. *Criminology, 33,* 451–481.

Snyder, H. N. (2004, September). Juvenile arrests 2002. In *Juvenile Justice Bulletin.* Washington, DC: Office of Juvenile Justice and Delinquency Prevention, U.S. Department of Justice.

Snyder, H. N. (2006, December). Juvenile arrests 2004. In *Juvenile Justice Bulletin.* Washington, DC: Office of Juvenile Justice and Delinquency Prevention, U.S. Department of Justice.

Sommers, S. R., & Ellsworth, P. C. (2001). White juror bias: An investigation of prejudice against Black defendants in the American courtroom. *Psychology, Public Policy and Law, 7,* 201–229.

Stalans, L. J., & Henry, G. T. (1994). Societal views of justice for adolescents accused of murder: Inconsistency between community sentiment and automatic legislative transfers. *Law and Human Behavior, 18,* 675–696.

Steinberg, L., & Scott, E. S. (2003). Less guilty by reason of adolescence: Developmental immaturity, diminished responsibility, and the juvenile death penalty. *American Psychologist, 58,* 1009–1018.

Stevenson, M. C. (in press). Perceptions of juvenile offenders who were abused as children. *Journal of Aggression, Maltreatment & Trauma.*

Stevenson, M. C. (2009, March). *Understanding jurors' discussions of a defendant's history of child abuse and alcohol abuse in capital sentencing trials.* Poster session presented at the annual meeting of the American Psychology–Law Society, San Antonio, TX.

Stevenson, M. C., & Bottoms, B. L. (in press). Does race shape perceptions of juvenile offenders in adult court? *Journal of Applied Social Psychology.*

Stevenson, M. C., Bottoms, B. L., Diamond, S. S., Najdowski, C. J., Stec, I., & Pimental, P. (2008, March). *Jurors' discussions of a defendants' childhood maltreatment during capital sentencing deliberations.* Paper presented at the annual meeting of the American Psychology-Law Society, Jacksonville, FL.

Sulzer, J. L., & Burglass, R. K. (1968). Responsibility attribution, empathy, and punitiveness. *Journal of Personality, 36,* 272–282.

Sundt, J. L., Cullen, F. T., Applegate, B. K., & Turner, M. G. (1998). The tenacity of the rehabilitative ideal revisited: Have attitudes toward offender treatment changed? *Criminal Justice and Behavior, 25,* 426–442.

Sweeney, L. T., & Haney, C. (1992). The influence of race on sentencing: A meta-analytic review of experimental studies. *Behavioral Sciences and the Law, 10,* 179–195.

Ugwuegbu, D. C. (1979). Racial and evidential factors in juror attribution of legal responsibility. *Journal of Experimental Social Psychology, 15,* 133–146.

Vidal, S., & Skeem, J. L. (2007). Effect of psychopathy, abuse, and ethnicity on juvenile probation officers' decision-making and supervision strategies. *Law and Human Behavior, 31,* 479–498.

Weiten, W., & Diamond, S. S. (1979). A critical review of the jury simulation paradigm: The case of defendant characteristics. *Law and Human Behavior, 3,* 71–93.

Widom, C. S., & Maxfield, M. G. (2001, February). An update on the "cycle of violence." In *Research in brief.* Washington, DC: National Institute of Justice, Office of Justice Programs, U.S. Department of Justice.

Woolard, J. L., Harvell, S., & Graham, S. (2008). Anticipatory injustice among adolescents: Age and racial/ethnic differences in perceived unfairness of the justice system. *Behavioral Sciences and the Law, 26,* 207–226.

Wordes, M., Bynum, T. S., & Corley, C. J. (1994). Locking up youth: The impact of race on detention decisions. *Journal of Research in Crime and Delinquency, 31,* 149–165.

Chapter 19

# An International Perspective on Juvenile Justice Issues

JOHN PETRILA

The U.S. Supreme Court ruled in *Roper v. Simmons* (2005) that the U.S. Constitution prohibited the execution of individuals who were younger than 18 years at the time of their offense. The Court's 5–4 ruling was striking in part because of the strong debate within the Court over the use of international law and standards in its jurisprudence. Justice Kennedy, writing for the majority, devoted three pages to reviewing the status of the death penalty for juveniles in international law and practice (*Roper v. Simmons*, 2005, pp. 1198–1200). Noting that the United States was the only country that officially sanctioned the execution of juveniles, Justice Kennedy observed: "It does not lessen our fidelity to the Constitution or our pride in its origins to acknowledge that the express affirmation of certain fundamental rights by other nations and peoples simply underscores the centrality of those same rights within our own heritage of freedom" (p. 1200). Justice Scalia, writing for the dissent, found the majority's reliance on the laws of other nations indefensible for a number of reasons, concluding: "More fundamentally, however, the basic premise of the Court's argument—that American law should conform to the laws of the rest of the world—ought to be rejected out of hand" (*Roper v. Simmons*, 2005, p. 1226). Whether the Supreme Court should utilize international sources of law in its opinions is a subject explored in detail elsewhere (Gerety, 2005; Sinnott, 2006). However, it is clear that international practice should be relevant to policymakers, practitioners, and scholars in the United States, in large part because, as with use of the death penalty, trends in many countries create an interesting counterpoint to the recent evolution of juvenile law in the United States.

This chapter, first, provides an overview of international standards for juvenile justice, primarily drawn from the work of the United Nations. Second, it discusses a number of interesting developments in juvenile law in countries from Australasia, Asia, Africa, Europe, and South America. This section includes a discussion of restorative justice, the animating philosophy for changes in juvenile standards in a number of countries and a philosophy with emerging impact in the United States. The chapter concludes with a discussion of the implementation and impact of juvenile justice reform internationally.

## INTERNATIONAL STANDARDS

The United Nations has created four principal sets of child-specific guidelines for juvenile justice. These include the United Nations Standard Minimum Rules for the Administration of Juvenile Justice (also known as the Beijing Rules; Office of the High Commissioner for Human Rights, 1985); the United Nations Standard Minimum Rules for Non-Custodial Measures (also known as the Tokyo Rules; Office of the High Commissioner for Human Rights, 1990c); the United Nations Rules for the Protection of Juveniles Deprived of Their Liberty (Office of the High Commissioner for Human Rights, 1990b); and the United Nations Guidelines for the Prevention of Juvenile Delinquency (also known as the Riyadh Guidelines; Office of the High Commissioner for Human Rights, 1990a).

The guidelines are derived from basic principles contained in the "hard" law of the International Covenant on Civil and Political Rights (Office of the High Commisssioner for Human Rights, 1966), which prohibits the death penalty for individuals younger than 18 when offending and which states: "In the case of juvenile[s] ... the [court] procedure shall be such as will take account of their age and the desirability of promoting their rehabilitation" (Article 14.4). Another relevant convention, with greater force on ratifying states than the Guidelines, is the United Nations Convention on the Rights of the Child (Office of the High Commissioner for Human Rights, 1989). The Convention on the Rights of the Child has been ratified by all countries except Somalia and the United States (United Nations Children's Fund [UNICEF], 1998).

Although a detailed discussion of each of these conventions, treaties, and guidelines is not possible, they articulate a number of important core principles that, in the aggregate, create the foundation for a nonpunitive juvenile justice system (for one of a number of detailed discussions, see Van Bueren, 1999). These principles include:

- Ensuring that child criminal justice issues are prioritized as part of the country's "national development process."
- Ensuring a focus on the family.
- Ensuring that the child's best interests are the foundation of legal proceedings involving children.
- Ensuring a focus on prevention and protection of children who are endangered or at "social risk."
- Ensuring that education is the foundation of interventions following involvement of a child with the legal system.
- Ensuring that diversion from the justice system and alternatives to judicial processes such as mediation are integral to the justice system for children.
- Ensuring that arrest, detention, and imprisonment are used minimally and that children are not detained with adults.
- Ensuring that legal processes for children are carried out as expeditiously as possible.

One U.S. commentator has described the broad adoption of these conventions and treaties by the vast majority of countries as "considerably revolutionary" and a challenge to "rethink fundamentally ingrained ideologies of childhood, families, rights, communities, and international law" (Levesque, 1996, pp. 1566, 1569). However, in an interesting historical juxtaposition, the conventions and treaties emerged during a period of rising juvenile crime. As a result, the principles embodied in these documents stand in stark contrast to developments in U.S. federal and state juvenile justice law since the early 1990s. Juvenile justice in the United States was governed since its inception by a commitment to the rehabilitation of the child (see Reppucci, Michel, & Kostelnik, Chapter 15, this volume). However, support for that philosophy began eroding in the mid-1980s, and by the 100th anniversary of the establishment of the first juvenile court, commentators observed "as the juvenile court approaches its 100th birthday ... its future is less secure than at any point in its history" (Geraghty & Drizin, 1997, pp. 2–3). Internationally, two trends appear to have emerged in the interim: Some countries, primarily western European nations, responded to perceived increases in juvenile offending by taking a more legalistic tack (similar to that taken in the United States), whereas other countries, particularly, although not exclusively, those attempting to create juvenile systems (e.g., China, eastern European countries), have used the principles enunciated by the United Nations as their foundation.

# RECENT INTERNATIONAL DEVELOPMENTS
# IN JUVENILE JUSTICE

The United States was not the only country to experience dramatic increases in juvenile crime in the 1980s and early 1990s, with rates falling off in many countries subsequently. Although some cautioned that specific examples of violent offenses committed by juveniles did not necessarily mean that overall rates of offending were increasing (UNICEF, 1998), it seems clear that the incidence of juvenile crime increased significantly in many countries, including Germany (Albrecht, 2004), the Netherlands (in violent crime; Junger-Tas, 2004), Canada (Reddington & Urban, 2006), some countries in eastern Europe following the fall of the Soviet Empire (UNICEF, 1998), and England, Wales, Sweden, Italy, Austria, France, Denmark, Switzerland, and Poland (Pfeiffer, 1998).

However, even as juvenile crime rates began to recede, the public perception generally continued to hold that it was increasing. For example, a comprehensive review of public opinion polls in Western countries revealed that, in nation after nation, the public overestimated, often significantly, the volume of crime committed by juveniles, despite the fact that juvenile crime, as measured by police reports and victimization surveys, was decreasing in the late 1990s (Roberts, 2004). The same was true in Australia, where youth crime was consistently perceived as increasing in volume and seriousness, although, in fact, such crime had been comparatively stable through the 1990s (Levy, 1999).

These developments did not occur in a political or demographic vacuum. Public fears regarding juvenile crime, changing demographics—particularly in Europe—resulting from low native birthrate and immigration from Africa and Asia and from eastern and central Europe to western Europe, and high-profile juvenile offenses covered extensively in the media combined to create a political environment in which "getting tough" on juvenile crime seemed to be the politically sensible thing to do (Roberts, 2004). As a result, in general, western European countries joined the United States in imposing harsher penalties for juvenile offending; however, in contrast to the United States, western European countries, with their richer historical commitment to welfare, also continued to focus on community-based alternatives, early identification of at-risk youth, and community reentry programs (Angell, 2004).

Although it is possible to generalize to some degree about the recent evolution of juvenile justice, particularly in Western countries, juvenile justice systems are embedded in larger cultural norms that may be specific to a particular country. For example, these larger cultural norms include basic decisions regarding the age at which children should be held criminally responsible. There is no uniformity among countries even on such a threshold issue, with the age of responsibility ranging from 7 to 18 (see also Reddington, 2002).

Given these factors, it is worth considering briefly the evolution of juvenile justice standards in a number of different countries to capture in a more nuanced way similarities and differences in national approach. As this brief and by no means comprehensive discussion suggests, several themes emerge. First, many developing countries have committed themselves, at least in theory, to the principles articulated by the United Nations, and in doing so have established the foundation for a less punitive approach to juvenile justice than that adopted by the United States. Second, restorative justice has been a philosophical benchmark in a number of countries that have chosen to favor community- and family-based interventions and prevention over the punitive sanctions adopted by many Western democracies in the 1990s. Third, there are many obstacles, including civil war, poverty, and broad exploitation and abuse of children, to implementing reform in countries that have committed to reform in theory.

## Australasia

In 1989, New Zealand enacted the Children, Young Persons, and Their Families Act, which marked a significant departure from the manner in which Western jurisdictions traditionally had handled juvenile justice issues. Prior to this legislation, there were two primary approaches: one a social welfare approach (used in much of continental Europe) and the other a more legalistic approach used in most English-speaking countries. As Maxwell and Morris (2006) have written, the restorative justice approach of the new legislation "recognizes and seeks the participation of all involved in the offending and focuses on repairing harm, reintegrating offenders, and restoring the balance within the community affected by the offence" (p. 243). Proponents of restorative justice posited it as a clear alternative to the retributive and rehabilitative philosophies that had dominated approaches to adult and juvenile justice in most Western countries (Zehr, 1990). Rather, restorative justice proponents "aim to create a way of 'doing' justice which would place victims at its centre, and which would empower stakeholders" (Zernova, 2007, p. 491).

In practice, the New Zealand juvenile justice system adopted a number of strategies to serve these goals, particularly the emphasis on repairing the harm to the community rather than focusing specifically either on the punishment or rehabilitation of the offender. These strategies included (Maxwell & Morris, 2006) taking into account the rights and needs of indigenous people, making families central to all decision making, giving offenders voice regarding disposition, giving victims a role in negotiations over penalties, and achieving decisions through group consensus. The use of judicial process was deemphasized in favor of the family group conference, a venue that permitted victims, offenders, family, and law enforcement to meet to decide on disposition.

Although restorative justice has been sharply criticized as creating unrealistic aspirations (Zernova, 2007) and its impact on practice in New Zealand has fallen short of its stated goals (Maxwell & Morris, 2006), it continues to lie at the heart of the New Zealand juvenile justice system. As the discussion later in this chapter suggests, it has also had influence in a number of other national and local jurisdictions since New Zealand first embraced it legislatively two decades ago.

In Australia, the first juvenile court was established in 1890 (Levy, 1999). Like the United States, Australia adopted a more punitive approach through the 1990s, as perceptions that juvenile crime was rising sharply came to dominate political discourse. At the same time, and despite a turn to more punitive practices, Australia simultaneously adopted strategies used in New Zealand, particularly "conferencing," or face-to-face meetings between offender and victim and their supporters. According to one commentator, the use of community conferencing before a case proceeded to formal adjudication resulted in the diversion from the justice system of many young offenders charged with minor offenses (Levy, 1999), although others have questioned its impact on diversion (Sarre, 2004). However, the approach continues to be used in a number of Australian jurisdictions.

## Africa

In 1990 the Organization of African Unity adopted the African Charter on the Rights and Welfare of the Child (University of Minnesota, 2007). The Charter is modeled on the United Nations Convention on the Rights of the Child. It has been adopted by a majority of African states. It defines a child as a human being younger than 18 years and seeks to protect the dignity and status of children, at the same time prohibiting exploitation such as the sale and trafficking of children.

There have been a number of efforts to convert these standards into practice. For example, a series of conferences was held in 2002 in Nigeria on juvenile justice with funding provided by the European Union and UNICEF. The conference proceedings urged adoption of the reforms outlined in the United Nations conventions and guidelines. Although the foundation of such reforms is a nonsectarian legal system, the proceedings noted that Sharia penal law, something of importance particularly in northern Africa, also permitted some flexibility in dealing with juvenile offenders (Juvenile Justice Administration in Nigeria, 2002).

At the same time, juvenile justice reform is nearly impossible in some parts of Africa for many reasons, including war and extreme poverty. In some countries, beatings and long-term imprisonment of juveniles continue to be the norm (Wines, 2006) A recent United Nations report noted the impact of a long-term war on Liberia's juvenile justice system (United Nations Office for the Coordination of Humanitarian Affairs, 2007). Africa, of course, is a continent with many nations, and there is evidence that in at least some parts of South Africa a restorative justice approach, emphasizing diversion and family and community involvement, may offer hope for broader reform (Raymond, 2004). An excellent discussion of the tension between retributive justice and restorative justice as philosophic underpinnings for South Africa's juvenile justice system can be found in Skelton (2002).

## Asia

Efforts to enhance the rights of children in a number of Asian countries reflect the manner in which different cultural norms influence legal and policy developments. In China, for example, the National People's Congress enacted the Juvenile Delinquency Prevention Act in 1999 (Zhang & Liu, 2007). Broad economic and social change in China was accompanied by rising crime rates, with juvenile offenses accounting for nearly 70% of total crime. China established its first juvenile court in 1984, but there were difficulties with the quality of justice for juveniles (Wong, 2001), and the 1999 legislation was an effort to regularize the administration of juvenile justice in accordance with Chinese cultural traditions regarding youth and family (Zhang & Liu, 2007). According to Zhang and Liu, the law has several important components. First, it emphasizes the role of parents and schools in the prevention of status and other minor offenses. Second (and similar to efforts in eastern Europe), the law emphasizes education as a major tool for prevention. Third, rehabilitation is emphasized even for comparatively major offenses, rather than the more punitive focus that has emerged in the United States and other Western countries since the 1990s. Finally, the law emphasizes what Zhang and Liu characterize as a "total-society approach" to delinquency prevention; this stands in contrast to the individualism that rests at the heart of many Western legal and philosophic traditions.

Like China, Vietnam and India have attempted reform of their juvenile justice systems against the backdrop of changes caused by accelerating economic growth and cultural change. Vietnam has adopted administrative alternatives to judicial proceedings for children charged with minor offenses and has attempted to incorporate the principles set forth in the Convention on the Rights of the Child (Salazar, 2005). However, such efforts have been hampered by a lack of adequate alternatives to detention as well as rules that place homeless children at a legal disadvantage primarily because children without an official residence can be sent immediately to a reformatory (Salazar, 2005).

India's child welfare movement goes back nearly as far as that of the United States, although India's was largely shaped by its colonial history (Kethineni & Klosky, 2005). In 1986, the central government enacted the Juvenile Justice Act of 1986. The Act was an attempt to create a national framework for juvenile justice, which historically had been the province of individual states. The Act was designed to provide care and rehabilitation for neglected juveniles, while at the same time creating an adjudicative structure for handling more serious cases. Although the Act maintained a "child-friendly" focus and emphasized alternatives to punitive sanctions, one review has found that implementation has lagged and that, in particular, many juvenile offenses are handled by adult criminal courts (Kethineni & Klosky, 2000, 2005).

In Pakistan, in contrast, there have been few apparent efforts at juvenile justice reform. At least one commentator reports that abuse of children in detention is widespread and doubts reform is possible, even if government were committed to it, because of the lack of resources and the absence of a judiciary free to act independently from the influence of nonjudicial entities (Geiger, 2000). The example of Pakistan illustrates one truism of juvenile justice reform: that such reform is almost impossible absent a tradition of and commitment to fair-minded judicial and administrative processes for dispute resolution and adjudication.

## Europe

Junger-Tas (2006) suggests that juvenile justice systems in Europe fall into three clusters. The first cluster comprises English-speaking countries (excluding Scotland but including the Netherlands). These countries adopt a "justice"-oriented approach, with a strong emphasis on the juvenile's accountability and a more retributive response to conduct. Evolution of juvenile justice in these countries more closely resembles changes that have occurred in the United States (for a further review of restorative justice in European systems, see Walgrave, 2004). The second cluster (mostly continental Europe) maintains a more "welfare"-oriented approach, although, as noted later, reactions to rising crime have created pressure to infuse these systems with more punitive characteristics. The third cluster is made up of the Scandinavian countries and Scotland, which rely on treatment and rehabilitation while still emphasizing personal accountability.

Two broader trends have also shaped juvenile justice in Europe in the last two decades. First, a number of countries (particularly in western Europe) have adopted a more legalistic and punitive approach to juvenile justice, while not abandoning the social welfare approach from which the juvenile justice system emerged. Second, eastern European countries that are no longer under Soviet rule have moved to create new justice systems that depend on legal principles rather than arbitrary decision making. The eventual success or failure of such efforts will establish the larger context in which juvenile justice reform will occur.

As noted earlier, much of Europe, like the United States, experienced rising juvenile crime in the late 1980s and 1990s as well as public perceptions that such increases were continuing long after rates of juvenile offending had stabilized. Historically, juvenile systems in many European countries emerged from deeply rooted social welfare systems, and so a commitment to education, treatment, and rehabilitation became a core value of juvenile justice (Junger-Tas, 2004). As juvenile crime rates rose, some countries responded with laws that made it easier to try juveniles as adults and made punitive sanctions more readily available. The result in countries such as the Netherlands has been social policy that "has been riven with ambivalences since the 1980s" (Junger-Tas, 2004, p. 293). However, even with a turn to a more legalistic juvenile system, the social welfare tradition has not been abandoned. For example, in Germany, one commentator has observed that, except during Nazi reign, German juvenile policy has been devoted to diversion, depenalization, and decarceration. Even after transfer to adult court became more readily available in Germany, it was rarely used (Albrecht, 2004). Restorative justice programs also continued to expand, for example, in countries such as Austria, Germany, and Finland.

Many of the democratic states that emerged in the early 1990s in central and eastern Europe attempted to rapidly enshrine constitutional and human rights by dramatically reforming existing legal systems. However, such efforts have been impeded in many countries by a combination of rising lawlessness, a lack of public confidence in the rule of law, and broader difficulties in maintaining democratic rule in the face of rising crime and economic dislocation (for an excellent review, see Siegelbaum, 2002). In addition, to the degree public opinion is now a politically relevant factor, punitive policies may receive broad support. For example, public opinion surveys in Russia revealed that, although there was significant support for a social welfare approach to some types of juvenile offending, public attitudes regarding juvenile crime mirrored to a significant degree the attitudes in England, Wales, and the United States that at least in part resulted in more punitive juvenile laws (McAuley & Macdonald, 2007).

In addition, there continue to be significant problems with basic access to justice in at least some countries in eastern and central Europe (Sesickas, 2000). Nonetheless, advocates have urged the expansion of education and other elements of a social welfare approach as an alternative to punishing juveniles (Henkes, 2000), and there is evidence that the principles of a welfare-based juvenile justice system have been embraced, at least legislatively, in countries as diverse as Poland, the Czech Republic, Slovenia, and Bosnia (Junger-Tas & Decker, 2006).

## South America

There is less written about juvenile justice in South America than any other continent. Although some countries (e.g., Brazil) have established juvenile courts, the United Nations has expressed continuing concern regarding the status of juveniles in South America. In its 2001 report, Human Rights Watch observed that conditions of detention for Brazilian youth fell far below international standards as well as Brazil's own Children's and Adolescents Statute and that, in fact, on the 10th anniversary of the enactment of that statute, there was "a wave of flagrant abuses against youths held in the detention centers ... Over the course of 2000, rights groups documented numerous cases of mass beatings; on several occasions, public prosecutors entered FEBEM (Sao Paolo's juvenile detention system, called the Foundation for the Well-Being of Minors) and also filmed the fresh wounds of dozens of detainees" (Human Rights Watch, 2001). The United Nations also urged reform of juvenile justice practices in a comprehensive report on children's rights (Committee on the Rights of the Child, 2004). The comparatively primitive quality of juvenile rights in at least some parts of South America is suggested by a 2001 report (Committee on the Rights of the Child, 2001) regarding Paraguay's treatment of children, where one of the recommendations was to "ensure that those officers implicated in acts of torture and ill-treatment against inmates are suspended from duty pending a full and impartial investigation and, if found responsible, brought to justice" (Observation 52.f). The Inter-American Court of Human Rights has also issued several opinions decrying the status of juveniles in many South American countries (Dohrn, 2006; Inter-American Court of Human Rights, 2002).

This is not to suggest that there have been no efforts at reform in South America. However, all available evidence suggests that it has been difficult to achieve progress and that, as in many countries in Africa, basic human rights issues, including the exploitation and abuse of children under government sanction, must be addressed before juvenile systems issues can be explored.

## IMPLEMENTATION AND IMPACT OF REFORM EFFORTS

It is clear from this brief overview that the treatment of children generally and juvenile justice particularly has been a focus of governments in every

part of the world. There has been a continuing commitment to a rehabilitative ideal, even in countries that have adopted more explicitly punitive
laws, and the notion of restorative justice appears to have an appeal that
transcends national borders. It is reasonable then to ask what the impact
of this ferment has been. As with most efforts at resolving complex social
problems, the evidence is mixed at best.

On the one hand, broad abuse of children, including juvenile offenders, continues to exist in many countries. UNICEF (1998) characterized the
situation in this way: "Given the importance placed on juvenile justice by
the international community, as evidenced by the scope and detail of the
international instruments it has adopted on the subject, it seems somewhat
paradoxical that the rights, norms, and principles involved are regularly
ignored and seriously violated virtually throughout the world, on a scale
that is probably unmatched in the field of civil rights implementation." In
some countries, as the earlier discussion of South America and Africa suggests, the threshold issue is a lack of adherence to basic human rights; in
societies where children are routinely abused, tortured, sold into slavery,
and otherwise exploited, one would not expect to find functioning juvenile
court systems. (It is worth noting, in this context, that the United States
has not been exempt from challenges to juvenile practices by human rights
organizations. Human Rights Watch, 2006, for example, has issued reports
condemning practices in state-run detention centers for juveniles. In addition, the U.S. Justice Department, 2005, has found horrific conditions in
such centers.)

In other places, reform efforts stumble on complex issues stemming
from broader changes in the form of government. For example, in parts of
eastern Europe and in Asia, the evolution of juvenile justice standards and
practice occurs against the backdrop of efforts to create the "rule of law"
in societies where authoritarian reign did not tolerate independent legal
processes and decision makers. In still other places with long histories of
separate legal processes for juveniles, barriers may be more prosaic but still
significant (e.g., a lack of adequate resources to provide rehabilitation and
care).

When reform has been implemented, it is not always clear that it
"works," at least according to the demands of the research paradigm. In
many ways, the most interesting development internationally has been the
emergence of restorative justice as the philosophical anchor for a number
of national efforts. Yet as Presser and Van Voorhis (2002) have pointed out,
restorative justice itself has a definitional elasticity that makes measuring its
impact difficult.

In addition, the studies conducted to date have been criticized on methodological grounds. Although these are not uncommon problems in trying
to assess the impact of new legal and policy developments (McGaha, Boo-

throyd, Poythress, Petrila, & Ort, 2002), they do make it difficult to generalize from existing studies. Data from Australia (Levy, 1999) and England
(Zernova, 2007) raise questions about the efficacy of a restorative justice
approach, but other evidence suggests that community-based alternatives to
incarceration can have a positive impact. For example, a multinational study
of 63 victim–offender dialogue programs, one type of program falling under
the rubric of restorative justice, showed a 9 to 27% reduction in recidivism among offenders based on their rates of offending prior to entry into
the program (Umbreit, Coates, & Vos, 2002). Other studies show similar
positive effects (Beale, 2003; Burkemper, Balsam, & Yeh, 2007; Walgrave,
2004). Although such studies are not definitive, they do provide empirical support for continuing to explore alternatives to punitive sanctions for
juvenile offenders.

## CONCLUSION

Juvenile policy clearly is a major issue for countries in every part of the
world. The state of justice for juveniles varies dramatically from nation
to nation. In some countries, internal strife and ongoing exploitation and
abuse of children make juvenile justice reform little more than an aspiration;
in other countries, juvenile justice reform is part of a larger shift to insti-
tutionalizing legal principles after years of totalitarian reign. In democratic
countries with long histories of separate juvenile systems, national policies
often reflect ambivalence between maintaining a rehabilitative focus while
responding to public demands for more punitive laws. However, even in
countries where more punitive policies have been embraced, there continues
to be strong support for prevention and alternatives to incarceration.

   Although the United States has been largely isolated in its unwillingness to ratify international standards articulated under the leadership of the
United Nations, there is evidence that international standards and practices
can exert significant influence. In juvenile law, the most striking example
is the Supreme Court's decision in *Roper v. Simmons* (2005), in which
the majority anchored its decision outlawing capital punishment for U.S.
offenders who offended before attaining the age of 18 at least in part in
international practice and conventions. Whether the narrow majority willing to entertain international law will survive future presidential elections
and changes in the Court's composition is yet to be revealed, but the Court's
decision in *Roper* is important in the broader debate over the role of international law in the Court's jurisprudence.

   There is also evidence that international practice is influencing policy in
some states. For example, there are a number of communities in the state of
Missouri (considered a leader in state juvenile practice) that have initiated

programs based on the principle of restorative justice (Burkemper et al., 2007), and even at the height of the move toward a more punitive paradigm, individual programs across the United States were maintaining a rehabilitative approach (Beale, 2003; Paye, 1999).

In short, juvenile justice in many countries is in a state of rich ferment. Although many in the United States often prefer to go it alone, participating in that ferment can only benefit policymakers and practitioners in the United States.

## REFERENCES

Albrecht, H. (2004). Youth justice in Germany. *Crime and Justice, 31*, 443–487.

Angell, K. M. (2004). The regressive movement: When juvenile offenders are treated as adults, nobody wins. *Southern California Interdisciplinary Law Journal, 14*, 125–149.

Beale, S. S. (2003). Still tough on crime? Prospects for restorative justice in the United States. *Utah Law Review, 2003*, 413–417.

Burkemper, T. B., Balsam, N., & Yeh, M. (2007). Restorative justice in Missouri's juvenile system. *Journal of the Missouri Bar, 63*, 128–134.

Committee on the Rights of the Child, United Nations (2001, November). *Consideration of reports submitted by states parties under Article 44 of the Convention. Concluding observations: Paraguay.* Retrieved December 11, 2007, from *www.universalhumanrightsindex.org/documents/829/502/document/en/text.html*.

Committee on the Rights of the Child, United Nations (2004, November). *Consideration of reports submitted by states parties under Article 44 of the Convention. Concluding observations: Brazil.* Retrieved December 11, 2007, from *www.universalhumanrightsindex.org/documents/829/277/document/en/text.html*.

Dohrn, B. (2006). Something's happening here: Children and human rights jurisprudence in two international courts. *Nevada Law Journal, 6*, 749–773.

Geiger, A. (2000). International law—Juvenile justice in Pakistan. *23 Suffolk Transnational Law Review, 23*, 713–745.

Geraghty, T. F., & Drizin, S. A. (1997). Foreword—The debate over the future of juvenile courts: Can we reach consensus? *Journal Criminal Law and Criminology, 88*, 1–14.

Gerety, C. D. (2005). *Roper v. Simmons* and the role of international laws, practices and opinions in United States capital punishment jurisprudence. *Chinese Journal of International Law, 4*, 565–582.

Henkes, B. (2000). The role of education in juvenile justice in eastern Europe and the former Soviet Union. *Constitutional and Legal Policy Institute.* Retrieved December 14, 2007, from *www.hrea.org/pubs/henkes00.html*.

Human Rights Watch. (2001). *World report 2001: Brazil.* Retrieved December 12, 2007, from *www.hrw.org/wr2k1/americas/brazil.html.*

Human Rights Watch. (2006, September). *Custody and control: Conditions of confinement in New York's juvenile prisons for girls.* Retrieved December 12, 2007 from *hrw.org/reports/2006/us0906/.*

Inter-American Court of Human Rights. (2002, August). *Advisory opinion OC-17/2002 of August 28, 2002, Requested by the Inter-American Commission on Human Rights: Juridical condition and human rights of the child.* Retrieved December 13, 2007, from *www.crin.org/docs/advisory-opinion17.pdf.*

Junger-Tas, J. (2004). Youth justice in the Netherlands. *Crime and Justice, 31,* 293–343.

Junger-Tas, J. (2006). Trends in international juvenile justice: What conclusions can be drawn? In J. Junger-Tas & S. H. Decker (Eds.), *International handbook of juvenile justice* (pp. 505–532). New York: Springer.

Junger-Tas, J., & Decker, S. H. (Eds.). (2006). *International handbook of juvenile justice.* New York: Springer.

Juvenile Justice Administration in Nigeria. (2002). *A report of three conferences.* Retrieved May 9, 2008, from *www.penalreform.org/a-report-of-three-conferences-on-juvenile-justice-in-nigeria.html.*

Kethineni, S., & Klosky, T. (2000). The impact of juvenile justice reforms in India. *International Journal of Offender Therapy and Comparative Criminology, 44,* 312–325.

Kethineni, S., & Klosky, T. (2005). Juvenile justice and due process rights of children in India and the United States. *International Criminal Justice Review, 15,* 131–146.

Levesque, R. J. R. (1996). Future visions of juvenile justice: Lessons learned from international and comparative law. *Creighton Law Review, 29,* 1563–1585.

Levy, K. S. (1999). The Australian juvenile justice system: Legal and social science dimensions. *Quinnipiac Law Review, 18,* 521–572.

Maxwell, G., & Morris, A. (2006). Youth justice in New Zealand: Restorative justice in practice? *Journal of Social Issues, 62,* 239–258.

McAuley, M., & Macdonald, K. I. (2007). Russia and youth crime: A comparative study of attitudes and their implications. *British Journal of Criminology, 47,* 2–19.

McGaha, A., Boothroyd, R. A., Poythress, N. G., Petrila, J., & Ort, R. G. (2002). Lessons from the Broward County mental health court evaluation. *Evaluation and Program Planning, 25,* 125–135.

Office of the High Commissioner for Human Rights, United Nations. (1966, December). *International covenant on civil and political rights.* Retrieved May 8, 2008, from *www.unhchr.ch/html/menu3/b/a_ccpr.htm.*

Office of the High Commissioner for Human Rights, United Nations. (1985, November). *United Nations standard minimum rules for the administra-*

*tion of juvenile justice (the Beijing rules)*. Retrieved December 12, 2007, from *www.unhchr.ch/html/menu3/b/h_comp48.htm*.

Office of the High Commissioner for Human Rights, United Nations. (1989, November). *Convention on the rights of the child*. Retrieved December 12, 2007, from *www.unhchr.ch/html/menu3/b/k2crc.htm*.

Office of the High Commissioner for Human Rights, United Nations. (1990a, December). *United Nations guidelines for the prevention of juvenile delinquency (the Riyadh guidelines)*. Retrieved December 12, 2007, from *www.unhchr.ch/html/menu3/b/h_comp47.htm*.

Office of the High Commissioner for Human Rights, United Nations. (1990b, December). *United Nations rules for the protection of juveniles deprived of their liberty*. Retrieved December 12, 2007, from *www.unhchr.ch/html/menu3/b/h_comp37.htm*.

Office of the High Commissioner for Human Rights, United Nations. (1990c, December). *United Nations standard minimum rules for non-custodial measures (the Tokyo rules)*. Retrieved December 12, 2007, from *www.unhchr.ch/html/menu3/b/h_comp46.htm*.

Paye, A. L. (1999). Communities take control of crime: Incorporating the conferencing model into the United States juvenile justice system. *Pacific Rim Law and Policy Journal, 8,* 161–188.

Pfeiffer, C. (1998). Juvenile crime and violence in Europe. *Crime and Justice, 23,* 255–322.

Presser, L., & Van Voorhis, P. (2002). Values and evaluation: Assessing processes and outcomes of restorative justice programs. *Crime and Delinquency, 48,* 162–188.

Raymond, L. (2004). *Transformation of the juvenile justice system: A paradigm shift from a punitive justice system of the old order to a restorative justice system of the new dispensation*. Unpublished thesis, University of the Western Cape. Retrieved December 10, 2007, from *etd.uwc.ac.za/usrfiles/modules/etd/docs/etd_init_8596_1175238405.pdf*.

Reddington, F. (2002). Age and criminal responsibility. *Journal of the Institute of Justice and International Studies, 2002,* 105–108.

Reddington, F. P., & Urban, L. S. (2006). Canada and the United States: A comparison of the approach to juvenile crime. *Journal of the Institute of Justice and International Studies, 2006,* 241–249.

Roberts, J. V. (2004). Public opinion and youth justice. *Crime and Justice, 31,* 495–542.

Roper v. Simmons, 543 U.S. 551, 125 S. Ct. 1183 (2005).

Salazar, C. V. (2005). 30 years after the war: Children, families, and rights in Vietnam. *International Journal of Law, Policy and the Family, 23,* 30–45.

Sarre, R. (2004). Impacting juvenile justice in Australia: The experience of family group conferencing. *Journal of the Institute of Justice and International Studies, 4,* 38–43.

Sesickas, L. (2000). Access to justice in Lithuania. *Fordham International Law Journal, 24,* 159–181.

Siegelbaum, J. H. (2002). The right amount of rights: Calibrating criminal law and procedure in post-communist central and eastern Europe. *Boston University International Law Journal, 20,* 73–124.

Sinnott, R. E. (2006). Universalism and cultural relativism in Roper v. Simmons. *Willamette Journal of International Law and Dispute Resolution, 14,* 132–153.

Skelton, A. (2002). Restorative justice as a framework for juvenile justice reform: A South African perspective. *British Journal of Criminology, 42,* 496–511.

Umbreit, M., Coates, R., & Vos, B. (2002). The impact of restorative justice conferencing: A multi-national perspective. *British Journal of Criminology, 1,* 21–48.

United Nations Children's Fund (UNICEF), Innocenti Research Centre. (1998). *Juvenile justice.* Retrieved December 14, 2008, from *www.unicef-irc.org/publications/pdf/digest3e.pdf.*

United Nations Office for the Coordination of Humanitarian Affairs. (2007, September). *Liberia: Juvenile justice system in tatters.* Retrieved December 12, 2007, from *www.irinnews.org/PrintReport.aspx?ReportId=74205.*

U.S. Department of Justice. (2005, September). *Investigation of the Logansport Juvenile Intake/Diagnostic Facility, Indiana. Letter from United States Attorney Susan Brooks to Governor Mitch Daniels, September 9th, 2005.* Retrieved December 11, 2007, from *usdoj.gov/crt/split/documents/split_indiana_logansport_juv_findlet_9-9-05.pdf.*

University of Minnesota, Human Rights Library. (2007). *African charter on the rights and welfare of the child.* Retrieved December 14, 2007, from *www1.umn.edu/humanrts/africa/afchild.htm.*

Van Bueren, G. (1999). A curious case of isolationism: American and international child criminal justice. *Quinnipiac Law Review, 18,* 451–468.

Walgrave, L. (2004). Restoration in youth justice. *Crime and Justice, 31,* 543–586.

Wines, M. (2006, December 24). For young, justice is as impoverished as Africa. *International Herald Tribune.* Retrieved December 11, 2007, from *www.iht.com/articles/2006/12/24/africa/web.1224africa.php.*

Wong, D. S. W. (2001). Changes in juvenile justice in China. *Youth and Society, 32,* 492–509.

Zehr, H. (1990). *Changing lenses: A new focus for crime and justice.* Scottsdale, PA: Herald Press.

Zernova, M. (2007). Aspirations of restorative justice proponents and experiences of participants in family group conferences. *British Journal of Criminology, 47,* 491–507.

Zhang, L., & Liu, J. (2007). China's juvenile delinquency prevention law: The law and the philosophy. *International Journal of Offender Therapy and Comparative Criminology, 51,* 541–554.

# Chapter 20

# Different Visions
# of Juvenile Justice

CHRISTOPHER SLOBOGIN

There are at least four distinct visions of how the legal system should deal with juvenile offenders. Phrased in terms of the well-known purposes of punishment, they might be said to focus on rehabilitation, adult retribution, diminished retribution, and individual prevention (the latter implemented through incapacitation, specific deterrence measures, and treatment targeted at reducing recidivism). Other visions of juvenile justice are possible (one of them—restorative justice—is briefly mentioned at the end of this chapter), but these other visions can all be seen as variants of one or more of these four models.

The rehabilitative vision, which probably comes closest to the original motivation for establishing a separate court for juveniles, views wayward youth as innocent and salvageable despite their antisocial behavior. On this view, disposition is designed to make the child a better person and confinement as punishment is to be avoided. This vision is most likely to apply to offenders who have not yet reached midadolescence, which was, in fact, the jurisdictional age limit in many of the first juvenile courts.

A second vision—the adult retribution model—sits at the opposite end of the spectrum. In vogue among many state legislatures in recent years, it sees most young people who commit crime as fully accountable individuals who should be punished in the same fashion as adults. This vision leads to broad transfer jurisdiction, adult-like sentences in juvenile court, or both. Note that if agreement can be reached on the appropriate age threshold, the first and second visions are not necessarily incompatible.

The third vision—diminished retribution—probably represents the consensus academic view as well as the practice in many moderate jurisdictions and sits somewhere between the rehabilitative and adult retribution approaches. It sees juveniles as neither innocent nor fully culpable but rather as beings whose responsibility is diminished because of youth. Dispositions are discounted proportionate to the degree of the juvenile's immaturity. This diminished retribution view can be compatible with the first two if only the youngest offenders are left unpunished and only the most mature adolescents are transferred to criminal court, with the middle group receiving more lenient sentences in juvenile court.

The individual prevention vision, which is sometimes incorporated into other visions but is never their principal focus, views youthful offenders not in terms of relative treatability or relative culpability but rather in terms of relative deterrability; its premise is that youth have a greater propensity to ignore the dictates of the criminal law. Dispositions are designed not to make the child a better person or to punish the adolescent but rather are individualized in an effort to prevent future antisocial behavior by the offender in question. Treatment is designed solely to reduce recidivism and thus is likely to be narrower in scope than under the rehabilitation vision, while resort to confinement occurs only if necessary to prevent bad conduct and thus may be less likely than under the second and third, retribution-oriented visions.

The first part of this chapter fleshes out the legal and policy implications of these differing visions. The second part discusses the other chapters in this part of the book within the framework developed in Part I. The third part compares the various visions of juvenile justice in light of the psychological knowledge about juveniles and the juvenile system that we possess today.

## THE FOUR VISIONS

The rehabilitative vision strongly informed the very first juvenile court, begun in the late 19th century in Chicago. Jane Addams, who helped establish the court, described its operation as follows:

> The child was brought before the judge with no one to prosecute him and with no one to defend him—the judge and all concerned were merely trying to find out what could be done on his behalf. The element of conflict was absolutely eliminated and with it, all notion of punishment. ... (1935, p. 137)

Ben Lindsey, an early juvenile court judge in Denver who wholeheartedly subscribed to this vision, opined that "our laws against crime were as inapplicable to children as they would be to idiots" (Lindsey & O'Higgins, 1909/1970, p. 133). In the eyes of these progenitors, juvenile offenders were blameless, and the goal of the juvenile court was not to punish but rather to help.

Under a rehabilitative model, then, the state is implementing its *parens patriae* power, not its police power (Tanenhaus, 2000, p. 18). Although no court, not even the one championed by Addams, consistently endorsed the youth-as-innocents concept, the rehabilitative model it spawned still heavily influences discussions of juvenile justice. The vision has both substantive and procedural implications, vestiges of which are visible today.

On the substantive side, the principal implication of the rehabilitative model is that the grounds for intervention are quite wide ranging. Prevention of recidivism is certainly one goal, because recidivism hurts the child as well as society. However, reduction of criminal behavior is not the main objective here. Judge Lindsey thought the court should ask, *inter alia*, "Is the child ... given to playing 'hookey' from school, or 'bumming' and running away, showing an entire lack of ambition or desire to work and settle down to regular habits?" (Platt, 1977, quoted in Steinberg & Schwartz, 2000, p. 12). From these types of sentiments rose an expansion of juvenile court jurisdiction beyond the law of (adult) crimes to include so-called status offenses, such as truancy, disobedience, and incorrigibility. One statute defined as "delinquent" any youth who

> knowingly associates with thieves, vicious or immoral persons; or, who, without just cause and without the consent of its parents or custodian, absents itself from its home or place of abode, or who is growing up in idleness or crime ... or who patronizes or visits any public pool room or bucket shop; or wanders about the streets in the night time without being on any lawful business or occupation; or who habitually wanders about any railroad yards or tracks or jumps or attempts to jump into any moving train ... or who habitually uses vile, obscene, vulgar, profane or indecent language; or who is guilty of immoral conduct in any public place or about any school house. (Tanenhaus, 2000, pp. 40–41)

Reminiscent of vagrancy statutes eventually declared unconstitutional by the Supreme Court (see, e.g., *Kolender v. Lawson*, 1983), these types of laws gave juvenile court judges discretion to intervene in the lives of vast numbers of youth.

On the procedural side, the rehabilitative model counseled against procedures that would limit judges' ability to learn everything about their charges. Judge Julian Mack, another early juvenile court judge, described his view of the ideal juvenile court procedure as follows: "Seated at a desk, with the child at his side, where he can on occasion put his arm around his shoulder and draw the lad to him, the judge, while losing none of his judicial dignity, will gain immensely in the effectiveness of his work" (Mack, 1909, p. 120). Because, as Addams (1935) put it in the statement quoted above, "the element of conflict was absolutely eliminated" in the parens patriae juvenile court, no formal conflict resolution process was necessary.

Most of the history of juvenile court in the past half-century has consisted of backing away from the substantive and procedural implications of the rehabilitation vision toward a more retributive stance vis-à-vis juvenile offenders. On the substantive side, observers from all points in the political spectrum expressed concern about the failure of the rehabilitative approach to hold kids clearly accountable for their actions, and much of the polity also felt that juvenile dispositions insufficiently protected the public. Indeed, even in the early days of the juvenile court, judges found ways to transfer to adult court juveniles who committed serious crimes or appeared to be particularly dangerous (Tanenhaus, 2000, pp. 20–21). Since that time, there has been a more or less steady progression toward harsher juvenile court sanctions and toward more expansive transfer jurisdiction, both in terms of the age at which it attaches and the types of crimes that can trigger it. Aside from baseless fears that crime committed by juveniles was continually increasing (Scott & Steinberg, 2003, pp. 807–809), the predominant motivation for these reforms appeared to be, in the words of one of their proponents, the perception that juvenile offenders "are criminals who happen to be young, not children who happen to be criminal" (Regnery, 1985, quoted in Scott, 2000, p. 297). In short, these reforms were based on a belief that juveniles who commit adult crimes should receive adult sentences.

Not all who believe youth should be held accountable for their crimes endorse this adult retribution stance, however. In the forefront of this group were the drafters of the Juvenile Justice Standards, promulgated in 1980. The Standards did recommend that juvenile court dispositions be based on the offense, not the offender, a position derived from retributive, just-desert principles (and, for the same reason, the drafters rejected status offenses; Institute of Judicial Administration, 1980). However, the drafters of the Standards also believed that juveniles' relative immaturity required lesser punishment than that meted out to adults who commit the same crimes. More recent writers, supported by empirical findings that adolescents are more impulsive, less future oriented, and more subject to peer influence than adults, have made an even more nuanced case for maintaining a separate juvenile system that is based on the understanding that youth who commit crime have diminished responsibility (Scott & Grisso, 1997; Zimring, 2000). These writers have also argued that treating juveniles like adults dims youths' prospects for becoming law abiding, because incarcerating adolescents with adults tends to exacerbate the criminal tendencies of the former group, which otherwise naturally tends to desist from crime by the late teens (Zimring, 1978). The standard conclusion of this view is that most youth who commit crime before age 18 should be tried and sentenced in juvenile court, with transfer limited to only the most serious, mature offenders.

The attack on the procedural aspects of the rehabilitative model was largely independent of the substantive upheaval just described. It began in the early 1950s, well before significant hostility to the rehabilitative goal or a strong movement toward holding children accountable developed (Tanenhaus, 2000, p. 30). Nonetheless, the importation of adult criminal procedure into the juvenile court—most conspicuously facilitated by the U.S. Supreme Court's decision in *In Re Gault* (1967) granting juveniles the rights to counsel at trial and other critical stages, to notice of one's charges, to confrontation of witnesses, and to remain silent—is closely tied conceptually to both retributive visions. A retributive system requires proof that a crime has been committed with the requisite degree of culpability, and it results in punishment commensurate with blameworthiness. Thus, in contrast to a rehabilitative model where conflict is, at least in theory, minimized, the retributive models represent the "criminal prosecution" referenced in the Sixth Amendment, which requires *Gault*-type rights in adult criminal court. Although *Gault*'s procedural reforms have not always been strictly implemented in practice, and in fact *Gault* itself cautioned that they should not be "ruthlessly administered" (p. 21), they have dramatically changed the way most juvenile courts operate (Feld, 2007).

All three visions of juvenile justice discussed to this point pay obeisance to public safety and prevention of recidivism. Judge Mack (1909) illustrated how the parens patriae position was at least partially cognizant of police power concerns when he famously stated, "The problem for determination by the judge is not 'Has this boy or girl committed a specific wrong' but 'What is he,' 'How has he become what he is,' and 'What had best be done in his interest *and in the interest of the state* to save him from a downward career'" (p. 110, emphasis added). The drafters of the Juvenile Justice Standards, although focused on just deserts, also recognized that protection of the public is a legitimate goal of juvenile justice. And the most punitive reforms of recent times were driven in part by the specter of the soulless juvenile "superpredator," who, unless confined, would routinely harm others (Bennett, DiIulio, & Walters, 1996). However, the central focus of these visions is elsewhere. The rehabilitative model hopes first and foremost to help the child, as Judge Mack's words indicate. The retributive models are, by definition, meant to punish for past acts, not prevent future ones, with the result that any achievement of the latter goal is an incidental effect of disposition.

The individual prevention vision, in contrast, has no other objective but to prevent future crime. In this sense, it is very similar to the sexual predator statutes considered by the Supreme Court in *Kansas v. Hendricks* (1997). There the Court upheld statutes that permit civil commitment of sex offenders considered to be "dangerous beyond their control" after they have served their time for the sex offense (p. 358). In other words, the Court held that individuals whose lack of volitional control makes them relatively unde-terrable may be preventively detained. By analogy, one can argue that the same indicia of immaturity in juveniles that reduce culpability—impulsivity, attraction to risk, and peer-driven behavior—also decrease deterrability and would permit preventive intervention (Slobogin, Fondacaro, & Woolard, 1999).

The substantive scope of an individual prevention model is likely to be significantly different from the other three models. Compared with the retributive models, it is likely to be both broader and narrower. Preteen children who might not be considered responsible, and thus not a just subject of retribution, might nonetheless be thought to pose a risk and thus in need of intervention in an individual prevention regime. At the same time, because the goal is prevention, not punishment, confinement in a detention facility would be the last resort under the individual prevention model, not the primary dispositional vehicle it is in a retributive scheme. Compared with the rehabilitative model, the scope of an individual prevention regime would probably be narrower, because the conduct underlying many status offenses and other "immoral" behavior is unlikely to be considered a serious risk factor. At the same time, the focus of an individual prevention model is corrective, not punitive, so, like the rehabilitative model, confinement simply for punishment's sake is eschewed (Slobogin, 2006).

The individual prevention vision of juvenile justice also has procedural implications. Because it is not punishment oriented, "criminal prosecution" is not involved. Of course, *Gault* held that adult criminal protections must be provided even in a purely rehabilitative regime. But that holding is not mandated by the Sixth Amendment. Rather, it is based on the Fourteenth Amendment's due process clause (which provides that government may not deprive individuals of liberty without "due process"), a much more flexible constitutional provision that does not necessarily require a full-fledged adversarial procedure (*Mathews v. Eldridge*, 1976). This is not to suggest that adult rights would be ignored in an individual prevention (or rehabilitative) regime, only that they are not as closely tied conceptually to the substantive liability rules as they are in retributive regimes and thus can be modified in ways that would be considered unconstitutional in adult court (Fondacaro, Slobogin, & Cross, 2006).

As noted early in this chapter, the four visions of juvenile justice can be reconciled, at least in theory. For instance, the rehabilitative model could govern disposition of children through age 12 or 13. The diminished retribution model could apply to youth from that threshold through 17 or 18 (or 20 or 25) but with the stipulation, consistent with the adult retribution model, that older offenders are transferred to adult court if sufficiently mature and their crimes sufficiently serious. Within the range set by diminished retribution principles the ultimate duration of intervention for those who remain in juvenile court could, in line with individual prevention goals, depend solely on risk assessment or adopt a "blended" sentence approach that imposes adult sentences after juvenile sentences are served only on those who reach 20 or so and are still considered a serious risk (Redding & Howell, 2000). Consistent with these substantive variations, relatively relaxed procedures might govern interventions for preadolescents, adult procedures could be required for trial of adolescents and transfer proceedings, and a hybrid process might apply in reviewing the postsentence status of adolescents retained in juvenile court. Any number of permutations of this basic framework can be imagined.

For the rest of this chapter, however, the four models are treated as competing visions. That approach allows one to tease out further the policy implications of each. The empirical findings described in the other chapters in this part of the book are used as a springboard for doing so.

## EMPIRICAL FINDINGS

Each of the chapters in this part of the book offers valuable empirical information about juvenile crime and the juvenile justice system. They are treated here somewhat out of sequence to facilitate discussion of related themes.

Cathy Spatz Widom and Helen W. Wilson (Chapter 13) thoroughly lay out the research testing the hypothesis that abuse of children contributes to later aggression by those children. The authors convincingly show a relationship between not only physical abuse and later violence but also nonphysical neglect and violence. They also provide a number of intriguing psychological and neurobiological theories as to why this relationship exists.

This research provides still another reason, besides the obvious one of preventing harm to children, for taking steps to prevent abuse. The key question for present purposes, however, is whether any of the findings are relevant to juvenile justice policy. In rehabilitative and individual prevention regimes, the answer would be yes. For advocates of the former approach, in fact, the distinction between prevention of abuse and prevention of harm caused by those who are abused is gossamer thin; in light of the evidence presented by Widom and Wilson, one can imagine a parens patriae proponent like Judge Lindsey, who considered it crucial to determine whether a child was "a victim of incompetent parents" (Platt, 1977, quoted in Steinberg & Schwartz, 2000, p. 12), opting for intervention even if the abused child had not yet committed any offense. In an individual prevention regime the fact of abuse or neglect might not be a significant enough risk factor to justify intervention. However, when combined with an offense, that factor might be a sufficient basis for exercising juvenile court jurisdiction.

Also relevant to both the rehabilitation and individual prevention regimes are the causal theories proffered by Widom and Wilson, which provide rich insight into how treatment might proceed. It should also be noted that, under either regime, this treatment would not have to take place in a detention facility. Several community treatment regimens have been shown to be effective at reducing criminogenic tendencies (including violent ones) by as much as 30%, while achieving "substantial cost savings from reduced incarceration, less restrictive placements, and other avoided social program and special education costs" (Tolan & Titus, this volume, p. 320; Hoge, Guerra, & Boxer, 2008).

Less clear is the relevance of Widom and Wilson's research in a retributive regime. In adult court, conviction is warranted if an individual commits a criminal act with the requisite mental state (e.g., purpose, recklessness, or negligence) and is unable to proffer a justification such as self-defense or an excusing condition such as insanity. These bare criteria are doubtless met in most cases in which individuals who were abused as children commit crime. Indeed, as Widom and Wilson say, "Many abused and neglected children do not become delinquent or violent youths" (p. 260), which suggests that abuse by itself does not have seriously debilitating effects on the cognitive capacities that mediate antisocial behavior.

The courts, in any event, generally take this view. Widom and Wilson mention the Caspi et al. (2002) study, which found that child abuse and low levels of MAOA significantly increased the probability of violent acts before age 26. Although this finding suggests that crime by these individuals is at least partially the result of factors over which they have no control, adult criminal courts have consistently refused to consider such evidence in support of a defense, and some have even held it is only trivially relevant at sentencing, on the ground that it at most shows a predisposition to aggressive action, not an impairment amounting to an incapacity to formulate intent or act rationally (Denno, 2006). Thus, this research is probably immaterial under the adult retributive model, properly construed.

It is probably also irrelevant under the diminished retribution model. Advocates of this model often analogize the immaturity of juveniles to the impairment caused by mental illness. But juveniles older than 10 who are not themselves suffering from mental disability are rarely as cognitively incompetent as people with schizophrenia and like disorders (Steinberg & Cauffman, 2000, p. 394). Moreover, even people with serious mental disability are convicted when they commit crime for rational reasons. The research may show that juvenile offenders who have been abused are "affectionless characters," attribute hostile motives to neutral actions, misconstrue other social cues, or are particularly prone to drug and alcohol abuse (Widom

& Wilson, p. 262–264). But none of this is usually considered sufficiently mitigating to reduce a sentence (Perlin & Gould, 1995), much less reduce the grade of the offense at trial.

James Garbarino, Kathryn Levene, Margaret Walsh, and Sacha Coupet (Chapter 17) catalogue a number of similar factors that can contribute to aggressive juvenile behavior, by girls in particular. Their research leads them to support an "early-starter" model of delinquency among girls. As they state, "Girls with an early aggressive history are, without effective intervention, increasingly at risk for engaging in delinquent offenses ... early school dropout, poor employment prospects, serious mental and physical health problems, early parenthood, and abuse and neglect of their offspring" (p. 343).

In rehabilitative and individual prevention regimes, this conclusion would counsel for intervention during preadolescence, and the state-of-the-art risk assessment and risk management techniques Garbarino et al. describe would play an important role in deciding which girls should be involved in treatment and what that treatment should be. One difference between the two models, again, would be the triggering event. As Garbarino points out, girls are more likely to be charged with status offenses. Although that fact would meld comfortably with the original impetus for the rehabilitative model, it could be problematic under a risk factor-driven individual prevention regime, depending on what the status offense is.

The early-starter concept brings out even greater contrasts with the retributive models. Intervention against a preadolescent might well be anathema in a regime based on maturity assessments; at the least, there would be no consequence for a status offense and probably only a slap on the wrist for conduct that would be criminal if committed by an adult. Thus, any treatment intervention that took place in connection with an early starter would not occur under the aegis of the juvenile court but would be left to other systems, such as schools and social agencies.

Chapter 16 by Patrick Tolan and Jennifer Anne Titus provides some additional factors to consider in this regard. First, the authors remind us that, although the type of research that Widom and Wilson, Garbarino et al., and they themselves report has improved immensely our understanding of juvenile crime, "even the strongest predictors of delinquency [have] modest capability to predict delinquency engagement" (p. 317). For example, the well-known finding, attributed primarily to Teri Moffitt (1993), that early-onset delinquency is the best indicator for serious and chronic involvement must be tempered by the fact that the majority of these early-onset children, even those who have elevated risk factors, do not go on to become chronic, violent offenders. Tolan and Titus also point out that specialized intervention systems designed specifically to reduce recidivism—juvenile drug courts, mental health courts, restorative justice programs, and teen courts—have been uneven in effectiveness. These findings reduce the attractiveness of rehabilitative and individual prevention regimes because of their reliance on risk assessment and management to succeed in their goals.

At the same time, Tolan and Titus's review of the relevant literature also casts doubt on our ability to make the culpability assessments necessary to retributive approaches. According to Tolan and Titus, although psychological and neuroscientific studies indicate that adolescents' decision-making and social judgment faculties "are more diminished ... than in adults," these studies "only set the stage for more careful work on how developmental needs and capabilities can be ... related to responsibility for self-control and social responsibility" (pp. 315–316). In short, as suggested previously, developmental immaturity does not necessarily nullify the relatively shallow capacities demanded by the traditional threshold for criminal liability.

In Chapter 15, N. Dickon Reppucci, Jaime L. Michel, and Jessica O. Kostelnik adopt a more confident appraisal of the research relating youth to diminished responsibility. They conclude that the research on developmental maturity "clearly suggests that adolescents younger than 16 years should not be treated as adults." (p. 308). However, they also report researchers' conclusions that "culpability is an elusive concept" and that "temperance (i.e., the ability to regulate impulsive and risky behavior) and perspective (i.e., the ability to evaluate the different perspectives in a given situation and place them in a larger context) [were] even stronger predictors of antisocial decision making than age," which indicates that many midadolescents, although immature, are no more immature than many adults (pp. 305–306). Given the absence, to date, of empirical research showing that immaturity prevents adolescents from possessing the capacity to formulate mens rea or to understand the consequences of one's actions, Reppucci et al.'s assertion that those under 16 ought to be handled differently from adults may be premature, at least when viewed from a just-deserts perspective. The best empirical argument against treating older adolescents like adults may instead come from the increasingly robust findings, also reported by Reppucci et al., that "transferring adolescents increases, rather than decreases, youth violence" (p. 308).

Reppucci et al. also describe empirical findings about the competency of juveniles to participate in the criminal process. Following Richard Bonnie's helpful characterization (1993), they divide this type of competency into two different capacities: adjudicative competence, or the ability to understand the criminal process and communicate relevant information to the attorney, and decisional competence, or the ability to make decisions about rights and other legal matters. The research Reppucci et al. report, supplemented by findings described by Thomas Grisso (2000), tends to show that juveniles younger than 14 are less likely than adults to demonstrate the ability to understand legal matters associated with adjudicative competence and much less likely to demonstrate the judgment associated with decisional competency. Juveniles 14 years of age and older are significantly better on both scores, although they improve with age, particularly with respect to decisional capacity.

In a retributive regime, with its Sixth Amendment-like process, these deficiencies are presumably very relevant. A lack of adjudicative competence undermines the dignity and reliability of the process by reducing the ability to attend to and confront one's accusers. Decisional competency is also important if juveniles are to be given the rights of adults, which include the right to (waive) counsel, the right to (waive) a jury, and the privilege against self-incrimination, which can be waived through a guilty plea or during the interrogation process.

In a rehabilitative regime, in contrast, a juvenile's incompetence might not matter, because the goal is to help the youth, not definitively determine guilt, and because youth are not assigned any decision-making role (Bonnie & Grisso, 2000, pp. 93–94). At most, a demonstration that the child is competent to testify (which courts have been willing to attribute to witnesses as young as 5; Melton, Poythress, Petrila, & Slobogin , 2007, p. 765), along with assurance that attorneys know how to deal with young clients, would probably suffice. An individual prevention regime would demand at least this amount of adjudicative competence, given the need to establish an offense has been committed. But it might not require much in the way of decisional competence. Its goal of effective risk assessment and management, based on evaluations by experts, could well render certain entitlements, such as the right to jury and the "right" to a reduced charge in exchange for a guilty plea, irrelevant or meaningless. Furthermore, given the fact that the adult right to self-representation is based on the Sixth Amendment (*Faretta v. California*, 1975), which need not apply in the individual prevention setting, the right to counsel could be deemed unwaivable, thus making decisional competence concerning this issue irrelevant as well.

The final issue addressed by Reppucci et al., which is also discussed in much more detail by Allison D. Redlich and Saul M. Kassin (Chapter 14), is the decisional competency required for waiving one's *Miranda* rights. Consistent with research relevant to other types of decisional competency, both of these chapters report that, compared with adults, youth younger than 15 years are significantly less likely to understand the content of the *Miranda* warnings and that even older juveniles are more likely than adults to waive their Fifth Amendment rights to silence and counsel during interrogation. Redlich and Kassin also note that false confessions from adults have been associated with suggestible personalities and lack of criminal justice experience and are perceived by law enforcement personnel to be associated with "evasive" behavior during interrogations (e.g., lack of eye contact; slouching), all tendencies that are even more likely to be associated with youth.

Research focused on juveniles tends to confirm that, compared with adults, children younger than 14 are more likely to yield to suggestions of wrongdoing and older adolescents are more likely to shift their stories in response to negative feedback. Yet, Redlich and Kassin also note, police do not seem to alter their interrogation techniques when interrogating young suspects.

These findings suggest certain policies designed to avoid false confessions, which could range from an unwaivable right to counsel during interrogation of juveniles, to exclusion of statements obtained using techniques that take advantage of adolescent vulnerability, to training of police officers to sensitize them to the greater suggestibility of youth. Adoption of these types of policies would be important under all four models, because all need reliable information about juveniles' antisocial behavior. However, consistent with the foregoing discussion, the legal basis for implementing these policies in rehabilitative and individual prevention regimes could be the Due Process Clause, not the Fifth Amendment (cf. *Allen v. Illinois,* 1986, which held that the Fifth Amendment does not apply in proceedings that do not result in "punishment"). Thus, juveniles in these two regimes would not have a "right" to remain silent, only a right to an interrogation that avoids techniques that tend to induce false confessions (which, of course, would include techniques that are physically coercive). The practical implication of this difference might be that juveniles subjected to interrogation in the latter two regimes would not be entitled to be told they have a right to silence (because such a right need not be required as a matter of due process— *Dickerson v. United States,* 2000) and the many technical rules that have developed around *Miranda* need not be followed by law enforcement and other officials.

Margaret Stevenson, Cynthia Najdowski, Bette Bottoms, and Tamara Haegerich (Chapter 18, this volume) also address procedural issues, but from the perspective of potential jurors rather than of juveniles immersed in the system. Although the Constitution does not mandate juries in juvenile delinquency cases (*McKeiver v. Pennsylvania,* 1971), the jury perspective is important because some states provide juries to juveniles, and many commentators have argued that juveniles subjected to transfer or adult-type dispositions are entitled to a jury (Ainsworth, 1991). Stevenson et al. note that laypeople are ambivalent about how to treat juvenile offenders, at times seeming to prefer treatment approaches and at other times "get-tough" approaches, depending, in part, on whether they visualize juveniles as wayward youth or superpredators. The authors also report research that indicates that various non-culpability-related factors such as juror or defendant gender, defendant race, juror empathy, and the perceived dangerousness of the defendant may heavily influence individual juror conclusions about culpability, conclusions that deliberations with other jury members may not budge. Although this research does not mean that juries should be abandoned as decision-making entities, it does open the door to consideration of alternative methods of determining facts, including the use of judges or experts who may be more attentive to the official culpability or risk criteria.

## WHICH VISION WORKS BEST?

As the foregoing discussion made clear, there are real substantive and procedural differences among the rehabilitation, adult retribution, diminished retribution, and individual prevention models. No effort is made here to resolve definitively which regime best conforms with and makes use of our current psychological knowledge (or whether, as suggested in other parts of this chapter, some combination of regimes works best). However, some preliminary observations as to the possible implications of the empirical evidence described in this part of the book can be made.

First, evidence is slim that nonmentally disabled adolescents who commit crime are congenitally or dispositionally impaired sufficiently to warrant an exculpatory or mitigating defense in an adult retributive system, at least as that system is presently constituted. This is not to say that there are no significant neurological and developmental differences between adolescents and adults in their 20s and 30s. Rather, the point is that, unless excuse and mitigation doctrines that currently operate in the adult system are broadened substantially, current psychological knowledge suggests that most adolescent offenders should not benefit from a reduced charge or sentence in that system. That fact undermines the premise of the diminished retribution model for those who offend during midadolescence or later; at the same time, it supports, at least weakly, the adult retributive model for these offenders.

Second, the developmental differences between juveniles and adults that do exist—primarily in the areas of self-control and temperance—appear to make juveniles less deterrable than adults, that is, less likely than adults to pay attention to the dictates of the criminal law. Whereas this reduced deterrability is not so great that it amounts to an excuse as defined by insanity doctrines such as the irresistible impulse prong of the insanity defense, it may be similar in effect, if not in cause, to the impaired self-control associated with sex offenders who are committed under the statutes upheld by the Supreme Court in *Kansas v. Hendricks* (1997). *Hendricks* is a controversial decision, and perhaps a bad one as applied to adults, but if the assertion just made concerning current empirical findings about juveniles is correct, its rationale may provide a theoretical basis for a separate juvenile court that is at least as strong as, if not superior to, the diminished retribution rationale (Slobogin, Fondacaro, & Woolard, 1999). To that extent, present psychological knowledge provides the individual prevention model at least a modicum of support.

Third, somewhat undercutting this last conclusion, the risk assessments needed for the individual prevention and rehabilitative regimes are not very accurate. Yet neither are the culpability assessments required for retributive regimes. The suspect nature of culpability determinations is often ignored, precisely because the criterion variable for determining the accuracy of a culpability assessment is so vague. In contrast, the validity of a risk assessment can often be gauged simply by determining whether the offender reoffends, thus making our incompetence at the latter assessment more blatant. This difference should not blind us to the possibility that psychological knowledge is no better at giving us answers about culpability than it is about risk. Further, juries, the principal procedural mechanism for assessing culpability under the Sixth Amendment, seem to be affected as much by empathy, gender, race, and risk as by the criteria the law prescribes for measuring blame, which does not bode well for the "accuracy" of culpability determinations.

Fourth, the treatment programs that are essential for an effective rehabilitative regime and important for an individual prevention regime are only modestly successful at reducing recidivism. However, research suggests that systemic and other types of therapies have vastly improved the therapeutic prospects of juvenile offenders. Moreover, imprisonment of juveniles, especially with adults, appears to be criminogenic. These two empirical findings suggest that community-based rehabilitation ought to be a component of juvenile justice, thus lending support to the rehabilitative or individual prevention models or to a retributive model that does not take just-deserts philosophy too seriously. Also relevant here, but unfortunately nonexistent at this point in time, would be research evaluating whether retributive regimes are better than the alternatives at holding juveniles accountable for their actions and whether doing so reduces recidivism.

Fifth, empirical research suggests that at least some of the procedural accoutrements of the adult system—decisional competence, the privilege against self-incrimination, and juries—are not necessary to ensure accurate results and the latter two may actually have the opposite effect. However, that statement must be tempered by the absence of evidence about the effectiveness of alternatives as well as the caveat that these procedural components can perform important systemwide symbolic and legitimizing functions as well as practical ones. To date, we simply do not have sufficient psychological information about the effects of various procedures and how they interact with substantive agendas to make any strong statements about their efficacy.

A final observation about the relative merits of the various regimes described here builds on John Petrila's chapter (Chapter 19) on the manner in which other countries deal with juvenile offenders. As he indicates, although many countries appear to maintain relatively punitive juvenile justice systems, international covenants and the law in other countries dictate that all proceedings regarding juveniles be in their "best interests," that children not be detained with adults, and that alternatives to "judicial processes" and to imprisonment be provided (Van Bueren, 1999). Petrila also describes the restorative justice movement, most prevalent in New Zealand, which emphasizes "repairing the harm to the community rather than focusing specifically either on the punishment or rehabilitation of the offender" (p. 373). This approach, which aims both at mending victims and at reintegrating offenders, often using victim–offender conferencing, could be seen as a fifth model of juvenile justice because of its focus on helping victims, or it could be folded into an individual prevention regime, given its emphasis on prevention. To date, Petrila notes, evidence is sparse as to its efficacy at achieving its aims.

## CONCLUSION

The chapters in this part of the book are rich both in information about juvenile offenders and in implications for the law. The authors of each have done a good job describing relevant empirical findings and those areas in need of further empirical work. Together, the chapters comprise a springboard for further improvement of the complicated system we call juvenile justice.

## REFERENCES

Addams, J. (1935). *My friend Julia Lathrop*. New York: Macmillan.

Ainsworth, J. E. (1991). Re-imagining childhood and reconstructing the legal order: The case for abolishing the juvenile court. *North Carolina Law Review, 69,* 1083–1133.

Allen v. Illinois, 478 U.S. 364 (1986).

Bennett, W. J., DiIulio, J. J., Jr., & Walters, J. P. (1996). *Body count: Moral poverty ... and how to win America's war against crime and drugs.* New York: Simon & Schuster.

Bonnie, R. J. (1993). The competence of criminal defendants: Beyond *Dusky* and *Drope. Miami Law Review, 47,* 539–601.

Bonnie, R. J., & Grisso, T. (2000). Adjudicative competence and youthful offenders. In T. Grisso & R. G. Schwartz (Eds.), *Youth on trial: A developmental perspective on juvenile justice* (pp. 73–103). Chicago: University of Chicago Press.

Caspi, A., McClay, J., Moffit, T. E., Mill, J., Martin, J., Craig, I. A., et al. (2002).

Role of genotype in cycle of violence in maltreated children. *Science, 297,* 851–854.

Denno, D. W. (2006). Revisiting the legal links between genetics and crime. *Law and Contemporary Problems, 69,* 209–239.

Dickerson v. United States, 530 U.S. 428 (2000).

Faretta v. California, 422 U.S. 806 (1975).

Feld, B. C. (2007). A century of juvenile justice: A century of progress or a revolution that failed? *Northern Kentucky Law Review, 34,* 189–256.

Fondacaro, M. R., Slobogin, C., & Cross, T. (2006). Reconceptualizing due process in juvenile justice: Contributions from law and social science. *Hastings Law Journal, 57,* 955–989.

Grisso, T. (2000). What we know about youths' capacities as trial defendants. In T. Grisso & R. G. Schwartz (Eds.), *Youth on trial: A developmental perspective on juvenile justice* (pp. 139–171). Chicago: University of Chicago Press.

Hoge, R. D., Guerra, N. G., & Boxer, P. (2008). *Treating the juvenile offender.* New York: Guilford Press.

In re Gault, 387 U.S. 1 (1967).

Institute of Judicial Administration, American Bar Association. (1980). *Juvenile justice standards, standards relating to juvenile delinquency and sanctions.* New York: Author.

Kansas v. Hendricks, 521 U.S. 346 (1997).

Kolender v. Lawson, 461 U.S. 32 (1983).

Lindsey, B., & O'Higgins, H. (1970). *The beast.* Seattle: University of Washington Press. (Originally published 1909).

Mack, J. (1909). The juvenile court. *Harvard Law Review, 23,* 104–130.

Mathews v. Eldridge, 424 U.S. 319 (1976).

McKeiver v. Pennsylvania, 403 U.S. 528 (1971).

Melton, G. B., Poythress, N. P., Petrila, J., & Slobogin, C. (2007). *Psychological evaluations for the courts: A handbook for mental health professionals and lawyers* (3rd ed.). New York: Guilford Press.

Moffitt, T. E. (1993). Adolescent-limited and life-course-persistent antisocial behavior: A developmental taxonomy. *Psychological Review, 100,* 674–701.

Perlin, M. L., & Gould, K. K. (1995). Rashomon and the criminal law: Mental disability and the Federal Sentencing Guidelines. *American Journal of Criminal Law, 22,* 431–458.

Platt, A. M. (1977). *The child savers: The invention of delinquency* (2nd ed). Chicago: University of Chicago Press.

Redding, R. E., & Howell, J. C. (2000). Blended sentencing in American juvenile courts. In J. A. Fagan & F. E. Zimring (Eds.), *The changing borders of juvenile justice* (pp. 145–179). Chicago: University of Chicago Press.

Regnery, A. S. (1985). Getting away with murder: Why the juvenile justice system needs an overhaul. *Policy Review, 34,* 65–69.

Scott, E. S. (2000). Criminal responsibility in adolescence: Lessons from developmental psychology. In T. Grisso & R. G. Schwartz (Eds.), *Youth on trial: A developmental perspective on juvenile justice* (pp. 291–324). Chicago: University of Chicago Press.

Scott, E. S., & Grisso, T. (1997). The evolution of adolescence: A developmental perspective on juvenile justice reform. *Journal of Criminal Law and Criminology, 88,* 137–139.

Scott, E. S., & Steinberg, L. (2003). Blaming youth. *Texas Law Review, 81,* 799–840.

Slobogin, C. (2006). *Minding justice: Laws that deprive people with mental disability of life and liberty.* Boston: Harvard University Press.

Slobogin, C., Fondacaro, M. R., & Woolard, J. L. (1999). A prevention model of juvenile justice: The promise of *Kansas v. Hendricks* for children. *Wisconsin Law Review, 1999,* 185–226.

Steinberg, L., & Cauffman, E. (2000). A developmental perspective on jurisdictional boundary. In J. A. Fagan & F. E. Zimring (Eds.), *The changing borders of juvenile justice* (pp. 379–406). Chicago: University of Chicago Press.

Steinberg, L., & Schwartz, R. G. (2000). Developmental psychology goes to court. In T. Grisso & R. G. Schwartz (Eds.), *Youth on trial: A developmental perspective on juvenile justice* (pp. 9–31). Chicago: University of Chicago Press.

Tanenhaus, D. S. (2000). The evolution of transfer out of the juvenile court. In J. A. Fagan & F. E. Zimring (Eds.), *The changing borders of juvenile justice* (pp. 13–35). Chicago: University of Chicago Press.

Van Bueren, G. (1999). A curious case of isolationism: American and international child criminal justice. *Quinnipiac Law Review, 18,* 451–468.

Zimring, F. E. (1978). *Twentieth century fund task force on sentencing policy toward young offenders: Confronting youth crime.* New York: Holmes and Merge.

Zimring, F. E. (2000). Penal proportionality for the young offender: Notes on immaturity, capacity, and diminished responsibility. In T. Grisso & R. G. Schwartz (Eds.), *Youth on trial: A developmental perspective on juvenile justice* (pp. 267–324). Chicago: University of Chicago Press.

# Index